Entrepreneurs
Talent, Temperament, Technique

Second edition

Bill Bolton and John Thompson

ELSEVIER
BUTTERWORTH
HEINEMANN

AMSTERDAM · BOSTON · HEIDELBERG · LONDON · NEW YORK · OXFORD
PARIS · SAN DIEGO · SAN FRANCISCO · SINGAPORE · SYDNEY · TOKYO

Elsevier Butterworth-Heinemann
Linacre House, Jordan Hill, Oxford OX2 8DP
200 Wheeler Road, Burlington, MA 01803

First published 2000
Second edition 2004

British Library Cataloguing in Publication Data
A catalogue record for this book is available from the British Library

Library of Congress Cataloguing in Publication Data
A catalogue record for this book is available from the Library of Congress

ISBN   0 7506 6128 3

For information on all Butterworth-Heinemann publications visit our
website at: http://books.elsevier.com

Typeset by Integra Software Services Pvt. Ltd, Pondicherry, India
www.integra-india.com
Printed and bound in Great Britain by
Biddles Ltd, Kings Lynn, Norfolk

Contents

About the authors

Bill Bolton

Dr Bolton is an international consultant in enterprise development and entrepreneurship. He has held a personal UNITWIN (UNESCO) Chair in Innovation and Technology Transfer. Dr Bolton was the Founding Director of the St John's Innovation Centre in Cambridge and taught engineering at Cambridge University. His twenty-five years' experience in business and industry has ranged from a Senior Executive role in a multi-national to starting a number of new enterprises. Dr Bolton is a Visiting Professor at the University of Huddersfield. His other publications include *The University Handbook on Enterprise Development* (1997) and, jointly with John Thompson, *The Entrepreneur in Focus: Achieve Your Potential* (2003).

John Thompson

John Thompson is Roger M Bale Professor of Entrepreneurship and Director of the Enterprise Network at the University of Huddersfield, as well as a Visiting Professor in Finland and New Zealand. Prior to this post, he was Head of the Department of Management at the same University, and he has previously held management posts in retailing and the steel industry. He has written a number of books and papers on strategy and entrepreneurship, including his textbook *Strategic Management*, which is now in its fourth edition. He raised the money to open the Huddersfield Business Generator for embryo businesses in the creative industry sector, and he plays an active role in supporting social enterprises in Yorkshire.

Figures

Tables

Preface

Why do a few people make it as entrepreneurs, whilst many of those who try, fail – often losing the family home and their marriage in the process? What distinguishes growth-oriented entrepreneurs from the enterprising people who run successful micro businesses? Why do well-intentioned programmes to promote high-growth businesses in a region have such uncertain results? Is the high failure rate of new businesses something that we just have to accept as a fact of life? Why do so many people believe entrepreneurs are only to be found in the world of business?

Understanding and identifying the entrepreneur is the most important key to answering all these questions, and it is the primary theme of this book. It is the entrepreneur who builds and grows the enterprise, often starting from almost nothing. It is the entrepreneur who transforms economies, when all seems lost. There are, of course, other support factors involved and, indeed, these are covered in Part Three of this book – but the over-riding consideration in matters of success or failure is the entrepreneur.

Research about entrepreneurs has told us that many are first-born males from families with some business background and a strong work ethic. Though these and other findings are reviewed in Chapter 1, they bring us no nearer to knowing whether anyone might have the potential to be a successful entrepreneur. There is little doubt that we know an entrepreneur when we see one, or more accurately, when we see what they have achieved, and Part Two is full of examples which demonstrate this point. Even so, the question of how to pick out those with entrepreneurial potential still remains open.

Since completing the first edition of this book in 2000, we have been working on this question. We have sought to find a way of identifying those with the potential to make it as entrepreneurs. We have considered how it might be possible to take a group of people, and find out those within that group, who should be encouraged to consider starting an entrepreneurial venture.

In Chapter 2, we describe the results of this work and present a methodology for identifying a person's entrepreneurial potential. It is based around the measurement of six character themes which conveniently form the acronym FACETS – these themes are Focus, Advantage, Creativity, Ego, Team and Social – the latter being a character theme exclusive to the social entrepreneur. As we explain in Chapter 2, a number of screening stages are involved but we are now able to make the first stage available over the Internet via our website www.efacets.co.uk. This first stage involves a balanced questionnaire, which when used in conjunction with the text provides an understanding of a person's entrepreneurial potential. Details of how to access the questionnaire are given on the website.

Whether or not you decide to try the questionnaire, we hope that this book will stimulate your interest in entrepreneurs, and help you to understand the central role that they play in the creation of wealth and prosperity. Above all, we hope that it will help you to seriously consider, if you might have the talent and temperament of the entrepreneur, and encourage you to take the necessary steps to make it happen.

Introduction

We believe that entrepreneurs create and build the future and that they are to be found in every walk of life and in every group of people. This book provides a wide range of examples of entrepreneurs that give substance to that belief.

We also believe that every community group, every public organisation and every private corporation has within it an entrepreneurial potential waiting to be released. There are far more entrepreneurs around than we realise but for many it is a talent that lies unrecognised, unused and undeveloped. Yet it is precisely these people that we need so desperately in today's world of change and challenge. In this book we want to show how this 'well of entrepreneurial talent' can be tapped and used for the benefit of all.

This book has many examples of successful entrepreneurs and so we want to begin with the story of an entrepreneur who never made it.

Cyril was the first entrepreneur I ever met. He was my brother-in-law. Cyril's enthusiasm and optimism for business were contagious. He was an exciting person to be with, always full of ideas. Cyril lived in Coventry and ran a precursor of what was to become the mail order business, except that in the late 1950s he sold his wares on the doorstep and his clients paid by instalments that he collected every week.

Cyril started the business after the Second World War when he served in the bomb disposal squad and learnt about risk! The business prospered and enabled him to buy his own home and support his family. Things were always going well; Cyril was an optimist and a great salesman. He had a generous and outgoing nature. His customers loved him.

Financing the business was obviously a problem because I can remember how pleased he was when a friend won some money on the football pools and put it into the business. This friend came with me on the money collection round one day – for I sometimes worked for Cyril at weekends – and when a customer made her final payment he simply thanked her for her business and walked away. 'Why didn't you try and sell her something else' I asked. This was an early warning sign that Cyril had a weak team.

Although Cyril was a brilliant salesman, he had difficulties in grasping the difference between sales and profit. Once when I returned after completing the Saturday morning round with a bag full of money he said 'Give the girls a fiver to go and get some fish and chips'. 'Aren't you going to check what I have collected first?' I asked, and then added 'Don't you realise that this money is not profit. You can't just go and spend it!' Was this another warning sign? Did he understand the financial side of business?

Cyril was keen to grow his business and decided he would rent premises and set up a shop to display his wares and to be his base. Until then he had worked from home but now with four children, space was becoming a problem. It was difficult to argue with Cyril about the wisdom of such a move because his optimism and confidence carried things along.

Just as the shop came on stream Cyril fell ill and was off work for about three months. Without Cyril at the helm things began to slide. When he recovered he had to try and rescue what was a dying business. He had built up large debts with his suppliers and with the extra cash flow demands of the shop he was not able to make repayments that were due.

The result was that the suppliers took legal action to recover their debts and the bailiffs moved into the family home. They stripped it of everything except a sewing machine that my sister was able to prove belonged to her. The house was also taken and Cyril, my sister and their four children were literally out on the street with nowhere to go. Cyril was declared bankrupt.

His family remained supportive throughout this catastrophe and to my surprise and delight Cyril bounced back and found a job in sales. He was so successful that he was awarded 'Salesman of the Year' for four years in succession and was finally given the silver trophy in recognition of his achievement. When one of his directors left to set up a rival company and invited Cyril to join him, he did so with enthusiasm. He enjoyed the challenge of moving from a secure job to a start-up business but he was never to launch his own business again. Cyril died in his mid-fifties after a severe asthma attack. His asthma had been getting worse over the years, no doubt triggered by the stress of his entrepreneurial activities.

(Bill Bolton)

This true story raises many of the issues addressed in this book, and our hope is that if Cyril had been able to read it, things might have been different.

Was Cyril really an entrepreneur or did he just aspire to be one? Was he more a self-employed businessman than a true entrepreneur? He had many of the qualities we associate with entrepreneurs. He was a dynamic hard-working person who got things done; he was an outstanding salesman. He was always optimistic and had great plans of what he was going to do. Cyril was an achiever. He was comfortable with risk and seemed relaxed about it as his wartime role in bomb disposal showed. Cyril enjoyed a happy married life with a family that always supported him. Despite all this he did not succeed as an entrepreneur – so what was missing?

Was it that Cyril just did not have the *talent* to be a successful entrepreneur? – possessing the aspiration but lacking the innate ability. Perhaps it was something in his personality that let him down? Maybe he had the wrong *temperament*. Or was it that he never received any formal training in how to run a business so that his business skills – his *technique* – were not sufficiently well developed?

In this book we use the three factors of *talent, temperament and technique* to open up the subject and reveal the entrepreneur. It may be that you are sceptical about the existence of *talent*, that you think *temperament* is too subjective a topic to be of practical use and believe *technique* has had so many books written about it that another is not needed. If you hold any or all of these views we would ask you to suspend judgement until you have read the stories and heard the arguments.

This book is in three parts. Part One deals with the *talent* and *temperament* side of the entrepreneur. Part Two provides real life examples that show how *talent, temperament* and *technique* combine to produce the complete entrepreneur. Part Three covers *technique* and the entrepreneur's environment.

In this second edition we take our understanding of *talent* and *temperament* to the next level of detail and break them down into their component parts. We can see the value of this approach if we look again at Cyril's case. The question of whether he lacked the *talent* to be a successful entrepreneur now becomes one of enquiring whether he was weak in any of the four talents of the entrepreneur. The *temperament* question is about the strength of his *inner ego* and *outer ego*. Here we use the terminology of Chapter 2, but the line of explanation is not difficult to follow.

Regarding *talent*, was Cyril missing the talent of *focus*? We think it unlikely. He was very hard working and made things happen. It was when he was ill that the business lost focus and began its decline. Maybe Cyril could not see true *advantage* in opportunities? Here the answer is less clear. He certainly had the opportunistic approach of the salesman but did not always appreciate what was best for the 'bottom line'. Perhaps it was an inability to be *creative* that let him down. We think not. He was always full of exciting new ideas. If anything, he had too many. Was Cyril weak in the area of *team*, unable to build a competent team that worked well together and unable to know when he needed outside help? We think this is closer to the mark and see *team* as his main area of weakness. Had he been stronger on *advantage* he may have carried the day. Had Cyril's business partner been able to build a team around him or provide the missing elements in the area of *advantage* the story might have had a happier ending.

What of Cyril's *temperament*? Did he have weaknesses in his *inner ego* or *outer ego*? We think not and believe he was strong in both areas. Within himself he was self-confident and strongly motivated and in dealing with the outside world he showed courage and carried responsibility well. However these strengths may have been a mixed blessing. When *temperament* is much stronger than *talent*, things can get out of balance. Decisions, for example, can be taken for *ego* reasons rather than for true *advantage* reasons.

We hope it is clear from this short case study that by taking *talent* and *temperament* to the next level of detail a deeper understanding of entrepreneurs and their performance can be achieved. As we explain in Chapter 2 it is possible to go further and use the approach to pick out potential entrepreneurs.

Of course this analysis of Cyril's entrepreneurial performance has not taken account of external factors. We do not know whether Cyril would have made it if he had not been taken ill or whether it would have simply delayed the inevitable. What is clear from Cyril's case is that even when events conspire against them entrepreneurs bounce back. It was the strength of Cyril's *inner ego temperament* that enabled him to do this.

On balance we think that given the right level of support and a good team behind him Cyril could have been successful. He had a strong *temperament* and sufficient *talent* for this to be the case.

We hope that this short example has shown the potential of the approach we present in this book.

How the book works

The three parts of the book are entitled:

- Part One – Entrepreneurs and the person.
- Part Two – Entrepreneurs in action.
- Part Three – Entrepreneurs and enterprise.

Part One is about the entrepreneur as a person. It deals with the 'who' questions. In Chapter 1 we give our own definition of the entrepreneur and then review what research has told us about this special kind of person. Chapter 2 describes our approach to the understanding of the entrepreneur and explains what we mean by talent, temperament and technique. We also present new material to this edition which provides a basis for the identification of potential entrepreneurs. Chapter 3 explores the strategic contribution of entrepreneurs. Part One thus enables the entrepreneur stories of Part Two to be seen in their strategic context and as demonstrations of how talent, temperament and technique can be combined and developed to produce 'elite entrepreneurs' similar to 'elite athletes' whose outstanding achievements we all recognise.

Part Two tells the stories of more than 100 entrepreneurs across many fields. It deals with the 'what' questions. What does an entrepreneur do? What actually happens in the real world? What do they achieve? We consider a wide range of entrepreneurs, from classic entrepreneurs such as Henry Ford, Walt Disney and Bill Gates to social entrepreneurs such as Cicely Saunders, who established the first modern hospice in the UK and inspired many others to follow her lead. There is a section on 'entrepreneurs in the shadows' where, amongst others, we look at unsociable entrepreneurs such as Robert Maxwell and Al Capone, who destroy some forms of capital to create financial wealth for themselves. Because Part Two adopts a story-telling approach, it is inevitably different in style from Parts One and Three.

Part Three sets entrepreneurs within the processes that are going on around them and of which they are part. It covers the 'how' questions. How do entrepreneurs do? What they do? How do the systems operate? This part deals with the practical issues of finding, developing and supporting entrepreneurs. We believe that releasing the entrepreneurial talent in a community, region or nation is one of the most untapped resources of our time, and Part Three explains how this can be done.

These three parts are laid out in a logical progression that we hope will appeal to the general reader. From discussing this topic with a wide range of people we recognise that some readers will want to focus on the results and will be more concerned with the 'what' questions than the 'who' and the 'how'. For these we recommend that they start with the entrepreneur stories in Part Two before moving to the 'who' and 'how' of Parts One and Three.

Others will prefer to consider concept before application and for these readers Parts One and Three should be read first and the examples of Part Two left to the end. It is important, if you follow this approach, that you do not get lost in the theory and ideas side of things. We want you to catch the excitement and buzz of the entrepreneur and to realise that there are entrepreneurs out there already making things happen. If you do not feel able to join them then at the least you can encourage and support them.

Outcomes

We hope for several outcomes from this book.

We hope that it will make you think differently about entrepreneurs and understand that not all of them are out there making money at other people's expense. We would like to redeem the word 'entrepreneur' and give it a more positive image linking it with concepts such as integrity and philanthropy. Our emphasis on entrepreneurial talent, as being something a person is given, promotes that end. People are more inclined to share their wealth if they see it as coming from their gifts rather than just their hard work. Equally others recognise that circumstances combined to give them an opportunity. Whether the gift is of talent or of opportunity, entrepreneurs often recognise that they owe a debt to the rest of us who are less fortunate. The two statements below, frequently heard from successful entrepreneurs, suggest that this is the case.

I have been very lucky. I was in the right place at the right time.
Life has been very kind to me and I would like to put something back.

These entrepreneurs recognise that it was not just their own efforts that got them there and so want to show their gratitude.

We want entrepreneurs to become both socially acceptable and academically respectable. Only when this happens will the culture barriers in society, in general, and in the academic world, in particular, come down. We hope that this book will help to make entrepreneurship a serious career option for the young graduate, with the right talent and temperament, through new courses and staff that support and enable this.

We want the unnecessary bureaucratic and financial hurdles that frustrate and impede would-be entrepreneurs to be replaced by mechanisms that actually facilitate their identification and development. We want to see all those with the potential to become entrepreneurs actually being given the opportunity. We recognise the fact that not all can become entrepreneurs but believe that many more people could start and run successful small organisations if they set their mind to it. Those who work in large organisations could be more enterprising. We hope that by providing greater insight into what entrepreneurs do and achieve, we will stimulate people to come up with new ideas and opportunities, and have the determination to follow them through.

We would like the role that clusters of entrepreneurs can play in economic and social development to be recognised. A few entrepreneurs can make a difference but when there are many of them and their number reaches a critical mass, a region or community simply takes off. Economic growth and social development become self-sustaining and an entrepreneurial culture develops. The Renaissance, the Industrial Revolution and today's High-technology Revolution are all examples of such entrepreneurial flowering. When the culture was right the entrepreneurs appeared as if from nowhere. Larson and Rogers (1986) explain how this happened in Silicon Valley:

> An agglomeration of spin-offs in the same neighbourhood as their parent firms is why a high-technology complex builds up in a certain region. The chain reaction of spin-offs from spin-offs is a kind of natural process, once it is begun.
>
> (Larson and Rogers, 1986)

These spin-offs were all the work of entrepreneurs. Entrepreneurs not only bring economic growth and social development, they also directly create jobs. Larson and Rogers (1986) calculated that in Silicon Valley each entrepreneur created 500–1000 jobs. By comparison, each technologist represents only sixteen additional jobs. There can surely be no stronger case than this for us to take entrepreneurs and the building of an entrepreneur culture much more seriously than we do.

Some may feel that these outcomes we seek are not relevant to the true entrepreneur and argue that entrepreneurs do not care whether anybody likes them or values them. They do not want life made easier and believe that things learnt the hard way are never forgotten. They are proud of their ability to beat the system.

We do not subscribe to this 'macho view' of entrepreneurship. Although it may be true that the harsher the environment the better the quality of entrepreneurs that emerge, there will be significantly fewer of them and it is the number of entrepreneurs that is the critical factor. There are many more potential entrepreneurs our there than we realise, and unlocking that potential is the key to the economic and social progress that we all seek. It is not a matter of government development programmes or major investment by the corporate sector. These can of course help but it is the front line troops – the entrepreneurs – that we need in order to make things really happen.

Finally, we hope that this book will stimulate your interest in finding the entrepreneurs in our midst, in considering whether you might be that entrepreneur and in supporting and enabling entrepreneurs as you have the opportunity. We want this book to be fun to read. We hope that the stories catch your imagination but we also hope that it makes you think and reflect on the entrepreneur in a new way. Above all we hope that it will lead to more winners and less losers amongst those who start and grow their business from scratch, especially if that person is you or someone that you are helping along that road!

We conclude this introduction with an analogy that shows just how buried talent can be.

The well of talent

The time has come to broaden our notion of the spectrum of talents. The single most important contribution education can make to a child's development is to help him towards a field where his talents best suit him, where he will be satisfied and competent. We should spend less time ranking children and more time helping them to identify their natural competencies and gifts, and cultivate those.

(Howard Gardner, Harvard School of Education, in Goleman, 1996)

When talent in sport has received serious attention the results have been outstanding. In the 1956 Olympics, East Germany gained only seven medals, of which one was gold. Twelve years later in 1968, they achieved twenty-six medals, including nine gold. Once their selection and training programme was in full swing the results were dramatic. In 1976 they won 90 medals, 40 of them gold, and in 1980 126 medals of which 47 were gold.

The East German Sports authority achieved this remarkable result by screening as many children as possible at age groups appropriate to the sport. For figure skating and gymnastics they started with children as young as 4–6 years. For sprinting and jumping the beginners' age was 9–12 years. They identified talent through training. The greater the talent, the quicker the learning. After the beginners' stage, people moved through to advanced, final and top performance stages. They started with many and ended up with a few who then achieved excellence (Harre, 1982).

We believe that the identification and development of talent is one of the greatest challenges facing education today. If it can be done in sport we see no reason why it cannot be done with other talents. Our educational methods and our culture are the main obstacles. The examples we give in this book are clear proof of this statement. Most have become entrepreneurs in spite of the system and not because of it.

Within any group of people there is an amazing mix of talent but we fail to harness it because in the main we fail to recognise that it is there. Talent remains buried and therefore untapped in our society. Offering training to everyone, regardless of their talent and likelihood of succeeding, can be a mistake. In any field where we want to develop excellence, we have to identify those people with the 'right' talent and temperament for the task in hand, and focus our endeavours and investment on them.

Figure I.1 shows our idea for a 'well of talent' with talents buried at different depths according to how difficult they are to get at and exploit.

We believe that *inventor* talent is the most deeply buried of all the talents in the UK although, of course, it is a talent that has great commercial value. Over the years, various government schemes have tried to promote invention and innovation but to little avail. One reason for the lack of success apart from simple bureaucracy is that a 'well of talent' approach has not been adopted. One inventor has suggested to us that if £20 million were made available across 200 inventors then we would see some remarkable results. In principle, he is right because it is a talent approach to the problem.

The *follower* talent is the least buried and most easily tapped because our educational system operates that way. We educate people to work for somebody else and equip them to be employees rather than employers. They become competent followers.

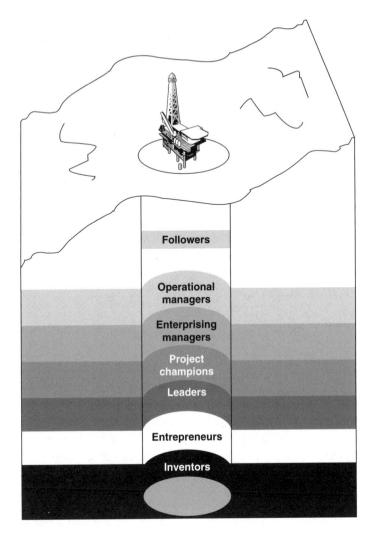

Figure I.1   *The well of talent*

Between the *follower* and the *inventor* we place *managers*, some of whom may be enterprising, *project champions*, *leaders* and *entrepreneurs*. Because we do not think in terms of talent, people become managers and leaders as they move up an organisation, often unrelated to whether they have the talent to do so or not. In fact we reward talented managers by making them leaders and wonder why they perform badly. For many, the so-called Peter Principle, promotion to a level of incompetence, then applies.

Entrepreneurs are in an even worse position because there has been no reason for an organisation to want them within a traditional hierarchy structure. When no one looks for them they are not found and remain buried. The move to flatter organisations and more dynamic flexible businesses means that entrepreneurs are now, finally, being talked about, though, even then we find we have to invent new words like intrapreneurs to describe entrepreneurs within the larger organisation.

Using the analogy of drilling for oil, if we could only tap the pool of entrepreneurial talent buried amongst us, then we would suddenly find an entrepreneurial pressure that we would need to cap and control. As it is, we are happy that it seeps out of the ground now and then.

References

Goleman, D. (1996). *Emotional Intelligence*. Bloomsbury.
Harre, D. (ed.) (1982). *Principles of Sports Training*. Sportverlag.
Larson, J.K. and Rogers, E.M. (1986). *Silicon Valley Fever*. Unwin Counterpoint.

Part One
Entrepreneurs and the person

1 Defining the entrepreneur

Defining anything is always a slippery business. In this chapter we propose a definition for the entrepreneur that we believe is robust and captures the personality, motivation and orientation of the entrepreneur. We explain the definition but leave the rest of the book to confirm substance and veracity. Next we summarise previous research and its findings about the entrepreneur as a person. We then consider ten things that entrepreneurs do – we call these their 'action factors' – and set them within the context of the entrepreneur process. Finally we describe the important work done by The Gallup Organisation on talent and roles.

On 25 February 1983, Nolan Bushnell, founder of Atari, Pizza Time Theatres and Catalyst Technologies delivered a speech at the National Engineers Week in Sunnyvale, California in the heart of Silicon Valley. He described the entrepreneur with this story.

> A guy wakes up in the morning and says 'I'm going to be an entrepreneur.' So he goes into work and he walks up to the best technologist in the company where he's working and whispers: 'Would you like to join my company? Ten o'clock, Saturday, my place. And bring some donuts.' Then he goes to the best finance guy he knows, and says, 'Bring some coffee.' Then he gets a marketing guy. And if you are the right entrepreneur, you have three or four of the best minds in the business. Ten o'clock Saturday rolls around. They say, 'Hey, what is our company going to do?' You say, 'Build left-handed widgets.' Another hour and you've got a business plan roughed out. The finance guy says he knows where he can get some money. So what have you done? You've not provided the coffee. You've not provided the donuts. You've not provided the ideas. You've been the entrepreneur. You made it all happen.
>
> (Larson and Rogers, 1986)

For Nolan Bushnell, an entrepreneur is someone who knows the right people, can pick a good team, act quickly and make it all happen. There is a dynamic about the entrepreneur that is captured well in this story; he or she is a person in a hurry.

The entrepreneur: a definition

The teacher asked his English class to write a sentence that showed the meaning of the word 'unique'. One pupil wrote 'My girlfriend is unique'. The
teacher's comment was 'Are you quite sure!'

Maybe you have the same reaction to any claim that entrepreneurs are unique. Yet
in many ways they are. They come in many different shapes and sizes. No two
entrepreneurs seem to be the same so that it is very difficult to pin down exactly *who*
is an entrepreneur. Some are extroverts and some are introverts, some have a family
history of entrepreneurs whilst others do not, some start from poverty when others
begin with wealth, some are young and some are old, some are men and some are
women. This ambiguity is found in much of the research into entrepreneurs and is
why it has been so difficult to build a clear picture of the entrepreneur as a person.

Entrepreneurs are certainly not like most of us. They are a minority group. From
experience with engineering undergraduates at Cambridge University in the 1980s
it was concluded that 10–15 per cent of this student group were potential entrepreneurs (Bolton, 1986). More rigorous assessments, by the late Professor Scott of Stir-
ling University, of the population at large came up with a similar figure. On making
this comment to many audiences we have been told that this might be the potential
number of entrepreneurs but the real number is more like 1 per cent. Others have
said that the potential number is much higher and have quoted figures for the US of
more than 40 per cent (Bygrave, 1998).

The difference between the number of potential and the actual entrepreneurs is
one of the central themes of this book. We believe that as with all talent, entrepreneurial talent was first to be discovered before it can be developed. Sadly our educational system and our professions – to name but two factors – not only inhibit the
flowering of entrepreneurial talent, they positively discourage it.

A professional psychologist whose business enterprise increased in value by
$50 million in its first year and achieved a 400 per cent return on invested capital has
commented that perhaps there is no greater punishment for psychologists than the
disapproval of their peers (Watts, 2000). As with other professional groups, psychologists prefer to stay with what they know and derive satisfaction from being
regarded as experts in their field. The would-be entrepreneur who breaks ranks is
often regarded with disapproval by others in the profession. If the venture fails they
are not likely to get their old job back.

Whilst the *who* of an entrepreneur may be difficult to prescribe, the *what* is easier.
This can be based upon what the entrepreneur does – the process – or what he
achieves – the results.

The origin of the word 'entrepreneur' is an important indicator of the process. It
derives from the French words *entre* meaning 'between' and *prendre* being the verb
'to take'. This would imply that it was another name for a merchant who acts as a
go-between for parties in the trading process. However the French economist Richard
Cantillon (1680–1734), who is reputed to have first used the word, related it to those
who carried the risk in the economy, so that it may have been the one who took the
risk between supplier and customer. The modern usage of the word in English is

broader and is focused more on results, although the original idea of the risk-taker is still there.

The French verb *entreprendre* means 'to undertake', as when undertaking a venture, but it can also be used in the relation to starting a new venture, and this is central to the use of the word 'entrepreneur' in English. In the French language the word *entrepreneur* means a contractor, such as a building contractor, but it is now also used in the same sense as it is in English. Hence the French bi-monthly magazine with the title '*le nouvel Entrepreneur* – le magazine pour créer et développer son entreprise'.

The entrepreneur, of course, goes back much further than the word we use today, to the merchants and traders who saw a commercial opportunity and turned it into profit. The following examples taken from the ancient and the medieval worlds show that the 'who' and the 'what' of the entrepreneur have not changed very much.

The ancient world example of an entrepreneur is Jacob in the Bible, perhaps better known as the father of Joseph and the provider of his 'coat of many colours'. Jacob is a classic example of the Arthur Daley car salesman type of entrepreneur, though he did reform later on in his career. In his long running dispute with his father-in-law, Laban (described in Genesis 30), he negotiates a spin-off from Laban's shepherding business with such words as 'Don't give me anything' and 'My honesty will testify for me in the future'. Jacob then puts his rather innovative veterinary methods into practice with the planned outcome that 'the weak animals went to Laban and the strong ones to Jacob'. The result was that Jacob 'grew exceedingly prosperous and came to own large flocks, and maidservants and menservants, and camels and donkeys'. Jacob was a successful entrepreneur.

A curious example of the entrepreneur merchant of the Middle Ages is provided in Umberto Eco's tale about the wanderer Baudolino (Eco, 2002). After various adventures Baudolino returns to his hometown and meets some of his old friends from childhood. He suddenly recognises one of them by the name of Ghini:

> It's true: you're Ghini! Weren't you the one who could sell anything, even the dung of your goats. Like that time when you passed some off on a pilgrim as the ashes of San Baudolino?
>
> That's right, I did! In fact, now I'm a merchant. Talk about fate!

Ghini was an entrepreneur.

In her book, *Worldly Goods*, Jardine (1997) develops a new history of the Renaissance which sees the fifteenth century as not so much as an age of outstanding artistic creativity as an age of entrepreneurs that then made possible the funding of great works of art. The immense wealth created at that time 'came from individual pieces of brilliant financial wheeler-dealing conducted at precisely the right moment' by entrepreneurs like the Fuggers and the Medicis. In reviewing the work of the painter Carlo Crivelli, Jardine (1997) comments that in his religious paintings 'celebrating global mercantilism is part and parcel of what is, after all, for him a commercial project – the entrepreneurial and the spiritual rub shoulders in this early Renaissance world'. It was a case of economic prosperity created by commercial entrepreneurs providing the financial resources to support talented artists, musicians and writers who in turn created aesthetic prosperity – people we describe as 'aesthetic entrepreneurs' in Chapter 8.

Although the Renaissance took some years to come to fruition, Tarnas (1996) sees it as the origin of a distinctive new Western personality 'Marked by individualism, secularity, strength of will, multiplicity of interest and impulse, creative innovation, and a willingness to defy traditional limitations on human activity'. This is not unlike a description of an entrepreneur and may explain the remarkable economic growth seen in the Western world.

These examples from the distant past are supplemented in this book by other more contemporary ones that tell the same story in different ways. There is certainly something special about the entrepreneur, but what is it? We start by first building our own definition and then considering what others have said on the subject.

In drawing up our definition we see the 'who' as a person and the 'what' as a process that is habitual and involves creativity and innovation and results in something of value that can be recognised by others. The building process, of course, first needs an opportunity to build on and this is something the entrepreneur is always able to spot.

Thus, we define an entrepreneur as:

A person who habitually creates and innovates to build something of recognised value around perceived opportunities.

'A person' can also be a group of people as it is possible to describe teams and even organisations as entrepreneurial, and we give some examples in this book. The word 'person' emphasises that a personality, rather than a system, is involved.

'Habitually' is an important characteristic of entrepreneurs that distinguishes them from business owner-managers or people who build a business simply to achieve a comfortable life style. The true entrepreneur just cannot stop being an entrepreneur.

> People ask me how to become an entrepreneur and I can't tell them.
> It's something innate. I couldn't stop even if I wanted to.
>
> (Bo Peabody, entrepreneur, millionaire
> and founder of Internet business, Tripod)

The word 'creates' is used to emphasise the fact that entrepreneurs start from scratch and bring into being something that was not there before. But entrepreneurs are not 'hey-presto' magicians, for they build as they create and fashion their venture. They are creators first and builders second but both are involved in the process.

True entrepreneurs 'innovate' as well as create. They see their ideas through to final application – they deliver. On the way, they use their innovative talents to overcome obstacles that would stop most people. For them every problem is a new opportunity.

'To build something' describes the output. The words 'habitually creates and innovates' refer to the process. 'To build something' is the aim of that process and for successful entrepreneurs this is their achievement. The word 'something' means that they build an entity that can be identified and is not just an idea or a concept, though it may start that way.

'Of recognised value' broadens the definition from the purely commercial. The traditional view of entrepreneurs is that they create financial capital. Whilst this is an important category of entrepreneur, we want to expand upon the use of the word 'entrepreneur' so that it also includes those who create social capital and aesthetic capital. For example, Dr Barnardo (1845–1905) was a social entrepreneur who created the now famous Barnardo's Homes that have a recognised social 'value' that is still current today. It is interesting to note that history describes Barnardo as a philanthropist rather than an entrepreneur. Whilst his motive may have been philanthropy, he was only able to achieve what he did because he was an entrepreneur. Andrew Lloyd Webber is an example of an aesthetic and business entrepreneur who has created financial capital as a result of first creating aesthetic capital.

'Perceived opportunities' are essential to provide direction and focus. The idea behind the opportunity may or may not be original to the entrepreneur, but spotting the opportunity to exploit the idea is a characteristic of the entrepreneur. Entrepreneurs see something others miss or only see in retrospect – the good idea seen with the benefit of hindsight.

Among the many thousands of things that I have never been able to understand, one in particular stands out. That is the question of who was the first person who stood by a pile of sand and said . . . You know, I bet if we took some of this and mixed it with a little potash and heated it, we could make a material that would be solid and yet transparent. We could call it glass. Call me obtuse, but you could stand me on a beach till the end of time and it would never occur to me to try to make it into windows.

(Bill Bryson, *Notes from a Small Island*)

We will return to our definition of the entrepreneur throughout this book to illustrate and expand upon its meaning.

Present understanding

We now summarise the main conclusions about entrepreneurs and entrepreneurship by several people who have studied the subject. Largely, it is an assessment of entrepreneurs from the outside. We group the findings into three sections:

- What entrepreneurs are like – the *personality* factors.
- Where entrepreneurs come from – the *environmental* factors.
- What entrepreneurs do – the *action* factors.

As a prelude, however, we would like to deal with three false assumptions often made about entrepreneurs. The first is that there is a formula which, if followed, will make a person an entrepreneur. Burns (1999) – and others who take a similarly prescriptive approach – believes that 'anyone who applies four key principles can become a successful entrepreneur' and develop a successful business. Burns's four principles are belief (in one's personal ability to succeed), focused knowledge (prioritised relevant learning), proactive approach (evaluating information deliberately and acting on the conclusions) and perseverance (working through the rough periods). These are important and relevant principles; but we do not accept that they explain entrepreneurs in the context of our earlier definition. Many people who might wish they could be entrepreneurs do not possess important elements of talent or temperament needed for success.

The second assumption that we question is that people who 'dabble in business' are entrepreneurs. Here we are thinking of people who are unemployed and are persuaded to do something themselves rather than look for another job, or people with some spare time on their hands who are looking to spend it in a meaningful way or people who invent something because they enjoy playing with ideas. We accept that wherever they find an activity or project in which they believe, and to which they can commit, 'dabblers' can achieve something that is useful and valuable. However they are not entrepreneurs by our definition. Nor are those people who start small businesses because they crave independence, and do not want to work for a large organisation, but who are content with something which stays small and provides them with a living. They might be described as 'lifestyle entrepreneurs' but they do not 'habitually create and innovate to build something of recognised value'.

The third assumption often made is that small business and entrepreneurship are the same subject. We see entrepreneurship in much broader terms. We believe that there are many people in the larger organisation who do possess entrepreneurial talent and temperament but prefer to stay employed, rather than start out on their own. This is particularly the case if they are encouraged to use their initiative and follow up their ideas. The word 'intrapreneur' has been used to describe such people. We compare and expand on the roles of the entrepreneur and the intrapreneur further in Chapter 3.

Thus, whilst many small businesses, though they may be successful, are not run by entrepreneurs we can find true entrepreneurs making a real difference championing causes and initiatives in larger organisations.

What entrepreneurs are like: the personality factors

Questions about personality are not special to entrepreneurs. Why we do what we do, why we are often alike and yet are so different are questions that psychologists have been studying for some time (Butler and McManus, 1998).

In this section we apply these questions to the entrepreneur and consider:

- motivation and emotion
- the born or made debate
- behavioural characteristics
- personality attributes.

Motivation and emotion   An engineer recently told us he felt real pleasure and satisfaction when he walked around his factory and saw it working like clockwork with raw material coming in and finished product going out. Even for the mechanistic engineer this was an emotional experience. Put together by his head, it stirred his heart.

For all of us our motivation comes from the heart as well as the head (Goleman, 1996) and so it is not surprising that psychologists link motivation and emotion together. In many ways it is the motivation and emotion of entrepreneurs that gives them a special kind of drive and purpose that marks them out from the rest of us. It is how they keep going and win through when lesser people would give up.

For some this can be very close to what the psychiatrist calls 'mania'. Whybrow (1999) comments that 'when the extraordinary energy, enthusiasm and self-confidence of the condition are found harnessed with a natural talent – for leadership or the creative arts – such states can become the engines of achievement, driving accomplishments much revered in human culture'. He lists Cromwell, Napoleon, Lincoln and Churchill as leaders in this mould.

Some entrepreneurs are also driven in this way as one sufferer recounts. 'I'll bet you that many successful businessmen, who have taken risks and almost lost their company, can describe something similar to my experiences in early mania. But they edit them out; they decide that such feelings have no relevance to anything but competition and risk, and they put them aside' (Whybrow, 1999).

A few, of course, are not able to put such feelings aside and suffer from what has been called 'entrepreneurial stress' (Buttner, 1992). This ranges from back problems and insomnia to more serious matters such as depression. We know of entrepreneurs who have driven past their offices rather than go into work because they could not face another day.

Other insights into motivation have been provided by McClelland (1961) who looked at the psychological and social elements that drove economic development. He saw motivation of individuals within a society as a crucial factor and linked it to three basic human needs: the need for achievement, the need for power and the need for affiliation. McClelland (1965) was particularly interested in the need for achievement because he believed that it was people with that need – the entrepreneurs – who drove economic development.

Various tests have been developed to measure these need-based drives. Roberts (1991) followed McClelland in using the Thematic Apperception Test (TAT) to assess the needs profile of technical entrepreneurs. (The TAT involves the verbal interpretation of fuzzy sketches.) Whilst McClelland (1965) concluded that entrepreneurs had a high need for achievement, Roberts found that on average technical entrepreneurs had only a 'moderate' need for achievement. However when he related his results to company performance he found that almost 80 per cent of the high-growth companies were run by entrepreneurs with a 'high' need for achievement.

Although this was an important finding it would be wrong to conclude that people with a high need for achievement would necessarily make good entrepreneurs. As sports psychologists have found, there is no clear correlation between the achievement motivation and the level of performance achieved (Woods, 1998). Other factors, most notably talent, have to be there as well.

Competitiveness is one aspect of motivation that is well-recognised in sports (Martens, 1976) but has received little attention in regard to entrepreneurs. In studies of entrepreneurship, competitiveness is generally set in the context of the external competitive forces on the business rather than the competitive spirit within the individual entrepreneur. Yet it is a character trait of entrepreneurs that they are people who do not like to be beaten; they want to be winners. This competitive streak is for many a main motivator. We recall an entrepreneur who competed with another entrepreneur all his life and this rivalry drove them both. When one died, the other remarked that he was pleased to have him finally out of the way. There was no sadness or remorse, only triumph.

Though entrepreneurs always want to win they do seem to have a remarkable resilience in defeat. They have the ability to bounce back. Cyril, in our introduction, picked himself up and found himself a job despite having no home, large debts and a family to support.

If motivational analysis is taken out of the psychological domain and entrepreneurs are simply asked why they started a business then the answers are clearer. Roberts (1991) found that for 39 per cent of a sample of seventy-two technical entrepreneurs the answer was that they sought independence, wanting to be their own boss. Thirty per cent were responding to a challenge and only 12 per cent were motivated by the possibility of wealth.

The low rating of money and wealth as a motivator with entrepreneurs is against the general perception of the entrepreneur. In reality money is a by-product for the business entrepreneur, but it is this that people see and so assume it to be the main motivator.

Many of the examples given in this book support Roberts's finding for technical entrepreneurs that the primary motivation for most entrepreneurs is independence. They want to be able to develop their own ideas in their own way without having to answer to anybody else. They want to be able to say 'I did it my way'. This is the entrepreneur's ultimate satisfaction.

The born or made debate   The concept of personality as something distinct and individual which directs a person's behaviour begs the same question that we consider here for entrepreneurs. Is personality 'born' or is it 'made'? Are we a product of 'nature' or 'nurture'?

Derlega *et al.* (1991) state that 'Personality refers to the enduring, inner characteristics of individuals that organise behaviour.' Some psychologists see these 'enduring, inner characteristics' (Hollander, 1971) as coming from an inner psychological core at the centre of our personality that is relatively permanent.

Such a model presupposes that a proportion of our personality is inborn and enduring. Hans Eysenck (1965) has suggested that we have two dimensions of personality that roughly correspond to motivation and emotion. He sees the two dimensions as related to biological differences in brain function (Butler and McManus, 1998) and on this basis has proposed that 75 per cent of our personality traits are due to genetic influence and 25 per cent due to environmental influence (Woods, 1998).

Research at the University of Minnesota on identical twins separated at birth and reared in different environments has built up a solid body of evidence that shows that many character traits are shaped by genetics. From this work it is estimated 'that the genetic contribution to "personality" is around 40 per cent' (Whybrow, 1999).

Individually, our genetic inheritance leads us to seek particular opportunities and tread particular paths. Our experiences on these journeys, and whether we are encouraged or discouraged in our endeavours and experiments, affect our personality and future behaviour.

Whatever the exact ratios are, it is clear that personality is now understood as having an inborn component and an environment component. In so far as the entrepreneur is a function of personality, we would conclude that entrepreneurs are both born and made. We come back to this idea in Chapter 2 when we consider talent and temperament.

Contrary to this finding from psychology, several books on entrepreneurship state that the argument is over and that entrepreneurs are 'made' (Kent, 1984; Burns and Dewhurst, 1989). One of the standard texts on entrepreneurship, now in its fourth edition (Kuratko and Hodgetts, 1998), says that it is a myth of entrepreneurship that entrepreneurs are born and not made. It states that entrepreneurship is a discipline that can be taught and mastered like any other. Whilst it may be true that the techniques of entrepreneurship can be 'taught' or more correctly 'learned', we do not believe that educators can make people into entrepreneurs. Whilst such a claim may fill the classroom we believe it to be irresponsible. We have seen too many failed entrepreneurs, who have lost the family home and whose marriage has failed, to believe otherwise. We are particularly concerned that such a standard text should recommend that those who score 25 out of a 103 in its Entrepreneur Quotient questionnaire should be advised 'You still have a chance. Go for it.'

We do however believe that educational programmes for entrepreneurs have their place – but they must recognise their boundaries. Whether the born/made ratio is 75:25 or 40:60, the environment is still an important parameter and one which those who wish to promote entrepreneurship can do something about.

Behavioural characteristics The behavioural characteristics of the entrepreneur have received the most attention from researchers over the years. After reviewing a number of sources, Hornaday (1982) drew up a list of forty-two characteristics including:

- perseverance and determination
- ability to take calculated risks
- need to achieve
- initiative and taking responsibility
- orientation to clear goals
- creativity
- honesty and integrity
- independence.

Although his full list was a long one, it is rather surprising that it did not include opportunity orientation, persistent problem-solving and internal locus of control which have been identified by others (Kao, 1991; Kuratko and Hodgetts, 1998).

The characteristics given in these lists are mainly straightforward but two require some comment. The first is to explain what is meant by 'internal locus of control'. This is a term used by psychologists (Rotter, 1966, 1971) to describe the extent to which people feel they are in control of what happens in their lives. People with an internal locus of control see themselves as being in control and believe that their own actions can dictate events, which of course is typical of the entrepreneur. Those with an external locus of control believe that their lives are controlled by external things such as luck and fate or the actions of others. Whilst entrepreneurs often acknowledge that circumstances did combine to give them a great opportunity and they were lucky, they believe that they were the ones who seized that opportunity and made it happen.

The second is to note the inclusion of honesty and integrity on the lists of Hornaday (1982), Kao (1991) and Kuratko and Hodgetts (1998). This is perhaps surprising given the image of entrepreneurs as people who take opportunities without too much thought as to the consequences for others. Some people think that there is no such thing as an honest entrepreneur and that you have to 'cut corners' and 'sail close to the wind' if you are to make it as an entrepreneur in today's competitive world. This is a view we do not share.

Of course there are dishonest people amongst entrepreneurs just as there are in all walks of life and when they are found out they receive a great deal of publicity. Robert Maxwell is an obvious case in point and is given as an example of an 'entrepreneur in the shadows' in Chapter 9. There are also particular temptations for those who acquire wealth and influence but there is no evidence that they 'fall from grace' more often than others. The main difficulty, particularly in the UK, is one of culture where we are suspicious of people who become wealthy. Like the story of the Englishman and the American waiting at a bus stop when a Rolls Royce drives by. While the Englishman comments 'I wonder who he cheated to be able to have a car like that', the American says 'Gee that's a great car, I wonder how I can get one'.

It is now generally recognised that ethical issues such as trust (Fukuyama, 1995) are important in a capitalist society and that business cannot function unless those involved can work together on a commonly accepted ethical basis. Entrepreneurs who like to move quickly and act decisively often build up a network of people they can trust rather than take the time on 'dotting i's and crossing t's'. They will shake hands on a deal and leave the 'legal boys' to sort out the details.

Social responsibility and business ethics are new and important topics in our business schools, and courses on entrepreneurship also include them. The standard text referred to earlier, includes a chapter on the 'Ethical and social responsibility challenges for entrepreneurs' (Kuratko and Hodgetts, 1998).

Personality attributes   Like a fingerprint, we all have our own unique personality. The question for us is whether there is a collection or cluster of personality attributes that distinguish the entrepreneur from the general public. Is there such a thing as the entrepreneur personality?

Personality attributes have been studied extensively and a wide range of tests have been developed to identify and even measure them. Such testing, termed 'psychometric testing', has become commonplace and is now a standard part of the interview process with many companies, particularly when the interviewee has to be part of a team. Jones (1993) lists nineteen such tests and describes them as 'Popular recruitment and career development tests'. One of the more popular tests developed by Cattell between 1946 and 1949 defines a set of sixteen personality factors (PF) and uses a questionnaire to evaluate them.

The Myers-Briggs Type Indicator (MBTI) is another popular test and a number of books are available which describe the test and its application (Keirsey and Bates, 1984; Goldsmith and Wharton, 1993; Kummerow *et al.*, 1997).

The MBTI was devised by Isobel Briggs Myers and her mother Katheryn Briggs and is based on four dimensions of personality proposed by the psychologist Jung, namely extroversion (E)/introversion (I), sensation (S)/intuition (N), thinking (T)/feeling (F) and judging (J)/perceiving (P). Combinations of the letters from each of the four dimensions give the personality indicator, making sixteen personality types in all. Goldsmith and Wharton (1993) state that ESTP types can be good innovators, negotiators and entrepreneurs, where E means that they are extroverted rather than introverted, S that they use their senses rather than intuition, T that they think rather than feel and P that they perceive rather than judge.

Roberts (1991) used a shortened version of the MBTI on seventy-three people who attended the Massachusetts Institute of Technology (MIT) Enterprise Forum and the 128 Venture Group. About two-thirds of the sample were known to be entrepreneurs and all were interested in entrepreneurship. Roberts found that as a group they were classed as ENTPs. The difference with the assessment of Goldsmith and Wharton quoted above is only in the sensation (S)/ intuition (N) dimension.

Before carrying out his research, and based on his personal experience of entrepreneurs, Roberts assessed entrepreneurs as ENTJ types. Keirsey and Bates (1984) describe ENTJs as 'the field marshal' which Roberts comments is 'perhaps an apt label for some entrepreneurs!'

Whilst this kind of personality test does not seem to point to a definable entrepreneur personality – they can be ESTPs, ENTPs or ENTJs – such tests can be useful in business start programmes.

From 1995 to 1997 we were involved in a programme in which new team-based businesses were set up around a business opportunity. The participants in the programme were drawn from the general public who had responded to advertisements in local newspapers. A personality and team profile was built up for each person using psychometric testing methods. The Occupational Personality Questionnaire (OPQ) developed by Saville and Holdsworth and Belbin's Team Role definitions (Jones, 1993) was used. This psychometric profile was then combined with the skill profile for each person, and teams selected to give an appropriate personality and skill mix. This methodology worked well and succeeded in producing balanced and effective teams, though of course they were not necessarily entrepreneurial teams.

Where entrepreneurs come from: the environmental factors

Here we consider the entrepreneurs' roots and their surrounding influences. These can be grouped under the following three headings:

- Family background
- Education and age
- Work experience

Though these can be powerful environmental factors they are essentially 'static'. They mould the entrepreneur, providing some of the attitudes and perceptions that are needed but they are certainly not prescriptive. Many entrepreneurs do not meet these norms and yet are successful. Often it is the 'dynamic' environmental factors, such as 'situation triggers', that have the strongest influence, as we explain in Chapter 11. These make the potential entrepreneur move into action. They provide the spark that lights the flame, the push that makes the entrepreneur jump. It may be a chance meeting with somebody, a sudden change of circumstances or an opportunity that simply pops up. Entrepreneurs have often told us that they were thinking of leaving their dead-end jobs when the decision was made for them and they were asked to leave. Redundancy is the most common 'situation trigger'.

Family background   Roberts (1991) has developed the idea of 'The entrepreneurial heritage' to describe the importance of the family background for the entrepreneur. This 'heritage' includes factors such as the father's occupation, the family work ethic and religion, family size and the first-born son, growing up experiences, and so on. Roberts was interested in entrepreneurs in high technology but many of his findings apply to entrepreneurs in general.

Roberts found that the strongest of these influences came from the father's career. His research showed that across several sample groups, the proportion of entrepreneurs whose fathers were self-employed was between 48 and 65 per cent, as compared with a figure of 25 per cent that would be expected if it was by chance alone. Although Roberts was looking at technology entrepreneurs, very few of the fathers were in technology. Typically they would own small retail stores, farms or small non-technical manufacturing firms. Roberts (1991) comments that 'indeed it may be that simply familiarity with a business environment, growing from "table talk" at home, is the key to increasing the probability that an offspring will later become an entrepreneur'. In a similar vein, Timmons (1986) speaks of entrepreneurial roots in which the parents provide the role model for the child.

Other researchers (Hisrich, 1990) have found similar figures for entrepreneurs in general. A study of 500 women entrepreneurs found that the majority of those in the sample had fathers who were self-employed (Hisrich and Brush, 1984).

We can thus conclude with Roberts (1991) that 'a disproportionate number of entrepreneurs are the sons of entrepreneurs', but we would also add 'daughters'.

Some have found that small families and being the first-born son are important for the emergence of entrepreneurs because in that environment they can develop a greater self-confidence (Hisrich, 1990). Research in Canada evaluated twelve personal and family variables among participants in an entrepreneurship programme and concluded that 'the characteristic most frequently associated with the entrepreneurial group was being the oldest child in the family' (Brockhaus and Horwitz, 1986).

The 'number one' son is an important consideration in some cultures, such as the Japanese, where there is a strong expectation on the first-born son (Fukuyama, 1995). This, of course, can be difficult when the son is not the entrepreneur his father was. Even in Western culture this can be a problem as the son either seeks to emulate his entrepreneur father or simply decides he would rather spend his father's money; the 'rags to riches and back again in three generations' syndrome.

Whilst these family factors can be important, they are by no means deciding factors. The research in this area often assumes that those who run their own business are entrepreneurs and, as we stated earlier, we do not believe that this is the case. Charles Forte was a first-born son and his father set up and ran a successful local business in Scotland. Charles's first-born son Rocco took over the empire his father Charles had built. All three were successful businessmen but a reading of Charles Forte's biography makes it quite clear that only Charles was a true entrepreneur (Forte, 1997). He was the only one of the three who 'habitually created and innovated to build something of recognised value'.

Education and age   Entrepreneurs seem to turn the importance of education and age upside down. Kevin Threlfall did not get enough A levels to go to university, but as a ten-year-old would go out with his father and learn about sales techniques. Today he has one of the larger retail businesses in the UK (T and S Stores, incorporating Supercigs, Buy-Wise and Preedy/Dillons) with sales of £500 million (Steiner, 1998).

It seems that entrepreneurs themselves do not generally rate education as having been an important factor for them. Studies of entrepreneurs appear to support this view. Comparing the educational level of entrepreneurs and managers, Brockhaus and Nord (1979) found that the managers had more than two years' extra education than the entrepreneurs. In an earlier entrepreneur sample from Michigan, Collins and Moore (1964) found that 60 per cent had not been educated beyond high school and this in a country where higher education is open to all. In the third-world countries where educational opportunities are limited, compared with the West, the charity Opportunity International that provides loans to the poor has found no shortage of entrepreneurs.

Thus we can conclude that the education of the entrepreneur does not exceed that of the average person in the community and may be lower. Our own anecdotal evidence with entrepreneur programmes for undergraduates in the UK suggests that too much education can actually deter entrepreneurs and bury their talent even deeper.

The exception to this conclusion, as one would expect, is in high technology. Roberts's (1991) work with technical entrepreneurs from MIT showed that 91 per cent had a bachelor degree or higher and 31 per cent had a doctorate. These were mainly in technical fields and so related to the expertise demanded by the product rather than their entrepreneurial activities. Roberts (1991) comments significantly that 'in fact relatively few of the technical entrepreneurs had ever taken business courses before company formation'.

Even this exception has its exceptions. Bill Gates spent most of his time at Harvard preparing the groundwork for what became Microsoft, that is, when he was not playing poker (Wallace and Erickson, 1993). Finally he dropped out and never graduated. Steve Jobs of Apple, and a millionaire before he was thirty, never made university. But Gates and Jobs were both into computers in their teens. Their hobby became a consuming passion and laid the foundation for two amazing companies. To them, further formal education was not important. They felt they knew more about computers than the teachers did and anyway they had a business to get off the ground. So even in the technology world, education may not be as important as some academics like to think.

Age is another interesting determinant for entrepreneurs. It is true that people start businesses at all ages but the real entrepreneurs just cannot wait and often begin in their late teens or early twenties. Two-thirds of the forty-two entrepreneurs, whose start-up stories were first reported in the *Sunday Times* and then summarised in a book (Steiner, 1998), set up their first business before they were twenty-five years old. In our experience with business start programmes around the UK we found that there were two age groups where entrepreneurs emerge. The first was between twenty-two and twenty-eight years. By this time people have had some experience and may have less family and financial commitments than in their thirties. The second was forty-five years and over when people often start a second career and, again, their family and financial responsibilities are less. We shall see in Chapter 4 how Ray Kroc was over fifty years old, and had worked for thirty years as a salesman, before he began McDonald's.

Roberts (1991) found that two-thirds of the MIT spin-off entrepreneurs (a sample of 119) were aged between twenty-eight and thirty-nine. Whilst this contradicts our view of UK entrepreneurs among the general public, it is consistent with our knowledge of the high-technology entrepreneurs in and around the Cambridge area. It is therefore likely that the special nature of high technology and the support structures that have been built around MIT in the USA and Cambridge, England make it possible and acceptable to spin-off a new enterprise despite a family and a mortgage.

In principle we do not believe that age is a determining factor for entrepreneurs except that the true entrepreneur is likely to do it sooner rather than later. We agree with Larson and Rogers (1986) who have experienced and studied the Silicon Valley story and conclude that 'anybody even an eleven year old can become an entrepreneur'.

Work experience   Several researchers have noted that entrepreneurs first gain some work experience in the line of business they later start up (Vesper, 1980). Studies have shown that as many as 90 per cent of entrepreneurs start their business in the same market and industry as they were working in (Brockhaus, 1982). The term 'apprenticeship' has been used by Timmons (1986) to describe this idea and he comments that most successful entrepreneurs 'have accumulated five to ten years experience or more of general management and industry experience prior to their first start-up'.

Entrepreneurs themselves, and those who study them, all agree that experience in the 'university of life' or 'the school of hard knocks' is what develops the entrepreneur (Collins and Moore, 1964). Some do this by starting a number of businesses over a period that do not grow and may even fail. Through this experience they learn lessons they never forget so that when the real opportunity comes along they are ready for it.

Others work for somebody else and learn that way. This has the advantage that they can learn at someone else's expense and get a feel of what makes a business successful before they have to carry the full responsibility themselves. At this point they are at their most receptive and objective. When they have their own business to run, things become rather more subjective and perceptions can get distorted.

A second advantage is that working for someone else often means that potential entrepreneurs find a role model. This can work both ways. If the role model is good then they will be inspired and much can be learnt. Role models can become mentors and often have a hand in getting the new entrepreneur started. If the role model is a bad one then the potential entrepreneur can find the experience so frustrating that he or she hops from job to job and then starts a business too early before having had enough experience.

So far, our consideration of the entrepreneur factors has been largely descriptive and, though they paint a general picture of the entrepreneur, there are many exceptions. Whilst we may be able to *describe* the 'typical entrepreneur' we do not feel that this brings us any nearer to being able to *identify potential* entrepreneurs. The fact that research has repeatedly shown that many entrepreneurs share certain background and personality characteristics, for example, does not mean we have a predictive cause–effect model. Others with the same characteristics do not become entrepreneurs.

The analogy of sport with entrepreneurship is relevant to this debate. The personality profile of an athlete can be defined in general terms as it can be for the entrepreneur. The motivational, emotional and personality characteristics of both can be assessed but when all this is done we are no closer to being able to identify potential winners either in sport or in entrepreneurship. Yet it is clear that there are winners and that their performances speak for themselves. We judge a successful athlete and a successful entrepreneur by their outstanding performance.

Recognising the limitations to this nevertheless valuable research, we now move on a stage and discuss what entrepreneurs actually do and then set this within the entrepreneur process.

What entrepreneurs do: the action factors

In this section we examine ten key action roles associated with entrepreneurs and entrepreneurship, regardless of the context:

1 Entrepreneurs are individuals who make a significant difference.
2 Entrepreneurs are creative and innovative.
3 Entrepreneurs spot and exploit opportunities.
4 Entrepreneurs find the resources required to exploit opportunities.
5 Entrepreneurs are good networkers.
6 Entrepreneurs are determined in the face of adversity.
7 Entrepreneurs manage risk.
8 Entrepreneurs have control of the business.
9 Entrepreneurs put the customer first.
10 Entrepreneurs create capital.

1 Entrepreneurs are individuals who make a significant difference

It is individuals who have always made the difference – not only in business, but in enterprises generally.

(Sir Clive Thompson, Chief Executive, Rentokil Initial)

Entrepreneurs translate 'what is possible' into reality (Kao, 1989). Put another way, they transform a simple, ill-defined idea into something that works (Kets de Vries, 1997). They have their own ways of dealing with opportunities, setbacks and uncertainties to 'creatively create' new products, new services, new organisations and new ways of satisfying customers or doing business.

Entrepreneurs disturb the status quo. They make a difference because they *are* different from most of us. They initiate change and enjoy it. For the entrepreneur it is always 'onwards and upwards'. Barriers and problems that would stop or hinder most of us are for them a spur and a challenge. They get involved directly in the whole operation, they are 'hands on' people, they 'push the cart'.

The remaining nine things on our list of ten that entrepreneurs 'do' all contribute to their ability to make a difference. Obviously not all entrepreneurs do these things equally well but they are all present to some degree and a few of them to an outstanding degree. It is the combination of these special strengths that enable the entrepreneur to make a significant difference.

2 Entrepreneurs are creative and innovative

My Golden Rule is that there are no golden rules.
(George Bernard Shaw, *Maxims for Revolutionists*)

The best way to forecast the future is to invent it!
(George Bernard Shaw, *Man and Superman, Act IV*)

Creativity and innovation are the distinguishing marks of the entrepreneur. This is why they disturb markets and can challenge the large established business. It is the entrepreneur who 'thrives on chaos', as Tom Peters (1989) describes today's business world.

Creativity is a continuous activity for the entrepreneur, always seeing new ways of doing things with little concern of how difficult they might be or whether the resources are available. But creativity in entrepreneurs is combined with the ability to innovate, to take the idea and make it work in practice. This, seeing something through to the end and not being satisfied until all is accomplished, is a central motivation for entrepreneurs. But once one project is accomplished, entrepreneurs seek another 'mountain to climb' because for them creativity and innovation are habitual, something that they just have to keep on doing.

After forty years as an entrepreneur, Armand Hammer was a wealthy man and needed a tax shelter – so he bought into Occidental Petroleum. With only dry oil wells this company was trading at a loss and had total assets of just $78 000. Thirty years later Armand Hammer had grown Occidental to rival the major oil companies of the world. His original investment of $100 000 was worth $11.5 million in a company valued at $16 billion. By then Mr Hammer was eighty-six years old (Hammer, 1988)!

3 Entrepreneurs spot and exploit opportunities

A story is told of a shoe manufacturer who, many years ago, sent two of his marketing graduates to the interior of Australia to see if they could come up with new product ideas for the undeveloped aborigine market. The first one responded: 'There's no business here; the natives don't wear shoes of any type!' The second one was more enthusiastic about the prospects: 'This is a great opportunity; the natives haven't even discovered shoes yet!'

People's perceptions about opportunities vary. How often do we only see an opportunity in retrospect? The 'good idea' was always there to be spotted, but for many of us it's a case of 'Why didn't I think of it first? It's so obvious!'

Entrepreneurs are able to see or craft opportunities that other people miss, even though the data or information that generates the idea is often there for all to see. They are able to synthesise the available information and clarify patterns that escape others. They are comfortable with ambiguity and they can bring clarity by piecing together previously unrelated messages and signals (McGrath, 1997). Not only do they see the opportunities they seem to know, as if by instinct, which of the many is actually worth pursuing.

In some cases the opportunity and need is widely recognised and talked about. We have been told that great wealth awaits the person who designs a reliable and low product-cost vending machine for French fries. The inventor might be the person who solves the problem but it is the entrepreneur who exploits that opportunity and turns it into a reality. Those gifted few who, like James Dyson reported in Chapter 4, are both inventors and entrepreneurs have a special edge.

4 Entrepreneurs find the resources required to exploit opportunities

Charles Forte did not have the financial resources to buy the Café Royal in London but he wanted it badly. His bankers would not advance the money under any circumstances and yet he found the resources, signed the deal and reported back to his colleagues 'We haven't paid for it yet, but we've bought it'.

(Forte, 1997)

The success of the entrepreneur is rarely due to a flash of inspiration or luck; rather it is the conscientious and disciplined exploitation of resources which are already to hand or which can somehow be found. Entrepreneurs are not put off by not having the resources they need; in some ways it seems to stimulate and challenge them. They are experts at exploiting contacts and sources, 'begging, stealing and borrowing', when necessary (Stevenson, 1997). In many cases, it is not necessary that resources are 'state-of-the-art' or the 'best available' but are simply ones that will perform satisfactorily. Entrepreneurs are pragmatists who find and put together the minimum resources required for the job.

5 Entrepreneurs are good networkers

The close networks that characterise Silicon Valley give the region an advantage over other areas.

(Larson and Rogers, 1986)

Entrepreneurs know 'where' to find resources (action factor 4) and 'how' to control a business (action factor 8) but they also know 'who' (Gibb, 1998). They are quick to build up networks of people that they know can help them. They have what has been called 'expertise orientation' (Clifton and Harding, 1986) – that is they know when they need experts and know how to use them effectively. Rather than exploiting such people they often become friends that stay with them over the years. When Charles Forte set up his first milk bar in London he used two young property agents to find him the premises he needed. 'They were even younger than I was, but had already established a considerable business. I was truly impressed by them and they remained life-long friends' (Forte, 1997).

Entrepreneurs are good networkers. When it comes to putting a team together, as Nolan Bushnell's earlier story illustrates, they know who to talk to. In Bushnell's Silicon Valley the bars and the restaurants were favourite places to 'talk shop'. The informal, no fee, no bylaws Homebrew Computer Club in Silicon Valley had a membership of 500 or so computerphiles almost as soon as it was started. It was a networkers' delight. Larson and Rogers (1986) reached the important conclusion that 'information exchange is a dominant, distinguishing characteristic of Silicon Valley'.

6 Entrepreneurs are determined in the face of adversity

People fall into three categories:
Those who make things happen.
Those who watch things happen.
Those who are left to ask what did happen.

If you think you can, you can.
If you think you can't, you're right.

(George Bernard Shaw, Reason)

Entrepreneurs are motivated to succeed; they possess determination and self-belief. On the one hand, this is a major reason for their success; they refuse to be beaten and persevere when 'the going gets tough'. On the other hand, this also explains why some would-be entrepreneurs fail. They have too much faith in their own ability; they believe they are infallible and can do almost anything; they refuse to accept they might be wrong; they fail to seek help when they need it.

Successful entrepreneurs are also able to deal with unexpected obstacles, the kind that cannot be predicted in a business plan. Most companies experience three or four life-threatening crises in their early years; to survive this period the true entrepreneur deals with these crises and wins through. He or she is an 'overcomer' who can resolve problems under pressure.

Entrepreneurs use their creative and innovation skills in these difficult times. Somehow they really do turn problems into opportunities. Allen Jones of AJ Restaurants comments 'I think I am a persistent devil. When things go wrong I generally go harder. I try not to be beaten and find another way to solve the problem' (Williams, 1994).

7 Entrepreneurs manage risk

There are two times in a man's life when he should not speculate – when he cannot afford it – and when he can.

(Mark Twain)

We invariably associate entrepreneurs with risk, but here we need to use our terms carefully. Entrepreneurs take risks, certainly, but risks they believe they understand and can manage. Whilst they may well take risks that other less-enterprising people would avoid, relatively few fall into the category of mere *adventurers*, very high risk-takers who take chances intuitively and with little analytical rigour. These ventures will sometimes pay off handsomely, but they are also prone to fail because they are always based more on hope than judgement (Derr, 1982).

In reality, many entrepreneurs will avoid this 'bridge too far' situation and instead prefer perpetual movement and improvement, continually hoping to find and exploit manageable risks and opportunities (Churchill, 1997). Their approach to strategy is a quick but careful initial screening of an idea, using only limited analysis to evaluate the quality of the idea. Their success lies in vigilance, learning, flexibility and change during implementation (Bhide, 1994).

Entrepreneurs are not risk averse, they prefer to find ways of saying 'yes' rather than 'no' and then are willing to accept responsibility for their decision.

8 Entrepreneurs have control of the business

I now learnt a lesson I shall never forget. I realised that until I could find the right balance between income on the one hand, and the cost of raw materials, wages, rent, rates and other overheads on the other, the sums would not add up. In fact there and then I worked out the essential ratios which would guarantee the profits.

(Forte, 1997)

It is easy for a business to get out of control and for the directors and managers to feel that the business is running them. Entrepreneurs do not allow this to happen. They are not 'control freaks' but they pay attention to detail and develop their own key indicators of performance that they monitor carefully. The *essential ratios* that Charles Forte worked out in his twenties were the same ones he used when he bought the Lyons Hotel group and turned it into profit. 'We used our tried financial formulae, the ratio of sales to gross profit that we knew was obtainable' (Forte, 1997).

Some entrepreneurs keep a loose rein on the business whilst others manage it very tightly but both know exactly the state of their business. They seem to have a knack for knowing what is important and what to keep an eye on. They *are* able to see 'the wood for the trees' but they also know which trees to watch. Thus it is that they are able to exercise strategic control over their business. Tim Waterstone of the Waterstone book chain tells us he has 'the gift of simplicity, of understanding how simple business is. I can lift out the only things that really matter' (Williams, 1994).

9 Entrepreneurs put the customer first

We always accepted that success is never based on a one-off transaction; it comes only by encouraging the customer to return again and again. It all sounds very simple; put like this, almost too simple. But it is true.

(Forte, 1997)

It is perhaps fairly obvious that entrepreneurs put the customer first and yet most of the studies of entrepreneurs do not mention it directly. Instead they speak of the need for market knowledge or observe that the best entrepreneurs are salesmen.

The market for any new enterprise is always a difficult place, with surprises just around the corner. But entrepreneurs thrive on this uncertainty and generally end up making a success of a product or of a market sector that was quite different to the one they started with. The reason they do this is that they listen to the customer, they are as quick to find out why they have won a sale and as to why they have lost one. They are able and willing to respond to what the customer is telling them.

10 Entrepreneurs create capital

> Society is always in deep debt to the entrepreneurs who sustain it and rarely consume by themselves more than the smallest share of what they give society.
>
> (Gilder, 1986)

Creativity and innovation, resource acquisition, control of the business, networking and the other 'action' factors are all part of the entrepreneur's intellectual and emotional capital. They are the currency that entrepreneurs bring to the table and which they use to generate new kinds of capital external to themselves. These are:

- financial capital
- social capital
- aesthetic capital.

The entrepreneur is generally associated with the first of these, financial capital, but we also want to include those who create social capital and aesthetic capital. This is because we see people operating in these areas who are clearly entrepreneurs by our definition. They create and innovate to build something of recognised value, but of course we do need to use measures other than pounds sterling or dollars to define this capital.

The measures of 'people helped' and 'jobs created' are used by the charity Opportunity International, which was set up by an Australian entrepreneur David Bussau. 'From 1981 to 1993 David and his partners in the Opportunity Network made loans to 46,000 entrepreneurs and created 77,700 jobs among the poor' (Sider, 1996). Their Annual Reports use 'the number of lives transformed' as a measure of social capital generated in the year. Bussau is discussed further under 'Social and environmental entrepreneurs' in Chapter 7.

The action factors and entrepreneur process   We have been considering what entrepreneurs do – their action factors. Actions are always part of a whole and so we now place them within the entrepreneur process. We do this using two process models. The first is specific to the action factors and the second is more general.

In the first model, shown in Figure 1.1, the starting point of the process is the motivation to *make a difference* (action factor 1). As we discuss later in this section there are other motivators for the entrepreneur but this we believe to be the most important. The ability to *create and innovate* (2) is the lifeblood of the process, without

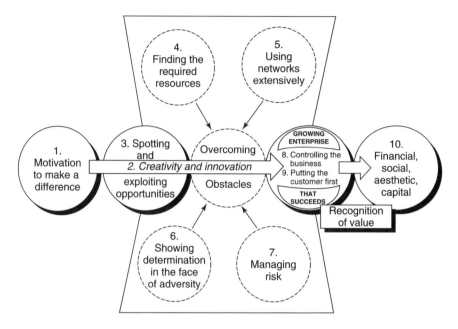

Figure 1.1 *The entrepreneur process diagram*

this vital blood flow the process would not happen. The first step in the process is to *spot and exploit an opportunity* (3) and then as things move forward obstacles appear. We group the next four action factors around the way in which entrepreneurs deal with these obstacles. They find *the required resources* (4), *use networks extensively* (5), are *determined in the face of adversity* (6) and *manage risk* (7). Using their creativity and innovation talent they turn the obstacles into opportunities. All these contribute to a growing enterprise that succeeds because entrepreneurs know how to *control the business* (8) and are consistent in *putting the customer first* (9). The outcome of the *entrepreneur process* is the *creation of capital* (10). Entrepreneurs seek recognition that they have created this outcome and really added value in line with their motivation to *make a difference* (1), which began the process.

The second entrepreneur process model has two distinct stages as indicated in Figure 1.2. These stages are expressed in terms of roles – the *opportunity-spotter* and the *project champion* – which together make up the entrepreneur.

The *opportunity-spotter* who sees or realises the potential for an idea may not be the originator of the idea; equally, the inventor of the idea may not appreciate how it might be exploited. Opportunity-spotters see the gap in the market. It could be an opportunity for making money, or for creating something of perceived value for the community (social entrepreneurship), or for adding to our artistic or aesthetic environment. The direction will depend upon the personal environment of the individual and the world in which he or she is looking for opportunities. Whilst business entrepreneurs will always emerge in a capitalist economy, people operating in a religious environment will find their opportunity there. This choice of environment is affected by personal values and interests – it is important in developing entrepreneurs that

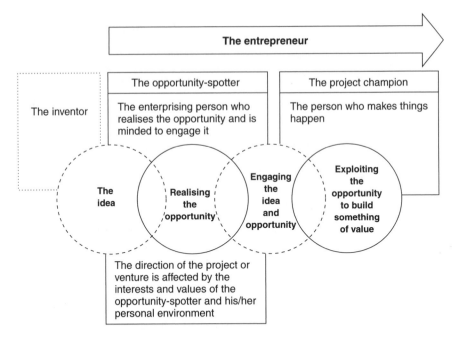

Figure 1.2   *The entrepreneur, the opportunity-spotter and the project champion*

they are able to work in the environment which is right and appropriate for their talents and interests. Whilst business entrepreneurs and some social entrepreneurs are responsive to external environmental opportunities and gaps, other social entrepreneurs and most artistic entrepreneurs are driven from within to search for ways in which they can exploit their personal gifts and talents.

Project champions are people who make things happen. They gather together the necessary resources, and they know where they can find help and support. They are completers. Opportunity-spotters may well be minded to engage the idea and take it forward but unless they possess the implementation capabilities of the project champion they will not succeed. The entrepreneur is successful because he or she combines the opportunity-spotter and the project champion in the one person with the ability to combine and execute both roles effectively.

Many of us do see opportunities to some extent – we might even be described as ideas people – but we do not possess either the abilities or the inclination to exploit the opportunity and build something distinctive and valuable. At the same time, others are extremely capable implementers. When provided with a challenge, a task or a project they can organise and lead a team, manage the necessary stages and bring everything to a successful conclusion. They simply need the good idea or a defined goal.

Whilst an individual's personal talents will affect whether he or she operates most comfortably as an opportunity-spotter in a business, social, religious or artistic environment, project championing skills and abilities are similar in every area of activity. It can be difficult, or even traumatic, when opportunity-spotters are not natural project champions but remain in charge of the project and fail to engage the necessary help and support. The story is told of Sir Christopher Wren over-running his completion deadline for St Paul's Cathedral by fifteen years. For the last two of these he was required to work without pay, in danger of imprisonment for alleged incompetence!

Small-business people spot a limited opportunity for something they can do, and choose to exploit it – but essentially that is where it stops. The opportunity does not have real growth potential. Or they do not behave habitually, finding further new opportunities to graft on to the business. They are not true opportunity-spotters.

Managers who champion change in larger organisations are often project champions acting on behalf of their organisations. Sometimes they are encouraged to come up with new ideas and see them through to fruition – as we shall see in Chapter 3. They are known as intrapreneurs, or internal entrepreneurs.

It will be appreciated that a study of the 'action' factors is vital for understanding the entrepreneur process, but again, like the personality and environmental factors, it does not help us spot those people with the potential to be successful entrepreneurs. Consequently we now move on to consider the important work of The Gallup Organisation that gave us the link we needed into our ideas of talent and temperament. It was from this starting point that we were able to develop our approach to identifying the potential entrepreneur that we describe in Chapter 2.

Gallup's 'life themes'

We review the general work of Gallup and their specific findings on entrepreneurs under the following headings:

- Gallup's 'life themes' and 'StrengthsFinder®'.
- Gallup's 'Entrepreneur Perceiver' Interview.

Gallup refers to The Gallup Organisation.

Gallup's 'life themes' and 'StrengthsFinder®'

> Every person can do something better than 10,000 other people. It's OK to be you.
>
> (Jill Garrett, previously Managing Director, Gallup UK)

Gallup, although better known for its opinion polls, has had a strong interest in personnel selection over many years and has developed its own approach based on role and talent (Buckingham and Coffman, 1999; Buckingham and Clifton, 2001). This side of their business was pioneered by Don Clifton, himself an entrepreneur, who was previously Professor of Educational Psychology at the University of Nebraska in the 1950s and 1960s. From his university base, Clifton set up Selection Research Inc (SRI) and became its full-time chief executive officer (CEO) in 1969. In 1987 SRI acquired Gallup with Don Clifton as CEO; a position now held by his son, Jim Clifton. Though Don Clifton has recently retired as Chairman of the Board he still chairs the Gallup International Research and Education Centre.

In this section we review the development of Gallup's understanding of life themes and their measurement.

Life themes   Gallup uses the term 'life theme' to describe a 'person's innate behaviour, thoughts and feelings' (Garrett, 1998). Don Clifton has defined it as 'a consistent and recurring pattern of thought and/or behaviour' (Clifton and Harding, 1986). More recently (Buckingham and Clifton, 2001) Gallup has used the term 'talent theme' rather than 'life theme' to describe the same 'recurring pattern of thought, feeling, or behaviour'.

Gallup's view that life or talent themes come from an inner psychological core that is inborn and enduring is similar to that of Hollander (1971) reported earlier. Figure 1.3 shows the underpinning model used by Gallup, with life themes at the centre, surrounded first by skills and then by experience.

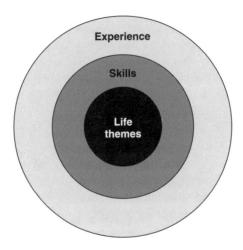

Figure 1.3   *The Gallup model*

When the life themes, skills and experiences are the right ones for the job, then we have a person who can fulfill a given role with excellence. Gallup is very specific about the need for excellence and about what it means by *excellence*. It is not just better than average, or simply the opposite of bad, but it is 'the capacity for recurrent high levels of performance' (Garrett, 1998). Individually we are all capable of high achievement in some area of activity. If we can identify this activity, based on our real strengths, then we can exploit them to build satisfyingly high outcomes – we can achieve excellence. But if we are not aware of our true strengths, then it is likely we will take on activities to which we are not suited. Not only will this be a deflating and stressful experience but a valuable resource will be wasted.

Gallup has determined the life themes required for a range of different roles. Using focus groups of people who were already performing to a high level in a particular role, they identified the set of life themes involved. Different roles have not only different life themes but the number of them is not the same. Thus the *leader* set has twenty different life themes and the *entrepreneur* set has twelve.

The potential to achieve excellence in a role does not require a person to possess each of the designated 'life themes' to the same extent. A typical profile for an outstanding leader, for example, would be three of the twenty themes at an unsuppressible level. They would be so strong that they would characterise the leader. They would be what people saw and recognised. Thirteen more would be habitual themes, strong enough to be there all the time influencing behaviour. The final four themes would be achievable with effort.

Gallup is not looking for outstanding strengths in all the life themes nor are they seeking average competencies across the whole set. The Gallup approach seeks to identify 'Mr or Ms Something Special' rather than 'Mr or Ms Average'. With only three or four of the possible twenty life themes having to be unsuppressible, there can be plenty of variety, which is why leaders can be so different from one another. Their personal style of leadership and the areas where they are found – from industry to the military, and from charities to exploration – are influenced by their profile of relative strengths across the twenty life themes, and by their circumstances that encourage them to follow certain paths. In exactly the same way, entrepreneurs can be found in industry, in the community, in music – and even in criminal activity as we discuss in Chapter 9.

Buckingham and Coffman (1999) have summarised the work of Gallup (SRI) over the last twenty-five years. They use the word 'talent' when referring to life themes and by way of example provide a list of thirty-nine talents, which they have drawn from the study of more than 150 distinct roles. They group these talents into the following three basic categories:

1 Striving talents that explain the why of a person.
2 Thinking talents that explain the how of a person.
3 Relating talents that explain the who of a person.

Table 1.1 is a selection from their list of thirty-nine talents to show the general spread but are not representative of any specific role.

Inspection of Table 1.1 shows that there are two sets of classification possible. The first is the one used by Buckingham and Coffman with talents or life themes being either striving, thinking or relating. The second is found within their description of talents as drives, needs or abilities. Of the two we consider that our words 'talent' and 'temperament' correlate more closely with the second classification. Thus 'talent' equals *abilities* and 'temperament' divides into *needs* and *drives* which are different sides of the same coin, the coin of 'temperament'. 'Technique' is not involved here because it is not a life theme but it does relate to the skill set that surrounds the life themes as Figure 1.3 indicates.

In a subsequent publication (Buckingham and Clifton, 2001) Gallup gave a list of thirty-four talents which, though slightly different to their earlier list of thirty-nine, is in principle the same. There is also a change in description from 'life theme' to 'talent theme' which we welcome and is more in line with our own thinking on talent. However a more important change is found in a shift in their approach. They move from their earlier focus on the set of life themes required for a particular role to consider the set of talent themes possessed by the individual. As before, excellence is achieved by building and developing these strengths but now it is more a case of the individual achieving excellence than of a role being performed excellently.

Table 1.1   *A selection of Gallup's life themes*

Striving talents (six selected from eleven)

Achiever	A drive that is internal, constant and self-imposed
Competition	A need to gauge your success comparatively
Belief	A need to orient your life around prevailing values
Mission	A drive to put your beliefs into action
Service	A drive to be of service to others
Vision	A drive to paint value-based word pictures about the future

Thinking talents (seven selected from fourteen)

Focus	An ability to set goals and use them every day to guide actions
Responsibility	A need to assume personal accountability for your work
Performance orientation	A need to be objective and to measure performance
Strategic thinking	An ability to play out alternative scenarios in the future
Problem-solving	An ability to think things through with incomplete data
Formulation	An ability to find coherent patterns within incoherent data sets
Creativity	An ability to break existing configurations in favour of more effective/appealing ones

Relating talents (seven selected from fourteen)

Woo	A need to gain the approval of others
Multirelator	An ability to build an extensive network of acquaintances
Interpersonal	An ability to purposefully capitalise on relationships
Individualised perception	An awareness of and attentiveness to individual differences (ability)
Team	A need to build feelings of mutual support
Activator	An impatience to move others to action (drive)
Courage	An ability to use emotion to overcome resistance

Gallup describes this set of strengths as a person's Signature Themes. These are the talent strengths that we lead with. 'No matter what the situation, they filter your world, forcing you to behave in certain recurrent ways' (Buckingham and Clifton, 2001). They define our habitual behaviour. We need to recognise our Signature Themes and then build on them.

Gallup makes two core assumptions about people (Buckingham and Clifton, 2001) which are the basis for this approach:

1 Each person's talents are enduring and unique.
2 Each person's greatest room for growth is in the areas of the person's greatest strengths.

Although we think that their talent list is a combination of both talent and temperament we do agree with their core assumption that talents are enduring and unique. Gallup is aware that their talent theme list can be put into various categories as with their earlier list but they now consider that the list stands on its own and would not benefit from being classified in line with current personality models (Buckingham and Clifton, 2001).

Their second assumption is perhaps more controversial. Gallup has found that most people do not accept that strengths should be the focus of personal growth. In Japan and China their research shows that just 24 per cent of the population believe that 'knowing their strengths will help them improve the most'. Even in the USA, which has an achievement culture, the corresponding number only rises to 41 per cent. Gallup makes the important observation that in cultures where there is a fear of failure, people are more likely to focus on their weaknesses than on their strengths (Buckingham and Clifton, 2001). Whilst this may be the natural thing to do, the best way to avoid failure is to recognise your strengths and then build on them.

Measuring life themes   Gallup's approach has always included not only the definition of life themes but also their measurement. In their early work they devised a series of questionnaires for different roles based on the set of life themes required. Trained interviewers took people through these role-based questionnaires, usually by telephone, to assess their strengths against the required life themes. The interviewers listened for particular responses and marked against their presence or absence. Gallup (SRI) termed these 'perceiver' interviews – the word 'perceiver' being used to emphasise the point that the questionnaire was about obtaining 'an understanding and not a score'.

The recent work of Gallup has taken this evaluation to the next stage. They now have a web-based questionnaire, termed StrengthsFinder®, which measures a person's strengths across thirty-four talent themes. As commented above, they are now measuring the individual. The role to which he or she is best suited is another matter. The questionnaire takes the form of 180 paired statements and the respondent has to judge between which of two statements describes them best. With 180 questions this is quite a lengthy procedure but there is a time limit on the response so that in all, the questionnaire takes about forty-five minutes to complete. Gallup then sends the respondent, by e-mail, a list of their five strongest talent themes with a description of each.

Gallup's book 'Now, Discover your Strengths' (Buckingham and Clifton, 2001) gives the descriptions of all thirty-four talent themes so that it is possible to do a self-assessment before completing the Internet questionnaire. In our experience there is an immediate correlation with either two or three of the person's top five talent themes. More careful reading of the talent theme descriptions confirms the remainder although there is often one surprise that had not been considered but which after reflection is thought to be correct.

Gallup's 'entrepreneur perceiver' interview

In 1986, SRI developed their 'entrepreneur perceiver' questionnaire. Focus groups and interviews with successful entrepreneurs identified twelve 'life themes'.

The questionnaire developed from this research comprised eighty-four questions, with seven questions for each theme.

The twelve entrepreneur 'life themes' are set out in Table 1.2 with brief descriptions of each theme based on more detailed descriptions provided to us by Don Clifton. The themes marked with an asterisk can also be found in Gallup's general list in Table 1.1, where the descriptions are slightly different.

In practice, these life themes rarely stand alone and their inter-actions are important. For example, *creativity*, *profit orientation* and *focus* come together in the entrepreneur so that the best ideas are generated, identified and targeted effectively. *Focus* enables *dedication* to bear fruit. The proverb 'necessity is the mother of invention' is another way of saying that *opportunity* drives *creativity*. We see *urgency* as the extreme end of *activator* and close to mania discussed earlier. *Team* and *individual perception* work together. *Ego drive* and *dedication* are the main motivators and give impetus and purpose to the entrepreneur.

Following the Gallup approach outlined earlier, the successful entrepreneur will have some *unsuppressible* life themes which will dominate. Others will be *habitual* themes and a few will be *achievable with effort*. In principle, this helps to explain the diversity we find among entrepreneurs. However, it is clear that some themes are more important than others. An unpublished study by Gallup of twenty entrepreneurs (Clifton and Harding, 1986) gives some indication of which these are. In the study entrepreneurs were taken through the 'entrepreneur perceiver' interview and the results evaluated statistically. When we compared the more successful entrepreneurs in the sample, the themes that came out the strongest for them were *creativity*, *profit orientation*, *courage* and *focus*, and in that order.

We develop further the idea that the entrepreneur possesses specific attributes or life themes in the next chapter where we provide a basis for identifying the potential entrepreneur. We also set it in the context of our three-part understanding of the entrepreneur as a combination of talent, temperament and technique.

Table 1.2   *The Gallup entrepreneur themes*

Entrepreneur life themes	Summary description
1 Dedication	Consumed by a goal or purpose
2 Focus*	Discriminates and targets
3 Profit orientation	Advantage-focused
4 Ego drive	Wants to make a recognised difference
5 Urgency	No time to waste, must take action now
6 Courage*	Determined in the face of adversity
7 Activator*	Wants to make it happen
8 Opportunity	Sees possibilities, not problems
9 Creativity*	Buzzing with ideas
10 Expertise orientation	Knows own limits and finds experts
11 Team*	Gets the right people together
12 Individualised perception*	Sees and uses strengths in others

References

Bhide, A. (1994). How entrepreneurs craft strategies that work. *Harvard Business Review*, March–April.

Bolton, W.K. (1986). Entrepreneurial opportunities for the academic. UK Science Park Association, Annual Conference.

Brockhaus, R.H. (1982). The psychology of the entrepreneur. In *Encyclopaedia of Entrepreneurship* (C.A. Kent, D. Sexton and K. Vesper, eds), Prentice-Hall.

Brockhaus, R.H. and Horwitz, P.S. (1986). The psychology of the entrepreneur. In *The Art and Science of Entrepreneurship* (D. Sexton and R.W. Smilor, eds), Ballinger.

Brockhaus, R.H. and Nord, W.R. (1979). An exploration of factors affecting the entrepreneurial decision: personal characteristics vs environmental conditions. *Proceedings of the National Academy of Management*. NAC.

Buckingham, M. and Clifton, D.O. (2001). *Now, Discover your Strengths*. Simon & Schuster.

Buckingham, M. and Coffman, C. (1999). *First, Break All the Rules*. Simon & Schuster.

Burns, P. and Dewhurst, J. (eds) (1989). *Small Business and Entrepreneurship*. Macmillan Education.

Burns, T. (1999). *Break the Curve: The Entrepreneur's Blueprint for Small Business Success*. International Thompson Business Press.

Butler, G. and McManus, F. (1998). *Psychology*. Oxford University Press.

Buttner, E.H. (1992). Entrepreneurial stress: is it hazardous to your health? *Journal of Managerial Issues*, Summer, 223–240.

Bygrave, B. (1998). Building an entrepreneurial economy: lessons from the United States. *Business Strategy Review*, **9** (2), 11–18.

Churchill, N.C. (1997). Breaking down the wall: scaling the ladder. In *Mastering Enterprise* (S. Birley and D. Muzyka, eds), Financial Times/Pitman.

Clifton, D.O. and Harding, R.E. (1986). A statistical analysis of the psychometric properties of the SRI Entrepreneur Interview. *Gallup Report*, September.

Collins, O.F. and Moore, D.B. (1964). *The Enterprising Man*. Michigan State University Press.

Derlega, V.J., Winstead, B.A. and Jones, W.H. (1991). *Personality: Contemporary Theory and Research*. Nelson-Hall.

Derr, C.B. (1982). Living on adrenalin: the adventurer-entrepreneur. *Human Resource Management*, Summer.

Eco, U. (2002). *Baudolino*. Secker & Warburg.

Eysenk, H.J. (1965). *Fact and Fiction in Psychology*. Penguin.

Forte, C. (1997). *Forte*. Pan Books.

Fukuyama, F. (1995). *Trust*. Hamish Hamilton.

Garrett, J. (1998). Gallup's discoveries about leaders. At work together, Spring Harvest Conference, Sheffield.

Gibb, A. (1998). In Management development for small and medium enterprises: setting out the challenge, *TEC National Council Policy Paper*, July.

Gilder, G. (1986). *The Spirit of Enterprise*, Penguin.

Goldsmith, M. and Wharton, M. (1993). *Knowing Me, Knowing You*. SPCK.

Goleman, D. (1996). *Emotional Intelligence*. Bloomsbury.

Hammer, A. (1988). *Hammer: Witness to History*. Coronet edn. Hodder & Stoughton.

Hisrich, R.D. (1990). Entrepreneurship/intrapreneurship. *American Psychologist*, February, 209–222.

Hisrich, R.D. and Brush, C. (1984). The women entrepreneurs. *Journal of Small Business Management*, **22** (1), 31–37.

Hollander, E.P. (1971). *Principles and Methods of Social Psychology*. 2nd edn. Oxford University Press.

Hornaday, J.A. (1982). Research about living entrepreneurs. In *Encyclopaedia of Entrepreneurship* (C.A. Kent, D.L. Sexton and K. Vesper, eds), Prentice-Hall.

Jardine, L. (1997). *Worldly Goods*. Papermac.

Jones, S. (1993). *Psychological Testing for Managers*. Piatkus.

Kao, J.J. (1989). *Entrepreneurship, Creativity and Organisation*, Prentice-Hall.

Kao, J.J. (1991). *The Entrepreneur*. Prentice-Hall.

Keirsey, D. and Bates, M. (1984). *Please Understand Me: Character and Temperament Types*, Prometheus Nemesis Books.

Kent, C.A. (ed.) (1984). *The Environment of Entrepreneurship*. Lexington Books.

Kets de Vries, M. (1997). Creative rebels with a cause. In *Mastering Enterprise* (S. Birley and D. Muzyka, eds), Financial Times/Pitman.

Kummerow, J.M., Barger, N.J. and Kirby, L.K. (1997). *Work Types*. Warner Books.

Kuratko, D.F. and Hodgetts, R.M. (1998). *Entrepreneurship: A Contemporary Approach*. 4th edn. Dryden Press.

Larson, J.K. and Rogers, E.M. (1986). *Silicon Valley Fever*. Unwin Counterpoint.

Martens, R.A. (1976). Competitiveness and sport. International Congress of Physical Activity Sciences, Quebec City.

McClelland, D.C. (1961). *The Achieving Society*. Van Nostrand.

McClelland, D.C. (1965). Need for achievement and entrepreneurship: a longitudinal study. *Journal of Personality and Social Psychology*, **1**, 389–392.

McGrath, R.G. (1997). The parsimonious path to profit. In *Mastering Enterprise* (S. Birley and D. Muzyka, eds), Financial Times/Pitman.

Peters, T. (1989). *Thriving on Chaos*. Pan Books.

Roberts, E.B. (1991). *Entrepreneurs in High-technology*. Oxford University Press.

Rotter, J.B. (1966). Generalised expectancies for internal versus external control of re-inforcement. *Psychological Monographs*, **80**, 609.

Rotter, J.B. (1971). External control and internal control. *Psychology Today*, **5** (1), 37–42, 58–59.

Sider, R. (1996). *Bread of Life*. SPCK.

Steiner, R. (1998). *My First Break*. News International.

Stevenson, H. (1997). The six dimensions of entrepreneurship. In *Mastering Enterprise* (S. Birley and D. Muzyka, eds), Financial Times/Pitman.

Tarnas, R. (1996). *The Passion of the Western Mind*. Pimlico.

Timmons, J.A. (1986). Growing up big: entrepreneurship and the creation of high-potential ventures. In *The Art and Science of Entrepreneurship* (D. Sexton & R.W. Smilor, eds), Ballinger.

Vesper, K.H. (1980). *New Venture Strategies*. Prentice-Hall.

Wallace, J. and Erickson, J. (1993). *Hard Drive*. John Wiley.

Watts, G.W. (2000). Psychologist-entrepreneurs: roles, roll-ups and rolodexes. *The Psychologist-Manager Journal*, **4** (1), 79–90.

Whybrow, P.C. (1999). *A Mood Apart*. Picador.

Williams, S. (1994). *Break-Out: Life beyond the Corporation*. Penguin.

Woods, B. (1998). *Applying Psychology in Sport*. Hodder & Stoughton.

2 Identifying the entrepreneur

In the previous chapter we defined the entrepreneur. Now we turn to the rather different task of identifying the entrepreneur. We first present a framework based on talent, temperament and technique which we believe provides a new way of looking at the entrepreneur. We then develop an approach to identifying the entrepreneur based on six attributes of the entrepreneur that conveniently form the word FACETS. The outcome of this approach is our 'entrepreneur indicator' with which we conclude the chapter.

A definition is about description, identification is about recognition. It is normally straightforward to go from definition to identification, but when the subject is a person, this is not the case. Identifying a particular kind of individual, such as the entrepreneur, is a subjective process no matter how well defined or understood. But it is not only subjectivity that bedevils evaluation and identification. There is the added difficulty that people change, develop and mature over time. When presented with the right opportunity or the right motivation, people often discover entrepreneurial talents they never knew they had. This is why identifying potential entrepreneurs is a different task from identifying practising entrepreneurs. Part Two describes more than one hundred of the latter and builds up a picture of the entrepreneur. There it is possible to see the key elements of our definition in operation. There are examples of creativity and innovation in action, and what the different entrepreneurs have built is clear to see. However, potential entrepreneurs cannot be treated in this way because they have yet to demonstrate their talents.

We see this identification of the potential entrepreneur as the real challenge in the field of entrepreneurship – not education, training, advice, finance or premises, important though these support elements might be. Programme after programme has been set up over the last twenty years to promote entrepreneurship and enterprise but the results have been disappointing. We believe that this will continue to be the case until we have some way of identifying those people with the potential to be successful entrepreneurs.

In this book and specifically in this chapter we offer a methodology that we believe meets this need. Our approach has two main elements or keys that unlock the puzzle. First there is the idea that entrepreneurs combine talent, temperament and technique to achieve excellence. This approach has a sports background but applies equally to business where entrepreneurs, leaders and managers each have their own set of talents, temperaments and techniques.

The second key is a set of six habitual attributes that are the talents and temperament of the entrepreneur. They conveniently form the word FACETS. Because these attributes can be measured they form a basis for identifying the potential entrepreneur. This material is new to this edition and is a summary of parts of our book 'The Entrepreneur in Focus: achieve your potential' (Bolton and Thompson, 2003).

We now consider these two elements in turn.

Talent, temperament and technique

Len Hutton was perhaps the greatest opening batsman that England has ever produced. He had a *talent* as a batsman that few possess, he was a natural. The coach who took Hutton under his wing when he was 16 years old and taught him the *technique* of batting commented that 'no instructor was ever blessed with a more voracious learner' – a sure sign of real talent. Yet Hutton rarely gave his talent free rein because of his obsession with batting technique. He was a perfectionist always striving to improve so that his natural ability was often inhibited.

Temperament was Hutton's area of greatest ambiguity. His ability to focus and concentrate was legendary. He once batted for more than thirteen hours to set a world record individual score of 364. His weakness was his caution and low risk approach. He found it difficult to cope with stress and believed that 'tension was the root cause of failure and the bane of cricket'. He knew this from bitter experience for in his first match in county cricket and his first at international level he failed to score.

(Tyson, 1987)

Len Hutton's story is an example of the interplay between *talent, temperament* and *technique*. It shows the importance that each has but also how they combine to produce or limit excellence as the case may be. This trinity of talent, temperament and technique is like the three-legged stool, if one leg is missing it will fall over and if they are not all in balance it will be uncomfortable and even dangerous to sit on!

In this chapter we will be talking mainly about talent and temperament but that does not mean that we relegate the importance of technique. We concentrate on talent and temperament because these are the areas where a case has to be made. The importance of technique for the entrepreneur is already well accepted, perhaps too much so for it cannot stand alone. Training courses and how-to-do-it books for entrepreneurs and those wanting to start a business are readily available.

We now consider two important aspects of our tripartite theme:

- Linking talent, temperament and technique.
- Talent, temperament and roles.

Linking talent, temperament and technique

In cricket, Tyson (1987) remarks that 'skill and success flow from the inner wells of temperament and character'. In athletics, Harre (1982) comments: 'The athlete must bring to bear not only his physical faculties, skill and intellectual abilities, but also his willpower and character, his moral convictions and traits.' It is, therefore, interesting to compare the prevailing media opinion about the current demise of the England cricket and football teams.

In 1998 a BBC Radio commentator, reviewing why England had again lost the Ashes series against Australia, commented that man for man both teams matched each other in talent and technique. The difference lay in their temperament. Australia had a will to win that the English team could not equal. In contrast, the character and commitment of English footballers is an acknowledged strength. Many of them repeatedly 'give everything' for the full ninety minutes of a match, but still the team fails to win. Passes go astray; shots fly past the post or go straight into the goalkeeper's hands; free kicks are conceded in dangerous positions. Few supporters will ever forget the team's failure in penalty shoot-outs at the end of important World and European Cup matches. 'Footballers with a high standard of technical ability and coaches with a sophisticated understanding of the technical requirements of the modern international game ... are missing' (Harverson, 1999). In other words, the weakness this time concerns talent and technique, not temperament.

On a more positive note, the appointment of Michael Vaughan as the England captain for one-day matches was greeted with the headline 'Vaughan has talent and temperament to handle pressure' (Martin-Jenkins, 2003).

Although we generally know what we mean by talent and temperament, and we can recognise them as different things, they remain difficult to define in a precise way. Yet, there is relatively little written about talent, and what there is often uses other words than 'talent' to describe the same thing. Thus Woods (1998) uses 'innate ability' which is closest to the dictionary definition. Others use words like 'strengths' (Clifton and Nelson, 1996), 'expertise' (Ericsson and Smith, 1991) and 'exceptional abilities' (Howe, 1990a). Psychologists often seem sceptical about the idea of 'gifts and talents' and see them as unscientific labels, though some are prepared to accept that there is truth in the claim that their origins are innate (Howe, 1990b).

Our view is that talent does exist, that we all have a collection of talents but that for a whole host of reasons we all too often fail to identify and therefore develop and exploit them. Sometimes the reason is found in our temperament, but on other occasions it is a matter of opportunity. By providing loans to the poor David Bussau (Chapter 7) shows that entrepreneurial talent does emerge when given the opportunity.

Temperament is a more 'academically respectable' word than talent and a number of recent books have brought new findings about temperament to the attention of the general public. Goleman (1996) tells us that 'temperament can be defined in terms of moods that typify our emotional life. To some degree we each have such a favoured emotional range; temperament is given at birth, part of the genetic lottery'. But he says that 'temperament is not destiny' and that life's experiences, particularly 'the emotional lessons of childhood, can have a profound effect on temperament, either amplifying or muting an innate predisposition'. Whybrow (1999) and Buckingham and Coffman (1999) describe temperament respectively in terms of an 'emotional landscape' and 'highways through the brain' that are formed as we grow up and learn from our environment and experiences, but relate back to a genetic template.

For our purposes, it is important to note that there is an inborn element in temperament that is later shaped by our environment, particularly in childhood. We can always act out of character in certain situations but our temperament defines our preferred emotional response.

We also see talent as inborn but with a potential to be developed. It is like a seed that needs the right environment if it is to flower and reach its full potential. By providing the setting for the talent seed, temperament becomes talent's emotional internal environment.

Miroslav Vanek who was President of the Federation of Sports Psychologists in the 1970s has suggested (Dick, 1997) that the talent and the motivation (a temperament issue) of an athlete correlate inversely in their early years. That is, the most talented are not as strongly motivated as those with slightly less talent. The former win easily, without having to try very hard whilst the latter have to push themselves and are the more competitive of the two groups. Over the longer term, the lesser talent with the stronger motivation wins over the greater talent with the lower motivation. Frank Dick, the British Athletics' Director of Coaching from 1979 to 1994, comments that 'it is no longer a case of talent spotting but also motivation spotting' (Dick, 1997). Thus talent and temperament must work together. But there is another ingredient, and that is technique.

These is clear evidence from sport coaches and from athletic performance that techniques develop and refine talent and build temperament in key areas. We once spoke with a person who had achieved international standard in his chosen sport of rifle shooting. He explained that excellence in his sport required two opposites. You needed the concentration to hold the rifle perfectly still and the relaxation to pull the trigger without snatching. After research in the laboratory that monitored impulses in his brain he found he was able to exert the mental control to be both concentrated and relaxed at the same time. This learnt technique enabled him to move up from national to international standard and represent his country in the Olympics.

In the search for excellence, the maturity over time of talent, temperament and technique and the way they work together are both important. We now present two models to explain the growth to maturity, Figure 2.1, and the inter-linking, Figure 2.2. Both apply to any area of activity or any role, though of course we have in mind the entrepreneur.

Figure 2.1 is a Nature–Nurture model in which the starting point is the inborn talent and temperament. For the entrepreneur, this starting point can be quantified as we describe later in this chapter. Subsequent improvements can also be measured so that the road to excellence is monitored. To achieve this, processes need to be in place that will develop and strengthen talents, manage and control temperament and impart and mature technique. These processes include both structured and unstructured learning and experiences so that there is a place for formal education and practical experience.

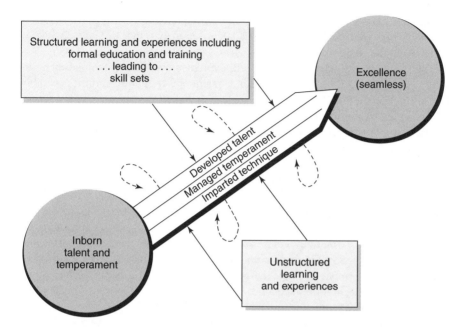

Figure 2.1 *The Nature–nurture model*

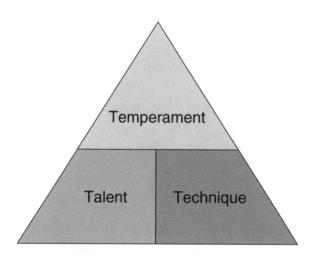

Figure 2.2 *The Performance triangle*

We believe that this represents an important model for achieving excellence in any area of activity or role. Sport has come the closest of any group to recognising that different talents, temperaments and techniques are required for different events. In comparison, the professions and particularly business have some way to go. The only area really understood is technique as the many business courses demonstrate. Temperament is now being recognised to some extent as the interest in personality typing and psychometric testing shows, but talent is almost completely neglected. The only work we have found that treats talent seriously is that by Gallup which we reviewed in the last chapter.

The 'performance triangle', Figure 2.2, expresses how talent, temperament and technique work together. The foundation is talent and technique and these combine to make possible a quality performance driven by temperament.

One of the indicators of talent is that people pick up technique issues very quickly. As the example of Len Hutton's coach given earlier and Fred Terman's comments on Hewlett and Packard in Chapter 14 show, techniques add value to talent. Because talent expresses itself through technique, it is extremely important that technique does not take over and block off talent. This can be the case with young entrepreneurs who have been through the university system and have had their entrepreneurial instincts buried and then substituted by analytical techniques and so-called best practice. Under such circumstances, talent finds it difficult to come through. Again we are not saying that technique is not important but that it has to build on and use talent. It is a partnership.

Temperament brings the motivation and commitment and is what most people notice about entrepreneurs. Their temperament leads but if it is not backed by real talent and sound technique, excellence will not be achieved. On the other hand it is temperament that drives talent and technique and gives it impetus.

Although Figure 2.2 shows a balanced picture, it is possible for one of the three elements to dominate. Temperament is generally the one most likely to do this and when very strong it produces the 'entrepreneurs in the shadows' of Chapter 9 with natural talent overwhelmed and important techniques and controls ignored or overlooked.

Ideally all three are well balanced, each playing its part in the pursuit of excellence.

Talent, temperament and roles

Talent and temperament are about the individual; their gifts, attributes and abilities. Roles are about what people do, about their job, their tasks and responsibilities. When these are well matched then excellence can be achieved but this does not mean there is a one-to-one correlation between talent and temperament and a given role. Experience shows that the same job can be done well in a number of different ways. Thus some talent and temperament issues will be about style and others about performance. The difficulty of course is in knowing which is which.

Another difficulty is that a role and a job are not necessarily the same. Different roles can be appropriate to the same job. Thus one company may need a CEO or Managing Director who is a leader to give direction to an unfocused business, another will require an entrepreneur to seize new opportunities and yet another will want a manager who can consolidate the business after a period of rapid growth. A study of electronics companies in the USA, under the title 'The Innovation Marathon', has shown how some companies change the role of the CEO on a regular basis with these different requirements in mind (Jelinek and Schoonhoven, 1990).

These links between talent, temperament, role and job relate to the approach adopted by SRI and subsequently Gallup that we described in Chapter 1. This approach began with a specific role and derived the corresponding life themes. This process of working back from role to life theme or talent is in our view a sounder process than trying to move the other way because it is essentially a converging methodology. Those who have started with an analysis of personality types, using Myers-Briggs for example, have found it difficult to link them to specific roles. As we saw in Chapter 1, not all entrepreneurs have the same personality type, nor is everybody with one of the three possible entrepreneur personality types an entrepreneur. This is clearly not a very helpful basis for identifying potential entrepreneurs.

In their recent publications Gallup has moved from its original focus on roles to one of identifying a person's key strengths (Buckingham and Coffman, 1999; Buckingham and Clifton, 2001). This is perhaps more a reflection of the current emphasis on developing a person's potential than of the link between roles and strengths per se. Whilst Gallup now say that 'whatever you set your mind to, you will be successful when you craft your role to play to your signature talents most of the time', they also speak of the need to build 'an understanding of the dominant talents necessary for excellence in a given role' (Buckingham and Clifton, 2001). We thus have two approaches. The original Gallup approach using a role-driven methodology which derives sets of life or talent themes for specific roles and the more recent approach which has a strength-driven methodology – Gallup's 'StrengthsFinder®' – to arrive at an understanding of a person's signature themes. These two approaches are inherent in the role/person relationship and have something of the chicken and egg debate about it. Certainly many roles have sufficient flexibility to accommodate different sets of 'signature themes' but others, and we would include entrepreneurs here, do have a set of talent themes necessary for excellence. We thus prefer the original Gallup approach as will be evident from our work on identifying the potential entrepreneur which we now consider.

Profiling the entrepreneur

Gryffindor, Hufflepuff, Ravenclaw and Slytherin are the four houses at Hogwarts, the school for witches and wizards in J.K. Rowling's books about Harry Potter. Gryffindor is the house for the brave and courageous, Hufflepuff for the hard working, Ravenclaw for the clever and Slytherin for the ambitious and those who seek power. New students are allocated their houses by a magic Sorting Hat which is placed on the head of each student in front of the whole school. The Hat first reads the mind of the student to assess personality and potential and then after due deliberation announces the chosen house in a loud voice to the rest of the school.

The task of the Sorting Hat is not too different from the one we attempt in this section of identifying people suitable for the house 'Entrepreneur'. We do so, not by magic, but by a matching process that is not dissimilar. We take account of a person's talents and temperament and match them with those of others in the same house. Like the Sorting Hat we want people to be happy and yet challenged in the house they are allocated and expect them to make a positive contribution consistent with the character and traditions of the house.

Our approach to identifying the potential entrepreneur is, like the Sorting Hat, essentially an interpretative one. It allows the behaviour and actions of the entrepreneur to be interpreted in terms of just six basic attributes. Once they are fully grasped it becomes relatively easy to pick them out in stories about entrepreneurs such as are found in Part Two. As this entrepreneur awareness develops, it becomes no longer such a difficult task to identify people who have entrepreneurial potential.

We term our six basic attributes, the entrepreneur's 'character themes'. We do so because 'attributes' is a rather general word and we wish to imply a specific meaning. We describe a 'character theme' as 'a personality attribute or characteristic that defines a person's normal expected behaviour' (Bolton and Thompson, 2003). Thus our 'character theme' has a similar meaning to Gallup's 'life theme' and 'talent theme' described in Chapter 1. We prefer the words 'character theme' because the word 'character' emphasises that we are dealing with a person's inner psychological core or make up, which we feel the word 'life' does not. We prefer not to include the word 'talent' because we see some of the themes as temperament issues. In essence, however, we are describing the same feature as Gallup has done with its terms 'talent theme', 'life theme' and 'signature theme'.

Our six entrepreneur character themes include and extend the twelve life themes identified by Gallup and described in the previous chapter, but consolidate them to a smaller number.

The FACETS entrepreneur profile

A convenient acronym, FACETS, is formed by the six character themes that we have identified and which define the entrepreneur profile. In terms of one definition of the word 'facets', they are 'aspects of a subject or personality' and in another they are 'the surfaces of a cut gemstone' (*Collins English Dictionary*, 1995). In that the first definition relates to aspects of personality it allows us to speak of 'facet character themes' or simply 'facet themes'. The second definition provides us with an interesting analogy to gemstones or crystals. Like the facet themes, the facets of a crystal are inherent in their chemistry. Thus, a quartz crystal has a hexagonal structure and a diamond a cubic structure. Even so, not all crystals of the same mineral look alike because the presence of trace elements gives them different hues. An amethyst is a purple or violet transparent variety of quartz and a diamond, though basically colourless, can be tinted yellow, blue and even black. In the same way, entrepreneurs have a particular facet structure but come in a variety of shades and are of different worth. Entrepreneurs, like Sir Richard Branson, Steve Jobs or Bill Gates, are in the gemstone category and highly valued. Most entrepreneurs are less well known yet still have the same basic structure. Others, like Jack Welch of General Electric, discussed under corporate entrepreneurship in Part Two, have additional facets that make them entrepreneurial leaders. Lord Andrew Lloyd Webber, described under music entrepreneurs in Part Two, has an artistic facet that supplements his entrepreneurial talent.

This analogy with crystals helps us to understand why entrepreneurs can be so different and yet be fundamentally the same. Thus:

- They have different trace elements due to their upbringing and experience.
- Some facets are more perfectly formed and stronger than others.
- Some have extra facets that supplement their entrepreneurial ones.

Three further important points come out of this analogy with the crystal. The first is that they occur naturally but need to be discovered. There are far more people with entrepreneurial potential than ever emerge. We are just not very good at finding them. One reason for this is that we do not really know what they look like and at first sight they may not seem too much like the real thing. Of course, the gem expert knows where to look and can pick out those that have true value without difficulty.

The second point is that the craftsman can add value to the raw crystal by cutting and polishing. It is the role of technique to take the 'rough diamond' and make it sparkle. Thus those who impart technique and help the entrepreneur along the road can make a real difference to the entrepreneur's performance.

The third point is that, as with all things of value, there will be counterfeits. Like the gem that is really only cut glass or the artificial diamond that, though it has many similar properties, is just not the real thing. Investors have met many such entrepreneur pretenders to their cost.

The six facet character themes are described below. In order to see the similarities and differences with Gallup's work on entrepreneurs that we described earlier and set out in Table 1.2, we cross-refer their twelve entrepreneur life themes.

1 *Focus* – the ability to lock on to a target and not be distracted, to act with urgency and not procrastinate, to get things done and not just talk about them. Our *focus* character theme includes Gallup's *focus*, *activator* and *urgency* themes, though we reserve the discrimination element to the next character theme *advantage*. The 'hard work' element in this theme links in with Gallup's *dedication* theme.

2 *Advantage* – the ability to select the right opportunity. It is this facet that enables entrepreneurs to pick winners and to know instinctively what 'falls to the bottom-line'. It is why they have no problem with finding the resources they need. It includes what Gallup has termed *profit orientation*.

3 *Creativity* – the ability to come up with new ideas habitually either simply as ideas in themselves or else translated into opportunities or solutions. This facet allows entrepreneurs to think differently, to 'break the mould', to see patterns others miss. It is the same as the Gallup theme *creativity*.

4 *Ego (inner)* – the ego that only the person knows. It provides confidence, creates passion and delivers the motivation to achieve and to win. It is what makes entrepreneurs 'mountain people' and not 'valley people' (Dick, 1997).
   Ego (outer) – the ego that others see. The ability to carry heavy responsibility lightly but not flippantly, to be openly accountable and to be instinctively courageous. Gallup's themes of *ego*, *dedication* and *courage* are included in this facet.

These four facets form another convenient acronym FACE and in many ways they are the face of the entrepreneur. Without all four of these facets a person just does not look like an entrepreneur and indeed cannot be one. Here we depart from Gallup's earlier approach that suggests it is sufficient to possess a few *unsuppressible* themes from a number of possible themes. We see the FACE themes as essential and that without them it is not possible to be a successful entrepreneur.

The last two facet character themes are not found in all entrepreneurs and are therefore optional. We know many entrepreneurs who are very difficult to work with. They are weak on *team*, the fifth facet. They create followers but not teams. The sixth facet *social* is unique to the social entrepreneur. Other entrepreneurs will have values and this will influence their businesses but those with a strong *social* facet character theme have espoused a cause that has become their passion. They are social entrepreneurs.

5 *Team* – the ability to pick the best people and get them working as a team, to know when you need help and to find it, and to build an extensive network of supporters. This facet provides the entrepreneur's multiplier effect. It includes three of Gallup's twelve entrepreneur life themes, namely *expertise orientation*, *team* and *individualised perception* but has the additional component of *networking*.
6 *Social* – the ability to espouse a cause and deliver on it. This facet invades the *ego* facet providing a motivation and passion all of its own. It is the distinguishing facet of the social entrepreneur. The closest Gallup entrepreneur theme is *dedication*.

The four facet character themes of *focus*, *advantage*, *creativity* and *team* are talents. They form yet another convenient acronym FACT that reminds us that they are inborn abilities. We have them whether we like it or not but they must be discovered, nurtured and developed if they are to achieve their full potential.

Ego and *social* are temperament issues. Some aspects are inborn and others are a matter of upbringing and experience. In many ways the temperament facets are the most crucial. There is just no point in starting along the entrepreneur road without a strong *ego* facet to keep you going and make the journey a fulfilling and successful experience. Equally without a strong *social* facet it is impossible to be an effective social entrepreneur. Belief and values alone are just not enough.

Whilst these six facet character themes are consistent with the earlier work of SRI/Gallup and take it on to a second stage, the link with Gallup's recent work and particularly their StrengthsFinder® questionnaire is less clear. This is firstly because of Gallup's shift from roles to talent themes and secondly because their thirty-four StrengthsFinder® talent themes are not easy to match with our six facets.

In developing and validating our approach we set up a research study with the support of Gallup in which more than seventy entrepreneurs or entrepreneur enablers selected by us completed the Gallup StrengthsFinder® questionnaire. Gallup then provided us with the top five talent themes of each respondent. We converted these talent theme results to our six facet character themes by appropriate grouping. Talent themes that did not fit with any of our facets were noted but excluded from the facet grouping. The first four most frequently found facets were in the order *creativity*, *advantage*, *focus* and *ego*. Interestingly, these results are similar to those of Clifton and Harding (1986) reported in Chapter 1. When converted to our facet character themes the strongest were *creativity*, *advantage*, *ego* and *focus*; the only difference being in the order of themes ranked third and fourth. *Team* showed up fifth in our results, with *Social* some way behind. As our sample contained only a few social entrepreneurs, this was not unexpected.

Identifying the entrepreneur

We now move from a general profiling of the entrepreneur based on the six facet character themes to a point where it becomes possible to identify the potential entrepreneur. First we consider the FACETS at their most basic. We call this the *foundation level* and go below the main character themes to their sub-themes. This is necessarily a lengthy section and is intended for future cross-reference as understanding develops. Next we look at some examples of how the FACETS work at an *operational level* as they interact with each other. Finally we outline a procedure for identifying the potential entrepreneur. Thus we consider:

- FACETS – the foundation level.
- FACETS – the operational level.
- Identifying entrepreneur potential.

FACETS – the foundation level

We now take a more detailed look at each of the six facet character themes. At first reading, they may seem an incomplete description of the entrepreneur. This is because although they are described alone, they do not stand alone but work together with other facets. That is, they are *foundation level* attributes. Thus when we describe *focus* we explain that entrepreneurs concentrate on a target but we do not say how the entrepreneur discriminates and knows which targets to go for. The ability to identify the right target is part of the *advantage* facet and is described under that facet. It is at the *operational level* which we cover later that they come together so that the entrepreneur successfully targets and discriminates.

Focus is a character theme required in many roles. It is not unique to the entrepreneur. Wherever something has to be delivered on, there you will find *focus*. Roger Black, the athlete, comments in his autobiography that 'my greatest strength is my ability to focus, to be cool under pressure' (Black, 1999).

Focus has three sub-themes that are important for the entrepreneur, namely:

1 Target focus.
2 Time focus.
3 Action focus.

Target focus is what most people understand by the word 'focus'. For the entrepreneur the more tangible and specific the target, the better. The leader may focus on an idea or a concept but the entrepreneur focuses on something concrete that can generally be measured. *Target focus* is also required of good managers. Both entrepreneurs and managers are people who like to have targets to deliver against.

An important part of hitting a target is knowing what and where it is. Because entrepreneurs are often operating in unknown territory it is not always possible for them to see the target clearly but they have an instinct as to where to find it and home in on things very quickly. Brian Souter, the entrepreneur who built the Stagecoach empire, 'concentrates on major issues, typically no more than three in any situation' (Wolmar, 1999). He is target-focused. Entrepreneurs are not people who juggle with many different things at the same time. Brian Souter's 'three in any situation' at any one time is probably the norm.

Gallup has identified *focus* as a major 'life theme' in all its studies. Thus we find it in Table 1.1 as one of their 'thinking talents', in Table 1.2 as an 'entrepreneur life theme' and in their StrengthsFinder® list of 'talent themes'. All of Gallup's descriptions include the idea of focus on a target. Gallup makes the important point that strength in this theme means that you filter out anything that does not help you get to your goal. You determine priorities on the basis of whether it helps you get to your destination. People strong on target focus always keep on track and do not wander off down false roads (Buckingham and Clifton, 2001).

Time focus allows people to concentrate and remain productive over long periods. People with this character theme are not easily distracted and there is an urgency to their work. Time matters to them. They enjoy deadlines and work very hard to achieve them. They do not procrastinate.

A sense of urgency is an important indicator of *time focus* – the belief that every moment has to be filled. It is not only entrepreneurs who feel like this. Brad Langevad the world's 'leading tennis biochemist' commented to a journalist 'I've got to improve my life management. I'm too manic. I've got to conquer the world by 8.00 a.m. As soon as I'm out of bed I down a cup of coffee and read my emails' (Johnson, 2003).

Urgency was picked out by Gallup as a life theme of the entrepreneur, see Table 1.2. This feeling of urgency can stimulate and drive the entrepreneur but it is possible to go to an extreme and suffer from 'entrepreneurial stress' and 'mania', as discussed in Chapter 1.

Entrepreneurs strong on *time focus* are often impatient and have a short attention span. They hate wasting time. Stimulated by an entrepreneur programme, some students at Cambridge University in the early 1980s set up businesses during the summer vacation and were running them in parallel with their final year. Whenever they thought the academic programme dragged this catch-phrase was heard – 'I haven't time to waste, I've a business to run!'.

Time focus has different time horizons for different roles. Gallup has identified that entrepreneurs have short time horizons, preferring to think only two months ahead. Others in the business world look further ahead. For most senior managers it is one to three years, and for investors it can be three years and more. These differences are one reason why entrepreneurs have trouble with bankers and investors. They cannot see the point of producing a three-year business plan when they know it is not possible to be certain of anything that far off.

Action focus is the third sub-theme. Entrepreneurs enjoy doing things. It is not simply a matter of their having a strong work ethic. Entrepreneurs just enjoy working hard; there is no compulsion or duty about it. Steve Wood who became the general manager of Microsoft in 1977 says of the early days at Microsoft 'we were just having fun and working really hard' (Wallace and Erickson, 1993). They were action-focused.

Entrepreneurs see themselves as doers rather than thinkers. They believe that actions speak louder than words. This 'action-man' approach gets things done but can make working with them difficult. Entrepreneurs give 110 per cent and expect everybody else to do the same. Nonetheless it is this ability to take action and to make things happen that is one of their distinguishing marks.

The three sub-themes just described work together differently depending on which sub-theme is dominant. This is because target is an end or outcome whereas time and action are the means and part of the process of getting to the target. Thus, if time or action are the strongest sub-themes it is very easy for them to take over so that the means become the ends and the true end, the target, is lost sight off. This produces 'busy fools' who rush around and work very hard but never seem to get anywhere.

In their 2001 publication, Gallup provided examples of people and roles to illustrate the different talent themes. An entrepreneur is given as an example of the *activator* theme. People with this strength, says Gallup, are 'impatient for action', they 'don't sit around until all the lights go green' but they also believe that 'only action makes things happen'(Buckingham and Clifton, 2001). *Activator* is a combination of *time* focus and *action* focus. These might be admirable qualities but without a target to go for, there will be activity but little result.

These comments about *time* and *action* are not meant to reduce their importance because without these strengths the target will not be achieved. The ideal is a strong *target focus* sub-theme that is served by the other two. The dictionary definition of the noun 'focus' captures this linkage well. 'A point (the target) upon which attention (time), activity (action) is directed or concentrated' (*Collins English Dictionary*, 1995). Gallup's description of the *focus* life theme given in Table 1.1 is even closer. 'Focus is an ability to set goals (target) and use them every day (time) to guide actions (action).'

The way in which the entrepreneur looks upon the completion of a task is an interesting example of the three sub-themes working together. 'Completion' means that a *target* has been met but entrepreneurs do not waste *time* admiring what they have just completed. Instead they go on to the next task and the next. For the entrepreneur completion is never an end in itself. It is simply the stepping stone to the next challenge, to more *action*. There is also an urgency about getting things completed that is independent of the job itself. *Time* matters. People who are focused never leave the job half-done. They enjoy *action*, completion is merely a consequence.

Advantage   is the one facet theme among the six that makes the entrepreneur really stand out. It is the basic talent of selecting opportunities with real potential. This facet theme refers to the 'perceived opportunities' of our definition of the entrepreneur in Chapter 1. When British Airways and Air France closed down their supersonic Concorde service in 2003, Richard Branson immediately saw this as an opportunity and commented 'I like a challenge, even if it's crazy'. At the time of writing we do not know the outcome but Branson has consistently come up with this kind of opportunity over the years, as we describe in Part Two.

Opportunity selection is the outcome of the *advantage* facet. It is what enables the entrepreneur to pick out the one opportunity among the many that will actually succeed. This is essentially a talent and instinct issue. No 'panel of experts' or 'due diligence' exercise can replace the entrepreneur with a strong *advantage* facet theme. Opportunity selection is simply not a mechanistic process; it requires vision and instinct. It was Akio Morita, one of Sony's founders, who picked out the opportunity that became the Sony Walkman – a clear example of the flair that the *advantage* facet brings. When he first suggested the opportunity he was met with opposition from the engineers who had a different product in mind and from the accountants who said it would never make any money. Even though they were sitting on what we now know was a very high-growth business opportunity only one man believed it, Akio Morita, the entrepreneur (Morita, 1994).

Most entrepreneurs have at least one example of an opportunity that was turned down by the investors or the bank manager but which then became the mainstay of the business. It always seems that the so-called professionals miss the big opportunities because they are too conventional and fear the unfamiliar and the new. Don Valentine, one of the most successful venture capitalists in Silicon Valley, once told us that when Steve Jobs first came to him with the idea of a computer in every home he thought he was 'off the wall' and sent him away. But Valentine did invest in Apple Computers the second time around and was very pleased he did so.

The *advantage* facet theme is just as important in the running of the business as it is in identifying the business opportunity in the first place. This is because in any successful business there are opportunities all around both internally in the way the business is run and externally in the marketplace and these have to be assessed and decisions made. It is an ongoing process.

The *advantage* facet theme is served by four sub-themes that work together and enable the entrepreneur to pick winners. These are:

1 Benefit orientation
2 Performance orientation
3 Resourcing
4 Vision.

Benefit orientation is the same attribute that Gallup has called *profit orientation* and which is described as 'advantage focused' in Table 1.2. The entrepreneur with this facet knows instinctively what 'falls to the bottom line' and what of several courses of action will bring the most benefit. It is this aspect of the *advantage* facet theme that enables the entrepreneur to discriminate and is the main criterion in the mental process of opportunity selection. They are attracted to an opportunity by what it can do for them and by the benefit it will bring. Benefit can have many interpretations from a strategic issue like market positioning to the day-to-day issue of cash in hand. Entrepreneurs do not select an opportunity just because it is technically clever or extremely novel. They want to know what benefit it will bring them.

This approach of 'what's in it for me' is a disposition and orientation that shows in every decision that entrepreneurs make and is why they are very good deal makers. Bill Gates did the biggest deal in his life when he got IBM to agree that Microsoft could sell its operating system to other hardware manufacturers. It appears that IBM did not realise the riches they were handing over but Bill Gates certainly did (Freiberger and Swaine, 2000).

When governments have deregulated industries or privatised them, people strong in *benefit orientation* have been the winners. In the UK there was Edward

Stobbart with the deregulation of the haulage industry, Brian Souter with public transport and Richard Branson with rail privatisation – all are now millionaires. Critics who said that the government was a soft touch missed the point. These men are exceptional deal-makers. Philip Green is an example of a private sector deal-maker. He acquired Bhs, previously British Home Stores, for £220 million in 1999 and in less than two years had increased its value to £1.2 billion. In reporting this, the press commented that Green had made the fastest ever £1 billion in retailing history and that to be able to do this kind of thing entrepreneurs needed a gambling streak in their make-up (The Times, 2002). We see this gambling streak as the *benefit orientation* sub-theme in action.

Some people have a benefit orientation which is merely selfishness. This is generally rather petty and is not what we mean by the term. They look for advantage at a personal level. Entrepreneurs on the other hand have a *benefit orientation* which comes from their *advantage* talent and which they use to the benefit of their enterprise. The general perception of the entrepreneur has confused these two types of benefit orientation, the one driven by self and the other by entrepreneurial talent. Certainly there have been entrepreneurs who have become very wealthy and used the money to indulge themselves but the vast majority have given far more to society in the form of jobs and standard of living than they have taken from it. Many donate generously to charities and some have their own charitable foundations.

Guy Kawasaki, Apple Computer's first software evangelist, has said of Steve Wozniak who co-founded Apple with Steve Jobs 'Woz has life all figured out: design a product you love, make a lot of money, retire young, and do something for other people' (Freiberger and Swaine, 2000). Clearly not all entrepreneurs are selfish.

Performance orientation separates entrepreneurs from people who are simply enthusiasts. The latter talk about opportunities but are never able to substantiate what they are saying. The entrepreneur on the other hand will provide a surfeit of information in addition to their enthusiasm. They will have the data to show that the opportunity is a real one and they will have gathered this information in the first place to convince themselves. They ensure that their instinct is always served by the facts, as far as they are available.

Although *performance orientation* is not included among Gallup's entrepreneur life themes nor in their latest list of StrengthFinder® themes, it is one of Gallup's original life themes given in Table 1.1. There it is defined it as 'a need to be objective and measure performance'. Generalities will not do for entrepreneurs, they need facts and figures. Some formal education and training can obviously be of help here. Brian Souter of Stagecoach is a qualified accountant but his interest in detail is something he has always had. A broker in the City of London has commented that although you would never pick Souter out in an identity parade as a man worth millions – he dresses casually and is famed for carrying his papers in a plastic bag – yet his grasp of details is 'unbelievable' (Wolmar, 1999).

Good sales people have this same *performance orientation* which they use in an opportunistic way to quantify the sales opportunities around them and measure their own performance. Cyril, who featured in the story in the introduction, was having a hard time selling fuel additives for diesel engines to a sceptical manager of a bus company. Cyril's solution was to spend a day following his customer's buses around, making a note of those that were emitting black smoke. When confronted with the long list of buses that Cyril had compiled the manager placed an order. This interest in detail and its use to quantify opportunities is an important indicator of the *advantage* facet theme and can be a useful tool to discriminate between people who have identified a real opportunity and those who think that every idea is an opportunity.

Once their company is up and running, entrepreneurs strong on *performance orientation* will gather information about how things are going on a day-to-day basis. Some we have known have had performance charts around their office wall and used them to keep a remarkably tight ship. Typically the entrepreneur owner will overrule the accounts people and tell them which cheques to pay and will be right. Involvement at this level of detail can be misinterpreted as checking up on people when in reality they are checking up on their own performance as we discuss further in the section on *outer ego*.

For the entrepreneur, *benefit orientation* and *performance orientation* must go together. People who are strong in only one of these will not make entrepreneurs. Either they will be carried away by the benefits of the opportunity or else they will get lost in its details.

Resourcing is a distinguishing mark of the entrepreneur and one of the entrepreneur's action factors in Chapter 1. It is the ability to find the resources needed for the task in hand, whether that be to exploit an opportunity or to solve a business problem. *Resourcing* is a basic talent of the entrepreneur and fundamental to success.

When people who have started their own businesses are surveyed they always give 'lack of resources' as one of the major problems. Our view is that most of these people are not true entrepreneurs because if they were they would find the resources and get on with it. *Resourcing* is one of the key differences between the small business owner who stays small and the true entrepreneur.

Anita Roddick had very little money when she started The Body Shop. Everything had to be done on a shoestring (Roddick, 2000). Roddick had a designer produce a logo for £25, used 'urine sample' plastic bottles because they were cheap, reduced the number of bottles needed by refilling them and painted everything green because it was the best colour to cover the damp patches on the wall. She went the franchising route because she did not have enough money to set up her own shops. Roddick possessed the entrepreneur theme of *resourcing* and used it to maximum benefit.

Support agencies need to be extremely careful in their approach to helping potential entrepreneurs. It is fairly easy to attract people who have the aspiration to be entrepreneurs if there is a generous resource package on offer. Unfortunately, this tends to attract people who lack this essential *resourcing* capability. The result is that they are never able to stand on their own feet and become increasingly dependent upon support.

Vision for the entrepreneur is essential. It is what lights up *opportunity selection* and brings passion to the opportunity. It is in some ways the business version of the *social* facet theme. It is what makes the entrepreneur believe in the opportunity and comes close to being the entrepreneur's 'cause'.

Some entrepreneurs find the idea that they might be visionaries rather difficult and prefer to use other words. Conrad Hilton has said 'To accomplish big things you must first dream big dreams.' He explains that he does not mean idle daydreams or wishful thinking. 'Nor is it the type of revelation reserved for the great ones and rightly called vision. What I speak of is a brand of imaginative thinking backed by enthusiasm, vitality and expectation' (Hilton, 1957). In 1931, Hilton was ruined. The Depression in the US had hit his hotel chain badly and he was heavily in debt. It was then at this low point that he saw in a magazine a picture of the brand new Waldorf-Astoria in New York. Despite his circumstances he dared to dream that one day he might own it. This became his dream, his vision. He cut out the picture and wrote on the back 'The Greatest of Them All'. When he had a desk again he placed it under the glass top so that, he said, 'it was always in front of me'. Fifteen years later, in October 1949, 'The Greatest of Them All' became a Hilton Hotel. His dream had been achieved (Hilton, 1957).

In Chapter 3 we describe the 'visionary entrepreneur'. This is the entrepreneur for whom vision plays a major role and is long term. However, for most entrepreneurs vision has a much shorter time scale in line with their shorter-term focus discussed earlier.

Vision is about the overall picture and relates to the strategic potential of the opportunity. Entrepreneurs are able to jump from this strategic and visionary dimension to the detail that is their *target focus*. They have before them an opportunity that they never lose sight of but at the same time they are practical people who want to deliver and not just talk. They are *vision* deliverers, and not just *vision* talkers.

Creativity is the facet theme that fuels the entrepreneur. It is the theme from which all else springs. It provides their raw material. Without creativity there would be no opportunities to select and no target to focus upon. Without creativity, problems would remain unsolved and the business would stall. Gallup identified it as one of their twelve entrepreneur life themes, Table 1.2, and as a 'thinking talent' in their general list of life themes, Table 1.1. Perhaps surprisingly it is not included in their thirty-four StrengthFinder® themes, though *ideation* – 'you are fascinated by ideas' – is in the right area.

The creativity of the entrepreneur is covered extensively in other sections of this book and so is only reviewed briefly here in relation to the *creativity* facet theme. Creativity is at the start of our definition of the entrepreneur – 'a person who habitually creates . . . ' and is one of our ten action factors discussed in Chapter 1. It is also discussed in the introduction to Part Three and in Chapter 11.

In the previous section, we said that *opportunity selection* was the output of the *advantage* facet theme and that it was supported by its sub-themes. Here the picture is different. All of *creativity*'s sub-themes are outputs and involve the same mental processes. There is the intuitive jump, the making of connections, the seeing of patterns, the link with past experience, the fresh insights, and so on. They cover a spectrum from the conceptual to the practical, moving from ideas, through opportunities and on to solutions. When *creativity* ties in with a strong *advantage* facet theme there is a powerful combination. Many of the examples given in Part Two show this combination at work.

The three *creativity* facet sub-themes then are:

1 Ideas
2 Opportunities
3 Solutions.

Ideas are what some entrepreneurs have all the time, especially the inventor entrepreneurs. They have a lively mind that can make connections and sees patterns that others miss. It is the fruit of this talent that evokes the comment from others 'why didn't I think of that'. They are one of the primary inputs to the entrepreneur process, as we describe in Chapter 11.

Scientists and inventors are not the only people who have 'eureka' moments. Mitchell Kapor, the founder of Lotus, the world's largest software company at the time, and Jerry Kaplan were returning to San Francisco in Kapor's private jet. He was already a millionaire at thirty-six years of age. They were discussing the idea of making computers much smaller and in a logical process went through each major component in turn, from disc drive to keyboard. They were moving logically towards the idea of a laptop computer. Then they had a break and as Kaplan dozed off he was thinking about the keyboard problem. He knew he always got his best ideas in his sleep. Kaplan woke up suddenly and challenged Kapor with the idea of using a pen rather than a keyboard, much as you write on a note pad. The idea gripped them both as they experienced a eureka moment. It was a powerful emotional experience that left them speechless (Kaplan, 1997).

What Kaplan and Kapor had 'discovered' was what is now the handheld computer or PDA (Personal Digital Assistant). Investors caught the vision of this powerful idea and the GO Corporation that Kaplan founded was able to secure $3 million of funding without a business plan or any serious financial projections.

Opportunities are ideas that have commercial potential and can be realised. It took some time before the technology caught up with Kaplan's idea and it became a true opportunity. In the meantime, the GO Corporation spent six years going through $75 million and then failed.

The ability to come up with viable opportunities is what distinguishes the entrepreneur from the pure inventor. In Part Two we give the example of Coca-Cola that has become world-famous through a succession of entrepreneurs who saw new opportunities in franchising the bottling process, in the use of crimped caps to seal the bottles and in mass advertising. John Pemberton, the inventor, gained virtually nothing (Pendergrast, 1996).

Not all opportunities have the commercial potential or are as viable as some imagine. In fact only about 2 per cent of ideas that are patented ever reach the marketplace. The ability to see opportunities is an important one but just coming up with opportunities does not make an entrepreneur. There has to be the talent to pick the winners, and that comes from the *advantage* facet.

Gallup identified 'opportunity' as one of the twelve 'life themes' of the entrepreneur. In Table 1.2 we defined it as 'sees opportunities not problems'. Gallup's more detailed description supplied to us by Don Clifton shows that they have in mind a combination of 'seeing opportunities', which is this sub-theme, and the *advantage* facet theme which helps the entrepreneur to identify the true opportunity.

Solutions are that part of the *creativity* facet theme that deals with problem-solving. It involves new ways of seeing things and the ability to see beyond the problem itself. This *solutions* attribute is particularly important in the running of a business where problems come along on a daily basis. When business owners complain about the difficulties and problems that they are facing they are showing that they are almost certainly not entrepreneurs.

Changes in Iraq have given fresh challenges to their business elite. An Iraqi entrepreneur from the Kurdish north who had been operating successfully outside his country for the last twenty-five years recently returned to his homeland. Speaking with a local businessman and a reporter from the Wall Street Journal he commented confidently 'One man's problems are another man's gold mine. I love a vacuum' as he enthusiastically outlined the many deals he had going through. The local businessman was not convinced. 'How can you do this when there are no laws?' he asked. 'You must make your own rules if you have to' was the quick reply. As the meeting ended, the entrepreneur commented to the businessman 'You are good at identifying the problems. But concentrate on solutions. That's what we're here for, to find solutions' (King, 2003). This ability to think in terms of solutions and to come up with them is what distinguishes the entrepreneur from the rest of the business world. This is why they make a difference in whatever situation they find themselves in – even if that is a country with no infrastructure and no laws.

Ego   is probably the most critical facet theme in that it controls the effectiveness of all the others. It is also always strong in entrepreneurs. Ed Faber, who in 1976 founded the retail chain ComputerLand in the USA, has commented of the early days in the industry – 'you were dealing with entrepreneurs mostly. Egos, a lot of egos' (Freiberger and Swaine, 2000).

The *ego* facet theme has two sides, rather like a coin. The *inner* private side that only the person knows and the *outer* public side that others see. It is quite possible to appear to outsiders to have a strong ego and yet to be less strong internally. Jack Welch was a strong, powerful and effective entrepreneurial leader at General Electric taking it to great heights and yet throughout his autobiography he continues to comment that his mother pumped self-confidence into him. It was as if he had to keep reminding himself of that fact because it did not come naturally to him. On his way up the organisational ladder, Welch had seen a blame culture destroy people's confidence and fill them with self-doubt. Even senior managers were involved and some never recovered. Welch termed this effect the 'GE Vortex' (Welch, 2001). The *inner ego* part is often more fragile than we think.

Inner ego   We divide this side of the *ego* facet theme into three sub-themes:

1 Self-assurance
2 Dedication
3 Motivation.

These factors were discussed in Chapter 1 when we reviewed what research had found out about entrepreneurs; so here we only provide a brief explanation of what we mean by them.

Self-assurance is the inner confidence that people have in their own abilities. Self-assured people decide a course of action and move forward never thinking that they might be wrong. Knowing you can do something is half way to doing it. Though some people may be naturally self-assured, upbringing plays an important part. Not only Jack Welch but Richard Branson and Anita Roddick all pay tribute to their mothers who built up their self-confidence. Roddick's father died when she was just ten years old and she helped her mother keep the family café business going. Her mother's advice was 'be special, be anything but mediocre' (Roddick, 2000).

True self-assurance has a degree of resilience that helps people bounce back from adversity. We have already given the example of Conrad Hilton who came back from failure to build one of the world's greatest hotel chains. This is an important attribute for entrepreneurs who can have every reason to feel that the world is against them and yet keep going with a remarkable confidence and determination.

Gallup includes *self-assurance* among its thirty-four StrengthsFinder® themes and says that people strong in this theme 'feel confident in their ability to manage their own lives. They possess an inner compass that gives them confidence that their decisions are right'. It is clearly an important theme for many roles, not only entrepreneurs.

Dedication is what gives entrepreneurs their inner passion and it affects directly how they do things. Entrepreneurs often have a passion about their customers and are dedicated to serving them. Edward Stobart, who made the Eddie Stobart trucking company one of the fastest growing businesses in the UK, had a passion to serve his customers and would never turn down a transport request, no matter how inconvenient. But he also had a passion for clean lorries. In the early days when he cleaned the lorries himself he said he could not relax at weekends if he knew they were dirty (Davies, 2001). Clean lorries was to became one of his company's hallmarks.

Gallup's list of twelve entrepreneur life themes includes *dedication* which we summarised in Table 1.2 as being 'consumed by a goal or purpose'. This summary is more what we mean by *vision* than by *dedication*. *Vision* is about the goal and purpose and its link to *advantage* whereas the idea of being 'consumed by' something is a key part of *dedication*. *Dedication* is more about a state of mind, about what really matters to the person. We see *vision* as a talent issue and *dedication* as one of temperament which is why we make the distinction between them.

Motivation is the entrepreneur's driving force. It has received more attention from researchers than perhaps any other entrepreneurial attribute, as we reviewed in Chapter 1. It is therefore a little surprising that *motivation* does not feature on any of Gallup's lists of talent or life themes. No doubt, this is because it underwrites so many of them.

As we have seen, entrepreneurs are motivated to make a difference, to leave their footprints. One of the strongest motivations is for them to be their own boss. They do not find it easy to take orders from other people. Entrepreneurs can often have their self-confidence dented by circumstances and be out to prove something to somebody; like the entrepreneur who was sacked by his boss and set up in competition nearby. Five years later he had the pleasure of buying out his old company and firing his ex-boss.

Some outstanding entrepreneurs have had very humble origins and want to show that they matter and have significance. For others it is a matter of necessity. They live in the poverty, their country has been in a war zone for years, they have had to leave their homeland – quite simply they are destitute. This group is of such size and economic importance that the Global Entrepreneurship Monitor (GEM) has termed them 'necessity entrepreneurs', as compared with the more usual 'opportunity entrepreneurs'. Survival is a strong motivator.

Outer ego We divide this outer side of the *ego* facet theme into three sub-themes:

1 Responsibility
2 Accountability
3 Courage.

Responsibility is the attribute that allows the entrepreneur to take charge and to be respected for it. People know that he or she is in control. The bank manager knows that the true entrepreneur will not just walk away when the going gets tough. It is this attribute that allows others to trust the entrepreneur. Sadly this is not the image of entrepreneurs and many people would want to score them down on *responsibility*. We believe that this is not justified by the evidence and that it is actually because they are prepared to take responsibility that they achieve so much.

J. Arthur Rank emerged from the shadow of his father, the miller, at the age of forty-one, to almost single-handedly build the British Film industry. Rank knew very little about acting or the theatre and yet he was the man who stepped forward and took the responsibility for the fledgling industry. Rank was to give the British Industry its finest hour and become a very rich man in the process. But the starting point was that he took responsibility for it all and people trusted him to deliver (Wakelin, 1997).

Accountability is something that entrepreneurs take seriously but they do so in a personal way. They are accountable to themselves above everybody else. They are their own hardest task masters. Athletes have the same kind of personal accountability which, like entrepreneurs, stems from their internal locus of control that we discussed in Chapter 1. The first person they blame is themselves. Others see this and often wonder why they are so hard on themselves. The answer is that they cannot help it. It is part of their nature, their ego.

Jonathan Edwards has been an outstanding holder of the triple-jump world record which he set in 1995. Three years earlier, he had failed badly at the Barcelona Olympics, not even reaching the finals. Edwards was very harsh in his judgement of his performance. His biographer comments that for top athletes 'there is a necessary harshness of self-judgement' in such situations. 'They work to a balance sheet with a bottom line that is defined as sharply as any financial institution in the City. There is one column marked "Win"; there is another column marked "Loss". The truth cannot be hidden' (Folley, 2001).

Accountability can put great pressure on the inner theme of *self-assurance*. Jonathan Edwards again provides an interesting example. Just before his world record achievement he went down with a serious virus and spoke with fellow athlete Roger Black who had had the same illness. Black comments 'I heard the tiredness and detachment in the voice, and became aware of his lack of confidence. You can always hear that doubt in an athlete' (Black, 1999). A person strong on *accountability* and weak on *self-assurance* can easily get caught in a downward spiral of guilt. With this kind of mismatch between the *inner* and the *outer ego*, it is difficult to live a happy life, let alone carry the pressures of the entrepreneur.

Responsibility and *accountability* are quite close to each other and a person strong in one is likely to also be strong in the other. Thus in Gallup's list of 'life themes' which we presented in Table 1.1 'responsibility' is defined as 'a need to assume personal accountability for your work'. The description of 'responsibility' in the StrengthsFinder® list is closer to our use of the word. People strong in this talent theme take psychological ownership of what they say they will do. They are committed to stable values such as honesty and loyalty.

Courage is what enables the entrepreneur to confront situations. It is one of our ten action factors in Chapter 1 and appears in Gallup's twelve entrepreneur life themes in Table 1.2 where it is defined as 'determined in the face of adversity'. This we term *practical courage*. Gallup's general list of life themes, Table 1.1, describes courage as 'an ability to use emotion to overcome resistance'. This we call *emotional courage*. We add a third *belief courage* and now review them briefly.

- Practical courage
- Emotional courage
- Belief courage.

Practical courage is the ability to face reality. People strong on *inner ego* can find this a particular difficulty. Their *self-assurance* and *motivation* can make it very hard for them to realise that they might actually be wrong. People who have never failed at anything in their lives can come to believe too much in themselves and find failure difficult to accept, let alone face up to.

Entrepreneurs need to be strong in *practical courage* if they are to cope with the difficult times. They need it to be able to make hard decisions. An entrepreneur achieved remarkable growth rates over several years and then decided to expand the business but it was at just the wrong time and he made some bad appointments in the process. The business took a nose-dive and reality had to be faced. Within a very short time the entrepreneur had dismissed the ineffective people that had been recruited, reduced the size of his operation to one that was viable and sold his family home and moved into a smaller house. He had demonstrated *practical courage*.

Emotional courage is this kind of courage required when people and personal situations have to be confronted. Entrepreneurs cannot afford to carry passengers and their expectations of performance are usually very high. People may have to be disciplined and hard decisions taken. Entrepreneurs who are not able to grasp this kind of 'person' nettle will be seriously disadvantaged. The ultimate is dismissing someone from their job and that takes real emotional courage, as anyone who has done it knows.

Emotional courage is also needed with customers, investors and people outside the business. It applies wherever trust is involved. There may not be the cash to pay a supplier, orders may have been promised and not come through, or the money promised by an investor may have been delayed. All of these can involve a call to people the entrepreneur has built up a good relationship with to explain that a promise cannot be kept or to point out that they have not met their obligations. It is much easier to delay the call and hope the issue resolves itself. Entrepreneurs strong on *emotional courage* bite the bullet.

Belief courage is the *outer ego* side of *dedication*. It is what helps entrepreneurs stamp their own beliefs and personality on their business. It is one thing to have beliefs but it is another thing to impose them on others. Entrepreneurs seem to do this without even thinking about it but it is still an important characteristic to recognise and often missed by investors. They expect a professionally led company and often find it difficult to cope with what they see as the style or even whims of the founder entrepreneur.

Anita Roddick and The Body Shop with its campaigning approach against injustice and exploitation is perhaps the classic case of *belief courage*. Some have questioned whether it is possible to run a successful business and at the same time get a 'belief type' message across. The entrepreneur does not really care. Like Roddick they just get on and do it. Those strong in *belief courage* stamp their beliefs on the business anyway. It is not in their nature to do otherwise.

Team   is an important facet theme for entrepreneurs that can enhance their performance significantly. We have already noted that in Gallup's early work on entrepreneurs that three of their twelve life themes were team issues, Table 1.2. We certainly agree with Gallup that team talents are important but we do not see them as essential. We know of entrepreneurs who are clearly successful and yet are not strong on *team*. They are aggressive, unpleasant individuals who never seem to consider how other people might feel. They think only about themselves and their business and treat people simply as a resource, hiring and firing at will. They do gather a team around them but it is not one that meets any of the sub-themes that we describe under the *team* facet.

Steve Jobs of Apple seems to be in this category. Steve Wozniak, his founding partner, has commented how abrupt Jobs was with people and says 'I couldn't be that way with people. But maybe that's what you need to run a business, to find things that are worthless and get rid of them' (Freiberger and Swaine, 2000).

What Jobs does have is the charisma of a leader. His return to Apple Computers announced at the Macworld Expo in San Francisco in 1997 was greeted with wild applause as the audience jumped to their feet in acclamation. Chris Espinosa, one of Apple's first employees, commented 'Finally in Steve we have a leader whom the people at Apple are willing to follow. All he has to do is bend his eyebrow the wrong way and people do what he wants' (Freiberger and Swaine, 2000).

Jobs is a leader entrepreneur who, though weak on *team*, has the leadership talent of 'charisma' that more than compensates. But his team is made up of followers, even disciples – they are not colleagues or co-workers.

Some entrepreneurs are weak on *team* but do not have Jobs's leader charisma. They too seem to find followers who develop a good understanding of what is wanted and are able to pick up the debris that the entrepreneur has left behind. They do not however contribute to the direction of the business and so are not effective in multiplying the talents of the entrepreneur.

Although the *team* facet theme may not be essential for the entrepreneur, it is certainly very desirable. Entrepreneurs will go further and higher with this facet than without it.

We have identified four *team* sub-themes. These include the three identified by the Gallup but under slightly different names to those used in Table 1.2. There is also an important addition, namely *networking*.

1 People selection
2 Team working
3 Using experts
4 Networking.

People selection is an important asset for anyone building a business. We began Chapter 1 with the Nolan Bushnell's description of the entrepreneur. The first step was to build the team. 'If you are the right entrepreneur, you have three or four of the best minds in the business.' Bushnell saw the entrepreneur almost entirely in terms of *people selection*.

Gallup's term 'Individualised Perception' comes closest to our *people selection*. It is included in their list of twelve entrepreneur life themes, Table 1.2, and their list of general themes, Table 1.1. The descriptions of this theme are respectively 'sees and uses strengths in others' and 'an awareness of and attentiveness to individual differences'.

Getting the right people is one of the most difficult and generally inefficient areas in business, and entrepreneurs just starting out do not generally have the money or time to use professional recruiting agencies. Instead they have to rely on their instinct which means they really do need to be strong in this sub-theme. Don Valentine, the Silicon Valley venture capitalist, has told us that he rates getting the right people as the most important success factor in business start-ups. He explained that he was always prepared to invest heavily to get the right person, and if that meant attracting the vice-president of a major company to the start-up then he would do what it takes.

Bill Gates knew the kind of people he wanted in his business. They had to be 'bright, driven, competitive, and able to argue effectively for what they believed in' (Freiberger and Swaine, 2000). But knowing the kind of staff you are after is not the same thing as being able to select them. In our experience, *people selection* is a rare talent.

Team working is about getting people to act as a single unit with everybody pulling in the same direction. Effective team work can be more important than the strength of individual members, as many sports have discovered. The English Football Association Cup consistently produces its 'giant killers' when clubs with international players are humbled by amateur teams.

Gallup's entrepreneur life themes include 'team', Table 1.2, as does their general list, of life themes, Table 1.1. Their descriptions are respectively 'gets the right people together' and 'a need to build feelings of mutual support'. Both relate to our term *team working*.

Team working is perhaps the *team* sub-theme most often found in the entrepreneur. There is something about a new venture that captures people's imagination so that they work together with a natural enthusiasm. The entrepreneur can build on this. We recall a visit to a small high-technology company in Cambridge where a notice board announced 'champagne for everybody in the board room'. They had achieved their best sales figures ever and this was the way the entrepreneur chose to thank his team – everybody was included.

In their StrengthsFinder® list Gallup combine our *people selection* and *team working* sub-themes under the word 'individualisation'. People strong in this talent theme 'are intrigued by the unique qualities of each person. They have a gift for figuring out how people who are different can work together'.

Using experts, the third *team* sub-theme, does not come easily to all entrepreneurs. It is the special talent of recognising when help is needed and then being able to select the right expert. Gallup uses the term 'expertise orientation' which Table 1.2 describes as 'knows own limits and finds experts'. Again, it is one of their entrepreneur life themes.

Two tasks are involved. The first is to be able to recognise when help is needed. This can be difficult if the inner ego is so strong that the entrepreneur thinks that he or she can do everything. Handing over a key area to somebody else is never easy and it is particularly difficult for the entrepreneur who wants to run the whole show. Some entrepreneurs are indeed remarkably competent but none can 'walk on water'.

The second task is selecting the right expert. This links in with the sub-theme *people selection* but is made more difficult because the entrepreneur is dealing with professionals outside his or her area of expertise. This is particularly a problem for entrepreneurs who are just starting out. They generally have no experience of lawyers, bank managers or accountants and assume that because these people are professionals they all have the same level of competence. This, of course, could not be further from the truth as many entrepreneurs have had to discover the hard way.

It can however have a positive side. One entrepreneur told us that when he started his first business he took advice from his bank manager and a business adviser allocated to him by a government agency. After a while he realised that he and they were just not on the same wavelength. They might have been older and more experienced than him but he found that he understood his business far better than they did. This gave him the confidence to make his own decisions and not to seek their advice. Even so, entrepreneurs do need professional advice and it is important they have someone whom they can rely on in the key areas. The entrepreneur who can select the right experts and knows how to use them has a great advantage.

Networking is vital to the entrepreneur and to the creation of an entrepreneur culture in a region. It is one of the entrepreneur's action factors discussed in Chapter 1 and, as we explain in Chapter 14, played a key role in making Silicon Valley what it is today.

It is perhaps surprising that *networking* was not among Gallup's original twelve entrepreneur life themes, particularly as *multirelator* – 'an ability to build an extensive network of acquaintances' – was included in their general list of thirty-nine themes shown earlier in Table 1.2.

Networking has long been recognised as a key business activity, as chambers of commerce and business associations demonstrate. But entrepreneurs give it a new and sharper edge. For them networking is not just about socialising with others of like mind. The entrepreneur with *networking* talent is always on the look out for people who can be of help. As Jack Welch of GE has commented 'everyone you meet is another interview' (Welch, 2001). Entrepreneurs always network with a purpose; a case of their *advantage* facet theme working with their *networking* talent.

One networking entrepreneur we have worked with gets a few of his contacts together from time to time with the comment 'I don't know if anything will come of this but I think you will find the other people interesting.' Invariably of course something useful does come from it. Networking is that simple but it is of vital importance.

Social is the facet theme of the social entrepreneur. We add this as a distinct theme because we believe that the social entrepreneur has an attribute that the business entrepreneur does not. We see it as more than having a social conscience or a generous disposition. This may be the starting point but social entrepreneurs have a cause that consumes them and is their passion. We discuss social entrepreneurs in detail in Chapter 7 with appropriate examples. Here we are concerned with the make up of the *social* facet theme. We construct it differently to the other themes. Rather than breaking it down into its sub-themes, that entrepreneurs possess in different strengths, we see it as a series of building blocks which together make up the facet theme.

These building blocks are:

1 Belief
2 Values
3 Cause
4 Service.

Belief is the basic building block. It is what a person builds their life around. If they build it around themselves then we have the *self-assurance* of the *inner ego* facet theme but if it is built around a faith or value system then we have the beginnings of the *social* facet.

In their general list of life themes in Table 1.1, Gallup describes 'belief' as 'a need to orient your life around prevailing values'. Belief and values are clearly linked but we prefer to start with *belief* and then move to *values*. This step from *belief* to *values* might seem self-evident but it is not the case. It is quite possible to have sincerely held beliefs without letting them interfere with business. This can be a case of simple hypocrisy but it can also be a conscious decision on the part of the entrepreneur to keep belief and business apart.

Brian Souter of Stagecoach has a sincerely held Christian faith but considers this is a private matter and that it is not practical to apply the Sermon on the Mount to business. He once told a newspaper reporter 'Don't misunderstand me, ethics are not irrelevant, but some are incompatible with what we have to do because capitalism is based on greed. We call it dichotomy, not hypocrisy' (Wolmar, 1999). Souter is also a socialist and sees capitalism as something he just has to live with.

Values, the second building block of the *social* facet theme, is more than business ethics or a set of behaviour standards, important though these are. It is a way of thinking about and understanding values that are internalised. They are values that the person has made their own and is prepared to live by even if it involves a cost to the venture. The Body Shop Charter drawn up by Anita Roddick has as one of its points 'The Body Shop's goals and values are as important as the products and profits'. Though City investors may not have been happy with this, Roddick stayed firm with this position over many years and grew a remarkable international business. We tell her story in Chapter 7.

Another part of the Roddick 'Charter' states 'Honesty, integrity and caring are core values and they should impact upon every activity' of the business. The wording here suggests that Roddick is trying to make the point that these values have to be internalised and made one's own. It is not just a matter of checking actions against a company handbook with a set of ethical rules or core values, they have to be lived out.

In their StrengthsFinder® description of the 'belief' talent theme, Gallup has the same overlap between belief and values that we have already noted. Thus Gallup describes 'belief' in terms of 'having strong core values that are enduring. Your belief theme gives meaning and direction to your life. Your work must give you the chance to live out your values'.

Many entrepreneurs have a *social* facet up to the level of *values* but not beyond. Nonetheless they are still able to make a significant social impact. In the late eighteenth century the Quakers created a remarkable entrepreneurial environment in Britain that combined business enterprise and social welfare. Their businesses spanned 'a huge section of British industry and commerce from brewing to banking, engineering to cotton, chemicals to china' (Kennedy, 2000). Names like Cadbury, Fry, Lloyds, Barclays, Price Waterhouse all have Quaker roots. In the nineteenth century George Cadbury built the town of Bournville for his employees and Elizabeth Fry pioneered prison reform. Their Quaker faith gave them values of honesty, fair dealing, hard work and social equality which they pursued diligently and with enthusiasm.

Whilst we would not call these business men and women full 'social entrepreneurs' we do recognise their valuable contribution to the creation of both economic and social capital.

Cause is the next building block of the *social* facet and marks the step to the true 'social entrepreneur'. Once people espouse a cause, life is rarely the same again. If that person has the *social* facet character theme within them, dormant or otherwise, the cause will bring it to life. Some people find their cause early in life but others have an experience that grips them and they find their cause. In Chapter 7, we tell the stories of Dame Cecily Saunders whose cause became 'care for the dying' when she nursed a dying man, and of Elliott Tepper who as an MBA student at Harvard got into drugs and then had a religious experience that changed his life. Tepper later found his cause while a missionary in Spain. It was drug rehabilitation.

Their cause is the basis of their mission. It digs deep into their *ego facet* and becomes their motivation. It strengthens their *courage* and they take on *responsibilities* they would never have thought possible.

Gallup lists 'mission' in their general life themes, Table 1.1, and describes it as 'a drive to put your beliefs into action'. We would want a stronger definition that included the idea of espousing a cause and following it through in service to others, which is our final building block.

Service to others is the outcome of the *social* facet theme. Social entrepreneurs take this last step. They are not prepared just to follow a cause and spend their lives lobbying in its favour. They want to take action and change things. William Booth, who founded the Salvation Army, did not just preach against the working conditions in the Bryant and May match factory. As we relate in Chapter 7, he set up his own match factory in competition which paid higher wages and did not use the unhealthy yellow phosphorus.

Gallup has 'service' as one of its general life themes, Table 1.1, and defines it as 'a drive to be of service to others'. For the social entrepreneur the *service* is much more focused. It is *service* in a *cause* rather than simply general good will. It is *cause* that motivates and *service* that delivers.

The three Gallup general themes of 'belief', 'mission' and 'service' come close to our model for the social entrepreneur. However we see them as one building upon the other and consider that the *cause* has a more direct impact on *service* than either the *belief* or the *values* that support it.

FACETS: the operational level

This section is concerned with how the six facet character themes of the *foundation level* work together at an *operational level*. There are many possible combinations of the six basic character themes that together explain how the entrepreneur operates. We have chosen to describe the three that we consider the most important but we would encourage you to think through other combinations for yourself. In that way the power of this approach will become clear.

Entrepreneurs do not think in terms of character themes nor are they likely to be aware of how they link together. But this approach does provide a basis for understanding how entrepreneurs operate and moves us closer to the point where we can identify the potential entrepreneur.

The three combinations we now consider are:

1 The talent chain.
2 The temperament challenge.
3 The social transformer.

The talent chain is the entrepreneur's main operational mechanism. It is how they 'create and innovate' and link together the first three facet character themes of *focus, advantage* and *creativity*.

Creativity is the first link in the *talent chain*. In some ways *creativity* is a servant or source talent expressing itself through other talents. In sport, in the arts and even in science, the interplay of *creativity* with other talents specific to the area results in excellence. The same is true for entrepreneurs. It is their *creativity* facet theme that helps them think differently and come up with new ideas, and for them it serves and fuels their *advantage* talent. Alone, the entrepreneur's *advantage* facet theme would have nothing to feed on.

Entrepreneurs are at home with uncertainty and chaos because they know they can always come up with an idea that will see them through. This happens because *creativity* and *advantage* work together. *Creativity* on its own would simply generate more ideas and increase the chaos but the entrepreneur's *advantage* facet theme is able to take these ideas and select the one idea that will make the difference. *Advantage* helps the entrepreneur to know which wave to catch.

In discussing *creativity* and *advantage* it is easy to think of them as standing alone, rather as the research and development department in a company stands apart from the marketing department. This separation is, of course, not in the interests of a company nor is it helpful in our considerations other than for the purpose of definition as in our *foundation level* descriptions. For the entrepreneur the manner in which these two facet themes come together is of crucial importance. The *ideas, opportunities* and *solutions* of the *creativity* facet theme will link in to the *advantage* facet theme differently depending on their strengths. For the entrepreneur, the most important link of the three is probably with the *opportunities* sub-theme.

In the study that we conducted with Gallup's help and reported on earlier, one of the respondents was found to be weak on *creativity* but strong on *advantage*. When we talked this over with him he agreed that he was not a very creative person but added that he was good at picking up ideas and opportunities from other people. It is thus possible for a weakness in *creativity* to be compensated for by strength in the *advantage* facet theme. Entrepreneurs who cannot create the opportunities simply go out and find them. In this sense, entrepreneurs can be 'opportunity predators' which is why inventors and others often resent their activities.

When we discussed earlier the *opportunities* sub-theme of *creativity* we gave the example of the entrepreneurs who helped to build up Coca-Cola in its early years. We could equally well have given this example under *advantage* since the entrepreneurs involved spotted, rather than created, most of the opportunities. In fact, several of them were 'opportunity predators'. This overlap between *creativity* and *advantage* is an important one which is why the chain is an appropriate analogy. Both facet themes intertwine at this point.

The *benefit orientation* sub-theme of *advantage* is what spots the opportunity and picks it up from the *creativity* link. The other *advantage* sub-themes work on the opportunity as it moves along the link towards *focus*. *Performance orientation* helps the entrepreneur to quantify the opportunity as *vision* begins to crystallise and sharpen. *Resourcing* enables the entrepreneur to service the opportunity. None of this process is quite as mechanistic as this description implies but the essential processes are there. As this interaction within the *advantage* facet theme takes place, the opportunity that was spotted becomes one that is either selected or rejected. This is the point at which the *advantage* and the *focus* links in the chain intertwine and the selected opportunity becomes the target that *focus* delivers against.

The mechanism that has been described, whereby *creativity, advantage* and *focus* all working together to take an idea through to practical application, is in effect the innovation process. For entrepreneurs, this process is involved in all they do. It is not just about one particular innovation. It is operating all the time, both on the large issues like building a company and on the small day-to-day matters that the entrepreneur has to deal with. Indeed, it is part of their make-up to be innovative. With the entrepreneur, 'innovation' is a person and not just a process.

We have been describing the ideal profile of the entrepreneur. We have said that a weakness in *creativity* is not serious as long as the *benefit-orientation* sub-theme is strong. *Advantage* and *focus* on the other hand are equally important facet character themes and unless a person is strong in both there will be no entrepreneur. Without *advantage* there would be no target and even an entrepreneur strong on *focus* would be unguided, unable to discriminate and prioritise. Equally, without *focus* the entrepreneur would not be able to grasp the opportunity and bring it to fruition. Neither of these facets can stand alone.

A chain is only as strong as its weakest link. The question therefore arises as to whether it is possible to strengthen areas where there is a known weakness. We do not believe this to be possible because we are dealing with a *talent chain*, and *talents* cannot be added on or trained in. As explained in Chapter 1, Gallup's research findings have consistently shown that efforts to correct weaknesses in areas that are talent-based do not work. Thus we see little point in a person who, for example, is weak on *advantage* enrolling on a course in marketing to try and strengthen this particular link in the *talent chain*. In the long term, the weakness will become all too evident.

The temperament challenge   is about moods and motivation, about self-worth and taking responsibility. It is about having the courage to face another day when things are tough. None of this is special to entrepreneurs but there is a particular temperament challenge for entrepreneurs. It is the challenge of using the temperament to enhance and galvanise their talents.

By temperament we mean what we have called the *inner ego* and the *outer ego* in our *foundation level* description. It will be recalled that *inner ego* is made up of three sub-themes: *self-assurance*, *dedication* and *motivation*. *Outer ego* similarly has three sub-themes: *responsibility*, *accountability* and *courage*.

These themes work together with the *talent chain* and with the *team* talent if it is present. The *inner ego* gives the confidence to exercise the talents and the drive to take action. The *outer ego* handles the consequences. The result is that the talent chain does not hang limp but is put under tension by temperament and things 'entrepreneurial' happen. *Team* provides an important multiplier, as we have already discussed.

However all this assumes that the character themes are equally strong and that is not always the case. A strong *ego* facet theme with a weaker *talent chain* or vice versa creates problems. The *advantage* facet theme is the most influenced. A strong *ego* with a weak *advantage* produces strong motivation and great enthusiasm that will be wasted on false opportunities. A strong *advantage* with a weak *ego* means great opportunities will be followed up indifferently and without commitment. Either way the entrepreneur will founder. When both themes are strong, however, *advantage* becomes even stronger. *Ego* brings the power and the passion to the opportunity which carries it forward and helps the entrepreneur to convince others of its viability most importantly, potential investors and customers.

Ego strengthens *creativity* and *focus*. *Creativity* is stimulated and encouraged. *Focus* is given drive and is empowered to persevere. *Ego* and *team* are more problematic because here the entrepreneur's *ego* theme meets other people's *ego* themes. Strong *motivation* can come over as pushiness and the desire for power. *Self-assurance*, *responsibility* and even *courage* of the entrepreneur can easily be mistaken for arrogance.

By way of example we now consider two specific linkages between the facets of the *talent chain* and the *ego* facet character theme.

- Motivation
- Courage.

Motivation provides the will and the power to do something with one's talents. Indeed, motivation can bring out talents that we never knew we had. This is certainly true of many entrepreneurs who have come from underprivileged or difficult backgrounds and have to do something just to survive. Often, to their surprise, they discover that they have the necessary talents and they do well.

Without motivation, talents can languish. Part of the succession problem in family companies is a matter of motivation rather than talent. The second generation enjoys the fruits of the first generation and decides to follow a life style pattern. They see no point in working as hard as their parent, usually their father, and decide instead to enjoy life. This does not mean they do not have the talent to be a successful entrepreneur but they certainly do not have the motivation.

The advent of high technology has created many young millionaires. Some were technologists in the right place at the right time rather than true entrepreneurs. It is therefore not surprising that they settled for a comfortable life style once they had made their money. However there are others whom one would have thought of as entrepreneurs but who have also settled for an easy life. We know a number of such people personally. The issue here is one of motivation. It is a weakness in their *inner ego* that prevents them from going further.

Because this is a temperament issue it is influenced by a person's experiences and by the prevailing culture. The current mood building up in our affluent western culture, that there is more to life than accumulating wealth, encourages a life style approach. We are not saying that this is wrong, but merely that it diminishes the motivation and drive of some entrepreneurs.

Courage is called into action when particular situations arise. Often these situations cannot be anticipated so that *courage* always has to be alert and ready for duty.

When Armand Hammer, the founder of Occidental Petroleum, was a young man he suddenly found himself in a corner. He was already a millionaire in his twenties, the son of a Russian immigrant and living in the USA. Hammer visited Russia to try and help with the severe famine of 1922. Seeing a completely unrelated opportunity he offered to set up a private venture pencil factory in competition with the state factory which was still at the project stage. He claimed he could set up a factory within one year producing $1 million worth of pencils. Quite a claim for a twenty-three year old who knew nothing about making pencils. His *advantage* and *ego* character themes were working overtime. He offered to back his claim with a cash deposit of $50 000, and the Russian Central Concessions Committee agreed the arrangement.

Hammer's plan was to go to a leading pencil manufacturer in Germany and offer them a deal. When he got there he found that they were not interested and he had no plan B. This was the corner he found himself in. Most people would have given up at this stage but Hammer was an entrepreneur strong in *advantage* and *courage*. In his biography Hammer admits that he thought of cancelling his contract but then 'a lucky chance opened the door for me' (Hammer, 1988). It might have been a 'lucky chance' but it was his *courage* that made him keep trying. Hammer met an engineer in a local bar – his *networking* talent in action – whom he discovered had been in the pencil manufacturing business in Nuremberg and had accepted an offer to set up a pencil factory in Russia. Then the war came and he was trapped in Russia. When he finally got back to Nuremberg his previous employers spurned him for being disloyal. Hammer found that there were many others in a similar position and within two months had recruited the workforce he needed. Almost exactly six months after signing the contract, the factory started production. Hammer knew how to make things happen. He was strong on *focus*. In the first year they produced $2.5 million worth of pencils well ahead of the target of $1 million and in the second year $4 million. They soon had a virtual monopoly on pencil production in Russia.

Each pencil was inscribed with the word Hammer. When Hammer met the Soviet leader Khrushchev in 1961 he was delighted to be told that Khrushchev had learnt to write using Hammer pencils (Hammer, 1988). Hammer's *inner ego* must have felt very pleased with itself but it was his *outer ego* sub-theme of *courage* that had made the difference.

This story not only shows the key role that Hammer's *courage* played when he was in a tight corner but also the interaction of *advantage, networking* and *focus*. With this example in mind, we would encourage you to read the stories in Part Two and note how the different character themes interact.

The social transformer is a way of describing the impact that the *social* facet character theme can have on the other facet themes. The transformation it achieves in the social entrepreneur goes right to the heart of what drives an entrepreneur. It challenges and redirects the *ego* facet giving it a new purpose and direction. But it also sharpens the talents and influences how they are used.

Transformation might seem too dramatic a word to describe the effect of the social facet but we feel it is actually what happens when a person takes on a cause and makes it their own. They may have been active in the social area for many years even approaching it in an entrepreneurial way, their belief and values providing the motivation and giving purpose. But once they engage a cause they move from the general to the particular and their whole life revolves around it. Elliott Tepper, as we said earlier, had a life-changing experience and became a missionary but he did not find his *social cause* until he met some drug addicts in Madrid.

We now consider in turn the transformation effects that the *social* facet can have on the entrepreneur's talent and temperament.

Talent transformation   The *social* facet works on talent in two ways. First it can help people to discover entrepreneurial talents they never knew they had. J. Arthur Rank had tried his hand at being an entrepreneur when he was younger but according to his biographer 'He made a complete hash of the business' (Wakelin, 1997). His father Joseph Rank was disappointed in his son but did allow him back into the family business. Then quite suddenly at the age of forty-one J. Arthur found his cause. 'He strongly believed God had given him the job of making good-quality religious films' (Wakelin, 1997). He was a staunch Methodist and a Sunday school teacher. Spreading the Gospel by films became his cause and his entrepreneurial talents blossomed. Over the years the cause developed and became broader but it had triggered his remarkable talents. Within ten years, he had a business worth £50 million owning film studios, cinemas and distribution rights.

The second way in which the *social* facet works on the talents is less dramatic but nonetheless important. *Belief*, the first element of the *social* facet, affects the way people view their talents. Many today simply see talents as something that they happen to have, and although we speak of people as being gifted in sports and the arts, this is not generally linked with a belief in any way. However, for people where the *belief* element is strong, the word 'gift' is understood quite differently. *Belief* provides an interpretation of talent that is strongly personalised and often interpreted in terms of a personal faith. Such people see talents as something special that they have been given and of which they are stewards. They believe that their talents must be used in the best possible way and certainly must not be wasted. Some would go further and see the exercise of their talent as a duty laid upon them.

Values has an effect across all the talents, bringing to them integrity and influencing them in different ways. It may put some areas of opportunity off limits; pornography or the arms trade, for example. Other areas will be stimulated. Guiness beer, for example, was developed by the entrepreneurial Guiness family in Ireland as a solution to the chronic problem of alcoholism, beer having a much lower alcohol content than spirits. Their motivation was a social one. As we have said, it is not only the social entrepreneur who can be strong on *values*.

Many of the day-to-day operational decisions of *focus* involve judgements that have a *values* element. For example, honesty in telling the customer the true state of an order or a supplier when the cheque is really in the post. These may be small issues but they make the point. Values have to work in practice. A psychologist who spent the first half of his career as an academic and then set up a successful business consultancy put it this way. 'People are most likely to be successful when they' have 'a well-thought-out and consistently applied set of business values' that 'then become an anchor for effective decision-making' (Langhorne, 2000).

People strong on *focus* do not just talk about values. They apply them and thereby bring an integrity to the way they operate in achieving their target.

Values can have an important impact on *team*, and specifically on the way that the entrepreneur works with other people. As with *opportunity* it can work both ways. Some may regard entrepreneurs strong on *values* as somewhat naive and so seek to take advantage of them. Others would respond positively, preferring to work with people who live by their *values*. Employees prefer a boss whom they can respect and trust. Trust is the chief result of *values* and *team* working together. It is trust that makes teams work well and gives them coherence. People are much more likely to encourage and help one another when there is a high level of trust.

Fukuyama (1995) has shown that trust within a people group has a direct influence upon the economic prosperity and well-being of that group. The extended family is an interesting example of this. They have shared values and mutual trust and they work very hard in support of each other. This makes for a very powerful and efficient economic unit which is why small businesses in places like Hong Kong and Singapore have been so successful.

Temperament transformation *Belief* and *values* can have an important influence on *ego*, the temperament facet theme. *Belief* tends to have its greatest impact on the *inner ego* whereas *values* affect more directly the *outer ego*. Thus *belief* can give *dedication* a stronger and deeper passion, and if it is a faith belief, both *self-assurance* and *motivation* can be affected. *Values* on the other hand can change the way the entrepreneur handles *responsibility* and give new and challenging criteria to *accountability*. *Courage* is influenced by both *belief* and *values*. *Belief* can actually give a person the courage to pursue a particular course of action that *values* have made the person decide to take.

In discussing *belief* and *values* we have used examples of the business entrepreneur as well as the social entrepreneur. This is because there is essentially no difference in the way that their *social* facet influences them, as far as *belief* and *values* are concerned. The situation with *cause*, the third building block of the *social* facet, is quite different and is an important dividing line between the business and the social entrepreneur. This is because *cause* has a profound effect on *ego*, the temperament facet, and brings about what is in effect a *temperament transformation*. It takes over and redirects the person. This happens whether a person is an entrepreneur or not because we all have an *ego* facet. Many who work in the more difficult areas of social need have the kind of commitment that espousing a cause brings. However, it seems from general observation that very few of them also possess the talents of the entrepreneur. Instead, most social entrepreneurs seem to be people who have taken on a cause and then discovered that they are entrepreneurs. In a few cases, business entrepreneurs are gripped by a cause and become social entrepreneurs. It is in such cases that a *temperament transformation* takes place, as the *cause* element of the *social* facet theme impacts the person's *inner ego*.

This impact is of two kinds depending on how strong the *inner ego* is in the first place. When it is weak the positive energy of the *cause* makes *dedication* and *motivation* come alive. *Dedication* has found something to commit to and *motivation* has an objective, as with J. Arthur Rank cited earlier. A weakness in *self-assurance* is not so easily transformed, and potential social entrepreneurs often lack the confidence to take the first step.

Lord Michael Young was probably the most outstanding social entrepreneur of his generation. Amongst thirty or more ventures he founded the Open University, the 'Which' Consumers Association and The School of Social Entrepreneurs. He was always telling potential social entrepreneurs to 'Go for it. You never know until you try.' One of them told us how Young had given her the confidence to take the first step and that was enough. Once she had started she gained more and more confidence and her *self-assurance* built up. 'It was as if I needed someone to give me permission' she told us 'but once I got going I really enjoyed it.'

People who are strong on *self-assurance* have a different problem. This is essentially a battle between their *inner ego* and their *cause*. The *ego* wants to do things for itself whilst the *social* facet wants to do things for others, and there is a basic conflict across *self-assurance*, *dedication* and *motivation*. A social entrepreneur deeply committed to social action has commented 'Selflessly we are motivated to serve God and people in need; Yet, despite our determination otherwise, self is not so easily defeated. Somewhere down the track all too often we start building our own empire' (Hawkins, 2001). He has clearly felt the tension between his *inner ego* and his *cause*.

He then describes the social entrepreneur's temptation. 'One of the root causes of this empire building tendency lies in self-worth. As we spend ourselves on behalf of the needy, a world that does not value them, thinks equally less of us. Result: we ourselves feel undervalued and become tempted to produce something that the world does value and recognise.'

This battle is a real one, as the example illustrates, and can only be won as the *social* facet finds strength in its *belief* foundation.

The final building block of the *social* facet theme is *service* to others. The *temperament transformation* has a direct effect on how this *service* is rendered in that the *inner ego* has a social *motivation* and the *outer ego* has social *values*. It is this that makes social entrepreneurs what they are and different from the business entrepreneur. In most cases the journey to the *cause* is the root of the transformation. It changes understanding and builds a feeling for the people who are served. Dame Cecily Saunders' 'dying man' and Elliott Tepper's own drug experiences meant that they could each relate effectively to those they served.

Identifying entrepreneur potential

Here we discuss a three-stage 'entrepreneur indicator' that we have developed based on the FACETS approach and conclude with a section on the 'entrepreneur enabler' who plays a key role in making all this happen.

The entrepreneur indicator   The FACETS approach described above considerably simplifies the task of identifying the potential entrepreneur. It is now a matter of assessing the presence or otherwise of the six facet character themes, and if we are concerned only with business entrepreneurs then that reduces to five. Even so the task is not a simple one when we are considering an individual's potential because some of the facet themes may be dormant. People are also very complex and it is never possible to assess them with certainty. We therefore prefer to think in terms of 'indicating' a person's potential rather than of identifying it. On this basis, we have devised a three-stage 'entrepreneur indicator' procedure. The first two stages screen or filter people through to the point where there is every indication that they are potential entrepreneurs. Stage three then works with them to further develop their talent, temperament and technique, so that they become true entrepreneurs.

- First screening – from the many to the possible.
- Second screening – from the possible to the probable.
- Third screening – from the probable to the actual.

First screening   This is designed to evaluate a group of people in as effective and efficient a way as possible. It is therefore necessarily short and approximate. It provides an indication of those within the group who may have the potential to be entrepreneurs. Typically the group being evaluated would be graduating students seeking some career direction or applicants for an entrepreneur programme such as a business start programme, an entrepreneur post-graduate course or an entrepreneur summer school.

Although designed with groups in mind this first level of screening is now available on the Web and so can be used by individuals who wish to assess their entrepreneurial potential. However it is important to remember that this is only a first screening and result should be checked out further. Details of the website can be found in the Preface.

The 'First Screening Entrepreneur Indicator' comprises a set of opposite statements designed around the facet character themes. Respondents choose between the statements on the basis of which describes them best. The respondent's strengths in each facet theme are then derived from these answers. When a weakness is indicated in a particular facet theme it is still possible that that person could be a useful member of an entrepreneurial team as long as at least one other team member is strong in that facet theme. Thus a team could comprise one person strong on *creativity*, another strong on *advantage* and a third strong on *focus*. In this case the roles within the team would need to match the facet theme strengths so that everybody is playing to their strengths.

Evaluations have shown that certain groups can possess higher or lower strengths than average because of some form of pre-selection or cultural influence. Thus a group of students specialising in media studies all scored highly on *creativity* whereas young graduates as a whole have tended to score low on *focus* but high on *ego*. These scores for young graduates suggest a relaxed approach to life together with a determination to succeed. This could easily be a case of student culture masking an innate ability to focus.

Second screening   This is a more detailed evaluation against all the facet character themes and can be conducted in a number of different ways. Whatever method is used, the aim is to produce as accurate as possible a measure of a person's strengths. The three methods that have been considered are:

- A comprehensive telephone or Internet-based questionnaire.
- A self-evaluation text-based procedure.
- A participative programme-based procedure.

The first of these options follows Gallup. Their early 'entrepreneur perceiver interview' is an example of a comprehensive questionnaire used with experienced telephone interviewers. Gallup's more recent StrengthsFinder® is an Internet-based questionnaire carefully constructed to evaluate strengths across thirty-four talent themes using paired questions. Our six entrepreneur facets themes have a total of twenty-five separate strength elements, if sub-themes are taken into account, and so would require something slightly smaller in scale than Gallup's StrengthsFinder®.

The self-evaluation text-based option is the one followed in our book 'The Entrepreneur in Focus' (Bolton and Thompson, 2003). The procedure involves a three-pass self-evaluation. The first pass is a short review of the six facet character themes to which readers give a quick response of their strengths. The second pass involves working through a descriptive and explanatory text, including questions to provide a self-evaluated score for each of the sub-themes. These are then combined to give a considered final score for each of the six themes. The third pass is an evaluation of the strength profile to identify operational strengths and weaknesses. Thus if the *inner* and *outer ego* scores are significantly different there could be a problem. Equally there could be an imbalance across the *talent chain*. If, for example, *focus* is stronger than *advantage*, which is stronger than *creativity*, then we have what might be termed an increasing or strengthening funnel. This is not as effective as when all are equally strong but it will mean that something is achieved as *focus* targets and takes action. If, however, the funnel is a decreasing one with *creativity* stronger than *advantage* which is stronger than *focus* then there will be a surfeit of ideas and little delivery.

The third evaluation option uses a learning environment with trained evaluators to take people through each of the facet character themes and explain the way that they work together, as we have done in this chapter. The learning environment should also include some entrepreneur exercises and the opportunity to evaluate stories of successful entrepreneurs against the six facet character themes. In this way, the participants will have begun to understand what is involved in being an entrepreneur and the evaluators will have formed their own judgement of each person's strengths. Each person then completes a self-assessment similar to the text-based procedure described above but with much more understanding. Because it takes place within a group setting there can be discussion so that the judgements made are more informed and less subjective.

The evaluation is completed by a one-to-one interview with an experienced evaluator at which both parties agree together on the candidate's strengths in each facet character theme. Ideally the outcome of this programme is that those who show that they have the potential then embark on a business-start programme of some kind. Here it is a case of *possibles* having become *probables*.

Third screening This is an ongoing measure of the person's entrepreneurial strengths and a record is kept over time. It continues to use the facet character themes, and evidence of the strengths is gathered by an assigned evaluator as the *probable* entrepreneurs go through the process of identifying and planning their business and then launching it. Here one would expect to see improvement as each strength is built on and develops.

Where strengths in a particular facet theme do not develop or improve as well as expected it is best to bring in other people who have the missing strengths. In this way an entrepreneurial team can be built up. Here the role of the evaluator is of vital importance. Not only is good judgement required but he or she must take on a coaching role to develop the person's or the team's entrepreneurial talents and work with them on their temperament issues. Technique input can be provided as and when necessary. The outcome is that *probables* become *actuals*.

This *three-screening* approach is not a short-term matter and takes time. People will drop out after the *first* and *second screenings* but that is to be expected. It is not that these people have failed but rather that they do not possess the necessary talents and temperament to be entrepreneurs. It is much better for them to find this out at an early stage than to have them learn the hard way when their business fails and there are heavy debts. Those who complete the first two stages and come out as *probables* will be those who have the potential to become successful entrepreneurs and will justify all the help that they are given.

The entrepreneur enabler The process described above relies on the ability and experience of people who are able to evaluate and thereby identify potential entrepreneurs. These people are part of a very special group which we term 'entrepreneur enablers'. We first identified this group when we looked at the way in which entrepreneur cultures develop in certain regions. We found that four components were required:

- An opportunity focus and resource – such as high technology.
- A number of spin-off points – places from which new businesses can emerge.
- A visible focus – evidence that something significant is happening.
- Entrepreneur enablers – people who find and encourage the entrepreneurs.

Much of the material presented in Parts Two and Three of this book are examples of these four components at work.

Fred Terman, of Stanford University, was a classic entrepreneur enabler. He encouraged a whole generation of students to think entrepreneurially and was a key player in the rise of Silicon Valley, as we explain in Chapter 14. Most notably he put Bill Hewlett and Dave Packard together and suggested they start a company. He helped them with start-up funding and was their coach and mentor.

'The Cambridge Phenomenon' had several entrepreneur enablers, particularly at the key spin-off points in some of the university departments and local research laboratories. But they were also two in a local bank and one was the head of an accountancy firm. In due course some of the early entrepreneurs also became entrepreneur enablers.

Entrepreneur enablers are 'hands-on' people who are able to spot potential entrepreneurs. They are like talent scouts but then go on to do the coaching, mentoring and training. Not all can cover the full range and there are signs that some specialisation is beginning to happen. Thus Leonard and Swap (2000) speak of 'mentor capitalists' as 'a special breed of adviser' who 'helps entrepreneurs with everything from recruiting talent to negotiating the first million in seed money'.

Most entrepreneur enablers seem to come from institutions or the professions. They have an entrepreneur's heart but are not themselves entrepreneurs. In terms of our six facet themes they appear to be strong in all except *advantage* and specifically the sub-theme *benefit orientation*. But they do seem to have an extra character theme which Gallup terms *developer*. Their StrengthsFinder® describes it in this way, 'you see the potential in others. Your goal is to help them experience success. Signs of growth in others are your fuel' (Buckingham and Clifton, 2001). We would also add the ability to enthuse with entrepreneurs whilst at the same time providing a reality check for them, thereby helping them to face the reality of a situation.

Entrepreneur enablers, like some entrepreneurs, simply emerge but others have to be encouraged to do so. Academics who are in touch with students, bank managers and accountants who meet with those who are thinking of starting a business and government and private agencies that promote business formation will all have entrepreneur enablers in their midst. Just as we need programmes to identify potential entrepreneurs so we need similar programmes to find the entrepreneur enablers. But it cannot be assumed that all those involved in helping people start businesses are entrepreneur enablers just as it cannot be assumed that everybody who runs a business is an entrepreneur. In one entrepreneur enabler programme for business advisers we estimated that only 20 per cent were entrepreneur enablers. It was a case of people being competent in the area of business techniques but not in the talents and temperament of the entrepreneur.

Today there is a constant search for potential high-growth businesses. They are seen as the key to regional economic development and millions are spent every year on trying to find and promote them. We believe that the starting point is not the ideas or the business model but the potential entrepreneurs and entrepreneur enablers. If these can be identified and put to work then high-growth businesses will simply spring up and local economies will be transformed.

References

Black, R. (1999). *How Long's the Course?* Andre Deutsch.
Bolton, W.K. and Thompson, J.L. (2003). *The Entrepreneur in Focus: Achieve Your Potential.* Thomson Learning.

Buckingham, M. and Clifton, D.O. (2001). *Now, Discover your Strengths*. Simon & Schuster.

Buckingham, M. and Coffman, C. (1999). *First, Break All the Rules*. Simon & Schuster.

Clifton, D.O. and Harding, R.E. (1986). A statistical analysis of the psychometric properties of the SRI Entrepreneur Interview, *Gallup Report*, September.

Clifton, D.O. and Nelson, P. (1996). *Soar with your Strengths*. Dell Books.

Collins English Dictionary (1995). HarperCollins Publishers.

Davies, H. (2001). *The Eddie Stobart Story*. HarperCollins.

Dick, F. (1997). *Winning: Motivation for Business, Sport and Life*. Abingdon Publishing.

Ericsson, K.A. and Smith, J. (1991). *Toward a General Theory of Expertise*. Cambridge University Press.

Folley, M. (2001). *A Time to Jump*. HarperCollins.

Freiberger, P. and Swaine, M. (2000). *Fire in the Valley: The Making of the Personal Computer*. 2nd edn, McGraw-Hill.

Fukuyama, F. (1995). *Trust*. Hamish Hamilton.

Goleman, D. (1996). *Emotional Intelligence*. Bloomsbury.

Hammer, A. (1988). *Hammer: Witness to History*. Coronet edn, Hodder & Stoughton.

Harre, D. (1982). *Principles of Sports Training*. Sportverlag.

Harverson, P. (1999). A surfeit of character, *Financial Times*, 10 September, p. 5.

Hawkins, P. (2001). Editorial, *In the Field*, Autumn.

Hilton, C. (1957). *Be my Guest*. Prentice-Hall.

Howe, M.J.A. (1990a). *The Origins of Exceptional Ability*. Blackwell.

Howe, M.J.A. (ed.) (1990b). *Encouraging the Development of Exceptional Skills & Talents*. British Psychological Society.

Jelinek, M. and Schoonhoven, C.B. (1990). *The Innovation Marathon: Lessons from High Technology Firms*. Jossey-Bass Management.

Johnson, R. (2003). A life in the day, *The Sunday Times Magazine*, 6 July, p. 58.

Kaplan, J. (1997). *Start Up*. Warner Books.

Kennedy, C. (2000). *Business Pioneers – Family, Fortune and Philanthropy: Cadbury, Sainsbury and John Lewis*. Random House Business Books.

King, N. Jr (2003). Iraq's business elite gropes in the dark, *Wall Street Journal*, 25 June.

Langhorne, J.E. (2000). From academe to business: a personal journey. *The Psychologist-Manager Journal*, **4** (1), 60–66.

Leonard, D. and Swap, W. (2000). Gurus in the garage. *Harvard Business Review*, November–December.

Martin-Jenkins, C. (2003) Cricket, *The Times*, 7 May, p. 36.

Morita, A. (1994). *Made in Japan*. HarperCollins Business.

Pendergrast, M. (1996). *For God, Country & Coca-Cola*. Phoenix Paperback.

Roddick, A. (2000). *Business as Unusual*. Thorsons, HarperCollins.

The Times. (2002). 16 January.

Tyson, F. (1987). *The Test Within*. Hutchinson.

Wakelin, M. (1997). *J. Arthur Rank*. Lion Publishing.

Wallace, J. and Erickson, J. (1993). *Hard Drive*. John Wiley.

Welch, J. (2001). *Jack*. Headline.

Whybrow, P.C. (1999). *A Mood Apart*. Picador.

Wolmar, C. (1999). *Stagecoach*. Orion Business Books.

Woods, B. (1998). *Applying Psychology in Sport*. Hodder & Stoughton.

3 Entrepreneurs and strategy

Strategy matters in entrepreneurship, but good ideas, in isolation, are inadequate – making things happen and implementing strategic ideas is a crucial element. In this chapter we look at how strategies are created, how they form, how they are implemented and how they are changed. We explore strategic positioning in relation to value-building opportunities and we consider how established organisations can promote and sustain growth through corporate entrepreneurship. Here we focus on intrapreneurship, the encouragement of internal entrepreneurs. We conclude with a section on strategic weaknesses. The points raised here are then explored in greater detail in the stories we feature in Chapters 4 and 5.

Introduction – entrepreneurs and corporate entrepreneurs

Strategies are means to ends. They are created and implemented in an attempt to fulfil the organisation's purpose. They are a metaphorical map of the routes which organisations follow; but those who undertake any journey are usually free to change their minds at any time and alter either the direction they are going in or the detailed route. From the map will emerge more specific tactics which provide a detailed guide to actions.

Some entrepreneurs set out on journeys which involve great distances; others have no great desire to travel very far. Some are willing to stretch themselves and move outside their previous experiences; others have only limited ambitions and prefer to stick with routes they know because they have travelled them before. Some set off because they want to go somewhere different; others are travelling because, for some reason or another, they have to. At the extreme are those who see themselves as explorers and who wish to 'chart uncharted waters'. Some will set off as lone travellers, perhaps hoping to meet up with fellow travellers and form a group to share the experience, whilst others will intend to stay on their own. Some, of course, only start out when they have found like-minded others. In these groups there will sometimes be harmony and sometimes friction. Some travellers will be remembered for their achievements and may even write about them; others will always be largely anonymous. Nobody will bother to tell their story. Some will exceed the expectations they have (and others have of them) when they set out; others will be disappointed and never achieve their final goal. Some will stumble or break down, failing to deal with the setbacks they encounter. As is the case with every journey, some travellers will be better prepared than others – they will try to make sure they set off with the resources they are likely to need, or at least with some knowledge concerning how to get hold of them. Some will have planned as much as they can, down to the finest detail; others will have a compass and leave a great deal more to chance.

If we take this metaphor and put it in the context of entrepreneurs in the general world of business, we can delineate three distinct layers. The importance of strategy is different in each case. We have:

- *The growth entrepreneur* – who creates a sustained high-growth business which will almost certainly add to the products, services and markets it begins with. The business is likely to diversify and become international, if not global, in scope. If the founding entrepreneur is to stay in charge of the business as it grows and prospers, he or she will need some leader characteristics. He will be a leader-entrepreneur who habitually champions new ideas which give the business a fresh impetus time and again.
- *The entrepreneur* – who creates a significant business by finding important ways to compete effectively and out-perform rival organisations. These entrepreneurs and organisations may diversify and globalise, but not on the same scale as growth entrepreneurs. In some cases, the growth potential is deliberately restrained because, for example, the entrepreneur wants to stay firmly in control. In some cases, entrepreneurs will opt to sell a business they have started once it reaches a certain size and, exhibiting serial behaviour, start another new one from scratch.
- *The enterprising person* – who establishes a small or micro business which will create a limited number of jobs, but which has only limited growth potential because it is not sufficiently different from its rivals that it is set apart.

The relation between these three levels is set out in the triangle featured in Figure 3.1. We have chosen a triangle to indicate that there are more enterprising people than there are entrepreneurs, and more entrepreneurs than growth entrepreneurs.

Basically, as people discover their talents and develop them, they can move up the triangle – as long as they have a good business idea and strategy. Developing ideas in Gibb and Ritchie (1982) we can argue there is a simple A-B-C key which determines the potential to move up the hierarchy.

- A represents ambition and certainly encapsulates the motivation element of the ego facet.
- B stands for the quality of the business model, which we discuss below.
- C is for capability, and this embraces ability and resources.

We can see that this A-B-C has two fundamental elements – the entrepreneur as a person and the business idea, the strategy. This is why it is essential to look at the entrepreneur and the strategy at this stage in our understanding. We can take this

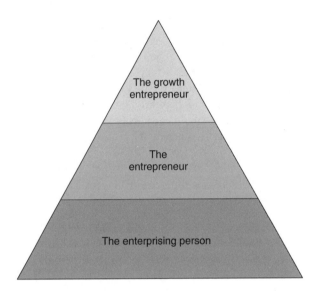

Figure 3.1 *The general business entrepreneur*

one stage further and create a measuring POLE for evaluating the basic worth of any business idea or proposal:

- P = Person
- O = Opportunity
- L = Leadership and championing the opportunity
- E = Exploitation of the opportunity, resourcing it and controlling the deployment of the resources.

Although we most commonly associate entrepreneurs with the general business sector, they are also found in the corporate sector and in the community and voluntary sectors. We can develop a similar triangle for entrepreneurs in the corporate world (Figure 3.2).

The levels in both triangles roughly correspond so that the intrapreneur is the enterprising person in the big company. The venturer is the equivalent of the entrepreneur, and the transformer is the growth entrepreneur of the corporate sector.

Transformers are those strategic leaders who succeed in either changing the rules of competition in an industry or dramatically changing the fortunes of a company that has fallen on hard times. Industry transformers force every rival organisation in an industry to take note of what they are doing and to respond in some way. Organisational transformers typically start by reducing costs and improving efficiencies (the so-called 'company doctor' role) but they follow this up by leveraging the resources at their disposal to create new forms of competitive advantage.

Venturing encapsulates a number of forms of new venture creation from inside an existing organisation. New businesses can be started up using corporate resources – maybe spare capacity, maybe an innovatory new idea. They can also be established

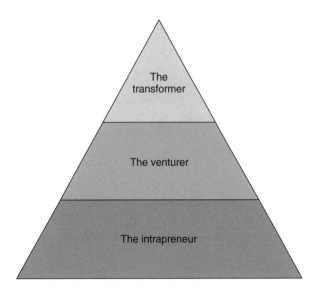

Figure 3.2 *The corporate entrepreneur*

by floating off a non-core activity as an individual business or by selling the business to its existing managers – what we call a management buy-out. Intrapreneurship involves encouraging those employees with entrepreneurial characteristics to be enterprising and to look for new and different ways of doing things.

We said earlier that growth entrepreneurs might be termed 'leader entrepreneurs'. In the same way we can use the expression 'entrepreneurial leaders' to explain the achievements of transformers and some venturers.

Explaining strategy

Entrepreneurs who succeed have a purpose and direction, and they build value. They accomplish this with successful strategies, which we have defined as 'means to ends' – ways of achieving objectives and fulfilling the purpose of the organisation. Strategies, then, are the things that businesses do, the paths they follow and the decisions they take in order to reach certain points and levels of success. The term *corporate strategy* is used for the range of activities, products and services embraced by the organisation. At the beginning of an organisation's life, there is likely to be only one or a very limited range of products or services, but this can expand considerably as the organisation prospers. The growth can be focused around related activities or show increased diversity, although contemporary strategic wisdom would counsel against too much diversification, as diversity often fails to deliver synergistic benefits. As well as a range of complementary – synergistic – activities which all benefit from being part of the same organisation, it is important that each activity is individually a strong competitor in its market or market segment. This implies it enjoys competitive advantage, an edge over its rivals, which comes from building values that customers appreciate and competitors find difficult to copy. These individual *competitive strategies* are themselves the result of a bundle or collection of functional activities and strategies, each of which relates to a particular aspect of, say, production, marketing, information or financial management. In this chapter we concentrate mainly on competitive strategy – reflected in strategic positioning – whilst recognising that suitable and carefully timed acquisitions and divestments which change the scope and diversity of the organisation can also be entrepreneurial and opportunistic.

As we have said earlier in the book, entrepreneurs see or realise where there is an untapped opportunity, engage it and make things happen. There is often a visionary element to this for the idea alone is clearly inadequate and indeed the idea might not be original to the entrepreneur. It is what entrepreneurs do and achieve which holds the key to success. Figure 3.3 suggests that an idea becomes an opportunity

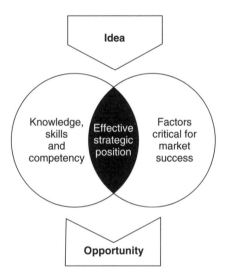

Figure 3.3   *From an idea to an opportunity*

when it promises an effective strategic position – which, in turn, implies a match between those factors which are critical for success with the customers in the targeted market and the knowledge, skills and competency the entrepreneur and the business can offer and provide. Figure 3.4 takes this argument further and relates it back to issues we discussed in Chapter 1. The opportunity-spotter realises where there is a gap in the market, and has or sees an idea to fill it. The project champion grasps the opportunity and builds the business which successfully fills the market gap. The entrepreneur, of course, accomplishes both.

This success then brings its own demands. Entrepreneurs need to build a team of appropriate key support people and they need to ensure a suitable organisation structure emerges – one which enables control as the business becomes more complex and the decisions that have to be made increase in magnitude. Whilst this happens the original idea and strategic position – the competitive strategy – will need constant refinement and improvement to sustain the growth and momentum, especially if

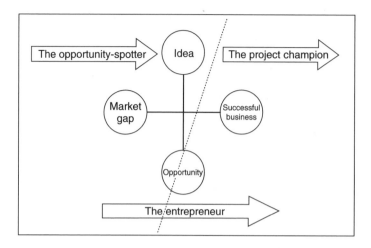

Figure 3.4   *The entrepreneur, the opportunity-spotter and the project champion revisited*

competition intensifies. On occasions, the relevant product or service may itself have to be abandoned and replaced by a new, fresh strategic idea and position. The emerging structure must not inhibit these changes; indeed it should positively encourage them.

As a summary of these points, Stevenson and Gumpert (1985) argue that entrepreneurs are opportunity-driven and that they constantly seek answers to a series of key questions, namely:

- Where are the opportunities?
- How do I capitalise on them?
- What resources do I need?
- How do I gain control over them? – we referred earlier to the fact that entrepreneurs use networks and contacts to 'beg, steal or borrow' suitable resources.
- What structure is best? – accepting that without this, renewal and growth is less likely to happen.

We can see these points brought together in Figure 3.5. The entrepreneur is placed in the centre of the diagram, the orchestrator of the whole process. His (or her) contribution is to input a vision, realise where there is an *opportunity*, engage it and stimulate action. To develop and grow effectively, the organisation needs to find a *strategic position* in the market where it can offer – and be seen to be offering – something which provides value for the customer. Either the product or the service is different from everything else, and different in a meaningful way, or it offers 'better value', perhaps by being cheaper but not of inferior quality. The idea for the winning position can start with ideas from inside the organisation, perhaps using new technologies to do new things, or it can be a response to issues raised by customers. Where it starts is less relevant than the need to bring together the customers' needs and the resources required to satisfy them. Finding this position, then, is the theme of *strategy creation*. Planning will play an important role in the process, but it may well be the actual implementation of the idea that is planned rather than the idea

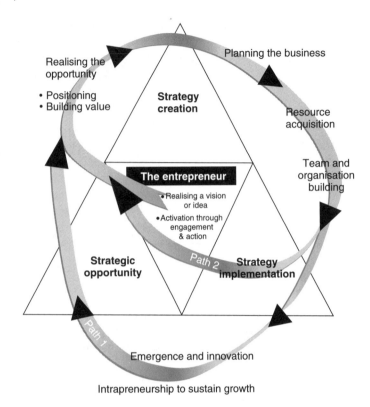

Path 1: Intrapreneurship/corporate entrepreneurship;
a flow of ideas from inside the organisation

Path 2: Fresh ideas from an entrepreneurial strategic leadership

Figure 3.5   *The entrepreneur: seeing and activating opportunities*

itself, which might have been realised more opportunistically, largely reliant on the entrepreneur's attentiveness and insight into the market. There are several planning techniques and models that can be utilised but it should always be remembered that a model is designed to support and assist the decision-making process, not to make the decision for people. Moreover, plans should be flexible rather than rigid, as implementation is a learning process. Ideas are refined with experience. It is impossible to foresee all the issues involved in activating the idea.

As we move further with *strategy implementation*, the team and organisation building we discussed above become increasingly significant. But, and again reinforcing points made above, strong and winning strategic positions will have finite lives, which in today's world can be relatively short ones. Successful companies attract competitors, who are themselves looking for new, profitable opportunities. Success is maintained by innovation and *strategic change* which keep an organisation perpetually one step (or even more) ahead of its competitors. The Path 1 loop in Figure 3.5

highlights how intrapreneurship can foster new ideas and improvements in a flexible and entrepreneurial organisation. Generally, here, we are implying changes to functional and competitive strategies. New ideas, of course, may well be input by the founding entrepreneur – Path 2 in the diagram. Sustained growth really needs more than one source of ideas; and, realistically, major changes to the overall corporate strategy will require a significant input from the strategic leader. Where there is a string of these 'giant steps', they are often linked to leader entrepreneurs.

The key message is that opportunity – strategy – implementation is a circular loop and it must be maintained with change. The successful entrepreneur will make sure there is a constant flow of new ideas and a commitment to try out at least some of these new ideas. If an organisation loses this momentum and the ideas dry up, perhaps because the developing structure promotes order and control rather than flexibility and change, the organisation will, sooner or later, hit a crisis point – as we will discover later in the chapter. When this happens, it is likely that a change of strategic leader will be needed before growth can be restored, always assuming it is not too late!

Where a company comes from is less important than where it is going.
As boundaries are erased, corporate birth certificates won't count for much.
(Ron Sommer, when President, Sony Corporation of America)

To conclude this section the following list cross-relates Figure 3.5 with some of the ten key action points on what entrepreneurs do, which we explained in Chapter 1.

- *Strategic positioning* – spotting and exploiting opportunities, prioritising customers' interests, creating value.
- *Strategy implementation* – finding the resources required, understanding and managing the risks involved.
- *Strategic change* – ensuring there is creativity and innovation in the business.

The business model

B stands for business model in our A-B-C criteria. The business model is fundamentally the logic behind the business idea – is it a product or a service with a clearly identified market? So, when we argue that an organisation needs a sound, or a winning, business model we mean that there is a need for a very clear picture concerning *what* the organisation is – and what it isn't – and *who* will buy its products and services, and *why*. The business model thus embraces three key themes – the product (or service), the market and the 'compelling reason to buy'. Invariably, products and services will be competing against others – there has to be some strong reason why customers should choose a particular one. Sometimes the reason will be price-related; quite frequently, it will be because it is different in a way that is attractive to customers. It represents value to them. Successful entrepreneurs understand customers; they know how to add value in a meaningful way.

It is important to remember here that strategy always involves choices. Organisations have to make decisions about what they intend to do, at the same time ruling out things less appropriate or desirable for them to do; maybe because competition is too intense; maybe because they do not possess the required competencies and capabilities. This picture then needs to be communicated and understood throughout the organisation. Moreover, the model – and the strategies which underpin it – needs to be reviewed constantly. The picture should embrace the business as it is now, and how it will be in the future – where and how it will change and grow.

In the interlude before Chapter 7 we discuss the rapid rise of Southwest Air, the pioneering no-frills airline whose model has been copied, at least in part, by Ryanair and EasyJet. Southwest was created with a very clear purpose which might be worded as follows – *make affordable travel available to everybody barred from exercising their freedom to fly by other airlines' high prices*. The fundamental underpinning to the model, then, is a low-cost culture with a constant search for savings to allow ever-lower prices, but without reducing passenger safety. This demands that only those aspects of the service that are seen as essential or important are included; others that are offered by the traditional full-service airlines are dropped. The market is anyone – business, holiday or general passengers – who wants low prices and will trade off certain aspects of service to get them. Their compelling reason to buy is price – as long as there is a basic level of service and no fears about safety. The model then has to be resourced, delivered and implemented; and this is where we come down to the operational details that support the model. The choice of a single type of aircraft and the selection of fringe airports are typical actions that make up the strategy to deliver the model. The no-frills airlines tend to use airports that are not main hubs and this is one of their ways of reducing costs. Because the purpose has always been clearly understood – and supported – by Southwest employees they have often been willing to 'go that extra mile' to provide a high level of service to their customers.

This model for the no-frills airlines has had a transformational effect on the airline industry, particularly in Europe. The full service carriers, such as British Airways, Air France and Lufthansa have all suffered as they have lost customers, revenues and profits. Another example of an entrepreneurial business model – but this time one from an existing market leader which consolidated its position rather than broke into an industry as a newcomer – would be disposable razors. Disposable razors have not displaced durable razors and disposable blades, but they have taken a sizeable market share. A completely different model would be one where an organisation builds its share of the market by a series of enterprising acquisitions of smaller competitors. In the case of funeral parlours, this is another strategy that was shown to work in America and brought over to the UK. It works because the basic product or service is identical in different towns and cities – implying there is the potential for scale economies and shared learning – but it remains important for the business to maintain a local presence.

Business models have finite lives, though the length of this life will vary tremendously. Whilst it is always important to be looking for ways to improve the existing model, it is also necessary from time-to-time to create a completely new and different model – as we saw in Figure 3.5; maybe in response to competition; maybe in response to changing customer expectations. Constant improvement demands an entrepreneurial culture in an organisation; transformational change requires an entrepreneurial leader to take charge and drive through the change.

The entrepreneur's environment

The future was predictable – though very few predicted it!
(Alan Kay, when Research Fellow, Apple Computer)

Hamel (1997) argues that a changing business (or external) environment opens up the possibility for finding new business and competitive opportunities all the time. There are opportunities for entrepreneurs and the entrepreneurially minded organisation; for the others there are threats. He cites globalisation, shorter product and service life cycles (linked to technology improvements and to consumer willingness to change more frequently than in the past) and faster, more sophisticated communication networks as typical sources of opportunity. He explains that there are known and visible areas of opportunity – such as gene-engineered drugs, non-branch banking and multi-media – but stresses the secret lies in finding the 'right' strategic position to exploit the opportunity. As we have already said, because of the constant environmental turbulence, any strategic position must be seen as temporary and sensitive to unexpected events; innovation is needed to reinforce and defend a position of strength.

Without constant improvement, renewal and intrapreneurship, there are obvious dangers in this changing environment, but alone this may well prove inadequate. The most entrepreneurial companies will, at the same time, be searching for new ways of competing. Linked to this is the difficulty for many organisations that future competitive threats are as likely to come from unknown or unexpected organisations currently outside the industry as they are from existing, known rivals. In the early 1980s it is highly likely that British Airways was particularly concerned with the possible actions over routes and fares by its main American and European rivals; it seems much more improbable that they anticipated the threat that Richard Branson and Virgin Atlantic were going to pose. British Airways may well have recognised the potential for new competitors as deregulation changed the air travel environment, but predicting the source was another matter. As we will see in Chapter 5, the outsider Direct Line had the same impact on the insurance industry.

Successful entrepreneurs find new products and new needs ahead of both their rivals and their customers. Market research can tap into issues that are important for customers, but it is unlikely to provide the answers. Creativity, insight and innovation stimulated within the organisation are more likely to achieve this. Entrepreneurs and entrepreneurial organisations thus *create proprietary foresight from public knowledge* by synthesising information and environmental signals and creating new patterns and opportunities.

This intellectual foresight has a number of possible sources, according to Hamel and Prahalad (1994):

- It can be a personal restlessness with the existing status quo – the Schumpeter view. In Chapter 5 we point out that the serial entrepreneur Paul Sykes was, from an early age, *not content with his lot.*
- It can be a natural curiosity – which the education system does not manage to stifle! – which leads to creativity. Sometimes the entrepreneurs concerned have a

childlike innocence in the questions they ask, and the process is stimulated by a wide network of contacts.

- It may be a willingness on the part of certain individuals to speculate and manage the risk of investigation. Invention has to precede learning.
- It is sometimes a desire to change things and 'leave footprints'.
- Often there is an empathy with the industry and market concerned.
- This can be coupled with the ability to conceptualise what does not yet exist . . . *you can't create a future you can't imagine.*

Three approaches to strategy

There are three distinct approaches to strategy and strategy creation. They should not be seen as opposing approaches, however, but as complementary approaches to opportunity finding. The entrepreneurial organisation will certainly take account of all three, placing an appropriate emphasis on each one. The three are:

- *Market-driven* – The market-based approach implies an active search for new product and marketing opportunities in the external environment. These might be found in industries in which the organisation already competes or in new ones.
- *Resource-based* – Here the organisation clarifies its distinctive core competencies and strategic capabilities – perhaps technologies and processes – which set it apart from its competitors in ways that customers value. It then seeks to build on these competencies and capabilities to build new values for both existing and new customers. This approach has the advantage of encouraging the organisation to focus on what it can do well – as long as there is a market for it.
- *Competitor-influenced* – This is a more tactical approach which implies short-term vigilance. Whilst seeking to build the future, an organisation must never lose sight of the present day. Its existing positions must be protected against active competition. This means an ability to react to competitor moves and proactive initiatives designed to surprise competitors. Of course, it is important not to become over-reliant on this tactical approach as this is likely to make the organisation more reactive rather than proactive.

Organisations should be looking for ways of being different from their competitors. This is unlikely to come from imitation, monitoring and copying what rivals do, although this approach can be seen in many organisations. In the end, such mimicry will make all competing organisations look remarkably similar, making it difficult for customers to distinguish between them and placing too much emphasis on price competition. Instead, organisations should be looking to innovate to achieve two purposes – one intention is to always be ahead of rivals with new ideas; the second intention is to draw apart from competitors with radical differences that they find hard to imitate in the short term. There are two important provisos. First, the differences should mean something positive to customers; it is not simply a question of being different for the sake of being different. Second, it should never be assumed that any gap or advantage is anything but temporary; all ideas can be copied eventually, and all good ones will be!

We now look at these in greater detail.

Strategic positioning

E-V-R congruence

Figure 3.6 develops ideas in Thompson (2001) and shows strategic positioning as an overlap between the business environment and the organisation's resources. In other

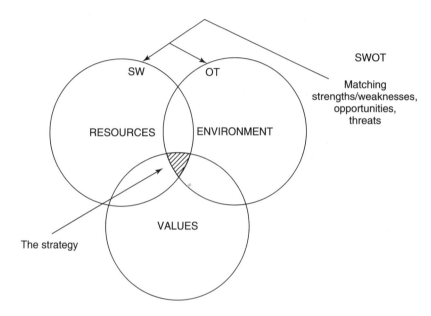

Figure 3.6   *E-V-R congruence*

words, the organisation possesses strategic or core competencies which enable it to meet the relevant environmental key success factors effectively – an analysis which, essentially, can be traced back to a SWOT (strengths, weaknesses, opportunities, threats) analysis. This accords with Porter's (1996) view that strategic positioning, per se, is not a source of competitive advantage. Positions can be understood by competitors and copied. The activities which create – and sustain with change – the position are the source of any advantage. It is through these activities that organisations build value. As we have said, positions must be seen as temporary. To ensure there is ongoing opportunity recognition, together with an ability and commitment to change, values is shown as a third circle, the overlap of this with the others creating an overall *E-V-R congruence*. It is useful to see 'values' representing the organisation culture and style of management, themselves dependent upon the style and approach of the strategic leader.

Readers who follow up the source material on E-V-R congruence will see that the concept can be applied to any size and type of organisation, and to individual parts of an organisation as well as to the whole. The search is for a position of congruency; the challenge is to maintain it in a dynamic environment. When the current situation is assessed, it is always worth conceptualising whether one would see the circles as 'overlaid' such that they can be easily slid apart, or ideally 'inter-connected', rather like the magician's three rings. If it is concluded that only two of the circles overlap, with the third one set apart, the particular pattern will provide an indication of the broad strategic route the organisation must follow if it is to generate congruency.

It is possible to re-label this basic model and show entrepreneurship as the key factor in balancing strategic competencies (resources) with windows of opportunity (the environment). Windows of opportunity are always opening in the environment, but to exploit the opportunity, organisations – and entrepreneurs – must first spot them and then capture them ahead of any rivals by obtaining and deploying the necessary resources in an appropriate way. Sometimes the resources needed will already be available; on other occasions they will have to be found. This is the market-based approach.

The alternative, and equally valid, resource-based approach to strategy emphasises that organisations must be aware of their main strengths, skills and competencies and be constantly vigilant for new opportunities for deploying and exploiting them. Prahalad and Hamel (1990) define core competencies as those distinctive skills which yield competitive advantage because they provide access to important market areas or segments, make a significant contribution to the perceived customer benefits of the product or service and, particularly, prove difficult for competitors to imitate.

Even if an organisation enjoys congruency it is clear that in a competitive environment rivals are metaphorically trying to force the circles apart – and that is why we need the magician's three rings. The competitor-influenced approach to strategy is an attempt to stop rival initiatives separating the circles and destroying congruency.

Competitive divergence

Porter (1996, 1997) concludes that strategy is *about doing things differently from your rivals*. It involves trade-offs and, in particular, critical decisions about what not to do and where not to compete. In this respect, Porter highlights the key need for strategic focus. However, he points out that in many industries there is more evidence of competitor *convergence* than there is of difference and *divergence*. Divergers – and entrepreneurs – create and build value where it can make a difference; they do not concentrate and focus on things which are only of limited significance to their customers. These rule breakers look to tread new grounds rather than copy what *everyone else is already doing*. They are creative innovators. They are likely to gain only limited benefit from those consultants who import ideas they have seen work elsewhere. In addition, they carefully select which customers and market niches actually matter to them and focus on these. Together, these issues and choices represent strategic positioning decisions.

Porter nominates Enterprise as a successful, different, divergent competitor in the car rental industry – with a business model that is distinctive. The main names we would recognise and recall are Avis, Hertz, Budget, National and Alamo. They all compete directly with each other for business. Their prices do vary, and different customers have different perceptions of their service, typically based on their experiences with the cars and, in particular, with their staff. But the services they offer are fundamentally the same. Around the world, much of their business comes from people on the move and their desks can usually be found in airport terminals. Enterprise is family-run, it is more profitable than either Avis or Hertz – although smaller – and it avoids airport locations. Instead, Enterprise has targeted customers whose cars are off-the-road for whatever reason. Perhaps they are being serviced or repaired; perhaps they have been involved in an accident. They access many of their customers through car dealers and insurance companies. They are willing to deliver cars to the customer (although clearly this does not make them unique) and they seem able to keep their cars longer – thus reducing their costs and allowing them to pass on these savings in competitive prices.

Strategic differences and divergence come from organisational activities and their unique bundling – which constitutes the way things are done in an organisation. We can see this as 'values' in the E-V-R congruence model above. It is an implementation issue. In the interlude before Chapter 7 we explain the long term, consistent success of Southwest Air in America, suggesting that whilst all Southwest's rivals know what the strategy is, it is the implementation, and the synergistic bundle of activities which support this, that make the difference.

Simon (1996) reinforces this point by separating three main levels of competitive difference and advantage. The first, and lowest, level is technology and products. Patents can help, but often these can be overcome and good ideas copied. The second level is the organisation itself, with its *operating* processes and systems. Although more difficult, these are again visible to some degree and can be copied. People comprise the third and highest level. The processes they utilise, individually and collectively, to deliver service are the hidden resource that provides the most potent competitive weapon.

Porter distinguishes between three positioning approaches:

1 Begin with the (different) product or service, built around important, core strategic competencies and offer the same product or service to anyone who might be interested.

   Bic pens are widely available. They are sold through a wide range of retail outlets; they are used by many organisations, such as hotel groups, for promotional items and low-cost give-aways.

   Southwest Air provides a no-frills, short-haul, point-to-point service between medium-size cities and secondary airports in large cities. Different groups of business and leisure travellers find Southwest's service and prices attractive.

2 Target a specific segment of the market and provide a range of products to meet a range of needs for the relevant target customers.

   > Ikea shall offer a wide range of home furnishing items of good design and function at prices so low that a majority of people can afford to buy them.
   >
   > (The Ikea mission statement)

Ikea's *main* target customers are young or first-time homeowners who are looking for modern styles at affordable prices. To satisfy this need Ikea has chosen to focus on certain strategies and ignore or sacrifice others – their carefully chosen trade-offs. There is only a limited choice of each product line (many competitors offer wider ranges); the majority of products are exclusive to Ikea and other brands are not available; expensive materials and style is traded off against affordable prices; customers self-select rather than find help from sales assistants; every store carries a large inventory, allowing for customers to buy on the spot – whilst many rivals carry only display items and rely on warehouse deliveries to people's homes.

3 Focus on a single product or service for a tightly defined niche. The small, footwear business which switched to focus on the fetish market – which we discuss in Chapter 5 – illustrates this approach.

New strategies and positions

To deal effectively with the challenges of the future, and to reinforce the points we have made earlier, Hamel and Prahalad (1994) argue that the organisation must go through three distinct but overlapping stages if it is to survive in a dynamic environment and capitalise on Path 1 growth opportunities. First, it must conceive a future position by competing for intellectual leadership in its chosen industry. To accomplish this it must understand the relevant technology, the market and the regulatory environment – and, in particular, any discontinuities that are likely to have an impact. Second, it must gestate the strategy by acquiring the resources and competencies which will be necessary to be a strong player and to be able to deal with the identified discontinuities. These resources will embrace technology and people and may be acquired with carefully selected alliance partners. Few companies possess all the competencies they will need. Nike, for example, developed competencies in product design and supplier sourcing and secured important endorsements from international sports stars. They realised that manufacturing was not an essential requirement if they worked with the right partners and suppliers. The resources must then be deployed to compete for position and market share. The third stage is to actually implement the strategy and deliver the promise.

Thompson (2001) offers the following criteria for evaluating proposed new strategies:

- *Appropriateness* – Is it a potentially winning strategic position?
- *Feasibility* – Can it be implemented? Are the necessary resources available or obtainable?
- *Desirability* – Is there a belief in it and a will to follow it through?

The virtuous circle

The successful organisation will have created a positive, virtuous circle. In true entrepreneurial fashion, it will have clarified what its targeted customers want and expect in the way of quality and service – and it will have set out to deliver this reliably and consistently and at a price that represents value-for-money. On the assumption that it has also got its costs right, this high level of customer satisfaction will yield superior revenues and profits. The organisation will use these to reward all its key stakeholders. It will pay sound dividends to its shareholders; it will reinvest a certain proportion to ensure it remains innovative and properly resourced; it will certainly reward its employees – after all, they are the people who deliver that service that satisfies, or possibly even 'delights', customers. In that way the circle is self-reinforcing. Only with change and innovation can the circle be maintained in a dynamic and competitive environment.

Corporate entrepreneurship

We have already shown how entrepreneurs are to be found in both the general business and the corporate worlds. Once an entrepreneur has built an organisation to a substantial size then the corporate world does, in fact, become its new home or new reality. It will need to find ways to change, and maybe even transform itself, in a dynamic environment. If it is to remain entrepreneurial it will have to sponsor intrapreneurship. However the entrepreneur who stays firmly in charge of this growing organisation – a person we call a leader entrepreneur – needs separating in our minds from the strategic leader who is appointed to head a large corporation. There is nothing to say that such a strategic leader has to be entrepreneurial himself or herself to be successful. Indeed, some corporate leaders have been extremely successful with a quite different personal style. Hence, some strategic leaders will be entrepreneurial leaders and others will not. They will have a different, perhaps more analytical or more financial style and approach. However, regardless of the style of leadership, the potential for venturing opportunities and the significant contribution of intrapreneurial managers is always relevant. We now look at these issues, bringing out both the strategy and the leadership aspects.

The visionary entrepreneur

In this section we are using the term 'visionary entrepreneur' to embrace both leader entrepreneurs and entrepreneurial leaders, those people who rise to the top of both the triangles that we explained earlier. Mintzberg *et al.* (1998) contend that for a visionary entrepreneur, strategy is a mental representation of the successful position or competitive paradigm[1] inside his or her head. It could be thought-through quite carefully or it could be largely intuitive. This representation – or insight – then serves as an inspirational driving force for the organisation. The vision or idea alone is inadequate; the entrepreneur must persuade others – customers, partners, employees and suppliers – to see it, share it and support it. Flexibility will always be an inherent factor; detail emerges through experience and learning.

Kets de Vries (1996) concludes that the most successful strategic leaders perform two key roles, a charismatic role and an architectural one, effectively. As a result, their strategies are owned, customers are satisfied, employees enjoy work and things can – and do – happen and change quickly. The charismatic role involves establishing and gaining support for a (winning) vision and direction, empowering employees and 'energising' them, gaining their enthusiastic support for what has to be done. The architectural role concerns building an appropriate organisation structure, together with systems for controlling and rewarding people. We can see that these arguments embrace visionary entrepreneurs and a process of intrapreneurship within the organisation. Simply some leaders will be more naturally architects whilst others will be more naturally charismatic. In each case it is necessary not to overlook the need for those contributions that are not their natural style.

Related to this latter point, Hamel (1999) distinguishes between stewardship and entrepreneurship. Stewardship concerns the continued exploitation of opportunities spotted in the past. Costs will be managed for efficiencies; some incremental changes and improvements will be made to reinforce the strategic position in a competitive environment. On its own, however, in an increasingly dynamic environment, this may well prove inadequate. Hamel uses the metaphor of Silicon Valley[2] to contend that organisations need to bring together new ideas, talented and entrepreneurial managers, and the resources they need in order to exploit new opportunities in an entrepreneurial way. The style of these people is dictated more by aspiration than by analysis – hence their link to the visionary entrepreneur.

We have extended these ideas in Figure 3.7. Here we argue that an under-emphasis on the visionary, charismatic role and an over-emphasis on structure

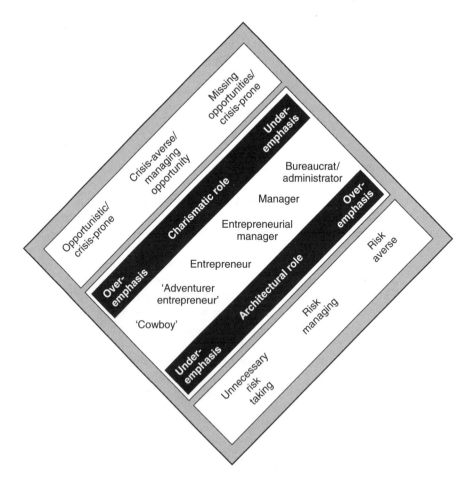

Figure 3.7   *Entrepreneurship, opportunity and risk*

and procedures results in a bureaucratic organisation which is risk-averse, likely to miss new opportunities and eventually, as a result, become crisis-prone. At the other extreme, an over-emphasis on the visionary role at the expense of adequate structure and systems implies an opportunistic 'cowboy' who takes unnecessarily high risks and again becomes prone to crises. The term 'adventurer entrepreneurs' has been adopted by Derr (1982) to describe people who take risks that others would perceive to be high ones. *They live on adrenalin; those who work with them live on valium.* They are able to exercise some control over the risks they perceive to be manageable. Entrepreneurs, entrepreneurial leaders and enterprising managers all balance the two roles in order to manage both opportunities and risks effectively.

For Mintzberg *et al.* (1998), visionary entrepreneurs often, but not always, conceptualise the winning strategic position as a result of immersion in the industry. They may simply have a genuine interest; equally they may have worked in the industry for some length of time. Their secret is an ability to learn and understand, making sense of their experiences and the signals they see. Whilst some people would never be able to make sense of a pattern of strategic signals pertinent to an industry, others learn very quickly.

> There are two types of people in the world – reasonable and unreasonable.
> A reasonable man adapts himself to the world; the unreasonable man persists
> in trying to adapt the world to himself.
>
> (George Bernard Shaw)

This quotation from Shaw appears to reinforce the relative merits of two schools of thought concerning what entrepreneurs are actually doing. Schumpeter (1949) believes that entrepreneurs disturb the existing market equilibrium and stability with innovation, whilst the so-called Austrian School of Economists (see, for example, Kirzner, 1973) contends that entrepreneurs actually create equilibrium and market stability by finding new, clear, positive strategic positions in a business environment characterised by chaos and turbulence. The Austrian perspective is that of the reasonable man who observes chaos and uncertainty and looks for an opportunity gap that others have missed. Schumpeter's innovators are unreasonable; they are trying to disturb the status quo, turn things upside down, find new strategic positions and make life hard for any existing competitors. Blanchard and Waghorn (1997) claim that Ted Turner (with CNN) and Steve Jobs (Apple) are unreasonable men who, like entrepreneurs in the mobile phones business, have been instrumental in changing the world we know.

Successful visionary, aspirational entrepreneurs, then, are not all the same. Simply, when they emerge from our so-called 'well of talent' they follow different paths. In Figure 3.8, hard entrepreneurship represents the paradigm of the independent, pragmatic, opportunistic and competitive entrepreneur. These achievement-oriented people are our typical managed risk-takers and natural networkers in search of a deal. Not every entrepreneur fits this pattern. Some present a softer image. They operate in a more informal manner; they are strong on communication and they sell their vision to engage and motivate others. The hard and soft approaches lead to quite different cultures, of course.

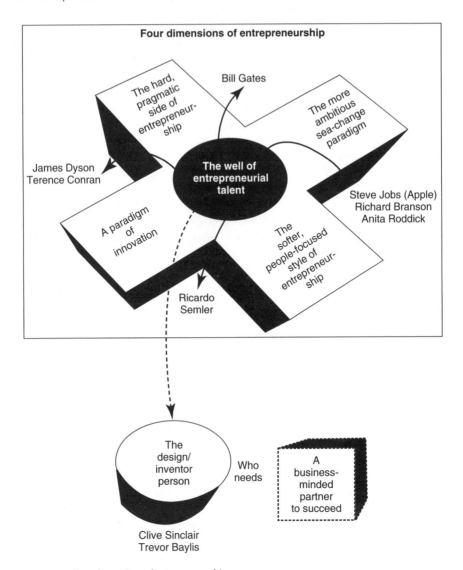

Figure 3.8   *Four dimensions of entrepreneurship*

Some visionary, adventurous entrepreneurs set out to change the world. These are people with a real ability to galvanise others; they work hard, play hard and operate at the leading edge. They have to have enormous energy and generally they would be described as 'having a presence'. Again this approach is not, and need not be, ubiquitous. The fourth arm, innovation, still requires imagination, creativity, passion and a commitment to bring about change (see Lessem, 1986, 1998).

We would suggest that Bill Gates is a typical hard adventurer – Microsoft has literally changed the world of computing – whilst James Dyson is a hard innovator. Steve Jobs, Richard Branson and Anita Roddick are certainly visionaries – their products have again had a major impact on our lives – but they have all adopted a softer style and approach. Ricardo Semler is a visionary, as far as management style is concerned, but Semco's engineering products – they include pumps and industrial dishwashers – are hardly revolutionary. He appears to typify the soft innovator.

There is a final category. The designer-inventor who lacks the necessary business acumen or interest to build the business on his or her own. Sir Clive Sinclair and Trevor Baylis fit here. All of these entrepreneurs are discussed in Part Two.

Corporate strategic change and venturing

Companies typically grow around a range of related products and services, at times extending the range or replacing models, and seeking new market opportunities. If growth ambitions start to exceed the growth potential from these somewhat limited strategies, they may look at more ambitious alternatives. Investing in their supply chain (by, say, acquiring a supplier or a distributor) is one possibility, but this invariably requires the subsequent development of new competencies. Acquiring a direct competitor or a related business is another possibility; here the organisation is seeking to build on its core competencies, normally in marketing or technology. The highest risk alternative is diversification into some unrelated activity. Ideally, with any acquisition or merger, some skills or resources will be transferable between the businesses to generate savings and benefits – which we usually term 'synergy'. But synergy is sometimes easier to promise than to achieve. Porter (1987) has identified three tests for a successful acquisition – and the more entrepreneurial businesses will score well against these. They are:

- The new industry should offer profit potential in excess of the cost of capital (debt or equity) involved.
- The entry cost (acquisition price) should not compromise the future profit stream.
- Both companies should be able to benefit from the merger. There should be true synergy from transferring skills or sharing resources.

Where a company fails against these tests, it is a reflection of a lack of entrepreneurialism in the strategic change. Most strategies, however, can be made to work if the implementation is handled well.

Reinforcing earlier points, some entrepreneurial businesses are very creative and opportunistic in their search for alliance partners to open up new market opportunities. In every case the challenge lies in fusing together two distinct cultures; where this fails to happen, E-V-R congruence can be lost.

When the growth decisions are misjudged – either the decisions taken are not appropriate and feasible, or good opportunities are missed – the organisation's performance can deteriorate and force disinvestment. This may simply require cutting back and retrenchment; it may, alternatively, require a sale of parts of the business to enable a renewed focus on core competencies. Organisations which fail to take the initiative and tackle the need for change with new, entrepreneurial ideas and ventures may be forced into this style if they are to survive – but it may turn out to be too late. Turnaround issues are discussed in the next section on strategic weaknesses.

vestment can also be a venturing opportunity for certain managers. ncerned might simply be floated off as a separate entity, raising capious parent as new investors buy in. Those managers who stay with it now find themselves in charge of their own venture. If the business is sold to its previous managers, who raise venture capital funding to become the owners, the same things happen but with a different financial model. We call this a management buyout. Where the business in question is sold to a different parent organisation, the managers who go with it may end up with more or less entrepreneurial freedom – it all depends on the style of the new owner.

Building the entrepreneurial organisation

Entrepreneurial leaders and leader entrepreneurs possess a number of leadership characteristics; they set direction and they inspire others. But their strong directional leadership should not throttle flexibility and learning by a resistance to trusting other managers and involving them in key decisions. The most successful entrepreneurs realise they cannot do everything on their own and build a team to whom they can delegate important decisions and contributions. Whilst some of these people will, by necessity, be specialists, professionals and technocrats, Horovitz (1997) stresses the importance of also recruiting or developing entrepreneurial managers to ensure the flow of innovation and change, and prevent entropy. He argues that one of the reasons Club Méditerranée (Chapter 8) lost momentum in the 1990s was the result of a failure to accomplish this back-filling effectively. Quinn (1980) also emphasises the importance of innovation and ongoing learning by this team because all the issues and difficulties that will have to be faced cannot be foreseen.

> The aim in a global business is to get the best ideas from everywhere. [In General Electric] each team puts up its best ideas and processes – constantly. That raises the bar. Our culture is designed around making a hero out of those who translate ideas from one place to another, who get help from somebody else. They get an award, they get praised and promoted.
>
> (Jack Welch, retired Chief Executive, General Electric)

Horovitz (1997) contends organisations should look for the problems before they even arise, by questioning what the (possibly very successful) organisation is doing wrong. At times it is important to abandon products, services and strategies which have served the organisation well in the past – they are not the future. Rosabeth Moss Kanter (1989) goes further still by arguing that the whole organisation holds the key to competitive advantage. She suggests that there are five criteria which are found in successful, entrepreneurial organisations. They are:

1 *Focused* on essential core competencies and long-term values.
2 *Flexible* – searching for new opportunities and new internal and external synergies with the belief that ever-increasing returns and results can be obtained from the same resources if they are developed properly and innovatively.
3 *Friendly* – recognising the power of alliances in the search for new competencies.
4 *Fast* and able to act at the right time to get ahead and stay ahead of competitors.

5 *Fun* – creative and with a culture which features some irreverence in the search for ways to be different; people feel free to express themselves.

In an earlier book, Kanter (1983) warned about the potential for stifling innovation by:

- Blocking ideas from lower down the organisation, on the grounds that only senior or very experienced managers are in a position to spot new opportunities. On the contrary, she argues, younger people with fresh minds are in an excellent position to question and challenge the status quo.
- Bilding too many levels in the hierarchy so that decision-making is slowed almost to a point of non-existence.
- Withholding praise from people who do offer good, innovative ideas, and instilling a culture of insecurity so that people feel too terrified to even question authority, policies or procedures.
- Being unwilling to innovate until someone else has tried out the idea – a fear of leading change.

In Chapter 4 we explain how Wal-Mart has benefited substantially from involving employees in new strategy creation.

Birkinshaw (2003) emphasises the importance for organisations of being clear about their venturing intentions. If they fail to clarify a proper strategy, the results are likely to be disappointing. He suggests four distinct but complementary approaches; organisations may focus on just one or adopt a mixed approach. The four are:

1 *Venture harvesting* – Creating a discrete unit to exploit spare organisational resources – such as spinning out new non-core businesses using technologies the organisation possesses. The organisation might simply go as far as patenting a new idea and then selling the patent. Some organisations have, in the past, spun out valuable service businesses built around processes they had developed to support their main activities.
2 *Ecosystem venturing* – Selective investments in complementary companies, possibly involving strategic alliances or joint ventures. Sony joined forces in a joint venture with Ericcson to develop mobile phones, for example.
3 *Venture innovation* – Some form of internal competition to generate new business ideas which the organisation then funds and supports. Shell has pursued this approach, calling its initiative 'Gamechanger'. 3M (Chapter 5) is another proponent.
4 *Corporate private equity* – Selective investments in external new start-ups that might ultimately support new directions for the organisation itself. Some organisations will provide hatchery space for these businesses to develop and grow – which allows a more hands-on involvement, as long as the corporate environment is not stifling.

Earlier comments from Brody and Ehrlich (1998) reinforce these arguments. They argue that established organisations should behave more like venture capitalists and be constantly on the lookout for new investment opportunities – finding ways to nurture them and then capitalise on their investment by withdrawing at an appropriate stage. Simply, established businesses have assets that they often fail to exploit as effectively as they might. Because they ignore anything that is non-core they fail to appreciate the potential value. However, it is important to find a suitable way of managing the new initiatives, so that attention is not drawn away from important core activities. The new ventures must not destroy the organisation's focus.

Whilst robust questioning and assumption-testing of any new ideas and initiatives is crucial, it is particularly important to remember that many people fear change, partly because of uncertainty about its impact on them personally. As a result, some people will seek to resist valuable change initiatives, and may even attempt to mount an active and orchestrated opposition. They are, in fact, enterprising and entrepreneurial, but they channel their energy in an unhelpful way. Their tactics may be aimed at preventing an idea ever taking-off; equally they may wait until it has taken root and is gaining some support and momentum. Managing change effectively, therefore, requires continuous effort and sometimes patience – reinforcing the significant contribution made by the project champion.

The process of intrapreneurship

Bridge *et al.* (1998) highlight the importance of recruiting, spotting and using people with entrepreneurial talent who are motivated to use their abilities and initiatives and do something on their own, but who may not want to start their own business. These internal entrepreneurs have been called *intrapreneurs* by Pinchot (1985) and they are instrumental in effective Path 2 growth. Intrapreneurship, then, is the term given to the establishment and fostering of entrepreneurial activity in large organisations which results in incremental improvements to existing products and services, and occasionally to brand new products. We can see an illustration of this with the example of 3M and Post-It Notes (explained in Chapter 5) but it is an extreme. The innovation is more likely to be a minor – but significant – improvement to a product or service or process – anything which makes a valuable difference. It has been commented that every one of us knows how we could do our job more efficiently or more effectively – it's just that we are not always asked or encouraged to explain how.

Intrapreneurs, typically, are strategically aware, ideas-driven, creative, flexible, innovative, good networkers, individualistic but also able to work well in a team, persistent and courageous. If frustrated by a lack of freedom they will under-achieve or possibly leave. But they are volunteers; intrapreneurship is not right for everyone.

According to Pinchot (1985), the key lies in engaging people's efforts and energy for championing, capturing and exploiting new ideas and strategic changes. This must stretch beyond the most senior managers in the organisation – who do not have a monopoly on good ideas. On the contrary, the potentially most valuable and lucrative ideas are likely to come from those people who are closest to the latest developments in technology or to customers. Suggestion schemes are linked in, but on their own do not constitute, intrapreneurship. The ideas need to be taken forward; and they can only be developed if the potential intrapreneurs are able to obtain the necessary internal resources – and, moreover, they are willing to do something. This in turn requires encouragement and appropriate rewards for success. People must feel involved in the process and comfortable they are being supported. Intrapreneurship cannot work where people feel 'frozen out' or 'dumped on'. Churchill (1997) summarises the philosophy as skills following opportunities. People in entrepreneurial businesses see the opportunities and set about acquiring the necessary resources. The whole process of change then becomes gradual and evolutionary. The momentum for change and improvement is never lost and the organisation is less likely to be exposed and weakened by its competitors, resulting in it having to cross a 'bridge too far'.

Finn (2002), who reinforces that fresh ideas are required for survival in competitive markets, cautions that many intrapreneurs are, by nature, mavericks. They are not easily handled. On the other hand, they do make others think and this, in itself, is important. Their enthusiasm for change can be highly infectious. Significantly, intrapreneurs do not think of themselves as either unusual or different – one problem is that many other people do. Finn concludes that the best manager for intrapreneurs is an entrepreneurial one – and one strong on entrepreneur team characteristics.

The intrapreneurial organisation

Fradette and Michaud (1998) describe four main elements to an organisation which succeeds with intrapreneurship. First, the strategic and structural environment is 'right'. The purpose and direction implies a realistic vision, and it is widely understood and shared. Formal systems and controls do not stifle innovation and people are free to make limited changes. Inhibitive internal 'chimneys' are pulled down so people can collaborate and share ideas readily. Second, an appropriate workforce has been built. Enterprising people – with entrepreneurial talent and temperament – have been recruited. They have been trained in key skills and there is an appropriate reward system. The organisation's main heroes are the entrepreneurial ones. Third, the workforce is backed by the necessary support systems. Teamworking is commonplace, people collaborate and network naturally, information is shared and learning is fostered. After all, several people in the organisation may be thinking along the same lines at the same time concerning future possibilities. Fourth, successes are visibly rewarded and mistakes are not sanctioned so harshly that people are dissuaded from further initiatives.

An intrapreneurial organisation will often feature a relatively flat structure with few layers in the hierarchy – too many layers tend to slow decision-making down. The culture and atmosphere will be one of collaboration and trust. The style of management will be more coaching than instructional, and mentoring will be in evidence. Ideally it will be an exciting place to work. The entrepreneur's enthusiasm will have spread to others.

Terazano (1999), however, reminds us that effective intrapreneurship is not that easily achieved, and that many organisations set off down the road but fail to reap the anticipated rewards. Balancing control (to ensure current activities and strategies are implemented efficiently) with flexibility (to foster and embrace changes to the same strategies) can imply different cultures, which are difficult to achieve without tension and conflict. Another difficulty frequently lies with finding the appropriate reward and remuneration systems to ensure fairness. It is a brave organisation which only awards bonuses to the visibly entrepreneurial people. Managers in established companies often find it difficult to handle setbacks and disappointments when initiatives fail. But there always has to be the risk of failure – albeit temporary – when experimenting with new and unproven ideas. Whilst intrapreneurs often have the security of large company employment, such that the penalty for failure is to some extent protected, the rewards for real success are unlikely to equal those of the true entrepreneur. Nevertheless, *increased competition in global markets and the pressure for innovation is forcing Britain's large companies to look for methods to stimulate ideas for new products.*

Hamel (2000) has pulled many of these themes together with his list of ten rules for *generating large consequences from small beginnings*:

1 *Unreasonable expectations* – stretching targets.
2 *Elastic business definition* – an open-ended mission and purpose that does not tie the business down too rigidly.
3 *A cause not a business* – developing the notion of the augmented product/service – visionaries build cathedrals; they do not simply make bricks.
4 *New voices* – remembering the need for a 'Council of Youth' as well as relying on experienced elders.
5 *An open market for ideas* – getting suggestions in, any time from anywhere.
6 *An open market for capital* – access to capital for intrapreneurs.
7 *An open market for talent* – giving people real opportunities to develop ideas and champion changes.
8 *Low-risk experimentation* – allowing trial and error before the bigger run-out; learning from experiences and events.
9 *Cellular division* – lots of small companies or units inside the large organisation, so small business flexibility can be simulated.
10 *Personal wealth accumulation* – give those who deserve it a share in the wealth created.

Strategic weaknesses

We have already mentioned two important strategic pressures which can leave the unprepared organisation weakened. First, competitive and other environmental pressures; second, focusing too much on controls at the expense of flexibility. Hurst (1995) has shown how management and control become increasingly necessary as organisations grow and become more complex, but, that this development contains the seeds of potential failure. We can see in Figure 3.9 that organisations often start life with an entrepreneurial vision but that the significance of this vision soon gives way to learning and emergence as the entrepreneur and the organisation learn to cope with the pressures of a dynamic and competitive environment. This flexibility maintains the momentum, and the organisation grows and

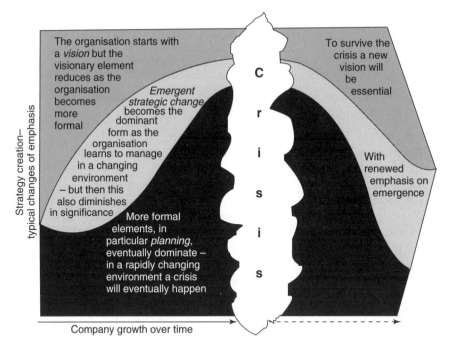

The organisation starts with a *vision* but the visionary element reduces as the organisation becomes more formal

Emergent strategic change becomes the dominant form as the organisation learns to manage in a changing environment – but then this also diminishes in significance

More formal elements, in particular *planning*, eventually dominate – in a rapidly changing environment a crisis will eventually happen

C r i s i s

To survive the crisis a new vision will be essential

With renewed emphasis on emergence

Strategy creation– typical changes of emphasis

Company growth over time

Figure 3.9 *Strategic change*

prospers. To ensure the organisation is managed efficiently, planning and control systems run by specialist professional managers become increasingly prominent – but this often reduces the flexibility which has proved so valuable. If the flexibility is lost, if the organisation fails to address what it is doing wrong whilst it is still succeeding, some of the momentum for Path 2 innovation is lost. Unless the entrepreneur and the organisation foresee the impending problem and find a major Path 1 initiative, a crisis is likely to happen. If the organisation is to survive the crisis it will need a new Path 1 opportunity – together with a renewed reliance on innovation and learning.

Businesses hit these crisis points when they run short of money, usually because they have failed to remain competitive and to attract sufficient resource contributions from customers and other important resource suppliers. Sometimes, turnaround is possible, frequently accompanied by a change of strategic leader to input the new vision and inspiration. On other occasions the intervention is too late, and the organisation either collapses or is taken over as a means of providing the necessary new leadership and resourcing.

Businesses in trouble, then, may be realistically non-recoverable, recoverable but only to a level of survival or capable of genuine renewal. The immediate need is to stop any financial haemorrhaging before new opportunities are sought and pursued. The first step does not need someone with entrepreneurial talent and temperament – it is largely based on technique, backed by a willingness to take tough decisions – but the second stage does.

Hurst further argues that on occasions it can be valuable to actually engineer an internal crisis and upset in order to drive through major changes in an organisation that has lost its dynamism and become too change-resistant. A controlled crisis is better than one resulting from external events as it can be used for positive change rather than constitute a more desperate reaction.

Another way of presenting these arguments is the following four-stage model of organisational progression and development:

- The first stage is a *creative* one, when new ideas are put forward.
- The second stage is *reflection and nurturing*, as the idea is crafted into a winning opportunity. We have already said that the person who has the original idea may not be the person who takes it forward in the most opportune way.
- The third stage is an *action* stage as the entrepreneur and the organisation develop the business from the opportunity. As the business takes off, and more and more products are sold, some element of order becomes vital if the organisation is to control events, manage its cash flow and deliver on time.
- The fourth stage then becomes one of *management* and administration with clear policies and procedures which deliver smooth running and efficiencies. This can become a dangerous stage if stasis sets in and new, creative ideas are not forthcoming.

Clearly, each stage has a downside. A constant stream of new ideas may not constitute entrepreneurial opportunities. Too much deliberation may inhibit action. An over-emphasis on 'doing' and competitiveness may mean inadequate attention is given to structural necessities. And finally, as we saw in Figure 3.7, too much bureaucracy can mean missed opportunities. The organisation begins to need a fresh input of creative ideas. Every one of us is different and our affinity and fit with each of these stages varies; some of us are not able to switch styles. Whilst the most successful and habitual entrepreneurs ensure there is a constant flow of activity between these stages and the potential downsides do not materialise, others need to recognise their relative strengths and weaknesses and recruit other people carefully to ensure there is a balance of skills and constant progression. Moreover, the positive organisation we are implying here will be in a better position to exploit and retain its most talented intrapreneurial managers.

Baden-Fuller and Stopford (1992) have proposed a four-stage model to explain the effective turnaround of an organisation in difficulty. First, the senior management is galvanised into action by the poor results and the obvious need to act. The team element here is critical; individual lone voices will be inadequate if they are baulked by other resistant colleagues who are opposed to the next step. Stage two demands that the crisis situation is simplified – by divesting loss-making activities in order to protect the organisation's core and preserve valuable resources. If there is a will, this stage is easy – at least at one level. The cutting back should not be indiscriminate; it should leave a new base upon which a fresh future can be built. It is all-too-easy to downsize and strip out important core competencies which weaken the organisation irredeemably. If the remaining core is strong, stage three, building new capabilities, can follow. This implies new strategic positions, which, if defensible and exploitable, are the basis for stage four – where new core competencies are leveraged to create further new and synergistic opportunities.

Business failures

Richardson *et al.* (1994) identify a number of business failure situations, and these are summarised in Table 3.1 and described below.

Poor strategic positioning can occur at various stages in the life of an organisation. Early on, it can reflect an organisation which might try very hard but is never really different in a meaningful way, or a business started by an inventor who is not an entrepreneur. At a later stage it implies an organisation which has been subject to strategic drift – an organisation which enjoyed E-V-R congruence at an earlier stage, but which has allowed its resources and values to drift away from a changing environment such that it is too reliant on past successes and is relatively unprepared for the future. One example might be ICI, once a leading world player in the chemical industry, but which eventually had to split into two parts, a bulk chemicals business and the more successful Zeneca, now Astra Zeneca after a later merger, which concentrates on pharmaceuticals and speciality chemicals. In recent years the new ICI has been changed further as some businesses have been sold or exchanged and others acquired to configure a radically different portfolio of products.

Villiers (1989) uses the metaphor of the boiling frog to describe this state. If a frog is dropped into a pan of boiling water, it will quickly feel discomfort and jump out. If, however, the same frog was placed in cold water it would not feel the same discomfort. When heat is introduced very gradually the frog remains comfortable and soporific, quite unaware of the developing threat as the water slowly reaches boiling point.

Table 3.1 *Business failures*

Reason for failure	Early stages	Later stages
Poor strategic positioning	No real differentiation	Strategic drift
Lack of innovation	Failure to see a niche can become a tomb	Inability or unwillingness to change in a bureaucratic structure
Other errors	Inability to take advice or build a strong team of managers	Over-ambitious growth, sometimes by ill-judged acquisitions and sometimes linked to a failure to understand why they are successful
and flaws	The entrepreneur takes too much money out of the business to support a personal lifestyle – leading to inadequate investment	Inability of the entrepreneur to delegate

In organisational terms, the problem issues build up gradually and are not dealt with properly. When difficulties arise, there is a tendency to look for a quick-fix resolution rather than, as entrepreneurs arguably do, looking for a more lasting solution which deals with the real issue and reduces the likelihood of recurrence in a fresh guise.

The second reason for failure is a lack of innovation. A small business often begins by targeting a niche and succeeds by offering something different. Without innovation, this niche can become a tomb. For larger organisations the crisis scenario, discussed above, can become a reality if planning and rigidity takes over from flexibility and emergent change. There are several reasons for this:

- Complacency – the entrepreneur loses the important urgency which once characterised the business.
- A lack of current awareness and strategic thinking.
- Inflexibility and a reluctance to abandon the past.
- A focus on growth rather than profitability such that issues of size draw attention away from more important performance indicators – true entrepreneurs understand profit.
- Inadequate investment to build new core competencies.

Leadership errors are often coincident with high ambition. Richardson *et al.* (1994) develop the frog analogy and suggest this is reminiscent of a drowned frog, one which tries too hard to be 'king of the pond' but lacks the necessary resources. In a small company environment this is the entrepreneur who 'knows it all' and either fails to look for advice, fails to take good advice or fails to build a strong team of support managers to help build the business. This entrepreneur fails to appreciate the strengths and potential contributions of others and believes himself – wrongly – to be infallible. Ironically this is sometimes the price of success. If a new business takes off very quickly and is instantly successful, the entrepreneur can be deluded into feelings of personal brilliance; but the success may be as much dependent on luck as judgement, and the *unconscious competency* must be understood by honest reflection and questioning.

In a similar vein, large and successful companies sometimes fail to diagnose just why they are successful, so they can build on very solid foundations. They again rely on assumptions, which tempt their strategic leaders to make poor strategic decisions, such as ill-judged acquisitions which fail to deliver the hoped-for synergies and benefits.

Leadership flaws reflect the wrong motivation and the bullfrog, the 'show-off' for whom status and power is more important than achievement. The person concerned enjoys being the 'centre of attention' and basking in personal glory from any success the business enjoys. Whilst he or she may well be the main reason behind the success, the future of the business will inevitably require additional inputs.

Some would-be entrepreneurs begin businesses with the main aim of supporting a particular lifestyle. Any early profits are invested in large cars and new houses rather than the business. This approach is even more indictable when the people spend money before the business has even earned it.

The large company parallel is the strategic leader who fails to delegate and build an appropriate organisation structure. Although it enjoyed several years of growth, success and prosperity, the mining and trading conglomerate, Lonrho, was unable to survive the entrepreneur behind the success, the late Tiny Rowland. For all the years he led Lonrho, Rowland maintained a tight hold on all key corporate strategic decisions allowable because he remained the major shareholder. Rowland's buccaneering style was loved by Lonrho's smaller shareholders, which enabled him to survive adverse criticism from both the larger institutional shareholders and the regulatory authorities – but eventually his own succession plan brought in a new entrepreneur who split the business into parts to realise its hidden value.

Behind these leadership failings are an over-reliance on a single person and a consequent failure to involve others in important decisions, which itself can reflect a flawed ego. The typical outcome is poor financial controls and inadequate measures of performance.

Signals of weak entrepreneurial leadership

We now conclude this chapter with a list of warning signals which draw together many of the points made earlier and signify failing entrepreneurship. They have been largely derived from Oates (1990) and Heller (1998).

1 The existence of (too many) *would-be's*. Something critical is missing. Possibly the interested people have a will to do something but lack a good idea; some key entrepreneurial competence or *talent* is missing – the person(s) concerned is unlikely to make it as an entrepreneur; there is a lack of true commitment to the idea/opportunity/venture – *temperament* is too weak.
2 The single dimension paradox. The start-up stage progresses well, but there is a lack of ability or opportunity to grow the business beyond the initial stages. The idea might only be viable in the short term; there may be inadequate funding; the entrepreneur may be unwilling to let go at the critical time; the initiative could simply run out of steam. The paradox is that the clear focus and individual drive that gets the initiative moving in the first place can be what brings it down – through a lack of necessary flexibility.
3 The business is a so-called *half-way house*. In other words it is a franchise or co-operative (or something conceptually similar) *and critically dependent upon the continued support and engagement of others who may be outside the business.*
4 The business is *impoverished*. Specifically it fails to achieve a winning strategic position – it is not sufficiently different. Funding is difficult or mismanaged and the business is under-capitalised. Insufficient attention is given to getting the quality right to 'delight' customers. The team is not developed in the appropriate way – such that key skills are missing. The business cannot cope when succession becomes an issue.
5 The business is blinkered. There is too much self-belief – perhaps driven by an orientation to production rather than customers – the *we know best* syndrome. The entrepreneur is unwilling to accept outside views and advice.
6 The business is technology-shy. There is a tension here . . . the business needs capital and technology, but it all costs money. The key questions are just when do you invest and how much do you spend?

7 The business has become smothered. Specifically, it has become over-bureaucratic – either because of Government or even European legislation/rules and regulations or because it has become bigger and more structured and has lost its creative spark.

8 The business is (now) run by a crisis manager . . . a manager who relies too much on an ability to deal (or not deal!!) with setbacks and crises as they arise, often implying the wrong trade-off between reaction and proactivity.

9 The business has started making (too many) mistakes. Possibly it has become too ambitious – say with misjudged diversification or acquisition. Maybe it has ignored warning signs such as a cash shortage. Maybe it is simply too greedy.

This concludes the first part of the book and provides a theoretical underpinning against which we can usefully explore the various stories and cases which comprise Part Two. In Chapter 4 we see the entrepreneur character themes illustrated in the stories of a selection of classic entrepreneurs. This is followed by a chapter on business entrepreneurs which encapsulates the themes of opportunity and change that we have discussed in this chapter.

Notes

1. We are using the word 'paradigm' here as it is commonly used in strategy literature to explain a view or perspective of a strong and advantageous competitive position. There is a case to be made that the word 'paradigm' should be reserved for a more significant and higher order context, and this argument will be debated later in the book – see Chapter 10.
2. We discuss Silicon Valley in depth in Chapter 14.

References

Baden-Fuller, C. and Stopford, J. (1992). *Rejuvenating the Mature Business: The Competitive Challenge*. Routledge.

Birkinshaw, J. (2003). Something ventured, much to gain. *Financial Times*, 5 August.

Blanchard, K. and Waghorn, T. (1997). *Mission Possible*. McGraw-Hill.

Bridge, S., O'Neill, K. and Cromie, S. (1998). *Understanding Enterprise, Entrepreneurship and Small Business*. Macmillan.

Brody, P. and Ehrlich, D. (1998). Can big companies become successful venture capitalists? *McKinsey Quarterly*, No. 2.

Churchill, N.C. (1997). Breaking down the wall, scaling the ladder. In *Mastering Enterprise* (S. Birley and D. Muzyka, eds), Financial Times/Pitman.

Derr, C.B. (1982). Living on adrenalin – the adventurer entrepreneur. *Human Resource Management*, Summer.

Finn, W. (2002). Managing Mavericks. *LiveWire*, October/November.

Fradette, M. and Michaud, S. (1998). *The Power of Corporate Kinetics – Create the self-adapting, self-renewing, instant action enterprise*. Simon & Schuster.

Gibb, A. and Ritchie, J. (1982). Understanding the process of starting a small business. *European Small Business Journal*.

Hamel, G. (1997). Address to the Strategic Planning Society Conference, London, November.

Hamel, G. (1999). Bringing Silicon Valley Inside, *Harvard Business Review*, September–October.

Hamel, G. (2000). *Leading the Revolution*. Harvard Business School Press.

Hamel, G. and Prahalad, C.K. (1994). *Competing for the Future*. Harvard Business School Press.

Heller, R. (1998). *Goldfinger – How Entrepreneurs Get Rich by Starting Small*. HarperCollins.

Horovitz, J. (1997). Growth without losing the entrepreneurial spirit. In *Mastering Enterprise* (S. Birley and D. Muzyka, eds), Financial Times/Pitman.

Hurst, D.K. (1995). *Crisis and Renewal – Meeting the Challenge of Organisational Change*. Harvard Business School Press.

Kanter, R.M. (1983). *The Change Masters – Innovation and Entrepreneurship in the American Corporation*. Simon & Schuster.

Kanter, R.M. (1989). *When Giants Learn to Dance*. Simon & Schuster.

Kets de Vries, M. (1996). Leaders who make a difference, *European Management Journal*, **14** (5), October.

Kirzner, I.M. (1973). *Competition and Entrepreneurship*. Cambridge University Press.

Lessem, R. (1986). *Enterprising Development*. Gower.

Lessem, R. (1998). *Managing Development Through Cultural Diversity*. Routledge.

Mintzberg, H., Ahlstrand, B. and Lampel, J. (1998). *Strategy Safari*. Prentice-Hall.

Oates, D. (1990). *The Complete Entrepreneur*. Mercury.

Pinchot, G. III (1985). *Intrapreneuring*. Harper & Row.

Porter, M.E. (1987). From competitive advantage to corporate strategy, *Harvard Business Review*, May–June.

Porter, M.E. (1996). What is strategy? *Harvard Business Review*, November–December.

Porter, M.E. (1997). Dare to be different, Interview for the *Financial Times*, 19 June.

Prahalad, C.K. and Hamel, G. (1990). The core competence of the corporation, *Harvard Business Review*, May–June.

Quinn, J.B. (1980). *Strategies for Change: Logical Incrementalism*. Irwin.

Richardson, B., Nwankwo, S. and Richardson, S. (1994). Understanding the causes of business failure crises, *Management Decision*, **32**, 4.

Schumpeter, J. (1949). *The Theory of Economic Development*. Harvard University Press. Original German edn, 1911.

Simon, H. (1996). *Hidden Champions*. Harvard Business School Press.

Stevenson, H.H. and Gumpert, D.E. (1985). The heart of entrepreneurship, *Harvard Business Review*, March–April.

Terazano, E. (1999). Fresh impetus from the need to innovate, *Financial Times*, 25 June.

Thompson, J.L. (2001). *Strategic Management: Awareness and Change*. 4th edn, Thomson Learning.

Villiers, C. (1989). The Boiled Frog Syndrome, *Management Today*, March.

Part Two
Entrepreneurs in action

4 Classic entrepreneurs

What can we see if we study a selection of classic names from the world of enterprise? We can sometimes see evidence of true vision and always the ability to see the potential of a real opportunity. Driven by an inner need to succeed and to make a difference in some way, the truly successful entrepreneurs focus on their opportunities and pursue them with great dedication and courage in the face of opposition and setbacks. Invariably we see the creative development of a business which looks after its customers and employees, one which grows by learning and finding new opportunities. We might say that they are 'off the scale' in terms of opportunity and team. Having wealthy parents and the benefit of a University education seems never to have been a pre-requisite for entrepreneurial success – but the ability to learn from the 'University of Life' is a critical factor.

One hundred and fifty years ago the UK prospered from the Industrial Revolution. The inventors and entrepreneurs who had contributed to this economic growth and global prosperity were popular heroes and heroines. Richard Arkwright (founder of the cotton mills), Richard Hargreaves (pioneer of the modern woollen industry), Thomas Chippendale (furniture) and Josiah Wedgwood (pottery) are still remembered for their differentiated, high-quality products. Samuel Cunard (shipping), George Stephenson (inventor of the first truly successful railway locomotive) and Isambard Brunel (pioneer of the Great Western Railway) left us a transport infrastructure. Rowland Hill made sure we have a postal service. Bankers such as Robert Fleming financed the growing businesses. Alongside some of these great achievements of the nineteenth century, social entrepreneurs also made an impact. Thomas Barnardo opened homes for homeless children, William Booth founded the Salvation Army, Elizabeth Fry pioneered prison reform, Florence Nightingale invented modern nursing and Robert Owen inspired trade unions and the Co-operative movement.

They were all visionary entrepreneurs who had made a difference, albeit in quite distinct ways. Many of them were leaders in their field, as well as entrepreneurs; and, to coin a popular phrase, *we will remember them*. Some of them accumulated huge personal fortunes (an outcome we invariably associate with entrepreneurship) but others remained relatively poor.

But who and where are the great heroes today? And will we remember them in centuries to come? Successive UK governments appear to recognise that prosperous economies need a constant flow of new businesses with high growth potential and offer some encouragement. The names Richard Branson and James Dyson are household names, associated with entrepreneurship and business success – we might almost call them business celebrities. Successful entrepreneurs can also still be found in other walks of life. But we often fail to properly appreciate all those who do succeed. People are still 'changing history' but arguably we have become less willing to celebrate their achievements. At the same time, and driven by the media, society certainly accords hero status to popular musicians and sports personalities, who invariably do build financial fortunes very quickly. Although other countries than the UK persist with these priorities, failing to appreciate entrepreneurs is not ubiquitous around the world. The 'geeks' and 'nerds' of Silicon Valley have become American cult heroes and, essentially, they are business entrepreneurs. Without doubt, greater visibility is one essential factor in understanding the contributions of the leading entrepreneurs.

But before we look at contemporary entrepreneurs in business and other sectors, it is useful to reflect upon the contribution of a number of classic entrepreneurs, business people who have been accorded legendary status. Many of them are associated with products, services and brands we still buy and use regularly. We begin with Carnegie and Edison. Carnegie did not invent steel, but he built the American foundries that supplied materials to the railway and construction industries. Thomas Edison did not invent electricity, but he used it to provide products which improved people's lives. The power stations he started are now part of the huge General Electric. Similar and later, Henry Ford did not invent the motor car but he was the first to make it affordable for less affluent consumers. The business he bequeathed to his descendants remains a powerful and dominant force in the industry. All these entrepreneurs saw a real opportunity to do something which would make a difference and, by harnessing the contribution of other people, actually made that difference.

Andrew Carnegie

Carnegie was a focused risk-taker who saw and seized opportunities. An insatiable learner all his life, he believed *the true road to pre-eminent success in any line is to make yourself master in that line*. Dedicated to pursuit, he claimed that *whatever I engage in I must push inordinately*. He made things happen (he detested speculators – *parasites feeding upon values but creating none*), he managed detail well and he was a team builder dedicated to bringing out the best in other people. He is probably remembered more for his philanthropic legacies of some $300 million to charities, arts, libraries and education – partially reflecting his strong ego and a pronounced social characteristic – than for his industrial achievements, though these were hugely significant.

Carnegie was a Scot, born in 1835; his father and grandfather were weavers. An astute opportunist from an early age, he bred rabbits and called them after his friends if they would help scavenge the rabbit food. Helping his father with his accounts, he learnt the principles of business at an early age. His family emigrated to America when he was thirteen and he was immediately sent out to work, where an uncle found him a job as a telegraph boy, delivering messages. Andrew taught himself to translate morse by ear, becoming the third person in the country able to do this. His skill proved useful for the developing railroad network, which Carnegie joined. Through the railroads he met several prominent businessmen, and acted on tips and information he picked up. He became a serial entrepreneur, starting when he saw an opportunity to be a supplier to the growing railroad network with Pullman railcars, so that passengers could rest and sleep on long journeys. When oil was discovered in Pennsylvania, where he lived, he became an early investor in oil field development. He then began to construct iron bridges for the railroads, to replace the less-robust wooden ones and, hearing of the new Bessemer steel-making process in the UK, he graduated into steel for manufacturing the rolling stock and the lines themselves. He was the founder of the American steel industry.

Whilst it is alleged he had flashes of inspiration and acted on them, he was at the same time a leading proponent of cost accounting. His father's teaching had ensured he was numerate and he believed in accounting for costs at every stage of production. It is generally acknowledged that his true genius was the way he was able to work with others for a common vision – an entrepreneur who was also a strong and charismatic leader. He believed *you must capture the heart of the original and extremely able man before his brain can do its best.*

Thomas Edison

Edison was a more reflective thinker who nurtured opportunities, many of which he stumbled on. Creative and innovative, he accumulated over one thousand patents, the most ever granted to one individual. *All progress, all success springs from thinking.* He was persistent and courageous, overcoming numerous hurdles and setbacks – *genius is one percent inspiration and ninety nine percent perspiration* – but his efforts and inventions were always focused firmly on commercial opportunities. He was also strong on advantage.

Edison was born in Ohio in 1847 and by the age of twelve he was selling newspapers on railway trains; three years later he was publishing his own weekly newsheet from a freight wagon. He was taught telegraphy by a local stationmaster as a reward for saving his son's life and, like Carnegie, telegraphy provided Edison with an opportunity he would not squander. Inquisitive by nature, he developed a number of technical enhancements, in particular devices for automating transmission and reception and for multiplexing, which enabled simultaneous multiple transmissions on a single telegraph line. Saving his earnings, he opened a laboratory and soon improved on the telephone, invented earlier by Alexander Graham Bell. Later, Edison's laboratory – an 'invention factory' – would pioneer the cylinder phonograph (1877), the first incandescent lightbulb (1879), the kinetoscope (the earliest rapid-motion projector of individual images, upon which the movie industry developed) and alkaline storage batteries. Income from the sale of some of his patents helped fund the laboratory. Edison also built power stations for transmitting the electricity needed for his lights.

Like Carnegie, Edison was committed to building a strong team of helpers, a network whose contributions were influential in ideas generation and development. Some of his work was greeted with great scepticism, as the *Scientific American* (June, 1879) confirms . . . *Six months ago popular attention was strongly drawn to the development of the electric light, and a panic prevailed among the holders of gas stock. That flurry has blown over. The electric light has not fulfilled its promises, and Mr. Edison's assertion that his latest lamp is a complete success falls on indifferent ears. The world is not so eager for the change as it appeared, and on all sides the disposition is to await developments patiently.*

Edison was essentially a technologist who made quantum improvements to what was already known, rather than discovering anything really new – with perhaps the exception of the electric light. For this, Edison discovered the potential of the flow of electrons from a heated filament, but this was not an instant breakthrough. He needed persistence and a 'half full rather than a half empty' philosophy. Even after some 10 000 failed attempts he refused to give up, and commented *I haven't failed . . . I've simply found 10,000 ways it doesn't work*! Focused on commercial opportunities, he believed there was an enormous potential for exploiting electricity to help improve the lives of ordinary people, and persisted. Fundamentally an inventor, Edison was a true entrepreneur because he understood the opportunities for exploiting his inventions, and followed them through to successful application. When we look at James Dyson later in this chapter we will see similar issues coming through.

Isambard Kingdom Brunel

Runner-up to Winston Churchill in a 2002 television poll to find the 'Greatest Briton', Brunel was, according to James Dyson, *unable to think small – nothing was a barrier to him*. He was the visionary engineer who built the Great Western Railway and the Clifton Suspension Bridge. A pioneer of steamships, his idea for a screw propeller was nevertheless greeted with criticism and great scepticism when he first suggested it. Brunel's family was wealthy, and he enjoyed the best technical education available in Europe. When his French father was commissioned to build a tunnel under the Thames, Brunel was able to gain early practical experience – he was employed by his father as an engineer. Whilst much of his work had enormous influence on the progress of other engineers and builders, Brunel was commercially unsuccessful, and when he died in 1859 (aged fifty-three) he left his widow impoverished. Fellow engineers accused him of pursuing novelty for the sake of novelty – he endeavoured to develop beyond the levels of current competency – and then stole many of his ideas! Brunel was certainly an engineer – almost certainly the UK's greatest engineer – and a risk-taker, but was he an entrepreneur? If accumulated wealth is the measure, the answer would have to be 'no'; but if a legacy of innovations that changed the world is the measure, the answer becomes 'yes'.

Brunel certainly saw several opportunities and followed them through. His Great Western Railway from London to Bristol has always been regarded as one of Britain's most significant infrastructure projects, but the vitally important railways were never enormously profitable. His Great Eastern, at its launch the largest ship ever built, was a commercial failure. Launched in 1859, and scrapped in 1889, the Great Eastern's hull was double-skinned and able to withstand external damage. Had the Titanic been built to the same design its story might well have been different! Brunel had dreamed of a ship that could carry enough coal to sail around the globe with 400 passengers in luxury accommodation. He built the ship; he had overestimated the demand. In reality the ship's greatest achievement was its success in laying the first telecommunications cable under the Atlantic. In the end, consumers have been the main beneficiaries from Brunel's work – he did not accumulate financial capital and wealth, but he did contribute enormous social and aesthetic capital. Moreover, his contributions helped other entrepreneurs make money. In Brunel's case, one might ask: *Who best deserves the laurels – he who achieves worldly success and contemporary acclaim by a safe route or he who risks failure for posterity to follow?*

Brunel was regarded as a perfectionist – *the best was never good enough* – who was also a poor delegator. He chose a broad gauge for the Great Western Railway, believing it to be so superior that others would follow. But (and here we can draw parallels between Sony's preference for the technically superior Betamax video which lost out to the perfectly satisfactory and cheaper VHS format pioneered by JVC) other railway companies developed with the lower cost narrower gauge. George Stephenson was his main rival and the two acted as a spur for each other – but their rivalry remained friendly and they willingly helped each other. Stephenson, for example, laid his rails on stone block sleepers, which were unsuitable for the speed Brunel wanted. It was the creative and innovative Brunel who pioneered hollow (not solid steel) rails on longitudinal timber sleepers.

Joseph Rowntree and William Lever

Rowntree and Lever were Victorian/Edwardian contemporaries who left a legacy associated with popular consumer products and brands which have been at the heart of the marketing revolution. There are similarities and differences in their stories. Both made fortunes; both left a significant social legacy.

Joseph Rowntree was born in 1834 in York, the son of a Quaker grocer. He left school at fourteen, with just five years' education and started working for his father – although he would soon spend time away in London as an apprentice. From 1859 he ran the family shop, but ten years later he opted to join his brother, Henry, who ran a Cocoa, Chocolate and Chicory factory employing thirty people. Henry died in 1883 and Joseph took full control. Capitalising on the success of its Fruit Pastilles and Fruit Gums, Rowntree now quickly became an international business, and by 1900 there were 4000 employees. The legendary chocolate products such as Aero, Kit Kat and Smarties were to follow. Although the business was always well-managed, the real brand building would begin in the 1930s, after the Rowntree family ceased to have managerial control. Joseph himself had died in 1925. Rowntree merged with Mackintosh (Rolo and Quality Street) in 1969, but was absorbed by Nestlé of Switzerland in 1988.

Joseph Rowntree has been described as paternalistic but an innovator of good working practices. He built a large new factory, where the workers had a say in who would manage them, together with a model village for his employees. A pension fund was set up in 1906. He was always active in public service and in 1904 he transferred a substantial proportion of his significant wealth into three separate trusts. One of them is now the Joseph Rowntree Foundation which funds social research to pursue the founder's dream of *seeking out the underlying causes of weakness and evil . . . in order to change the face of England*.

William Lever was also the son of a grocer, but a Lancastrian rather than a Yorkshireman. He was born in Bolton in 1851. In 1885 he opened his first factory, in Warrington, making soap. Working in the family shop, he had seen how people bought soap as a commodity, having a slab cut off a large block. Manufacturing was largely in localised cottage industries. Lever pioneered soap bars, individually wrapped – which he branded Sunlight. By 1900 he was the largest producer in the UK, selling 40 000 tonnes. Like Rowntree, Lever built a modern factory linked to a model village – at Port Sunlight on The Wirral – and started the charitable Leverhulme Trust. But unlike Rowntree, he sought to exploit the potential power of branding and aggressive marketing from the beginning. He grew by acquisition (a leading rival, Pears, was one company he bought), investing overseas (palm oil plantations in Africa), new product development (Lifebuoy soap, Vim cleanser and Lux flakes were examples) and diversification into foods. After his death in 1925 (the same year as Rowntree) Lever merged with the Dutch Margarine Union to create Unilever, which is still a powerful global business.

Henry Ford

Rowntree and Lever left a social legacy through their charitable trusts. Henry Ford left a different social legacy. By building *a motor car for the multitude, so low in price that the man of moderate means may own one*, he transformed Western civilisation. With a motor car people could travel where and when they wanted; they had greater freedom over where they lived; young people gained greater independence from their parents. Without the car, modern shopping malls and drive-through restaurants, now a feature of modern life, could not have happened.

Henry Ford was a visionary dedicated to the pursuit of his vision. His vision was for what the car could do for people. Possessor of a very strong ego, he was nevertheless a businessman with a conscience. He activated his vision by exploiting production line techniques but paid his workers above the average going rate, increasing wages when his profits grew. He adopted a five-day working week and employed handicapped people for jobs they could handle satisfactorily. Greater output led to lower costs and, in turn, lower prices fuelled demand. What Ford had been able to do with great success was borrow ideas from elsewhere and combine them in a different and very potent way. Interchangeable parts had been pioneered in the manufacture of sewing machines; continuous flow production already existed in soup canning; slaughterhouses already had assembly line techniques.

Ironically Ford's failure to appreciate that customers might prefer other colours than black is also legendary! His choice was based on the fact that black paint dried faster, therefore providing a cost saving. It was Alfred Sloan at rival General Motors that saw the potential in giving consumers as wide a choice as possible. It was this, of course, that meant the motor car was also a pioneer of planned obsolescence and the desire to replace based on fashion more than life expectancy. Ford was focused on costs and efficiencies; in turn this affected his strength in advantage.

Ford's father was an immigrant Irish farmer and he was born in Michigan in 1863. Brought up on a farm, the young Henry was a 'tinkerer' and he soon proved to be a natural at repairing farm machinery. Presented with a watch at the age of eleven, he proceeded to take it apart and then started making his own – which he sold for $1 each. At the age of twelve he was absorbed when he saw that an agricultural steam engine mounted on a wagon could cause the wagon to move forward without a horse pulling it. He had experienced his trigger. With hindsight we can see that his life's work was then dedicated to the production of a motorised replacement for the ubiquitous horse and cart, and a tractor to do the work of the horses on the farm. His experimenting continued after he left the family farm and started working in a steam engine workshop at the age of sixteen – a job he soon left in order to work for Thomas Edison. Ford became manager of one of Edison's power-generating plants. Edison was aware that Ford was using and refining the gasoline-driven internal combustion engine invented by Daimler and Benz in Germany to produce early motor cars, and he encouraged him in this endeavour. The two men never lost touch and Edison's laboratory has been reconstructed for Ford's world-famous Greenfield Village Museum. Henry built three cars in his own workshop in his spare time and then moved on to racing cars before branching out as a manufacturer.

In 1907 Ford drew up plans for the largest automobile factory in the world, intending to build just one car in it, the Model T. He intended to use the production line, which he had seen being used for less complex products such as sewing machines, bicycles and guns. Ford's unique contribution was to go for minute division of labour and a methodological arrangement of the machine tools. In this ability to transfer ideas he resembles James Dyson, as we shall see later. Interestingly this ability to transfer was crucial in the Second World War. In 1941, the Consolidated Aircraft Company was failing to achieve its production target of fifty B-24 Liberator bombers every month. This four-engined aeroplane had 500 000 separate parts in its assembly. Ford was asked to help, and within a year his engineers had built a mile-long factory which could complete planes at a rate of more than one every hour.

For all his successes, Henry Ford made mistakes. He was an autocrat who failed to build a strong team of managers, which inevitably hindered his progress. His ego was particularly strong, and it is reported that he was so taken by the adulation he received that he stopped listening and taking advice. He did not replace the Model T as quickly as he should have, and thus lost new opportunities. He first thought that all his production should be concentrated in one huge plant, before realising that separate and dedicated plants were more efficient.

Bill Gates

Henry Ford was fascinated by cars and believed others would be the same once they could afford them. Bill Gates had a similar vision for transforming the lives of ordinary people, foreseeing *a single operating system for every personal computer around the world* to complement Steve Jobs' (Apple) vision of *a personal computer on every desk in every home and office around the world*. Dedicated pursuit of this focused vision through Microsoft has made him the world's richest person. Like Ford, he had a strong ego; and like Edison, but unlike Carnegie and Ford, Gates was born to wealthy parents. Again like Edison, he was only concerned with tight control mechanisms once his business had grown, he was energetic and inspired to work *ridiculously long hours*, and he has inspired criticism.

There are several reasons behind Gates' phenomenal success. Among them are his ability to absorb information quickly and his technical expertise – he can actually write computer code. He understands consumers and is uncannily aware of market needs. He has an 'eye for the main chance' coupled with an ability and will to make things happen. Moreover he is an aggressive defender of his corner, which has caused tension in his dealings with the American and European Anti-Trust Authorities.

Born in 1955 in Seattle, Gates quickly became interested in science fiction and unusually went to a school which had a computer students could use. A 'nerd' from an early age it has been said Gates *preferred playing with computers to playing with other children*. He nevertheless teamed up with his friend, Paul Allen, and together they *begged, borrowed and bootlegged* time on the school computer, undertaking small software commissions. Gates and Allen went to Harvard together, where Gates proved to be an unpopular student because of his high self-opinion. Surreptitiously, using Harvard's computer laboratories they began a small business on the campus. Gates later left Harvard to start Microsoft – never completing this formal part of his education. Allen was his formal partner in the venture, but Gates always held a majority control. Bill Gates' visionary contribution was the realisation that operating systems and software (rather than the computer hardware) held the key to growth and industry domination.

Gates took risks in the early days, but, assisted by some good luck, his gambles largely paid off. When the first commercial micro-computer (the Altair) needed a customised version of the Basic programming language, Gates accepted the challenge. His package was later licensed to Apple, Commodore and IBM, the companies which developed the personal computer market. He had exhibited inspired opportunism; he proved he had the courage to fail. When IBM decided to seriously attack the personal computer market, Gates was commissioned to develop the operating system; innovatively improving an existing off-the-shelf package and renaming it MS-DOS (Microsoft Disk Operating System) Gates was now 'on his way'. Since then Windows has become the ubiquitous first-choice operating system for most PC manufacturers.

By-and-large his success has depended on his ability to create 'standard products', the benchmark against which others are judged. Interestingly, one of the biggest threats to Microsoft is Linux, the open source operating system which users can acquire at far lower cost.

Gates has clearly not needed to work for several years now, but he is driven to continue. He is a serial, habitual entrepreneur. His strong focus and ego are demonstrated by his determination to gain a stranglehold of the industries he competes in – and to sustain this. In pursuing this he has demonstrated advantage by ensuring new versions of his software are backwards compatible – users don't have to throw everything away and start from scratch. Having said that, he has stepped down from being the CEO to a more focused technical role. Gates hires the *best and brightest* people, and he has made many of them millionaires. He claims to prefer a college-style working environment with a culture dedicated to learning, sharing and overcoming hurdles; but at the same time he allows his brightest people to fight each other for supremacy. Gates himself personally thrives on combat and confrontation. His colleagues have to be able to stand up to him – but it does generate creative energy. However, he is also seen as enormously charismatic, and employees desperately *want to please him*. In his younger days he was branded a risk-taker; stories are told of his love of fast cars and his tendency to leave late for meetings in order to provide him with an excuse for driving fast.

Microsoft has diversified in recent years – into software for servers and the X-Box games console which has yet to seriously challenge the market leadership of the Sony PlayStation.

Walt Disney

The talent we will always associate with Walt Disney is creativity. He was also very clearly opportunistic, focused, dedicated, courageous (overcoming several setbacks) and visionary. Although it was Walt's drive and charisma that built Disney, the Corporation has survived his death and continued to grow and prosper, testimony to a robust organisational legacy. He left a strong team of people and a culture which has enabled Disney to continuously improve its existing activities and, at the same time, build in new directions.

Walt Disney was born in 1901 and raised on a small farm. Chasing work, his father moved the family to Kansas City, where he obtained a newspaper distribution franchise. He forced Walt to work for him without pay at the age of nine, but the canny Walt quickly realised he could earn pocket money (to buy the sweets he was forbidden at home) if he found his own customers without telling his father. His 'University of Life' education continued when he went to France in 1917 (lying about his age) to help the Red Cross. He started doctoring German steel helmets recovered from the battlefields to make it appear as if the soldier had been shot in the head. He found a ready market for his souvenirs.

The artistic Walt dreamed of being a newspaper cartoonist, but could not find employment. Joining forces with another talented artist, Walt formed a small advertising business and persuaded the publisher of a low-price throwaway paper that sales would improve with illustrated advertising. The business succeeded, but when he was offered a job as a cartoonist with a film company, Walt unhesitatingly sold his share of the business to his partner. After developing the necessary skills, Walt left to form his own cartoon production company, persuading local citizens to invest in shares. The cartoons may have proved popular but the business was not profitable. After it collapsed in 1923 Walt left for Hollywood, where his elder brother, Roy, was working.

Partnered by Roy, Walt started again, adding sound and colour to his cartoons. Eventually his Mickey Mouse creation reached the cinemas, and this success persuaded Walt to gamble everything on a version of Snow White and the Seven Dwarfs. When he made this in 1937 it cost ten times the normal amount for a feature film – a huge risk. It succeeded, to be followed by Pinocchio, Bambi and Fantasia – all produced over budget! As he had before, Disney failed to control his costs and was forced to sell stock to stay in business. Like Richard Branson, as we shall see later in the chapter, he did not enjoy being accountable to external shareholders, but he persevered. Quite simply, Walt Disney was an extraordinary story-teller who understood his market. Adopting Mark Twain's philosophy of his own books, Disney was never a classic film maker. If classic films are like wine, Disney's films are like water. But everyone drinks water!

The creative Disney worked in three separate areas. His most creative work was accomplished in a colourful open-space area, with illustrations on every wall. Planning and organising was relegated to a formal office, whilst a third, darkened room with comfortable furniture was reserved for discussions and opportunities for colleagues to question his ideas and thinking in a more intense atmosphere.

Disney diversified into non-cartoon family films and then Walt had the idea for a theme park. He could see a new opportunity for exploiting his characters – he had always been able to tell stories and he now wanted to provide a live stage for his characters. But would he be able to convince others with his vision? His brother Roy was sceptical and persuaded investors not to back the project. Undeterred Walt struck a deal with ABC Television. For $5 million, ABC could use Mickey Mouse. Walt had the money for Disneyland, which eventually opened in Anaheim, south of Los Angeles, in 1955. A winner from day one, the theme park was contributing 30 per cent of the Corporation's revenue in its first year of operations.

Disney died in 1966 but the growth and success has continued. Magic Kingdom opened in 1971, followed later by Epcot (1982) and Disney-MGM Studios (1989) – all in Florida – and EuroDisney in 1992. Disney Corporation bought ABC Television in 1995, thereby merging its content with a key distributor. Through its Touchstone Pictures, Disney also produces restricted-audience films. Character licensing and astute marketing of videos of the cartoon feature films are major revenue generators. Headed for the last eighteen years by Michael Eisner, Disney has experienced 'ups-and-downs' but proved it understands service and how it is delivered through people – a competency it shares with McDonald's, Wal-Mart and Virgin, as we shall see.

Sam Walton and Wal-Mart

If Walt Disney was a truly great entertainer, Sam Walton was a truly great retailer. His Wal-Mart stores provide huge ranges and choices of household goods; they are the largest retail chain in the world. Prices are kept low through scale economies and a first-class supply chain network. Despite their size, the stores seem friendly and Walton employed people simply to answer customer queries and show them where particular goods are shelved. Again a visionary, he was focused and dedicated. He worked long hours and *talked retailing outside work*. Strong on the people and team elements, and willing to take measured risks, Walton sought to learn from other organisations. In this respect he was opportunistic, but reflective. He never claimed to be an original thinker and he networked widely to find his new ideas.

Born in 1918 in Missouri, and raised in relative poverty, Walton started earning money from selling newspapers when he was very young. As a footballer he showed he was highly competitive, a trait which again proved valuable when he started his career in retailing. After he graduated in 1940 he began selling shirts in a J.C. Penney store. Because of a minor heart murmur he was not drafted for the war effort and instead worked in a gunpowder factory. Afterwards, and in partnership with his brother, he took on the franchise for a Ben Franklin five-and-dime store in Arkansas. The two brothers bought additional outlets, abandoned counters in favour of self-service, established central buying and promotion and quickly became the most successful Ben Franklin franchisees in America. In 1962, the same year that K-Mart began opening discount stores in larger cities, Walton began with discount stores in small towns. Both had seen the concept pioneered elsewhere. Walton's principle was simple – mark everything up by 30 per cent, regardless of the purchase cost. This proved to be a winning formula. He toured, observed, absorbed and learned to develop his *buy it low, stack it high, sell it cheap* strategy. Walton's first Wal-Mart store opened in Arkansas in 1962; turnover now exceeds the figures for McDonald's, Coca-Cola and Disney combined! Yet the wealthy Sam Walton is alleged to have driven himself around in a pick-up truck and to have been a mean tipper!

Growth was gradual in the early years, but there were thirty Wal-Mart stores by 1970. Once Walton opened his own distribution warehouse (another idea he copied) growth would explode. In addition, Wal-Mart was the first major retailer to share sales data electronically with its leading suppliers. *We got big by replacing inventory with information.* Wal-Mart has always been careful to contain the risk by *not investing more capital than is justified by results*. But Sam Walton was always willing to try out new ideas, quickly abandoning those which did not work. He successfully combined emergent strategy with his vision to create a potent organisation and formula.

Walton's very strong ego, team and advantage was manifested in three guiding principles: respect for individual employees, service to customers (*exceed their expectations*) and striving for excellence. An intuitive and inspirational retailer, Walton was also a cheer-leading orator and inspirer. He preached that *extraordinary results can come from empowering ordinary people*. His showman style was also reflected in *glitzy store openings*. He created a *culture that in many ways represents a religion – in the devotion it inspires amongst its associates and in the Jesuit-like demands it makes on its executives.* Following the lead of the John Lewis Partnership in the UK, Walton called his employees 'associates' and personally spent much of his time in stores exchanging ideas with them. Profits were shared with employees. *Ownership means people watch costs and push sales.* Like Andrew Carnegie, Walton provided support for many good causes, but largely anonymously. Recognising his own weaknesses, Walton recruited an analytical businessman, David Glass, to be his number two. Glass commented once that Walton *wasn't organised – I saw one store he was running with water melons piled outside in temperatures of 115 degrees.* Glass has continued as Chief Executive after Walton's death.

Founded by individual entrepreneurs, Disney Corporation and Wal-Mart have become entrepreneurial businesses; their growth and prosperity has continued after the death of the founder. Wal-Mart has expanded selectively into other countries. In 1999, Wal-Mart acquired Asda in the UK.

Before concluding this chapter with a review of two contemporary but quite different classic entrepreneurs, Richard Branson and James Dyson, we next look at three other entrepreneurial organisations: McDonald's, Sony and Coca-Cola. Whilst McDonald's was the inspiration of a single entrepreneur, Ray Kroc, Sony was founded by two entrepreneurial partners. Coca-Cola has benefited from a series of entrepreneurial inputs. All three have become hugely powerful and influential brands, which have touched the lives of millions of people around the world.

Ray Kroc and McDonald's

Ray Kroc has been described by *Time Magazine* as *one of the most influential builders of the twentieth century.* Few children refuse a McDonald's burger! – and its golden arches logo symbolises American enterprise. Kroc was a truly opportunistic and focused entrepreneur who built an organisational network of dedicated franchisees. Yet his entrepreneurial contribution began late in life and the McDonald's chain of hamburger restaurants was certainly not his own invention. Instead he saw – really he stumbled on – an opportunity where others missed the true potential for an idea. Once he had seen the opportunity he rigorously applied business acumen and techniques to focus on providing value for his customers. By standardising his product and restaurants he was able to guarantee high and consistent quality at relatively low cost. Kroc was also wise enough to use the expertise his franchisees were developing.

In 1955, at the age of fifty-two, Ray Kroc completed thirty years as a salesman, mainly selling milkshake machines to various types of restaurants across America, including hamburger joints. His customers included the McDonald brothers, who, having moved from New Hampshire to Hollywood but failing to make any headway in the movie business, had opened a small drive-through restaurant in San Bernadino, California. They offered a limited menu, paper plates and plastic cups – and guaranteed the food in sixty seconds. When their success drove them to buy eight milkshake machines, instead of the two their small size would logically suggest, Ray Kroc's interest was alerted and he set off to see the restaurant. Kroc's vision was for a national chain which could benefit from organisation and business techniques. He bought out the McDonald brothers and set about building a global empire. After he officially retired from running the business, and until his death in 1984, Ray Kroc stayed on as President and visited two or three different restaurants every week. He saw himself as the 'company's conscience', checking standards against his QSCV vision – *q*uality food, fast and friendly *s*ervice, *c*lean restaurants and *v*alue for money.

McDonald's has always been a focused business, never straying from fast foods. For many years its products were the same everywhere they were served, but local variations have developed. Branches opened in hospitals, military bases, airport terminals, zoos and roadside service areas as well as in towns and cities. Success depends on a strong supply chain, careful control over production and employee engagement. Many employees are young part-timers but they must still deliver a high-quality service enthusiastically. Like Disney, McDonald's was an early pioneer of its own corporate university for training its staff.

It would be a mistake to underestimate the contribution of Ray Kroc's franchise and supplier 'partners', who have always been encouraged to contribute their ideas and expertise. The Big Mac, introduced nationally in the US in 1968, was the idea of an entrepreneurial Pittsburgh franchisee who had seen a similar product in a rival hamburger restaurant, and who was allowed to trial the product in his own restaurant. Its success allowed McDonald's to strengthen its appeal to adults. The launch of Egg McMuffins a few years later was a response to a perceived opportunity – earlier opening times and a breakfast menu. It took McDonald's four years to develop the product to a satisfactory standard, using a new cooking utensil invented by a Santa Barbara franchisee. When Chicken McNuggets were launched in 1982, it was the first time these small boneless pieces of chicken had been mass-produced. The difficult development of the product was carried out in conjunction with a supplier and there was immediate competitive advantage. The product could not be copied readily. From being essentially a hamburger chain, McDonald's quickly became Number 2 to Kentucky Fried for fast-food chicken meals.

By the mid-1990s there were 20 000 McDonald's restaurants around the world. The company held 40 per cent of the US market for its products and yet its burgers were not coming out as superior to Wendy's and Burger King in taste tests. McDonald's continued to grow into a chain of 30 000 restaurants serving forty million customers every day. But the company suffered its first ever trading loss in 2002; some restaurants closed. Some newer stores had been cannibalising sales from long-established units nearby. Was this the beginning of the end? New products with a healthy eating focus are amongst the strategies adopted in an attempt to turn the company around. For the moment, although Ray Kroc has been dead for almost twenty years, his legacy lives on in a brand name that is recognised and revered – albeit a little tarnished – around the world.

Sony

Sony truly deserves its reputation as a creative, innovative business. A pioneer of new consumer electronics, it has been instrumental in the development of several important products and, unusual for a Japanese organisation, it has been described as *a young, maverick company* by the Financial Times. Sony was only started after the Second World War. Its two complementary founding partners, Masaru Ibuka (a passionate inventor) and Akio Morita (a business-minded member of a leading brewing family), wanted to build consumer products. *We started with the basic concept that we had to do something no other company has done before.* Driven by inventions, Sony, like Thomas Edison, has rarely lost sight of its customers and their needs. Elements of opportunism and risk, and a mixture of good and poor judgement, characterise its growth.

After its first new product, a rice cooker, was a failure, Sony's breakthrough came with tape recorders. Ibuka had seen the large American reel-to-reel machines used by the Occupying Forces and envisioned a small consumer version. True resourcefulness was required to overcome a shortage of plastic for the recording tapes – importing plastics was prohibited. Instead Sony created a smooth calendered paper which could be coated with magnetic powder. Ibuka then visited America and saw a potential for transistors the American inventors were missing. He licensed the patent and went on to create the first portable radios. In reducing these to pocket-size, Sony began to develop a ground-breaking competency in miniaturisation. Televisions – Sony pioneered its Trinitron system for better picture quality – and video recorders followed. Here Sony took a risk that proved to be a misjudgement – backing its own higher quality Betamax system and initially ignoring the cheaper but perfectly satisfactory VHS system pioneered by its rival, JVC.

In 1979 Sony's legendary status was secured with the Walkman, an idea of Akio Morita which *changed the lifestyle of a generation*. There was nothing new about the technology involved in these miniature personal listening devices – Morita saw an opportunity for a cassette player which allowed people to listen to music anywhere through personal headphones without disturbing anyone else. Unlike other cassette players, recording was not possible, and more recently new radio and CD versions have been spawned. Really the opportunity had existed for a while, and the product was feasible – it needed an entrepreneur to spot the gap in the market. Sony has followed later with pioneering contributions to the popularity and success of compact discs, camcorders, computers and floppy discs.

A different form of risk and entrepreneurship was evident when Sony chose to acquire CBS Records and Columbia Pictures and link its own expertise in electronics hardware with American competency in software and entertainment. This brave move forced structural and cultural changes, and for a long time the 'jury remained out' concerning whether this was an appropriate move for a Japanese company, even though many Americans came to believe Sony is actually American. The value of this diversification was delivered with PlayStation. Sony had avoided the computer games industry in its early years, but a Sony executive won a Nintendo console in a competition, became hooked and championed the development of a rival – the PlayStation. Sony's position of market leader came about through a mixture of powerful hardware and a wide range of games, which in turn depend on suitable software. A number of games have been linked to successful films.

Coca-Cola

Coca-Cola is the world's premier soft drink; the company's global market share for carbonated soft drinks exceeds 50 per cent. In recent years, consumption of carbonated soft drinks has fallen as consumers drink more and more bottled water. Coca-Cola also markets branded bottled water. The company's success cannot be attributed to one person, but rather to a series of individual entrepreneurs, all of whom saw different but important opportunities.

The original syrup for Coca-Cola was invented in 1886 by an Atlanta pharmacist, John Pemberton. Records do not clarify how carbonated water came to be added to his medicinal syrup to produce the *delicious and refreshing drink* that soda fountains sold for 5 cents a glass. It is known, however, that the brand name was suggested by Pemberton's partner and book-keeper, Frank Robinson. Pemberton never realised the potential for his invention and readily sold more and more shares in his business until, in 1888, all rights to the product were owned by a businessman, Asa Candler. Pemberton had earned some $2300 for his product.

Candler understood merchandising, and this was to provide the foundations for the real early growth – he gave away free-drink coupons, advertised the product and introduced Coca-Cola souvenirs. More recent advertising slogans such as *It's The Real Thing*, *Things Go Better With Coke*, *Coke Adds Life* and *Always Coca-Cola* are testimonies to Candler's legacy. By 1895 there were production plants and sales into every state in America. The second important entrepreneur was a soda fountain owner in Vicksburg, Mississippi – Joseph Biedenhorn. Impressed by customer reaction, Biedenhorn installed a bottling machine and started taking bottled Coca-Cola out to plantations and lumber camps. But really this was the extent of his ambition and his idea was copied by two Chattanooga businessmen, Benjamin Thomas and Joseph Whitehead, who, in 1899, secured exclusive rights to *bottle and sell* Coca-Cola in most American states. Candler was willing to 'almost give the rights away' because he was not convinced that bottling was the answer. A wide variety of different stoppers were being used, none of which was ideal. The solution lay with the crimped cap, which, although invented, was slow to gain wide acceptance because of the need for huge investments in new machinery and new bottles. Thomas and Whitehead timed their move perfectly. These partners set up a network of franchised local bottlers, and thus established a pattern ubiquitous in soft drinks distribution to this day. *They gave birth to one of the most innovative, dynamic franchising systems in the world.* The distinctively shaped contour bottle first appeared in 1916, a design the company ultimately patented in 1960.

A new era began when the Candler family sold Coca-Cola to another businessman, Ernest Woodruff, for $25 million in 1919. Ernest's son, Robert, took over the business in 1923. Under his innovatory leadership came the six-bottle pack, exports of the syrup to other countries (1926), metal-top open coolers for selling ice-cold Coca-Cola in retail stores (1929) and automatic fountain dispensers (1933). In 1941, with sugar rationed and the Americans at war, Woodruff instructed his managers to *see that every man in uniform gets a bottle of Coca-Cola for 5 cents, wherever he is and whatever it costs the company.* This led to the opening of new bottling plants wherever troops were stationed and eventually to the new intent . . . *always have Coke within an arm's reach of desire.* Both Woodruff and General (later President) Eisenhower realised the power of the Coca-Cola brand – more than anything else it symbolised America and reminded the troops of just what they were fighting for. Woodruff continued the earlier emphasis on marketing such that Coke calendars, desk blotters, napkins and the like became ubiquitous. He also insisted that the secret formula for the concentrate was only known to two people at any one time, and that they never flew together. In itself, this was never really an important issue, but the mystique it conveyed proved invaluable.

Distribution has always been the key to success. The company has always retained control over the syrup, but not seen it essential to own the bottling plants, as long as the supply arrangements were robust. There is little logic in transporting the canned or bottled product over great distances – its main constituent is water! There are special Coca-Cola aisles in Wal-Mart stores and exclusive supply arrangements for certain products with McDonald's.

Coca-Cola was first canned in 1964, and plastic bottles came on the scene in 1969. Different sizes and packs have followed, as have related new products – Fanta, Tab (sugar-free Coke), Fresca, Diet Coke, Vanilla Coke and Minute Maid (fruit juices, and a business which Coca-Cola acquired). Nonetheless there have been strategic misjudgements, which arguably reflect the dangers in losing focus on what a business is really about. The 1982 acquisition of Columbia Pictures culminated in its sale to Sony when the hoped-for synergistic benefits did not accrue; and the decision in 1985 to change the flavour with *New Coke* was quickly reversed when customer reaction was hostile. Ironically, Robert Woodruff, who had maintained an active involvement with the company after his retirement and until his death in 1984 (at the age of ninety-four), had always been steadfast in his refusal to countenance a change to the formula. It was not that he believed the taste was incapable of improvement, but because of the symbolism of the original. He always realised that Coca-Cola has never been just a soft drink!

Richard Branson and Virgin

Richard Branson is unquestionably a legend in his own lifetime. His name and presence are associated closely with all the Virgin activities and businesses, and he has demonstrated a unique ability to exploit a brand name and apply it to a range of diversified products and services. He *is* Virgin – so, will he leave a lasting business legacy like Ray Kroc has done? Could this company out-live its founder? Or would Virgin be split up into its many constituent businesses without Branson to lead it?

Branson is creative, opportunistic and dedicated to those activities he engages. Possessed of a strong ego, he is an excellent self-publicist. Popular with customers and employees, he has created a hugely successful people-driven business. His determination to succeed and his willingness to take risks are manifest in his trans-Atlantic power boating and round-the-world ballooning exploits. Although he has said that he *wouldn't do this if I didn't think I'd survive*, the *Financial Times* has commented that *all those associated with Mr. Branson have to accept that he is an adventurer . . . he takes risks few of us would contemplate*. He has chosen to enter and compete in industries dominated by large and powerful corporations. Having challenged British Airways, for example, Coca-Cola has been a more recent target. Significantly, and not unexpectedly, his name comes up frequently when other business people are asked to name the person they most admire.

Now, over fifty years old, Branson has been running businesses for over thirty years. He began *Student* magazine when he was a sixteen-year-old public schoolboy, selling advertising from a public phone booth. Ever opportunistic, he incorporated a mail order record business, buying the records from wholesalers once he himself had a firm order and cash in advance. Thwarted by a two-month postal strike, Branson decided to enter retailing. Realising the importance of location, he started looking for something along Oxford Street in London. Spotting an unused first floor above a shoe shop, he persuaded the owner to let him use it rent-free until a paying tenant came along, on the grounds that if he was successful he would generate extra business for the shoe shop! *He had a queue stretching 100 yards when it opened and never looked back* – characteristically he had turned a threat into an opportunity. The London record shop was followed by record production – Branson signed and released Mike Old-field's *Tubular Bells* after Oldfield had been turned down by all the leading record companies. Branson was always an astute and visionary businessman, carefully recruiting people with the necessary expertise to manage the detail of his various enterprises. His main skill has been in networking, finding opportunities and securing the resources necessary for their exploitation. In this he has had to show courage and flexibility.

Virgin Atlantic Airways was started after an American businessman suggested the idea of an all-business-class transatlantic airline. Branson rejected this particular strategy but was hooked on the idea. Initially he minimised the risk by leasing everything, and he was able to compete with the larger airlines by offering a perceived higher level of service at attractive prices. Over many years he has successfully marketed a range of products and services by systematically applying the Virgin brand name. The products and services may have been diversified – holidays, consumer products such as Virgin Vodka and Virgin Cola, cinemas, a radio station, mobile phones, financial services and Virgin Railways are examples – but the customer-focused brand image has remained constant.

Virgin was floated in 1986 but later re-privatised. Branson had been uncomfortable with the accountability expectations of institutional shareholders. Since then he has used joint ventures, minority partners and divestments (such as the sales of his music business and record shops) to raise money for new ventures and changes of direction. In 1999 Branson sold a 49 per cent stake in the airline to Singapore Airlines, partly to strengthen its competitiveness, but also to raise money for investment in further new ventures. Later, 49 per cent of Virgin Railways was sold to bus and rival train operator Stagecoach. Describing itself as a *branded venture capital company* Virgin had already created over 200 businesses, and Branson had decided to target electronic commerce and the Internet, believing a vast range of products and services can be sold this way under the Virgin umbrella.

Branson's business philosophy is built around quality products and services, value for money, innovation and an element of fun. *I never let accountants get in the way of business. You only live once and you might as well have a fun time while you're living.* By focusing on customers and service, he has frequently been able to add value where larger competitors have developed a degree of complacency. *The challenge of learning and trying to do something better than in the past is irresistible.* Branson always realised that this would be impossible without the appropriate people and created an organisation with a devolved and informal culture. Business ideas can – and do – come from anywhere in Virgin. Employees with ideas that Branson likes will be given encouragement and development capital. Once a venture reaches a certain size, it is freed to operate as an independent business within the Virgin Group – and the intrapreneur retains an equity stake. Branson runs Virgin from a large house in London's Holland Park, having out-grown the canal narrow boat he used for many years. There has never been a traditional head office infrastructure.

James Dyson

Dyson is another entrepreneur who challenged the industry giants, in his case with a revolutionary vacuum cleaner. His dual cyclone cleaner now has a UK market share in excess of 50 per cent and international sales are prospering. A Hoover spokesman has said on the *BBC Money Programme*: *I regret Hoover as a company did not take the product technology off Dyson . . . it would have been lain on a shelf and not been used.* Hoover has since had to pay £4 million in damages to Dyson for patent infringement. Dyson has been compared by Professor Christopher Frayling, Rector of the Royal College of Art, with *the great Victorian ironmasters . . . a one-man attempt to revive British manufacturing industry through design.* Dyson is creative, innovative, totally focused on customers and is driven by a desire to improve everyday products. His dedication and ego is reflected in the following comment: *the only way to make a genuine breakthrough is to pursue a vision with a single-minded determination in the face of criticism . . .* and this is exactly what he has done. Clearly a risk-taker, he invested all his resources in his venture. In the end, his rise to fame and fortune came quickly, but the preceding years had been painful and protracted, and characterised by courage and persistence. They reflect the adage that *instant success takes time.*

James Dyson's father, who was a schoolmaster, died of cancer when he was just nine years old. The public school to which he was then sent *made him a fighter.* At school he excelled in running, practising by running cross countries on his own, and it was on these runs that he began to appreciate the magnificence of the railway bridges constructed by Brunel in the last century – an experience which helped to form his personal vision. An early leap in the dark came when he volunteered to play bassoon in the school orchestra, without ever having seen a bassoon! Naturally artistic, he won a painting competition sponsored by the *Eagle* comic when he was ten years old. Art became a passion and he later went on to complete a degree in interior design – Dyson may be an inventor, but he has no formal engineering background. His story is one of courage in the face of adversity and setback.

Dyson's first successful product and business was a flat-bottomed boat, the Sea Truck. At this time he learnt how a spherical plastic ball could be moulded, an idea he turned to good use in the wild garden of his new home. His wheelbarrow was inadequate as the wheels sunk into the ground, so he substituted the wheel with a light plastic ball and thus invented the Ballbarrow. Backed by his brother-in-law on a 50:50 basis, Dyson invested in his new idea. Made of colourful, light plastic, the barrow was offered to garden centres and the building trade, both of whom were less than enthusiastic. With a switch to direct mail via newspaper advertisements, the business took off. A new sales manager was appointed but his renewed attempt to sell the barrow through more traditional retail channels was again a failure. The financial penalty was the need for external investors, who later persuaded Dyson's brother-in-law to sell the business.

A second painful experience came when the sales manager took the idea and design to America, where Dyson later failed with a legal action against him.

Dyson's idea for a dual cyclone household cleaner came in 1979, when he was thirty-one years old. Again it was a case of a need creating an opportunity. He was converting his old house and becoming frustrated that his vacuum cleaner would not clear all the dust he was creating. Particles were clogging the pores of the dust bags and reducing the suction capability of the cleaner. Needing something to collect paint particles from his plastic spraying operation for the ballbarrows, Dyson had developed a smaller version of the large industrial cyclone machines, which separate particles from air by using centrifugal forces in spinning cylinders. He believed this technology could be adapted for home vacuum cleaners, removing the need for bags, but his partners in the ballbarrow business failed to share his enthusiasm. Out of work, when the business was sold, his previous employer, Jeremy Fry (for whom he had developed the Sea Truck) loaned him £25 000. Dyson matched this by selling his vegetable garden for £18 000 and taking out an additional £7000 overdraft on his house. Working from home, risking everything and drawing just £10 000 a year to keep himself, his wife and three children, he pursued his idea. Over the years he produced 5000 different prototypes.

When he ultimately approached the established manufacturers, his idea was, perhaps predictably, rejected. Replacement dust bags are an important source of additional revenue. A series of discussions with potential partners who might license his idea brought mixed results. Fresh legal actions in America for patent infringement – *with hindsight I didn't patent enough features* – were only partially offset by a deal with Apex of Japan. Dyson designed the *G-Force* upright cleaner which Apex manufactured and sold to a niche in the Japanese market for the equivalent of £1200 per machine, from which Dyson received just £20. At least there was now an income stream, but this had taken seven years to achieve. Finally, in 1991, Lloyds Bank provided finance for the design and manufacture of a machine in the UK. Several venture capitalists and the Welsh Development Agency had turned him down. Dyson was determined to give his latest version the looks of NASA technology, but further setbacks were still to occur. Dyson was let down by the plastic moulder and assembler he contracted with, and was eventually forced to set up his own plant. Early sales through mail order catalogues were followed by deals with John Lewis and eventually (in 1995) with Comet and Curry's. In this year, a cylinder version joined the upright. Dyson continues to improve the designs to extend his patent protection. By 1999, his personal wealth was estimated to be £500 million.

Dyson has always seen himself as more of an inventor than a businessman. He set up two separate businesses, both in Malmesbury, Wiltshire – he keeps Dyson Manufacturing and Dyson Research (design and patenting) apart. The dress code for employees is perpetually informal and communications predominantly face-to-face. Memos are banned and even e-mails discouraged. Every employee is encouraged to be creative and contribute ideas. Most new employees are young – *not contaminated by other employers* – and they all begin by assembling their own vacuum cleaner, which they can then buy for £20. Reflecting both advantage and a willingness to confront situations, Dyson incurred criticism when he switched manufacturing of the dual cyclone cleaners – and later his new washing machines – to Malaysia to save money. 865 jobs were lost to the UK. This reduced the head-count in the UK to 1200, 400 of whom are scientists and engineers. Designers work on improvements to existing products as well as new product ideas. At the same time, Dyson has demonstrated that his social characteristic extends beyond his style of management in the workplace. He developed and marketed a special limited edition cleaner to raise money for cancer research.

In early 2000, Dyson was ready to launch a robot version of the dual cyclone cleaner, which is battery-powered, self-propelled and able to manoeuvre itself around furniture. The retail price would have been £2500, which was seen as too expensive to drive the market, and a lower price version was due for launch in 2003. Dyson has also launched a superior, but currently premium priced washing machine with short wash cycles and an ability to spin clothes almost dry – another challenge to the manufacturers of both washing machines and tumble dryers. This time, however, Dyson had his own resources to launch the product! Moreover Dyson controls 100 per cent of the shares in the business. He has learnt some painful lessons but is now enjoying the rewards of his dogged determination.

In this chapter, we have looked at a number of classic stories of legendary individuals and businesses to illustrate the key points introduced in Chapters 2 and 3. Entrepreneurs have the ability to see a potential opportunity and obtain the resources required to exploit it. Sometimes things happen quickly; sometimes it takes longer. The most robust and entrepreneurial businesses sustain their growth with renewed innovation – but rarely do they lose sight of the essential values upon which the business has been built. Understanding – and satisfying – the needs and expectations of customers and the development of committed employees are both essential. Our truly successful entrepreneurs have this ability to focus on key issues and remain dedicated to the business, creatively overcoming the inevitable setbacks and hurdles. Sometimes they are visionary, but not always. They are, however, all possessed by a desire to achieve. We take these points further in the next chapter by showing how entrepreneurs and entrepreneurship can be found in all types of business and business activity.

5 Business entrepreneurs

Entrepreneurship is about opportunity and risk. Successful entrepreneurs first spot opportunities, often where others fail to see the same idea at the same time, although the same information is available to them. This is merely the beginning of a process; the good idea has to be made to happen. The project has to be championed. Customers have to be found and consumers satisfied. Service has to be delivered. Changes, modifications and improvements will be required to sustain a competitive advantage. To achieve all this an organisation and a strong team of people has to be developed. There is uncertainty and risk in this implementation process; entrepreneurs embrace the uncertainty and deal with the challenges. In this chapter we look at the successful execution of this process in the context of a wide range of different business ideas and opportunities. The focus of this chapter is the wide range of opportunities that can be found and the process of exploiting them.

Entrepreneurs recognise opportunities – they may or may not actually invent the ideas personally – and then exploit these opportunities by creating and building successful operations or organisations. They may enter the process because they spot an opportunity and are minded to do something about it. They may well have been searching for just that opportunity because they are instinctively entrepreneurial. Others enter the process through necessity. They live in a country where self-sufficiency is a key to survival; they have been made redundant and cannot find work.

It was commented at the beginning of Chapter 4 that the truly successful entrepreneurs are 'off the scale' in terms of opportunity and team. Some of their activities and behaviours are the result of training (which enhances their technique), but talent and temperament are critical. In fact, it has been suggested that *if Thomas Edison had gone to Business School, we would all be reading by larger candles!*

Reinforcing points made in Chapter 3, strategy matters in entrepreneurship. Businesses cannot grow and prosper without an underlying 'good idea' or business model which creates and adds value for customers and consumers, positions the company distinctively in terms of its competitors and represents a valuable competitive edge. This added value and difference generates the all-important profit. But the idea alone is inadequate. It must be implemented successfully, and then the advantage must be sustained with flexibility, innovation and change. For this to happen, the support and contribution of people is essential to create a virtuous circle. Committed and motivated employees deliver satisfaction to customers; with loyal and satisfied customers, companies are able to grow and prosper. To complete the circle, employees have to be rewarded accordingly to maintain their contribution.

In this chapter we look at several examples of successful entrepreneurs in various types of business situations and consistently see evidence of these achievements and of the virtuous circle. In addition, we see *habitual entrepreneurship* in action, where entrepreneurs create and maintain a momentum and do not stand still. The majority of successful entrepreneurs find new opportunities to add different values in their existing businesses, changing flexibly to sustain competitive advantage. Others retire from one business and start another, but largely staying focused at any one time. A minority of successful entrepreneurs will be active in more than one activity at the same time.

Being creative and spotting an opportunity is not enough. In fact, the world is full of people with 'good ideas'. The secret lies in delivery and implementation. These arguments are confirmed by research by Charan and Colvin (1999), which showed the average survival rate for Chief Executives in large US corporations is under five years. The problem is generally not one of shortcomings in the strategy or vision, but rather the inability to implement. Good strategic ideas soon become public property. The secret of success lies in the way the idea is implemented and changed for sustained advantage. Moreover, we can see evidence of a number of entrepreneurial themes in those strategic leaders who are most successful. They are dedicated and focused with the strategy; they are able to activate and make things happen; they are profits- and results-driven, and they work hard to develop individuals and teams. *Not putting the right people in the right jobs* is the key reason for chief executive failure.

Although our emphasis in this chapter and in the book as a whole is on entrepreneurial growth businesses, we should never forget the important economic role of the millions of enterprising people around the world who similarly spot opportunities for micro businesses and run them successfully. In this chapter we include the Starbucks and Subway stories – we could also have told a story about the enterprising car repair business near the author's University. Witnessing considerable building activity all around him, the owner moved a large caravan onto his land and opened a café – for the building workers and students. It is busy, successful and profitable. It works because of its location. It is not different in any other significant way and will therefore not branch out into a huge growth business.

This chapter shows how entrepreneurial business opportunities can be found 'everywhere'. Some are genuinely new; others are innovatory improvements on a theme. Some are limited-growth ideas; others can be used to build global businesses. They only succeed and grow if they are different in some meaningful way and executed effectively. We first explore a range of different opportunities – niche market opportunities, the creation of new markets, transposing good ideas, opportunities through privatisation. We look at individual and team entrepreneurs, and at examples of successful entrepreneurs who operate on the fringe of other businesses. We discuss corporate entrepreneurs at three different levels – transformers, venturers and intrapreneurs.

There is, then, an infinite set of possibilities for people with the talent and temperament to become successful entrepreneurs to choose from. But, as we have said, spotting the idea and the opportunity is only the start! The cases and examples reported in this chapter also provide insight into and a number of valuable lessons in implementation.

The world of business opportunities

Niche market opportunities

David Bruce   In the late 1990s Allied Domecq had been opening forty new *Firkin* pubs every year, and expanding into Europe, before it sold the chain to Punch Taverns. Allied had bought the name and concept in 1991, but the first *Firkin* pub had been opened in 1979 when David Bruce, with a background in the brewing industry, realised there was an opportunity for a pub which brewed its own real ale on site. Bruce bought the lease on an existing pub which was about to close down at the Elephant and Castle in south London. Renaming it the *Goose and Firkin*, he remodelled it as an old-fashioned drinking house – with bare floorboards. Some beer was bought in, but most was brewed in the cellar. His own brews were all strong and distinctive – and with unusual names such as *Bruce's Dog Bolter* and *Bruce's Earth Stopper*. The pub was an instant success, and in 1980 he opened a second one. By 1987 he had eleven pubs in Greater London, all with *Firkin* in the name and nine with on-site brewing. His creative tongue-in-cheek promotions became increasingly outrageous. The *Flounder and Firkin* was *a plaice worth whiting home about* and you could *spectre good pint when you ghost to the Phantom and Firkin* – for a pint of *Bruce's Spook!*

The structure was not developed in line with the growth, however, and the entrepreneur was stretched. Bruce had lost focus and there was an absence of performance orientation. When this became apparent, Bruce's reaction was to recruit a microbiologist and an accountant, and he put a manager into every pub – but he remained personally responsible for ensuring his vision and concept were delivered consistently. He believed in the personal touch. In 1988 he decided to sell his chain to Midsummer Leisure, netting a personal sum of £1 million. He then established a charitable trust to provide canal holidays for disabled people, but returned to brewing in 1990. This time he kept his organisation smaller, focusing on just two pubs. They were both named the *Hedgehog and Hogshead*; one in Hove, Sussex, and the other in Southampton. The concept was the same one as his original *Firkin* pubs, none of which would eventually brew on site.

He later moved to other ventures before entering a joint venture with WH Brakspear in September 1999. Brakspear has brewed in Henley-on-Thames since 1779. One of Bruce's other ideas has been the Bertie Belcher brand, *pubs that brew the beer you'll want to repeat*. The name for the new venture was Honeypot Inns; David Bruce was chief executive. Brakspear put seven managed pubs into the venture (six more would be added every year) and they were to be retained as independent pubs which reflect the character of the building and their local communities. They were designed to be a loose chain, linked by a common brand name but they were all individual. The new additions would be unusual sites rather than typical high streets.

Brakspear believed Bruce had *tremendous skills for identifying opportunities for the development of retail operations that catch the imagination of consumers.* He is certainly a master of the weak pun. Bruce asserts that *creating the right ambience is an innate skill – not something I can explain.* He fully intended to move on again when the venture is properly up-and-running . . . *I put my all into these ventures for up to five years and then I have to do something else.* He is a serial entrepreneur.

Yo! Sushi   The first Yo! Sushi restaurant was opened in London in 1997 by Simon Woodroffe. Woodroffe left school at sixteen and worked in the rock music business, eventually televising concerts. He recruited Robin Rowland as CEO two years later. With experience in systems and service in the leisure industry, a man with commercial acumen had joined one with big ideas. Now the business is successful; the founder puts in just three days a week, handling marketing, PR and product development. As for the rest of the time, he plays polo, writes, speaks and acts as the CBI Ambassador of Entrepreneurism.

The idea is based around Japanese food – focusing on fish, rice and vegetables – served from a moving conveyor belt. Customers eat (and pay for) whatever they fancy and just take it off the moving belt. It works in carefully selected locations. Customers stay on average twenty-two minutes and so the restaurants have been opened in streets where people are constantly on the move. Success is dependent on energetic staff and close attention to detail. Woodroffe was always able to network and generate publicity, and so the venture has been widely visible. He has also not stood still. In addition to the chain of restaurants, there are Yo! Below beer and sake bars, a Yo! ToGo home delivery service and Yo! ToWear merchandise as well as pre-packed Yo! Sushi boxes in Sainsbury's, a joint venture with Geest.

Steve Pateman   A more bizarre niche opportunity was found by Steve Pateman, the owner and manager of a family shoemaking business in Northamptonshire. His business, like many other British companies in this industry, had become uncompetitive against cheaper imports – so he adapted his machines and began to manufacture boots and kinky leather goods for the fetish market. To boost sales – and after shaving his legs! – Pateman turns up personally at erotica shows to demonstrate his products. Local people think *he is from another planet* but he has been described differently by Sir John Harvey-Jones . . . *that man is an absolute hero . . . people laugh, but he was going to fight for his business and his people, no matter what. You have to produce something that is different. You can no longer compete just by being better at what you do.*

Opening up new markets

Occasionally a new, innovatory, entrepreneurial idea changes the nature and the rules of competition in an industry. When this happens it is by no means certain that the idea comes from an existing competitor – the idea may well provide an opportunity and a springboard for a new competitor to break in and steal market share from existing players.

Direct Line which was launched in 1985, had this impact on the established insurance industry. The idea belonged to Peter Wood, who secured financial backing (of £20 million) from the Royal Bank of Scotland. Wood's background was in information technology. Direct Line used information technology to sell motor insurance directly to customers over the telephone, without the need for expensive offices and brokers. The savings in overheads and commissions could be passed on to customers in the form of lower prices. Wood thus *shook an industry that was not used to revolutionaries* and forced many existing businesses to follow his lead and change their ways of operating. Wood made sure he had a strong, albeit small, team of insurance actuaries and IT experts to run Direct Line, and within a year he had secured 1 per cent of a huge market. Within ten years, this share had grown to 10 per cent. At the end of the 1990s, Direct Line was UK market leader for motor insurance and seventh for homes and contents. It had three million customers and Peter Wood sold his share of the business to the Royal Bank of Scotland.

In 2001, Wood returned with another new venture – Esure, on-line insurance. Backed by a £150-million investment from the Halifax, Wood's model is built around *attract on price; keep on service.*

Car Phone Warehouse With the Car Phone Warehouse, Charles Dunstone saw his opportunity in the rapidly growing new market for mobile phones. Dunstone had been a sales manager with the electronics company NEC, and he used £6000 of his savings to open his first store. In just ten years the business grew to 450 stores, including the 270 Tandy computer stores that Dunstone bought. Car Phone Warehouse has become Europe's leading mobile phone retailer and, after a flotation in 2000, Dunstone still owns half the business. Sales exceeded £1 billion in 2002 from 1000 stores. He has sustained his leading position by finding new ways to add value in a rapidly changing market. He was quick to appreciate that customers can be persuaded to upgrade their phones as specifications improve, even though their existing model works perfectly well. He was an early national advertiser, using classic FM radio to target specific customer groups. His theme is based on reassurance and expert, objective advice to help people select a phone and payment system which is right for them. The market is complex and potentially confusing with a huge array of choices – and, for many potential customers, a lack of knowledge about the alternatives on offer. Dunstone has also diversified – into both fixed line services (through acquisition) and billing services.

Federal Express provides an excellent example of an organisation and an entrepreneur who opened up an unrealised market opportunity and began a new industry. *The greatest business opportunities arise when you spot things your customer didn't have a clue they needed until you offered it to them.* The idea is simple. It is to provide a speedy and reliable national and international 'overnight' courier service for letters and parcels based upon air cargo. *We invented the concept of overnight delivery, creating a whole new market where previously there was none.* FedEx is, however, unusual in a number of ways. Before it could even begin, FedEx needed a nation-wide (North American) distribution system with a fleet of planes and trucks – a huge investment in resources.

The business was the idea of Fred Smith, whose father was also an entrepreneur who had founded and built a successful bus company. When Fred was a student at

Yale in the 1960s he wrote a paper outlining his idea for a freight-only airline which delivered and collected parcels to and from a series of hubs. Traditionally parcels were shipped on scheduled passenger airlines as normal mail, whilst Smith proposed flying at night when the skies were relatively quiet. His paper was graded as a C. After graduating, Smith served as a pilot in Vietnam before he bought a controlling interest in Arkansas Aviation Sales, a company which carried out modifications and overhauls. Determined to implement his idea for a courier service, he invested a $10 million family inheritance and raised a further $72 million from various sources based on a number of independent but positive feasibility studies.

FedEx took to the skies in 1973, offering a service in and out of twenty-five East coast cities with fourteen jet airplanes. The demand was there, as he had forecast. Unfortunately the rise in the OPEC oil price made FedEx uneconomical almost as soon as it started. Two years of losses and family squabbles – Smith was accused of *squandering the family fortune* – were followed by profits and Smith's belief, courage and persistence were rewarded.

FedEx is successful because it delivers on time and speedily, and because it has a sophisticated tracking system for when something does go astray. There are now 600 FedEx aircraft flying one million miles every two days. The central hub is in Memphis but the flights are international. Three million packages from 200 countries are handled every night. FedEx's courier vans cover another two million miles every day collecting and delivering these parcels. To ensure FedEx can maintain its service it flies empty aircraft every night, which track close to the pick-up airports and which are brought into service if they are needed.

In 2003 FedEx bought Kinko's a chain of 1200 stores which provide document printing services to mainly corporate customers. FedEx has had drop boxes in Kinko's for several years.

New opportunities based upon existing ideas

Kwik Fit   The phenomenally successful Kwik Fit outlets in the UK were transplanted from the US, but again the potential for the idea had to be seen and exploited. Tom Farmer (now Sir Tom Farmer) was born in 1940, the seventh child of a shipping agent who lived in a two-bedroom house in Leith, Edinburgh. Slightly built – Farmer is just over five feet tall – Tom grew up a Roman Catholic in a largely Protestant city. At the age of fifteen he began working for a tyre replacement business. Eight years later he borrowed £200 from his bank to start his own tyre business. Reflecting an entrepreneur's attitude to resourcing, he painted his shop with bright blue and yellow paint – selected simply because he could get these colours free – and began selling tyres at discount prices. He acquired the tyres on a sale-or-return basis. When new, tighter tyre regulations gave a boost to the tyre replacement market, Farmer quickly expanded to four shops. Before he was thirty years old he had sold up and retired with his family to California (where one of his sisters lived) with £450 000 in his pocket.

By 1971 he was bored and in need of a fresh challenge. He had seen the localised success of fast-change tyre and exhaust shops in America, and returned to Scotland with the idea. He claims the name Kwik Fit came to him in a dream. He re-employed a number of his old friends and loyal employees and again adopted the distinctive blue and yellow colours. Under Farmer, Kwik Fit grew to 1900 outlets, 10 000 employees and eight million customers a year. Kwik Fit also diversified into insurance to exploit its name, image and customer database; and Tom Farmer sold his business to Ford for £1 billion in 1999.

Tom Farmer was always a committed workaholic with a strong sense of community. He was focused and dedicated and keen to look after his people. Kwik Fit has always been perceived to offer a high level of integrity in an industry often thought to involve dubious commercial practices. *All sound businesses are built on good Christian ethics – don't steal, don't exploit your customers or your people, always use your profits for the benefit of your people and the community.*

Starbucks   In under fifteen years Starbucks grew from a single store on the Seattle waterfront to a chain of over 1600 across America, spawning competitors in the US and elsewhere. Now, apparently, three new ones open every day. As part of its drive to expand internationally, Starbucks bought its smaller UK rival, The Seattle Coffee Company, in 1998. Starbucks succeeded because it found the right way to blend sales of top-grade fresh coffee beans with sales of cups of coffee to drink. Coffee bars have existed for a very long time, but rarely have they featured the strong and distinctive aroma found in stores which sell fresh coffee. The individual drinks are relatively expensive, and some aficionados think they are relatively sweet, but they are individualised and made-to-order. There is a wide range of piping hot and iced-cold variants to choose from. Although coffee-to-drink is very much the leading product, fresh coffee beans and a range of related products, such as cakes, biscuits, mugs and coffee makers, are also on offer. Customers include shoppers and working people from local stores and offices at lunchtime and teatime on their way home – people who take time to relax and converse over their coffee – as well as people who pop out from work to their nearest outlet when they have a short break because the coffee is perceived superior to the instant they might otherwise have to drink. Outlets can also be found at airport terminals and in those bookstores where people go to browse and relax. Essentially, Starbucks *sells an emotional experience* and not just a commodity product. It thus adds value.

The success is down to Howard Schulz, who grew up the son of a blue-collar worker in Brooklyn. Schulz became a salesman, and when he was working for a houseware products company he visited Seattle and was introduced to the Starbucks Coffee Company, a business which sold imported coffee beans. He joined the business in 1982 with the title of Marketing Director. Enthused by the espresso bars he found on a business trip to Italy, and convinced a similar concept could be developed for America, he attempted to sell the idea to his bosses. The family declined to go along with him and he left to start up on his own. He managed to raise enough money to open one outlet – within two years he was in a position to buy out Starbucks.

Schulz claims that his mission has always been to *educate consumers everywhere about fine coffee.* Customers who visit Starbucks must feel relaxed and enjoy *a sense of wonder and romance in the midst of their harried lives.* People will pay *arguably outrageous prices* for their coffee whilst ever it is seen as an indulgence. If this is to be achieved, staff attitudes and behaviours are going to be critical. Service, therefore, is everything. Schulz set out to create Starbucks as *living proof that a company can lead with its heart and nurture its soul and still make money*. Employees are called partners. Including part-timers, they all enjoy free health insurance, stock options (known as bean stock), training programmes and wages above the industry average. Although many are young and fit, students who will not stay long enough to earn stock options and who will not need health care, Schulz wants them to feel valued and consequently deliver the desired service. We have already seen these 'virtuous circle' themes in some of the organisations included in Chapter 4 and we will see them repeated in other successful organisations featured in this chapter. They matter.

It is interesting at this point to consider what constitutes good service. Starbucks manage to persuade customers to queue twice – once to order and pay and once to collect their order. In addition, and in the authors' experience, some Starbucks outlets are not as clean and tidy as some of the other fast food chains.

Embracing a social theme, all unsold beans over eight days old are given away free to local food banks. Nevertheless the company has also been criticised for exploiting cheap labour in coffee-growing countries. Very recently, and ignoring advice from a number of people he consulted, Schulz set out to conquer Japan. Starbucks is now ubiquitous in Tokyo! His motivation and ego is also reflected in the following quote . . . *It is those who follow the road less travelled who create new industries, invent new products, build long-lasting enterprises and inspire those around them to push their abilities to the highest level of achievement.*

Our next two stories are from the same industry. The market for bras is global. Sometimes bras are worn purely as functional garments for support and comfort. On other occasions glamour and fashion comes into the equation. The leading manufacturers are, predictably, powerful and global. Sally Robinson distributes their products whilst Michelle Mone has taken them on as a direct competitor.

Sally Robinson   is, in many respects, a 'necessity entrepreneur'. She is a farmer's wife with 200 acres in North Yorkshire that struggles to sustain the family. Knowing they needed to diversify she first started offering bed and breakfast. It was one of her B&B customers who helped her solve the problem of what to do with an empty barn – use it for a mail order business selling bras to women with large or small busts who need unusual sizes not easily obtained in the high street stores. Amplebosom.com is not at the high fashion end of the market. Her target customers are aged 40 plus.

Catalogue sales began in 1999, quickly followed by on-line sales. The company offers a huge range of sizes from ten manufacturers, including the leading brands. Originally the business absorbed just two hours a day; now there are three full-time and two part-time employees. There are three catalogues a year and the company has diversified into swimwear. Following the notoriety and film of the enterprising Rylstone Women's Institute members – also from North Yorkshire – who posed in the nude for a calendar to raise money for cancer research, there are plans to make a film of Sally Robinson's story.

Asked why she has been successful, Sally offers the following thoughts:

- She was always clear about the need for systems and measurement – *performance orientation* – as the number of problems grew as the business expanded.

- Customers come first.
- She always got someone else to do what she struggled with – *team* – because not only do they do it better than she can, they also enjoy it.
- She has been an active *networker* and courted publicity.

Michelle Mone MJM International, the business started by Michelle Mone, competes in the same industry, but in a quite different niche. Michelle left school in Glasgow at the age of fifteen to become a fashion model. Her father had been confined to a wheelchair and she wanted to help out with family finances. Earlier she had made money from newspaper rounds – taking on the responsibility for a number of rounds and sub-contracting the work – and distributing an Avon catalogue through school. She moved on to work for a brewery and became head of sales and marketing. When she was made redundant in 1996, she was twenty-four years old and a mother of two.

Supported and encouraged by her husband, she started marketing silicone breast enhancers under licence from an American manufacturer. Her heart was in this business – not wafer thin herself, she was always complaining about not being able to find comfortable bras to wear on formal occasions. Unlike Sally Robinson, it was always her intention to design her own products and have them manufactured for her. This was achieved with the Ultimo gel-filled bra which she was able to launch in 1999. By this time £1 million had been invested in developing the business. Entrepreneur and business angel Tom Hunter – who had made a fortune from the sale of his chain of sports shops – had bought 25 per cent of MJM. Her Ultimo bra was worn by Julia Roberts for the movie 'Erin Brokovitch'. In 2000 she was declared 'Young Business Achiever of the World'. A firm believer that her *wee Scottish company can take on the world* she secured distribution through big-name retail outlets in the UK and abroad and diversified into related lingerie and swimwear products. Her products are now available in Debenhams, for example. Mail order distribution was also part of the plan. It was never going to be easy, though. There is intense competition in the 'cleavage enhancement' sector of the market.

The Michelle Mone story is one of advancement and setback. Determined to succeed and willing to accept responsibility, she signed her house over to a bank in exchange for a loan when she was pregnant with her third child! Always strong on ideas and with great self-belief and determination Michelle Mone has come up with a series of creative, customer-focused ideas; her setbacks have tended to come at the implementation stage. She has relied on others, especially people overseas, who have on occasions let her down and not fulfilled her expectations. When her first call centre was opened, things were fraught. But when she has intervened personally, her creativity and focus have generally turned things around. But she cannot always be hands-on. Her creativity and resourcefulness is manifest in Michelle persuading Penny Lancaster, high-profile girl friend of Rod Stewart, to model her lingerie.

The accidental opportunity

Lonely Planet Tony Wheeler, the founder of the hugely successful and influential Lonely Planet travel guides, did not set out to be either a publisher or an entrepreneur. He was used to travel; his father had worked in the airline industry after a career in the RAF. Wheeler was an engineering graduate who worked in the car industry *but didn't enjoy it*, and so he went to London Business School and completed his MBA. Afterwards, aged twenty-six, he and his wife Maureen set out to travel through Asia on a tight budget. They finished in Melbourne and got jobs. Wheeler had kept a detailed diary of their experiences and decided to write a backpackers' guide in his spare time. He recognised there was a real value in the material he had accumulated. From this grew the world's largest independent travel publisher. Wheeler's books may make him the backpacker's guru but he has always realised there was potential in making his publications attractive to all types of travellers. City guides, cycling and walking guides supplement the country guides. Prior to 11 September 2001 Lonely Planet employed 500 people in Melbourne and sub-offices in countries around the world. Post 9–11 there have been redundancies and some contraction. At this time, he was admonished in the US for prioritising Australian employees and is reported not to have enjoyed being criticised in this way.

The business has always been a partnership, though, with Maureen providing the pragmatism. Wheeler himself was described by a business school colleague as *a shy, nervous ball of energy . . . too uneasy to be a business mogul . . . he didn't appear to have the desire to succeed*. Perhaps he came to entrepreneurship by chance. But it appears that once he found and seized his opportunity he was driven to succeed. *He had tried something and found he loved it*. His restless spirit and determination to succeed must have been affected by the deaths of both his father and brother from heart attacks at relatively young ages.

Wheeler has been approached by Microsoft who first asked him to supply material for a series of CD-ROMs (which he declined) and then offered to buy the business, which he also declined. Like Howard Schulz he will defy other people's opinions on occasion. Advised not to publish a guide on Burma because of the political unrest he went ahead and did it. *Politics will change*.

The next cases in this chapter look at other effective entrepreneurial teams, where people find good, appropriate partners with complementary strengths which allow them to focus on their own personal strengths and not worry unduly about overcoming their weaknesses.

The team opportunity

Ben and Jerry's Ice Cream is an idiosyncratic but very entrepreneurial business. Ben Cohen was a college dropout who had become a potter. His friend from his schooldays was Jerry Greenfield, a laboratory assistant who had failed to make it into medical school. They had become *seventies hippies with few real job prospects*. They decided to do something themselves and *looked for something they might succeed at*. They *liked food, so food it was!* They could not afford the machinery for making bagels, but ice cream was affordable. In 1977 they opened an ice cream parlour in Burlington, Vermont, where there were *lots of students and no real competition*. They fostered a relaxed, hippy atmosphere and employed a blues pianist. Their ice cream was different, with large and unusual chunks.

They were instantly successful in their first summer – but sales fell off in the fall and winter. They realised they would have to find outlets outside Vermont if they were to survive. Ben went on the road. Always dressed casually, he would arrive somewhere around 4.00 am and then sleep in his car until a potential distributor opened. He was able to *charm the distributors* and the business began to grow. Ben and Jerry's success provoked a response from the dominant market leader, Häagen Dazs, owned by Pillsbury. Their market share was 70 per cent of the luxury ice cream market. Häagen Dazs threatened to withdraw their product from any distributors who also handled Ben and Jerry's. The two partners employed a lawyer and threatened legal action, but their real weapon was a publicity campaign targeted at Pillsbury itself, and its famous 'dough boy' logo. *What's the Dough Boy afraid of?* they asked. Their gimmicks generated massive publicity and they received an out-of-court settlement. More significantly, the publicity created new demand for luxury ice cream, and the company began to grow faster than had ever been envisaged. A threat had been turned into a massive opportunity. Soon, Ben and Jerry's had a segment market share of 39 per cent, just 4 per cent behind Häagen Dazs. The company has expanded internationally with mixed success. They enjoyed only limited success in the UK *because there was only limited marketing support.*

Perhaps not unexpectedly, given their background, Ben and Jerry have created a values-driven business; some of their ice creams have been linked to causes and interests they support and promote. Rainforest Crunch ice cream features nuts from Brazil; the key ingredients for Chocolate Fudge Brownie are produced by an inner city bakery in Yonkers, New York; and they always favoured Vermont's dairy farming industry. When the business needed equity capital to support its growth, local Vermont residents were given priority treatment. Ben and Jerry argued they were committed to their employees who *bring their hearts and souls as well as their bodies and minds to work* but acknowledge their internal opinion surveys showed a degree of dissatisfaction with the amount of profits (seven and a half per cent) given away every year to good causes.

The two realists with an unusual but definite ego eventually dropped out of day-to-day management . . . *the company needed a greater breadth of management than we had . . .* and remained *two casual, portly, middle-aged hippies.* In 2000 they agreed to sell the business to Unilever, a huge global business that would, on the face of it, appear to have completely different values. And yet, as we saw in Chapter 4, William Lever had demonstrated social characteristics. During the take-over negotiations, Unilever gave $5 million to Ben and Jerry's Foundation and another $5 million to set up a venture capital fund for ethical start-ups – called 'Hot Fudge' – which would be run by Ben Cohen.

Nantucket Nectars is another unusual business started by two friends. When Tom First and Tom Scott graduated from Brown University in Rhode Island they decided they wanted to live on Nantucket Island, off the New England coast, and find some way of earning a living. In the summer of 1989 they started a small business for servicing the yachts belonging to visitors to the island. This was always going to be seasonal. They travelled around the harbour in a distinctive red boat, delivering newspapers, muffins, coffee, laundry and any other supplies, for which there was a demand. They also washed boats, emptied sewage and shampooed dogs. This seemed to lead naturally to them later opening the Nantucket Allserve general store – which still exists. They used the following promotional slogan in the early days – *Ain't nothing those boys won't do.*

Once the summer was over, demand for their services fell as the yachts disappeared. They decided to experiment with fruit juices, mixed in a household blender. They first sought to replicate a peach-based nectar they had sampled in Spain. During the following summer they sold their bottled juices from their red boat. They always produced distinctive flavours from the best-quality ingredients. By investing their joint savings they were able to hire a bottler to produce 1400 cases. Overall though, the business merely struggled on for a couple of years – until one wealthy yacht owner offered them a $500 000 loan to develop the business. They seized the opportunity. Nantucket Nectars then expanded quickly to cover a number of states on the American east coast. Initially they did their own bottling, but this is now subcontracted.

> If I were on the outside looking in, I'd say Nantucket Nectars was an overnight success. Being on the inside, it's been a long, long time. We almost went out of business a thousand times.
>
> (Tom Scott)

The company grew to employ 100 people with sales in over thirty American states and a number of selected export markets. Values were always a key element, the partners remained determined to *create the best quality product in the juice market*, and yet the company remained enigmatic. The bottle labels state *We're juice guys. We don't wear ties to work*; folksy radio commercials have been utilised extensively; but the new head office is in an old Men's Club near Harvard University. It is furnished with antiques, and managers have private offices instead of the open-plan arrangement which is increasingly popular in many informal organisations. First and Scott have typically taken their dogs into work. Each week every head office manager focused on talking personally with one of their salespeople in the field, staff who would otherwise have little contact with head office.

The founders claim the company was always run on gut instinct and trial and error. Few people had any formal business qualifications. In 1997 Nantucket Nectars was awarded a contract to provide juice for Starbucks, and later that year Ocean Spray – leading manufacturer of cranberry juices and other products – acquired a 50 per cent stake. The companies believed they could make extensive savings on supplies if they joined forces. First and Scott continued to run the business they founded.

The BayGen Radio A completely different example of team entrepreneurship can be found with the BayGen Radio, which was the idea of the English inventor, Trevor Baylis, in the early 1990s. Unlike other portable radios, this one does not use batteries; instead, it is powered by clockwork. Baylis developed the idea for the Third World, where batteries are prohibitively expensive, after watching a television documentary on Africa which suggested that the spread of AIDS was affected by the lack of effective communications. He experimented until he had a spring which could power a small generator by releasing energy at a constant rate. Typically springs release energy at a reducing rate. Baylis failed with his early attempts to gain backing and financial support to develop the idea further. However, his prototype was shown on BBC Television, on *Tomorrow's World*, where it was seen by Christopher Staines, the then director of mergers and acquisitions with a leading accountancy practice. Staines was gripped with the potential, worked all night on a business plan and faxed it to Baylis the next day. Within forty-eight hours Staines had secured the worldwide development rights and, after raising financial support from the Overseas Development Agency, he took the idea to South Africa, where he had family connections. The idea was endorsed by President Nelson Mandela, seed capital was duly raised and a new factory with a capacity to build 20 000 radios a month was ready in September 1995. Refinements to the original generator produced forty minutes listening time from twenty seconds winding. Many of the employees are disabled, and the first customers included the Red Cross and UNICEF who then sell them into Third World countries at reduced prices. Trevor Baylis was – and remains – essentially an inventor who provided the idea and the technology; Christopher Staines is the entrepreneur who saw the opportunity for the idea, championed the project and exploited it to great effect.

The location opportunity

Infosys was started in 1981 with 10 000 (Indian) Rupees, equivalent to some US$1200; it is now one of India's most dynamic wealth generators. The story illustrates the focus, advantage and social characteristics. The company was floated in 1993; within six years, and after growing by some 50 per cent per year, the share value had increased eighty-five times. Infosys would become the fifteenth largest company quoted on the New York NASDAQ and the first Indian business to be listed there.

Founder Narayana Murthy, who was around thirty-five at the time, left an American computing business, together with six Indian colleagues, and they started Infosys in Murthy's home in Poona, near Bombay. Infosys would write software for established businesses in the G7 countries, and also provide systems integration and consultancy services. Murthy was the son of a teacher, and although he had been working abroad extensively, particularly in Paris, he was to be the only one of the seven to stay based in India. The others would work in America, close to their key clients. The business would be global from 'day one'; there was no local market of any consequence for what they were doing. Their first major client was Reebok.

> The market for the idea did not exist in India . . . we had to embrace globalisation.
> I believe globalisation is about sourcing capital from where it is cheapest, producing where it is most cost-effective and selling where it is most profitable, all without being constrained by national boundaries.
>
> (Murthy)

India was able to offer well-educated, English-speaking staff who were proficient in IT. They had a strong work ethic and the prevailing salaries were well below those of their client countries. America has generally provided two-thirds of the company's revenues. Infosys was able to offer very competitive prices for high-quality work.

But things were not altogether smooth. *It took one year for a specialist telephone connection, two years to get a license to import a computer and two weeks every time we needed foreign currency to travel abroad.*

In 1987 Infosys began a joint venture with a management consultancy based in Atlanta. The US staff would seek out business; Infosys would provide the skilled personnel to deliver the product. This gave Infosys market credibility and opened up a host of fresh opportunities. New clients included Nestlé, General Electric and Holiday Inn.

The joint venture was abandoned in 1995 when Infosys felt it was sufficiently established and well known to open its own offices in the US. In 1991, back in India, Infosys had moved from Poona to a new 55-acre complex in Bangalore, home of India's burgeoning software industry.

There was now to be a focus on a broader product range with an extended set of staff skills and competencies; this would involve selective acquisitions. The company was restructured around strategic business units. The emphasis would be on service and customer focus. Additional business from existing clients was sought energetically – it amounted to 80 per cent of revenues – as well as the active search for new clients.

Infosys has not been without its critics in India. Its 'social perspective' on working conditions and rewards has not endeared it to everyone. Murthy has proclaimed that *all profitable exporters should give 20% of their earnings before interest and tax to help fund higher education in India*, which has detractors as well as supporters. As for Murthy himself, he has stepped down from the Chief Executive position he held for over twenty years but he remains as Chairman. In 2003 he became the company's 'Chief Mentor' responsible for helping to 'create future leaders' within Infosys.

The privatisation opportunity

Stagecoach   The privatisation of a number of businesses by the Thatcher and subsequent governments provided opportunities for several entrepreneurs in the UK, including Richard Branson with Virgin Rail. The greatest success story is undoubtedly Stagecoach, which also provides an illustration of effective team entrepreneurship and entrepreneurial growth through acquisition.

Founders Brian Souter (born in 1955) and his sister Ann Gloag (twelve years older than her brother) were the children of a Perth bus driver. They became the richest people in Scotland until Harry Potter author, J.K. Rowling, achieved fame and fortune. Souter is a dealmaker, who had earlier worked as a bus conductor to finance his university education. Gloag provided the underpinning management; she was previously a nurse. After graduating, Brian Souter worked as an accountant. *I had a terrible time [finding a job] because a lot of the people I got interviewed by are terrible snobs. I didn't go to the right school, didn't live in the right street and my father wasn't in the right occupation.* Possessing a strong ego, this early struggle made Souter determined to succeed.

The first (1980) Thatcher Transport Act deregulated express and excursion coach services. Seeing an opportunity in an industry they understood, Brian Souter and Ann Gloag began a Dundee to London 'Stage Coach' overnight service. Their level of service was absolutely basic and they succeeded by undercutting everyone else. They found a niche and exploited it. They had used their father's redundancy money (after forty years of driving a bus) to purchase two second-hand coaches. Further growth was possible when a rich Canadian uncle invested an additional £25 000. By 1981 Stagecoach was offering several express services. The 1985 Transport Act heralded the deregulation of local bus services and this was the springboard for the real expansion.

Bidders could only bid for a maximum of three designated franchises in England (1987) and later (1991) two in Scotland. Stagecoach won three in England – Hampshire, Cumberland and United Counties (Bedfordshire, Cambridgeshire and Northamptonshire) but later acquired East Midlands, Ribble (Lancashire) and Southdown (Hampshire, West Sussex and Portsmouth). By 1989 they were spread all over the country, and duly expanded into Scotland in 1991. All the buses are instantly recognisable with their distinctive red, blue and orange colours. Stagecoach carefully recruited experienced senior managers from other bus companies to create a strong management team. But they operate with a lean structure and relatively flat hierarchy. Expansion has continued with the acquisition of bus operations in Hong Kong, Malawi, Kenya, Canada and New Zealand and a rail franchise – South West Trains – in 1992. In 1998 Stagecoach became a substantial shareholder in Virgin Rail. In 1999 Stagecoach paid a premium price to acquire Coach USA, a diversified transport conglomerate. Divestments and poor financial results suggest this was not a good strategic move.

There has been controversy as Stagecoach has more than once been referred to the Monopolies and Mergers Commission for the way it has competed in certain areas, pricing aggressively and allegedly driving weaker competitors out of business. Whilst it has always remained focused on transport and a clear industry leader, Stagecoach has been flexible and very responsive when new opportunities have come along. Souter has suggested that *tunnel vision is a great disaster for businesses and often inventors are the worst people to admit that their inventions aren't working.*

Neither Souter nor Gloag is described as an easy person to work with. Critics argue Souter is not a good delegator and team builder. However he certainly has target focus (he is a master of detail), strategic vision (constantly searching for new opportunities), profit orientation and a Christian work ethic linked to a modest personal lifestyle.

Ann Gloag has been described as a *driven woman . . . even when her business tactics were being criticised she was convinced she had done no wrong.* However her dedication to the business cost her marriage. Later, in 1999, her son committed suicide and that prompted her to walk away from executive responsibility at Stagecoach. She opted, instead, to work for Mercy Ships, a charity that provides free ship-based medical services and dental care to the world's poorest regions and people. She donated £4 million to buy a new ship but she also wanted active involvement and returned to front-line nursing on one of the ships. Her brother has managed to separate his business and personal interests in a different way – Souter spent hundreds of thousands of pounds campaigning to retain Clause 28 of the Local Government Act, a clause which bans the promotion of homosexuality in schools. The cause was lost.

The franchising opportunity

Subway Many entrepreneurial businesses and fortunes have been built with franchising – McDonald's is an excellent example. However, by 2003, McDonald's had been overtaken by Subway in terms of the largest number of fast food outlets in America. The company is also growing overseas – and all of it through franchising.

The company, which sells freshly made sandwiches and salads to order – its trademark is the long 'submarine' roll – was started in 1965 by the seventeen-year-old

Fred Deluca, in partnership with a family friend – and nuclear physicist – who invested $1000. The first sandwich shop struggled, but it survived and was joined by a second and then a third. By 1968 Deluca owned five outlets. In 1974 he switched to franchising. Rapid growth followed such that 200 outlets in 1981 became 5000 in 1990 and 11 000 in 1995. In 1983 all Subway outlets began baking their own bread.

Subway is successful for a number of reasons:

- It is simple – an easy model to replicate.
- It is innovative. Menus are changed constantly with new breads as well as fillings.
- There is distinct advantage in the healthy option sandwiches and salads.
- It has a very clear focus and business model. Franchisees are not creators of new ideas; rather they are there to deliver products and service. Their overheads are low because the franchiser supplies most of the equipment they need. Franchisees organise their own local food purchases – which is quite different from the way many franchised fast food outlets are supplied with centrally sourced materials.

Opportunities built from resources

When entrepreneurs spot new opportunities they find the resources required to exploit them. Sometimes they have relatively straightforward access to many of the resources they need – premises, money and know-how – and that is, in part, why the opportunity makes sense for them. Other entrepreneurs find opportunities to exploit particular talents or skills that they possess. Some sports personalities have built important networks and they enjoy notoriety – these are exploitable assets. Some academics have very specialist knowledge and know-how that can be commercialised.

David Lloyd was a British tennis star who played at Wimbledon and in the Davis Cup; he was visibly competitive and aggressive. His brother and fellow player, John, however, always enjoyed the higher profile. Their father was a businessman in Essex who had been successful for a period before he failed. At school and playing tennis, Lloyd was always involved in a deal of some sort. Once he had finished playing full-time Lloyd opened a leisure club which grew into a chain that he eventually sold to Whitbread for £20 million. He had spotted the opportunity when he was playing, but it was slow going at first. He had not made enough money as a player for what he needed and many financiers felt he lacked any proven business ability. The clubs he started were successful because he paid attention to detail and provided what he *knew would be popular with customers*. They still bear his name but he no longer has any involvement. After the sale he did stay on for a time but became critical of Whitbread, accusing it of *massive central control . . . no empowerment*.

More recently he has started a second chain of leisure clubs, called Next Generation, which are deliberately different from what he calls the *leisure sheds* he first opened. He has courted controversy and unpopularity in Hull, where he was looking to merge the football club with one of the two rugby league clubs. He has also reportedly fallen out with the Lawn Tennis Association, for whom he coached the Davis Cup team for a number of years. An ex-employee calls him *driven and ambitious . . . but the cleverest man with figures I've ever seen*. He has a notoriously short fuse and could be baited as a tennis player. Clearly very focused and strong on advantage, his very strong ego could, on occasions, work against him.

Filtronic   David Rhodes, at the time a Lecturer at the University of Leeds and aged in his thirties, established Filtronic as a campus spin-off company in 1977. Rhodes had a research background in microwave engineering and he had worked at Universities in both the US and the UK. His intention was to develop a series of electronic and mechanical devices for separating and processing microwaves and which had a commercial potential. In the early days Filtronic secured a contract from the US military to develop products which would jam enemy radar. The company also worked on the Stealth Bomber project. Filtronic's products could identify aircraft by their radar signatures and communicate with space probes. Real growth, however, came in the late 1980s/early 1990s when Rhodes was able to capitalise on the fast-growing market for mobile phones. Filtronic could supply products which separate signals to and from mobile phones, increasingly useful as the radio wave space available to the various system providers becomes ever more congested. It became a leading supplier of antennae – both internal and external – supplying the leading manufacturers. By 2000 Filtronic employed 2500 people in the UK, the US and Australia. Annual sales are now nearly £300 million, with 20 per cent of the revenues being generated in the UK and 50 per cent in America. David Rhodes remains Chairman and Chief Executive of the company he started, and he retains a 10 per cent shareholding in the business. In addition he still lectures part-time for the University of Leeds; students on an MSc programme in Microwave Engineering have several of their lectures at Filtronic, whose headquarters is just a few miles away. The company is, in fact, based in part of what was Salt's Mill, a restored Victorian mill in Saltaire, and which is now a World Heritage Site. This story is told in the Interlude preceding Chapter 7. Many of his senior managers are ex-academics and students.

Rhodes' judgement has sometimes been questioned. He agreed to buy a microprocessor plant that Fujitsu had built but could not operate profitably. Located in Prime Minister Tony Blair's constituency, he bought it cheaply. It has taken a number of years to make it profitable. He is also a substantial shareholder in Bradford City Football Club, which had a period in administration and mixed fortunes in the game itself. Businessmen are invariably criticised for investing in football clubs! He is sometimes called *bombastic* and he has shown he can irritate the press who have commented *he is not a man who takes criticism with equanimity*. He is also said to *suffer rather than enjoy* the City. He has a strong ego.

Opportunities on the fringe of business

Warren Buffett

The very existence of businesses provides opportunities for other businesses – and not just those which are direct suppliers and distributors. We look first at Warren Buffett, an entrepreneur who has built a hugely successful business empire and become a multi-billionaire by careful investment in other companies. Buffett began by acquiring Berkshire Hathaway in 1965, when it was focused in insurance. Shares which were then worth $18 each are now valued at over $70 000. The annual return on equity has consistently been between 20 and 30 per cent.

His strategy was to invest long term in carefully selected businesses. He is not a speculator, nor does he seek to acquire and control a business. Instead he is interested in *good companies with good managers* and seeks to buy shares at favourable, low, market prices and then *hold them for life*. He *bets on managers who love their business and not the money* and he never buys without tracking a company and carrying out extensive research to determine its true value. He prefers low-risk investments . . . *I don't jump over seven foot bars . . . I look around for one foot bars I can step over*. Consequently Buffett has invested in insurance, candy stores, newspapers and the Dairy Queen fast-food outlets amongst many others – as well as buying a large stake in Coca-Cola.

Buffett follows a number of key principles when choosing where to invest. He looks for strong brands and he avoids products which *don't travel well*. Food, for example, does not provide the foundation for a strong global business as tastes vary so much between countries. What works in one may not be successful in another. He is also extremely careful with high-technology businesses. Reflecting this philosophy, his Managing Director has commented: *If I taught a strategy course, I would set the following examination question . . . 'Evaluate the following Internet company . . .' and anyone who gave an answer would be failed!* Buffett counsels against investing in something *you don't understand . . . always look in detail at the product, its competition and its earning power*. Then . . . *never rely on stock market valuations . . . look for the real value . . . look carefully at Annual reports for openness, honesty and cover-ups.*

Like many other successful people, Buffett has underpinning values, ones which closely embrace certain key entrepreneurial characteristics . . . *My principle is to leave enough money for your children that they can do anything they want, but not enough they can do nothing.*

Donna Sammons Carpenter

Donna Sammons Carpenter is quite different, but also very successful on a more modest scale. Her company, Wordworks, provides ghostwriters for many well-known management authors – but not including the writers of this book! Tom Peters is probably the most successful author she works with, and her name can be found in the acknowledgement section of a number of his books. It is the author who takes the risk when commissioning Carpenter. There is a negotiated fee for the work, and if significant sales of the subsequent book are not achieved, the author may well be out of pocket. However, the chances of success are clearly improved with a contribution from a strong and experienced writing team. Moreover, a successful management book can be *a calling card to high earnings from speaking engagements!*

Mark McCormack

Mark McCormack, who died in 2003 at the age of seventy-two, has written a number of popular management books, but his success has come from the International

Management Group that he established. McCormack has been described as *the most powerful man in sport*; he saw an opportunity for bringing together big business and sports personalities. Originally a lawyer and recreational golfer, he acted for Arnold Palmer in a legal capacity. He was then offered the opportunity to widen his portfolio, which he seized, and followed up with representation for other leading sports personalities, including golfers Gary Player, Jack Nicklaus and Tiger Woods, tennis stars Pete Sampras and André Agassi, skiers and Formula One racing driver Michael Schumacher. Opera stars José Carreras and Kiri Te Kanawa, together with several top models, can be added to the list. McCormack specialised in merchandising deals, licensing the star's name and negotiating television appearances. Nicknamed 'Mark The Shark' he was very driven, very focused and a hard dealmaker. He was not universally liked, and he was often outspoken if any stars left him for other managers. But he was a true opportunity-spotter, always on the lookout for the next deal. He had time focus – every day was broken down into fifteen-minute slots – target focus and performance orientation. He used 'to do' lists on yellow legal pads and completed them all before his day's work was complete. He rose at 4.30 a.m. every day and was a renowned workaholic. *He really liked what he did and never stopped.*

When he died, his business was turning over $1 billion and his 3000 employees worked from eighty-five offices in thirty-five countries. He had transformed sports management. Reflecting his views on talent and temperament he commented: *the only thing worse than not finding your genius is finding it and wasting it.*

The stories told so far in this chapter concentrate on entrepreneurs who have started and largely remained focused on a particular business. A minority start something and then make an exit once the venture is prospering – to start again with something new and sometimes completely different. Either through lack of interest, or by knowing where their real skills lie, these entrepreneurs are creative, innovative and opportunistic but less concerned with maintenance and nurturing.

The serial entrepreneur

Paul Sykes

Paul Sykes was born in Barnsley in 1944, the elder son of a Yorkshire coal miner. He left school at fifteen and worked initially as a tyre fitter. His success as an opportunity-spotting serial entrepreneur is testimony to the value of the *University of Life*. Asked whether he regretted leaving school at the age of fifteen, Sykes has responded: *Yes I do. I wanted to leave at eleven; the extra four years cost me a lot of money!*

Paul quickly got tired of working for other people and started out on his own at the age of eighteen. He began cutting up buses for scrap, something he had already been doing part-time for a friend at weekends. He had just £170 to invest, which he used to buy his first bus and a second-hand pick-up truck; he made sure he could return to his job as a tyre fitter if the venture failed. An ability to manage the downside risk is one of the secrets of his success. Spotting potential opportunities for adding value in the Far East, he began reconditioning bus engines for export, mainly to Hong Kong, where many were used to power junks. Some of the second-hand buses were also supplied to Asia in kit form, whilst others were refurbished for lease in the UK. These business interests grew and prospered such that by the early 1970s Sykes was buying some 3500 buses a year from the National Bus Company, approximately half the number it was scrapping and replacing. But eventually the number of buses available for recycling declined and at the same time Japanese competitors began to move in to his markets. Typically intuitive, Paul concluded he should come out of bus recycling and he made a swift exit, selling some interests to his younger brother and a cousin. Already a multi-millionaire he turned his eyes to coaches and property. His coach distribution and leasing company was later sold for £20 million.

Paul Sykes now changed direction, opting to invest £30 million of his personal wealth in property development, his initial achievement being the UK's first out-of-town cinema complex in Salford Quays. He soon became convinced that the trend for out-of-town developments in America would spread to the UK; his prediction was correct. An early entry into London's Docklands was, however, followed by a quick exit – he was sceptical about the adequacy of the support infrastructure and worried about escalating rents for the freeholds. He saw a downside risk. This was followed by a realisation – arguably a vision – that derelict land in Sheffield's Don Valley (vacated as steel firm after steel firm closed down) could be used to create wealth and jobs. The outcome was the Meadowhall shopping centre, begun in 1986, and whose success has spawned a raft of further developments, including sports stadia, the Sheffield Arena (entertainment venue) and a new airport. Planning permission from an initially doubtful local authority was a major and time-consuming hurdle, but it was eventually granted. Sykes' persistence had been rewarded. As the embryo idea developed and borrowings of over £350 million became necessary, Sykes formed a partnership with fellow property-developer, Eddie Healey, whose holding company took over management of the shopping centre. Sykes retained a 40 per cent shareholding in Meadowhall which was valued at £1.2 billion when it was sold in 1999. At this time, Sykes' wealth was estimated to exceed £400 million. Again showing prescience and skills in timing his exit, Paul Sykes has not been seriously affected by the recent rises and falls in property values, and Meadowhall was his last *major* development.

A true opportunity-spotter, Paul later turned to information technology and helped form Planet Online, which grew to become Britain's largest commercial Internet provider (for business to business transactions), employing 350 people and with a base in Leeds. He had been introduced to the man with the idea at a football match. Peter Wilkinson already ran a computer business and understood the technology. Sykes was able to appreciate where the real opportunity lay, realising that Britain *needs information highways more than it needs tarmac highways*. The transport system is heavily congested and information technology has the potential to streamline the distribution of both goods and services. At the same time, if organisations can outsource information management, they can focus their efforts on the heart of the business. Having committed himself within forty-eight hours of the first meeting with his new partner, Paul sold his majority shareholding in 1998 to create a fund – or war chest – which he would dedicate to his campaign to keep Britain out of the Single European Currency in order *to protect our sovereignty and democracy*. With this campaign he has found a cause to which he was willing to dedicate considerable time, energy and resources – mirroring many of the social entrepreneurs we feature in Chapter 7. His Internet investment of £10 million had earned him a profit of £37 million in just three years. At the moment, Europe is his leading interest and passion, but he retains a limited portfolio of business and property interests.

Paul Sykes has always been energetic, tenacious and was *not content with his lot* when he was young. Leaving school at the earliest opportunity, and with no formal qualifications, he was committed to working hard – characteristics he inherited from his mother. Throughout his business life he has exhibited vision, opportunism and timing; he has been careful to manage any downside risk and has *earned a profit every month and every year*. He has used his wide network of contacts for mutual benefit and he has been willing to form suitable partnerships. His experiences have taught him that successful businesses must be kept simple. *Success depends on value-for-money products and services which address customers' needs – and a stream of future potential customers if growth is to continue.*

Opportunities for corporate entrepreneurs

So far we have concentrated on entrepreneurs who have built something substantial from scratch; we now move on to look at entrepreneurs who work inside existing corporations, including those who successfully turn around companies in difficulty. The umbrella term for these people is corporate entrepreneurs, and three distinct types can be identified – transformers, venturers and intrapreneurs. There are occasions where an existing business introduces new strategies which lead to transformational changes in its industry. When Ted Turner launched CNN, it heralded the start of twenty-four-hour news broadcasting, which in turn has had a major impact upon the way the world is briefed on key events as they unravel. Another aspect of transformation is the renewal of existing and under-performing organisations with hidden values. We look at the entrepreneurial style of Jack Welch, who has ensured the diversified American conglomerate, General Electric, has prospered when many similar organisations have become increasingly focused. Venturers spin off businesses from those they are currently involved with – the story of Silicon Valley features many examples – or buy out businesses from their current owners. The third type is the creation of new businesses within existing organisations, where we look briefly at the 3M approach. When corporate entrepreneurs are successful, it is because they appreciate how to add value, create differences and thereby improve the competitive position of their business. They create a new opportunity.

Transformer entrepreneurs

Ted Turner was a risk-taker and an acquisitive entrepreneur. He is 'off-the-scale' as an opportunist, *living life on the edge*, but he has shown an unusual approach to delegation and people. He was one of the first to see the opportunities cable television would bring.

Turner was born in 1938; his parents were wealthy and he was always competitive. He chose to focus on competitive sailing when he found he was not outstanding at more popular sports. His dedication later paid off when he won the 1977 America's Cup race and the 1979 Fastnet race in the Solent, the year several competitors died in the severe weather conditions. Turner had earlier inherited a $1-million billboard advertising business when his father committed suicide, and he used this as a base to acquire more advertising and radio businesses. Aggressively seeking growth, he was willing to accept large debt commitments and once claimed: *I've won more awards than anybody my age; I've probably also got more debt than anyone else in the world.* He first moved into television when he bought a station in 1969 and used it to establish the first national network by beaming signals via satellite to other cable stations. This proved valuable for covering the 1981 assassination attempt on President Reagan and the 1986 space shuttle disaster. His CNN (Cable News Network) twenty-four-hour news station really 'came of age' during the 1990 Gulf War.

Turner's uncanny success in starting high-risk ventures is not accidental. He is a workaholic who always retained personal control over key decisions. He employed five senior managers but *would not let the five go out and have a beer together, let alone run the company.* In 1986 he failed to take-over CBS in a costly and acrimonious battle, but he fought back by acquiring MGM Studios, with its extensive film library, which he used to establish network cable movie channels. He did acquire CBS some years later, before selling out his business empire to Time Warner – retaining a personal stake of 10 per cent in the world's largest entertainment company. Reflecting his interest in sports, he has retained ownership of the Atlanta Braves (baseball) and the Atlanta Hawks basketball team. With an estimated net worth of $2 billion, he has established the second largest foundation in America, to support needy causes.

Reflecting a strong ego and his attitude to risk, he once said . . . *basically I am in business because it gives me a good feeling about myself. You learn a lot about your capabilities by putting yourself on the line. Running a successful business is not only a financial risk, it is an emotional risk as well. I get a lot of satisfaction from having dared it – and done it – and been successful.*

Jack Welch and General Electric   The diversified conglomerate General Electric is one of the most successful, admired and powerful companies in the world. It is also innovative and entrepreneurial. General Electric manufactures aircraft engines, defence electronics and household consumer goods, provides financial services and owns NBC Television in the USA. Until 1994, GE owned the Kidder Peabody Investment Bank, but now invests in a wide range of other businesses through its GE Capital subsidiary. Jack Welch was the Chief Executive Officer from 1981 to 2002 and he pursued a strategy of focusing on market segments where the company could be Number One or Number Two and ambitiously emphasised high-growth industries.

The company he left behind is decentralised and employees are encouraged to speak out and pursue ideas. External contacts and sources are constantly monitored for new ideas, leads and opportunities. *At Head Office we don't go very deep into much of anything, but we have a smell of everything. Our job is capital allocation – intellectual and financial. Smell, feel, touch, listen, then allocate* (Welch). In 1995, NBC was anxious to win the television rights for the Sydney Olympic Games in 2000. Pre-empting its competitors, NBC bid jointly for these games and the next Winter Olympics in Salt Lake City and presented the IOC (International Olympic Committee) with a take-it-or-leave-it deal before any bids had even been invited. When Welch was asked to support the proposal – and the huge sums involved – he took just thirty minutes to give his agreement. Within a week the deal had been struck. The IOC commented afterwards that *the reaction of NBC's rivals was one of disappointment but reluctant admiration for the initiative that NBC took.*

General Electric's structure is decentralised and systems such as regular briefings and meetings for senior managers at GE's corporate training centre seek to ensure best practices are shared. Managers move from one division to another to gain promotion and there are cross-business teams always working on new ideas *in an organisation without boundaries* – but the turnover of divisional heads is low. *Put the right people in the right jobs . . . leave them . . . and things get better not worse* (Welch). Welch is proud of his ability to *spot people early on, follow them, grow them and stretch them . . . we spend all our time on people!* Rewards are carefully varied between businesses, to reflect the different levels of risk.

It is significant that Welch built an organisation where there were three strong candidates to succeed him. Only one could have the job; perhaps inevitably the others left. Larry Johnson became CEO of Albertsons, the second largest supermarket group in America, but struggling a little. He has successfully turned around its fortunes. Robert Nardelli did exactly the same at Home Depot, which had enjoyed extremely fast growth as a DIY warehouse chain but had lost its focus. Both were able to give their new businesses a fresh vision and strong operational strengths to deliver.

The Anglo-Norwegian consultancy, The Performance Group, concluded in a 1999 Report that GE's success has been built on *continual 'breakthroughs' in every area . . . from product development to corporate culture, from sales and marketing to labour relations.* This report concludes that *a company that avoids upheaval and change is not long for this world.*

Kim Winser and Pringle

Winser, once a manager at Marks and Spencer, was recruited by Scottish knitwear manufacturer, Pringle, when the company was experiencing falling sales and profits. Design misjudgements had compromised the once-famous brand and its previous owner, Dawson, had sold the business to two brothers from Hong Kong.

Could manufacturing survive in the UK? Winser introduced new products, found new suppliers, terminated contracts with some retail outlets and found new ones, and demanded new trading terms. The business was turned around and profits restored. The *Financial Times* described her as a *perpetual innovator . . . who takes tough decisions and is then completely committed and determined.*

Kim Winser is a growth entrepreneur at the head of an established business, giving it a new direction and a new future. Our next story is about another serial entrepreneur. Steve Jobs would be forced out of the company he started, only to return later and turn it around – an entrepreneur and then a corporate entrepreneur.

Steve Jobs and Apple

Entrepreneur Steve Jobs joined forces with a computer 'nerd', Stephen Wozniak, to start Apple in 1976, a company which has made a major and profound contribution to the personal computer industry. Begun in a garage, this creative and innovative company was a world leader by the end of the seventies. By 1983, and with just a number of variants of a single model, Apple was turning over $1 billion a year. Wozniak had, however, left to find a new challenge and the Apple structure and management systems had not developed sufficiently. Steve Jobs persuaded John Sculley, then chief executive of PepsiCo, to come and help him run Apple, freeing himself up to concentrate on developing Apple's new product, the Mackintosh. *Do you want to spend the rest of your life selling sugared water, or do you want a chance to change the world?* was allegedly the challenge from Jobs which had the most influence on Sculley's decision.

At this time, Jobs' attention and interest was focused entirely on the new product. He had been allowed access to the Palo Alto Research Centre owned and run by Xerox; it was there he saw the first graphic user interface on a computer screen. *I knew this was the future!* he claimed afterwards, although Xerox itself chose not to develop along these lines. Whilst the Mackintosh was a pioneer of the mouse-driven screen display, and remains to this day a high added-value, premium-price product and the first choice of designers, Microsoft's Windows software grew to dominate the mass market. By focusing on the top end of the market, Apple provided Bill Gates with his opportunity – and his success was clearly damaging to Apple as time went on.

Jobs, by this time, had clashed with the Apple Board of Directors and left to 'pursue other interests', enjoying mixed fortunes in the following years. A software business had some success; his new film animation company, Pixar, worked with Disney to produce the lucrative *Toy Story* film.

Struggling to compete with Microsoft's market dominance, Sculley then left. He was replaced initially by Michael Spindler and later by Gil Amelio, but Apple remained fragile. In 1997, Jobs returned as interim chief executive, insisting he would not take the job permanently; Wozniak was retained as a consultant. With a new Mackintosh as its lead product, and with an investment of $150 million from Microsoft, Apple made a comeback under the leadership of Steve Jobs. We discuss Apple further in Chapter 14.

This second time around, Jobs has championed a lower price version of the Mac, the E3 and the iMac, an integrated computer and monitor to which a keyboard and mouse can be attached in an instant. Design and image are key features; the 'futuristic' housings for the latest Apple machines are produced in colourful translucent plastic. Jobs has deliberately targeted those users *who like individuality*. The most recent and hugely successful product is the iPod, which allows users to download and copy their favourite music tracks and play them at leisure, through personal headphones.

Venturer entrepreneurs

Buy-outs (where the existing management team acquires a business from its present owners) and buy-ins (where a new, external, management team buys an existing business) are turnaround opportunities for entrepreneurial managers. These entrepreneurs create new value with a business that has typically been under-achieving – which often arises when the business concerned has a poor strategic fit inside its existing parent organisation. The results are often quite startling. Some famous brand names have been bought-out – including Hornby Hobbies (electric trains and Scalextric) and Parker pens.

Premier Brands was formed in 1986 as a result of a management buy-out from Cadbury's. Cadbury's drinking chocolate, biscuits, Smash instant mashed potato,

Marvel and Coffee Complement, Chivers and Hartley's products and TyPhoo tea were the main brands involved. Cadbury's had decided to focus on its main chocolate products and, through its merger with Schweppes, on soft drinks.

The new chief executive of Premier Brands was Paul Judge. Within a few years the spin-off company was floated on the Stock Exchange. Judge, who was now a rich man, opted to retire. He funded the Judge Institute of Management at Cambridge University with some of his newly acquired wealth.

Microcell In contrast, Microcell is an ideal example of a spin-off business. Jyrki Hallikainen worked in R&D for Nokia in Finland but left to start his own business in 1997. By this time the once-diversified Nokia had focused on mobile telephones and become the world's leading supplier of handsets. Filtronic is one of its leading suppliers. Microcell was *profitable from day one* and Hallikainen recruited his team from people he knew at Nokia. He had spotted an opportunity in the market and set out to exploit it. Microcell is Europe's leading ODM (original design manufacturer) in the industry. They design, develop and manufacture mobile phone handsets. Their customers – who include Sony Ericsson, Siemens and Philips – market them under their own brand name.

Intrapreneurs

Our 3M story provides a valuable illustration of a relative American strength and corresponding British weakness highlighted by Sir John Harvey-Jones (Ashworth, 1999). Sir John argued the UK *has a very unforgiving [business] environment . . . we have a low expectation of people, so far too many people can survive just by not making a really big screw-up. In America, they don't even consider you're a businessman unless you've screwed something up, because, by definition, you're not pushing the frontiers . . . almost everything in this country is an endeavour to avoid making a mistake, and if you avoid making a mistake you are never in front . . . I don't long to employ masses of people who screw everything up, but if a guy makes a mistake because he's really stretching for the stars, that's different.*

In this context, Archie Norman, Conservative MP and a proven corporate entrepreneur at Asda, argues that a *failing organisation is almost invariably an organisation that ceases to innovate and to experiment because innovation and experimentation are risky.*

3M The Minnesota Mining and Manufacturing Company (3M) is based in St Paul, Minnesota and has developed a leading reputation for being innovative and creative. The story of 3M's Post-It Notes is really 'the stuff of legends'. The internal entrepreneur in this case was an employee called Arthur Fry, who had become annoyed that pieces of paper he placed inside his Church hymn book as markers kept falling out when he was singing. Fry was a 3M chemical engineer who knew about an invention by a scientist colleague called Spencer Silver. Silver had developed a new glue which possessed only a very low sticking power, and for this reason was being perceived as a failure! Fry saw the new glue as the answer to his problem – when he applied it to his paper markers, they stayed put but they were easily removed. Realising that many others also shared the same problem, Fry sought approval to commercialise his idea – but initially he met with scepticism. The idea took hold when he passed samples around to secretaries within 3M and other organisations. The rest, as they say, is history!

Over the years the company has developed over 60 000 new products, including everything that bears the Scotch brand name, including sellotape and video cassettes. 3M also manufactures heart-lung machines. Employees are actively encouraged to work on developing new ideas and products. They can legitimately spend 15 per cent of their working time on new projects that they initiate and they can apply for internal company development grants of up to $50 000. When ideas are taken forward they also have the option of championing the new business in its later development stages. There is an understood tolerance of both opt-out and failure, but employee bonuses depend on new product development. A supportive management accounting system is used to advise on the cost implications of bringing new ideas to market, assessing the impact on existing businesses and establishing realistic targets and milestones. This enables effective prioritisation.

This chapter has provided an insight into the wide and varied range of opportunities used by business entrepreneurs to build organisations and create financial capital, and also highlighted how many of them have actually translated the idea into a successful business. The idea alone is inadequate; it must be engaged, captured and exploited. Successful ideas and opportunities imply added value and differences which are attractive to potential customers, who then reward the entrepreneur with their custom. The successful business needs structure, organisation and, above all, supportive, committed people – who actually create the value. We have seen how many of the entrepreneurs featured in this chapter have understood the strategic importance of their people and ensured their competencies and endeavours have been harnessed effectively to create the virtuous circle of growth we mentioned in the introduction.

The next chapter looks at more business entrepreneurs – those who are active in the dot.com industries – and then we feature examples of entrepreneurs who have used and exploited their talents to prioritise the creation of social and aesthetic capital. In some cases, but not all, profit-seeking businesses are involved – but in these examples, whilst the profit is an important element, it is not the key focus for the business.

References

Ashworth, J. (1999). Looking for Trouble? Interview with Sir John Harvey-Jones, *GNER* (*Great North Eastern Railways*). *Travel Magazine*, July.
Charan, R. and Colvin, G. (1999). Why CEO's fail, *Fortune*, 21 June.
The Performance Group (1999). *Breakthrough Performance Through People: Report.*

Further Readings

Some of the material in the Lonely Planet story has been sourced from: Davidson, A. (2002). Putting his foot in it? *Financial Times*, 1 June.
Some of the material in the David Lloyd story has been sourced from: Davidson, A. (2002). Lloyd looms, *Financial Times*, 15 June.

6 The new Internet entrepreneurs

Internet-related businesses are a phenomenon of the last ten years. At one level e-commerce businesses require only limited start-up capital. Developing the idea and a website is not prohibitively expensive; the problem – and the expense – lies in establishing the procurement and distribution systems. The other key issue is making sure web users visit the site of the business, a problem which intensifies all the time as more and more sites are put up. However venture capitalists have at times been investing in these businesses, often accepting risks and uncertainty not normally associated with venture capitalists. A number of professional firms (consultants, lawyers and public relations specialists) have opted to waive their fees in exchange for equity in these new ventures. The reason – things have been moving very quickly and people were afraid of being left behind in the race! But some interesting and sometimes expensive lessons have had to be learned.

As we progress further into the new, third millennium, cyberspace and e-commerce is *providing another Klondike gold rush . . . it is not just another fad*. The use of the gold rush metaphor is both interesting and meaningful. It conjures up thoughts of huge fortunes. Sixty-four new millionaires every day in Silicon Valley alone was a headline just a few years ago. But we must not forget that only a small percentage of those prospectors attracted to Alaska really made their fortune. Most failed to find very much gold – and many perished in the harsh conditions. The Internet is a wonderful and attractive opportunity, but it is proving disappointing, even cruel, to many of those would-be entrepreneurs it attracts. The commercial potential of new creative, innovative ideas is difficult to evaluate, and consequently the ability to persuade a venture capitalist to back a venture – difficult as this may prove to be – is certainly no guarantee of success. An infrastructure and a market both have to be built.

There are broadly two types of Internet business. First, those *providing* a service – such as a search engine, on-line auction facilities or weather information – and largely paid for by advertising. Second, those *selling* either a product or service commercially – known as electronic or e-commerce.

As these businesses are knowledge-based and often begin with a creative, innovative, novel idea, market entry can seem tantalisingly simple. After all, there are no effective barriers against putting up a website. But attracting adequate finance to develop the idea, buy or access the necessary powerful web servers, establish a supply chain and then attract customers from the 'busy electronic highways' is not quite so straightforward. *The net is all about execution . . . things being done on time and with great service*. Shoeless Joe, in the film *Field of Dreams*, said: *If you build it, they will come* – but whilst new websites may attract interest, the implementation and project management of a new Internet business is complex, expensive and hazardous.

Electronic commerce can change the economics and customer proposition of an industry; exploiting this real opportunity is the challenge for many Internet entrepreneurs. Distribution costs can be reduced as less stock is required in the system. Prices can be truly flexible, ideal if last-minute price reductions are being considered for non-storable services such as airline and theatre seats and hotel rooms. Demand can be matched with supply more effectively for the benefit of both suppliers and customers who are willing – or need – to wait until the last minute. The range of choice can be improved dramatically – a virtual store can have almost limitless size whereas physical stores are inevitably restricted. Extensive background information can be provided very easily. In addition, suppliers can use the information they acquire about their customers to carefully target special promotions. However, e-commerce can only work properly if the goods or parcels can be delivered efficiently and effectively. Amazon.com, for example, has a marketing partnership with the US Postal Service, and similarly valuable opportunities have arisen for specialist parcel carriers such as Federal Express, who we discussed in Chapter 5.

The fundamental principle, then, behind many new e-commerce businesses is trading without either manufacture or long-term inventory. E-commerce cuts out the retail store element. New organisations dedicated to e-commerce are similar in principle but yet distinctly different from the situation where established organisations (including, for example, leading retailers such as Tesco and Waterstone's) have experimented with selling via the web as well as through their own high street outlets. Some large retailers have, of course, increasingly moved in this direction because of the impact the specialist e-commerce companies have had on customer buying habits. It may not be automatically necessary for them to choose to follow this route, but they should nevertheless have a clear strategy for how they are going to embrace the potential opportunities and threats from the Internet.

Whilst the new businesses may own warehouses for collecting stock for onward transmission and holding limited numbers of fast-moving items, there will rarely be any need for them to employ either sales or production staff – and, of course, this element can be outsourced to specialists in logistics, leaving the e-commerce company to focus on creating and maintaining a successful website, once the supply chain is set up. Simply, they are a virtual company.

Their fundamental advantage is their ability to reach a wide customer audience at low cost – as long as they can be attracted in the first place and then retained as a regular customer. Relatively specialist items can thus be made available to people who find it difficult to visit the shops which actually sell them directly. One key disadvantage is that the goods cannot be touched and inspected, which matters more for some customers and products than it does for others. The main infrastructure requirements for a successful e-commerce business are appropriate managerial and technical skills, venture capital to set up a sophisticated supply chain and secure payment systems. They also need customers who can and do access their site, recognise the convenience and benefits being offered, and believe the payment systems are private and secure.

In this chapter we look at organisations we might categorise as winners, survivors and fallers. The 'winners' tend to be those providing a service with a business model that is heavily dependent on advertising, rather than those selling either a product or a service. It is from this second category that we have drawn our survivors and fallers. Prominent and visible companies such as Amazon.com can only be categorised as survivors as they have yet to record any consistent profit figures, however large they might have grown.

Warren Buffett (2000), America's richest investor as we saw in Chapter 5, has predicted the Internet will *create no more wealth than a chain letter . . . for society the Internet's a wonderful thing, but for capitalists it's probably a net negative*. He was arguing that people at the start of a chain letter do make money – but no money is actually created. Some investors have appeared to believe that the Internet was a magic money-making machine – but this has not proved to be the case across the board. Internet businesses have a huge potential to burn cash.

As we tell these stories, it is worth bearing this view in mind. It is also significant to look at the backgrounds of the entrepreneurs themselves. Many of them are well educated and well connected – this is their gateway to securing the money required. Finally, it is useful to measure the companies against the following six themes that Gwyther (1999) offers as evaluation criteria for Internet businesses:

Three factors which determine the extent and value of the opportunity:

1 The concept or idea

- How value is created and built.
- The potential for profit, based on costs and revenues.
- The size of the potential market.
- The potential to establish an advantage and reap the rewards – specifically the presence of effective barriers to entry by direct competitors.

2 Innovation

- The initial difference and the potential to build new values and thus sustain any early advantage.

3 Engagement and implementation

- The ability to set up the infrastructure and the business – which inevitably depends upon the people behind the business.

Three further factors which reflect the project or business outcomes:

4 Traffic

- Numbers of customers generated – linked to the extent of repeat business, which in turn is dependent upon service levels achieved.
- Although Web congestion can be a constraint, the fact that people recommend websites by word-of-mouth is a major opportunity.

5 Financing

- Financial resources secured, to fund continued expansion as well as start-up.
- Setting up a robust business and infrastructure on the Web is expensive.

6 Visibility

- The critically important brand identity and image.
- Public profile and visibility – which can also act as a barrier to entry.
- This will often be in the form of media coverage for either an exciting new idea or the recognition of a new, successful entrepreneur or even a Web millionaire.

We also think the quality and strengths of the entrepreneurs themselves are important, and the stories bear this out. People criteria as well as business criteria must be considered.

Winners

Sabeer Bhatia and Hotmail

Sabeer Bhatia, joint founder of Hotmail, arrived in America – in Los Angeles – in 1988. His father had served as an officer in the Indian Army before entering public service; his mother worked as an accountant for the Bank of India. Sabeer had won a scholarship to study in America and possessed just $250, the maximum he had been allowed to bring out of India. His scholarship for Cal Tech was no ordinary scholarship – he was the only student in the world that year to have reached the qualifying threshold on the brain-teaser tests. In a typical year, 150 people try and the best scores above the threshold qualify for a scholarship. He came with no intention of staying; he assumed he would obtain his degree and return to India to work as an engineer in a large corporation. At the time he had not realised that America is the land of opportunity!

An enthusiastic student, he regularly attended lunchtime seminars at Stanford, when entrepreneurs from Silicon Valley came in to talk about their experiences. They all told their audiences: *You can do it too.* Sabeer began to listen. After all, they seemed like ordinary people to him – something he had not expected to find. Eventually, after successfully completing his Master's degree, and freshly armed with a Green Card, he took a job at Apple, at the time thinking that he would pursue a career path in a large American corporation. At the same time he began to network extensively; he joined an association of Indian entrepreneurs, most of them much older than he was. Soon they began to seem like men he could emulate.

His best friend at Apple was fellow hardware engineer, Jack Smith, a shy young American with a wife and two children. Sabeer was single. Sabeer kept telling Smith that if they worked together closely they could make it on their own. On the face of it, he had less to lose. But Smith was finally persuaded. Now all they needed was a good idea.

Their first idea (in 1995, when they were both twenty-six years old) was for a net-based personal database, which they called Javasoft. They wrote a business plan, but every time they approached a venture capitalist they were rejected. At this time a typical venture capitalist would be receiving 12 000 plans a year, from which they might see 500 and invest in 15. Their plan contained flaws, a reality they began to accept when the same shortfalls were repeatedly pointed out to them. In December 1995 Smith had the germ of an idea for a free-of-charge e-mail network that users could access anonymously on the Internet from anywhere they were in the world. The moment he shared the idea with Sabeer and they began to discuss its potential, they knew they were on to 'something special'. They believed the idea was so power-ful, but easily copied, that they needed to keep it under wraps until all the necessary funding was in place. Both Sabeer and Smith had personal e-mail accounts with AOL (American Online) but they were unable to use this system from their comput-ers at work, which meant that any personal e-mail messages they shared during working hours were on an organisational intranet and therefore insecure. They drafted their business plan – and deliberately avoided making any spare copies.

In the next two years they would build a company's subscriber base at a faster rate than any other media company had ever achieved. By 1998 they would reach twenty-five million active e-mail accounts and 125 000 new members every day. Sabeer's personal wealth was about to reach $200 million. At this time he was still single and living in a rented apartment. *Houses [here] are over-priced. . . I think I'll save a little money if I wait until they come down.* Simply, they had found a way to overcome a problem they were facing. Like many good ideas, it had been under their noses all the time.

Early in 1996 Sabeer, sometimes on his own, sometimes with Jack Smith, con-tinued to seek appointments with venture capitalists. Still obsessed with secrecy, Sabeer cannily presented his Javasoft business plan and waited for a reaction. If he felt he was being treated dismissively, he simply went way. If he received objective and helpful feedback on the Javasoft flaws, he followed up with the business plan for Hotmail. Whilst Sabeer was doing this, Smith fixed them a fall-back seed capital fund of $100 000 from his friends and family, although they were always realistic that this would never be enough to bring the project to fruition. Their twenty-first venture capitalist was interested. Nevertheless, Steve Jurvetson of Draper, Fisher, Jurvetson, regarded Sabeer's growth projections as totally unrealistic. In the event, Sabeer would be proved correct. His instincts for Hotmail were right, but he was always in danger of being seen as *arrogantly optimistic*.

Jurvetson was genuinely interested in a deal, although so far there was nothing beyond a well-documented idea committed to paper. There was no proof of concept or confirmation of early customer interest. Despite the fact that nobody else was expressing any interest, Sabeer was determined to hold out for the deal he wanted. He was willing to release up to 15 per cent of the equity; the bankers first demanded 30 per cent. At one stage, he simply walked out of the negotiations. Hiding the real business plan and walking away when someone is offering a considerable sum of money to a completely unproven entrepreneur with an untested idea, reflect true self-belief and a substantial ego. But having been rejected over twenty times, Sabeer and Smith were even more determined to prove they could succeed.

Sabeer and Smith persisted with the name Javasoft for their business – they con-tinued to believe the Hotmail idea was worth stealing and someone could beat them to launch. Every day for six months they checked the Internet to make sure someone else had not marketed the idea ahead of them. They also worked from non-descript offices with the name Javasoft on the door to try and avoid any unwanted attention. In exchange for 15 per cent of their equity, Juvetson had provided $300 000, ostensibly for proof-of-concept work. Sabeer and Smith began to employ people and to build their embryo business. Fearful of having to release more equity to financiers, they were determined to stretch the $300 000 as far as it could possibly stretch. They bought cheap or second-hand equipment wherever this was feasible. Their essential paper shredder cost just $15. But by June 1996 money was very tight. Sabeer somehow managed to persuade a bank to loan them a further $100 000 unsecured and a public relations agency to represent them in exchange for stock options. Sabeer also took up a suggestion that he persuade his first fifteen employees to accept stock options in lieu of wages.

They launched Hotmail on 4 July 1996, Independence Day, a public holiday. Although e-mail was well-established, computer users immediately saw the value of being able to access their e-mail from any remote terminal anywhere in the world. Word-of-mouth recommendations were instantaneous. One hundred subscribers in the first hour that Hotmail was available were joined by 200 more in the second hour. Simply, as soon as someone received a Hotmail message they became a subscriber themselves. The growth was so rapid that no promotional advertising of any consequence was required. Hotmail began to deliver news and advertising material directly to its subscriber mailboxes – always for a fee. Sabeer had no intention of paying for the news, which was the normal procedure. He argued his users would read the news and then visit the relevant origination site – so he was providing a gateway service. He began to convince everyone of his vision.

The company was now growing quickly – and its people were growing with it. Sabeer and Smith continued to recruit *strong, smart people* and give them all the responsibility they would accept. *Sabeer got everyone in the company totally focused . . . harmonised . . . telling the same story. People trusted each other and believed in the business.* Hotmail enjoyed a six-month window before anyone attempted to compete with it directly. Serious competition, in the form of Rocketmail, took a full year. Sabeer and Smith continued with their external networking with renewed energy and vigour – and the momentum increased. More capital was raised and used to develop both the concept and the business. Jack Smith's invaluable contribution from behind the scenes was a system which did not crash as it absorbed more and more users and activity.

For some reason, Microsoft – who many had predicted would launch a rival service – left Hotmail alone for eighteen months. By this time Hotmail, with twenty-five employees, had signed up six million subscribers and was clearly entrenched as market leader. A rumour grew that Microsoft would invest in Hotmail and offer it to Microsoft Network subscribers, but in Fall 1997 Microsoft offered Sabeer and Smith $350 million to take over Hotmail. The partners would have made *tens of millions each* but they turned it down as inadequate. They were invited to Seattle to meet Bill Gates. Initially in awe, Sabeer grew in confidence when he realised that Gates was asking him *very predictable questions about the strategy*. He realised Gates was *smart but not superhuman*. Now supremely confident, Sabeer demanded $500 million for the business. Angry Microsoft negotiators responded that he was *crazy*. External analysts agreed, convinced that Microsoft was also negotiating to buy Rocketmail as an alternative. Urged to settle by most of his employees, and advised to be careful by his financial backers, Sabeer continued to hold out for more money. Steve Jurvetson even began to joke that he should wait until he was big enough to counter-bid for Microsoft. Whilst ever the negotiations continued, the subscriber base grew remorselessly. Finally, on 31 December 1997, Microsoft acquired Hotmail in exchange for shares valued at around $400 million.

Some analysts and journalists seemed truly amazed that a two-year-old e-mail company could be worth this amount of money. Sabeer and Smith *did not deserve their success and wealth*. Ex-Apple colleagues were said to be particularly resentful. A business colleague from the Indian community, however, reached a different conclusion. *Sabeer had never had an opportunity to raise money . . . to run a company or even a division. But . . . he did an outstanding job. Nothing in his background prepared him for it . . . it must be something innate in him.* Specifically he had the talent and the temperament.

Restrained by 'golden handcuffs', Smith and Sabeer stayed on to run Hotmail, which then had around 150 employees and forty-five million subscribers. Sabeer was appointed as General Manager of Hotmail and Jack Smith as Director of Engineering. Sabeer went straight on to level three in the Microsoft hierarchy, *reporting to someone who reported to Bill*. The company remains devolved and empowered. Some have even dared to argue that the selling price of $400 million was still too low.

In March 1999, having at last bought an apartment and a Ferrari, Sabeer Bhatia left Microsoft and Hotmail. He was reportedly frustrated by the bureaucracy he found. He has since started a number of new businesses, the majority of which have succeeded.

Google

Google is an Internet search engine that handles some 2000 queries every second, amounting to 200 million searches a day. In just five years it has become the world's most popular Internet search engine and the 'world's best known brand'. Begun in 1998, it has always been fast, reliable and profitable. Its revenues amount to some $500 million a year.

Now located in Mountain View in California's Silicon Valley, Google began life in the dormitories at Stanford University before being moved out initially to a garage in Menlo Park. The founders were two young computer science graduates who had written a paper on search engines. The Chairman is Fergey Brin, whose parents are Russian immigrants to America – his father was a mathematician and his mother a scientist. The CEO and co-founder is Larry Page. Between them they were able to raise $1 million in loans from friends and family to start the business. They have since raised $36 million in venture capital funding but left much of it untouched.

The business has succeeded for a number of reasons:

- It has always been fast and reliable – arguably more reliable than its competitors.
- Google's on-screen advertising has never been overly obtrusive.
- The website and pages have always been kept simple – no unnecessary graphics.
- Google stayed firmly focused on search and, unlike some of its competitors, did not diversify into being an Internet portal as well.

- The founders sought two sources of revenue – advertising and fees for specialist search facilities from corporate and media clients.

Google has a cubicle culture typical of Silicon Valley. Casual dress is the norm and some employees bring their dogs to work. Almost 20 per cent of the 260 employees have PhDs, and Google has been described as *more technological than entrepreneurial*. The Director of Machine Learning is a leading expert on artificial intelligence and he joined Google from NASA, where he was in charge of a team of 200 scientists.

Ebay

Ebay has overtaken Amazon (which we discuss next) as the world's favourite e-commerce website. It is fundamentally an on-line auction house, dealing in almost anything. The most popular products are cars and motor cycles, computers, books, music and electronic goods – but Ebay once sold a Gulfstream jet aircraft for $4.9 million. Altogether there are 16 000 categories and it is not unusual for five million items to be featured a day.

Described as an on-line flea market in the late 1990s, Ebay had actually started life in 1995 when its founder, French-born computer programmer Pierre Omidyar, set up a site so that his wife, who collected Pez sweet distributors, could make contact with other collectors around the world. It was not the first on-line auction house – and, unlike a number of its rivals, it has always charged a commission rather than provided a free service. Omidyar was another Silicon Valley resident and he also went in search of venture capital to expand the business in 1997. He raised $6.7 million for a third of his business. Similar to Google, most of this has never been used. The company was and always has been profitable. By 2002 it could boast thirty-eight million customers and deals amounting to $9.4 billion a year. Ebay's revenue target is $3 billion by 2005.

Head-hunters found Meg Whitman for Omidyar and she joined as CEO in 1998. Whitman had a corporate background – she had been working for Hasbro, the toy company, where she was running the Mr Potato Head franchise and masterminding the import into America of the Teletubbies. She recalls that she found a black and white website with a single typeface – courier. Despite the fact the company was successful and growing, she believed the website was 'confused'. She set about changing all this. She built up a fresh, strong management team and prepared the business for an IPO. When this happened late in 1998 it was the fifth most successful ever in US corporate history. Whitman has made the company international – it trades in eighteen countries. Where sales have been disappointing – the case in Japan – she has simply closed the country site down. Ebay arrived in the UK in December 1999. Its competitors now include Yahoo and Amazon, powerful names in Internet commerce.

On-line auctions have an interesting business model. There are no supply costs and there is no inventory. Goods are never handled – they simply move from seller to buyer. Once established, there is little need to advertise. Overall, very little capital expenditure is required. Regular customers spend an average of ninety minutes when they are surfing the site – but they will make other quick visits to check progress when they are bidding for an item. Countless small businesses have found Ebay a useful opportunity for selling their products. Success has to depend on satisfied customers and Ebay invests in customer feedback, which is collected for every transaction and made available as data for other customers to access. Whitman is strong on performance orientation. Ebay maintains that it has always listened to its customers and responded whenever appropriate. Interestingly there is little evidence of dishonest customer activity. Very few cheques ever seem to bounce, for example. Moreover, customers are very quick to respond if they notice any apparently rogue products being offered for sale – alleviating the need for Ebay to invest heavily in security monitoring.

Approximately 40 per cent of the transactions are now on-line and Ebay has had to develop the necessary competency. In July 2002 Ebay bought PayPal, the world's largest on-line payment system. It is clearly possible to expand the scope of the business by offering the facility for customers to offer their products at a fixed price through the site – but this is different from the concept of an auction.

Survivors

Jeff Bezos and Amazon

Jeff Bezos is a highly successful growth entrepreneur who has been able to 'change the rules of competition' in an industry. Amazon.com, the *Earth's largest bookstore*, pioneered bookselling via the Internet and, in the process, changed consumer-buying habits and forced the existing major booksellers to react and also offer electronic sales and postal deliveries. Paradoxically, this has happened in an environment where – and in parallel – *good bookstores have become the community centres of the late twentieth century* by providing comfortable seats, staying open late and incorporating good coffee bars.

Amazon.com was founded in 1994 by Bezos, the son of a Cuban immigrant, who once dreamt of being an astronaut and consequently went on to graduate in electrical engineering and computer science from Princeton. Whilst a teenager, a paper he wrote on the effect of zero gravity on the common housefly won him a trip to the Marshall Space Flight Center in Alabama. But after Princeton he became a successful investment banker on Wall Street. He was, in fact, the youngest senior vice-president ever at D.E. Shaw, which he joined from Bankers Trust. Intrigued by the speed of growth of the Internet in the early 1990s, he decided to *seize the moment*. He had experienced his trigger and left the bank with the straightforward intention of starting an e-commerce business.

At this stage he had no specific product or service in mind, and so he began by drawing up a list of possible activities. He narrowed down his first list of twenty to two – music and books – before choosing books. In both cases, the range of titles available was far in excess of the number any physical store could realistically stock. In 1994 there were 1.5 million English language books in print, and another 1.5 million in other languages. Yet the largest bookstore carried 'only' 175 000 titles. Moreover,

Bezos appreciated that the distribution was fragmented. He believed there was scope to offer books at discounted prices and wafer-thin margins to seize sales from existing retailers, whilst also boosting the overall size of the market. The secret of Bezos' success lay in his ability to establish an effective supply chain. Warehouses have been strategically located and Amazon makes sure it can deliver either from stock or from publishers within days of receiving an order electronically.

His second fundamental decision, then, was location. He quickly narrowed the field to Boulder, Portland and Seattle before selecting Seattle. In theory, he could have picked anywhere, but he believed there were a number of important criteria which had to be met. A ready supply of people with technical ability was essential – and other key members of his management team would need to find it an attractive place to live and work. As the firm has grown, a number of experienced people have been recruited from nearby Microsoft. In addition, it had to be a relatively small state. Bezos would have to charge a relevant sales tax to residents of any state where Amazon.com had a physical presence, but others would be exempt.

He rented a house and started in the garage, using the coffee shop in the nearby Barnes and Noble bookstore to interview potential staff. He personally made the first desks they used from old, recycled doors – and he still uses his! After raising several million dollars from venture capitalists and private investors he knew, he moved into a 400-square-foot office and began trading on the Internet in July 1995. Bezos was adamant that he warned his investors of the inherent risks in his ambitious venture. Sales began immediately, and within six weeks he moved to a 2000-square-foot warehouse. Six months later he moved again. This time he set up Amazon's head-quarters in a twelve-storey former hospital.

Music, computer games, toys and pharmaceuticals are just some of the products Amazon now supplies as well as books. In addition, Bezos has formed alliances with numerous other businesses which could sell books as an adjunct to their own goods – for a sales revenue percentage their sites are hyperlinked to the Amazon site. In 2001, Amazon absorbed the on-line book retailing business started by the UK's leading specialist bookseller, Waterstone's, which opted to re-focus on its stores.

Within its first year, Amazon.com earned revenues of $5 million, equivalent to a large Barnes and Noble superstore, the leading American high-street bookstore. Sales have since grown dramatically as the company has expanded rapidly – but so too have the costs. By 1999, sales had reached $1.5 billion and they topped $3 billion in 2001. By 2001, accumulated losses amounted to $2.3 billion and Amazon had debts of $2.1 billion. Its first *quarterly* profit came late in 2001, but the business has yet to post an annual profit. In 2001, some staff had to be laid off. The company went public in May 1997. Not unexpectedly, its share price and market valuation are very volatile, but Amazon has, at times, been valued at more than Wal-Mart. There are now some 8000 employees around the world, with 800 in Seattle.

Bezos, himself, remains infectiously enthusiastic and firmly at the helm. He is noted for two personal quirks – his loud and frequent laugh and his tendency to always have to hand a small camera. His closest colleagues confirm he is *sometimes goofy*. A noted workaholic, he believes *that if he works over 60 hours a week he gets tired – but under 60 he gets bored!* He also believes that *successful entrepreneurs are both flexible and stubborn simultaneously . . . the secret is knowing when to be flexible and when to be stubborn*. Where a successful entrepreneur does not possess leadership qualities, or does not wish to act as the strategic leader of a large corporation, he or she will often make a timely exit and move on to a fresh challenge. Jeff Bezos, like a number of the other entrepreneurs we have featured in the book, is a *leader entrepreneur*. In other words, he possesses key leadership talents to complement his entrepreneur character themes.

There are four value propositions to Amazon.com: convenience, selection, service and price. Clearly, there are no books to touch, open and read. All communications are through the worldwide website pages or via the e-mail. The website allows customers to search the extensive (one million plus titles) book catalogue by topic and author, to read explanations and summaries from authors as well as reviews from other readers, specialist reviewers and Amazon's own staff and to order with a credit card. Leading titles are held in stock but others have to be ordered from their publishers. Books are despatched very quickly after Amazon receives them into stock. Delivery to the customer of a non-best seller, therefore, is normally around a week, with more unusual titles taking longer. Stock titles take around forty-eight hours.

All books are discounted – originally best-sellers by 30 per cent and others by at least 10 per cent of the jacket price. Now, however, 30 per cent discount on any book costing $15 or more is typical. This has, to some extent, been inevitable as bookstores have discounted more aggressively as a response to Amazon. The 'store' is open twenty-four hours every day and is accessible from anywhere in the world.

Lastminute.com

Lastminute.com mainly deals with products and services with a finite shelf-life that are close to their sell-by date and are sometimes candidates for distress pricing. Seats for flights, sporting events, theatres and holidays would all qualify. Providers often prefer for the distress prices to be offered by an intermediary rather than direct from them. Products and customers include:

- Airlines – BA, Virgin and Lufthansa.
- Hotels – Bass and Forte.
- Tour operators – Kuoni and Thomas Cook.
- Car rental – Avis.
- Entertainment – English National Ballet and several West End theatres.
- Restaurants – ones owned by Conran.
- Gifts – CarPhone Warehouse.

Events in the UK, France and Germany are included and Lastminute can also provide services such as babysitters. It is a simple business model; Lastminute.com brokers a deal and then takes a commission. Clearly, this Web company is not the only potential outlet for the products in question, and consequently its success will depend on the variety it can offer, the extent of the business it can generate through its site and its ability to finally bring buyer and seller together. One of the main reasons Lastminute has been successful is the range of suppliers it has been able to sign agreements with. The target market is cash-rich, time-constrained professionals who would like a bargain but who cannot invest the time and effort to find it personally. No direct American equivalent could be identified when the business was set up, although there are some very successful American sites selling cut-price travel.

The company was founded in November 1998 by two ex-consultants in their late twenties, Brent Hoberman and Martha Lane Fox. The basic idea was Hoberman's – he had become increasingly irritated with the process of price haggling with individual hotels and airlines when he was travelling. In 1999, Lastminute.com claimed 300 000 registered subscribers with an average of almost fifteen site visits per month. Revenues amounted to some £6 million. In 1999 it was being anticipated that the company would be floated in 2000. A potential valuation of £400 million was featured in the reports. The two partners were able to retain 45 per cent of the equity. Midway through 1999 they had raised over £6 million from, amongst others, Intel, Sony and Deutsche Telekom, and they were constantly seeking new backers to help develop the scope and extent of the business.

The company was floated successfully in March 2000 with a share price of 380 pence. In fact, the offer was forty times over-subscribed; there was no shortage of willing investors. At the end of the first day's trading this had risen to 488 pence and the company was being valued at £732 million. However, the collapse of other dot.com businesses 'burst the bubble' and Lastminute's share price has never reached this figure since. By May it had fallen to 245p. In October 2001 it stood at just 18p, although it has since risen to 118p in May 2003.

To date Lastminute has accumulated losses in excess of £70 million. The figures for 1999–2002 respectively are £5 million, £35 million, £30 million and £7 million. All this time, the company has been growing. Lastminute did manage to post a quarterly profit for the fourth quarter of 2002 (the run up to Christmas) but the first two quarters of 2003 have seen this reversed again.

Lastminute has acquired a number of smaller competitors along the way, most of these continental businesses. In October 2000 Allan Leighton, one of the people responsible for the successful turnaround of Asda before its sale to Wal-Mart, joined as non-executive Chairman. Leighton is also Chairman of Consignia, known to most as the Royal Mail.

The name 'Lastminute' was allegedly not chosen to reflect the company's business, but rather to describe its founder, Brent Hoberman. Recognised as an extensive networker and socialite, Hoberman comes from a line of successful entrepreneurs in South Africa, but he attended Eton and Oxford. He was part of the founding team of QXL, the successful UK on-line auction business. He is not naturally strong on focus. He has been described as disorganised, readily jumping from one thing to another. He is always 'on the last push', indicating low time focus. But he is strong on creativity and advantage. He has ideas and he can sell them. He is also strong on ego – determined and ambitious are words associated with him. He always believed he could make Lastminute work, despite the inherent risk.

His business partner, Martha Lane Fox, who he met when they were both consultants, has complementary character themes. Another Oxford graduate, she is focused and good with detail. She has operationalised Hoberman's idea. How well do they work together? *He tells me what to do and sometimes I do it*. Martha Lane Fox chose to leave Lastminute in late 2003 to find a new challenge.

Thinknatural.com

Carol Dukes is the creator of Thinknatural.com. Dukes graduated from Oxford in 1983 and then, unusually, embarked on a secretarial course. She later worked as a strategic planner for Emap and at Carlton, where she was involved in Internet developments. Specifically she helped launch three on-line businesses in film, food and entertainment. Before these large companies, she had worked for IUS, a five-person micro business supplying in-house movie systems to hotels in the Middle East. When IUS was an early mover into cable franchising in the UK, Dukes was involved in raising money from venture capitalists. Her experience then was already helping map the route ahead for her. At the end of the 1980s she completed an MBA at London Business School.

In 1999 Carol Dukes raised substantial venture capital funding to start Thinknatural.com, Europe's first site for natural health and beauty products. One investor was Kingfisher (owner of Woolworth's and B&Q) which injected £4.5 million for a 12.5 per cent stake. The money, again unusually, but similar to the experience of Hotmail, was secured on the strength of the business plan and a confidence that she was 'the right person' for this sector. *Thinknatural will make money because we have this weird business model where we sell things for slightly more than we pay for them.* Dukes has a partner, Emma Crowe, who worked with her on Internet projects at Carlton.

Dukes summed up her views on collateral and risk as follows: *my flat was not available as security . . . there is an old fashioned attitude among **some** UK venture capitalists that things have got to hurt . . . remortgaging my home would have made me risk averse, whereas with the Internet you really have to go for it.* The reality for many start-ups is, of course, double jeopardy. The founders' business loans are secured against their main assets, and yet the business remains their only source of income. To overcome this, venture capitalists will need a deep-seated belief in the ability, talent and temperament of the potential entrepreneur.

Unlike Amazon.com, where discounting is essential for building sales, Thinknatural can charge full prices for its distinctive products, ranging from vitamins to aromatherapy oils and beauty products. Whilst the range is far wider than that of Body Shop, Thinknatural.com has adopted one of Anita Roddick's key strategies. The website offers a wealth of information on products and therapies and a facility for customers to exchange ideas. As well as funding the development of the site, the venture capital was required to fund a physical warehouse for over 5000 different lines.

Whilst Thinknatural did manage to lift its annual turnover to £2 million, this was inadequate to meet its financial commitments. It was also significant that the bulk of these sales had been made through catalogues rather than on-line. In November 2001 Thinknatural merged with Greenfingers, which sells plants and garden furniture on-line and by mail order. The two had *a similar customer base used to home shopping.* The businesses would have separate and distinct websites, but they would share warehousing, finance systems and back-office administration. The ex-Great Universal Stores executive who ran Greenfingers was to be the new CEO; Carol Dukes withdrew to a non-executive director role. Looking ahead, she commented that she *would not rule out starting another Internet business.*

Fallers

Boo.com

Boo.com had a physical base in London's Carnaby Street, home of 1960s' fashion, and it was set up to sell sportswear. The idea was to widen the availability of the more exclusive designer-label items, which are typically only available in large cities. It is significant that these tend to be high-margin items at premium prices. The business had three founders; the most prominent two were both Swedes. Ernst Malmsten had originally been a book critic; Kajsa Leander was a former fashion model. But two of the three had been involved in a successful Internet bookstore start-up.

It has been estimated that Boo.com was able to raise £75 million in venture capital, but this is still far less than the amount required to set up a physical retail infrastructure which could provide customers with these items on a wide scale. After a number of well-publicised false starts, the company went on-line in November 1999, offering deliveries in eighteen countries from warehouses in Cologne and Kentucky. Boo.com did not own these warehouses but had a dedicated staff working there and an alliance with the actual owners. Goods were delivered to the warehouses by their manufacturers and then repackaged in distinctive Boo boxes before being posted on. Linked to a high-profile advertising campaign, the founders were able to obtain extensive publicity and the site was launched with a massive fanfare. Whilst this was good in one respect, the delay and subsequent hiccups were equally visible and damaging.

The website offered 40 000 items. Each had been photographed at least twenty-four times such that browsers could examine them from every angle. Clothes could be seen on their own and on particular mannequin figures. Product descriptions were available in eight languages and sales were in local currencies. There was a sophisticated internal checking system to ensure customers were never sold anything which was not immediately available from the relevant manufacturer.

By January 2000 discounts of up to 40 per cent were being offered and it was reported the company had already started to lay off staff. That did not come as a surprise to a number of commentators who believed the company was overstaffed from the beginning. Boo.com had *set up the most expensive call centre in the world*. It transpired that customers were having trouble accessing and downloading the complex website. Limited specification computers without sophisticated 3D tools were simply inadequate. A revised website was required and initiated. Boo.com had also misjudged the return rates. They had predicted 10 per cent returns in an industry where 30 per cent is the norm. These problems brought about an early defection of certain key people and the company was into a downward spiral.

In May 2000 it was apparent that Boo.com required a fresh cash injection of at least £30 million, and when this was not forthcoming the company went into liquidation. It had £300 000 in cash but had been burning twice this amount every week.

Malmsten summed up the story as follows: *We have been too visionary. We wanted everything to be perfect and we have not had control of costs.* He is perhaps indicating weaknesses in advantage, specifically resourcing and performance orientation. Others commented that *on-line flair is never enough . . . conventional off-line business skills remain critical to success.*

Etoys

Etoys closed down in March 2001. At its height this American Internet business employed 1000 people, including seventy-five in London, Swindon and Liege. The site retailed a huge range of games and toys, including computer games, prominent best-sellers such as Barbie and Lego, character toys popular at that time, such as Bob the Builder, niche products such as Meccano and up-market variants like Steiff teddy bears. The site offered advice and recommendations. Targeted at those adults who buy toys as presents and who do not enjoy the experience of working their way around toy superstores, logic said it should be successful. In many ways it was, but it reflected the general trading pattern of the toy industry which is seasonal and skewed. Predicting sales levels proved tricky and investors began to get wary.

Webvan

The year 2001 also saw the collapse of Webvan, the American on-line grocer which had received huge funding. On its first day of trading in 1999, the company was valued at $8.7 billion; within two years it would have burned $1 billion and cost 2000 people their jobs. This was not an e-commerce offering from an existing supermarket business; this was a dedicated and focused Internet company. Interestingly, it had been conceived (in 1996) by an experienced retailer – Louis Border of Borders Books, America's leading bookstore chain.

Webvan was a very ambitious punt at a huge market. The average US family shops for groceries twice every week and spends some $5000 a year – equivalent to £3000. The intention was to set up twenty-six distribution centres within three years. Each one would have around eighteen times the floorspace of a large supermarket and service homes within a 50-mile radius. They were heavily automated and with an extensive conveyor belt system.

It is a difficult business model to implement. The massive overheads mean that fixed costs are huge and variable (handling and delivery) costs less significant. At the same time, the vast majority of items are competitively priced and low margin. This means a high break-even and great sensitivity around break-even point. Customers have to buy-in to the concept and buy repeatedly. But deliveries can only be when people are at home, and for working families this was always tricky.

In this chapter we have looked at a handful of successful and less-successful new, Internet businesses. Some service providers have generated huge wealth in a short space of time; but those in e-commerce often 'exist on a precarious precipice'. There are some interesting lessons. However good the idea and the opportunity, championing the project is essential. Establishing the supply chain and maintaining the marketing expenditure in a dynamic and competitive environment absorbs enormous sums of money. It is hard to generate revenue to compensate for the cash burn. Venture capitalists have at times been willing to back these start-up businesses, accepting that some will fail, but always assuming that a few will earn huge returns and fortunes. The jury remains out on whether companies like Amazon and Last-minute will eventually deliver these profits. If there are genuine success stories, with success measured by profitability as well as size, this investment capital will continue to flow. If there are too many failures because of the industry dynamics and uncertainty, the situation could become increasingly sticky. Without substantial sums of money, these businesses can never build a realistic base from which to launch a potentially successful venture. The key question for e-commerce in the retail sector is whether enough people will change their buying habits and move over to the Internet. On this issue, Warren Buffett may, in the end, be proved correct.

References

Buffett, W. (2000). Speech to Berkshire Hathaway investors, reported in A.E. Johnson, Buffett discussed spurious net wealth, *Financial Times*, May.
Gwyther, M. (1999). Jewels in the web. *Management Today*, November.

Further Readings

Bronson, P. (1999). *The Nudist on the Late Shift – and Other Tales of Silicon Valley*. Secker and Warburg.
Kotha, S. and Dooley, E. (1998). Amazon.com. Case study included in C.W.L. Hill and G.R. Jones, *Strategic Management: An Integrated Approach*. 4th edn. Houghton Mifflin.
Saunders, R. (1999). *Business The Amazon.com Way*. Capstone.

Interlude: An introduction to social, financial and aesthetic capital

In the introduction to this book we defined entrepreneurs and stressed that they build value and capital. In Chapters 5 and 6 we have discussed a number of classic and business entrepreneurs who, in the main, have created and accumulated significant wealth and financial capital. They have achieved this by building successful businesses which have made money for their owners by providing value for their customers, and in the process also rewarding their employees and other stakeholders. In Chapters 7 and 8 we move on and look at entrepreneurs who, rather than focusing on financial wealth and capital, have instead been principally motivated by a desire to build social and aesthetic – or artistic – capital and, in some cases, to preserve environmental capital.

The term *social entrepreneur* is being used more and more, but it is clear that people are using it to embrace a variety of subtly different activities. Businesses started by an entrepreneur with a very strong social facet, or run by an entrepreneurial leader with a marked social orientation, are social entrepreneurship in action. But they are, fundamentally, businesses. They produce products or create services in order to generate revenues. Simply, the products and services, and the ways in which they are marketed, feature a strong social dimension which is sometimes a defining element of the business. Anita Roddick is a prime example of this type of social entrepreneur. When they are deemed successful it is because they are, on the one hand, profitable, and, at the same time, clearly 'doing good' in the world. Organisations we term 'social enterprises' generate revenues from their activities, but define themselves as non-profit because all the surpluses are given over to a specified cause. They are organisations with a 'double bottom line'. The chain of charity shops run by Oxfam would fit here.

Liam Black, CEO of the Furniture Resource Centre in Liverpool, defines social enterprises as *organisations that invent commercially viable trading activities in order to achieve their social purpose*. Social Enterprise, London, argue *social enterprises are financially viable and sustainable businesses that trade in the market to fulfil social aims such as employment creation and the provision of local services*. They bring people and communities together for economic development and social gain; they exhibit three common characteristics:

- they are enterprise-oriented
- they have social aims
- they have social ownership.

The successful actor, Paul Newman, comes from a family where it is traditional to give away bottles of home-made oil and vinegar salad dressing at Christmas and Thanksgiving. Newman joined forces with a friend, A.E. Hotchner, to pursue his idea of making this into a business and giving all the profits to charity. The idea was successful – with the Newman's Own brand prominent on the bottles – and the range was extended, always using top-quality no-additive ingredients. In its first year of existence, $1 million was donated to charities. After twenty years, some $125 million had been raised. It is *shameless exploitation in pursuit of the common good*.

But social entrepreneurship is also manifest in the myriad of community initiatives that make up the so-called third sector; some of these are run by entrepreneurial leaders driven by a cause. But these initiatives do not generally produce products. They clearly provide services, but quite often either make no charge or charge at a rate below their full cost. The necessary subsidy comes from grants and, in fact, many of these initiatives are grant-dependent. Much of the entrepreneurship in the activity is channelled into finding new sources of grant money!

For all of these 'social organisations' there is a potential problem of perspective. It is all-too-easy for social enterprises (businesses with a social focus) to lose sight of the key *business* indicators because they are too focused on the cause they serve. Equally, some community initiatives are less business-like than they should be because they believe 'the cause is all'. As a result, there is sometimes an expectation of second-best quality in this sector and this is fundamentally inappropriate.

Fukuyama (1995) has defined *social capital* as *the ability of people to work together for common purposes in groups and organisations*. Leadbeater (1997) has refined this to suggest the building of something of real value to local communities or society. The realisation that these 'builders' use one form of social capital – relationships, networks, trust and co-operation, which we might alternatively call *human capital* – to gain access to physical and financial capital which is then redeployed to build something of value for the community, appears to reconcile the two variations. This form of community-based social entrepreneurship typically – and importantly – addresses unmet social needs which a nation's welfare system does not, cannot or will not meet. It seems inevitable that there will always be a gap between a society's welfare needs and the ability of the state to provide help and support. In some countries the gap is wider than it is in other parts of the world. Social capital of this type (like aesthetic capital, which we discuss later) is more intangible than financial capital. Consequently, we believe that the critical test or effectiveness measure for many of these initiatives is the extent to which they would be missed if they were lost. Until they happen, there is simply a gap and an unmet need, the significance of which is dependent upon individual perceptions. Once the gap has been filled, or at least partially filled, the significance of the need becomes more widely apparent. Where social entrepreneurship involves the use of under-utilised community resources, such as derelict buildings, these often provide a visible and identifiable artifact with which people can relate.

Social entrepreneurship is frequently attractive to people who feel committed to a cause. Many people are willing to donate money to causes they support, but when an individual with entrepreneurial talent or character themes feels a true commitment to a particular cause or need we are likely to see social entrepreneurship as, in effect, the need seems to find the person who will engage it and make something happen. A number of people – often people with entrepreneurial character themes – have been driven to significantly high levels of achievement by their commitment to a cause. Whilst the sector attracts a considerable number of unpaid, volunteer helpers, without doubt the most successful ventures invariably feature an identifiable champion, someone who will possess the character theme profile of an entrepreneur, but who chooses to use his (or her) talents to build social, rather than financial, capital.

We have seen in earlier chapters how entrepreneurship comprises an (often opportunistic) idea and the ensuing actions which bring about desirable outcomes. Particularly relevant for social entrepreneurship is Sykes' (1999) delineation of three key contributions to the growth of organisations: *envisioning* a future state in an uncertain environment, *enacting* the vision by giving it direction and purpose and acquiring the necessary resources and *enabling* it to happen by harnessing the support of other key people. Clearly entrepreneurship – as a process – embraces all three. The entrepreneur – the person – will invariably perform the enacting role and at least initiate the enabling role, but may not always be the envisioner. The vision could be 'bought-in' from somewhere else, replicating a good idea that others have proved can work. The growth of the modern hospice movement and the systematic restoration of steam railways throughout the UK provide excellent examples of this.

Leadbeater and Goss (1998) have also differentiated social entrepreneurship from civic entrepreneurship, where, for example, a local authority, either individually or by joining forces with the private sector, sponsors innovative new products and services. An example of an alliance would be where a local authority employee spots a need, a gap and an opportunity, and then engineers the appointment of an entrepreneurial person to establish the activity which can fulfil the need and close the gap. Schools which take greater responsibility for their own resourcing – with the active support of parents, school governors and the education authority – would be described as entrepreneurial and their heads as civic entrepreneurs.

Aesthetic or artistic capital brightens or enriches peoples' lives. There is an element of the 'feel-good factor' involved. People enjoy and gain a variety of benefits from an imaginative urban landscape and architecture, for example. People choose designer clothes to help fashion an image for themselves – which in turn can yield material benefits as well as the feel-good factor. People are stimulated by certain films, pieces of music and examples of art and design. The relevant architects, directors, designers, musicians and artists who have this effect on our lives are quite often entrepreneurs. In addition to making an aesthetic difference, they often build very successful and lucrative businesses and become personally wealthy. In order to achieve this notoriety, of course, they have to market their talents. Some aesthetic entrepreneurs, such as architects, may be driven by causes, but the majority possess artistic and creative talent, and they are driven by a desire to exploit their talent. Entrepreneurial character themes help them identify and exploit opportunities for realising their creative potential.

In some noteworthy cases, aesthetic entrepreneurs transform something that has become redundant into something with a completely new and desirable use or function. Old sailing ships now compete in Tall Ships competitions and they also provide a useful base for team-building programmes. Steam railways have been restored and provide a mixture of leisure and nostalgia for both those who work and ride on them; they do not exist purely to move people from one place to another. Ghirardelli Square in San Francisco demonstrates how disused factories can be transformed into popular shopping centres.

Social and aesthetic capital concerns people and their impact on their environment or the world in which they live. When we discuss *environmental capital*, we are really looking at the relatively small number of entrepreneurs who are primarily concerned with *sustaining* important global resources – rather than *building* capital, as most entrepreneurs do. Their commitment to an environmental cause constitutes a primary motivation for their business or project. However, it is perfectly feasible – and important – for other (business) entrepreneurs to seek to build financial wealth and capital without destroying greenbelt countryside, rainforests or other natural geological or ecological resources. In Chapter 5, for example, we saw how Ben and Jerry's has drawn attention to a number of environmental concerns with its sourcing policies and with its choice of names for some of its ice creams. It is important that entrepreneurs see sustainability as an opportunity rather than a cost. For some businesses, such as mining and tourism, the issue is a particularly significant one.

Figure Int.1 pulls these themes together. In the main diagram we can see how business enterprises are dedicated to the creation of financial capital. Similarly,

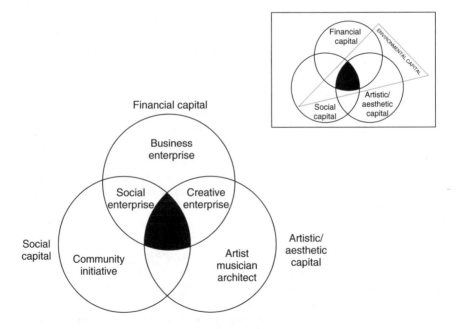

Figure Int.1 *Financial, social and artistic capital*

community initiatives generate social capital while artists, musicians and architects, aesthetic or artistic capital. Social enterprises produce a blend of financial and social capital, creative enterprises generate both financial and aesthetic capital. With social and creative enterprises, there is always the potential for tension between the conflicting pulls of the two different and desired outcomes. Which is the dominant paradigm? Is Terence Conran fundamentally a designer or a business entrepreneur, for example? And what impact might this have? We explore this issue in Chapter 8. In Chapters 7 and 8 we also look at a number of leaders of community initiatives and at examples of artists, musicians and architects respectively – seeking those who clearly possess entrepreneur characteristics which they use to create social and aesthetic capital by finding opportunities for exploiting their talents.

There is a common theme which links all the people we discuss – they affect the world around them. The small inset to Figure Int.1 shows how environmental capital overlays financial, social and aesthetic capital. Entrepreneurs in all walks of life can – and will – impact in either a positive (arguably desirable) or negative (relatively undesirable) way on the wider environment and the world in which we all live. We separate environmental capital in this way, rather than see it as a fourth circle in the diagram, as generally it is managed, rather than created.

It will be apparent that we are arguing that financial capital is essential for building social and aesthetic capital and preserving environmental capital, and that ideally businesses and organisations will act positively in all four areas. We have to realise, however, that the accumulation of one form of capital can be at the expense of one or more of the other forms. The relative weight and importance which should be attributed to each will always remain an issue of perception and judgement, but there is a notional dividing line and those businesses which cross it are behaving in a societally unacceptable manner. Businesses – and entrepreneurs – who focus on financial capital without fair regard to social, aesthetic and environmental issues are, in effect, destroying other forms of capital to build financial wealth. Sometimes, this happens with deliberate strategies and policies; at other times it is the result of oversight or ignorance rather than malicious intent. In Chapter 9 we look at this shadow side of entrepreneurship.

Similarly charities can sometimes appear financially cynical in the ways they aggressively chase donations and legacies. They do need people to give – and to give generously – for their cause. But they are also in competition with innumerable others, and donors often have to make choices. Charities have to appear efficient and professional; but some also look 'slick'. This has partially resulted from the changing background of many of the social entrepreneurs involved. In the past, the majority of charities were set up by people who cared and wanted to donate or give to a cause. Increasingly many newer ones have been set up by the potential beneficiaries who are seeking help for something which is personal to them. This inevitably affects the culture and outlook.

Blending financial, social and aesthetic capital

We end this interlude with a series of stories which all illustrate how the three capitals can sometimes come together in an inter-related, inter-dependent way.

Herb Kelleher and Southwest Air

Our first story explains how Herb Kelleher has built a hugely successful and influ-ential business that has been exceptionally profitable – and his achievements have encouraged others to follow in his footsteps. Southwest Air could well have been included in Chapter 5 because of the way in which it changed the rules of competi-tion in the airline industry. It did this with both a new business model and an unusual culture based on fun and irreverence, which are acknowledged sources of innovation. It created a virtuous circle of committed employees, satisfied customers and superior profits. Kelleher realised the significance of internal social capital and aesthetic capital in the product offering. Ryanair and EasyJet have adopted the busi-ness model but not all the values and beliefs!

Herb Kelleher began Southwest Air in 1971 with a simple intention – *fly people safely, cheaply and conveniently between Dallas, Houston and San Antonio*, three key cities in Texas. Kelleher set out to compete against coach and car travel rather than the other airlines. In over thirty years as a low-price, no-frills airline, Southwest has prospered and grown to become the fifth largest carrier in the US. By the late 1990s it was serving over 50 cities in 27 states, with some 2500 flights every day, and still looking for new growth opportunities. Kelleher's strategy, competitive advantage and success is based on a number of factors:

- Frequent and reliable departures
- Relatively short journeys by American standards, now averaging something over 450 miles, but with the average having increased as the airline has grown in size and destinations
- Where relevant, the choice of smaller airports nearer to City centres in preference to International airports which are further away from the centre
- Very low prices
- Automated ticketing and direct bookings (without travel agents), and now using the Internet extensively
- Limited frills, with no seat assignments, no videos and just one class of seating – as people board in the order they check-in at the airport, early check-ins are encouraged and it is rare that a plane is held up waiting for stragglers
- No hot drinks on board – cleaning up empty sugar packets and milk sachets takes time and delays the plane on the ground
- Fast gate turnarounds, to maximise the time the planes are in the air
- A standardised fleet of Boeing 737s, to simplify maintenance.

Southwest is now America's most significant short distance, point-to-point carrier. Others have certainly tried to compete, but have been unable to make the equivalent impact. It has won the US Department of Transport's coveted 'Triple Crown' award of best on-time record, best baggage handling and fewest customer complaints on several occasions. Every new route and destination is immediately popular and, as a result, Southwest has been consistently profitable for the whole of its life, a unique record for an American airline.

Kelleher was a champion college athlete and a successful Texas lawyer before he started the airline when he was forty years old. The idea for Southwest came from a client (and co-founder of the business) who spotted the gap in the market. He is a renowned 'people person'. Through profit-sharing schemes, employees own over 10 per cent of the company's stock, and he has made *working in the airline industry an adventure*. Southwest is dynamic and responsive; employees accept empowerment and are motivated to work hard and deliver high levels of service consistently. Rules and regulations are minimised to allow staff the freedom to deal with issues as they arise. *Ask employees what's important to them. Ask customers what's important to them. Then do it. It's that simple* (Kelleher). The frequent flyer programme, unusually, rewards passengers for the number of individual flights, not the miles flown.

But it is never that simple! Southwest is also renowned as *one of the zaniest companies in history*. From the very beginning, Kelleher encouraged flight attendants to crack jokes during in-flight emergency briefings, but, at the same time, operate with very high safety standards. He was determined passengers would enjoy their flights. Some of the planes are decorated externally to reinforce the fun image. Three of them, promoting major sponsor Sea World, are flying killer whales; one is painted with the Texas flag; another is christened Arizona One, a spoof of Air Force One. Flight attendants have been known to hide in the overhead lockers as passengers come on board, startling them as they open up the lockers. Kelleher himself has often appeared in fancy dress for certain flights and special occasions. A special prize for the passenger with the biggest hole in his sock would be quite typical.

Consequently, a sense of humour has become a key element in the recruitment process. During their training, employees are given a book with sections on jokes, games and songs – but they are all encouraged to develop an individual style. *At Southwest we don't want clones – everyone is expected to colour outside the lines.* Kelleher is dedicated and focused and in possession of a strong ego. He is creative and innovative and he understands the contribution people can make. He has always had the courage to be different. When introduced to an idea he appreciated the opportunity and activated it. Truly profit-oriented, he has been extremely successful in a dynamic and cruel industry, where many competing airlines have failed.

William Randolph Hearst and Hearst Castle

Hearst Castle, near San Simeon in California, is actually a stunning and wholly idiosyncratic building designed on Spanish-Moorish lines and built part-way up a 1600-foot mountain overlooking the Pacific ocean. The architect, Julia Morgan, had to build an underground reservoir to provide a water supply before construction could even begin. The original owner, William Randolph Hearst, was a successful entrepreneur and newspaper magnate, who had been born to wealth. He had been given his first newspaper by his father when he was twenty-four years old. He had used this base to build a business empire and had served as a United States Congressman. He was flying aeroplanes only seven years after the Wright Brothers' first flight and he was the producer of over 100 silent films in Hollywood. He built his castle with two main motives. First, he was an insatiable collector of art and antiques and sufficiently wealthy to indulge himself throughout Europe. His possessions (Hearst accumulated a multi-million dollar collection of antiques and works of arts) needed a home. The castle has 115 rooms, the size of some of them being determined by the antiques they were to house! Antique ceilings, wall tapestries, choir stalls and mediaeval dining tables required rooms of particular dimensions. Second, Hearst liked to entertain the rich and famous, especially movie stars from Hollywood, and needed a suitable estate with accommodation (there are a number of guest houses in the grounds), swimming pools (there is one outdoor and one indoor) and tennis courts. Begun in 1919, used extensively in the twenties and thirties, yet still incomplete when Hearst died in 1951, the castle thus represents a mixture of artistic and social capital. Since his death his descendants have transformed the estate into a hugely popular tourist attraction. Visitors can only enter the grounds on organised tours; there are four different daytime tours which operate at regular intervals every day and evening tours during the winter months. Clearly the castle now generates substantial financial capital.

Sir Ernest Hall and Dean Clough

Sir Ernest Hall was not born to wealth. One of thirteen children, his parents were mill workers in Bolton. But he became wealthy through business, and he has then used this financial wealth to create social and artistic capital in the form of Dean Clough Mills in Halifax. He is a serial entrepreneur, who has achieved in different fields at various stages in his life. *To be a successful entrepreneur, one needs a vision of greatness for one's work. If we dream extravagantly, we will be motivated to forge a reality beyond the straitjacket of practicalities.*

His first passion was music, developed when he heard classical music played on a gramophone at his primary school. He was eight years old at the time, and he then set off on a quest to listen to more and more music. He also persuaded his parents to buy a piano, which he practised playing with great enthusiasm. In 1946 he became a student at the Royal Manchester College of Music; his parents were sceptical and suggested the only way he would ever make money would be as a player in a dance band – playing music he hated! Although successful, the astute Ernest was aware of fellow students with more natural talent, and he looked to develop a career outside music. He found a job with a small textile mill in Yorkshire. From a starting belief that *commerce was ugly* – but necessary – he found industry to be *satisfying and exciting . . . designing fabrics and running a business was a creative process, similar to composing music or writing poetry.* By the early 1960s he was running his own textile business, a management buy-out. Over the next twenty years the business prospered and he became a wealthy man.

His awareness of the declining fortunes of many Northern communities – fuelled by industrial decline – intensified during these years, and he became determined to do something meaningful to help arrest the decline. Because many people and communities had lost their confidence and any belief that the area could once again be great, his task was daunting. Undeterred, he used his wealth and connections to acquire Dean Clough Mills, an integrated complex of sixteen nineteenth-century mills in Halifax. The mills had been built by the Crossley family and had grown to be one of the largest carpet factories in the world. The business was closed in 1982. He dreamed of a restored complex where *commercial success could be used to support a wide range of activities in arts and education*. He was seeing an opportunity – and, significantly, a cause – where most others saw an insoluble problem – and he possessed the determination and project championing skills to make it happen. By 1994 he had created his dream, with over 100 companies operating alongside professional painters, sculptors and printmakers. The number of companies has since doubled, and over 3500 jobs have been created. Some of the companies have always been small start-ups, but Halifax plc also occupies office space. In addition, there are six galleries showing contemporary art together with the prestigious Slade School of Art, a theatre and a theatre company. Dean Clough is the home base of the Northern Ballet Concert Orchestra and the Northern Brass Band Federation.

This momentous achievement was not enough to satisfy the entrepreneurial Sir Ernest – in his sixties he resurrected his musical ambitions. He played the piano for classical recitals and recorded the music of both Bartok and Chopin. At the same time, encouraged by his second wife, a renowned equestrienne, he started riding horses. He has since become a champion dressage rider. Possessor of a strong ego, and a conviction that wherever people believe in themselves and their potential, they can achieve, he has used his considerable entrepreneurial talent to build financial, social and artistic capital – and has shown how they can all work together harmoniously. The local environment has benefited as a once derelict mill complex is now a thriving community. In 2003, Ernest Hall decided to relocate to Lanzarote and set up an artists' colony.

Jonathan Silver, Titus Salt and Salt's Mill

The story of Jonathan Silver and the restoration of Salt's Mill in Saltaire, a short drive from Halifax, has many similarities. But to understand the significance of this we need to know its history. Titus Salt, often described as a Victorian philanthropist, was one of a special and important group of entrepreneurs who seem able to operate in the business and the social world at the same time. Although Salt amassed his fortune from producing worsted and alpaca cloth, opening several mills, he became an entrepreneur by chance and necessity. He started as a wool trader, but he had a problem when he bought a large quantity of Donskoi wool for which he could not find any buyers. Local mill owners did not believe the wool could be spun and woven. Determined to prove them wrong, Salt rented a mill. He succeeded and rented two more before opening one of his own.

Salt started with alpaca in a similarly opportunistic way. By chance he saw some open sacks of alpaca at Liverpool docks. They were awaiting return to Peru – there had been no buyers for them. He bought a small quantity, found he could use it to make an unusually lightweight cloth and bought the rest of the consignment cheaply. As his business grew, Salt built over 800 buildings in Saltaire, including mills, schools, public baths, a library, a chapel and homes for his employees. Everything was to a higher standard than the norm of the day. Saltaire is now a World Heritage Site; many of the buildings remain intact and used. The fact that the main mill complex is occupied comes down to Jonathan Silver.

Silver's father was a Bradford Jew who had a number of small shops and restaurants. Whilst at school Silver bought and sold antiques – he was always passionate about paintings – as well as selling fresh farm eggs door-to-door. He studied Textiles and Art at University and by the age of thirty had built up a chain of thirteen clothing stores. He was certainly creative and exhibited strong advantage and ego characteristics. Ernest Hall has commented that he was not an outstanding businessman because *he didn't think things through*. He was not a logical thinker. He was not really strong on team because he preferred to just get on and do things, very much leading from the front and *making things up as he went along*. He was resourceful. He was linked to Dean Clough at the beginning but he and Ernest Hall did not always see eye-to-eye; although they remained lifelong friends, their business interests became separated. Silver 'retired' in his thirties and took his family around the world for three years. At the age of thirty-seven he bought the derelict Salt's Mill complex, dreaming of turning part of it into a world class Art Gallery. Today it is home to the world's largest collection of works by David Hockney (whose story we tell in Chapter 8) and a number of pieces by Lowry. This has been financed in part by the restoration of other parts of the complex to create accommodation for Pace (microelectronics) and Filtronic, whose story we told in Chapter 5. Silver died in middle age, but he did manage to see his restoration completed.

References

Fukuyama, F. (1995). *Trust – The Social Virtues and the Creation of Prosperity*. Hamish Hamilton.

Leadbeater, C. (1997). *The Rise of the Social Entrepreneur*. Demos.

Leadbeater, C. and Goss, S. (1998). *Civic Entrepreneruship*. Demos.

Sykes, N. (1999). *Is the organisation encoded with a 'DNA' which determines its development?* Unpublished paper presented at *The Visioneers* conference, Putteridge Bury Management Centre, April.

7 Social entrepreneurs

In the last two chapters we discussed a wide range of business entrepreneurs who have built financial wealth and capital. In this chapter we explore how entrepreneurs can also build social capital and present examples of people who have made a difference by helping others. These people are entrepreneurs because they possess the character theme profile of an entrepreneur; they identify and engage an important opportunity; they gather the necessary resources; they start and develop an initiative; and they have an important impact on our lives. They simply have a strong social facet which affects their other characteristics in an important and meaningful way.

We begin this chapter with three classic social entrepreneurs, before discussing a series of quite different contemporary examples of entrepreneurs behind both social enterprises and community initiatives. A number of the social entrepreneurs we include have religious connections, and consequently we also include one specifically religious entrepreneur. The chapter concludes with a short section on environmental entrepreneurs.

Classic social entrepreneurs

Florence Nightingale

Florence Nightingale was born in 1820, the daughter of well-off and well-connected parents. Her parents and society had expectations for the way she would grow up and spend her adult life – but Florence was determined to be different. As a child she was *exceptionally intelligent*, and at the age of seventeen she began to believe she was called to the service of God in some way or another. However, the next five years of her life comprised foreign travel. She returned to England in 1842 to find a country in the grip of an economic depression, where poverty, starvation and disease were manifest and widespread. She upset her family and friends by opting out of the social life she was expected to enjoy, turning down offers of marriage, and ultimately deciding that her vocation lay in hospital work and in helping sick people. In the 1840s *the only qualification required for nursing the sick was to be a woman.* Nursing was not perceived to be a worthy occupation for Florence. No skills or training were required; the women nurses were *frequently drunk and an occasional prostitute with the male patients.* Her parents were horrified and opposed her choice. Nevertheless, Florence was determined and persistent. Whilst caring for sick members of her family and their friends, she started studying both medicine and administration.

In 1851 she was able to visit Kaiserwerth, a dedicated training centre for nurses in Germany. In 1853 she finally persuaded her parents to support her application for the honorary post of Superintendent at the Institute for the Care of Sick Gentlewomen in Distressed Circumstances. She used this opportunity to transform nursing practices. One year later she helped nurse cholera patients at the Middlesex Hospital during a major epidemic. Florence's vision for a new form of nursing care to support doctors was becoming clearer. She became determined to make nursing a respectable profession for women who were skilled, trained and professional. She believed this would provide a foundation for higher standards of hygiene in hospitals; at this time hygiene was inadequate except for the hospitals where nuns provided nursing care. But, of course, the nuns were again not trained in any formalised way.

Drawing on family connections, she obtained permission to form a team of nurses who would travel out to the Crimea and care for the war casualties. In first obtaining the permission, and then when she was out there, she exploited the fact that this was the first overseas war where journalists were providing newspapers back home with regular reports on progress and conditions. Finding it difficult to recruit the volunteers she wanted, Florence ended up with twenty-four nuns in a group of thirty-eight, and at Scutari she found a field hospital *where a soldier was more likely to die than if he were fighting on the battlefield.* She was also resented by senior army staff and had to overcome a series of obstacles. Tackling issues of diet, supplies, sewers and drainage, and the actual physical handling of the casualties, she was still able to demonstrate a real difference in just six months. Through her persistence, she succeeded in transforming the perception people had of nurses and nursing care. Suddenly Florence Nightingale had become a national heroine!

After the Crimean War she initially withdrew from public life and devoted herself to taking her campaign to senior politicians and the Royal Family. Afterwards she was again active in the establishment of new civilian hospitals and training schools for civilian nurses. In essence, her work and inspiration provided the foundation for the modern nursing profession. The entrepreneur character themes of dedication, focus, courage, opportunity-taking and picking good people are clear in this short commentary on her life.

William Booth

William Booth was a contemporary of Florence Nightingale. Born as the son of a Nottingham builder in 1829, he moved to London after the death of his father and found work as a pawnbroker's assistant. He had already been converted to

Christianity and he became a revivalist Methodist preacher, arguing that church ministers should pursue a strong social role as well as their pastoral one. He was later to practice what he preached! Not atypically, he saw women as *the weaker sex*, but married a strong, self-willed woman, Catherine Mumford, in 1955. Outraging many Christians, Catherine herself began preaching in 1860. Soon supported by an originally sceptical husband she was *outstanding and inspirational*.

As a preacher in Nottingham, Booth attracted socially deprived converts to Christianity at his open-air meetings, but those who were particularly dirty and smelly were not always welcomed in Chapel by other Methodists. In 1865, and working together, William and Catherine opened a Christian Mission in Whitechapel, in the squalid East End of London, to help feed and house the poor. Their trigger had been the poverty and social deprivation they had witnessed. At this time they had seven of their eight children, and their eldest son, Bramwell, soon joined them in the Mission work, as did Booth's second key assistant, George Scott Railton, a Christian businessman from Middlesbrough, who had read of the Mission and come to London specifically to work alongside Booth. William Booth had now built a strong central team. When the Mission was reorganised along military command lines in 1878, with the preachers called officers and William Booth the General, the Salvation Army was formed. Influenced by Catherine, the Salvation Army gave equal preaching and welfare responsibilities to women. The services were informal and *joyous music* played a significant role. Again, not unexpectedly, there was hostility from the established Church of England. Army members were imprisoned for open-air preaching and Booth was declared the 'Anti-Christ' for his support of women preachers. But the Army prospered – more and more people joined and opened Citadels up and down the country. Booth started his own newspaper, The War Cry, and wrote a book about social conditions in England, offering his personal suggestions for overcoming poverty.

Booth's entrepreneurial characteristics were clearly demonstrated when he became determined to improve the working conditions for women at the local East End Bryant and May match factory. Pay was low, but more significantly the women's health was being damaged by Bryant and May's preference for using yellow phosphorus for the match heads. Toxic fumes caused skin discolouration, followed by discharging pores and ultimately death from necrosis of the bone. Other European countries had begun to use harmless red phosphorus as an alternative, but the campaigning Booth was told this would prove uneconomical. Consequently, in 1891, the Salvation Army opened its own match factory in competition. Workers were paid double the Bryant and May rate, but using red phosphorus, Booth was soon producing and selling six million boxes a year. Members of Parliament and journalists were encouraged to visit the *model factory* and *compare the conditions with other sweat shops*. In 1901 Bryant and May also switched to red phosphorus. An invitation to attend the Coronation of King Edward VII in 1902 confirmed that William Booth's contribution had been recognised.

The Salvation Army became established abroad – Booth himself travelled widely throughout the UK, America and Australia. He died in 1912, at the age of eighty-three, twenty years after his wife. Railton died very shortly afterwards and consequently

Bramwell Booth succeeded his father as General. The growth and significance of the Salvation Army has clearly continued.

Dame Cicely Saunders

Dame Cicely Saunders is the founder of the modern hospice movement. Founding the St Christopher's Hospice in Sydenham in 1967, she established new methods in pain and symptom control and inspired others to raise funds, find premises and open over 200 new hospices all over the country. At the time, she was forty-nine years old. The dream had taken several years of effort and persistence, and in some ways reflects the dedicated pursuit of a dream that we saw evidenced in James Dyson.

Again, Cicely's parents were well-off and she had begun studying at Oxford when she left to train as a nurse at the beginning of the Second World War. She served at St Thomas' Hospital in London. Hampered by a back condition, she had to abandon nursing as soon as the war was over and return to Oxford to complete her degree in philosophy, politics and economics. At this time she converted to Christianity. Her next move was to train and become a hospital almoner, the equivalent of a modern hospital social worker. At work she became friendly with David Tasma, a Polish Jew who had escaped from the Nazis. Tasma was dying, but it was their short friendship which helped her *realise and appreciate the needs of the dying patient*. His death spurred her to help as an evening volunteer at St Lukes' Hospital in Bayswater where *effective pain control, not practiced in other hospitals* was used on terminally ill patients. Simply, pain-killing drugs were being administered at regular, controlled intervals before pain levels could rebuild. Now determined to improve the quality of care for the dying, Cicely Saunders was persuaded to retrain as a doctor. Her non-scientific background was a hurdle, but she persisted and succeeded. Totally focused, she qualified in 1957 and then obtained a research fellowship to study pain in the terminally ill. Combining her medical qualification with her experience at St Lukes' she was able to trial new pain controls for cancer patients at St Joseph's Hospice, which was run by Irish nuns in Hackney.

Later she had a vision for 'The Scheme', a one-hundred-bed home for terminally ill patients, where spiritual care would be combined with the best methods of medical care available. She also saw it as a training base for doctors and other qualified carers. She worked out that she would need £200 000 to build 'The Scheme' and documented her plans in detail. In 1961 she circulated it widely and dedicated herself to bringing 'The Scheme' to fruition. She obtained her site in 1963 and the hospice opened four years after that. During this six-year-period she *pushed ahead with faith* and 'eleventh-hour' donations became quite normal. In many respects the vision was fulfilled. The 100-bed size was always too optimistic, but the true measure of her contribution is the influence she has subsequently had on others. It remains interesting, though, that whilst 'everybody' recognises the name Florence Nightingale and many would be able to associate William Booth with the Salvation Army, outside medical circles, few would appreciate the contribution of Cicely Saunders to the hospice movement they support financially. In aggregate terms, hospices became the most successful charity fund-raising organisation in the UK in the 1990s.

Social entrepreneurs in business

We begin this section with the story of a business run by a social entrepreneur before we look at social enterprises. We conclude with the stories of two businesses that emphasise the importance of human capital in a very significant way.

Anita Roddick and The Body Shop

The Body Shop, which sources and retails (mainly through franchises) natural lotions and cosmetics, has been a highly successful business with a price to earnings ratio which stayed well above the retail sector average throughout the 1980s, before declining as a result of expansion and acquisition. Until 1999, mainly through a series of acquisitions, Body Shop also manufactured at least half of the products it sold. In many respects its success has been linked to the brand and the values with which it is associated.

Body Shop was started in England in 1976 by Anita Roddick and her husband, Gordon, who used their savings of £12 000 to open the first shop, partially to help provide an income for Anita and her two daughters. *It was never meant to be serious – it was just to pay bills and the mortgage.* Shortly after the business was started, Gordon took a sabbatical leave to fulfil a lifelong dream and rode a horse from Buenos Aires to New York. Stores have subsequently been opened in over forty countries – there are now over 1200 stores – and Body Shop was floated on the UK Stock Exchange in 1984. Well-renowned for its environmental and ethical stance and strategies, Body Shop has made an impact around the world. *'If you think you are too small to have an impact, try going to bed with a mosquito'* (Anita Roddick).

As the business began to grow, Anita was increasingly influenced by her personal commitment to the environment and to education and social change. Simply, her talent for business was channelled into a cause. *I am, in my skin, an activist. I am trying to free guys in prison in America and stop sweatshops. When I went into business, I didn't think you had to leave yourself and your beliefs at the door.* The business and its financial success has been a vehicle to achieve other, more important, objectives. *Profits are perceived as boring, but business as exciting.* Body Shop's declared 'Reason for Being' *dedicated the business to the pursuit of social and environmental change.* Anita Roddick was concerned to do something which was *economically sustainable, meeting the needs of the present without compromising the future.* Her ideas were the outcome of her world travels. She had visited many third-world countries, *living native,* and had seen how women used natural products efficaciously and effectively. She noticed how women in Tahiti rubbed their bodies with cocoa butter to produce soft, satin-like skin despite a hot climate. She realised women in Morocco used mud to give their hair a silky sheen. She also saw Mexicans successfully treat burns with aloes, the slimy juice from cactus leaves. From these observations and experiences she conceptualised – and realised – her opportunity. She would use natural products from around the world to produce a range of new products. People in third-world villages were asked to supply her with the natural ingredients she needed – a form of *trade not aid.*

Body Shop has always aroused enthusiasm, commitment and loyalty amongst those involved with it. *The company must never let itself become anything other than a human enterprise.* Much of this has developed from the ethical beliefs and values of Anita Roddick, which have become manifested in a variety of distinctive policies. Gordon Roddick was the one responsible for the operational aspects of the business. Body Shop is very strong on environmental issues, offering only biodegradable products and refillable containers. Posters in the shops have been used to campaign, amongst other things, to save whales and to stop the burning of rain forests. Packaging is plain, yet the shops are characterised by strong and distinctive aromas. The packages, together with posters and shelf cards, provide comprehensive information about the products and their origins and ingredients. This has created a competitive advantage which rivals have at times found difficult to replicate. The logo and the packaging were redesigned in 1995.

The sales staff are generally knowledgeable, but they are encouraged to not be forceful and not to sell aggressively, generally offering advice only if it is requested. Marketing themes concern *health rather than glamour, and reality rather than instant rejuvenation.* Body Shop chose to avoid advertising for many years in fact, preferring in-store information to attempts at persuasion. More recently, and especially in the USA, informative advertising has been used. In 1995, in the UK, Body Shop introduced an in-store radio station, transmitted by satellite. Body Shop states that all ingredients used in its products are either natural or have been used by humans for years. There is no testing on animals. However there have been accusations to the contrary, and Body Shop was forced into litigation (which it won) in 1992. The business has always been controversial is some circles and attracted hostility. *When the first shop opened morticians were horrified at the name: The Body Shop!*

Employees are provided with regular newsletters, videos and training packages. Anita Roddick contributes regularly to the newsletters, which concentrate on Body Shop campaigns. Employees and franchisees can attend the Body Shop training centre in London free of charge. All the courses are product-centred and informative – they do not focus on selling, marketing or how to make more money. Employees are given time off, and franchisees encouraged to take time off, during working hours, to do voluntary work for the community.

Body Shop was initially able to effectively integrate manufacturing and retailing, and was efficient and operationally strong. Fresh supplies were typically delivered to its stores with a 24-hour lead time. These strategies, policies and beliefs generated substantial growth and profits in the 1980s. In the year which ended on 28 February 1991, turnover exceeded £100 million, with trading profits of some £22 million. When these results were announced, the UK share price exceeded 350 pence. Between 1984 and 1991, against the Financial Times All Share index of 100, Body Shop shares rose from an index figure of 100 to 5500. However, by mid-1995 the share price had fallen to 150 pence. Profits had fallen; new professional senior managers had been brought in to add strength. One dilemma concerned whether the culture and quirky management style was still wholly appropriate as Body Shop became a much bigger multi-national business. Global scale brings global competition. *As the business grew it lost some of its entrepreneurial spirit.*

In addition, Body Shop had attracted more and more competition. Leading UK retailers such as Boots, Marks and Spencer and Sainsbury's introduced natural products in their own label ranges; a further threat was posed by the US Bath and Body Works, whose early trial stores were a joint venture with Next. Bath and Body Works is renowned as a fast-moving organisation, quick to innovate new ideas – and aggressive at advertising and promotion. Amongst its responses in the UK, Body Shop began trials of a party plan operation. The Bath and Body Works chain was also growing faster than Body Shop in the USA, and that prompted the Roddicks to expand rapidly, opening new stores very quickly. The costs had a dramatic impact on profitability. UK retailers are generally perceived to be less slick than their US competitors at managing rapid change; Body Shop was no exception. In 1994, Body Shop also began to face criticism concerning the reality behind its ethical stance; a full publication of its social audit – then being commissioned – was promised.

In October 1995 Body Shop announced its intention to reprivatise the company by buying back shares at a price of 200 pence. The objective was to escape the constraints of the City institutions, which Anita Roddick had earlier called *the pinstriped dinosaurs.*

> I think business reporters only know a language of profit and loss. I think one of the great myths is that business can't be ethical. It's a lie. The Quakers were enormously wealthy while building schools and helping the community. They never lied and never stole. Can you imagine that happening today?

The plan was to place the shares in a charitable trust, which would be able to make donations to humanitarian and environmental causes. It was abandoned in March 1996 because of its loan implications; Body Shop would have had to borrow heavily to finance the plan, arguably leaving it too exposed. In 1998, with shares trading at under 100 pence, Anita joined Gordon as a co-chairman and a new chief executive was recruited from outside the company. The loss-making US stores were separated out and a joint venture business was established; a non-executive director injected $1 million in exchange for 49 per cent of the US business. Nevertheless, profits did grow steadily throughout the 1990s, reaching almost £40 million in 1998. In 1999, Body Shop withdrew from manufacturing and established a strong supply network instead *enabling it to return to its roots as a fast-moving entrepreneur.* Neither Anita nor Gordon now has any executive responsibilities in the business with which they remain irrevocably linked.

Body Shop is an idiosyncratic and unusual business; Anita Roddick, like Richard Branson, is an entrepreneur who has made a very individual contribution. She has shown how financial and social capital can be created in harmony – at the same time helping, rather than destroying, the environment or having no impact on it. It has not been easy and has required courage in the face of criticism, hostility and setback.

Aspire

Aspire is, in some ways, reminiscent of *The Big Issue*, in that it is a business set up to help the homeless. Paul Harrod and Mark Richardson grew up together in Bristol, where their fathers both taught at the same Methodist Theological College. They both attended Oxford, where the idea for Aspire started. They were aware that 85 per cent of homeless people in Bristol are long-term unemployed, and they set out to provide work for homeless people via a fair trade catalogue. A range of imported products would be sold door-to-door and through faith communities. There would be no hard-sell and the sellers would be guaranteed a wage; here is where Aspire differs from *The Big Issue*. In the beginning they relied on personal loans and small grants, and the business succeeded, spawning a number of regional offices throughout the UK.

The partners share the same ethical view of business that Anita Roddick has – but they are dissimilar characters who work well as an entrepreneur team. Harrod is based in London and he networks extensively, building up the contacts the business needs. He does not see himself as *outstanding on detail*. Richardson describes his partner as single-minded and determined – clearly focused. He is allegedly good at turning ideas into reality – advantage. Meanwhile Harrod describes Richardson – who has chosen to remain in Bristol – as a creative strategist who is also strong on implementation. It is Richardson who liaises with the regional offices which employ the homeless distributors. Whilst the business has taken off and grown substantially, the partners have struggled with the issue of how much it is a business and how much it is a vehicle for helping the long-term unemployed homeless people they employ. It became necessary to strengthen the controls and make Aspire more business-like.

Charlotte Da Vita and Trade Plus Aid

Trade Plus Aid began more by chance than design in 1991. Charlotte Da Vita, then aged twenty-five, was in Ghana when drought ruined thousands of farms. Wanting to help in some way, she had an idea. She suggested to local tribal chiefs that she would spend her £800 savings on seed for them if they would make her 800 pendant-size carvings. The deal was struck. Back in London, and calling on her friends to help her out, she began selling the pendants at Portobello Market, plucking a price, of £6.99 each, out of thin air. Somewhat to her surprise, the carvings sold quickly and easily. The risk she took had paid off, and she was encouraged to want to do more. She envisioned a seed bank from which local farmers could borrow seed without any payment until they harvest their crops. To progress her idea, she negotiated an alliance with an established mail order business in Japan – and pendant sales were strong once the infrastructure and supply chain was in place. Her seed bank was started in 1995. The venture grew rapidly with a comprehensive Japanese mail order catalogue, which included jewellery, clothing and toiletries from various countries in Africa and South America. Unfortunately, the 1995 earthquake at Kobe, in Japan, destroyed the warehouse that Da Vita's partner owned; the mail order company was in trouble and the Japanese market disappeared overnight. Exhibiting the courage character theme, she managed to survive and rescue the business by spending hours and days searching out new mail order buyers in America and Germany – but they would only buy her supplies at cost.

Many of the third-world village supply groups she helped establish are now trading independently; they no longer need her help. *A good year is seeing my groups become self-sufficient, not increasing my turnover.* The ever-creative Trade Plus Aid, however, continues to experiment with new initiatives. Da Vita has been able to raise money from business people around the world – who believe in what she does – to establish a 140-employee factory in China for producing hand-enamelled teapots. She sells these at the Victoria and Albert Museum and various up-market department stores. Underestimating demand once forced her to resort to airfreighting; and the operation breaks even rather than making a surplus. A similar venture produces wind chimes in South Africa. In the UK, Trade Plus Aid relies more on volunteer helpers than it does on paid employees, and Da Vita herself takes only a limited salary from the operation.

We might describe the next two social entrepreneurs as 'way-of-life entrepreneurs' for they are people who have chosen to run their organisations in a different, people-centred way. They are more concerned with human capital than the external impact with which Anita Roddick is associated. Again, they have shown how a business can be driven by social concerns without sacrificing profitability. Yet many people remain sceptical and true way-of-life entrepreneurs like Ernest Bader, or like Ricardo Semler remain a small, but nevertheless significant, minority. Neither would be regarded as the 'arbiter of normality'.

Scott Bader

Scott Bader is a private industrial chemical company with a radically different approach to both ownership and management. It was started as a private company in 1923 by Ernest Bader to be the sole agent in the UK for a Swiss manufacturer of celluloid. At this time celluloid was being moulded into colourful knife handles, combs and cases as well as table tennis balls. It is of course the base product for film. Part of Bader's early success came down to the popularity of the small plastic windmills children used to play with at the seaside! Other products in the paint industry were later imported from Germany and America, but the depression of the 1930s squeezed these merchanting activities. Bader moved into manufacturing, concentrating on paint pigment pastes, a specialist niche within the chemical industry. *He had a strong, entrepreneurial ability to select leading product lines . . . industry buyers kept close to Bader to see what he would come up with next.*

In 1940, at the beginning of the blitz, the company was moved from its central London offices and dockland factory to the old Wollaston Hall in Northamptonshire. The hall itself provided office accommodation, the stables became laboratories and a new factory was built on the 44-acre site. Manufacturing could be extended on the new site, but the company has always remained relatively small, reaching a maximum of around 450 employees in the UK, a number which has declined and risen with trade recessions and strategic changes.

A production plant was opened in Amiens, France, in 1966; in 1972 Scott Bader acquired a manufacturer of glass reinforced plastic products, for which it supplied the raw materials, and a major distributor in 1978. Other acquisitions have followed, and by 1997 Scott Bader owned three plants in France, seven distribution centres in the UK, and distribution centres in Ireland, Sweden, the Czech Republic, South Africa and the Middle East, as well as its main site in Northamptonshire. The company has always been profitable in a very competitive industry. Again, in 1997, total group turnover amounted to £100 million (with £5.3 million operating profits) from 650 employees. The figures for the UK are £60 million turnover, £4.4 million profits and 365 employees.

However, Scott Bader is not a typical company in terms of philosophy and governance. It is innovative with its style of management, seeking to achieve E-V-R congruence – see Chapter 3 – with a distinctive emphasis on values. Whilst it is, in effect, a values-driven business, it must still satisfy its customers with differentiated products and controlled costs. Ernest Bader, a Quaker since 1944, believed that *men should employ capital rather than capital employ men*, and as a result he established the Scott Bader Commonwealth in 1951 as a charitable trust. This belief, which he was willing to act on, became his cause. Bader and his family gave 90 per cent of the company shares to the Commonwealth, holding back the remaining 10 per cent (which carried over half the voting shares) until 1963, when they too were transferred. All employees who have completed a probationary period with the company can apply for membership of the Commonwealth and thus share in the ownership of the company, although shares are never individually theirs to trade.

The Commonwealth has a Board of Management with members elected from company employees, and its prime functions are concerned with social guidance, support of charitable causes and encouraging similar forms of common ownership elsewhere. Scott Bader has a proper management structure with a Board of Directors, similar to that of other companies – except for the equivalent of four employee directors.

The Community Council with elected members from all parts of the company can investigate and discuss any matters referred to it by any individual or group and can recommend a course of action to the Company Board. In the past, members of the Community Council have been actively involved in the selection of a new managing director for the company. In addition, there is a Board of Trustees, two Directors, two from the Community Council and three external to the company, to deal with such things as constitutional changes.

No group has overall authority, so that ultimately they have to move together as one body even though they may push and pull against each other in representing particular interests.

The principles of the Commonwealth include:

- Opportunities for personal growth and development.
- Releasing the best in all employees.
- Recognising and sharing talents.
- To render the best possible service as a corporate body to one's fellow men.
- To produce goods beneficial to the community.
- Management by consent, and not coercion.

People are allowed to serve on Boards for limited periods of time only and are not allowed to stand for re-election, so that individual power bases cannot be developed. Newly elected members have often had to be trained for their new roles. Things have not gone completely smooth, however. Whilst many employees have participated, some have chosen not to. It has been claimed that the company has at times lost dynamism because there has been too much concern with the quality of working life.

One significant change happened when Scott Bader bought a Unilever subsidiary, Synthetic Resins (Speke, Liverpool) in 1982. Although some Scott Bader employees are members of trade unions, the unions are not active within the company. But Synthetic Resins was different. It was conventionally managed and traditionally unionised. Despite efforts to integrate the companies and introduce common ownership at Synthetic Resins, Scott Bader failed to persuade the Liverpool workers to accept the new culture. Synthetic Resins was closed in 1985 and the essential parts of the business were transferred to Northamptonshire. After this experience, any possible acquisition has had to offer the potential for participation in both work (delegated responsibility) and governance.

Ernest Bader himself died in 1982, at the age of ninety-one. His son, Godric, acted as Chairman from 1969 to 1989, when he became Life President. He continues to encourage other organisations to adopt aspects of common ownership.

Ricardo Semler and Semco

Ricardo Semler was just twenty-one years old when he took over as chief executive of his family's business, Semco. This Brazilian company manufactures pumps, food mixers, meat slicing equipment and dishwashers. Brazil is, of course, a country characterised by high inflation and a massive relative wealth gap between the rich and the poor. His father believed that if he handed over the reins when Ricardo was still young, *he could make his mistakes whilst he was still around to fix them!* His father had run the business along traditional and autocratic lines; Ricardo was to change everything – and the company has thrived and prospered.

Although he has an MBA from Harvard, Ricardo Semler's stated business philosophy is: *follow your intuition.* He inherited a company where *people did not want to come to work* and managers *watched everything and everybody constantly, trusting nobody* – and transformed it into one which is *ultimately democratic* and based on *freedom, respect, trust and commitment.* Things did not happen instantaneously; many new approaches and experimental methods were tried and abandoned. However, in a ten-year period, from the mid-1980s, Semco achieved 900 per cent growth.

There is no reception area, no secretaries and no offices. Managers walk around constantly to provide help and assistance when it is requested; the workers organise their own flexible working time arrangements. Employees work in small clusters, and they can also rearrange their working space and environment as they wish. Semco has come to believe that clusters of no more than ten are required if this approach is to work effectively. Twelve layers of a management and supervisory hierarchy have been reduced to three. The appointment of any manager has to be approved by the workforce, and managers are subjected to regular assessment by their subordinates and shopfloor employees. People talk openly and *when someone says they'll do something, they do it.* Consequently, managers also feel they can spend time away from the plant – with customers and suppliers. Recently people have been allowed to take every Wednesday afternoon off if they accept a 10 per cent salary cut – the time is made up by retired employees working on Wednesday afternoons.

Profit-sharing is by consultation and negotiation – 23 per cent of after-tax profits is available for the workforce – and all employees are trained to ensure they can read the company accounts. There was no longer a formal chief executive post for

Ricardo, who became President. Instead, there is an informal board of six associates (the most senior managers) who elect a nominal chief executive for a six-month period. Ricardo continued to attend their meetings – as an adviser.

Ricardo began to take his ideas further, encouraging employees to consider starting up satellite supply companies and sub-contracting for Semco. Those who have opted for this entrepreneurial route have been allowed to take Semco machines with them, leasing them on favourable terms. One advantage for Semco is the fact that it is no longer responsible for the maintenance and safety of the equipment. In addition, there is an opportunity for the machinery to be used more effectively as the satellite companies are free to work for other organisations; their efficiency gains can be passed through in the form of lower prices. If the venture fails, Semco takes back the equipment and the men. It is a relatively low and managed risk for all concerned.

Ricardo Semler has not been a man who has hidden his achievements! He has written the story of his role at Semco with the title *Maverick*, and he has become a recognised member of the management guru circuit around the world. He has also campaigned against corruption in Brazil and exposed government officials who have been demanding bribes for domestic planning permission. As a result, he has generated hostility from certain prominent people in his country. He makes sure he puts time on one side every day to sit, relax and think.

Successful companies will be the ones that put quality of life first. Do this and the rest – quality of product, productivity of workers, profits for all – will follow. Ricardo Semler, like Ernest Bader before him, is an entrepreneur because he has pursued a vision, courageously persevered against resistance and challenges, and made things happen.

In the next section on community initiatives, many of the names will be 'unknowns' to the majority of readers. This is partly due to the fact that some of the initiatives are small and localised but it is also affected by the reality that this form of social entrepreneurship does not receive the publicity that successful businesses do.

Social entrepreneurs in the community

Elliott Tepper

Elliott Tepper is an American missionary who lives in Spain. He has an MBA but has chosen to channel his not inconsiderable energies into helping alcoholics and drug addicts. He started Betel, a not-for-profit Christian rehabilitation centre, in the early 1990s. At any one time Betel now houses over 500 young addicts, both men and women, in homes in ten Spanish cities, in Birmingham in the UK and in Brooklyn, New York. Half of the people on Betel's programme are HIV-positive. Most of the single-sex houses or 'communities' – a number of which have been obtained by initially squatting and then 'doing up' – are run by volunteer ex-addicts.

In return for a place to live and an opportunity to break their addiction, the residents have to turn their backs on alcohol, cigarettes and drugs – and work, mainly with their hands. Within the houses the rules are strict, and any resident who breaks the rules is likely to be thrown out without undue haste and ceremony. Betel provides cleaners, plumbers, painters and bricklayers as well as running charity shops which sell used clothes and household items they have been given. Most of their food is donated by local supermarkets – it is typically food which is close to its sell-by or use-by date and which otherwise would be wasted. Betel's goal is self-sufficiency but it does receive financial donations from City councils and the Red Cross and looks for free materials its workers can use.

5000 people passed through in the first seven years. Half stayed for at least six months. Tepper believes people need to stay for at least a year if they are to beat their addiction; and of this 5000 some 17 per cent left fully cured. Of those who accept the Christian faith, the success rate seems to be as high as 90 per cent. The ratio of men to women was 4:1. Three per cent were aged under twenty, 54 per cent between twenty and thirty, leaving 43 per cent over thirty years old. Currently the annual revenue – donations plus income earned by the resident workers – comfortably exceeds £3 million.

It is interesting to see how Elliott Tepper's early experiences brought out his inherited entrepreneurial talents. His father was President of an electronics firm in New York and a partner in two other businesses. *A man of vision, he tried to do the impossible and I inherited that from him.* At the age of fourteen, Elliott's world began to unravel when his parents divorced and his father lost his fortune. His college education began at Lehigh University and was paid for by a wrestling scholarship that he won – he was the New York State champion. This was followed by a Cambridge (UK) MA in Economics and an MBA at Harvard. *In my last year at Harvard I joined a commune and took part in all-night discussions about politics and philosophy. That was when I started taking hallucinogenic drugs, hashish and marijuana.* This was followed by a life-changing experience which encouraged Tepper to become active in his local church once he returned home after Harvard. He subsequently attended Bible College in America and worked as a missionary in Mexico before going to Spain.

In Elliott Tepper we can see that an obvious need is being addressed by someone with a vision who is able to gather together the financial, people and other resources required to operationalise the vision. On this occasion, and not unusually, that person is a Christian Minister. At the heart of the initiative are buildings, without which the venture would be impossible. Like the partial reliance on charity shops all these issues are commonly found in community social entrepreneurship. Three other factors, however, make Betel distinctive and unusual – and different from many charities. First, in order to benefit from the rehabilitation programme, people have to do something; the support they receive is not a free gift. Second, part of Betel's income comes from the beneficiaries actually working and earning. Third, and like the modern hospice movement, the original idea has been grown into a major initiative which has broken out of a single community identity.

The next three examples illustrate social entrepreneurship in the UK in the 1990s. They are all important and significant in their own way – and their non-existence would leave a gap – but we see three quite different levels of impact.

Andrew Mawson

Andrew Mawson is a Yorkshire-born United Reform Church minister who was moved to London's East End in 1984. His church in Bromley-by-Bow had a leaking roof, poor heating, a damaged piano and just a small congregation of mostly elderly people. Radical change seemed the only obvious way forward! The new Bromley-by-Bow Centre reflects a complete transformation inspired by Mawson and implemented by the community it serves. The church itself was redesigned to generate more open, flexible space and offered to the local community for appropriate daily use on weekdays. In the early days one local woman used it to build a boat! Local artists soon realised it could provide useful studio facilities. Word-of-mouth brought in a dance school, a nursery and a café. A disability group offered to landscape the gardens. In effect, the building became a community centre in the week and a church on Sundays – with a growing and active congregation.

On the back of these developments, Mawson helped raise money from Royal and Sun Alliance and NatWest to fund projects for combating youth crime in the area and for supporting local young entrepreneurs. In addition, there is now an adjacent health centre for the local community. The area still has high unemployment and deprivation, but the community can boast a centre of excellence and achievement. Mawson always set deliberately high targets to spur extra effort. One of his main contributions has been to build a central team – who have imparted a mission and values – and then involve and encourage enterprising members of the community. Involving artistic people from the beginning ensured consistent creativity and there has always been an emphasis on building value for local customers.

Andrew Mawson has since been instrumental in establishing The Community Action Foundation with a remit to identify examples of effective social entrepreneurship and help sponsor new developments throughout the UK.

Margaret Handforth

The Castleford Community Learning Centre in West Yorkshire provides an excellent example of the need drawing in the entrepreneur. Margaret Handforth, miner's wife, ex-secretary and mother of three sons, had demonstrated her latent talent by founding a local playgroup but had never thought of herself as an entrepreneur before the 1984 Miners' Strike. Forming a small group, she set up a soup kitchen to help people survive the traumas of the time. Invited to speak to students at local universities in exchange for a collection, the women set foot on university campuses for the first time in their lives. They began to realise that education can broaden horizons and Margaret Handforth had a vision of a better life through self-improvement. She had *no idea how to do it, just a determination to start something off*. Although the venture has grown remarkably, most of the founding team have no current involvement. Margaret has recruited a new team to help her.

The Castleford Women's Centre – as it was called in the beginning – started gradually in humble premises they were able to restore with the help of a small grant. Support and counselling was supplemented with tea dances and craft classes, *really anything that would bring people in*. Additional contacts led to additional grants, and the venture took off. It was really *growth out of necessity* – the need had found the right person to fill the gap. Known locally as the University of Life, the Women's Centre has moved into new premises with a new name. A wide raft of courses up to degree level, and validated by local colleges and universities, is now available, usually at low or no cost to women in this economically deprived area. It has succeeded because it has always been flexible, opportunistic and close to its customers. *I daren't go out for a sandwich at lunchtime as people [I would meet] would keep stopping and talking to me . . . I'd be out for two hours (Margaret Handforth).*

Genya Johnson

A few miles down the road, in Rotherham, the Get Sorted Academy of Music also makes an important social contribution, but on a smaller and more limited scale. Genya Johnson was a full-time special needs teacher whose Russian father had moved to England after the Second World War and opened a chain of small shops. She inherited his entrepreneurial talent, but chose to use it for helping others in her spare time.

Get Sorted occupies the upper floors of what was a motor cycle shop; it was set up to provide soundproof rehearsal rooms for teenage bands. Originally called The Get Sorted Crew the young beneficiaries were organised to do most of the building and restoration work themselves. Rehearsing was soon supplemented by access to recording facilities, the organising of gigs for the bands in order to raise funds and a management agency for those bands good enough to secure independent bookings. Genya Johnson first appreciated the need gap and the opportunity when she was recruited by the local police force to help with a drugs awareness campaign. She helped the first band by allowing them to practice in her own home, before setting out to find appropriate premises. She has relied more on free handouts (such as spare tins of paint) and volunteers' time than on financial assistance. Nevertheless she was personally awarded a small, recurring grant to reimburse her for her time as a form of youth leader. She opted to give the money to a younger helper – an ex-band member – so he could work full-time for Get Sorted. She herself took no reward for her part-time commitment, which amounted to every evening and weekends! Over one-hundred bands and five-hundred young people, from a range of social backgrounds and with some from several miles away, made use of the facilities in the early years, for which they always had to pay a token rental. Friends of the musicians also used the centre and help with promotional material and renovation work. In one important respect, Get Sorted became a social centre which keeps young people off the streets and often out of trouble.

Get Sorted's reputation spread and Genya was invited to take on more and more. This often happens to community social entrepreneurs and there is always a danger that they can lose focus as they are not people who like to say 'no'. Now called an Academy of Music, Get Sorted provides one-to-one special needs teaching, based on a theme of music, during school hours to those children who are typically disruptive in mainstream schools. Outside school hours it provides music teaching for a variety of instruments. Genya Johnson is now fully employed – and fully occupied – by the initiative she started. Although her husband works with her, it is hard to imagine its survival without her.

David Bussau

David Bussau is a business entrepreneur who invests in the poor; his story is different from the social entrepreneurs we have considered so far. Bussau became a millionaire from a series of business interests and then focused his not inconsiderable talents on helping poor people around the world. Many millionaires do give generously and set up foundations to help create social, and sometimes aesthetic, capital – but Bussau set out to help people help themselves. In this respect he has a similar ethos to Charlotte Da Vita.

David Bussau spent the first sixteen years of his life (1940–1956) in an orphanage in New Zealand and the next nineteen years making his fortune as an entrepreneurial businessman. When he left the orphanage with *no family, no close friends and no money* he managed to start a hot-dog stand. Within six months he had six other people leasing stands from him. With his profits David bought (and later sold) a small bakery and then a biscuit factory and a pancake restaurant. He never had any formal business education; he was simply able to grow businesses!

In his mid-twenties, after marrying, he sold up and moved to Australia. His wife was ill at the time, and they believed that for her particular condition the medical facilities in Australia were superior to those in New Zealand. He got a job in construction. Perhaps inevitably he was soon to become a partner in the business he joined – before he bought the business outright and used it as a base to set up a whole series of construction firms. He was a millionaire before he was thirty-five. *It was clear that I was an entrepreneur and that whatever business I chose to take on, I was going to make a success of it.*

On Christmas Day in 1974 Darwin (in the Northern Territory) was devastated by a cyclone. A committed Christian, Bussau set off with twenty of his employees to help – short term – with rescue and rebuilding activities. This experience changed his philosophy of life. A year later, David sold a number of his businesses, leaving managers in charge of the others, and moved with his wife and family to Darwin to continue helping with the rebuilding programme. In 1976 the whole family moved on to Bali, to help there in the aftermath of an earthquake. Here he organised the construction of a dam, a bridge, a clinic and an irrigation system. He earned nothing from this – in reality he invested in the projects. Travelling around Bali he sensed potential entrepreneurs who were being held back by a lack of money at affordable rates of interest. He started making small, short-term loans to very poor people. Some would buy tools which they would use to boost their family income. Others would buy basic ingredients and bake them into saleable products.

He returned to Australia, but was persuaded to return to Bali in 1980. With the help of others he set up a church-based revolving credit scheme to provide short-term loans. Local banks were not interested in loaning small amounts, such as $50 (Australian dollars), which was all that new, small businesses required to start up, because their processing costs made the rates of interest prohibitive. Bussau's idea was for small loans, paid back very quickly so the money can be re-lent to others. A first loan could, of course, be followed by subsequent, and usually larger, loans as the businesses began to grow. The interest charged covered the operating costs and nothing more. Project officials also provided advice to the small businesses whilst ever they had a loan. Ten years later – and under the umbrella organisation, Opportunity International – there were forty-seven similar agencies in nineteen other countries around the world. Some 50 000 small entrepreneurs had been provided with the limited financial support they needed to either get started or grow their business. Although Christianity is at the heart of the programme, two thirds of the loans have been made to non-Christians. In recent years Bussau has concentrated on persuading other Christian business leaders in developing countries to *use the gifts and skills God has given them to help the poor*.

The story of businessman David Bussau is an excellent example of someone following the Christian preaching of John Wesley: *make as much as you can; save as much as you can; give away as much as you can*. We have also seen religious themes coming through in several of the other stories we have included. William Booth founded the Salvation Army; Andrew Mawson is a vicar and Elliott Tepper a missionary; Florence Nightingale and Cicely Saunders both believed they had been called by God. In this section we develop the religious connection further and look at another Church minister who has been able to use his position to raise substantial amounts of money which has then been redeployed to help others through socially entrepreneurial ventures. Whilst Andrew Mawson relies on corporate donations, and Elliott Tepper's clients have to work, Television evangelists in America have learned how to use the power of the media to capture the hearts and minds of a large congregation and to generate huge donations. Occasionally there has been evidence of corruption. What we see in evidence here is entrepreneurship which addresses two opportunities simultaneously and brings them together in a powerful and synergistic initiative. The first opportunity is creative fund-raising – social entrepreneurs can only spend what they can raise! The second opportunity concerns identifying appropriate causes for redirecting the funds to create demonstrable benefits for the more needy. The social capital, and the need it addresses, can, on the one hand, constitute a cause which provides a focus for the fund-raising. At the same time they constitute the measures which justify the effectiveness of the venture.

Pat Robertson

Pat Robertson was the founder of the American Christian Broadcasting Network (CBN) in 1960. The first Christian television network, it grew to become one of the world's largest television ministries and the heart of a major business empire. It is still popular as a family channel with a strong religious heart, and its daily flagship programme attracts an audience of 1.5 million viewers in America alone. There are countless more in the ninety other countries where it is broadcasted. The CBN incorporates an extensive call centre; viewers can ring up at any time to either make donations or seek advice on any problems they have. A parallel family entertainment channel set up by Robertson was sold to Rupert Murdoch in 1997 for $1.9 billion. The stations were established on land in Virginia Beach, which Robertson owns, and where he has developed other activities and businesses. He created the private Regent University where entrepreneurship is included as a key feature programme; and his other business interests include diamond mining, chemicals and banking. In 1978 Robertson also founded a non-profit organisation – Operation Blessing – for providing humanitarian aid in the form of food, clothing, medicine and financial support to disadvantaged people and disaster victims. In twenty years $500 million was raised via CBN and dispersed through Operation Blessing.

Pat Robertson was born in 1930 in Lexington, Virginia. His father was, at different times, a member of both the House of Representatives and the Senate. His direct ancestors include a signatory of the Declaration of Independence and two American Presidents. After military service in Korea, Pat Robertson qualified as a lawyer before choosing to study theology. A Southern Baptist Minister from 1961 to 1987, he eventually resigned from the Ministry to seek the Republication nomination for the Presidency. A series of successful books has contributed to his considerable wealth.

Despite his ancestry, religious calling and clear success as a social entrepreneur, Robertson is a controversial man. In March 1999 it was announced that the Bank of Scotland was teaming up with him to establish a joint venture organisation which would provide telephone-banking services (in which the Bank of Scotland has expertise) for the millions of Americans who watch CBN. Direct telephone banking was yet to develop in the US to the extent it had in the UK. This, therefore, appeared to be an excellent and ideal opportunity for the two partners, who would bring distinct but complementary skills to the venture. Deposits and savings accounts were to be followed by credit cards and loans. By June the deal was off. Over many years Robertson had earned a reputation for strong right-wing views; he has long been forthright about his hostility towards *homosexuals, feminists, liberals, Muslims and Hindus*. When, in May 1999, he described Scotland as *a dark land that panders to homosexuals and which has lost its morals*, many Royal Bank customers were incensed. Bank executives felt they had to withdraw *to save further embarrassment*, even thought they would have to pay compensation to buy out Robertson's share in the joint venture.

Environmental entrepreneurs

In this last section we look first at two small businesses which provide 'green' energy, both of them started by entrepreneurs who are dedicated to the preservation of the natural environment. This is their cause, and for them it is far more important than the building of financial wealth. We finally look at a Scandinavian entrepreneur who has taken on some of the largest consumer products companies in the world.

Dale Vince

In 1996 Dale Vince, together with two friends and £10 000, set up The Renewable Energy Company, then *Europe's largest, dedicated supplier of green electricity*. Within a year, turnover exceeded £4 million, with £400 000 pre-tax profits. The energy was generated initially from landfill gas (methane) but more recently supplies have been obtained from purpose-built wind farms, specifically clusters of windmills. The early success with methane generated the cash to invest in the new windmills. One opportunity was exploited to allow another opportunity to be seized. In the long term the company must be able to keep its prices in line with those of the major, established suppliers who use gas, oil and coal – and not open itself to criticism for building wind farms which are eye-sores in the countryside.

Jeremy Leggett

Jeremy Leggett was an environmental campaigner in charge of Greenpeace's global warming campaign before he became an entrepreneur. Convinced of the potential of solar energy he installed solar panels on the roof of his home in Richmond, Surrey. The panels generated 68 per cent more energy than the household needed; and over their life the panels *should prevent more than 30 tonnes of greenhouse gas emissions.* Leggett set up his business, Solar Century, in March 1999 to promote solar energy and distribute panels manufactured by a range of alternative suppliers. Architects are seen as a key target audience, but early orders have been received from individual homeowners. At the moment the panels remain expensive, but if a mass market can be generated Leggett believes the price can be brought down to a competitive level.

Marlene Sandberg

Marlene Sandberg was a Swedish lawyer before she became an entrepreneur after the birth of her second child. She went into business to produce an environmentally friendly disposable nappy – made from a biodegradable thermoplastic˙comprising corn, wheat and potato starch. Her business was named Naty and her product Nature Boy and Girl. She had no business or manufacturing experience, but she was still determined to challenge an industry dominated by names such as Procter and Gamble with its Pampers brand. She would quickly seize 2 per cent of the Swedish market and contract licensees in America, Australia and New Zealand.

Sandberg had a network of useful contacts which she used to track down three key people. She found an inventor who had designed a nappy with greater absorbency through special ducts and channels for redistributing the fluid. She was put in touch with an Italian entrepreneur who had developed a biodegradable plastic. A former director of Volvo (who had earlier worked in the disposable nappy industry) invested in her business (taking 4 per cent of the equity) and helped her find the venture capital she needed. He also acted as her coach and mentor. Her success has also depended on her ability to reach lasting distribution agreements with selected retail chains. Sandberg started out with the intention of manufacturing everything herself, but early problems and setbacks caused her to have a change of heart and strategy – as an alternative she found a German company with spare capacity.

Of course, although her nappies use renewable materials they are not completely disposable and they still end up on landfill sites. Sandberg wants to find a suitable material that is fully biodegradable and which can be composted.

This chapter has been about entrepreneurs who have elected to focus on social and sometimes environmental wealth and capital rather than on financial wealth. Some of the stories have been about people with entrepreneurial talent and temperament who have chosen to use their abilities to pursue causes that have been important to them – and for many others. Society has benefited substantially from their efforts and contributions. It would be quite normal not to think of some of the people we have featured in this chapter as entrepreneurs – simply because their initiatives have not been motivated primarily by financial wealth creation – but they are entrepreneurs. They possess the character themes of an entrepreneur. They have been able to spot, engage and exploit an opportunity for doing good and helping others. They have been able to recruit the support and commitment of others in their endeavours. They have built important capital and made an impact. The difference in most cases is that they have been driven by their commitment to a cause and it is this commitment that has drawn their energy in a particular direction. In the next chapter we consider another group of people who possess entrepreneurial character themes, but who are particularly talented in design, art or music, and are driven to find opportunities to pursue and express their creativity – and, in this way, have a significant influence on the lives of others.

Further Readings

Some of the material on Anita Roddick has been taken from her autobiography:

Roddick, A. (2000). *Business as Unusual*, Thorsons/HarperCollins and from an interview with web-based Startups.co.uk.

8 Artistic and aesthetic entrepreneurs

Some financially very successful businesses are built around the creation of artistic or aesthetic capital. Fashion design and musical entertainment are two obvious examples. Arguably the entrepreneurs behind them would prefer to be remembered for their creative contributions rather than for their business acumen. In this chapter we look at examples of these and other artistic entrepreneurs. Some gifted artists and musicians have always been able to generate financial wealth through the development and exploitation of their natural, creative talents, and we explore the presence of entrepreneurial character themes in the way they create and chase opportunities.

In this chapter we look at entrepreneurs whose main wealth contribution is artistic or aesthetic – the merit and value of which is linked to people's perceptions and which consequently needs to be assessed qualitatively rather than wholly quantitatively. Some would argue that the main legacy of a generation to successive generations lies with the architecture, art and music it bequeaths. At the same time, people do pay premium prices for designer clothes and quality food in good restaurants, for seats at concerts and to buy recorded music and works of art. Here a quantitative value is being attributed, and, as a result, certain designers, artists, restaurateurs and musicians become very wealthy – although monetary wealth is rarely their main motivation. Britain, of course, is often thought to excel in creative industries such as advertising, architecture, design and fashion, computer software, books, entertainment and media. We have already seen how important social entrepreneurs are for building community-based capital; here we see how many aspects of our 'general well-being' are dependent upon artistic and aesthetic entrepreneurs.

The true entrepreneurs in this field are generally 'off the scale' with their creative talent; the most outstanding are sometimes described as eminent or 'truly great'. After all, a good proportion of the population can read music or play an instrument – but how many can write or perform inspirationally and produce a work that people want to hear over-and-over-again? Similarly, most of us can mix colours and use a paintbrush, but rarely do our efforts genuinely 'move' other people.

Highlighting the parallels between the outstanding business people we normally associate with entrepreneurship and eminent people in all walks of life, Ludwig

(1995) argues that true greatness requires a special ability, gift or talent but that not everyone who is gifted becomes eminent. They must be identified and trained to exploit their gift. Rachmaninoff, for example, played music by ear at the age of seven; as did Bix Beiderbecke. Judy Garland was performing at the age of two. How many of the business entrepreneurs we have described started with some entrepreneurial venture at a very young age? Parental support, together with access to necessary resources, is essential, despite the fact that the talent is typically accompanied by an equally critical willingness to challenge existing norms and paradigms. Raymond Blanc told the first chef he worked for that his food was too salty. His reward – a flying pan which broke his nose and jaw! Those destined for greatness possess a need to accomplish something distinctive (ego) and a determination to achieve, often despite hostile criticism. Sigmund Freud similarly believed that their driving force is a desire for fame and public recognition.

Truly great people do enjoy a prolonged appreciation and reputation which stretches beyond their death – as do our classic social and business entrepreneurs. Some, of course, are only appreciated properly after they are dead. They produce original, imaginative and innovatory work – often, but not always, sustained for many years – which influences others. Although blessed with a natural talent, this still demands intense effort and persistence – reflecting the right temperament. Whilst it cannot ever be easy to bring into existence something of high perceived value that has never before existed, the most creative people do not necessarily see what they do as difficult. They do what they do, either because they enjoy doing it or because they are unable to stop themselves. They are driven. In addition, great artists and composers have not always enjoyed the very best formal training that was available. Instead they have shown a tremendous ability to develop their own talent, inspired by the work of other eminent people. It is an interesting parallel that although an increasing number of large corporation chief executives are MBA graduates, the MBA degree remains relatively uncommon amongst the most successful business entrepreneurs. We have already stressed that with certain exceptions, such as new Internet businesses, formal education to degree level or beyond is not a prerequisite for entrepreneurial success.

In this chapter we begin with the classic story of a legendary entertainer, P.T. Barnum, and then consider a number of designers who have built successful businesses and business entrepreneurs who have seen the potential in creative ideas. We next look at several entrepreneurs in different sectors of the entertainment industry. Whilst creativity is inherent in every successful entrepreneurial venture, we have chosen to describe these as creative enterprises in Figure Int. 1. We next tackle the question 'Were artists like Michelangelo and musicians like Mozart actually the artistic and aesthetic entrepreneurs of their time?' They focused on the most appropriate opportunities that were available to them for exploiting their talent, building significant artistic capital and leaving a priceless legacy for the world to enjoy.

Jensen (1999) re-emphasises the importance of these entrepreneurs who contribute to *the dream society, based on emotion,* as distinct from *the information society, based on rational thinking.* He believes the emphasis will continue to shift from the latter to the former as future consumers will be increasingly affected by the stories of the image and branding of products and services. Jensen argues, for example, that the success of expensive outdoor clothing and shoes is affected by a desire for adventure by some people, and he shows how the intellectual capital lies in the design and image, and not manufacturing capability. In some industries, arguably including music and cars, retro-designs provide *peace of mind from an idealised past*; and, as we saw in the previous chapter, businesses linked to causes often succeed because they impact upon our convictions.

P.T. Barnum – another classic entrepreneur

For many, the name Barnum is a reminder of a popular musical show which starred Michael Crawford in the title role in the 1990s. Always enterprising himself, Crawford learned to walk a tightrope for this role! But P.T. Barnum is unquestionably a creative business entrepreneur. Reminding us of the less-than-ideal image that entrepreneurs sometimes have, Barnum's name is often associated with the phrase *There's a sucker born every minute* although it appears highly doubtful that he ever said this. Born in Connecticut in 1810 he was destined to be America's second millionaire.

In his youth he sold lottery tickets and ran a newspaper. He would later produce New York's first illustrated newspaper and build a circulation of 500 000 regular customers. He became an incredible networker, befriending the rich and famous around the world. He knew Abraham Lincoln very well; Mark Twain was a close friend; he went hunting with General Custer. During his life he had to deal with the aftermath of five serious fires, each of which wiped out either a home or a business. Each time he simply started again and built something more substantial. He experienced something similar with business decisions, losing a fortune on more than one occasion through poor investment. His autobiography was perhaps aptly called 'Struggles and Triumphs' and, revised several times, it eventually sold over one million copies.

At heart he was an entertainer who succeeded by taking unknowns and making them into international stars. Examples of these stars were Tom Thumb, a tiny boy that he taught to sing and dance, Joice Heth, a black slave who was allegedly 160 years old and Jenny Lind, the Swedish soprano. His American Museum, which attracted over forty million visitors, was *the Disneyland of the 1800s* and, of course, he started the Barnum and Bailey Circus, which still exists today. He is credited with inventing both beauty and beautiful baby contests; he was also a significant property developer. An astute dealer, he would acquire a piece of land, divide it into plots and secure planning permission. His regular donations of common land to City councils seemed to help here! He would then sell non-adjacent plots and help the purchasers finance the buildings they put up. He would hang on to the other plots until the buildings were complete and then release them at inflated prices.

His general success is put down to a number of factors:

- He was always customer-focused.
- He 'thought big'.
- He chased and created publicity and advertised widely in magazines, newspapers and posters; some see him as the real creator of modern advertising.

- He gave people 'more than their money's worth'.
- He rewarded his employees.
- He never let setbacks pull him down, always setting out to recover as quickly as he could.
- He had an unshakeable faith that everything happened for a reason.

The following quotes reveal something of his entrepreneur characteristics:

Engage in one kind of business only and stick to it faithfully while you succeed – or until you conclude and abandon it (Focus).

Every man's occupation should be beneficial to his fellow man as well as profitable to himself. All else is vanity and folly (Advantage).

I believe hugely in advertising and in blowing my own trumpet . . . but I never believed that any amount of advertising or energy would make a spurious article permanently successful (Ego and advantage).

We cannot all see alike but we can all do good (Social).

Creative business entrepreneurs

Terence Conran

Terence Conran is a habitual, serial entrepreneur, albeit that design has been a key element of all his businesses and activities. He is a rich and successful business entrepreneur – but he will be remembered more for his creative design talents than for his business acumen. Conran is an innovator who has applied his entrepreneurial talents to furniture making, designing, retailing, publishing and restaurant management. He has had many successes and some notable setbacks. Still, fully active in his seventies, he continues to work seven days a week and appears to have no thoughts of stopping.

Born in Surrey in 1931, his background and upbringing were middle class. Interested in crafts from an early age, he set up a workshop at home. As a young boy he spent some considerable time at a local pottery, and at school he specialised in chemistry, engineering and art. Encouraged by a friend, he then went to college and studied textile design, where he became intrigued by the possibilities of screen-printing. In partnership with an architect, he also started making furniture to his own designs, mainly for his friends.

His first paid employment, in 1949, was as a librarian at a design centre – but he left to join forces with his architect friend, and together they produced designs for the 1951 Festival of Britain. They continued with their furniture – which they were able to have displayed in selected London department store windows – and they were commissioned to produce textile designs for Myers Beds. In addition, his architect-partner was specifying Conran furniture for the offices, hotels and hospitals that he designed. Realising that he was *terribly inept at the business side*, Conran began to address marketing and selling issues, employing someone to sell and to produce a brochure for him.

The growth of his business was helped by cash injections as he bought, renovated and sold premises, systematically improving his base.

To help raise additional money to buy new machinery, he joined forces with another friend, a psychiatrist, to open a café-cum-soup kitchen in 1953. This developed into a chain of four before they sold it in 1954. By the mid-1950s he had set up a textiles conversion business, buying cloth or having it woven and then selling it on. He was also designing exhibition stands and accepting shopfitting contracts. Aided by a grant, he then moved his business activities – and his eighty staff – out of London, to Thetford. In 1956 he established Conran Design as a consultancy and architects practice – the practice still exists, and is one of the largest of its type in Europe, but Conran himself withdrew in 1992 after a majority shareholding was acquired by a French competitor. Terence Conran immediately began a new design consultancy partnership.

In 1962, and in a brand-new factory, he began to manufacture domestic furniture, which he sold through eighty retailers in the UK. When he visited these outlets he was typically *appalled by the display and presentation* and decided to open his own shop. In 1964 the Habitat concept was born, first in London and then in Manchester, selling Conran furniture together with kitchen utensils, lighting and floor coverings and targeting various ages and socio-economic groups. His strategy was to fill the shops with stock, rather than force people to order and wait. The theme was complementary designer products, many of them bought in – but from a single-eye perspective – and presented in a colourful environment. Before the 1960s were over the Habitat chain had expanded considerably and Conran had acquired Ryman's office furniture. The merger was not a success and Ryman's was sold to Burton. In 1973 he opened the more exclusive Conran Shop in London, selling high-quality, superior design furniture and household goods which were being rejected for Habitat on the grounds of price.

Habitat was floated on the Stock Exchange in 1981; a year later Mothercare was acquired. Conran knew the Mothercare founder, Selim Zhilka, and was aware the business *was in need of a new direction – it had slipped downmarket with lacklustre merchandise*. Finance was available from a Dutch bank which believed the conceptual ethos of Habitat was readily transferable to other retail concepts. Subsequently Heals (furniture retailer, 1983), Richard shops (clothing, 1984) and Blazer (also clothing, 1987) were acquired. When Habitat was merged with British Home Stores in 1986 the retail consortium was renamed Storehouse, and Conran became Chairman and Chief Executive. However, he resigned his chief executive post in 1989 and the Chairmanship in 1990, buying back The Conran Shop and using it as a base for a small chain of exclusive stores in the world's leading cities. There are now nine shops in four countries.

In parallel to his retailing activities, Conran had published his first book, The House Book, in 1974. In effect, this was a published version of his in-house training manual for designers. Others followed before he joined forces in 1983 with Octopus Books to produce a range of lifestyle publications. At the same time, and being *a keen cook and gastronome, Conran had begun to transform the experience of eating out in London.* After the sale of his share in the Soup Kitchens chain (1954) he began opening a series of specialist restaurants, mostly in London. His main projects include Quaglino's (originally fashionable in the 1930s and renovated to serve over 1000 people a day),

Mezzo (the largest restaurant in Europe, serving 700 people at any one time) and Bluebird (a complex incorporating a restaurant where the food is cooked in a wood-fired oven, a flower market, a fresh food market, a private dining club and an exclusive furniture shop). There are now over a dozen exclusive Conran restaurants in London, and others in Paris, New York and Stockholm. Very recently he returned to designing moderately priced furniture in an alliance with the manufacturer, Christie-Tyler.

In this story we can see clear evidence of several entrepreneur character themes. Terence Conran is creative and innovative; he is dedicated to design; he has a strong ego and is clearly action-focused; he is advantage-driven and benefit-oriented; he is able to build the teams necessary to drive his various ventures forward. Significantly he chose to draw back from the large corporation leader position. His current business interests have a combined turnover in excess of £100 million and he reputedly checks the figures every day.

He himself says 'I have always seen myself as a designer first, rather than a businessman, although I've made things happen and enjoyed making them happen . . . businesses are ways of putting my ideas and products in front of the public'.

Mary Quant

Mary Quant was a contemporary of Terence Conran and a *trailblazer behind the swinging sixties scene in London*, but she chose to use her design talents in a different way. Her story is one of focusing on what one can do best, understanding customers and team entrepreneurship – working with partners who can provide other skills and abilities, ones which are either natural weaknesses or which would only be achievable with considerable effort.

Mary Quant's first business was a boutique in London's Kings Road in 1955; her second outlet in Knightsbridge (1957) was designed by Terence Conran. Mary Quant was initially in partnership with her husband, Alexander Plunket-Green, who she had met at art school. The two were later joined by fellow-entrepreneur Archie McNair, who had opened the first coffee bar in London and who had premises over the road from Mary's Bazaar boutique in the Kings Road. Initially Bazaar incorporated a small workroom; Mary Quant employed machinists and bought her fabrics mainly from Harrods. McNair was convinced that design, and not manufacturing, was the platform for growth, and this was the model they followed. Stock was manufactured under licence by other independent companies to Mary's designs. When Quant mini-skirts were worn in America by the Beatles' girlfriends in 1964, a new fashion was born and the business simply took off. This key invention opened the door to her success and prosperity. The creative and innovative design skills were systematically transferred to other products. Dresses and coats were followed by swimwear and tights (1963), bold cosmetics (1966), household furnishings and domestic textiles (in conjunction with Du Pont and ICI, 1968), bedwear and curtains (with Carrington Viyella, 1972), sunglasses (with Polaroid, 1977), Axminster carpets (1978), shoes (1982) and finally stationery (with W.H. Smith). In 1971, Mary Quant formed a joint venture in Japan; and there is still a Quant shop in Manhattan, selling cosmetics, leather goods, T-shirts and jewellery.

Paul Smith

The story of the contemporary fashion designer Paul Smith illustrates a number of the same points, but here we have someone who needed substantial courage, to overcome the obstacles and hurdles he faced. It is the story of a person who, once he had an idea, sought opportunities and proved he had project championing qualities. Again, though, we must ask the question – Will he be remembered more as a businessman or a designer?

When he left school, Paul Smith had no qualifications of any consequence and no plans for his future. His father was able to find him a job as a 'gofer' in a clothing warehouse in Nottingham. His interest was immediately engaged, and by the time he was twenty (in 1966) he was managing Nottingham's first boutique for a friend. Smith had helped his friend find a site, paint the shop and choose the stock – but all the time he was now dreaming of his own business. His problem – he had no money. He had, however, got to know Douglas Hill, a local tailor, and kept telling him 'I can be a success'. Hill provided Paul Smith with his next opportunity – he offered him the use of the back room of his shop. In 1970, Paul had his own business. The room was only twelve square feet, but Smith transformed it into a small shop with its own entrance, opening it only on Fridays and Saturdays at first. He sold expensive, stylish clothes, some of which he bought from known designers and others he designed himself and had manufactured locally. He did receive both help and encouragement from his then girlfriend, a graduate in fashion design – they are still together over thirty years later. After three months, Hill increased his rent from nothing to 50 pence a week! On the other days Paul Smith started to study fashion design himself. Inside four years, the business had developed into a full shop unit which he was able to open six days a week. His reputation for unusual designs had spread, and customers were coming to Nottingham from Leeds and Manchester to buy clothes that otherwise were available only in London.

Borrowing £3000 from Douglas Hill, supplemented by a loan from his father, Paul Smith next moved to London to focus on designing clothes – from his bed-sit. He still had to work part-time for the International Wool Secretariat and for an Italian shirt manufacturer. His early customers were buyers from Bloomingdale's in New York City and from Seibu in Japan. Cannily negotiating a reduced and deferred rent agreement for an empty unit in Covent Garden, Smith opened his first London shop in 1979. Within one year he was employing fifteen assistants, such was his popularity. He quickly expanded into the unit next door and set up in Japan where *he is now a cult figure* with some 200 licensed outlets. His 'retail empire' has since expanded to eight London stores, together with others in Manchester, New York, Paris, Hong Kong, Singapore, Taiwan and Manilla – and, of course, Nottingham. His fabrics are mainly Italian, French and British and most of his products are manufactured in the UK. There are now eight clothing collections, supplemented by watches, shoes, spectacles, toiletries and bags. His style is *simple and practical, characterised by wit and humour . . . his clothes provide excitement in offbeat fabrics and colours.*

Despite the size and spread of the business, Smith remains the chief designer and also takes responsibility for all wholesaling and retailing activities. This is rare for a designer who has risen to this level of success. Smith comments 'I have never gone down obvious routes . . . the key [to my success] has been in exploring alternative routes that no one else has thought of'. His story reflects focus, dedication, persistence and courage. He has built an important network of contacts and helpers – including his girlfriend! – and in the early days he 'begged and borrowed' the resources he needed to start and expand.

Sarah Doukas

Another important element of the fashion industry is modelling. In fifteen years Sarah Doukas would build the Storm Model Agency from nothing to 30 employees, 350 models and a turnover of £75 million. Her leading models include Kate Moss, Sophie Dahl, Elle Macpherson and Eva Herzigova. Storm is not the biggest or the most profitable but it is recognised as *visible, idiosyncratic and entrepreneurial*. Doukas was the eldest of three children; their father was a successful gynaecologist. Her younger brother, Simon Chambers, works with her in the business; their sister, Emma Chambers, is an actress who has appeared in 'The Vicar of Dibley' and the film 'Notting Hill'.

Doukas attended public schools, but she was never *outstanding academically* and she left without taking her A levels. She worked in Kensington Market and as a part-time model before marrying the American lead singer of a rock band. After spending time 'on the road' with her husband and daughter – who also now works for Storm – she returned to London and started work in a model agency. Eventually she set up on her own, encouraged by her second husband. This was in 1987 and she was thirty-three years old. Having discovered Kate Moss, then aged fourteen, in a transit lounge in New York, Doukas realised the value of *scouring streets and airports looking for fresh talent*.

Doukas needed to raise external capital to start the business and she received backing from Richard Branson – she had known his sister from her schooldays. She had already been turned down by pop musician, Miles Copeland, who she thought *would want less equity than Branson*. In 2002 she was able to buy Branson out. Her brother, eight years younger and with a short career in merchant banking after university, joined her and he *handles the money side of the business*.

Model agencies act as managers, arrangers, agents and confidantes for their models, many of whom start when they are very young and potentially vulnerable. Doukas was always *determined to try and protect them from the more exploitative, dark side of the industry*. She builds work portfolios for the models, finding and paying suitable photographers – and then seeks to find the right opportunities for them. Her key talents are her drive and determination together with her natural ability to relate to the models. She nurtures and enables them. Apparently she does not see herself as ambitious, but those close to her believe she is. Her credo is 'You are going to meet with rejection . . . you deal with it . . . you move on . . . you keep pushing.'

Gilbert Tregano

Entrepreneur Gilbert Tregano developed Club Méditerranée to be *an organized melange of hedonism and back to nature*. Club Med was originally founded in France in 1950 by Gérard Blitz as a non-profit camping organisation – Trigano supplied the tents.

He saw the real opportunity, and under him Club Med grew unchallenged in its niche for over thirty years, pioneering the all-inclusive holiday and featuring *beautiful people playing all sorts of sports, white sand beaches, azure sky and sea, Polynesian thatched huts, free and flowing wine at meals, simple yet superb food* (Economist, 12 July 1986).

By the mid-1980s, however, occupancy rates had fallen, and profits declined and then stagnated. While the underlying concept was still sound, people's tastes were changing – and Trigano had 'taken his eye off the ball'. Holidaymakers increasingly sought higher-quality facilities than the straw huts provided. Many Americans wanted televisions and telephones – yet *it was the absence of these which had helped make Club Med unique*. Building on the original concept and strategy, Club Med now developed new products in order to better satisfy selected audiences around the world. In addition to the traditional villages, where in some cases straw huts were replaced by bungalows, there were now both cheaper, half-board holidays available in newly acquired hotels and villages, and more expensive properties with superior facilities. This latter development was pioneered at Opio, near Cannes, which opened in 1989. Opio was built with expensive rooms with facilities, and, unusually, was open twelve months of the year. The international conference trade was being targeted. Attempts were also made to attract more American visitors, but there was always some scepticism. Americans are more puritanical in their tastes and expectations, and *Club Med's sexy image* has not proved as successful in the USA.

In 1993, Gilbert, then aged seventy-two, partially retired and was succeeded by his son, Serge, who also stepped down in 1997, after they had both failed to properly turn the organisation around. Profits had in fact turned to losses, and the need for stronger management had been acknowledged. Smart cards replaced beads which were used as currency in the villages; a cruise ship was sold, along with the budget villages; the other villages were systematically improved – and prices reduced. Phillippe Bourguignon, recruited from Euro Disney began to restore Club Med's lost fortunes – but it was not to last. His decision to diversify into gyms and leisure centres was not popular with some leading shareholders and he too resigned in 2002 as the company slipped back into losses.

There can be few better-loved children's characters than Thomas the Tank Engine, created originally by the Reverend W. Awdry in his spare time. As well as this series of illustrated books for children, Awdry also wrote serious, adult books on steam railways. Thanks to an entrepreneur who saw the real opportunity – and was determined to pursue her ideas when even Awdry himself was sceptical – Thomas' popularity continues through television, advertising and licensing deals.

Britt Allcroft

The entrepreneur in question, Britt Allcroft, a producer of television programmes, had been to the same school at the same time as Anita Roddick. She had always had a passion for story-telling. In her younger days she had written several short stories, but had never been published. Instead she had found her way into television, and in 1978 she was making a film about the British passion for steam engines. Awdry was invited to appear in the film; he agreed, but inclement weather held up the project for several days. Awdry and Allcroft spend two days talking to each other. Although others had tried unsuccessfully to animate Awdry's characters – essentially a fleet of steam engines with distinctive faces and personalities – Britt Allcroft became determined to succeed where others had failed. Together with her business partner, who at the time was her husband, she approached venture capitalists, but the general reaction was that the time for Thomas had passed. Eventually a bank loan from Barclays – supplemented by a second mortgage – allowed her to agree a licensing deal with publishers Reed Elsevier, who owned the master rights to the character, and make her first film – which was broadcast on network television in 1984. Supported by a range of toys and clothing, the film was an instant success.

Her business now grew rapidly. More films were completed, with ex-Beatle Ringo Starr doing the narrating, the books were all reissued and character merchandising mushroomed. The films found an audience in forty-three countries, including America – where, for political correctness, the Fat Controller was renamed Sir Topham Hat! When Britt Allcroft's company went public in 1996, it was valued at £31 million. In 1998 she posted a profit of £3 million, roughly 10 per cent of this coming from the films and 90 per cent from merchandising. 1800 different items – books, videos, toys, clothes, bags, party supplies, bakewear, computer games, puzzles, models and carpets – were being manufactured by 400 sub-licensees. Thomas himself had become the seventh most valuable toy brand in America.

In 1997, Britt Allcroft had also acquired the worldwide rights to another past-glory character, Captain Pugwash, for £1.5 million and had set about resurrecting a programme which had first appeared on television in 1957 and disappeared in 1975. In the following year she bought all the rights to Thomas from Reed Elsevier (for £13.5 million) and no longer had to pay an annual license fee. In 1999 Britt Allcroft formed an alliance with the two venture capital businesses which owned the rights to Sooty, a hugely popular puppet character since its creation by Harry Corbett in 1952. Allcroft would merchandise the characters around the world and receive a management fee.

Allcroft now had three hugely valuable characters for pre-school children and she set about acquiring others that would appeal to older children. She acquired the TV programme Art Attack and then she bought Guinness World Records.

Britt Allcroft stepped down from the Board of the business she founded in September 2002 and moved to Los Angeles, where she would provide creative television and film inputs from their American office. The business was renamed Gullane Entertainment.

Allcroft sums up her courage, focus and dedication with the following comment 'You need courage when people tell you you are off your head . . . Thomas is much more than just a steam train having adventures – it is a way of life for me'. It is also clear that her motivation and self-assurance (her ego) have made her very determined.

Anne Wood

Related, but quite different, are the Teletubbies – the first ever children's television programmes to be targeted directly at two- and three-year-olds. The opportunity lay in the reality that children watch television from a very early age – yet nobody was really thinking of them as viewers. Ironically, and despite the obvious success, nobody was then tracking how many people actually watched the programmes – UK audience research ignored anyone under four years of age! The Teletubbies programmes are popular and successful because they creatively combine fun and entertainment with the serious tasks of nourishing young children's thinking skills, teaching them to listen, helping arouse their curiosity and developing their imagination. They were made for the BBC by Ragdoll Productions, founded in 1984 by Anne Wood, a 'reluctant entrepreneur'.

A mother of two, and originally a teacher, Anne Wood was working on children's programmes for TVam – for whom she created the infamous Roland Rat – when she was sacked. She was then in her forties and spent two years failing to find another job. *Financial necessity forced me to set up my own production company.* In fifteen years Anne Wood accumulated a personal fortune of £55 million and established a £20-million-per-year business. The Teletubbies are popular around the world, and merchandising naturally accompanies the programmes. In the Millennium Dome, the four characters were described as *one of Britain's greatest industrial achievements.*

This is the story of a creative person who saw an opportunity – or gap in the market – that others were simply failing to realise was there and found a way of filling the gap. Anne Wood attributes her success to her ability to *find my way back to how it felt to be a three year old and perceive the world from that standpoint.* She thus has the ability to be close to her customers.

Thomas Kincade

Little known outside his native America, Thomas Kincade – known as 'the painter of light' – is America's most-collected living artist. Kincade paints a mixture of old buildings and landscapes and blends summer daylight scenes with winter snows and evening darkness. He gives his work a historical perspective by using old cars and horse-drawn carts. His paintings can sometimes be bought as originals, but most sales are limited editions and lithographic copies. They are mainly available from several specialist Thomas Kincade Galleries, and they have been made affordable for the less-wealthy enthusiast as well as the wealthy collector. His work is also available in the form of Christmas and gift cards, cookie tins, calendars, books and mugs. The Thomas Kincade Collectors' Society is carefully engineered to encourage people to own more than one painting or print. In other words, Kincade is a popular artist who has turned himself into a very lucrative business by successfully exploiting the marketing opportunities which have not been available to earlier painters. A deeply religious family man, Kincade *credits God for both the ability and the inspiration to create his paintings.*

Thomas Mangelsen

The Kincade strategy is certainly not unique to him. It has also been adopted by Thomas Mangelsen, one of the world's most talented nature photographers. Trained in wildlife biology, Mangelsen began filming wildlife in northern North America over twenty years ago, spending time in both winter and summer in Alaska, Yukon and the Hudson Bay Area. His initial subject was birds, but he later chose to specialise in polar bears. His first published collection, *Images of Nature*, was very successful, and when he followed up with *Polar Dance* (a unique collection of polar bear images) in 1996 he had accumulated over 85 000 pictures of bears and other Arctic wildlife. His work has been exhibited in galleries and museums, and he has accepted commissions from various magazines, including National Geographic. Like Kincade, Mangelsen has turned himself into a prosperous businessman. He has opened a number of Images of Nature Galleries which sell his photographs as framed and unframed, limited and unlimited editions – in various sizes from gift-card to large wall-size. Selected images are also available as CD-ROMs.

Kincade and Mangelsen are clearly artistic creative entrepreneurs because they have successfully linked art and business. Later in the chapter we look at one leading contemporary artist and four legendary painters from the Middle Ages to see if we can trace entrepreneur character themes in the ways they have exploited their talents and blended imagination with superior technical skills.

Music and entertainment entrepreneurs

Andrew Lloyd Webber

Lord Andrew Lloyd Webber is easily Britain's most successful modern composer – in a world where popular music lyrics are increasingly being viewed as the contemporary equivalent of the poetry of old. He has composed the music for a series of hugely successful stage musicals, including Joseph and the Amazing Technicolour Dreamcoat, Jesus Christ Superstar, Cats, Evita, Starlight Express and Phantom of the Opera. He has also written a more classical Requiem. He is the only composer to have ever had three musicals running simultaneously in both London and New York. Millions of people around the world have seen his shows and listened to his music – which has been recorded by the world's leading performers. He has built both aesthetic and financial capital by providing people with entertainment and enjoyment.

He was born in 1948 and has been described as *small, dark, intense and nerdish*. Like his brother, the cellist Julian Lloyd Webber, he has been a natural musician all his life. They inherited their musical talent from their father. Andrew was seventeen when he started looking for a *with-it writer of lyrics* to work as his partner, and he was contacted by Tim Rice. A friendship of opposites developed – Rice was older and more outgoing. The two experimented with a number of projects before writing Joseph for a local boys' school concert in 1968. The performance was noticed, and its success was instant. The two young partners were soon being talked about. Although many see Jesus Christ Superstar (1971) as their best work, their real fame came later in 1976 with Evita. Before this, a musical based on the fictional character, Jeeves (more recently reworked by Lloyd Webber) was less successful. By the late 1970s there were tensions between Rice and Lloyd Webber and they chose to go their separate ways and find new partners. Tim Rice eventually switched to film scores, with which he has had a number of hits. Lloyd Webber has since worked with several other lyricists, most notably Don Black and Charles Hart, who individually and as a pair have written the words for Phantom (Hart), Song and Dance (Black) and Aspects of Love (in partnership). He has demonstrated expertise in finding strong, suitable partners, but although his most recent projects have been successful, his earlier musicals have generally enjoyed greater popularity.

Lloyd Webber set up a public company, The Really Useful Group, as an umbrella organisation for his various activities. The company has staged his shows and other shows, and is also involved in music and book publishing, CD, television and video production. It also owns theatres. Similar to Richard Branson, Lloyd Webber later bought back the company from its various shareholders, and then sold a 30 per cent stake to PolyGram. In 1999 he regained total control again by acquiring this 30 per cent stake from Seagram, who in turn had acquired PolyGram.

It is interesting to debate whether composers such as Andrew Lloyd Webber should be termed entrepreneurs because they are able to exploit their natural talents – but there can be no question that those people who successfully produce and stage the musical shows are entrepreneurs. They see an opportunity for the work in question and they champion the project.

Cameron Mackintosh

Sir Cameron Mackintosh is *King of the stage* and one of the most important influences in British and American theatres. Taken to the theatre at the age of eight, he decided there and then that he wanted to produce musicals – he had experienced his trigger, and as he grew older he dedicated himself to making it happen. Working his way through provincial theatres, he finally made it to London's West End with a production of Anything Goes when he was twenty-two. It lasted just two weeks, but he persisted and returned. In the 1970s his major achievements were with innovative new productions of Oliver!, My Fair Lady and Oklahoma. He was even more successful with ones he helped create from scratch in the 1980s. In 1981 he collaborated with Andrew Lloyd Webber to stage Cats, and he followed this with Phantom of the Opera and then Les Misérables. Again we can see evidence of focus, dedication, activation, creativity, opportunity, benefit orientation and team building – all key entrepreneur character themes. Singer Michael Ball has commented that he has an instinctive appreciation of what audiences like, that he can spot talented performers and know exactly which role they are suited for.

Lew Grade

Lord Lew Grade was known as *Mr Showbusiness* for his contribution to films, television and the theatre. One of his greatest achievements was an ability to understand the *preferences of the man in the street*. He understood his customers. Originally a dancer, but never a star, he became a theatrical agent before joining commercial television in its infancy. *The stars*, he once said, *keep 90% of my money* – he was profit-oriented.

He was one of three brothers who were born in Odessa – he in 1906 – before the family moved to England. His brothers were also successful entrepreneurs; it was in the blood. He was nearly thirty – and dancing – when he was offered the opportunity to join a theatrical agency. He seized the chance. Eight years later, and in partnership with one of his brothers, he had his own agency. The brothers became close friends with Val Parnell, then the manager of the London Palladium, and as a result, they were always able to secure high-profile bookings for their star clients, who included Bob Hope. Sensing an opportunity, Parnell and Grade joined forces and became involved in the creation of ATV (later Central Television) in 1955. They remortgaged their houses, but succeeded in winning one of the first commercial television franchises. Their initial strategy was popular game shows and imported American action programmes – as well as the legendary Saturday Night at the London Palladium. Recruiting a strong creative team, they introduced popular series such as The Persuaders, Danger Man and Robin Hood. By the late 1960s Lew Grade was selling more programmes overseas than all the other independent television companies and the BBC put together.

Had Lord Grade retired in 1971 – when he was 65 – he would be remembered as Britain's most successful showbusiness entrepreneur. Instead he had other mountains he wished to climb. He was a habitual entrepreneur. He turned to film-making, and although he had some successes, he will always be remembered for one of the greatest and most expensive flops – Raise The Titanic. One banker commented that *it would have been cheaper to lower the Atlantic.* The 1990s' success of James Cameron's Titanic makes this story seem even more ironic.

The Lord Grade story is an excellent reminder that people can learn from their experiences and from their mistakes and improve their mastery as a project champion – but seeing and exploiting winning new opportunity after winning new opportunity in an industry dictated by taste and fashion is inherently difficult.

Bob Geldof

Some entrepreneurial ventures, of course, are one-off projects. The Live Aid concert at Wembley Stadium in 1985 was just that, although others have since borrowed the idea from Bob Geldof. An Irish singer with the Boomtown Rats, and possessing a questionable reputation, Geldof would not have been seen as a natural entrepreneur – but he saw an opportunity to use pop music as a vehicle to raise money to help famine-stricken countries in Africa. His trigger had been a television news documentary. He channelled his energy into making it happen, using his network of contacts. Fellow stars appeared without charging a fee. The media were quickly engaged in helping publicise the innovative project which caught the imagination of the public. 70 000 paid to attend the concert itself, and 1.4 billion viewers saw it on television in 170 different countries. £70 million was raised and spent.

Harvey Goldsmith

One of Bob Geldof's team for Live Aid was the impresario Harvey Goldsmith, who project-managed the actual concert event. Goldsmith's rise to fame and fortune had begun as a student at Brighton Polytechnic, where he booked bands for student dances to help pay his way. During the 1960s, 1970s and 1980s he promoted the UK tours of several leading American artists and became the *biggest impresario of the age*. He later diversified into classical music and brought Pavarotti to Hyde Park. Concert promotion is, however, a low-margin business – the stars themselves pocket most of the proceeds – and so there is little room for error. Mistakes may not be forgiven. In 1999, Harvey Goldsmith's business went into receivership – *he had tried to change with the times but had not quite managed it*. The 'straw that broke the camel's back' was his Total Eclipse Festival in Cornwall, which like the eclipse itself, failed to attract the anticipated audience.

George Lucas

If people were reluctant to brave the West Country traffic jams to get a view of the total eclipse of the sun, they were certainly not reticent about the fourth and fifth Star Wars movies. They had, after all, been waiting sixteen years. The success of the Star Wars phenomenon is down to creator, writer, film director and entrepreneur, George Lucas.

Lucas was born in California in 1944, and grew up a typical teenager of that time. He was hooked on adventure television and spent time cruising in his car. He drifted. His *perspective on life changed* when he was involved in a freak car accident in 1962. He survived because his seat belt snapped. This experience made him determined to do something with his life – he had experienced his trigger. He chose to study film at the University of Southern California, where he won a major award for a short film. In turn this won him a scholarship with Warner Brothers, and through this he met Francis Coppola. The two decided to make a movie together; it was named THX-1138 and was an extended version of Lucas's award-winning short film. The film was popular with audiences but not critics and the two separated. Whilst Coppola began his Godfather trilogy, Lucas set about raising money to make American Graffiti, which starred Harrison Ford. Premiered in 1973, it was another financial success and it provided him with the funds to launch his Star Wars project, which had been inspired by Flash Gordon. In the next few years, and together with Harrison Ford, he made three Star Wars films and three Indiana Jones films and *rewrote box office records*. Although the Star Wars films were released by Twentieth Century Fox, Lucas has always retained the rights and ownership of merchandising licenses. He also controls the distribution of the films. Lucas is, quite clearly, both an opportunity-spotter and a project champion.

We complete this section with two more individual entrepreneurs who have found winning personal opportunities in the fickle and complex world of entertainment – but are both controversial characters.

Michael Flatley

Michael Flatley has been christened 'Lord of the Dance' and cynics have said he would only appear at the biggest venues because the others are *too small to accommodate his ego*. Flatley counters that he is merely self-confident. He was a modestly successful Irish dancer in America when he was recruited to choreograph Riverdance to fill the interval at the Eurovision Song Contest in Dublin in 1994. A window of opportunity had been opened for him. The short sequence was hugely popular and quickly spawned a full-length production. After successful performances in Dublin and London, Flatley increased his personal demands for future appearances, but negotiations with the promoters broke down. Flatley was sacked and his understudy took over at short notice; the popularity of Riverdance – The Show was largely unaffected.

Believing in his own ability, and determined to exploit the still-open window of opportunity, Flatley immediately set about devising a new Irish dance show, which he intended should be more ambitious than Riverdance. He recruited a strong management, musical and choreographic team – and contacted promoter Harvey Goldsmith. He was investing his reputation as well as his savings – he had to succeed. The team work intensely and all hours to create the new show, which Flatley called Lord of the Dance. Publicity was easy, as the media were anxious to compare the relative merits of the two competing shows. The new show was another instant success, capitalising on the new-found popularity of traditional Irish music and dance. Shortly after it opened, Flatley did not appear personally in a number of the shows because of torn leg muscles. Once his understudy began to receive standing ovations for every performance, Flatley fought hard to regain his fitness! Lord of the Dance has been successful; at the same time Riverdance – the show has filled theatres and sold successfully in video format.

In Michael Flatley we can see a focused and determined entrepreneur in action. We see clear evidence of the ego, opportunity, urgency, activating, creativity, expertise and team-building character themes.

Chris Evans

The previous owner of Virgin Radio, Chris Evans, is another determined individualist who has been described as *utterly single-minded*. Brought up on a council estate in Warrington, Evans organised a squad of delivery boys for his local newsagent and an unofficial school tuck shop. He was devastated when his father died of cancer when he was fourteen years old. His ego and attitude are summarised in the following comment 'I believe absolutely in one man having one vision for the way something should be done'. Following a spell as a Tarzanogram in Manchester, he secured minor opportunities on local radio stations before eventually becoming a regular morning disc jockey on BBC Radio One. Invariably controversial, he walked out when he was refused a four-mornings contract – he wanted Fridays off so that he would have more time to prepare for his Friday evening television show on Channel Four.

Recognising his public popularity and attraction to the media, Richard Branson offered him the prime morning slot on Virgin Radio, where he quickly increased the number of listeners from 1.8 to 2.6 million – helped in part by the publicity generated by his move. Once he realised Branson was willing to sell Virgin Radio, in true entrepreneurial fashion, he used his show to appeal for financial support to buy it. Allegedly an act of impulse, Evans is normally perceived to be someone who knows exactly what he is doing. He did succeed in persuading Branson to sell the station to him rather than to Capital Radio – and he was able to raise £85 million to secure the acquisition. Branson retained a 20 per cent stake in Evans' personal holding company, Ginger Media. Virgin Radio was later sold to the Scottish Media Group (SMG).

Without question, Evans possesses many strong entrepreneur character themes – he also has characteristics which work against him. *People don't like Evans because he's about changing everything . . . [yet] his greatest gift is that he wants to do everything differently, and better, all the time.* He is a driven man and an innovator, *never satisfied with himself or other people's performances.* He has always been seen as a control freak, and he is prone to use his media access to air personal views and grievances. He was fined by the Radio Authority for giving out private mobile phone numbers on the air and he once commented that *half the BBC's staff are on drugs.* He was thwarted in a bid to buy and take over a daily newspaper, the Star, when the vendor pulled out. It was intimated that Branson was less than happy at the time, fearing that a link between Virgin Radio and a perceived downmarket tabloid newspaper might tarnish his own personal image. In 2001 Evans was sacked from Virgin Radio by its new owners – he had been drinking heavily and failed to turn up for work. Evans sued for wrongful dismissal; SMG counter-sued for breach of contract. Evans lost the court action and had to pay both damages and costs. The judge, when summing up, used the following phrases to describe Evans . . . *management nightmare . . . temperament of a prima donna . . . lied when it suited his purposes.*

If we return to our talent–temperament–technique triangle, we can see here evidence of an extremely strong temperament that can exploit natural talents but which, in the end, is so dominant that it is destructive.

Artists, musicians and architects

The commercial opportunities that have been available to artists and musicians in the twentieth century are, of course, markedly different from those that were available to artists, painters and composers in the past. Although we do not naturally think of great artists as entrepreneurs, the ability of some of them to exploit the far more limited opportunities that were available to them – in order that they might utilise and exploit their natural gifts and talents – is testimony to the fact that they did possess a number of critically important entrepreneur character themes. Typically they would have to look for commissions and patrons – which demanded networking skills. The legacy of the great artists is their work, which has endured and sells for huge sums of money, even if they themselves failed to accumulate significant wealth when they were alive – although some of them did become wealthy. Their creations, simply, help us to see things differently. Particularly relevant in this context are many Renaissance artists who symbolically interpreted important religious themes and gave them meaning. In reality, many of them had to overcome a wide range of obstacles, especially the envy and hostility of their rivals, in order to pursue and complete their work – indicating the presence of ego, dedication and courage. Parental position and connections mattered far more than they do today, of course. To succeed, they had to have 'know-how and know-who' and know where they could obtain patronage and resources.

Michelangelo Buonarotti

Michelangelo Buonarotti was *a genius who few have challenged since*. He succeeded as a sculptor, an artist, an architect and a poet, and he became a legend in his own lifetime. *He raised the status of artists by his achievements.* He was born in Italy in 1475 and lived until 1564, a long and productive life. By the age of thirteen he was apprenticed to a master sculptor, where he came under the influence and patronage of the de Medici's. The Medici family had earned enormous financial wealth from trading, which they used to acquire power, to influence and support the Papal Monarchy and other regional Dukes and to *commission great art as an expression of their wealth and status in the world . . . the whole economy revolved around them.* Michelangelo's Statue of David was commissioned in 1501 by the new Republic of Florence. The marble block he used had been reserved for this purpose since 1462. The work took three years and established him as a great sculptor. In 1508 Pope Julius II brought him to Rome to paint the ceiling of the Sistine Chapel. He accepted the commission, but, bravely and very unusually, questioned the Pope's design. In the end, the imagery was Michelangelo's and it was quite different from that which Julius II had planned. It took Michelangelo four years of intense, dedicated, focused effort, for throughout he worked largely unaided by anyone. It was a truly momentous and creative achievement and reflected enormous self-belief and ego. After 1513, the new Medici Pope, Leo X, sent Michelangelo back to Florence where he mainly worked as an architect and sculptor. In the next decade, he built the Medici Chapel in San Lorenzo and the Laurentian Library. Eventually he was to return to Rome as chief architect for St Peter's.

Leonardo da Vinci

Whilst we can readily see both the opportunity-spotter and project champion in Michelangelo, the same cannot be said of his famous contemporary, Leonardo da Vinci, who was *not noted for completing all his ideas.* Some great artists are more entrepreneurial than others. Leonardo, born in 1452, was the illegitimate son of a lawyer, and through his family he too was able to gain the patronage of the de Medici's. Commissioned by the Duke of Milan (in 1497) he painted The Last Supper; the Mona Lisa followed in 1500 after Milan had fallen to the French. Eventually he would remove to France *to investigate the nature of the world around him.* He believed an artist should be a *contemplative and creative thinker, similar to a saint or philosopher.* He was certainly a man of ideas and very innovative; he was interested in aerodynamics and flying, hydraulics and canal building, astronomy and human anatomy. At one stage in his life he was employed as a military engineer. He left a legacy of 19 notebooks and 3500 pages of sketches and notes on various topics. Included was da Vinci's conceptual diagram for the modern helicopter. Perhaps, da Vinci might be better described as an artist and an inventor rather than an entrepreneur.

El Greco

Another Renaissance painter was the religious artist, El Greco, who was born in Crete in 1541 and who, after some time in Italy, settled in Spain. *Arrogant and uncompromising, proudly aware of his own merits and originality amongst an army of imitators, El Greco gave offence more than once . . . he made disobliging comments on [the paintings of] Michelangelo.* Using contacts he had made in Rome, El Greco was commissioned to paint for the cathedral in Toledo, and from this base he set out to secure Royal patronage. However, King Philip II simply did not like the result of the work he commissioned, and, although it was paid for, the painting was not hung. A resourceful El Greco turned instead to the wealthy people of Toledo. His son became his main collaborator and *his last contracts always provided for assistance with the work.* Typically he would start a work and then others would complete it. There were many stories of his impropriety in his use of assistants, enterprising though it was.

El Greco was a great and talented artist – he also *let it be known that there was nothing in the world superior to his paintings* – but he illustrated the 'shadow side' of entrepreneurship. He earned a great deal of money, but *spent extensively and excessively on maintaining his household.* He died in 1614 with many unpaid debts and he left 200 paintings which had all been commissioned and started but which needed completing.

Diego Velázquez

Diego Velázquez was entrepreneurial in yet another way. Born of nobility in Seville in 1599, he has been described as *one of the greatest painters of all time.* Through family contacts he was accepted at Court and was the established Royal painter for thirty-seven of his sixty-one years. Moreover he persuaded King Philip IV to make him chief buyer of paintings. For this he was paid a retainer and a travel allowance – he was thus able to spend time in Italy and elsewhere and observe at close hand the style and approach of his renowned contemporaries. He was an early benchmarker. He became a rich man in his lifetime, although he was not personally prolific. After his death – and the protection of the Royal family – he was *pursued by envy.*

David Hockney

Yorkshire-born David Hockney is Britain's most successful living artist. *He is one of the only British artists this [twentieth] century to have become internationally renowned in the same way as pop and film stars.* He is a millionaire. In true entrepreneurial fashion he too has found lucrative commercial opportunities for exploiting his talent – but he is different in both style and strategy from the American artist, Thomas Kincade, who we discussed earlier. Born in Bradford, Hockney was encouraged to exploit his natural talents by his parents, *from whom he inherited energy and imagination.* His father was seen by some as eccentric; he was certainly idiosyncratic and enterprising. He notably once sold a billiards table by placing a newspaper advertisement and using the telephone number of a nearby public call box. He sat outside the box for hours waiting for a potential buyer.

Although some artists only become truly famous after their deaths, Hockney was well known by the time he was twenty-five. He had been noticed for work he submitted to the 1962 Young Contemporaries Exhibition, and his paintings began to sell in London. Appreciating the value of publicity and notoriety, he immediately bleached his hair and took to wearing gold lamé jackets and large spectacles. Magazine articles made him into a celebrity figure. He was soon to move to Los Angeles where he has lived for over thirty years. However, as we saw in the Interlude before Chapter 7, the largest collection of his work is in Saltaire, near Bradford, the town built in the nineteenth century by philanthropic mill owner, Titus Salt, as the *perfect industrial community* with houses, schools and hospitals built specifically for the mill workers. Hockney's early work featured people, sometimes in portrait form, more often in simple domestic settings – but for many years he has diverted his attention to experiments with other art forms. He has produced photo-collages by mounting several dozen small – and related – photographs to create a large image, and also experimented with fax and photocopier machines to produce a different finished image. He has earned a substantial income from designing opera stage sets, and he has generally produced the posters for promoting his own exhibitions.

In 2001 Hockney published a remarkable book – from which a television programme was made – on mediaeval artists. He had conducted extensive research to show how the 'old masters' had used optics, specifically mirrors and lenses, to project images and thus make tracings of their subjects, rather than simply paint onto a blank canvas. His experiments demonstrated how artists such as Van Eyck, Caravaggio and Velázquez had been able to reproduce incredibly fine details in their work. He commented 'this does not diminish their skill . . . it reveals their technical expertise and creativity as being even more extraordinary'.

David Hockey is wealthy and famous because he has proved himself able to exploit a number of artistic, marketing and commercial opportunities that have been available to him and thus manage both his prolific output and his natural talent. In this way he has successfully blended the project champion role with that of the opportunity-spotter.

We saw earlier how Andrew Lloyd Webber is a very wealthy modern composer. He has produced some extremely popular musicals and overcome a number of disappointments, systematically teaming up with a series of talented partners. He understands contemporary taste for musical theatre and, showing great creativity and innovation, he has found and exploited a series of opportunities. It is not difficult to accept that he is an entrepreneur. But was *the greatest composer who ever lived* – Wolfgang Mozart – also an entrepreneur? Certainly the same commercial and marketing opportunities were not available to him! Neither was the technology and computer software which is available to help modern composers. Arguably Mozart had a number of entrepreneur qualities, such as focus, dedication, activation, determination, creativity and innovation – but, try as he did, he was never able to completely overcome the obstacles he faced. *A kind and gentle man, he was never spoilt by his genius* – but, instead of being rewarded in his lifetime for his outstanding ability, he was affected by the envy of his rivals.

Mozart

Mozart was born in 1756 in Salzburg. His father was a violin teacher and a musician at the Court of the Prince-Archbishop. He was a genius – *music came to Wolfgang Mozart as natural as did breathing* – and as a result he was denied a normal childhood. He was playing the harpsichord by ear at the age of three; he was taught musical theory and composition by his father, who was determined to exploit his talent. His father was loving but tyrannical, and a major influence for a number of years. At the age of six – a child prodigy – he was playing the concert platforms in the leading European cities – his own compositions as well as the work of others.

In his early teens he was given the post of Concert Master for the Archbishop of Salzburg – *for a pittance of a salary*. He was never offered a permanent position in a leading European Court, the opportunity his father dreamed of securing for him.

Already jealous rivals were preventing his music being played in Vienna. He was criticised and dismissed by several contemporary musicians in Rome and Paris on the grounds of his age and immaturity. Though his concert performances and his music continued to receive audience acclaim, at this time artistic success was no guarantee of financial wealth. He eventually settled in Vienna after he married, but events continued to work against him. He was an active freemason and seen by some to be frequenting the wrong social circles; he championed social causes, which also cost him friends amongst the aristocracy. But he continued to receive commissions from counts, merchants, aristocrats and opera-goers – and the music flowed. *No other composer has been able to equal his range and variety of output.* When Austria went to war with Turkey in 1788, many aristocrats left Vienna and a number of financial opportunities left with them.

Ironically, other contemporaries, who did not provoke the same envy and jealousy, were more successful – Haydn in particular. Haydn and Mozart, however, were firm friends and Haydn actively promoted Mozart's work. Mozart's greatest compositions came in his later years – he died in 1791 at the age of thirty-five. Some have speculated that he was poisoned, but this has never been proved. Between 1786 and 1790 he wrote four outstanding operas – The Marriage of Figaro, Don Giovanni, The Magic Flute and Cosi Fan Tutte. They were enormously popular when they were performed. At this time he was also writing his best-known symphonies and a series of concertos for solo instruments. *He pushed every instrument to its limit.* Yet, and only in part because he liked to live comfortably, Mozart found himself having to beg for financial help from his friends. Freelance musicians without court appointments did not become rich, however successful and acclaimed their work. He died a pauper, still composing his Requiem, and mouthing the words to his sister-in-law from his death bed. The Requiem had been commissioned anonymously by a wealthy count, who later claimed he had composed the work himself.

With Mozart, then, we have an entrepreneurial paradox. In the context of his music, he was both a genius and an entrepreneur. He pushed out the boundaries and was creative at a level others will only ever dream of attaining. His work remains popular and unrivalled, except perhaps by Beethoven. Various polls of classical music enthusiasts have confirmed that both experts and listeners consider him to have been the greatest composer who has ever lived. Although recognised by some in his life, his genius attracted enemies who were able to deny him key opportunities. If financial reward was of great significance to him, partly as a measure of his success, he would surely have been personally disappointed and seen by others as an under-achiever. Had he not had a number of entrepreneur character themes, though, he may never have left the legacy he did.

Frank Gehry

The new Guggenheim Museum was opened in 1997 in Bilbao in Northern Spain. Described as *one of the century's greatest buildings* – it blends titanium and stone in a *collision of forms* – it soon attracted one million visitors a year. *It has transformed a city once known mainly for industrial decline and Basque terrorism into a cultural landmark.* It did for Bilbao what the Opera House had earlier done for Sydney, and it thus provided an important route to urban regeneration. Arguably its American architect, Frank Gehry, is an entrepreneur – for he 'habitually creates and innovates to build something of recognised value'. Now, over seventy years old, and sometimes seen as a controversial and artistic architect, Gehry has always experimented. *He takes chances, he pushes boundaries beyond previous limits. There are times when he misses the mark and times when he alters everyone else's vision.* Much of his work has been inspired by the motion of fish. His imitators *are legion.* Interestingly the Guggenheim success won Gehry the commission for a new Management School along similar lines at Case Western Reserve University in Cleveland, Ohio. The University hopes that *creative architecture will inspire the imagination of business students.* Another important Gehry building is the Walt Disney Concert Hall in central Los Angeles, where again it is hoped this can have something of a transformational impact upon a crime-ridden inner city area.

In this chapter we have told the story of a wide range of creative entrepreneurs, many of whom have had very marked effects on our lives – and in quite different ways. Some of them have created great works of music and art which have 'stood [and will stand] the test of time' whilst others have used creative design to build significant businesses. We have seen how entrepreneurs are present in the world of entertainment, using their entrepreneur character themes to build financial wealth around enjoyment and pleasure. At the same time we have seen how some entrepreneurs also possess certain character themes which mean there is a shadow side to their activities and personality. With the ones featured in this chapter, this element has merely qualified their achievements; in the next chapter we consider those entrepreneurs whose darker side brings more damaging results. We see how capital can be destroyed as well as built.

References

Jensen, R. (1999). *The Dream Society.* McGraw-Hill.
Ludwig, A.M. (1995). *The Price of Greatness – Resolving the Creativity and Madness Controversy.* Guildford Press.

Further Readings

Some of the Barnum material has been sourced from:
Vitale, J. (1998). *There's A Customer Born Every Minute – P T Barnum's Secrets of Business Success,* AMACOM.
The Storm material has been summarised from:
Davidson, A. (2002). The storm forecast, *Financial Times,* 18 May.

9 Entrepreneurs in the shadows

In this chapter we switch emphasis from the positive to the potentially negative side of entrepreneurship. Inevitably, amongst the most notorious stories of famous entrepreneurs, we find a limited percentage who have either failed or who have destroyed capital which was important to others. Some reflect errors of strategic judgment while others reflect over-ambition – promises that were realistically always too good to be true. Some of these stories, of course, are of criminal behaviour. Some of the entrepreneurs we feature were always in the shadows; others ended up there for a variety of reasons. There is an important message underpinning this chapter – the more we relax the controls on entrepreneurs, in order to encourage more entrepreneurial behaviour, the greater the potential for the shadow side of entrepreneurship to prosper.

So far in this book we have extolled the virtues of entrepreneurship, suggested we need more entrepreneurs in all walks of life and used a wide range of examples to support our case. We have described our so-called 'well of talent' and argued that we must learn how we might better tap the rich seam of entrepreneurial talent that lies hidden. But, once we tap the seam we must also be able to control the flow. We cannot sensibly give every entrepreneur a totally 'free rein'. In some ways, this is a paradox, because entrepreneurship is encouraged by relaxing controls and constraints. Fewer regulations, less 'red tape', easier access to finance and so on, are the accepted way forward. Yet these are the very constraints which regulate against excess by people whose ethics or honesty can be called into question. Metaphorically this is like an oil well – once the seam is found, the oil gushes up in free flow and the well must be capped to regulate the flow and exploit the yield most effectively.

Simply, there is a shadow side to entrepreneurship. In its extreme form it destroys capital as well as creating it. Some entrepreneurs direct their efforts to their own personal benefits at the expense of others, who, as a result, suffer in some way. It is, of course, no coincidence that, for many people, the term 'entrepreneur' is synonymous with fictional characters like Arthur Daley and Derek Trotter – people we might call 'likeable rogues', 'wide-boys' or 'wheeler-dealers'. We read about property developers who appear to disregard the concerns of environmentalists and preservationists. We hear of 'cowboy' tradesmen, who target vulnerable old people, take their money and fail to deliver an acceptable product or service in return. There has been no shortage of bogus mail order businesses. The opportunities are always there for the people determined to find them – but that is no excuse for making it easy.

In addition, entrepreneurial journalists have been known to destroy people's lives with the way they have handled sensitive material. Terrorist bombers are entrepreneurs who destroy social and aesthetic capital at the same time. In Summer 2003 a British entrepreneur and arms dealer was arrested in America and charged with arranging the import of a surface-to-air missile from Russia – which allegedly was to be used in an attempt to bring down a commercial airliner. The organised football hooligans who can outsmart the police and engineer gang fights with local fans are proven project champions. Can we live comfortably with the entrepreneurial finance company manager in Japan who demanded that a client in arrears sell one of his eyes or kidneys in the black market in order to help pay off his debt? One important implication of this is that the whole notion of entrepreneurship needs redeeming to ensure people relate it to the beneficial financial, social, aesthetic and environmental capital it can generate.

People with the strongest entrepreneur character themes are very driven, very ambitious and very profit- or achievement-oriented. When the desire to succeed is particularly strong, these entrepreneurs may well take exceptionally high risks – which sometimes do pay off. But not always. Something as-it-were 'boils over'. In a business context the company grows too quickly and the bubble bursts when there is no spare resource capacity to deal with the inevitable setbacks or crises. This can be made worse by an unrealistically optimistic belief in one's ability to handle the crisis and a refusal to seek help. Strategic errors can be made by egotistical entrepreneurs; shortfalls can be ignored or covered up. Sometimes this is accidental, but it can be negligent and, on occasions, dishonest. Some entrepreneurs do cut corners, bend rules, behave unethically and generally 'over-step the mark'. Some are fundamentally criminal.

In this chapter we look at examples of:

- opportunist entrepreneurs who either adopt a flawed strategy or fail to deliver;
- empire-builders who grow too quickly and lose control – sometimes involving a creative cover-up strategy;
- corporate entrepreneurs – or entrepreneurial strategic leaders – whose greed and ego leads to inappropriate decisions and behaviour;
- entrepreneurs who make mistakes, or whose business fails, but who determinedly make a come-back;
- inventors who become failed entrepreneurs as they lack key project championing capabilities;
- dishonest entrepreneurs.

In the stories, we see entrepreneurs who are extremely good at publicising their activities in order to attract customers and finance, and entrepreneurs who believe their failure is not their fault. Other people, resentful of their success, have set out to destroy them. This is not uncommon in entrepreneurs and it helps explain why a number who have failed start all over again – determined not to fail a second (or even a third) time. The habitual, serial element. The real issue is whether they have been able to learn from their experiences.

It is also significant that many of our entrepreneurs 'in the shadows' have a very visible and often flamboyant lifestyle. They enjoy their wealth and they flaunt it. This is not saying, of course, that a flamboyant lifestyle is, in itself, an indication of a shady person!

We conclude the chapter with a section on criminal entrepreneurs. We have seen in earlier chapters how some individuals, with strong entrepreneurial character themes, are driven from a very young age to enterprising behaviour – such as a pocket-money business. Parental and other encouragements or discouragements affect their learning from this. Arguably, some young people with these entrepreneurial character themes who also possess particular qualities such as impulsiveness, fearlessness, aggression and/or hyperactivity may seek to develop their enterprise 'in the shadows', at the expense of others. If they succeed, and if they are not discouraged, we have our shadow entrepreneurs in the making.

Some of the stories go back several years; they have been selected because the entrepreneurs they feature are well known and often very colourful characters. The failings in these stories will have been repeated in many other less-publicised cases.

Entrepreneurs who failed

John de Lorean

The case of John de Lorean goes back some twenty years, but provides the ideal example for justifying the need to control the activities of entrepreneurs. In 1978 the UK (Labour) government was completely behind de Lorean's ambitious plan to build a radical new car in Northern Ireland. Whilst de Lorean was ultimately the architect of his own downfall, the appointed receiver to the business later commented that *a more robust project* could have succeeded. Anxious to secure the car plant for the troubled Belfast region, the government was pushed into acting quickly, arguably over-hastily, and failed to investigate all de Lorean's past business experiences. They were persuaded by his public image and salesmanship. In the event, £80 million of public money and 2600 newly created jobs were lost.

John de Lorean was born in 1925, the eldest son of a Detroit foundry worker. He obtained degrees in music, industrial engineering and business administration; his first employer was General Motors, where he rose through the ranks. By 1970 he was General Manager of GM's Chevrolet division and he was being tipped by some as a future GM President. Tall, elegant, stylish and charismatic he was *unparalleled as a salesman* and hugely popular with the company's extensive and powerful dealer network. Whilst his career progressed rapidly and seemingly trouble-free, his high-profile personal life was different. In 1969 he was divorced from his first wife and quickly re-married to the nineteen-year-old daughter of a football star. Two years later he was divorced again and was dating film stars from Hollywood. He had been attracted by the glamour of the movie industry and his position in GM allowed him to socialise accordingly. His third wife was a New York fashion model. At this time he grew his hair and took to dressing in trendy clothes, which was seen as unusual for a prominent corporate executive. His whole lifestyle was *expensive and flamboyant*.

Nevertheless, he was incredibly focused and worked long hours – and, partly for this reason, other 'skeletons in his cupboard' were largely ignored. Over a period of years he had made substantial personal investments in businesses which had all folded with acrimony and litigation. These activities, which included motor racing circuit franchising and car radiator manufacture, were related to automobiles. In 1973 he resigned from GM and announced his vision for an innovative and radical new car built in a state-of-the-art production facility. He blamed *restrictive management controls* in GM for his move. There had been a number of signals and indicators that de Lorean might be a high-risk investment for the UK government, but they were largely over-looked.

The dream car would be built of stainless steel and feature distinctive gull-wing doors, hinged at the top. There were *innovations to improve safety and driveability . . . an emphasis on style and quality . . . all at a reasonable price.* Part of its ultimate fame would come from its starring role as a time machine in the three *Back to the Future* films. John de Lorean was able to secure $175 million to finance the venture and finally chose Belfast in preference to Detroit, Puerto Rico and the Republic of Ireland – influenced by grants and a speedy decision. His outline concept was translated into a production model by Group Lotus under a sub-contract arrangement. Both John de Lorean and Colin Chapman of Lotus agreed to handle the financial arrangements through a Swiss-based third-party organisation. It later transpired that this company was in reality also a convenient vehicle for siphoning UK government funds and moving them back to the US to cover personal loans to de Lorean himself.

The deal was struck in 1978, and within two years cars were coming off the line. A 72-acre field – with two rivers running through it – had been transformed into an advanced production facility. A dealer network was in place across the key market of North America, where most of the cars were destined, and various personalities were signed up for endorsement advertising. de Lorean made things happen; but the controls were inadequate. Costs were escalating; production difficulties were emerging; de Lorean began to talk about prices 20 per cent above the original estimate. He needed more money than he had forecasted, and he began to seek funds from every source he could identify. Attempting to hide the severity of the problems, he continued to insist that the funding stream was secure. Flying across the Atlantic on Concorde on at least a weekly basis, and maintaining his expensive lifestyle, de Lorean successfully covered up the precarious state of his personal and business finances. The extra funding was never in place and the company went into receivership in 1982. The plant ultimately closed; the dream was over. Nevertheless, 8000 cars had been made and sold. Early in 1999, some 6000 of these were still on the road. Judged on the sales record after its launch, the car was clearly a success. Customers liked it and bought it. John de Lorean understood his market.

However, to compound matters further in 1982, de Lorean was charged with attempting to broker a $24 million cocaine deal in an endeavour to raise money. Whilst he was acquitted on the grounds of federal entrapment, his credibility was finally shattered. It seems an ultimate irony that de Lorean described his factory as *the world's first ethical car company* and chastised GM managers as *men of sound personal morality, but all too capable, as a group, of reaching business decisions which were irresponsible and of dubious morality.*

Freddie Laker

Freddie Laker, who became Sir Freddie in 1978, was an entrepreneur and a pioneer in the competitive international air transport industry. He was a well-quoted self-publicist whose commercial exploits brought him fame and recognition. He introduced cheap transatlantic air travel, providing travel opportunities for many people who previously had not been able to afford the fares; but his business collapsed in the early 1980s. At the time he blamed others for his demise and, whilst there is substance in his argument, the fact remains that he had personally sown the seeds of his downfall with a flawed strategy. But he would later bounce back again.

Laker was born in 1922 in Canterbury. His trigger for a life in aviation was a sight of the *Hindenberg* and a Handley-Page bi-plane flying over his house when he was still a boy. He subsequently learned to fly and served with the Air Transport Auxiliary in the Second World War. In 1953 he began his first business, Channel Air Bridge Ltd, to sell air transportation of vehicles, passengers and cargo (including live animals) on the same aircraft. He was involved in the design and development of Gatwick Airport, before he helped develop and run British United Airways in 1960. At this time BUA was the largest aircraft company in the private sector. His next venture – Laker Airways in 1966 – was a small independent company *operated on a shoestring* which offered inclusive package holidays and provided charter flights for organisations who could book all the seats on a plane and flights for tour companies who did not own their own airline. He was the first all-jet carrier in the UK. Laker's stated intention was to stay small 'If we get any bigger than six planes you can kick my arse'. From a marketing perspective, Laker was always pioneering new ideas.

In the 1970s his ambitions changed and he became determined to *try a new market and offer transport to a lot more people*. At this time the only cheap air fares across the Atlantic were charter flights, whereby travellers had to be a member of some sponsoring organisation for at least six months before flying. The international carriers operated a price-fixing cartel organised by the International Air Transport Association (IATA) with the connivance of all governments concerned. Charter flight regulations tended to be abused and, consequently, the major carriers fought for stricter monitoring which brought about a decline. Laker conceived Skytrain, a *no booking, no frills* operation with prices significantly below those offered by the major airlines, who naturally opposed his idea.

Laker applied to the Civil Aviation Authority (CAA) for a licence first in 1971 and was refused. In late 1972 he was given permission as long as he flew out of Stansted, although his base was at Gatwick. Delaying tactics involving British and US airlines, the UK Labour government, the US government and the American equivalent of the CAA meant that the first flight did not take place until September 1977 when Skytrain was launched with enormous publicity, this time from Gatwick. In this period oil prices had increased dramatically and Skytrain, although still under £100 for a single fare, was double the price estimated in 1971. In turn, the Skytrain fare was well under half the cost of the cheapest fare offered by IATA carriers who subsequently had to reduce their fares in the face of this new competition.

Although they claimed they did this reluctantly, it had a devastating impact on Laker – who accused them of adopting a predatory pricing strategy purely to try and drive him out of business. Skytrain's competitive strategy – and apparent advantage – was its low price resulting from its low cost base; its service package was clearly inferior to that of the major carriers. When the price gap was narrowed, Skytrain became less attractive to customers; its early competitive advantage was not sustainable.

Skytrain made £2 million profits in its first year of operation, but difficulties experienced when it was extended to Los Angeles in 1978 effectively wiped out the profitability. In 1979 Laker became a fully licensed transatlantic carrier and for the first time was able to pre-sell reserved seats. Laker's confidence grew, and anticipating that he would be given permission to fly more routes around the world he ordered ten Airbus A-300s and five McDonnell Douglas DC10s at a total cost of £300 million. Eventually this was to bring his downfall. Laker was already using DC10s for Skytrain and when the US government grounded all DC10s for checks in 1979 Laker lost £13 million in revenue. In 1980 he failed to win licences to fly Skytrain in Europe and to Hong Kong, although he did begin services from Prestwick and Manchester to Miami.

Profits of £2.2 million were reported for 1980–1981, but significantly three-quarters of this came from favourable currency movements. By 1981 the pound was falling against the dollar, demand was declining, revenue was down, but the debt interest payments, mostly in dollars, were rising. There were, in effect, too many planes and not enough passengers flying the Atlantic. The major airlines wanted fares to rise, but Skytrain remained the force which kept them low. Laker did manage to renegotiate some interest payments and a cash injection from McDonnell Douglas, but he also had to increase fares and sell his Airbuses. He was left with a break-even level of virtually all the seats on every Skytrain, but was able to fill only one-third of them. When the receiver was called in (February 1982) Laker had debts of some £270 million.

Laker had pioneered cheap transatlantic airfares, which have stayed in different guises since his collapse, but he made the mistake of becoming over-confident. The man who originally intended to stay small went for growth. At the same time he was determined to retain total control of his company and therefore raised loan capital against very limited assets rather than seeking outside equity funding. The interest payments brought him down, particularly as he raised most of the money in dollars without adequate cover against currency fluctuations. Finally, as something of a buccaneering character described by one airline executive as a man who *a few hundred years ago would have brass ear-rings, a beard and a cutlass*, he underestimated the power of the vested interests who opposed him. Had their opposition not delayed the introduction of Skytrain by six years, maybe things would have turned out differently.

A bitter Sir Freddie moved to Florida, but by the early 1990s he was back. In 1992 he began regular flights to and from the Bahamas from his new hub; and then, in 1996, he returned to the UK with return charter flights to Gatwick from Orlando. This time he intended to compete on service as well as discounted prices – he had learned a hard lesson. He negotiated convenient take-off and landing times and offered above-normal baggage allowances. His drinks (in crystal glasses) and food (served on china with stainless steel cutlery) were to be superior to most other charter flights. Would the package prove sufficiently different and would he be able to fly his small fleet of DC 10s reliably? Yet again, all would not go smoothly and he would be criticised for flights not taking off and landing on time.

Pierre Levicky

The first Pierre Victoire restaurant was opened in Edinburgh in 1988 by the French chef, Pierre Levicky. It was his first new venture. Within eight years he would own eighteen restaurants and another eighty-three franchised outlets. *I didn't envisage this success. It has happened because it is a charming concept* (Levicky). Unfortunately this rapid growth coupled with a lack of innovation and inadequate controls from the beginning would bring the business down.

His successful idea was based on quality French food and wine at reasonable prices with a simple decor (originally this was by necessity) of whitewashed walls, wooden floors and sometimes second-hand furniture. Levicky produced a cookbook of 500 recipes to guide the other chefs in the chain.

In the early days Levicky was very hands on, doing most of the cooking himself. When he opened a second restaurant he did not worry himself with management controls. He was soon in debt, but his bank helped him to set up the necessary structure and controls. On a firmer financial footing, he set up two new restaurant concepts, one a vegetarian restaurant, and grew rapidly through franchising. With hindsight his selection of franchisees was inadequately robust. 'Some business experience and acumen' mattered more than direct experience in the restaurant business. Levicky helped the franchisees recruit continental chefs, and in a number of cases this resulted in personality conflicts.

The corporate team initially comprised loyal employees Levicky promoted, although later he did recruit external specialists. It was 1996 before the chain benefited from a centralised information system. In that year there was a planned flotation, but it never happened, and 10 per cent of the business was sold to an investment trust. Undercapitalised, Pierre Victoire went into voluntary receivership in 1998 with undisclosed debts.

As the early novelty of Levicky's French restaurants had worn off, and he had failed to develop the concept as competition had grown, and as quality across the chain was inconsistent because of the variations in skills and experience, there wasn't a business to rescue.

Bill Rooney

Bill Rooney (born in 1941) created and built Spring Ram kitchens and bathrooms. Once dubbed the best manufacturing company in Britain, it became crisis-prone and Rooney was ousted by the institutional shareholders when it became clear that financial and stock controls had collapsed. Before starting up on his own, Rooney had worked for Cavenham Foods (owned by the entrepreneurial James Goldsmith) and Hygena Kitchens. He began in 1980 in a disused mill in West Yorkshire. At this time he had a strong minority partner, Bill Murray, who stayed with the company until 1990. Whilst Rooney was always the power behind the ideas and the marketing,

Murray maintained effective controls. Murray's successor as financial director was never as able to restrain both Rooney and the business' propensity to grow.

When Murray departed, Spring Ram had built a 20 per cent share of the bathrooms market (second only to Armitage Shanks) and 12 per cent of kitchens, where it was out-performing all its main rivals. There had been a mixture of organic growth and acquisitions. Pre-tax profits had been growing at an annual rate of 50 per cent whilst most rivals had seen profits decline; Spring Ram seemed to be resistant to the forces of the economic recession which was gripping Britain. Analysts concluded that Spring Ram was simply able to produce market-led products with guaranteed quality and lower prices. Its delivery times of forty-eight hours were uncharacteristically short. Its plants were heavily automated and featured the most advanced technology; Spring Ram had bought land at favourable prices and, paying only low dividends, had invested its past profits in new factories. Good at forecasting both sales and supply requirements, Spring Ram took seventy days credit but gave its customers just twenty-eight days. The product ranges and their distribution were wide and comprehensive. The products appealed to the cost-conscious and the quality-conscious segments of the market and were available from DIY superstores, builders' merchants and specialist independent retailers. Bill Rooney and the company had accomplished a great deal and had made a number of sound decisions, but future problems were already rooted inside the business. Spring Ram had decided to expand into related products such as Artisan ceramic tiles and interior doors (Regency Doors) and again committed investments in large, new factories. With these new activities in the early 1990s, Spring Ram *began trading without definite business plans, and without adequate appreciation of the technical, production and marketing issues surrounding the early development of a business*. In addition, Stag Furniture had been acquired – realistically an unrelated product dependent largely on a separate distribution channel.

The 'bad news' began to emerge in November 1992 when it came to light that the accounts for a Spring Ram subsidiary business (Balterley Bathrooms, which had been acquired in 1986) overstated both stocks and sales. Order bookings, rather than deliveries, constituted the sales figures, and distributor returns were not being recorded. In Spring 1993 Spring Ram asked for its shares to be suspended – in advance of an announcement that profits had fallen, mainly because previous result-boosting presentations in the figures had been prohibited but also because the new activities were losing money. Typically grants had been booked earlier than was legitimate; product development costs had been recorded as assets; depreciation was being understated. Spring Ram had always made a virtue of the way it *motivated the entrepreneurs who ran its subsidiaries*. Rooney had always operated a very devolved structure; each subsidiary had its own directors and considerable independence. When the head office had continued to demand growth results when the housing market was clearly in recession, essential to maintain its 'good news culture', *aggressive accounting* had become more commonplace throughout the whole business. The institutional investors pressed for Rooney's resignation. He was joined by forty of the sixty subsidiary directors and the company's auditors. Rooney commented wryly 'There was a hiccup at the time institutional shareholders generally were getting macho'.

Despite management changes and new systems, the company has never recovered. Attempts to properly turn it around have failed. Artisan Tiles was closed in 1994; Regency Doors was sold to a competitor. Factories have closed, with resultant job losses. The housing market continues to rise and fall; Spring Ram, after all, was not recession-proof. In 1999 the business was sold to US Industries for £82 million; at its peak in 1992 the company was valued at ten times this amount.

Meanwhile, Bill Rooney, a habitual entrepreneur, has prospered. He resettled in Barbados, where he already owned property, and he began to develop a prestigious golf and leisure complex which attracts both golf and media celebrities. Alongside the championship golf course are villas which sell for between US$700 000 and $2.5 million. He has planning permission for 270 units on the land he owns. He originally invested £2 million to buy 75 per cent of a sugar plantation while he was still with Spring Ram, and has subsequently bought the remainder. As well as the villas, he is building a new hotel with 950 bedrooms, the largest on the island. He has a parallel property rental organisation. The villa owners typically stay in their properties for about two months every year. For a commission, Rooney organises lets for the remaining ten months.

Estimates of Rooney's personal wealth come out at around £200 million, and three of his sons are involved with him in the property business. Again he saw an opportunity and he has made it happen. He has been able to attract wealthy British tourists to Barbados – important because Americans prefer the Bahamas. He claims to be *the catalyst who helped restore Barbados' flagging tourist industry*. He is a popular figure there.

The story of Ratner's recounts another business which has managed to survive the fall from grace of a high-profile entrepreneur, who has himself again made a comeback. This time the company did not suffer as significantly as did Spring Ram.

Gerald Ratner

Gerald Ratner was born in 1949 and became Joint Managing Director of the family business (jewellery retailers) in 1978. By 1984 he was sole Managing Director, and Chairman in 1986. He saw a real opportunity in critical mass and in product standardisation across a range of stores for low-cost, lower-quality fashion jewellery. He realised that some people, with some products, will treat jewellery as discardable rather than a lifelong investment. A major competitor, H. Samuel, was acquired to yield the critical mass. To ensure standardisation, everything was sourced centrally. Staff at head office experimented with window designs and layouts, and when they were satisfied they took photographs which were sent to every branch. The exact layout, down to the position of an individual ring on a tray, must be replicated in every branch. The business invested in advertising and promotion. Later Ratner's bought other retail outlets – such as Zales (jewellers) and Salisbury's (principally leather goods) which were acquired from Next. Ratner was very aggressive. *I was a complete megalomaniac, very ambitious, very competitive. If another jeweller opened, I'd do anything to put him out of business.* The strategy worked, but it was always replicable. His rivals could follow – and some did, even if they were smaller and less profitable. He was never a major threat to the expensive and exclusive specialist, of course.

Speaking at an Institute of Directors' Conference in 1991 Gerald Ratner claimed that his company was able to sell sherry decanters at really low prices because they were *total crap*. He is also on record as saying that his gold earrings, priced at under

£1, were *cheaper than a prawn sandwich from Marks and Spencer but they won't last as long*. Ratner's continued success relied on its reputation for slickness and efficiency; denigrating his company's products in this way would prove a 'bridge too far'. The tabloid newspapers seized on the comments, were very critical, and the company's previously strong image was damaged. The group name has subsequently been changed to Signet, and although the company still trades profitably, the name Ratner's has disappeared from the high street. Gerald himself was forced to resign, devastated by the reaction to what he saw as a light-hearted, throw-away comment.

He spent four years recovering from this setback – *my esteem was low for a long time*. He did find work, though. One job was letting office space for a property developer in Canary Wharf. In 1996 he spotted that one of the richest towns in the country, Henley-on-Thames, did not have a health club. The sixth bank that he approached was willing to back his proposed new venture; he also had financial support from friends. Reflecting his project-championing skills, he advertised for members and signed up 500 prospects before he committed himself to a lease on a warehouse he planned to convert. He planned a luxury, up-market health club – and he knew he needed to open without delay. Once other property developers realised there was a gap in the market they might try and beat him by being the first to open. He began work with a colleague/partner, who was destined to be the General Manager after it opened. In the end there were tensions, and Ratner took over control of day-to-day responsibilities. Changes to the specification were made as the conversion progressed; Ratner decided to add both a creche and a pool. The target break-even increased from 700 to 900 members. On the day of the official opening the complex was not completely ready, but Ratner went ahead anyway. It was re-opened two months later, when it was fully complete, and very quickly the membership topped the thousand mark.

Ratner said he was determined that this time his style and approach would be more restrained. 'My ambition has gone', he claimed. Well, maybe not altogether, because he was soon talking about the prospect of opening more clubs – and in 2002 he announced his return to the jewellery industry.

Ratners Online – as he intended to call his new venture – would sell branded watches and other jewellery items at discounts of up to 30 per cent using the Internet. Argos Online had already shown there was a market. He had forged links with high street jewellers, Goldsmiths, who would provide warehousing, invoicing, dispatching and returns and repair services in exchange for a royalty. Ratner planned to float the business immediately with an Ofex listing, but Signet intervened and obtained an injunction against him using the Ratner's name for his new venture. In the end he had to settle for Gerald Online, and the year's delay cost him his Ofex listing. Instead, he formed a joint venture with SB&T International, a diamond jewellery business based in Bombay. The joint venture was a 60:40 deal – Ratner was the minority owner.

John Ashcroft

John Ashcroft did not start Coloroll; he was recruited to be its Managing Director at the age of thirty in 1978, and he immediately set the business on a fast expansion path which ultimately would cause it to fail. He was an entrepreneurial strategic leader. After graduating, Ashcroft had started as a management trainee with Tube Investments before working in marketing management for Crown wallcoverings, the market leader in its field. Coloroll was a competitor to Crown. It was based in Manchester, and after John Ashcroft became Managing Director (and subsequently Chairman) it first increased its share of the UK wallpaper market from 3 per cent to 30 per cent, and later diversified into pottery and earthenware, bed linen and finally carpets (Kosset) with the acquisition of John Crowther in 1988. Ashcroft deliberately recruited a new and youthful management team to support him – they were described by one analyst as *MBA barrow boys.*

The company was very market-oriented and concerned to give the customer *what he wants when he wants it. . . . I've geared the business towards generic growth, which means exploiting market trends and knocking out competitors by pushing them off the shelf* (Ashcroft). There was a clear and coherent strategy. Coloroll targeted the growing DIY retailers who were beginning to build large out-of-town units; delivery lead times (from stock) were reduced to a very competitive two days, and manufacturing costs were reduced with investments in new machinery. After securing market leadership for wallcoverings from Crown, Coloroll successfully identified and exploited an opportunity to provide a range of attractive and affordable household products for young consumers who were either first-time home owners or removing for the first time. The Coloroll brand name was now being stamped upon some famous and well-established products including Denby pottery and Edinburgh crystal glassware.

Acquisitions were implemented with a clear three-stage process: *assessment, reconstruction* and *rehabilitation.* Companies were acquired if Coloroll believed they could improve the performance, and they began by changing the culture. *Symbols are regarded as important in making the change of culture. Staffordshire Potteries had a wood-panelled boardroom and a directors' snug complete with bar. Both were ripped apart by Coloroll (alcohol is not allowed anywhere within the group) and turned into meeting rooms for the workforce. At Fogarty [duvets and bedlinen], where there were three grades of toilet – one for the chairman, one for the other directors, and one for the ranks – there was a similar ritual demolition* (Ashcroft).

Reconstruction was designed to simplify the job of management, accelerate decision-making and reduce unnecessary overheads. Structures were altered, and Coloroll ensured that managers understood the objectives that were being set, and offered incentives to make them worthy of achievement. The most senior managers from the acquired company were likely to be replaced, often by managers from within the company, and Coloroll introduced tight financial monitoring systems. Clear targets were set for key financial measures. Up-to-date sales and financial information was collected weekly, and any variations from budgets were acted upon quickly. His style was ruthless, radical and charismatic. He made a difference.

We have a very small head office team of four directors. The rest of the company is divided into businesses that all have their own managing directors who operate autonomously. These MDs have big salaries, big bonuses, big cars and big prestige positions, and they are the people who make all the decisions. . . To operate smoothly, I need to have a clear perception of where the business is going. Every year we debate it, but once I decide, then everybody has to go along with it. There's a lot of nonsense talked about democracy. I believe management democracy is everybody agreeing to do what the leader wants.

(Ashcroft)

Sales of £6 million in the late 1970s increased 100 times in ten years. Profits grew at a comparable rate and exceeded £50 million in the 1988–1989 financial year. There were misjudgements, nevertheless. A move into retailing – when Coloroll opened its own store in London in 1986 and planned another in Manchester – was abandoned when Marks and Spencer and other leading customers threatened to cancel orders. However high rates of interest in 1989 led to a slowing down in the rate of growth of Coloroll's sales, aggressive pricing policies by both Coloroll and its competitors and substantial increases in the cost of borrowings. The financial difficulties were compounded by Coloroll having paid too high a price for John Crowther. Interim profits for the six months to September 1989 collapsed. Ashcroft's strategy had proved extremely successful in buoyant market conditions, but growth was too fast. The company was not sufficiently robust financially to withstand adverse trading conditions. *We got carried away with the concept and lost sight of the cash* (Ashcroft).

In March 1990 John Ashcroft resigned, and his replacement was described as a 'doctor handed an incurable patient'. Within weeks Coloroll was in receivership, and the business was subsequently offered for sale either as a whole or up to eleven separate parts. Finally, five divisions were sold to their respective managers, three to other companies and three were closed down.

Ashcroft himself started a new business – Survival Aid – in the Lake District in 1991, selling outdoor clothing by mail order, but with plans to expand into retailing. This again grew very fast and experienced cash difficulties. Ashcroft did not seem to have learned all the lessons from Coloroll. Once described by Mrs Thatcher as a 'shining example of British entrepreneurship', and appearing to be just that, he was actually an ambitious corporate empire builder with an extremely strong ego. Many of his decisions were sound strategically, but the growth was too rapid and too ambitious, and the company's resources were too over-stretched to deal effectively with the inevitable crises. He was not strong enough on all the aspects of advantage.

Inventor entrepreneurs

John Edgley

It is not the case that all inventors are entrepreneurial failures, simply that some never manage to establish and grow the business that their invention promises. The unique Optica spotter plane was designed by John Edgley, who built the prototype in a house he owned in North London, before taking it for final assembly and testing to an airfield in Bedfordshire. The plane received substantial publicity when the first production model, under test by the Hampshire Police for observation duties, crashed on its maiden flight in May 1985. The subsequent investigation cleared the Optica of any design faults – but really the business never recovered from this slice of bad luck.

The Optica was revolutionary, having a three-seater observation cockpit at the very front, with the engine, propeller and wings all behind. It could cruise at slow speed and turn tightly. It was designed to compete with helicopters, and it promised a substantial cost advantage for both purchase and running. The business was design-led, with the market investigated properly only after the prototype was flying. Forecasts for potential demand always proved over-optimistic. Throughout its history, interest in the aircraft and indications of possible future orders were frequently described as firm orders to imply an exaggerated and unrealistic level of acceptance and success. It is, of course, quite conceivable that Edgley actually believed they were orders and he was simply waiting for final confirmation.

In 1974 John Edgley was a thirty-year-old designer *who wanted to build, own and run an aircraft factory*. Originally a civil engineer, he also had a post-graduate degree in aeronautical engineering. His company was begun with family savings, topped up with loans from relatives, and the first Optica was built on a shoestring budget. Its maiden flight was in 1979; one year later, Mrs Thatcher described it as *a triumph of British enterprise and technology*. At the Farnborough Air Show, painted in bright yellow, it was a *show stopper*. Without any firm orders, Edgley set out to raise money to grow the venture. Using a network of friends and contacts in the city, he was successful.

Edgley and his institutional backers invested an estimated £8 million in building a sophisticated production facility, using computer-controlled machine tools, at Old Sarum Airfield near Salisbury, still before any definite orders were received. Hoping for interest to be translated into firm orders, they began building aircraft. Edgley had his factory. However, and typically, it had taken longer than he expected, and cost more than the original budget. Many obstacles had been overcome, such that Edgley commented they had become blasé about their ability to deal with problems and setbacks. The Optica won a major Design Council award in 1984 and a full airworthiness certificate at the beginning on 1985. Edgley had been committed for ten years by this stage. In October 1985, and just five months after the fatal crash, Edgley Aircraft (the company) went into receivership, was sold, and renamed Optica Industries. At this time John Edgley ceased to have any personal involvement in either the aircraft or the business – but there is more to the story.

The wisdom of building a capital-intensive production facility without orders for aircraft was questioned when the new owners had to accept sub-contract and 'metal-bashing' work to utilise their spare capacity. The premises, however, was destroyed by a mysterious fire early in 1987, and subsequently re-built. The company was re-named Brooklands Aerospace. The first actual order for an Optica, in March 1988, came nine years after the prototype had first flown. In July 1989 an American order for 132 Opticas was received, and the company also diversified into manufacturing additional light aircrafts under licence.

But in the end, the Optica has never been developed commercially – financial difficulties led to a second receivership in April 1990. It is another good idea which never came to fruition. Light aircraft manufacture is, by its very nature, a difficult and high-risk business to enter as substantial up-front investment is required to secure full certification to fly. Whether the Optica could have been successful if the unfortunate crash in 1985 had not occurred, or if the business had not accumulated huge overheads by building state-of-the-art production facilities, will never be known. Edgley appeared to know the risks and accepted them – but he failed. Afterwards he reflected that he had failed to realise that he was developing a product and building a business simultaneously, and that they are not one and the same. He was simply not a project champion. He was certainly an inventor, and maybe a good opportunity-spotter.

Clive Sinclair

Clive Sinclair also promised but never ultimately delivered. He is not remembered for his early successes but for his later failures. Like John Edgley, he is a mixture of the inventor and opportunity-spotter who never managed to build a successful long-term business. Sinclair was born in 1940 in Surrey; his father and grandfather had both been engineers. His grandfather was a renowned and innovative naval architect, and his father had started and run his own business. Whilst Clive was still at school, his father suffered a major business setback and had to start all over again. Entrepreneurship seemed to be in the blood.

Clive Sinclair was always a voracious learner – with *ways of thought and speech beyond his years* – who preferred the company of adults to children. Keen on mathematics, he discovered electronics and began to experiment at home. Like the founders of Sony, he was naturally drawn to the challenge of miniaturisation. He was still at school when his first articles were published in *Practical Wireless*. At the same time he was always looking for opportunities to supplement his pocket money and finance his experiments.

Despite being qualified, he chose not to go to university and instead found employment as an editor with *Practical Wireless*. Through the contacts he was able to nurture, he was next invited to work in publishing – writing, editing and commissioning books for hobbyists. But all the time he was dreaming of owning his own business once he had the financial resources to start it. In his early twenties, and thinking he had a private backer for a radio construction business, he resigned from his job. When the backer pulled out he had to return to technical writing – but this setback actually provided him with a valuable new expertise. In his new job he became knowledgeable about semi-conductors. Eventually he was able to begin a business, initially designing and assembling miniature radios and amplifiers from bought-in components. His early successes were all down to innovative, breakthrough ideas and his natural tendency to seek and obtain publicity. Generally his success continued through the 1970s, but not without setbacks. He skimped on the quality of metal connectors in his calculators, for example, and they simply exploded and stopped working.

He established small assembly units in Boston, St Ives and Cambridge, where he based his headquarters, and in 1980 he launched the ZX80, *the world's smallest and cheapest computer*. It measured just 9" × 7" and retailed at under £100. There were design issues – for example, the raised-surface touch key-pad was difficult to use – but the 'man in the street' was attracted by the thought of ownership and sales, through both mail order and high street stores, were buoyant. Although the rate of return for shoddy workmanship was relatively high, the low price continued to tempt customers.

As a result, the ZX80 was followed by an improved version, the ZX81, and then the more sophisticated, but still low-price and miniature, Spectrum. At this stage in the company's development, the Timex (watch) factory in Dundee was a major sub-contractor for much of Sinclair's assembly work. Without doubt, by 1983, the innovative, buccaneering and successful Clive Sinclair appeared to be the *very epitome of the new Elizabethan technologist*. Moreover, 1984 was to be the year of the advanced, and much heralded, Sinclair QL miniature computer. QL was derived from quantum leap. Although the launch was announced and planned, the deliveries simply did not materialise. For the first time, the Sinclair bubble had been truly burst, and thereafter the story becomes one of largely unfulfilled promises.

Sinclair already had the technology and designs for thin flat screen televisions, which could potentially be mounted on walls and thus take up much less space in homes – but he has never been able to produce at a cost which would create a market. His real demise, however, came with the electronic tricycle, the C5. Promoted as the safe, easy and clean way to beat traffic congestion, its batteries were inadequate – it quickly ran out of power and stopped. Both Sinclair and the C5 were scorned and became the subject of comedians' jokes. Overwhelmed by debt and unsold stock, Sinclair sold his computer business – and all his patents – to Alan Sugar (Amstrad) for £5 million in 1986.

Clive Sinclair was an opportunity-spotter and, to a degree, an inventor. Although he had a business partner, this proved insufficient to overcome the relative failings which ultimately brought him down. Whilst cynics would dismiss him as an assembler, this seems unjust. He had obsessions (rather like social entrepreneurs have causes), but allowed these obsessions to push him into actions and decisions which were not sound business sense. He was not noted for accepting the blame when things went wrong or for learning from his misjudgements. He was willing to compromise on quality and engineering to keep his prices low, and this has to be an unsustainable strategy. He was not a businessman or true entrepreneur – because he was not a project champion. Sadly, Sinclair is not the only loser. Some potentially great ideas have been lost because of his failings – customers and society are also losers.

Dishonest entrepreneurs

Robert Maxwell

The story of Robert Maxwell is too complex to recount in full, but a number of key points show how he was a successful and extremely able entrepreneur, but unethical and dishonest. Physically a big man, he had a matching ego and reputation; even in death he remains mysterious. What we see in Maxwell is the danger of extreme character themes. He was extreme on advantage and certain aspects of focus as well as ego; he was possibly also extreme on creativity. He was very charismatic and was able to attract followers. He built teams of people who obeyed him and generally carried out his wishes; he did not build true entrepreneur teams.

Maxwell was born in real poverty in a small village on the Czech–Romanian border in 1923. His real name was Jan Hoch, and he was Jewish. His father, like his father in turn, *wheeled and dealed in cattle*. Separated from his family at the outbreak of the Second World War Jan Hoch somehow found his way to England, where he joined the Pioneer Corps. He was useful because he spoke fluent German. During the war he adopted a number of different aliases before choosing Robert Maxwell for his new name. A brave soldier, he won several promotions and decorations. At the end of the war he was determined to become *rich and famous – and to belong*. He began trading scarce commodities, and in 1947 he secured a position, and later a partnership, with the German scientific publisher Springer-Verlag, which was struggling to find export markets for its scientific books and journals. Even at this time, Maxwell was always involved in several simultaneous activities, which he generally managed to separate and compartmentalise. Whilst the constant disarray that seemed to surround his activities might have suggested he was more an opportunity-spotter than a project champion, he was able to get things done. In the end, however, his business affairs became too complex.

Maxwell soon established a publishing house of his own, which he called Pergamon, and used it to publish some of the valuable scientific work he was beginning to acquire, much of it from Russia. Breaking with Springer, after agreeing certain concessions for Pergamon, he immediately broke his agreement and poached work from his previous partner. Charging unpopular high prices for his journals, he was a millionaire by the early 1960s. He was elected as a Labour MP in 1964, but, much to his disappointment, he was not offered an immediate Ministerial post. When Rupert Murdoch 'pipped him to the post' in an acquisition battle for *The News of the World* he commented that *the British will never let me succeed*.

His first major setback came when he sought to merge Pergamon with an American publisher. Creative accounting practices which overstated profits were discovered during due diligence. The eventual outcomes were that Pergamon was sold to America, Maxwell lost his parliamentary seat and a DTI enquiry concluded that his *fixation with his own abilities causes him to ignore the views of others . . . the concept of being responsible to a Board was alien to him . . . he could not be relied on to exercise proper stewardship of a public company*.

But he did not earn the nickname *the bouncing Czech* for nothing. One year later (in 1974) he controlled Pergamon again, having ingratiated himself with its new owners, the Scottish Daily Express. Pergamon now grew rapidly, and on the back of its success, Maxwell first regained full ownership and then used it as collateral to acquire the leading, but troubled, printer BPC (British Printing Corporation) in 1980. The vendors commented 'he was the greatest wheeler-dealer we'd ever met'. Although closure of this struggling business had earlier seemed a real possibility, Maxwell's autocratic and robust style quickly returned it to profit. In 1982, and allegedly bored, he began juggling and trading a whole network of businesses. Amongst other things, he bought a stake in Central Television and acquired Oxford United Football Club. In 1984, and fulfilling his dream of owning a newspaper, he bought *The Daily Mirror*. The paper was in trouble, but its owners, its employees and the Labour government (which the paper supported) all expressed dismay at the news. Despite protestations to the contrary, he interfered with the editorial policy and content. By this time, five of his seven children were working in managerial positions in one or other of his companies – but under his tight control and authority.

A bid for Waddington's (games) foundered when details emerged about the complex ownership arrangements of the companies that Maxwell controlled. It transpired that they were ultimately registered in Liechtenstein, where disclosure requirements are more limited. It did not seem to matter to Maxwell that some of these were public companies with shareholders. At his death, in 1991, there were 400 registered businesses in the Maxwell empire. His companies constantly traded in each other's shares, a convenient method of moving money around and, at the same time, propping up share prices and inflating their worth.

Maxwell was now rich and famous but he still felt he was not accepted. He became even more determined to satisfy this outstanding ambition by building a global communications business. He set out to purchase the American publisher, Macmillan. Trading shares between his various businesses, he was able to boost the paper value of Maxwell Communications (the new name for BPC) and thus guarantee a bank loan for the acquisition. After his early bids were all refused, he eventually triumphed, but he had paid a very high price. *The battle had not been about commercial sense, but over a man's place in history.* This all took place in 1988. When the cash needs of his various businesses began to soar in the following economic recession, Maxwell was forced to adopt increasingly desperate strategies. The sale of Pergamon in 1991 helped, but it was not enough. Maxwell secretly transferred shares held by the Mirror Group Pension Fund and pledged them as collateral for further loans. They did not belong to him, of course. He simply knew of their existence and whereabouts and was initially able to cover up his clandestine activity.

In 1991 a BBC Panorama team began to investigate some of his activities, not appreciating at first what they would uncover. They had been tipped off that his high-profile Bingo game in the Mirror was rigged to prevent anyone winning the main prize. The public were at last beginning to learn the truth about Robert Maxwell. In November 1991 his body was found floating in the sea alongside his yacht. His death has never been fully explained. It soon became apparent that his cumulative business debts were unrepayable and his empire was in a *meltdown situation*. Once he was no longer in a position to cover up his wheeler-dealing, more and more of the facts came out.

How had he got away with it? Alongside his huge ego, he had real ability. He was able to overcome obstacles. He was also hugely charismatic and – when he wanted to be – charming. Determined and plausible, he told people what they wanted to hear, regardless of whether or not it was true. When haggling and dealing he simply made promises he had no intention of keeping. Had he been driven only by a profit motive, maybe he would have been more restrained. But he wanted, it seemed, unlimited power and prestige. His background – he never ceased to trade on his reputation for being *a Jew who had escaped the holocaust* – and his perception that he was rejected by the British establishment, were instrumental in his behavioural extremes. Yet he was always able to court other famous and influential people and trap them in his web. Life with Maxwell could be highly rewarded, and it was certainly exciting. Ideas flowed from him continuously, but he failed to build strong and robust businesses for all his activities. Senior managers who worked for him, and who suspected at least some of the truth, were very clearly afraid to expose him.

Nick Leeson

'Rogue-trader' Nick Leeson is the plasterer's son from Watford who brought down Baring's Bank – although he never set out to do so! Initially a City settlement clerk, he had moved to Baring's and transferred first to Jakarta and then to Singapore in 1992. He enjoyed a *star trader* image and reputation and he was noted for his high-risk deals. By 1994, at the age of twenty-eight, he was General Manager of Futures Trading for Baring's in Singapore. Convinced the currently depressed Japanese market was about to turn the corner and start to rise, he began investing heavily. His guess was wrong, and the Japanese market actually continued to fall. Leeson increased his investment – some would say naively – still believing in the upswing. Dealer losses are, of course, not unusual in this speculative business – the problem here was that he had no trouble covering up the truth about his predicament. Unusually, he was allowed by Baring's to control his own 'back office' where all the deals were settled, and where he simply set up dummy client accounts into which money was able to disappear. He was empowered with too much freedom and he exploited it. He deceived his employer and systematically dug himself into an ever deeper hole. Of course, if the market had turned upwards, Baring's would have made huge profits and Leeson would have been in line for a substantial bonus. In the event, he was regarded as a criminal and no longer a hero of the dealing floor.

In January 1995 an earthquake in the Kobe and Osaka regions caused the Japanese market to plunge even further and very rapidly. At last it came to light that Leeson had accumulated losses of $1.3 billion, over twice the level of reserves held by Baring's. Leeson went on the run with his wife, but he was caught in Germany, extradited back to Singapore and sentenced to a period of imprisonment for fraud and perjury. Now released he is able to earn money for his story, and he may have managed to stash away some money. At the same time, he has suffered from colon cancer during his spell in jail and his wife has divorced him.

Alan Bond and Christopher Skase

Our stories of Maxwell and Leeson highlight the need for effective controls over strong entrepreneurs, but this has typically been talked about more than acted upon. It was, after all, hardly a new phenomenon, and it was something that could be found everywhere in the world. Alan Bond, the British-born high-profile Australian entrepreneur, who, in 1983, was the first sailor ever to wrest the prestigious America's Cup from long-term holders, America, was jailed twice during the 1990s, the second time for that country's biggest ever corporate fraud. Another well-known Australian entrepreneur would die in exile in Majorca in 2001. Christopher Skase was fifty-two at the time and he had succumbed to cancer. He was *Australia's most flamboyant fugitive*. Originally a financial journalist he had bought a tin mine and turned it into a media and leisure empire. At his height he controlled two-thirds of Australian television and owned a number of London theatres. He enjoyed a visibly lavish lifestyle, but when he went bankrupt in 1991 his debts exceeded his corporate assets by a ratio of 2:1. His acquisitions had been made with money borrowed too easily during a financial boom.

However, in recent years, the scandal surrounding financial practices at the American energy trader, Enron, has drawn serious attention to corporate fraud and dubious financial practices. The story of Tyco is an ideal example of corporate excess brought about by a mixture of greed and extreme ego. It shows how a loss of trust can bring about the downfall of a successful leader. The leader in question was a corporate entrepreneur who had transformed the fortunes of the company he eventually led.

Dennis Kozlowski

Tyco began life in 1960 as a research laboratory doing experimental work for the US government. Its founder was Arthur Rosenburg. Tyco quickly diversified into producing high-technology materials and energy products for commercial sale. Its steady growth resulted in a listing on the New York Stock Exchange in 1974. In the mid-1970s Tyco began to grow more rapidly and acquire other businesses. Dennis Kozlowski, the son of a New York policeman and a trained accountant, joined the company in 1975; by 1992 he would be its CEO. He presided over a decade of remarkable expansion and growth.

Between 1992 and 2002 Tyco spent over $50 billion on acquisitions, taking it to 200 businesses and operations in 100 countries. There were 182 000 employees. The most high-profile and defining deal was the acquisition of ADT home security systems, a successful business which had been built up by the former UK Tory Party Treasurer, Lord Ashcroft. Kozlowski's style was to surround himself with like-minded people – mainly corporate climbers who came from relatively humble backgrounds.

He was highly remunerated. Between 1998 and 2002 the average value of his package, including bonuses and stock options, exceeded $100 million a year. This funded a lavish lifestyle. He flew helicopters and raced yachts. Employees reportedly saw him as highly demanding but fair. By 2002 Tyco was based in Bermuda and diversified into a variety of different business clusters, including electrical connectors, home security and fire protection, commercial finance and health care, which included both pharmaceuticals and medical equipment. But, post-Enron, it was attracting attention for what some regarded as aggressive accounting practices. Tyco's acquisitions had generally been funded through equity rather than cash – this is only realistic if the share price remains buoyant. Tyco ensured this by demonstrating its ability to strip out costs, but at the same time, apparently, using charges related to the acquisitions to obscure the true financial performance. There was a lack of transparency and this became problematic for Tyco.

In January 2002 Kozlowski announced the business would be split into four separate companies to help generate its true worth. Rather than boosting the share price it had the opposite effect. By April it had fallen from $60 a share to $20 and it would continue down to $10. Eventually the corporate split would be abandoned. It hardly helped that Kozlowski was charged with tax evasion in June 2002! He was being accused of not paying sales taxes on private art deals. He resigned. More details began to emerge, implying that he had used company money improperly. In fact, it was suggested, he used company money as if it was his own. He would engineer loans which would later be written off. His houses and apartments were all bought using company funds; he entertained lavishly on the back of the business. With hindsight there seems an element of irony that he used Tyco funds to endow a Chair in Corporate Governance at Cambridge in the name of Tyco Director, Robert Monks.

Kozlowski was replaced and it seemed as if the company's reputation was slowly being restored. However, in January 2003 more financial irregularities – dating back some six years – were unearthed. These concerned the inappropriate booking of bad debts, inventories and reserves. Can total confidence and trust in Tyco ever be restored?

Criminal entrepreneurs

Nick Leeson became dishonest as he became increasingly desperate; Robert Maxwell turned from unethical and questionable practice to dishonesty in his increasingly desperate attempts to save his cracking business empire. We don't yet know exactly what happened with Dennis Kozlowski. In this section we look at a different group of dishonest entrepreneurs – those for whom crime is their business.

Most criminal activity implies an absence of the social character theme. Criminals are taking something from others and from the society. They are destroying lives and destroying social capital. As we have seen, some successful business entrepreneurs are successful in part because they have broken the law. Other people, with a number of the entrepreneur character themes present, choose to focus their talents and energy on criminal activity instead of business. In many ways, successful gangsters are entrepreneurs. To spot a criminal opportunity – and to carry it out successfully – needs an entrepreneur with project championing skills. It implies someone with strong entrepreneurial character themes who simply chooses to deploy these talents in illegal acts. After all, if there is such a thing as the 'perfect crime', the following abilities would seem to be required:

1 Carrying out the crime with some degree of ruthless precision, making sure nothing or nobody gets in the way – *focus*.
2 Spotting a lucrative opportunity and an appreciation of how to achieve the desired outcome without detection – *advantage and creativity*.
3 Extensive press coverage of the achievement, and admiration for the daring involved – *ego*.
4 Pulling together, and controlling, all the resources required to execute the crime – *team*.

The more we consider aspects of criminal behaviour, the more we see evidence of the entrepreneur character themes in some form. Many minor criminals – rather than the true professionals who are very focused – are impulsive, which implies a lack of self-discipline and someone who is very low on focus. At the same time, serious criminals are often fearless, which would represent an extreme form of courage, part of the ego facet. Some are aggressive, which we can easily link to a need for domination, again an extreme form of ego.

Entrepreneurs, of course, have long been a feature of criminal fiction. Arguably, both Sherlock Holmes and James Bond possessed a number of obvious entrepreneur character themes, and many of James Bond's adversaries were unquestionably entrepreneurs. Auric Goldfinger, for example, was an opportunity-spotter and a project champion. He did not intend to steal the gold from Fort Knox – he would never have been able to move it all! Instead, he planned to contaminate it with a small nuclear device. If it was untouchable for several years, his own stock of gold would increase in value. Poisoning the guards with spray from light aircraft – to facilitate the break-in – was creative and innovative.

In the story of The Godfather we can again see clear evidence of entrepreneurship. The story is about Mafia control of rackets, gambling, bookmaking and labour unions. The Godfather himself, Don Vito Corleone, carefully avoids drugs – *society does not accept drugs as readily as it does liquor, gambling and prostitution*. The family-based network of contacts brings in all the necessary resources – and there is superb succession planning. The profit orientation is clearly visible. Things are made to happen; setbacks are not allowed. Anything or anyone who stands in the way of the Godfather is dealt with. There are no barriers which cannot be surmounted. The Godfather is a popular book and movie. People even feel sympathy for the Don, because there is visible evidence of worldly wisdom, insight and relative good in activity that is fundamentally evil. And, is it wholly fictional? The Mafia exist. Moreover, they are not the only manifestation of organised crime.

At the same time, legitimate businesses have to learn how to deal with both organised crime and more random corruption if they wish to trade with many developing – and some developed – countries in the world. It has been estimated that at the very least, European and American businesses spend around \$50 billion a year on dealing with criminal activity and corrupt officials.

Sometimes, of course, entrepreneurial criminals are countered by equally talented entrepreneurs working on the side of law and order. The true story of Al Capone (who found his most valuable opportunity in bootlegging and illicit brewing during the years of prohibition in America) and Eliot Ness is an excellent illustration of this point.

Al Capone and Eliot Ness

In the late 1920s Al Capone was one of the best-known, most feared and most successful criminals in America. *His power in the Chicago area was as awesome as his intrinsic cruelty.* Involved in a wide range of criminal activities, most notably his illicit brewing, he nevertheless wanted to be seen as a legitimate businessman. Somewhat ironically, he was recruited by the President of the Chicago Crime Commission to ensure an honest Mayoral election in a local county. In accomplishing this, Capone achieved something most observers had believed was an impossible task. Outraged at being labelled 'Public Enemy Number One' he also opened a soup kitchen for people without jobs in the depression. He was an entrepreneur as well as a crook. He understood profit. But to call him a social entrepreneur would not be realistic. It took three other enterprising men, and a series of creative and innovative moves, to finally bring him to justice.

Eliot Ness was totally focused and dedicated to the fight against organised crime, and in 1928 he was invited to focus his energies on defeating Capone. He had been born in 1903, the son of a Norwegian immigrant who had become an entrepreneur in the bakery business. After graduating in business and law, he surprised his family and friends by choosing a career in federal law enforcement. Apparently he had *always admired the resourceful, albeit fictional, Sherlock Holmes*. To some he was an ego-maniac who craved attention – but the more popular view is that he was motivated by risk, excitement and danger. Taking on the most ruthless criminals provided the ideal opportunity for him to prosper.

The arrogant and egocentric Capone felt he was outside the grasp of the law. The City law enforcement officials in Chicago were not actively seeking his prosecution. They tolerated his activity – after all, most of them were on his payroll. The President, Herbert Hoover, however, had a different view, and in an enterprising move, chose to target Capone for federal offences and ignore City and State issues. Capone was leading an extravagant life style and appeared to be wealthy – yet he had no apparent means of support and had not filed an income tax return for several years. The Federal Authorities believed that this offence, together with his bootlegging activities – both Federal offences – could be used to nail him.

Employed by the Federal Prohibition Bureau, Ness was invited to build a team of agents to tackle Capone – a group which became known as The Untouchables. Every member of this team had to be unquestionably honest and reliable – as well as dedicated and brave. Whilst Ness' Untouchables started to look for the illegal breweries, IRS (Internal Revenue Service) officials started digging for firm evidence of his real sources of income. There were, in fact, over twenty breweries yielding a weekly sales revenue in excess of $1.5 million. Hard liquor, purchased from the Mafia, was also being delivered through Capone's extensive distribution system. Ness started to gather information via phone tapping, but on his first brewery raid, the staff managed to escape. It had taken too long to break through the security pro-tection system. Undeterred, and learning form this experience, Ness fixed a snow plough on to the front of a ten-ton truck and ram-raided the other breweries he was able to identify. His approach was that of the *wild west frontier lawman*.

At the same time, Elmer Irey, senior IRS investigator, managed to implant two undercover agents in Capone's organisation, and they were able to gather priceless intelligence. At the time, this was seen as a remarkable achievement. Ness, then delib-erately baited Capone by publicly parading the forty-five brewery trucks he had sys-tematically captured and impounded. Capone's brewing empire was being destroyed, and he seemed unable to counter Ness' daring and enterprise. As his breweries closed and his income fell, he had fewer resources for bribing key officials.

Meanwhile, and due largely to the leads provided by the undercover agents, suffi-cient evidence was gathered to bring Capone to trial for several counts of tax evasion. A wholly successful prosecution could get him a 34-year jail sentence, but this looked very optimistic. A confident Al Capone and his lawyers attempted to plea bargain for a confession and light sentence. He even let it to be known he was discussing the script for a movie of his life. The government was actually willing to accept the proposed deal – but Judge James Wilkerson was not, and the trial went ahead. Demonstrating his enterprise, and exploiting his network of contacts, Al Capone was able to bribe every prospective juror sequestered for the case. The equally enterprising judge – when he heard rumours of this achievement – waited until the very last moment and then switched juries with a fellow judge who was trying a similar case. Capone was found guilty and sentenced to eleven years imprisonment. Already ill with syphilis, he *finally emerged from jail little more than a cabbage*. His career was over.

Having made his contribution, Eliot Ness later took over – and systematically cleaned up – the corrupt and apparently incompetent police force in Cleveland, Ohio, another haven for gangsters. Again he was able to build a team of trusted undercover agents who were dedicated to the task in hand. Eliot Ness clearly possessed many leadership character themes, but he was an entrepreneur because he made a difference by being different. His tactics – his daring raids on illegal gambling joints and his willingness to go head-to-head with the most hardened criminals – were innovative and imaginative. He was always an above-average risk-taker as his life was constantly in danger – but he was able to cope with this.

James Munroe

In 1999 James Munroe launched a new motor racing team in the UK at a well-publicised and lavish press reception. Apparently a multi-millionaire, he actually worked in the finance department at publishers, McGraw-Hill. Munroe had set up a series of companies, which were regularly sending invoices to McGraw-Hill, where he was in a position to ensure they were paid. Estimates for his scam varied from £2 million to £3 million. Initially he used the money to fund a lavish personal lifestyle before moving on to racing-car ownership. He courted publicity for his racing activities and was featured in magazines and on television. He was also noted for organising lavish corporate hospitality events, which he did in his spare time through one of his illegally funded companies.

Martin Frankel

In September 1999, America's most wanted financial fugitive, Martin Frankel, was arrested in a Hamburg hotel, *surrounded by a bank of computers, a bag of diamonds and a female accomplice*. Previously at odds with the regulatory authorities, Frankel had managed to set up a bogus securities business which he ran from his house in Connecticut. He had been able to obtain control of eight small insurance companies – across six southern states – and then siphon money from these businesses, apparently as legitimate investments in funds he managed. His capture came down to a lucky tip-off; he had effectively escaped the detection of the FBI.

George Reynolds

Our final story concerns a criminal who changed and reformed. The company started by George Reynolds manufactures chipboard in County Durham. Reynolds himself is a convicted criminal who now uses his entrepreneurial talents for more legitimate – and lucrative – ends. Sixty-three years old in 1999, he was born in Sunderland; his father was a deep-sea fisherman. He describes himself as *dyslexic, illiterate, backward and brainless*. The first may be true, and the second partially correct, but he is neither backward nor brainless. His childhood was deprived, and he followed years in institutional care with three jail sentences, the last for safe-breaking. In prison he was a *bootlegger and bookmaker, lucky not to be caught*. A trigger happened during his last jail sentence when a Catholic priest asked him 'If you are such a good thief, how is it you were caught yet again?' The priest suggested he should go into business, and he heeded the advice. It turned out to be good advice; Reynolds does possess strong entrepreneur character themes.

Borrowing money from his mother (which he was initially able to supplement with some illegally earned savings) he opened an ice cream business, a night club and a shop before he began manufacturing. As well as chipboard (which he started in 1981) he has an engineering business and a share in a shipping company. Worth over £250 million, some of which he spends on a lavish lifestyle, he also owns Darlington Football Club. His managers work closely together with no secretaries – a *type of prisoner camaraderie*. Long hours are a norm and Reynolds is proud of his reputation for being a fast and decisive decision-maker. Employee discipline is tight, misdemeanours are fined, but the rewards are high. Reynolds is reputed to be a tough negotiator and *intolerant of suppliers who let him down*. One close colleague comments 'In 1981 he would have made rash decisions . . . now he makes devastating decisions . . . he has learned a lot'.

In this chapter we have looked at a wide range of entrepreneurs who operate in the shadows. Some are unlucky, some are rash and over-reach themselves – but others are simply dishonest. In every case we have considered, the mistakes were realised and a penalty was paid. There are many similar stories which have passed largely unreported, and other entrepreneurs whose crimes and misdemeanours have so far not been detected. Sometimes these people are colourful, fun characters with a very visible and lavish lifestyle; on other occasions they are, to some degree, evil. They will always exist and they will always find or create opportunities. For them, shadowy or even illegal behaviour becomes unsuppressible. But we must never make things too easy for them by misjudging the controls we need.

Part Three
Entrepreneurs and enterprise

Having looked at entrepreneurs in some detail in Parts One and Two we now consider the enterprise process of which they are part and the environment in which they operate. In Chapter 14 we use Silicon Valley as an example of how amazing things can happen when the process and the environment come together in the right way. The final chapter provides an introduction to the third of our entrepreneurial factors – technique.

The link between entrepreneurs and enterprise might sound like a simple case of cause and effect. Entrepreneurs produce enterprises. If only this was true! Sadly many would-be entrepreneurs never succeed in building an enterprise. As with Cyril in our Introduction there can be a host of reasons for this. There may be shortcomings in the entrepreneur's make up; perhaps a weakness in some of the talent character themes or difficulties with temperament. Or it may be lack of training and know-how giving weaknesses in the area of technique.

Equally, the reasons may not be of the entrepreneur's making. The business support infrastructure may be weak so that finding start-up money and getting help is very difficult with the result that few entrepreneurs emerge, and many that do, never quite make it. There can be practical things in the infrastructure that are just not there or are at least not in the quality or quantity needed. The educational and financial sectors may not be geared to the needs of the new enterprise. Basic facilities like transport, postal system and telecommunications can be a major problem for the start-up entrepreneur who has to learn his way around before he can find out the best deal. There is the simple Catch 22 situation of organising credit accounts with suppliers. In the UK a supplier will not set up a credit account with a new business unless it has references from other suppliers where the new business already has a credit account. As a new business has no suppliers when it starts, it has no credit accounts either, and so cannot provide any references. Whilst the new business is resolving this Catch 22 problem it has to pay cash on delivery, and its cash flow is hit immediately.

Most likely, the environment in which the entrepreneur has to operate is hostile. Despite all the regulations and controls, the marketplace still has its cartels that shut out new entrants. Government bureaucracy and taxation systems and the economic situation can strangle a business before it starts, not to mention problems of corruption and extortion. Worst of all, there can be a culture that rewards dependency and discourages risk-taking.

With all these problems to cope with, it is no wonder that the link between the entrepreneur and the enterprise cannot be taken for granted.

Even in the other direction there are difficulties. Just because there is an enterprise it does not mean that there is an entrepreneur around. There may have been in the early days but when the entrepreneur goes he leaves behind an enterprise that is soon intellectually bankrupt, even if it is not financially bankrupt. Such businesses join the ranks of the business community run by well-meaning people of moderate competence but without the innovation and dynamic of the entrepreneur. Apple Computers was never the same once Steve Jobs had been ousted (Carlton, 1998).

In Chapter 1 we defined an entrepreneur as *a person who habitually creates and innovates to build something of recognised value around perceived opportunities*. It is our belief that entrepreneurs are the people who possess the imagination and flexibility to ensure that there is a causal link between the entrepreneur and the enterprise. They are the ones best-suited by talent and temperament to deal with the challenges of today's turbulent and uncertain world. Their minds and behaviours are agile, and they are willing to experiment with new ideas in their attempt to make a difference. In an entrepreneurial society, ideas, talented people, finance and opportunity all come together. In this section of the book we explore the challenge for us all if this potent combination of forces is to be brought and fused together.

However, it is also important to remember that entrepreneurial behaviour in established organisations, or intrapreneurship, needs the same synergistic forces – as we discussed in Chapter 3. There is really no reason why this should not happen in large companies – if those who run the business are willing to sponsor and champion it. People everywhere in the organisation can be encouraged to contribute ideas, as we saw with the story of Wal-Mart in Chapter 4. There is rarely a monopoly of good strategic ideas at the most senior levels in the hierarchy. Within most, if not all, organisations, if they are sought, identified and encouraged, there are people with the talent and temperament to be internal entrepreneurs. The organisation simply has to create the mechanisms and opportunities for exploiting this talent and provide the necessary resources to finance and implement their projects. After all, new products are vital for most organisations, and the new product ideas, people might provide, can have a major impact upon the organisation. Witness the impact upon spirits manufacturer, Diageo (previously known as Grand Met), of a range of alcopops based upon Smirnoff vodka. Sony had deliberately not entered the computer games industry and it was only by chance that a senior manager won a games console in a competition. He tried it and became convinced it was something Sony should develop. The PlayStation was the outcome and it has been a hugely significant product for Sony.

In reality, intrapreneurs ought to be able to find the resources from inside a large, established and successful organisation more easily than an entrepreneur trying to start-up a new business from scratch. But the culture has to be right. Moreover, the larger companies should be ensuring they retain and reward their most talented people (in this context) if they are going to foster this intrapreneurship. A hostile or unwelcoming culture, which demands conformity and fails to recognise or reward initiative, will have the opposite effect. People with entrepreneurial talent will underachieve, and they may very well leave. In this context it is worth remembering that new products and innovation invariably take time to come to fruition and deliver results. It took Guinness several years to develop Draft Guinness and 'get it right'. Philips allegedly spent twenty years developing compact discs. Individuals who are determined to make their mark inside organisations and see promotion as their natural reward – either with their current or a new employer – will realise that it is quicker to show results from cost cutting and efficiency drives.

In the remaining chapters of this book, we focus mainly on the start-up situation and consider the key issues. However the principles and lessons are easily transferred to the creation and championing of innovative new ventures and projects inside the established organisation. The stages of the process are broadly similar. Simply the relevant environment is internal to the organisation itself rather than external.

Creativity, innovation and entrepreneurship

Before we explain the structure of Part Three it is important to clarify further certain key terms in our definition, and the links between them.

> Ideas don't make money.
> Products don't make money.
> Businesses make money.

> (Frank Martin)

As we argue above, it is important for businesses to search for opportunities to *do* something *new* and *different*, in part because consumer expectations, and sometimes consumer spending, grow faster than the speed of innovation in many industries. The words do, new and different are significant. 'New' demands creativity; 'different' requires innovation; 'do' is a verb that implies enterprising behaviour.

Creativity

Creativity implies conceptualising, visualising or bringing into being something which does not yet exist. It is about curiosity and observation. In the history of science there are interesting examples of creativity occurring at the same time with no contact between the individuals involved. The mathematics of calculus was created by Newton and Leibniz in the seventeenth century, quite independent of each other, despite their allegations of plagiarism. Creativity seems to come 'out of the blue' triggered by a problem to be solved or an idea to be expressed. Its roots and origins are mysterious and unknown but its existence cannot be denied. This metaphysical aspect has meant that science has shied away from the topic though it is now becoming a subject *of serious study among cognitive scientists and experimental psychologists* (Finke *et al.*, 1992).

Entrepreneurs are familiar with ideas that suddenly come to mind and are not too concerned with their origins. This is the starting point of the entrepreneurial process. We see creativity as a talent, an innate ability, though we recognise that it can be developed and that there are techniques that promote creativity and problem-solving. Creativity is also a function of how people feel. Some are more creative under pressure whilst others need complete relaxation. Some use divergent thinking in their creativity whilst others prefer convergent thinking. For many there is a 'Eureka moment' when something important is discovered.

One thing that seems common to all forms of creativity is joy. Einstein comments that the idea that *the gravitational field has only a relative existence* was *the happiest thought of my life* (Pais, 1982). His creative genius had come up with the idea of relativity and it made him happy. There is an intense personal satisfaction in having come up with something new and novel.

This is one reason why entrepreneurs see their activities as fun. There is the joy of creativity all around them. For the entrepreneur, creativity is both the starting point and the reason for continued success. It is the secret formula by which he or she overcomes obstacles and outsmarts the competition.

Arguably every one of us has the ability to be creative – but do we all use and exploit this ability? Many of us simply do not act creatively much of the time. Possibly we are not motivated and encouraged; maybe we do not believe in ourselves and the contribution and difference we could make. There is certainly a skills and technique element to creativity – in a business context, for example, we can be taught creative thinking and behaviour in the context of decision-making – but this is clearly only part of the explanation. The issue of meaning is also a critical element.

Many people have the ability to play a musical instrument. They have a skill – and possibly natural talent – and they can be taught more skills and techniques, whilst ever they are willing to persevere and practice. Furthermore, some people who play music naturally appreciate the meaning the composer was trying to convey when he wrote the work. Others have to be taught this interpretation. Some people simply see things that others cannot until they are given a detailed explanation. The same applies to opportunity-spotting. People who miss the valuable opportunities that others see first often have access to the same information – but it means something different to them.

> Discovery consists of looking at the same thing as everyone else and thinking something different.
>
> (Albert Szent-Gyorghi, Physician and Nobel Prize winner)

In just the same way, many young people can dribble, head and pass a football, and their skills can be improved with coaching. But when they watch a football match – or play in one – are they able to 'see the whole game'? Can they spot goal-scoring opportunities and positions and get there ahead of a defender? Most people who watch team sports such as football simply follow the movement of the ball, exactly as the television camera tends to do. They ignore or miss the emerging patterns as the other players move off the ball in search of good positions. This partially explains why we do not all seem to see the same game evolve, even though we were present at the same match.

Innovation

Innovation builds on creativity when something new, tangible and value-creating is developed from the ideas. Innovation can be focused on the theme of being 'better' – incremental improvements – as well as the theme of being radically different. The former will often form the world of the intrapreneur, who is attempting to make his or her organisation better and stronger than its rivals. The latter is often, but certainly not always, reserved for the true entrepreneur, who is more concerned with doing something genuinely new and different rather than improving on ideas which have gone before.

Schumpeter (1949) argued that entrepreneurs occasionally stumble on something which is radically new or different and which is disruptive in unpredictable ways. He called this 'alpha innovation'. It triggers secondary, 'beta', effects as new opportunities are opened up for other entrepreneurs who come in and either change or develop new industries. Steam, railway engines, petrol engines and micro-processors are alpha innovations in Schumpeter's view.

Innovation is about seeing the creative new idea through to completion, to final application, but, of course, this will not necessarily be a business. It is the *entrepreneur* who builds a business around the idea and the innovation. Both can be difficult roads and require courage and perseverance, as well as creativity and imagination. These are attributes that the entrepreneur brings and his role in innovation is crucial.

There are three basic approaches with innovation, which are not mutually exclusive, and which we have seen illustrated in the stories in Part Two. First, it is possible to have a problem and to be seeking a solution, or at least a resolution. Edwin Land invented the Polaroid camera because his young daughter could not understand why she had to wait for the pictures to be printed when he took her photograph. Second, we might have an idea – in effect a solution – and be searching for a problem to which it can be applied. 3M's Post-It Notes happened (as we saw in Chapter 5) when a 3M employee created a glue with only loose-sticking properties, and a colleague applied it to a need he had for marking pages in a manuscript. Third, we might identify a need and design something which fits. James Dyson's innovatory dual cyclone cleaner came about because of his frustration with his existing machine, which was proving inadequate for cleaning up the dirt and dust he generated when he converted an old property.

Generating opportunities from ideas requires us to attribute meaning to the ideas. Ideas form in our minds and at this stage they mean something to us, personally. Typically, they become a real opportunity when we expose the ideas and share them with other people, who may well have different perceptions, attribute different meanings and see something we miss initially. This process of exploration is fundamental for determining where the opportunities for building new values are. In other words, innovation comes from the way we use our ideas. Crucially the person with the initial idea may not be the person who realises where the real opportunity lies. An inventor is not always an opportunity-spotter, and often not a natural project champion. Picasso claimed that *great people steal ideas and create opportunities where others cannot see the potential.*

Creativity is the talent of the inventor and innovation is the talent of the project champion who turns ideas into reality. The entrepreneur does both these things but he does more. He does not just complete the successful application of an idea; he builds something of value in the process.

The Sony Walkman provides an excellent illustration of what happens. The idea came to Sony co-founder Akio Morita when he was questioning why he was finding it difficult to listen to music when he was in public places or walking round a golf course. The idea became an innovative new product – and a valuable opportunity – when Morita shared his idea with other colleagues in Sony, and existing technologies and competencies were used to develop the compact personal cassette player with adequate playing time from its batteries and individual headphones. The project was championed, resourced and implemented. The original cassette player has systematically been joined by personal radio and CD players. It was simply a great idea which rejuvenated Sony at the time it was conceived, and it has brought value and affected the lives of millions of people around the world.

Figure P3.1 endeavours to pull these strands together. Creativity (the idea) is the starting point whether it is associated with invention or opportunity-spotting. This

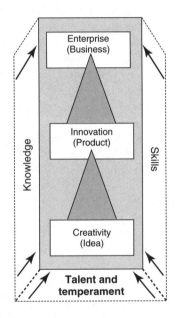

Figure P3.1   *Creativity, innovation and entrepreneurship*

creativity is turned to a practical reality (a product, for example) through innovation. Entrepreneurship then sets that innovation in the context of an enterprise (the actual business), which is something of recognised value.

To be exploited fully and effectively, they need to be supported by certain talents and aspects of temperament. We also need a base of knowledge, which we use to help generate and develop our new ideas. In part, this is developed through our experiences but it also needs to be supplemented further by certain key skills.

In very simple terms,

- Talent and temperament combined with knowledge helps us find out and discover new possibilities.
- Key skills can enhance the discovery process, whilst other skills help us design and craft new opportunities from the ideas.

The enterprise process

To repeat our definition: *an entrepreneur is a person who habitually creates and innovates to build something of recognised value around perceived opportunities.* In Part Three we look at how the entrepreneur actually does this. As the earlier comments show, the link between the entrepreneur and the enterprise cannot be taken for granted. We therefore set the actions of the entrepreneur within a process model that captures this link. In Part One we spoke of the entrepreneur process and now we turn to consider the enterprise process. This is an important distinction. The former is concerned with entrepreneurs and the way in which their attributes and personal qualities contribute to the things that they do. The latter is concerned with the process whereby entrepreneurs build the enterprises.

The *enterprise process* has as its setting what we have called the *enterprise paradigm*. Figure P3.2 illustrates this setting and gives some of its characteristics. In many

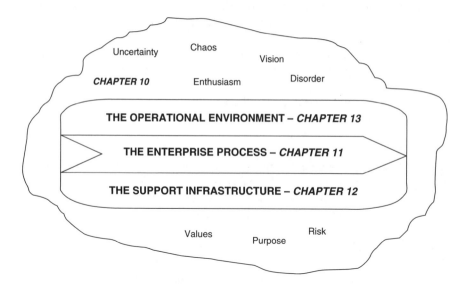

Figure P3.2   *The enterprise paradigm*

ways this is the entrepreneur's natural habitat. Entrepreneurs are at home with its fuzzy boundary and its uncertainty and chaos, seeing them as the fertile soil of new opportunities. The vision and values of this new paradigm emphasise that it is the domain of social and aesthetic entrepreneurs as well as economic entrepreneurs, though for them too issues of vision and values are becoming increasingly important. All this is a refreshing change for the entrepreneur, who for centuries has had to live within a deterministic world that is suspicious of the new and hates risk. In Chapter 10 we consider *the entrepreneur's world* and show how today's world of the *enterprise paradigm* is moving in the right direction. Hopefully this will mean that more of the latent entrepreneurial talent will emerge and we will learn to value the entrepreneur more highly in our society.

The centre and focus of the model is *the enterprise process*. It is this process that is served and promoted, whether by the entrepreneurs themselves or those who are trying to educate, encourage and support them. In Chapter 11 the *enterprise process* is broken down into its component parts as we consider *how the entrepreneur operates*. The *getting ready* stage prior to start-up is considered first followed by the *building* stage in which the enterprise grows and develops. Although we deal mainly with the entrepreneur who creates economic capital the principles are similar for those who employ their talent in other areas such as society and the arts. We therefore use *enterprise* in its widest sense to mean *a piece of work taken in hand, an undertaking; especially one that is bold, hazardous or arduous*[1] rather than as simply a *business firm, company.*[2]

In Figure P3.2 the *support infrastructure* is set beneath the *enterprise process* because it is the infrastructure that supports the process and carries it forward. The *support infrastructure* can be thought of as a boat that carries its passengers or freight to its destination. A boat that is not strong or large enough or takes in water will hinder the process and may even sink. The elements that comprise the *support infrastructure* are the subject of Chapter 12 as we consider *how the entrepreneur can be helped and supported*. Each element of the infrastructure has a specific job to do and must link together effectively. Thus, if a university or research laboratory is a source of business ideas then there has to be a means of accessing that technology. There must be mechanisms for capturing the intellectual property and funding resources for its commercialisation.

The *operational environment* is placed above the *enterprise process* in Figure P3.2 because the process has to operate under this environment and be subject to it. In our analogy it is the weather or climate through which the boat has to sail. If the weather is hostile the boat will have a difficult journey and may not survive but if there is sunshine and gentle seas then progress will be rapid and the mission successful. In Chapter 13 we review the main elements that make up this environment. It includes elements such as the market and the economy that entrepreneurs cannot influence in the short term. These are things that they have to learn to live with if they are to *survive and win*.

The distinction between infrastructure and environment is based upon the degree to which the entrepreneur or the economic developer can control the elements involved. The infrastructure is under short to medium control but the environment takes much longer to change. It may be possible to set up a seed capital fund or build a business incubator but there is little that can done about interest and inflation rates.

In terms of our analogy it is possible to design and construct a boat that is seaworthy. This kind of activity can be organised. Mechanisms and facilities can be put in place in the short and medium terms. Even if it is not be possible to do everything at once, a strategy can be developed for a region that puts the most important elements in place first. On the other hand there is little that can be done about the weather. We can watch the weather forecast and either steer out of the way or take precautions as best as we can. A company that is holding on to its cash in a recession is taking the right precautions. It is battening down the hatches.

Chapter 15 considers *Techniques for the Entrepreneur* and presents a number of technique summary sheets with references to where further information can be found.

In summary, then, Part Three considers how the entrepreneur:

- sees the world
- operates
- can be helped and supported
- survives and wins
- makes it happen.

Underlying all of these *How* questions is the make up of the entrepreneur – his or her talent and temperament. Two of the questions considered are more specifically about technique and know-how and have a body of knowledge and experience associated with them. These are *how the entrepreneur can be helped and supported* and *how the entrepreneur makes it happen*. In presenting this material we want to repeat the point that the acquisition of this knowledge does not make a person an entrepreneur. We acknowledge that someone may be able to turn a failing business into a successful one when they have learnt about cash flow and market share but unless the right talents and temperament are there to be developed they will never be able to *build something of recognised value*.

Most of us are able to run. Some can sprint to catch a train, others are fitter and jog regularly or even run a half or full marathon. But we reserve the word *athlete* for the person who runs competitively on a regular basis and describe the outstanding performer as an *elite athlete*. We believe that the word *entrepreneur* should be used in a similar way – it is too important an issue to apply the word generally to the enterprising business person or worse still to the small business person.

Notes

1. Definition from the *Shorter Oxford English Dictionary*.
2. Definition from the *Shorter Oxford English Dictionary*.

References

Carlton, J. (1998). *Apple*. HarperCollins.
Finke, R.A., Ward, T.B. and Smith, S.M. (1996). *Creative Cognition*, MIT Press.
Pais, A. (1982). *'Subtle is the Lord' – The Science and Life of Albert Einstein*, Oxford University Press.
Schumpeter, J. (1949). *The Theory of Economic Development*, Harvard University Press.

10 The entrepreneur's world

Today, entrepreneurs are in a world that perhaps for the first time ever has close resonances with their own world. Uncertainty and opportunity have come together. Here we examine and critique today's world to arrive at an intellectual framework that helps us to understand why the entrepreneur has such a central role, both economic and social, to play in the society of the future. We conclude by considering the factors that present entrepreneurs with a unique opportunity to realise their true destiny as agents for positive and creative change.

Opportunity and action

How we see the world is important. Some see threats where others see opportunities; for some the cup is always half-empty, for others it is half-full. Entrepreneurs have two linked perceptions of the world. Firstly they see it is a world full of opportunities and secondly as a world of actions in which they can make things happen. It is as if entrepreneurs have two eyes seeing *opportunities to grasp* and *actions to take*, as illustrated in Figure 10.1. The brain links these perceptions to give a single view of the world. If the opportunity side is not linked with focused action then in the worst case we have a *butterfly* that hops from one opportunity to another, never settling for very long. If the action side is not linked with the right opportunity then we have a *beaver* that builds a perfect dam but in the wrong place.

The link between these two perceptions is important. The mature entrepreneur moves from opportunity to action without difficulty, but for the potential entrepreneur the link may not be so straightforward. The first sign of entrepreneurial talent is generally the ability to spot opportunities but the circumstances may be such that the potential entrepreneur does not have the confidence to go forward and take action. Lack of confidence in the early days is not a sign of lack of talent. This is seen in other areas when a talent is discovered. Gifted public speakers often admit that they found it extremely difficult when they first addressed an audience. After a while they discover that public-speaking comes naturally to them and they begin to enjoy it as their talent blossoms. It is the same with entrepreneurs when they discover that they are

Figure 10.1 *Linked perceptions*

able to spot an opportunity and take it to fruition. Once they find they can do this they gain confidence and very soon it becomes something that they do naturally, even habitually – they have discovered that they are entrepreneurs.

The challenge then is how to create an environment in which people are able to come forward and test their abilities as entrepreneurs. The educational approach would suggest some form of school or academy, such as is found in cricket and tennis, that is geared to identifying and developing talent at an early age. Although this is a possible approach the world view of the entrepreneur is often anti-academic – they are doers rather than thinkers. There is certainly no correlation between IQ level and success as an entrepreneur. Entrepreneurs are often strongly individualistic and difficult to work with in groups. They learn best by doing and not talking.

Whilst the entrepreneur school approach is discussed under 'developing and supporting' the entrepreneur in Chapter 12, hopes of tapping the well of talent lie much more with the developments that are taking place in the world around us. Today's world is characterised by change and uncertainty, and for the entrepreneur this is fertile soil. It is an opportunity generator in which nothing is impossible. The *Berlin Walls* of the large multinational are no longer as impregnable as they once appeared. Richard Branson has championed the cause of the entrepreneur against the big monolithic business empires by first taking on the record companies and then the might of British Airways. Many of these same organisations are now seeking ways of replicating this entrepreneurial spirit. British Airways' response to the low-cost airlines was to set up their GO company and staff it with a very entrepreneurial team. The title of Rosabeth Moss Kanter's book (1990) *When Giants learn to Dance* captures this point well. At that time, now more than a decade ago, she saw a revolution taking place in business management which she termed 'post-entrepreneurial because it is taking entrepreneurship a step further, applying entrepreneurial principles to the traditional corporation'.

Tom Peters' books have targeted the same area. His *Thriving on Chaos: Handbook for a Management Revolution* (1989) became a best seller as the corporate world tried to come to terms with uncertainty in which markets changed almost overnight and competitors emerged out of nowhere. As we report in the Silicon Valley story in Chapter 14, IBM disregarded the idea of the mini-computer allowing a new start-up, DEC, to make the running. Both companies then disregarded the PC opportunity allowing Apple and others to take the lead. It was a credit to the new thinking in IBM that they later put together an entrepreneurial team to develop the IBM PC that caught up and overtook the early leaders.

The entrepreneur is at home in this turbulent world where he can see opportunities and can take action. It is not a matter of being *post-entrepreneurial*, as Kanter (1990) put it, but rather of being entrepreneurial in a business environment that has suddenly become uncertain and turbulent, whether that is in the large corporation or the start-up company. The dynamic of the entrepreneur has not changed. It is simply that the business environment has now moved on enabling the entrepreneur to make the difference. Sadly, many years of neglect have resulted in entrepreneurs either staying away from the large corporation or else having their talent unrecognised and undeveloped, but times are changing and intrapreneurs are now seen as a valuable asset.

The situation in the small business sector has not been a great deal better. This is partly because they serve the large company and end up very like them in attitude or become so disillusioned that they never want to work for a big company again. Some big-name companies take a year to pay their bills and believe that their suppliers should regard it as a privilege to have their business!

The importance of the small business sector has been championed in the UK since the Bolton Committee of Enquiry on Small Firms published its report in the early 1970s (Bolton, 1971). The contribution of the small business is the same in most of the world's developed economies. Ninety-nine per cent of all businesses employ 100 people or less and 95 per cent of them employ less than ten people. Half of the entire workforce and half of the sales come from firms with 100 people or less. These figures make the importance of the small business sector no longer a matter of debate.

With the recognition of the importance of the small firm, the UK government introduced schemes to encourage their growth and development. Despite the money spent, businesses have not grown and small firms have remained small. The reasons for this are at the centre of our theme. The schemes are focused on almost everything except the entrepreneur. They look at product development and innovation, at new manufacturing initiatives, at quality improvement, at providing advice on marketing and IT and so on. To the real entrepreneur all these issues are peripheral. Entrepreneurs know when they need help and they know where to get it, as we discussed in Chapter 2. In principle they just want to be left alone to get on with the job. Government efforts would be better spent on reducing the bureaucracy that start-up businesses have to deal with than trying to intervene in what is, after all, a natural process.

The small business has stifled the potential entrepreneur almost as much as the big firm, but times are changing, thanks to the turbulence in technology and markets. Young potential entrepreneurs who see an opportunity and are told that they can expect promotion in a couple of years are no longer prepared to wait. They leave and set up their own business, often taking the opportunity with them. If government must intervene then it is these kinds of entrepreneurial aspirations that should be encouraged. The challenge is to unlock the entrepreneurial potential in our midst. The Thatcher government took an important step in this direction when it withdrew the exclusive exploitation rights held by the British Technology Group on government-funded research in British universities. Unfortunately, in most cases, this control was then taken over by the universities themselves, showing a complete failure to recognise the importance of the role of the entrepreneur in the process of commercialisation. Cambridge University was an important exception to this and its liberal policy on intellectual property was certainly one of the factors behind the remarkable growth of technology-based businesses in the Cambridge area over the last twenty years. It is significant that there is now pressure on Cambridge to tighten up on this approach and come more into line with other universities.

These comments reflect the situation in the UK and Europe. In the USA the role of the entrepreneur is well recognised and some of the government schemes to help small business growth are excellent. The US 'Space Race' budget provided a major cash injection into the companies of Silicon Valley, as we explain in Chapter 14. When the US government specified that a percentage of all defence contracts should be placed with small firms it gave the small business sector a real boost. This experience suggests that a main task of government is to open up opportunities that entrepreneurs can identify and exploit.

The situation in those economies which have had years of central control is particularly difficult for the entrepreneur. The countries that previously composed the USSR, including Russia itself, have a huge task before them. Speaking to a young Russian entrepreneur we were told that it was impossible to grow a business in Russia because if there was any degree of success there would be visits, first from the Mafia and then the government tax police. We know of a successful business incubator in Moscow that was eventually closed down because of the actions of the tax police. In such an environment it is not surprising that some people use their entrepreneurial talents on the dark side of society. It is the easier route, though somewhat risky!

The Third World is an interesting place for the entrepreneur. Although most businesses are small and serve a local market the owner-managers seem to show more entrepreneurial characteristics than their counterparts in the developed world. Many of the new aid programmes are linking in to this entrepreneurial talent and provide start-up funding and resources. In 1998 a fish-farming project in Cambodia provided 800 000 baby fish to eight local villages and thereby enabled them to take a significant step out of poverty and into self-sufficiency. Run by a Christian charity on a not-for-profit basis the project was set up as a commercial venture. The local farmers had to pay for their fish, often on credit terms, but they were given help and advice so that they could learn how to run their farm as a profit-making business. This type of hands-on project helps to reveal the potential entrepreneurs and provides an excellent opportunity for them to develop their talent for the benefit of the rest of their community.

The next section develops further the idea that we are moving into a world that puts the entrepreneur centre-stage but first we must make an important distinction between the way the entrepreneur sees things and the prevailing world view within a culture. Entrepreneurs like Jacob and the artistic entrepreneurs of the Renaissance mentioned in Chapter 1, are no different from the entrepreneurs of the Industrial Revolution or of Silicon Valley. They all see opportunities and build upon them. Jacob's world of sheep and goats was very different from the sophisticated world of the Renaissance and yet the essential characteristics of the entrepreneur remain the same. In our experience entrepreneurs are the same the world over, from the Central African Republic to Silicon Valley. Entrepreneurs have a particular view of the world that they see through the two lenses of opportunity and action and is independent of the world in which they find themselves. The world around them simply determines the opportunities that are there for them to see and the resources that are available for them to use.

The enterprise paradigm

In the 1960s a young concert pianist from Mexico won a scholarship to the USA. During her concert tour she met Dizzy Gillespie, the jazz trumpeter. She was impressed by his amazing ability to improvise his music, which she found alive and exciting. When Gillespie asked her why she played 'dead music' she had no answer and abandoned her musical career. She saw no hope that she could be so spontaneous and creative. Later on she began to study how jazz musicians like Gillespie made their music and learnt that they improvise within a structured framework. It might have appeared spontaneous, and it was, but there was a framework behind it. Today's world of uncertainty and turbulence is a place where the creativity and improvisation of the entrepreneur can flourish but it does so within a framework that is both conceptual and practical. This chapter deals with the conceptual aspects, and Chapters 11 and 12 with the practical.

We choose the term 'enterprise paradigm' to describe this framework. The word 'enterprise' is used because it catches the spirit and provides a positive focus towards a more prosperous society. The word 'paradigm' suggests a framework that has content and embodies a new way of thinking. We choose this word with some hesitation because it is now over-used and often misapplied. The term came into common usage following the publication in 1969 of Thomas Kuhn's *The Structure of Scientific Revolution*. In a subsequent edition (Kuhn, 1975) he comments on two meanings of the word. 'On the one hand, it stands for the entire constellation of beliefs, values, techniques and so on shared by the members of a given community. On the other hand, it denotes one sort of element in that constellation.' We use the word paradigm in the former sense so that a 'paradigm shift' is a major change in the way we think about and understand the world in which we live. As we shall argue, the present paradigm shift moves us into a paradigm in which the entrepreneur has a central role to play, but we must remember it is not his paradigm, it belongs to all of us. Hence we call it the 'enterprise paradigm' and not the 'entrepreneur's paradigm'.

Kuhn's approach to the history of science was based around the idea that scientific thinking develops within a particular intellectual envelope or 'paradigm' which it fills out until it reaches a block when there is a 'paradigm shift' and a new paradigm takes over. A given paradigm has its own set of rules and understandings that are accepted as true because they are consistent within themselves. Inside the paradigm there is still debate but there is an essential harmony because people all think in a similar way with the same norms and reference points. Kuhn argued that a paradigm breaks down when it fails to answer the questions of the day. At first these questions are few and not seen as important but gradually, as more and more unanswered questions arise, the intellectual pressure builds. Finally the dam bursts as the old paradigm can no longer sustain the pressure and the new paradigm takes over. 'The resulting transition to a new paradigm is scientific revolution' (Kuhn, 1975).

The Greek understanding of science lasted well into the Middle Ages in Europe and was a very successful paradigm. Then scholars like Copernicus (1473–1543), Kepler (1571–1630) and Galileo (1564–1642) began to come up with observations and ideas that challenged it. Although this has been seen by many as a challenge to the Church, it was in fact a challenge to the science of the day which quite simply failed to explain the new discoveries. The intellectual pressure for a new scientific paradigm was building up.

'More than any other, it was the Copernican insight that provoked and symbolised the drastic, fundamental break from the ancient and medieval universe to that of the modern era' (Tarnas, 1996). Although in hindsight this was a defining moment it was by no means obvious at the time. The scientists, as much as the churchmen, found it difficult to accept this insight. Even Copernicus was not happy with his new theory because it made the orbits of the planets much more complicated (Koestler, 1989). It was only later when Kepler showed that the orbits of the planets were ellipses and not circles that the whole thing simplified. But it still required Isaac Newton born in 1642, the same year that Galileo died, to put all these ideas together. He was in his twenties when he produced the mathematics that explained these discoveries and the new paradigm was finally born. Surprisingly it took the persuasion of the astronomer Halley some twenty years later before Newton told the world what he had done and published his now famous *Principia Mathematica*.

The nature of this scientific revolution was well expressed by the Cambridge historian Sir Herbert Butterfield when he wrote:

> It outshines everything since the rise of Christianity and reduces the Renaissance and Reformation to the rank of mere episodes, mere internal displacements, within the system of medieval Christendom. It changed the character of men's habitual mental operations. It required a different kind of thinking cap, a transposition in the mind of the scientist himself.
>
> (Butterfield, 1957)

Over time, this shift in the way scientists thought became the basis for our Western culture and the way we think today. In scientific, social and economic terms this paradigm has been a great success and has provided the basis for the Western world, as we know it. The emphasis on the individual that was a feature of this paradigm was also a help to the emergence of the entrepreneur. People's lives were no longer governed by fate and the gods but by man's own efforts. The Protestant work ethic was an important motivator (Weber, 1905) and drove many successful entrepreneurs. It brought economic prosperity to certain parts of Europe. Successful groups such as the Huguenots and the Mennonites were driven out from where they settled as much from economic envy as for their religious beliefs (Reaman, 1963). North America benefited from these upheavals in Europe as entrepreneurs flooded in. Waves of immigrants have continued to top up the entrepreneurial stock, as the story of the Cuban refugees in Miami described in Chapter 11 indicates. It is therefore not surprising that the USA has created the most successful and largest economy the world has ever seen.

At the beginning of the twentieth century the Newtonian paradigm was beginning to feel the pressure, just as the Greek paradigm had done 400 years earlier. Experiments concerning the nature of light and moving bodies in space were giving some strange results that were not explained by what we now call 'Classical Physics'. Then, in 1905, Albert Einstein, at that time an examiner in the patent office in Switzerland, published his first paper on relativity. This proved to be the door to a new paradigm. Not only was it able to make sense of the strange results that classical physics could not explain but it opened up a new world of relativity and quantum mechanics. It was the world of the New Physics. Without this breakthrough, the modern world of nuclear energy and IT would not have been possible. High technology, as we know it today, is a product of this new paradigm.

Central to an understanding of the New Physics are two theories put forward in 1927; Heisenberg's Uncertainty Principle and Bohr's Principle of Complementarity. They represent the mind-set of the new paradigm and show a complete break from the deterministic thinking of the Newtonian Paradigm. It is not a matter of more complete scientific knowledge; it is about seeing things in a new way, about putting on a 'different kind of thinking cap'.

To illustrate this new way of thinking we consider what one of these theories, the Principle of Complementarity, meant in practice. Since the time of Newton a debate had raged between scientists as to whether light was a wave or, as Newton believed, a stream of particles. Throughout the eighteenth century the particle or corpuscular theory, as Newton called it, was believed to be the right answer, which conversely meant that the wave theory had to be wrong. At the beginning of the nineteenth century this view was challenged by ThomasYoung and later in that century by James Clerk Maxwell who showed beyond doubt that light was indeed a wave. It was part of the electro-magnetic spectrum of waves that start with Gamma rays and X-rays of very small wavelength and move through to the visible range called 'light' and on to radio waves of much longer wavelength. By the time Einstein came on the scene, light was understood as a wave and not as a stream of particles. Einstein stunned the scientific world by showing that the photo-electric effect could only be explained if light was a stream of discrete bundles of energy called photons. This put Newton's corpuscular theory back on the agenda. So was light a wave or a stream of particles?

Separate experiments could be performed, some of which demonstrated the wave characteristics of light and others which showed that light behaved as a stream of photons. The Classical Physics paradigm of Newton could not come to terms with these two explanations because it required that one must be right and the other must be wrong. Bohr's Principle of Complementarity in the New Physics Paradigm offered a completely different understanding. Both explanations of the nature of light were right; they were complementary and, not contradictory, answers. This was not a scientific fudge, it was simply a different way of looking at things.

As this example illustrates, a fundamental shift has taken place in the way scientists think. Science now has a new intellectual framework that can handle ideas of uncertainty and chaos found at the level of atoms and particles. The interesting thing is that this thinking did not stop with the scientists. Whilst an essay by Bohr entitled 'Causality and Complementarity' shows they were still debating the issue in 1958 (Ferris, 1991), general Western culture had its watershed in the 1960s when it too embraced uncertainty and chaos at the human level. It was a time of great upheaval with the hippy free love movement, psychedelic drugs and protest marches. Much of this emanated from California, and the entrepreneurial culture of Silicon Valley is closely linked with the values and thinking that started at that time.

> But there was more to the Valley than electronics: The free- speech movement at Berkeley, the summer of love in Haight-Ashbury, flower power, the Grateful Dead, the birth of a counterculture. Apple was a technological manifestation of its environment.
>
> (Rose, 1989)

Members of the Homebrew Club of the mid-1970s in Silicon Valley, described in Chapter 14, grew out of this culture. As one of the main spin-off points in the Valley, this club spread a new approach to business. When Apple Computers began to be featured in Business Week and Fortune Magazine the rest of American industry took note. In 1984 when Apple challenged the supremacy of IBM in a famous Superbowl TV commercial it was clear that the business world would never be the same again. Uncertainty and chaos had entered this world too.

This paradigm shift in culture and then in business is described in rather robust terms by Alvin Toffler:

> A new civilisation is emerging in our lives, and blind men everywhere are trying to suppress it. This new civilisation brings with it new family styles; changed ways of working, loving and living; a new economy; new political conflicts; and beyond all this an altered consciousness as well. The dawn of this new civilisation is the single most explosive fact of our lifetime.
>
> (Toffler, 1981)

In *Future Shock*, ten years earlier, Toffler had pointed to the 'Death of Permanence' and the change and turbulence that was becoming a characteristic of our society. 'Change sweeps through the highly industrialised countries with waves of ever accelerating speed and unprecedented impact' (Toffler, 1971).

Toffler's themes were picked up by business. Hammer and Champy who introduced the idea of 're-engineering the corporation' comment that, 'Suddenly the world is a different place. In today's environment nothing is constant or predictable. Adam Smith's world and its way of doing business are yesterday's paradigm' (Hammer and Champy, 1993).

Porter observed in his *Competitive Advantage of Nations* (1990) that 'there is a growing consensus that the dominant paradigm used to date to explain international success in particular industries is inadequate'. He found that classical economic theory could not explain the emergence of the newly industrialised countries, such as Taiwan and Korea.

It is as if the physicists were the first to feel the pressure and broke through into their new paradigm in the early part of the twentieth century to be followed by general culture in the Western world in the 1960s and by business and industry in the 1970s and 1980s. What is significant is that they all have change, uncertainty and turbulence as key characteristics. In some ways it is one huge paradigm shift encompassing science, society and business.

Many writers have picked up these themes. Some have done this under the heading of post-modernism (Lyon, 1994) and others have applied it to their special area of interest such as business (Handy, 1993). Lyon uses the film *Blade Runner* to pick out three elements of post-modernism; the debate about reality, an industrial order based on 'new organising principles structured around knowledge' and a consumer society 'where everything is a show and the public image is all'. In his *Age of Unreason* Handy (1993) argues that we need 'creative upside-down thinking in today's world of discontinuous change' and uses shamrocks, doughnuts and portfolios as models to help us think differently.

Toffler has put these themes in a historical perspective with a three-wave model which has parallels with our use of paradigms:

> The First Wave – the agricultural revolution – took thousands of years to play itself out. The Second Wave – the rise of industrial civilisation – took a mere three hundred years. Today history is even more accelerative, and it is likely that the Third Wave will sweep across history and complete itself in a few decades.
>
> (Toffler, 1981)

Whilst Toffler's waves relate to society as a whole there is a correspondence between his 'Second Wave' and the deterministic world of the Newtonian Paradigm and his 'Third Wave' and the world of the New Physics Paradigm of Einstein. John Sculley (1987) has applied Toffler's wave model to business and used it to compare his very different experiences at Pepsi Cola and Apple Computers. Under the heading 'Contrasting Management Paradigms' he compared 'Second Wave' Pepsi Cola with 'Third Wave' Apple. Table 10.1, taken in part from this analysis and similar listings by Kawasaki (1992), compares some of the characteristics of Second- and Third-Wave companies. Kawasaki was a 'software evangelist at Apple Computer Inc from 1983 to 1987'.

The Third-Wave company is the entrepreneurial business with its flat and flexible management structures and its ability not only to embrace change but to stimulate it. People in Third-Wave companies are valued as persons and are not seen simply as a human resource. It is the new that is important and not the institution, so that for the potential entrepreneur the Third-Wave company is a natural habitat.

The main motivation in the Third-Wave business is to make history. As reported earlier, John Sculley's decision to leave the security of Pepsi Cola for the roller

Table 10.1   *Two management paradigms*

Parameter	Second wave	Third wave
Structure	Hierarchy	Flat and flexible
Ability	To organise	To embrace change
Output	Market share	Market creation
Personnel	Human resource	The person
Focus	The institution	The new
Motivation	To make money	To make history
Status	Title and rank	Building the new
Working environment	Formal, regulated	Informal, chaotic
Culture	Tradition	Genetic code
Philosophy	Fit into roles	Build on strengths
Mission	Goals/strategic plans	Identity/direction/values
Where	Clubhouse	Anywhere
When	9.00 a.m.–5.30 p.m.	Anytime

coaster, that was Apple, was based around the one question from Steve Jobs. 'Do you want to spend the rest of your life selling sugared water or do you want a chance to change the world?' Status and rank are not important. The big office and access to the managers' dining room do not matter anymore. Third-Wave companies, like entrepreneurs, want to build something, to do things that have not been done before. They are not interested in the status quo.

The working environment is completely different in Second- and Third-Wave companies. Rules, regulations and tradition are important to the former but have no place in the latter. The board meetings at Second-Wave Pepsi Cola and Third-Wave Apple Computers could not have been more different. Sculley (1987) tells us that at Pepsi Cola:

> Everyone wore the unofficial corporate uniform: a blue pin-striped suit, white shirt, and a sincere red tie. None of us would ever remove his jacket. At Apple all of us dressed casually, sans ties and jackets. Steve Jobs sat on the floor lotus style, in blue jeans, absent-mindedly playing with the toes of his bare feet.

Table 10.1 gives the options for culture as tradition or genetic code and is from Sculley's list. Tradition is derived from the past. Companies like Pepsi have their legends and heroes. They have their own way of doing things. Almost their only business indicator was their market share compared with Coca Cola's. Apple in contrast was a living dynamic organisation driven by elements deep in its culture that like the genetic code are always present but express themselves 'differently in different organisms'. Sculley believed that the company's vision and direction derived from this.

In Chapter 2 the role of talent and temperament was discussed and related directly to what a person does best. Sculley's genetic code analogy makes the same point. Third-Wave companies allow people to discover what they are good at and then help them to do it. They build upon the strengths of their staff. Second-Wave companies put people into pre-determined roles and if they do not fit then they have to adapt or leave. Personal development is focussed on strengthening weaknesses rather than building on strengths.

The relevance of all this to entrepreneurs is that they suddenly find themselves in a world that is far more in tune with their approach to life than was the old deterministic paradigm. The turbulence of the new paradigm throws up many more opportunities than the previously slow-moving and fairly predictable world. Risk and uncertainty is now inherent in the system, so entrepreneurs have less to lose. Today in the USA if you fail in business it is seen as a qualification and not a handicap. Creativity and doing things in new and innovative ways are now seen as positive and are encouraged. Those who say something cannot be done because it has never been done before are living in the old paradigm. Networking, market creation, values, making a difference and building, are all things that warm the entrepreneur's heart. The Third-Wave characteristics listed in Table 10.1 are central to the entrepreneur's view of the world so that, perhaps for the first time in history, the entrepreneur and the rest of us live in the same world. It is for this reason that we believe the future is more in the hands of the entrepreneur than it is of any other group or profession.

How true is it? A critique

Some important assertions have been made above and it is important to evaluate the basis on which they are made with some care. So how true is all this?

Whether or not we are moving into a new paradigm there is little doubt that times are changing, and changing very rapidly. The pace of technology alone brings a momentum that seems unstoppable. Computers, telecommunications and the World Wide Web are changing the world in which we live. But this was also true of railways, sanitation, telephones, motor cars, tarmac roads, mass production, electrical power, aeroplanes, plastics, the jet engine, TV and supermarkets. These innovations only produce a discontinuity when people just cannot cope with the rate at which they come along. It is certainly true that new technology is being adopted more rapidly than in the past. Cell phones and PCs took thirteen and fifteen years respectively to reach 25 per cent of the US population compared with the telephone that took thirty-five years. But thirteen years is still quite a long time and hardly worthy of the word 'revolution'. Even if these technology 'adoption times' were to reduce further, as seems to be the case with the World Wide Web, there is no evidence that society will not be able to cope with such changes.

The key question is not whether times are changing but whether the Western world is experiencing a major intellectual and social transition. This is the real issue. Is society moving from the deterministic paradigm brought in by Newton into a new one where change and turbulence are the way it is? If so then it is good news for entrepreneurs but if not it will be just as much a struggle for them as it has always been. Is Toffler right when he describes the three waves that have swept over humanity or is the division between Second- and Third-Wave companies just a convenient way of explaining a few differences? Is it yet another management fad that will soon be replaced?

There has certainly been no shortage of new approaches to management over recent years. Management book titles tell their own story. Examples are *In Search of Excellence* (Peters and Waterman, 1982), *When Giants Learn to Dance* (Kanter, 1990), *Thriving on Chaos* (Peters, 1989), *The Innovation Marathon* (Jelinek and Schoonhoven, 1990) and *Reengineering the Corporation* (Hammer and Champy, 1993). Other books offering a new approach include *Competitive Advantage* (Porter, 1985), *The 80/20 Principle* (Koch, 1997), *The Fifth Discipline* (Senge, 1990) and *Principle-Centred Leadership* (Covey, 1990). Books on successful individuals and their way of doing things have also been common: *Making it Happen* (Harvey-Jones, 1988), *Talking Straight* (Iacocca, 1989), *Business the Bill Gates Way* (Dearlove, 1999), *Direct from Dell* (Dell and Fredman, 1999) and *In Sam We Trust* (Ortega, 1999). Is this plethora of such books a sign that things really are different now or is it simply that we are 'dedicated followers of fashion'?

Certainly there are signs that some have had too much of these fashions and want to get back to basics. Titles like *Managing without Management – A Post-Management Manifesto for Business Simplicity* (Koch and Godden, 1998) and *The Power of Simplicity: A Management Guide to Cutting through Nonsense and Doing Things Right* (Trout and Rivkin, 1998) show this trend.

Whilst this view is understandable it is surely a sign of turbulent times when so many new solutions appear to the old problems. Thanks to mass communication the world is a much smaller place and conversely the marketplace is suddenly much bigger. Combine this with the advances of technology and one has a major shift in the economic and social environment. Even the large multinationals cannot assume a 'business as usual' approach. 'In the 1960s, it took twenty years to displace the top 35 per cent of the top 500 American companies; now it takes four or five years' (Bygrave, 1998).

In our view there is little doubt that the world is entering a new paradigm as profound as that identified by Thomas Kuhn (1975) for the scientific world. What is less sure is the model proposed by Toffler that sees the old replaced by the new as a Third Wave sweeps in. This just does not accord with the facts. As every secondary school student of mathematics and physics knows, the Scientific Revolution of the sixteenth and seventeenth centuries did not throw out Euclid's geometry, the Pythagoras theorem or Archimedes' principle. The Newtonian paradigm certainly did embody a major shift in the way scientists approached their science but not all of the findings of Greek science were rejected.

The same thing is seen with the present shift to the world of Einstein and his colleagues. Although the way of thinking has changed profoundly, Newton's Laws of Motion are still taught and engineers still design things using these principles. The difference is that it is now known that Newton's Laws and similar findings of deterministic science have their limits.

This carry-over from one paradigm to the next is important to recognise. A paradigm shift idea is a new envelope of thinking but not everything in the envelope is new. As Butterfield put it 'there is a new kind of thinking cap' but the content of the paradigm is a mixture of the completely new and some of the old that has been carried over. It is rather like moving into a new house when most of the furniture is new but there is also furniture from the old house. Both sets of furniture are arranged to fit in with the new setting.

Applying this to the analysis of the Second- and Third-Wave companies in Table 10.1 the modern company has to take on board the new and yet keep some of the old, and see both in a new light. Whilst 'management by objectives' may have had its day, the goals and targets of the Second Wave are just as important as the direction and vision of the Third Wave. The difference is that the goals and targets can no longer be set in stone. They must be flexible and serve the direction and vision of the organisation. Management structures that are strongly hierarchical are not likely to survive and will need to be replaced by flexible networks, but at the same time responsibility, authority and accountability must be retained.

Any company that has only the Third-Wave elements will have serious problems, as Apple Computers discovered to its cost. Their experience was the result of focusing on market creation and ignoring market share, considering only direction and not targets (Carlton, 1998). But acceptance of the contradictions of the Second- and Third-Wave characteristics of Table 10.1 is not easy and there is generally a polarisation of view around the board room table. It is market share *versus* market creation rather than market share *and* market creation. Under the old way of thinking these are a contradiction as much as was the description of light as both a wave and a particle. In the new paradigm, using the scientist's Principle of Complementarity, both are of equal importance.

This understanding has been articulated by Charles Handy (1995). In *The Empty Raincoat* he argues that with all the old certainties gone and change and turbulence about us we must accept the 'paradoxes of our time' and learn to live with them both in society and in business. Jelinek and Schoonhoven (1990) in the *Innovation Marathon* report on how the best US electronics companies are able to survive and grow in a fast-moving industry. They have learnt how to hold in balance the stability of the Second-Wave company and the change of the Third-Wave business. This same point is found in *In Search of Excellence* by Peters and Waterman (1982). Among the characteristics of top performing companies they identified the ability to manage both tight and loose structures at the same time. Successful companies are able to manage this paradox within a Third-Wave context.

From this critique it is concluded that the developed world and its way of doing business is indeed entering a new paradigm but it is one which includes elements of the old set in the context of the new. It does require a new way of thinking and specifically calls for the ability to hold opposites in balance and to manage paradox. Kuhn (1985) has called this 'the essential tension'. Handled in the right way it can be highly positive and creative but handled badly it can be destructive.

The key ingredient in managing paradox is the level of trust between those who hold opposing views. All organisations, whatever the corporate approach, are a combination of Second- and Third-Wave people and this produces tensions. Within an organisation, the level of trust will decide whether this inherent tension works for good or ill. If a sufficient level of trust is achieved then the paradox of stability and change and of tight and loose structures can be handled. This is where the network organisation is so important because it has a much greater potential to generate and build trust than does a hierarchy. 'The ability of companies to move from large hierarchies to flexible networks of smaller firms will depend on the degree of trust and social capital present in the broader society' (Fukuyama, 1995).

Entrepreneurs have this same dichotomy within themselves. Their creativity and advantage talents are Third-Wave characteristics whilst their focus and ability to get things done belong to the Second Wave. As in the case of a company, there is, within entrepreneurs, a tension between these two sets of characteristics which they must be able to hold within a Third-Wave context. The context side is not normally a problem for the entrepreneur because it is entrepreneurial in nature. But handling the tension is more difficult, as we described in Chapter 2, when we considered the talent chain and the temperament challenge. It is the inner ego, where internal trust and self-confidence reside, that decides if the talent chain is effective and whether the tension can be held in a positive and productive way.

Entrepreneurs have a Third-Wave temperament which works with their talents, both Second and Third Wave, to produce excellence. In the room and furniture analogy used earlier the Second-Wave characteristic of focus has to move in to the Third-Wave room of the entrepreneur working with creativity and advantage which are already there.

The entrepreneur's opportunity

Today's world is a time of special opportunity for business entrepreneurs. If they are able to seize this opportunity then there will be a remarkable explosion of entrepreneurial activity and, thereby, a new level of prosperity for all.

Prosperity, of course, is primarily a statement about economics and the creation of wealth. It is not about contentment and happiness. People can be very prosperous and also very miserable. The role of the social and the aesthetic entrepreneurs will be important here although the opportunities will be less obvious and more demanding of the entrepreneur. For this reason it will be important to encourage them so that they come forward and provide a balance against the excesses that follow from a pursuit of prosperity. This suggests that special efforts should be made to identify and promote social and aesthetic entrepreneurships in our universities and that entrepreneurship courses should not be limited to those studying business, economics and the technologies.

It is also important that as wealth is created it is distributed across the population and not held by a few. This is a difficult social and political issue but it is also an entrepreneurial issue. The old idea that entrepreneurs comprise a wealthy élite is now being challenged by the facts. *Forbes Magazine* published their 1999 list of America's 400 richest people under the heading 'A century of wealth'. In that issue an article entitled 'The billionaire next door' commented that today's billionaires 'seem fanatically determined to appear middle class'. They argue that this is because most of them were not born into wealth and want to stay with their middle-class values. Fifteen years ago 40 per cent of the Forbes 400 made their wealth and 60 per cent inherited it. In 1999, 63 per cent of them had made their own wealth; a figure that seems set to increase in the future. Below billionaire level the picture is even more remarkable. In 1989 there were 1.3 million dollar-millionaires. Just ten years on there were five million and it is estimated that in the next ten years there will be twenty million. The article concludes that:

In the past 200 years, the great achievement of the modern West was to create a mass middle class, allowing the common man to escape poverty and live in relative comfort. Now the United States is ready to perform an even greater feat. This country is well on its way to creating the first mass affluent class in world history.

In the USA the terms 'the rich', 'the middle class' and 'the poor' no longer mean what they used to.

For some of these 'overclass', as the Forbes article calls them, their sudden wealth makes them uncomfortable. 'They know they are doing well, but they also want to feel like they're doing good'. Wealth is being seen as something to be shared rather than indulged in. A British television programme in October 1999 featured a wealthy trader in the City of London who decided what he and his wife required for a reasonable standard of living and then gave away the rest of his earnings. When interviewed he suggested that a millionaire should be someone who has given away a million pounds rather than one who has acquired a million.

With these caveats about the social and the aesthetic entrepreneurs and the distribution of wealth we now consider the opportunities that make today's world so special for the entrepreneur. In some parts of the world the time of the entrepreneur has already arrived. A decade and a half ago it was commented that:

What has emerged here, [the USA] primarily in only the past two decades, is a community of a few hundred professional investors with entrepreneurial management and advanced technology to create new products, new companies and new wealth. This has sparked the greatest burst of entrepreneurial activity the world has ever seen.

(Wilson, 1986)

The same 'burst of entrepreneurial activity' has been experienced in Cambridge, England with the 'Cambridge Phenomenon' (Segal *et al.*, 1985) and in Bangalore, India (Singhal and Rogers, 1989). These are the first signs of a phenomenon that could encompass the whole world. This belief is based on two things. First the theme that underlies this book – 'that entrepreneurial talent is to be found in people everywhere, whether they are rich or poor or in an advanced or a developing society' – and second the new Enterprise Paradigm that is spreading around the globe creating the right conditions. The match between the entrepreneur's world and the real world has never been closer. 'In the 21st century, the winners will be those who stay ahead of the change curve, constantly defining their industries, creating new markets, blazing new trails, reinventing the competitive rules, challenging the status quo' (Gibson, 1998).

The three characteristics of today's world that make this a time of special opportunity are:

- new and converging technologies that create and disturb markets
- products and services with low market-entry costs
- more entrepreneurs.

Technology and markets

Entrepreneurs thrive on change, but only within certain boundaries. In the past, change, both economic and social, has come about by wars and conflict and by politics and colonisation. This has been the time of the leader rather than the entrepreneur. The only entrepreneur to appear consistently throughout history has been the merchant entrepreneur. For many centuries the Great Silk Road was an entrepreneur's highway linking different worlds driven by the Roman's demand for silk and China's interest in wools, gold and silver – it was a market-driven highway. Then there were those who plied the oceans of the world bringing back exotic products to a curious western world. The cost of mounting such expeditions was perhaps the world's first example of venture capital.

When a period of peace has been achieved the entrepreneur took the opportunity to be more than just a merchant trader. As cited in Chapter 1, Jardine (1997) sees the Renaissance as being as much an entrepreneurial opportunity as a period of great artistic flowering. Great wealth was accumulated by the entrepreneurs of the day whilst the kings were living off credit and, in reality, had huge debts. The entrepreneurs were beginning to build something of recognised and substantial value.

Entrepreneurs have never really been accepted as a factor in economic growth. Economists have virtually ignored their existence. 'Until the mid-nineteenth century most economists held a relative indifference to the entrepreneur, focusing instead on the dynamics of capitalism and industrial development' (Buckingham, 1987). 'As recently as 1985, very few economists paid any attention whatsoever to entrepreneurship' (Bygrave, 1998). Whilst a few voices were raised amongst the economists in support of the entrepreneur, they were rare. Jean Baptiste Say (1767–1832) the influential French economist was one. With his business background he was able to appreciate their importance. He commented that 'the man who conceives or takes charge of an enterprise, sees and exploits opportunity is the motive force for economic change and improvement' (Galbraith, 1991). The subsequent experience of the US economy was to prove this point. By 1890 America had more than 4000 millionaires and the number was growing fast (Pendergrast, 1994). Industrial giants like Andrew Carnegie and Cornelius Vanderbelt were the champions of this new world of wealth.

In the early decades of the twentieth century the link between economic growth and invention and technology was being made. The evidence for this was there for all to see. In his *Theory of Economic Development*, published in 1911, Joseph Schumpeter (1883–1950) put entrepreneurs centre stage seeing them as those who introduce new ideas and 'challenge the established equilibrium with a new product, a new process or a new type of productive organisation' (Galbraith, 1991). Asa Candler (1851–1929) was such a man who became a self-made millionaire thanks to a new product called Coca-Cola. There were many entrepreneurs around, like Candler, for Schumpeter to observe. As we described in Chapter 4, Candler was not the inventor but he made it happen. John Pemberton, its inventor, died in 1888 virtually penniless but 'if the Pemberton's had not sold the formula it would have stayed an old drink somewhere and been lost in time' (Pendergrast, 1994). It was Asa Candler, the entrepreneur, who made it all happen.

Although Schumpeter made the connection between the entrepreneur and the innovation, others chose to focus only on the innovation. They saw science and technology as the driver of economic progress and gave the entrepreneur a back seat. In 1919 Kondratieff proposed his 'long wave' theory of economic growth and technological innovation. Working from the 1700s he identified cycles of growth and decline of approximately fifty years. Growth arose from a cluster of innovations that led to the creation of new industries giving prosperity to certain regions. Other groups would pick up the next wave of innovations, and using this competitive advantage would overtake the rest that would then go into relative decline. Thus the invention of the power loom created the cotton industry and steam power made possible the iron industry. These made Britain the 'workshop of the world' (Malecki, 1997) in the first of Kondratieff's waves from 1787 to 1845. The Bessemer steel process, the steamship and the railways were the innovations that led to new industries now on a large scale in the period from 1846 to 1895. Despite Mr Bessemer inventing his process in Britain and entrepreneur engineers like Brunel building steam ships and railways this period saw Germany and the USA challenging Britain's supremacy.

The third period from 1896 to 1947 was underway when Kondratieff put his idea of 'long waves' forward. This was picked up by others (Hall and Preston, 1988; Ayres, 1990) who have brought the analysis up to date. The exciting new sciences of chemistry and electricity, and the technology of the internal combustion engine all gave rise to huge industries to the benefit of the economies of Germany and the USA. The fourth period from 1948 to 2000 saw science and technology merge as the transistor and microprocessor led to the electronics, computer and telecommunications industries.

This model not only gives some interesting historical insights but also shows that science and technology are important drivers and sustainers of the economy. It is clearly a necessary condition for the present world's economy, as we know it. As Malecki (1997) puts it 'Technology is central to regional change, positive and negative, and to economic change, job-creating and job-destroying. It is the most obvious cause and effect of the cumulative wealth of rich nations'.

In introducing a government White Paper in 1999 on the knowledge-driven economy the UK's Prime Minister Tony Blair commented that 'The Modern world is swept by change. New technologies emerge constantly, new markets are opened up. There are new competitors but also great new opportunities' (UK government, 1998). This link between technology and markets is a key point. Technology alone cannot create a viable opportunity; only the market can do that. It is the response of the customer to the technology that creates the market. Internet Service Providers (ISPs), like Compuserve and America On-Line (AOL), had been around for a few years but it was when the retailer Dixon's launched its free ISP, Freeserve, in 1998 and scooped a million subscribers in just nine months that the market really took off. With the imagination of the entrepreneur, technology becomes a great disturber of markets and even more opportunities are created.

Opportunities are also coming from the convergence of different technologies. Computers and telecommunications have come together to produce a huge wave of opportunities linked with the World Wide Web. With digital television and the Internet linked up, the face of retailing could change for ever as on-line shopping establishes itself. The technology of the mobile phone is picking up a number of different technologies to offer the customer more and more services, from e-mail to knowing your exact location in an emergency.

All these trends result in more and more opportunities for the entrepreneur so that we are on the threshold of a period that could perhaps one day be truly the age of the entrepreneur. For the first time, an age will be described, not by a science or a technology as was the atomic age and the computer age but, by the exploiter of that technology, the entrepreneur.

Low market-entry costs

The science and technology that led to the major industries identified in Kondratieff's 'long waves' had increasingly high entry costs. The power loom and steam power of the late eighteenth century was too expensive for the cottage industry to take up, so the first factories were formed and people began to 'go to work'. The price that had to be paid for capital equipment continued to increase and the small factory was replaced by larger and larger ones as economy of scale was pursued. By the end of the Second World War the scientific and the technical talents of the UK was being absorbed by large sectors such as the chemical and aircraft industries and the potentially large nuclear power industry. These sectors had huge entry costs so that for graduates and others at that time the idea of setting up one's own technology-based business was simply not an option. Even when the computer industry began to take shape it was dominated by large mainframe manufacturers like IBM. Everything was big and appeared to offer secure jobs with promotion guaranteed for the career-minded graduate.

In the 1960s and 1970s the inventions of the semi-conductor, the integrated circuit and the microprocessor came together and changed everything. With the personal computer and its software, an unprecedented period with low market-entry costs had begun. Individual entrepreneurs could actually think of starting their own business without a family fortune behind them. This is one reason why the majority of millionaires in the world today have made their money in their own lifetime.

Of course, as these industries have grown some big players have emerged and have created their own market-entry problems for the new business. Microsoft represents the large company that has maximised its hold on the marketplace. Yet even as they were being charged with taking unfair advantage of their monopoly position, a young man from Finland, Linus Torvald, was offering a new operating system, Linux, free of charge on the World Wide Web. Linux is fast becoming a serious competitor to Microsoft's Windows operating system yet it had no venture capital backing and was not supported by a large company. Torvald wrote the operating system at home and sent it around on the Web, only asking that users sent him a postcard. Torvald's secret was to offer to software developers low-cost entry to a new and powerful operating system.

Biotechnology is another new industry that has opened over the past twenty years. Although entry costs are not high, special laboratories are needed and the time to market is significantly longer than in other technology sectors because of the regulatory nature of the drug industry. This means that the start-up company often spots the opportunity and takes it through to the proof of principle, and even working prototype stage, but goes no further. By this time it can have created sufficient intellectual property for the company to have real value. Some have been able to achieve huge stock valuations on this basis or have been bought out by one of the big pharmaceutical companies.

Although some of the early start-up companies, such as Microsoft and Intel, have risen to dominate their sectors, and biotechnology start-ups have a longer road to travel than in other sectors, the opportunities for technology-based start-ups just go on increasing and the low-cost market-entry situation still prevails. This was recognised in the UK Government White Paper on the knowledge-driven economy (UK government, 1998) which concluded that it:

- gives small firms new opportunities to access international markets without the need for a global marketing network
- permits more contracting out of activities, particularly those based on codified knowledge, and creates possibilities for new forms of organisation such as 'virtual' companies.

Information technology, the knowledge-driven economy, the Internet age and the e-commerce era are all terms used to describe this new world of opportunity but it only works to the benefit of the entrepreneur if he or she can enter that world at low cost with limited resources. It is this fact that is central to the present opportunity. The Internet boom came about because of this. As Steve Bennett of Jungle.com has commented 'The beauty of the internet is that the cost of entry is really low. Someone can sit in their bedroom and look like a massive company' (*e-business*, 1999). A strong profitability record is no longer needed to appear successful. Some of the major players like Amazon books and Yahoo! have billion-dollar valuations and have not yet made consistent profits. This is a new world for the financial community who are having to invent new ways of valuing a business. The ISP, Freeserve, was valued at £1.5 billion when it was launched on the stock exchange in July 1999 because its one million customers who paid no fee were each valued at £1500.

More entrepreneurs

Science and technology with its turbulent markets and low-entry costs is, however, only part of the story. As Schumpeter observed, the entrepreneur is needed to turn the opportunities that science and technology bring into an economic reality. Malecki (1997) comments that 'the process of entrepreneurship may be more important to regional and local economies than the process of technological change'. In many ways new technology and the entrepreneur are made for each other, both are about change in the marketplace. It is science and technology that makes possible this turbulence but it is the actions of the entrepreneur and the entrepreneurial business that actually create the turbulence and upset established markets and open up new ones. Often these changes can be enormous and produce completely new markets.

The personal computer market came out of nowhere in the 1980s, the result of clever science and a host of entrepreneurs. The mobile phone market was a variant of the existing telephone market but now has a life of its own. Its driver was the miniaturisation made possible by modern electronics and the microprocessor and the entrepreneurial companies of the early days, notably Vodafone and Nokia.

There is no diminution of today's turbulence in the marketplace as science and technology continue to bring us new opportunities at an ever-increasing rate. The entrepreneur has 'never had it so good'. The real question is whether there are enough experienced entrepreneurs to make the most of this abundance of opportunity. This is a key factor in international competitiveness. As Porter (1990) has put it 'Invention and entrepreneurship are at the heart of national advantage'. The country that encourages and stimulates its entrepreneurial talent will be the winner. We already have the technology and the low cost of entry but do we have the entrepreneurs?

Though entrepreneurs are emerging in increasing numbers it is taking some time for their role in economic development to be really accepted. Much effort and a great deal of money are spent trying to get hold of promising technology with commercial potential but a similar effort is not made on the entrepreneur side of the equation. As long ago as 1982, the *Investors Chronicle* presented a version of this equation on its front cover:

Academic + Entrepreneur = Profit

It then commented 'Dragging commercial products out of ivory towers is the latest twist to the venture capital boom'. Whilst an understandable comment, it does show that the old attitudes were still there. The academics were seen as living in ivory towers remote from reality, and the venture capitalists were the entrepreneurs who extracted and exploited, for profit, the commercial products that were there for the taking. This polarised view is one reason why it has taken so long to forge an effective partnership between those who generate the technology and those who can take it on to commercial reality. There was also the erroneous assumption that venture capitalists were entrepreneurs.

The UK situation has improved since 1982 and an effective liaison is developing between the academic world and the venture capitalist but the entrepreneur's position is still not recognised. In a MORI poll conducted in 1989, after the Thatcher government's promotion of enterprise and wealth creation had had time to make an impact, only 32 per cent of people thought that the entrepreneur contributed a great deal to society. A similar percentage thought that the plumber made an equal level of contribution (*The Economist*, 1994).

In the USA there is a better picture. The Gallup Organisation polled sixteen- to eighteen-year-old high-school students and found that 70 per cent would like to have their own business. Bill Bygrave, Professor of Entrepreneurship at Babson College in the USA, believes that 'Most young Americans want to be entrepreneurs: entrepreneurs are highly rated in their society and being an entrepreneur is a very respectable career and an honourable profession' (Bygrave, 1998). In the UK the recognition of the entrepreneur achieved in the USA has yet to arrive.

Despite this difference with the USA there are grounds to hope that the role of the entrepreneur will gradually achieve its rightful recognition in the UK. One key reason is that the career aspirations of young people are changing. In 1973 Schumacher's influential *Small is Beautiful* (Schumacher, 1973) was published and young people particularly began to develop attitudes that were against big business. The idea of a job for life was also being challenged as companies began to lay off workers. Staff with qualifications were at first spared but then cuts were made across a company at all levels, including the board. In the 1980s the Thatcher government began a massive privatisation policy which soon spread around the world as other governments took on the idea. Then in the 1990s came the notion of downsizing and concentration upon the core business. These changes have all contributed to a distrust of the large enterprise and a feeling that 'I might as well be in control of my own destiny as be dictated to by others'.

This enthusiasm for the small and the arrival of low-cost entry opportunities should mean that starting one's own business is now an option being considered by more and more people, as they begin their careers. Whilst the logic is there, society attitudes still need to change before this happens on a large enough scale. In 1994 *The Economist* featured on its front cover a picture of the TV character Arthur Daley with the heading 'How Britain sees its entrepreneurs'. The editorial commented that Daley was 'a symbol of a country where "trade" is a bit disreputable, where starting a firm that fails is worse than not starting one at all'.

This caricature is the image that many have of the entrepreneur and it is in serious need of correction. The entrepreneur should hold a position of respect and value in our society. To do this the word 'entrepreneur' needs to not only be given its rightful place, it needs to be redeemed. Its image needs to be cleaned up and brought back from its 'dodgy' past. Entrepreneurs like Richard Branson, Anita Roddick and others we have described in earlier chapters are helping to change the public perspective. The fact that the *Sunday Times* has continued to run its regular series of articles on how entrepreneurs got started is a sign of the increasing interest in the entrepreneur.

The entrepreneur is the third of the factors with technology and low-entry costs that give us today's special opportunity. It is difficult to say which of the three factors is the most important because they inter-link. It is technology that makes the low-entry costs possible and it is the entrepreneur who takes up the opportunity that this combination presents. But it should be understood that technology does not have to be leading edge. The computer and the Internet should now be regarded as tools that can be applied in many sectors to create competitive businesses. The sectors themselves do not need to be high technology. The tourist industry, for example, is the biggest industry that there is and is set to become even bigger. 'It employs one out of nine people in the world. But apart from a few big players like the airlines, who provide the infrastructure, tourism is made up of millions and millions of entrepreneurs' (Naisbitt, 1998). Technology has given us all the tools that entrepreneurs need to operate in the world market, whatever his business; they simply have to learn how to use them.

References

Ayres, R.U. (1990). Technology transformations and long waves. *Technological Forecasting and Social Change*, **36**.

Bolton, J.E. (1971). Report of the Committee of Enquiry on Small Firms. Cm 4811. HMSO.

Buckingham, M.W. (1987). Entrepreneurship. Dissertation, Faculty of Social and Political Science, Cambridge University.

Butterfield, H. (1957). *The Origins of Modern Science*. 2nd edn. Bell & Hyman.

Bygrave, B. (1998). Building an entrepreneurial economy: lessons from the United States. *Business Strategy Review*, **9** (2), 11–18.

Carlton, J. (1998). *Apple*. HarperCollins.

Covey, F. (1990). *Principle-Centred Leadership*. Simon & Schuster.

Dearlove, D. (1999). *Business the Bill Gates Way*. Capstone.

Dell, M. and Fredman, S. (1999). *Direct from Dell*. HarperCollins Business.

e-business (1999). Jungle fever. December, 71–73.

Ferris, T. (ed.) (1991). *The World Treasury of Physics, Astronomy and Mathematics*. Little, Brown.

Fukuyama, F. (1995). *Trust*. Hamish Hamilton.

Galbraith, J.K. (1991). *A History of Economics*. Penguin Books.

Gibson, R. (1998). Rethinking business. In *Rethinking the Future* (R. Gibson, ed.), Nicholas Brealey.

Hall, P. and Preston, P. (1988). *The Carrier Wave: New Information Technology and the Geography of Innovation 1846–2003*. Unwin Hyman.

Hammer, M. and Champy, J. (1993). *Reengineering the Corporation*. Nicholas Brealey.

Handy, C. (1993). *The Age of Unreason*. 2nd edn. Century Business.

Handy, C. (1995). *The Empty Raincoat*. Arrow Books.

Harvey-Jones, J. (1988). *Making it Happen*. HarperCollins.

Iacocca, L. (1989). *Talking Straight*. Bantam Books.

Investors Chronicle (1982). Academic + entrepreneur = profit?, 23 April, 190–191.

Jardine, L. (1997). *Worldly Goods*. Papermac.

Jelinek, M. and Schoonhoven, C.B. (1990). *The Innovation Marathon*. Blackwell.

Kanter, R.M. (1990). *When Giants Learn to Dance*. Unwin Paperbacks.

Kawasaki, G. (1992). *Selling the Dream*. HarperBusiness.

Koch, R. (1997). *The 80/20 Principle*. Nicholas Brealey.

Koch, R. and Godden, I. (1998). *Managing without Management*. Nicholas Brealey.

Koestler, A. (1989). *The Sleepwalkers*. Arkana Penguin.

Kuhn, T. (1975). *The Structure of Scientific Revolutions*. 2nd edn. University of Chicago Press.

Kuhn, T. (1985). *The Essential Tension*. University of Chicago Press.

Lyon, D. (1994). *Postmodernity*. Open University Press.

Malecki, E.J. (1997). *Technology and Economic Development*. 2nd edn. Longman.

Naisbitt, J. (1998). From nation states to networks. In *Rethinking the Future* (R. Gibson, ed.), Nicholas Brealey.

Ortega, R. (1999). *In Sam We Trust*. Kogan Page.

Pendergrast, M. (1994). *For God, Country and Coca-Cola*. Phoenix Paperback.

Peters, T.J. (1989). *Thriving on Chaos*. Pan Books.

Peters, T.J. and Waterman, R.H. (1982). *In Search of Excellence*. Harper & Row.

Porter, M.E. (1985). *Competitive Advantage: Creating and Sustaining Superior Performance*. The Free Press.

Porter, M.E. (1990). *The Competitive Advantage of Nations*. Macmillan.

Reaman, G.E. (1963). *The Trail of the Huguenots*. Frederick Muller.

Rose, F. (1989). *West of Eden*. Business Books.

Schumacher, E.F. (1973). *Small is Beautiful*. Blond & Briggs.

Sculley, J. (1987). *Odyssey: Pepsi to Apple*. Collins.

Segal, N., Quince, R.E. and Wicksteed, W. (1985). *The Cambridge Phenomenon*. Segal Quince Wicksteed and Brand Brothers.

Senge, P.M. (1990). *The Fifth Discipline*. Century Business.

Singhal, A. and Rogers, E.M. (1989). *India's Information Revolution*. Sage.

Tarnas, R. (1996). *The Passion of the Western Mind*. Pimlico.

The Economist (1994). The unloved entrepreneur, 28 May, 105.

Toffler, A. (1971). *Future Shock*. Pan Books.

Toffler, A. (1981). *The Third Wave*. Pan Books.

Trout, J. and Rivkin, S. (1998). *The Power of Simplicity*. McGraw-Hill.

UK government (1998). *Our Competitive Future: Building the Knowledge Driven Economy,* White Paper Cm 4176. HMSO.

Weber, M. (1905). *The Protestant Ethic and the Spirit of Capitalism.* Unwin Counterpoint.

Wilson, J.W. (1986). *The New Venturers.* Addison-Wesley.

11 How the entrepreneur operates

Entrepreneurs operate within a process that starts with the entrepreneur and a perceived opportunity and outputs something of recognised value. Within the process the entrepreneur creates, innovates and builds. In this chapter we present our model of the enterprise process and describe the key elements involved. Its focus is the enterprise that is being built in and the various stages it passes through. It is a practical model against which the progress of the enterprise can be measured and any remedial action that may be required can be identified.

The enterprise process model

Entrepreneurs are individuals with very different ways of doing things but the things that they do are similar. They all identify an opportunity, put together the necessary resources and build something of recognised value; but how do they do it? What stages do they go through in the process? Figure 11.1 is a model of the enterprise process that seeks to answer these questions (Bolton, 1993, 1997).

The model identifies the inputs, the process itself and the output. People and ideas are the raw material that feed the process. In this chapter the people side is

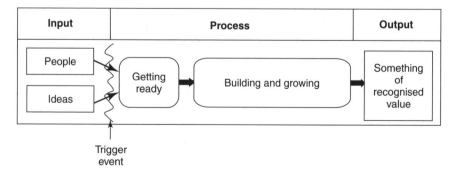

Figure 11.1 *The enterprise process model*

considered first, as the roles of the *entrepreneur*, the *manager* and the *leader* are examined. This distinction is important because all three are often involved with starting enterprises when it is really the province of the entrepreneur. On the ideas' side, the *sources of ideas* available to the entrepreneur are outlined.

The *enterprise process* is often set off by some form of trigger event. As Larson and Rogers (1986) put it when describing entrepreneurship in Silicon Valley 'Setting off the initial spark is the key'. This chiefly affects the *people* input and examples of the important triggers are given. Most *idea*-based triggers link directly with the *people* input, as when the entrepreneur suddenly has a bright idea. An important exception, when the idea side is not linked with the people side directly, is the trigger associated with a particular sector of technology. The Silicon Valley story in Chapter 14 shows how a series of technology triggers came along and fuelled the entrepreneurial process. The Internet linked to the World Wide Web is the latest of these triggers and its effect is being felt across the world. It has given birth to its own type of entrepreneur, the *Netpreneur*, for whom the key issue is not profitability but branding and customer service. Steve Bennett believed that the Internet would come down to two or three brands and he intended his company Jungle.com to be one of them (*e-business*, 1999).

The *enterpise process* is considered as two stages. A *getting started* stage and a *building and growing* stage. Each is broken down into a series of elements or sub-stages through which the process passes. The real entrepreneurs are often unaware that they travel this road but its features and milestones are described so that they can recognise the road and be encouraged. Its true value is in guiding the inexperienced and the less-confident travellers so that they can chart their progress and understand what to expect on their entrepreneurial journey. It also provides a useful framework for those who would encourage and support the potential entrepreneur. It enables an intervention strategy to be developed for the promotion of indigenous businesses in which specific stages of the process can be targeted.

The output from the *enterprise process* is something of recognised value. For the economic entrepreneur, part of that recognition is achieved by the creation a viable business and sustainable jobs. For the social and the aesthetic entrepreneurs the recognition comes from the group they serve, and ultimately the general public.

The inputs

People: the entrepreneur, the manager and the leader

The characteristics and personality of the entrepreneur have already been discussed in Chapters 1 and 2. Here the entrepreneur is considered in relation to managers and leaders, since all can be involved in starting up and running enterprises, whether for business, social or aesthetic reasons. It is, of course, the entrepreneur whose talents suit this process best.

When managers are involved, it is important that they are not the driving force. In a business-start programme run in the UK one of the teams that was put together consisted of three well-qualified professional managers. This combination proved to be a mistake. The team talked and debated a great deal and produced many excellent plans but they never started a business. The entrepreneur spark was missing. By contrast, a team of four which did include an entrepreneur started their business before the programme was finished. In fact, they did not really need the programme, other than to help them form into a team and give them basic advice.

Using the earlier point that a project manager is an entrepreneur, but without the ability to see opportunities, it could be argued that managers can be entrepreneurs as long as somebody else provides the opportunity. It is certainly true that managers can set up businesses if someone else gives them the idea but they will be managed businesses and not entrepreneurial ones. This is because issues such as creativity and opportunity-spotting are something that characterise an entrepreneurial business all through its life and not just at start up.

Leaders are a different group to managers and are much more in tune with the entrepreneur. This is because a number of their life themes overlap. As discussed in Chapter 1, the Gallup Organisation has studied both groups in great detail and identified twenty life themes for the leader and twelve for the entrepreneur, with seven common to both. In comparing these life themes in Figure 11.2, some simplifications have

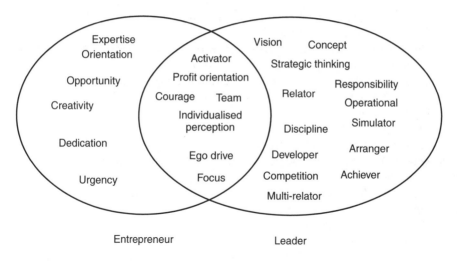

Figure 11.2 *Entrepreneur and leader envelopes*

been made. The performance orientation of the leader and the profit orientation of the entrepreneur have been taken to be the same, although they are slightly different. There are also some differences when the same life themes have a slightly different meaning for the entrepreneur and the leader. Thus, as we discussed in Chapter 2, 'focus' for the entrepreneur has only a two-month horizon whereas for the leader it has five or more years. Accepting these small differences, Figure 11.2 indicates that there is a clear overlap between the entrepreneur and the leader, and that depending upon the life theme mix there are entrepreneurial leaders and leader entrepreneurs.

Fifty-eight per cent of the entrepreneur's life themes are shared with the leader but only 35 per cent of the leader's are shared with the entrepreneur. Whilst more life themes could be added for the entrepreneur, as discussed in Chapter 2, it is probably true to say that the entrepreneur has more in common with the leader than the other way round. The entrepreneur is not a sub-set of the leader because the points of difference are extremely important. What makes the entrepreneur different are the life themes of opportunity, creativity, dedication, urgency and expertise orientation. In terms of our facet character themes these correspond to advantage, creativity, inner ego (dedication), focus (time) and team (using experts). These are key talents unique to the entrepreneur. The advantage and creativity character themes are particularly important and explain why an entrepreneur, rather than a leader, is the best person to start an enterprise in the turbulent market conditions of today.

Another way to see the difference between the entrepreneur and the leader is to compare definitions:

> An entrepreneur is 'a person who habitually creates and innovates to build something of recognised value around perceived opportunities'.

> A leader is 'a person who, by word and/or personal example, markedly influences the behaviours, thoughts, and/feelings of a significant number of their fellow human beings'. (Gardner, 1995)

Thus, the entrepreneur is concerned with building something whilst the leader influences people. Leaders appear in the same domains as the entrepreneur. There can be leaders in business, in society and in the arts but they are the influencers, they affect the way people behave, think and feel. Entrepreneurs may do this but they are essentially builders of something that is tangible and real. Entrepreneurs who successfully start a trend or a new approach to a product have this leadership ability to influence people. Anita Roddick changed the approach to selling cosmetics. In the process she embraced a cause and changed the way people think about her product. Guy Kawasaki (1992) of Apple Computers was not selling a product; he was 'selling the dream'. He put into words what Steve Jobs was really trying to do with Apple. He influenced the way people thought about computers. Even today, the Apple computer and the PC are thought of differently. The former is an experience, the latter a piece of equipment.

The distinction made between an entrepreneur, a manager and a leader is often seen as a convenient shorthand for roles that people play. Some fit the role well, others find it more difficult. This idea needs to be turned around so that, like the definitions quoted above, the words describe 'a person who . . . ' rather than 'a role that . . . '. Thus, the enterprise process starts with a person who is an entrepreneur, rather than with someone who merely fulfils that role to the best of their abilities. Most leaders and all managers who try to take on the role of the entrepreneur are likely to fail.

Hickman (1990) has studied managers and leaders and used the Myers Briggs Indicator to describe their personality characteristics. Of the possible sixteen personality types, he assigns one half to the manager and the other half to the leader. The difference rests on whether a person is an S-type, a Sensing person, or an N-type, an iNtuition person, with the S-type being the manager and the N-type the leader. To explain the differences further, Hickman presents a number of lists of what managers and leaders do. Table 11.1 is based on Hickman's manager/leader comparisons but includes our own column for the entrepreneur.

Table 11.1   *What entrepreneurs, managers and leaders do*

The entrepreneur	The manager	The leader
Has fun	Manages	Leads
Innovates	Administers	Innovates
Creates	Maintains	Develops
Focuses on the business	Focuses on systems	Focuses on people
Builds his team	Relies on control	Inspires trust
Sees opportunities	Sees problems	Sees the future
Asks how and when	Asks how and when	Asks what and why
Acts short term	Acts medium term	Thinks long term
Does the right things	Does things right	Uses his influence

These lists show that there are similarities as well as differences. Thus the entrepreneur and the leader both innovate whilst the manager administers. The entrepreneur and the manager are doers, they take action, whereas the leader is a thinker. In other respects the entrepreneur, the manager and the leader are each different. The entrepreneur sees opportunities, the manager sees problems and the leader sees the future. In summary, the entrepreneur builds something based on a perceived opportunity, the manager runs organisations and the leader influences people to follow a dream.

Ideas: where they can come from

The true entrepreneur has ideas all the time. As Victor Kiam puts it 'Entrepreneurs are simply those who understand that there is little difference between obstacle and opportunity and are able to turn both to their advantage'. He bought the Remington company after it had turned in losses of $30 million over five years with the simple maxim 'I liked the shaver so much, I bought the company'. Soon Remington became a leader in the shaver market.

The entrepreneur sees opportunities all around and knows which are the best to go for. It is not a matter of analysis but of instinct. Bernie Ecclestone, the man behind the success of Formula One racing, believes 'You have an instinct. You can't learn business' (Steiner, 1998). His first business move came at the age of nine when he exploited wartime food shortages. He sold Chelsea buns to his school friends in the lunch break. He saw the opportunity and it was obvious to him to take it.

Ideas come from many sources. In this section a number of common ones are considered.

Our own needs   Because we understand them well, needs that we have discovered for ourselves often provide the business opportunity. In 1984 Tom Hunter was an unemployed graduate in marketing and economics living in Ayrshire, Scotland. He liked to wear training shoes and found that there was no shop around where he could see a good selection. 'I noticed a growing demand for training shoes. I thought maybe I could do something in this area of business.' He borrowed money from his father and the bank to buy stock and rented space from a retail group that had stores in Aberdeen, Leeds and Sunderland. Soon he had fifty such outlets. He then set up his own shops and by 1995 he had forty-five with annual sales of £36 million. The acquisition of a competitor moved his company Sports Division to top spot in the UK with annual sales of £260 million. Some fifteen years on Tom Hunter sold the business and became a millionaire. Since then he has been involved in a number of ventures, often in a business angel role, as with Michelle Mone's MJM that we mention in Chapter 5. Hunter is the classic habitual entrepreneur.

New inventions are often spurred by this recognition of a need. As reported in Chapter 4, James Dyson's invention of the 'dual cyclone' cleaner came out of a problem he had with his old reconditioned Hoover Junior vacuum cleaner. It was not working very well because the bag was full. When he found that there were no new bags in the cupboard he began to improvise. His inventive talent finally led him to a complete redesign of the vacuum cleaner.

Niche spotting   is a major provider of opportunity. Two examples from the pages of the *Sunday Times* and subsequently published in a book (Steiner, 1998) illustrate the point. 'It set me thinking there was a niche, Indian restaurants being so popular.' This niche was to provide Indian beer for Indian restaurants. Karan Bilimoria set up Cobra Beer and became the largest bottler of Indian beer in Britain. Laura Tenison found a niche in the clothing market with the obvious thought that 'Just because women become pregnant it doesn't mean they suddenly do not want to look good'. She set up Jojo Maman Bébé Ltd, selling mainly by mail order. In 1993 she won the British Telecom Retailer of the Year Award.

Not all niches can sustain viable businesses. Indeed, a niche can become a tomb. Niches are, by their nature, small and self-limiting in terms of company growth, but they are a good place for the entrepreneur to gain experience before moving up to something larger. Often, niche markets can suddenly expand to be quite big ones. Ink jet printing on irregular surfaces was a niche market until government regulations required sell-by-dates to be printed on all food products. Domino Printing Sciences in Cambridge was ready when this opportunity came and grew rapidly. Oxford Instruments had a similar experience when the body scanner was invented and their niche market in small high-powered magnets suddenly opened up.

Niche markets can also provide access to a customer base that has niche opportunities in addition to the one identified. An entrepreneur who provided music and lighting for discos was asked by the manager of a hotel if he 'did security lighting'. When he finally said 'Yes', he soon found he had the security lighting contract for a major hotel group. His business grew so rapidly that he abandoned his disco work. One niche had led to a much larger one via the customer.

Hobbies   It was computer hobbyists in the USA that created the personal computer industry. Bill Gates's hobby was writing software! Most hobbies are not in this league though they can be the basis of a successful business. Hobbyists, however, have some of the characteristics of the inventor – they are in love with their hobby. This often makes it difficult for them to approach things in a commercial way because it takes the joy out of their hobby. It is no longer such fun.

Artists have a similar difficulty. They often feel that to produce things commercially devalues their art and kills their creativity. Titian, one of the great Renaissance painters and an entrepreneur, had no problem with this. He employed assistants to do most of his painting for him, filling in the sky, the landscape and the drapery. El Greco who was apprenticed to Titian was at first appalled by this because Titian always signed the finished canvas – but he 'learnt from the Master', as we saw in Chapter 8. By 'the end of the year he saw how impossible it would be for one man to produce the number of paintings that Titian sold; and he conceded that what Titian did contribute transformed a routine canvas into a masterpiece' (Braider, 1967).

Inventions and the application of technology This is an area full of opportunities that seem to be never ending. Inventions and research discoveries can open up huge markets but spotting the application is the secret. This is one of the entrepreneur's real talents.

The world would not be what it is today if the microprocessor had not been invented. It has created many new markets moving from calculators to personal computers to telecommunications and the Internet. But it was when a pair of Apple fanatics at MIT invented the Visicalc spreadsheet programme and gave it a real life application that the personal computer entered the American office (Rose, 1989) and a billion-dollar market was born. It was when Tim Berners-Lee in 1989 proposed the World Wide Web as a means of sharing physics research information that the Internet gold rush began. Communications between computers had found their application.

Laser Scan plc came out of nuclear research at the Cavendish Laboratory of Cambridge University. The commercial application was spotted when somebody made the connection between a research apparatus that could digitise images of particle tracks and the opportunity to digitise the contour lines on maps. Twenty years later, the company has a full stock exchange listing and is the largest quoted Geographic Information Systems Company (*Cambridge Science Park Newsletter*, 1996).

Vertical integration offers the opportunity to expand from one activity in the production and supply chain to others.

'It was in 1883 the Essex farmer, Arthur Charles Wilkin, was driving a consignment of his strawberries to the London-bound train. Returning home with groceries and jam for his wife, he mused that quite possibly the jam contained his own fruit . . . ' Wilkin had seen the opportunity of making the jam himself and the now-famous Tiptree range of jams, preserves and jellies came into being in June 1885. His great-grandson Peter Wilkin is chairman of this privately owned company which now has annual sales in excess of £10 million and exports to more than sixty countries.

Downsizing is the opposite of vertical integration and is more popular today as companies concentrate on their core business. This can mean the closure of whole departments but with it comes the opportunity for teams with experience to spin-off almost intact from the parent. This is similar in principle to the management-buy-out (MBO) when an existing team is able to buy out the whole company and run it for themselves. Downsizing however carries less risk because it usually has its previous owner as the first customer.

The UK manufacturing plant of an international tractor company was closing down its apprentice training shop and its component manufacturing activities to concentrate on its core business of tractor assembly. With support from the local Training and Enterprise Council the apprentice training shop was able to spin-off as a separate business and provide a service to several companies in the area, including its parent.

Demerging   is a variant of downsizing in which a whole activity is spun-off from the parent. In 1999 Hewlett-Packard demerged its test and measurement division as a company called Agilent. In 1997 IBM demerged its printer division as Lexmark. The chief justification for demergers is to reduce costs and increase competitiveness but part of the reason can also be to bring the entrepreneurial advantages of the smaller business. It is surprising in such situations how previously frustrated managers suddenly discover that they have entrepreneurial talent, and they and the spin-off enterprise find that they have a new lease of life.

Sub-contracting   Large companies usually have thousands of suppliers, and the advent of just-in-time (JIT) procedures has made them seek out local suppliers to reduce delivery uncertainties. In a study conducted by a company in north-east England, it was found that 70 per cent of their suppliers were located outside the region. This company then set about helping potential entrepreneurs to create local businesses to which they could sub-contract the manufacture of the components they required.

The Ford Motor Company recognised the same need at their Dagenham plant. A £500-million investment plan announced in May 1999 included a purpose-built 'supplier park' to house component manufacturers locally (*Financial Times*, 1999). Unfortunately, Ford later decided to end car production at Dagenham and the scheme was not implemented showing that the idea of a 'supplier park' is only really valid if more than one major client is supporting it.

Franchising   For many would-be entrepreneurs franchising is an obvious opportunity. It provides a readymade business and offers them and their staff appropriate training. This may be a good starting point to gain valuable experience but the real entrepreneurs are those who start the franchise in the first place.

One of the earliest into this field was Coca-Cola and its bottlers. In 1899 Asa Candler missed a trick when he signed away all bottling rights to two entrepreneur lawyers, Thomas and Whitehead. He agreed to sell them syrup at $1 a gallon and provide all the advertising. This simple contract was to revolutionise the Coca-Cola business, giving birth to one of the most innovative, dynamic franchising systems in the world. To become a bottler franchisee required an investment of $2000 for the bottling equipment and another $2000 for a horse and wagon and working capital. The special syrup had to be bought from Thomas and Whitehead who provided an expert bottler, bottle caps and advertising. Half of the plant's profits went to Thomas and Whitehead. Although many bottlers failed, the entrepreneurs amongst them did well. By 1919, there were 1200 plants; virtually every town in the USA had a Coca-Cola bottler (Pendergrast, 1994).

Sectors Opportunities can often be identified by focusing on sectors where the prospects look good such as tourism, leisure, security, the Internet or something similar. These are all large and growing sectors with entrepreneurs already operating in them. This means competition but if the entrepreneur has some inside knowledge of a particular sector this need not be an obstacle.

Young Charles Forte had some inside knowledge of the catering industry from working with his father. When he saw an article in the London Evening Standard about a milk bar, recently opened in Fleet Street, he went to take a look. Instead of the ornate furnishing of the cafés of the day there was a large serving counter and a minimum of stools, chairs and tables. What Charles Forte saw in 1934 was a fast-food outlet and recognised the innovation at once. He comments in his autobiography 'It was certainly an original approach to catering, and one which appealed to me' (Forte, 1997). It took him five years to establish five milk bars in London but they were all in prime sites and he had taken his first step to becoming a hotel and catering multi-millionaire.

The trigger event

In order for the inputs of *people* and *ideas* to come together and start on the road, some form of *trigger event* appears to be necessary. This is as true for the large entrepreneurial movements that have taken place throughout history, as it is for individual entrepreneurs making their own decision.

Displacement trigger This is probably the most important type of trigger because of the large number of people involved and the whole new economies that it can generate. The history of the United States provides many examples of immigrant waves that became entrepreneurial waves. Gilder (1986) documents the case of the Cuban refugees who settled in Miami, Florida. In 1961 the economy of Miami was in a bad way and more than 1000 homes lay empty in the inner city area. Then, 200 000 destitute immigrants arrived over a period of two years. Their tragic dislocation acted as a trigger to those with entrepreneurial talent, and an economic miracle ensued. By 1980 there were 10 000 Cuban-owned businesses and at least 200 Cuban millionaires.

A similar example in the UK was the forced displacement of the Indian business and professional community from Uganda by President Amin in the 1960s. Many of this group came to the UK and brought their entrepreneurial spirit with them and built significant businesses.

Culture change is a trigger that also affects a large number of people and can transform economies. In this case it is the change to an entrepreneurial culture that provides the trigger. It is not just a matter of removing the inhibitions of the previous culture but also of replacing them by positive stimulation. In Chapter 14 we review the history of Silicon Valley and show how it developed an entrepreneurial culture in which it became 'natural' for people to think about starting their own business.

In the 1980s the Thatcher government in the UK endeavoured to promote the idea of an 'Enterprise Culture' (Young, 1990) but failed to trigger entrepreneurship. Significantly during this same period and without any government intervention an entrepreneurial culture was developing in the Cambridge area of East Anglia. It mirrored what had happened in Silicon Valley decades earlier. In March 1981, *Computer Weekly*, under the headline 'The Cambridge Phenomenon', commented that 'over the last decade a phenomenon with a good deal of significance for British industry has occurred in Cambridge. Forty-one computer-based firms have been established there during the period and are now flourishing' (Levi, 1981). The 'Cambridge Phenomenon' (Segal *et al.*, 1985) gave the East Anglia region the fastest growing economy in the UK throughout the 1980s. The culture change trigger was amazingly effective in revealing the entrepreneurs within the academic community.

Opportunity trigger   Turning to individual entrepreneurs, perhaps the most important trigger is the opportunity trigger. Would-be entrepreneurs see an opportunity that they cannot resist and decide to go for it with the feeling that if 'I don't do it soon somebody else will'. Opportunity triggers often include place and time factors that combine with the opportunity to give the necessary impetus. As the entrepreneur stories recounted earlier show, it is a matter of being in the right place at the right time with the right opportunity. The skill of the entrepreneur is to recognise that this is the true situation and then to take action.

Crisis triggers   have an important role to play for those whose entrepreneurial talent has been buried or suppressed. Redundancy is a major trigger for many, particularly, as redundancy payments can be quite generous and can provide the start-up money for a business. Such people often comment 'I wish had done this earlier'. For others, of course, it can be a serious mistake and they should have tried to find another job.

Dame Cicely Saunders, reported in Chapter 7, experienced a trigger that was both a crisis and an opportunity. The crisis was the death of her friend, David Tasma, and that then led her to see the opportunity of setting up the first hospice in the UK.

Most of these trigger events are unplanned interventions, as far as the entrepreneur is concerned. Castro may have planned the exit of people who did not like his regime but it was certainly not part of his plan to create millionaires and restore the economy of Miami. Similarly, most people do not plan their own redundancy; it is something that happens to them to which they respond. This, of course, does not mean that people have to sit around waiting for a trigger event before they do anything. True entrepreneurs make their own trigger or at least do not need much of a push to get going.

The enterprise process

The enterprise process model set out in Figure 11.1 has two stages: the *getting ready* stage and the *building and growing* stage. These are now reviewed in turn.

Getting ready

In this first stage the people and the ideas come together and the necessary preparations are made to launch the enterprise. Both have important backgrounds that come with them. People bring the influence of family, upbringing, education, age and work experience, as discussed in Chapter 1, and the talent and temperament qualities, of Chapter 2. It has been assessed that 70 per cent of entrepreneurs can identify some significant shaping event in their childhood (Cooper, quoted in Steiner, 1998). Richard Branson (1998), one of the classic entrepreneurs of Chapter 4, recalls that his mother kept giving him challenges to develop his independence. When four years old she left him on a roadside and told him to walk home across the fields. When under-twelve she sent him on a fifty-mile cycle ride to Bournemouth, leaving home in the dark, one January morning. These experiences built his sense of independence and strengthened his self-confidence so that he was in the right frame of mind to do something about the opportunities that he later saw around him.

Ideas also develop and form. Most ideas are 'half-baked' to begin with and new markets always take time and effort to open up. However the rapid rate of technological progress and of market change today means that the development time for ideas is now probably less than the preparation time for people.

Sometimes it is during this preparation period that the people and the ideas come together. This is often the case with the social entrepreneur where the final vision takes time to mature. William and Catherine Booth started their work in the east end of London some thirteen years before the Salvation Army was formed. Their experience of working amongst the very poor shaped their thinking and the development of their vision.

Figure 11.3 shows the steps of the *getting ready* stage and indicates its precursors of a preparation period and a trigger event.

Figure 11.3 *The elements of the* getting ready *stage*

The activities of 'training and assessing' and 'research and evaluation' are areas of expertise in their own right represented respectively by the 'education and training sector' and the 'research and development sector'. As these fit more appropriately into the *support infrastructure*, they are discussed in Chapter 13, but some comment is required at this stage on the more difficult 'training and assessing' of potential entrepreneurs and on how the people and the ideas come together.

Training and assessing   Training is important because it is the first formal step in developing the entrepreneur's technique and know-how. Potential entrepreneurs need to learn the basics of business at this *getting ready* stage. This is not easy because most of them prefer to learn by doing and do not respond well to formal training sessions, especially when they are in a hurry to start their business. This poses its own problems but the real difficulty is the assessment side. We see the identification of the potential entrepreneur as the weakest link in the enterprise process. This is why Part One of this book is devoted to the entrepreneur as a person and why we spend a complete chapter, Chapter 2, in explaining our approach to the identification and assessment the potential entrepreneur. We now present three approaches used by others to assess entrepreneurs and which have links with the methodology we have proposed.

The questionnaire approach   This appears to be the simplest and the most straight-forward approach to assessing the potential entrepreneur. The difficulty is that such questionnaires are difficult to validate. There are a number of questionnaires available but most are a list of fairly self-evident questions with little or no theoretical underpinning. Psychometric testing has a sounder base and a well-developed methodology, as we discussed in Chapter 1, but it fails to give a clear picture of the entrepreneur. Gallup's life themes approach is better because it considers talents and sees them as inherent strengths on which to build. A life theme is a 'talent that fits a role' so that the question becomes 'What talents and temperament do entrepreneurs need?' rather than 'What personality type should they be?' The question that then follows is 'Can these attributes be measured?'

Gallup has done work in both these areas, though it has been with people who are known to be entrepreneurs or who are already running businesses. However it has been a useful starting point for the approach and methodology of Chapter 2 where we offer a procedure for identifying the potential entrepreneur, part of which involves a questionnaire.

Of course, there will always be difficulties with a questionnaire-based approach when applied to the entrepreneur who tends to be something of a maverick by nature. Questionnaires should therefore be used with care, especially if there is no one-to-one intervention. Even so, as we propose in Chapter 2, a questionnaire is useful as a first level screening procedure to evaluate groups of around a hundred people. This would cover the case of people involved in a major redundancy programme where there was a need to identify those who could seriously think of starting their own business. It also allows the initial screening of people who apply for a business start programme or an entrepreneur introduction programme.

Interview approach   The main difficulties with this approach are that it is time-consuming and can be rather subjective. It puts a practical limit on the number of people who can be taken through this process and depends critically upon the skills of the interviewer.

Interviews are best used as a second screening procedure where there are less people but its practicality depends very much upon what first screening procedure has been used. The more effective this is, the better yield there will be from the interviews. In most business start programmes in the UK, the initial screening is done not by a questionnaire but by a carefully worded advertisement and an evaluation of application forms, often involving a telephone conversation with the applicant. The real difficulty with this procedure is the advertisement. If it is too enthusiastic or offers too much it will attract one kind of person and if it is dull and factual it will attract another. The answer lies somewhere in between but it is not easy to get it right.

Once there is a group of people that are genuinely interested in starting their own business, then an interviewer can assess their entrepreneurial potential by talking them through a number of areas. Discussion about their early childhood noting any examples of entrepreneurship and what motivated them to do things is an important starting point. It is always relevant to see how much of this has extended into adulthood and if not, why not. Most people who apply for courses about running their own business have already thought about it and some even have gone as far as writing a business plan. This is another important area of discussion.

A person's work ethic and their approach to obstacles that they have met in life are key indicators of entrepreneurial potential and need to be probed at length. The lazy person who panics at the first sign of trouble clearly has little potential. Failure is also an area to explore as it gives a good indication of their inner ego strength and how they see themselves.

Creativity should be explored in the interview and examples from the applicant's own experience discussed. Finally, it is important to find out what they enjoy doing most. This is another way of asking what are they best at doing.

Interviewers need training before they embark on this kind of interview because the right prompts and knowing when to speak and when to listen are so important.

In Chapter 2 the second stage of our *entrepreneur indicator* offers a structured approach to interviewing based on our six facet character themes. The context of the interview is important and we believe the best option is to conduct it within a formal programme in which candidates are taken through the self-evaluation procedure with the assistance of trained evaluators.

Discovery approach   The alternative to searching for the potential entrepreneurs by external screening methods is to set up mechanisms that will reveal them. Mechanisms can be cultural, enabling or educational in nature.

When a region or organisation develops an entrepreneurial culture, it acts as a mechanism for revealing entrepreneurs. They simply emerge out of the woodwork. The Cambridge Phenomenon that began in the 1980s brought with it an entrepreneurial culture and there were many examples of successful entrepreneurs for all to see. When an entrepreneurial professor arrived at the Engineering Department in a new red Porsche others noticed it! This kind of cultural peer group influence helped to develop the idea among the academics that 'If he can do it, I can do it!'

Enabling mechanisms tend to be situation- and organisation-specific. Experiences in Silicon Valley and with the 'Cambridge Phenomenon' show that entrepreneurial businesses are one of the best mechanisms for revealing entrepreneurs and generating spin-off businesses. The classic case in Silicon Valley was Fairchild Semiconductor, as we describe in Chapter 14. Also some organisations take specific steps to encourage the emergence of the entrepreneur. Cambridge University, for example, has introduced a scheme whereby academics can take leave of absence for five years. This allows them to get involved in start-ups on a full-time basis with the knowledge that they still have a job back at the university if things go wrong.

Educational mechanisms for revealing entrepreneurs are discussed more fully in Chapter 12. The ideal situation is that students with entrepreneurial potential are revealed within the context of the normal courses across all disciplines. Those revealed in this way can then enrol on specific entrepreneur programmes. It is, of course, not easy to embed entrepreneur issues within already overcrowded curricula and there are often not the staff available to communicate entrepreneurship effectively. These difficulties aside, mechanisms built into the teaching programmes can be extremely effective and provide high-quality candidates for more specialist entrepreneur programmes.

The potential entrepreneur and the probable opportunity The two activity blocks of 'training and assessing' for the people input and 'research and evaluation' for the ideas input are an important part of any intervention strategy to promote the generation of new enterprises. Whatever the influence of the earlier events, the unproven inputs of people and of ideas need to be processed to assess and improve their quality. If this is not done then the odds are heavily stacked against success, as the following arithmetic shows.

Assuming that among the general population 10–15 per cent of people have the potential to be entrepreneurs and that 1–2 per cent of unscreened opportunities appear to be viable then the chance of combining a potential entrepreneur with a probable opportunity is between 0.1 per cent and 0.3 per cent.

If some evaluation is done beforehand then the situation is improved but the odds are still not high. For example, if we only consider people who say they want to have their own business rather than with the general public, the percentage of potential entrepreneurs could be increased to around 20–25 per cent. Similarly if a panel of experts screened the ideas then the percentage of probable opportunities could rise to 20 per cent or even 40 per cent depending on the ability of the panel and the information they have available. With these figures the chance of a successful combination rises to between 4 per cent and 10 per cent, which is still a low figure.

A more helpful approach is to evaluate the person/idea combination on a case-by-case basis and plot the results on the diagram shown in Figure 11.4. Whilst the percentages discussed above put most *people plus idea* combinations in the bottom left quadrant, the diagram shows the advantage of working on either the people or the ideas side to increase the yield.

A typical example of a project in the upper left quadrant would be where there is an individual or team with some entrepreneurial experience but the idea is not proven. This could be a group that has spun out of an existing business and has a good track record but their idea needs working on. The lower right quadrant has a well-developed low-risk opportunity but the individual or team is new and the entrepreneurial skills have not been tested. A franchise opportunity could be in this quadrant. The upper right quadrant carries the best chance of success with a potential entrepreneur and a probable opportunity. The management buy-out would fit here, as would the team that spins out from an existing company as a result of downsizing.

This methodology can also be used to decide which of a number of different projects to support. This is a problem often faced by economic development agencies with their

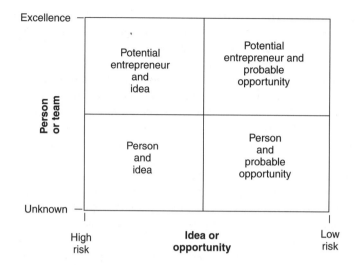

Figure 11.4   *People/ idea combination*

limited resources. In one study, in the rural areas of western Scotland, some twenty projects were identified and plotted on Figure 11.4. Most were in the lower left quadrant but there were three in the upper right quadrant to which priority was given. Steps were also suggested to improve the position of some of the weaker projects in the lower right and upper left quadrants by working on the people and the ideas respectively to improve their chances of success and move them into the upper right quadrant.

Another aspect of the relation between the person and the idea that the model highlights is the assumption that the people with the ideas are the right ones to run the enterprise. Many schemes, often promoted by the public sector, make this assumption when they offer training programmes to help people who have good ideas, to get into business. One of the important points from the models in Figures 11.1 and 11.3 is that the people and the ideas are separate inputs. They come together in the true entrepreneur but for everybody else they are distinct. The inventor with the great idea and the academic whose research has shown up an opportunity are almost certainly not the right people to translate the opportunity into a business. Roberts (1991), who studied high-technology entrepreneurs in the USA, has termed this problem the 'Founder's Disease, the diagnosed inability of the founding CEO to grow in managerial and leadership capacity as rapidly as the firm's size'. Some people recognise their limitations right from the start. They prefer to remain as inventors or academics and are happy to be advisers to the business and not get further involved. Others either find it very difficult to hand what they see as 'their baby' on to somebody else. Some never quite feel their idea is ready and continue to add 'bells and whistles' when the product is already marketable.

The people and the ideas are more than inputs to the process. When the person is a potential entrepreneur and the idea a probable opportunity then we have two intertwined strands, rather like a double helix, that together have the real possibility of creating and building something of recognised value. Other resources such as money help the process forward but they are the basic constituents. The entrepreneur is not just the director or manager of a process, he is part of the process itself.

The enterprise model also applies to the social and the aesthetic entrepreneurs and is not just the domain of the business entrepreneur. The difference lies in the nature of the link between the entrepreneur and the opportunity. Business entrepreneurs often start with an opportunity that they originated and so have an emotional attachment to it. With experience, they learn that any viable opportunity is as good as another and will respond to their entrepreneurial talent. Social entrepreneurs are different. One opportunity is not as good as another. Social entrepreneurs are driven by a cause or a need. It may be the need to help the marginalised in our society into jobs or to lift the poor out of poverty in the Third World. Whatever it is, social entrepreneurs have a strong calling to meet a need that they have perceived and they cannot be moved from it. This helps them to focus well and gives them exceptional courage. Temperament plays a key role in the make-up of social entrepreneurs who feel a real burden for the task they have committed to. This often means they are misunderstood by their contemporaries who cannot see why they are wasting their lives in such a cause. Florence Nightingale, William Booth and others described in Chapter 7 all illustrate this point.

Aesthetic entrepreneurs are driven by their talent, which means that they have to express themselves through their art or music. For them, their talent represents their opportunity. Artists often express the fear that their talent may desert them. For many this can be a cause of real depression. They see the ideas that come to them as external, from somewhere outside themselves that they cannot control. There are similarities with the business entrepreneur who can spot opportunities. He does not know when he will see his next opportunity and, as with artistic inspiration, it can just come out of nowhere.

Enterprise start-up activities   With the quality of the inputs now improved, the process moves forward to engage directly in the enterprise start-up activities. It is the stage at which preparations are made to start the enterprise. The potential entrepreneur completes the evaluation of the opportunity and decides to go for it. A detailed business plan is prepared and the required resources put together. The potential entrepreneur decides the company name, legally constitutes the business, talks to the banks, finds premises and so on. Many do this in a frenzy of activity. They cannot wait to get started, in fact they often start before they have the formalities in place, such is their enthusiasm.

Figure 11.5 presents a formal version of this stage breaking it down into three elements or sub-stages.

The entrepreneur and the opportunity   In the first sub-stage the potential entrepreneur takes on a probable opportunity as the basis for the enterprise. The true entrepreneur is not always conscious of this, for it appears self-evident. Sometimes the trigger event can happen at this point rather than earlier, when the potential entrepreneur suddenly realises that the opportunity is now ready to run with. It has moved from an idea to a probable opportunity in the perception of the entrepreneur. In January 1975 Bill Gates and Paul Allen stood in Harvard Square eagerly reading the description of a kit computer in the magazine *Popular Electronics*. Bill Gates (1995)

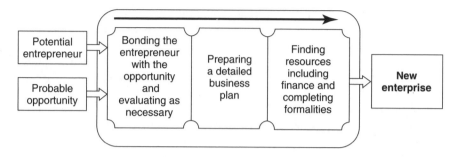

Figure 11.5 *Enterprise start-up activities*

comments 'As we read excitedly about the first truly personal computer, Paul and I didn't know exactly how it would be used, but we were sure it would change us and the world of computing. We were right'. Immediately they set about writing a basic language for this computer, and Microsoft was born.

This first sub-stage is often the point at which many would-be entrepreneurs come to a halt. They may have been on a business training programme or completed an entrepreneur course of some kind but they now have to take steps to make something happen. Perhaps they have difficulty in being sure of the opportunity or they have too many to choose from. Some people enjoy lingering at this early stage and never make a commitment to go forward. Others can do the same thing at the business plan stage and produce endless variations of their plan.

Often a level of planned intervention is helpful at this point so that people can focus on a decision or complete a specific task within an agreed timetable. The planned intervention helps to move people along so that they feel that this is the best opportunity they are ever likely to get to start their own business. Intervention can be in the form of a business start programme or of an assigned mentor or adviser. Most regions of the UK have business start programmes of one kind or another provided by both the public and the private sectors and some of these also involve the assignment of a mentor. For young people, the Prince's Trust in the UK has done an excellent job over the years in providing those who want to start their own business with grant money in the context of a business plan and an experienced business adviser.

The team-based business start programme is an important example of the planned intervention. It takes people who have an interest in being part of a business team and puts them together around a business opportunity. The results have been mixed but yet encouraging. Three or four small businesses are usually generated per programme, and now and again one hits the jackpot. Within four years of start-up, one business was employing 700 people (*Financial Times*, 1995). The main lesson learned from these experiences is that the intervention has to be clear and decisive so that people are put into teams and have a limited choice of carefully researched business opportunities. In line with Figure 11.4 the aim is to reduce the risk as far as possible on both the people and the idea sides.

Most programmes now employ some form of psychometric testing and put the teams together on the basis of people's personality and skill set to give a good mix and balance in the team. It is helpful to include elements in the programme that will build the commitment and focus in the team. One route that has been used is to get the team members to discuss and agree at the outset how much money each would be able to put into the venture. This can then link in with the equally important discussion about share ownership. A team that comes out positively from these discussions will be well-bonded.

Some business start programmes have offered the availability of a business idea as a major feature of the programme. This kind of offer attracts the type of candidates who naively think that 'get rich quick ideas' actually exist and then are very critical when the ideas do not meet their unrealistic expectations. Generating a sufficient number of quality opportunities for such a programme is extremely difficult because good ideas do not remain open long enough to bridge the time between their selection for the 'ideas bank' and their take up by one of the business start teams.

In this first part of the 'start-up activities' in Figure 11.5 the individual or team takes on board the opportunity and begins to *own* it both intellectually and emotionally. For the entrepreneur who sees the opportunity and makes it happen this is not a difficulty, but with the intervention approach to business start-up, it is one of the problem areas. If it is difficult to put a business team together; then getting it to adopt a business opportunity adds another level of difficulty. The earlier analysis of the probability of finding an entrepreneur and an opportunity needs to include an additional factor to cover the probability of the entrepreneur accepting the opportunity. This further reduces the probability of a successful intervention in the process.

An important part of this first stage is for the entrepreneur or team to conduct a formal evaluation of the opportunity before moving to the business plan stage. This is a re-run of the original evaluation that took the *idea* on to become a *probable opportunity* but now it is carried out by those who hope to make it happen. This sharpens the evaluation, and as it proceeds it should build confidence that it really is a viable opportunity for them. If this does not happen then the process can be repeated with another *probable opportunity* or changes can be made to the original idea to make it viable. It is far better to drop the opportunity at this early stage as the further through the process it is done the more difficult and expensive it becomes.

Market research is an important part of the evaluation. It needs to be practical and relevant to the business. When Charles Forte was thinking of starting his milk bar project his research involved standing outside the milk bar of his competitor in Fleet Street, London and counting the number of people going by and the number who went in. When he had identified a possible site for himself near Regent Street Polytechnic he carried out the same counts and compared the two. On this basis he rented the shop and started his first milk bar.

The business plan stage   Once the individual or team is comfortable with the enterprise opportunity the process moves forward to the second stage in Figure 11.5, the preparation of a detailed business plan. The business plan has two purposes; for the potential entrepreneur or team it is to confirm that the enterprise has a good chance of success and for the financial backers it is to convince them that the proposal is worthy of their investment. These are not quite the same thing. The first priority must be for the team to be quite sure that the project is viable. If the business plan throws up doubts or seriously questions the viability of the project the matter should be dealt with there and then and not left till later. It is the belief and commitment of the entrepreneur that convinces the backers as much as the business plan itself. They are experts at exposing doubts and watch for the integrity of the answer; so it is important that the entrepreneur has sorted out anything in the business plan that he or she is not fully convinced about.

The business plan for the backers will not be the same as the one produced for internal use. For example it will need to be simplified so that it is understood by people who are less familiar with the details of the opportunity and its application. An outline for a business plan is provided in Chapter 15.

Mentors and advisers can play an important role at this point and they can be a useful bridge to the third stage in Figure 11.5 where resources and finance are put together. Rather like the athletic or football coach, the mentor can use these early stages to bring on the talent and develop technique and know how. He or she can also watch for signs of temperament problems. Some entrepreneurs will want to run before they can walk, others will not meet deadlines or simply treat the whole exercise as a game.

The identifying and training of mentors is just as important an issue as identifying and training entrepreneurs. People who take on this role often have a banking or big company background, and are available because they have taken early retirement. Whilst there are obviously exceptions, this is not an ideal experience-base from which to draw mentors. They will need to have been through the process of starting up and growing an enterprise for themselves, and probably to have failed a few times.

Finding resources   The final stage is in two parts: finding resources, including finance, and completing the formalities. Both require contact with the outside world, so from this stage on others know what is being planned. At this point the decision to make a start has been made whether the entrepreneur is aware of it or not, although the exact date will not be known. It is important to tie this down in order to avoid drifting into a level of commitment without realising it. The resource side is another reason why setting a start date is important. There will never be a time when the potential entrepreneur has sufficient resources to start the business. It is a chicken and egg situation in which risk and judgement are involved. The resource issue, more than any other, is what separates the entrepreneur from the rest. The ability to handle this stage well is one of the clearest indicators of entrepreneurial talent. The spotting of opportunities gives some indication but the resources issue shows whether the potential entrepreneur can link opportunity with implementation. If he or she can, then, the enterprising person and the project champion are present in the one person and there is a true entrepreneur.

The resources issue is even more of a challenge for social and aesthetic entrepreneurs than it is for business entrepreneurs because their focus is on their vision or their art and resources, like finance, come some way behind. Entrepreneurs working in these areas need to have the 'resourcing' talent in abundance. Social entrepreneur Elliot Tepper, discussed in Chapter 7, is one such. He always has visions well beyond his current financial resources but seems to be able to find the money from somewhere. When we visited him in Madrid he drove us around a large building he planned to buy. With his MBA and economics training, he quickly went through the financial advantages of owning rather than renting property and added that he needed the extra space anyway. His confidence in finding the money was remarkable. As Tepper put it 'The Lord will provide the money if he means me to have the building'. When that is combined with his entrepreneurial talent the combination is unbeatable!

If the social or aesthetic entrepreneur is weak on this resources side or is simply not an entrepreneur then there is a role for the agent entrepreneur to come alongside. This is already an established mechanism in sport and music. The Beatles was certainly a very talented band that brought in a new era of pop music but it was the partnership with the entrepreneur Brian Epstein, their agent, that really made them so successful (Geller, 1999). There are signs that this agent idea is beginning to be applied to social projects. The first step was to use professional money raisers but amongst them have been some entrepreneurs who have really driven the project rather than simply helped with the funding.

Completing formalities in this final stage covers all the things that have to be done to set up and run a company. It involves contact with banks, solicitors, property agents, government offices and suppliers like printers and stationers. Many forms have to be completed and signed as the entrepreneur enters the world of bureaucracy. These things take a great deal of time and become quite complicated, but they are tangible and real. For this reason some people prefer to sort these areas out before they have completed the business plan and made a real commitment to go forward. This, of course, is a mistake and is often a sign that a manager, rather than an entrepreneur, is at work. Managers enjoy this involvement with practical things, whereas most entrepreneurs find them a chore and only do them when they have to.

The above has set out the *getting ready* stage as a series of activities through which the entrepreneur has to pass. In practice, it is unlikely that he or she will do so in such a structured and linear way but each activity will need to take place in some form. If they are not done before the enterprise is launched, then they will have to take place afterwards which is likely to be less efficient and could even seriously hinder the early progress of the business.

Comments have been made throughout about the difficulties with business start programmes that try to replicate the start-up process. Despite these factors, interventions that follow through the stages of the model are being run successfully and at a cost per job created which compares well with other job creation schemes. The proviso is that businesses created in this way will not necessarily be entrepreneurial and therefore are most likely to remain small. The entrepreneur business will only emerge consistently when entrepreneur selection procedures, such as the *entrepreneur indicator* we describe in Chapter 2, are applied.

Building and growing

The *getting ready* stage leads on to the *building and growing* stage. This is where the enterprise really happens and entrepreneurial talent comes into its own. It is characterised by a number of phases or stages that the enterprise passes through as it grows and builds to something of recognised value. Various models based on research studies define the process as a series of stages (Greiner, 1972; Churchill and Lewis, 1983; Scott and Bruce, 1987; Jolly, 1997). The model (Bolton, 1987, 1989, 1993, 1997) presented in Figure 11.6 uses a similar approach and is based on practical experience. The growth stages follow those found in the natural world, from embryo through to adulthood and full independence. The output is a viable and growing enterprise that has recognised value.

Figure 11.6   *Building and growing*

Before describing the growth stages of the process, a major objection to this kind of linear sequential model needs to be considered. It has been common in recent years to dismiss such models as too simplistic because of the considerable overlap and feedback between the stages of the process (McKinsey Report, 1991). The argument is not so much with the stages themselves as with how they relate to each other. The concern is that a linear model does not allow for feedback or for activities to run in parallel with each other and interact. Whilst these points have some validity, the essential feature that a linear model tries to capture is that the process has a beginning and operates in real time. The purpose of the model in Figure 11.6 is to help entrepreneurs understand the stages that their enterprise can expect to pass through. Without this understanding, the entrepreneur is likely to drift from one stage to the other unaware of what is happening, with a consequent loss of focus. The transfer from one stage to another offers a time to stop, reflect and plan the next stage. Next to finance, the handling of time is the most critical issue facing the growing enterprise so that a model based on time as its axis is clearly of value.

In setting out stages on a time base it is easy to imply that there is a pattern to how long each stage will take. Whilst the stages would be expected to increase in length, as the process goes forward from perhaps a few months to three or four years, there are so many exceptions that it is difficult to generalise. The problem is that it is easy to get stuck in one of the stages because things have not gone according to plan. In this case it is often necessary to go back to the start of the stage or even to the one before.

The growth stages described   The description of the stages is taken from the natural world. The bird makes a good analogy because it finally takes off and becomes independent.

Embryo stage   The 'embryo stage' is the starting point in Figure 11.6. It begins with conception and ends when the egg hatches and the chick appears. This is a very formative stage and determines what the enterprise will look like and its direction. It is its potential that is being developed. The embryo stage is crucial for any enterprise whether it is a commercial business, or a social or aesthetic undertaking. The arrow from the *getting ready* stage is shown running into this stage because the founders and the opportunity may have already come together and, as happens in conception, the characteristics of both will be found in the embryo. The point at which a legal entity, such as a company, is set up will depend upon the local circumstances. In principle, it is best to do this as soon as possible because it ties the founders into the project and makes for a sharper focus by all concerned. It also helps to resolve any questions of commitment before they become a problem.

Nurture stage   The 'nurture stage' was a later addition to the model (Bolton, 1993) but came out of the experience of working with start-ups. Many enterprises find it difficult to take the step that finally gets a reliable product out of the door to a real customer. Like the chick that has to be fed and nurtured by its parent, the enterprise needs to be helped along through this stage. This is the point at which the business incubator described in Chapter 12 can be so important in providing a supportive and nurturing environment. It is a very formative time for the entrepreneur and the team as the business becomes a reality. Their learning curve is probably at its steepest in this stage.

Fledgling stage   In the 'fledgling stage' the chick loses its down and grows real feathers as the enterprise begins to look like a serious business. The dependency on outside help is steadily reduced as the young bird learns to fend for itself. It is able to fly greater and greater distances and find more and more of its own food. Here, there are fewer new tricks to learn but the enterprise has to become proficient at doing them. Speed of response and finding resources become second nature. Staying alive becomes much easier and the enterprise is less vulnerable to predators or accident.

Take-off stage   The final stage to becoming a viable and growing business is what we have previously called the 'maturing stage' (Bolton, 1997) but now prefer to call the 'take-off stage'. This is because it is in this stage that the enterprise either takes-off or else remains as a small business. The difference between the real entrepreneur and the life-style entrepreneur is now revealed. The life-style person is quite happy to settle down, maybe in a niche market, and the enterprise remains static. The true entrepreneur, one the other hand, is stimulated by what has already been achieved and is now ready to race ahead. Once Charles Forte had grown his chain of milk bars he went for hotels and never stopped. As explained further in Chapter 13, it is in this stage that the product/service offered by the enterprise is taken up or adopted by the marketplace. It is here that a market share is achieved that puts the new business among the leaders, if not in the lead.

A critique

Flamholtz (1990) and others see the entrepreneurial process as the first stage in a company's progression to being a professional business. He defines seven growth stages. The first two, the 'new venture' and the 'expansion stages' correspond with those covered by the model in Figure 11.6 and take the business to a sales level of $1–$10 million. The 'take-off stage' extends into what Flamholtz calls the 'professionalisation' stage with a limit of $100 million annual sales. He sees this as the final stage to organisational maturity with the remaining three, 'diversification', 'integration' and 'decline and revitalisation', as simply stages in a company's life cycle.

There are two issues that Flamholtz's model raises for the entrepreneurial enterprise. The first is the transition from the entrepreneurial enterprise to the professional business. Does this really have to happen? Experience certainly shows that some company founders are often not the right people to take the company through to maturity but then these founders were probably not true entrepreneurs. If they had been they would have grown and developed their business just as many of the entrepreneurs, described in this book, have done. These true entrepreneurs have been able to keep their businesses entrepreneurial and yet at the same time have very professional operations. The question is not whether a company has to stop being entrepreneurial and become professional but how it can be both at the same time. Handling this paradox is the key.

The second issue that this transition model raises takes us back to the discussion about Second- and Third-Wave companies in Chapter 10. Flamholtz describes the need 'for a fundamental transition from the spontaneous, ad hoc, free-spirited enterprise to a more formally planned, organised and disciplined entity'. That is, the organisation has to change from a Third-Wave to a Second-Wave company. This conventional wisdom is not supported by the facts. Second-Wave companies can only survive in well-structured non-changing markets so that professionalising a business and dropping the entrepreneurial culture will be the kiss of death for most companies in today's changing business world. Apple Computers replaced Steve Jobs, the entrepreneur, with John Sculley, the corporate man, and failed to compete in the turbulent computer market. Professionalising an entrepreneurial company did not work.

The real issue is not whether the transition to professionalism should be engineered but how one can stop it happening. In reality, there is a kind of bureaucratic gravity that pulls companies into structure and system. The fun and excitement that was there in the company's early days is lost and is replaced by its exact opposite: routine and boredom. The entrepreneurs cannot survive in such a business and leave to be replaced by administrators. In today's world, Third-Wave companies that have gravitated to the Second Wave find it very difficult to survive, let alone grow and develop. Far from engineering this transition, we should seek ways of keeping the entrepreneurial spirit alive. Certainly, systems and discipline are required as a company grows but this should serve the business and not strangle it.

The growth stages defined

The enterprise growth model of Figure 11.6 describes what is in reality a natural progression. The entrepreneur moves steadily through these stages as he builds the enterprise. The value in structuring the growth is that it provides an understanding for less experienced entrepreneurs and tells them what to expect. Those who work with entrepreneurs can use it to plan how they will support and promote the process.

To be of real value, the growth stages need definitions that are practical, with a minimum of ambiguity. Figure 11.7 gives criteria for the break point between the stages. They are based on the development stage that the product/service offered by

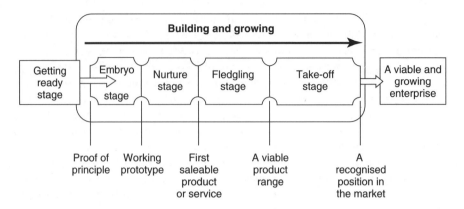

Figure 11.7   *Growth stage criteria*

the enterprise has reached. The benefit, when compared with other possible criteria, is that they can be quantified. There is either a prototype of the product or service that can be demonstrated or there is not. There is either a saleable product or there is not.

One problem with this approach is that it can be confused with the ongoing development of new products that often run in parallel as the company itself develops. This model is about the growth of the business and uses the development of its first product line as an indicator of the stage the business has reached. The terms for each stage refer to the embryo, nurture, fledgling and take-off stages of the enterprise itself, and not the product/service. Using the development of the first product as the indicator has the advantage of focussing the team on which product that actually is. Often it is not clear in the early days, exactly the product or market to really go for, and focus can be achieved by linking this with consideration of what stage the company has reached. Another advantage of these criteria is that they are easily understood by inventors, engineers and technologists, and the link with business development makes sense to them.

The criterion to enter the *building and growing* stage is 'proof of principle'. That is to say, the idea upon which the business opportunity is based must actually work and there must be no areas of uncertainty that could kill the opportunity. The term arises in the context of technology where the science behind it has first to be proved before it can be applied. This is done in the research and development stage that precedes the embryo stage. Because science and technology has an increasingly strong commercial focus, it may become appropriate to include a 'pre-embryo' stage in the model. For opportunities that do not involve technology, the proof of principle would involve proof that a market does really exist and that the product or service that will be offered to that market can actually be delivered. Proof of principle is the entry point to the process and requires the opportunity to be researched and evaluated, as described in the 'getting ready' stage. Ideally there will be some form of demonstration of the proposed product or service. Something tangible is far more telling than any document or verbal presentation, though a business plan should be available to back up the commercial claims of the opportunity.

In the embryo stage, the enterprise gives the opportunity life by developing it to the point where it can be shown to potential customers and users. Several prototypes might be required during this stage as the opportunity takes on its final form. It may not be like the finished article but its potential should be clear to the customer and not just the enthusiastic team behind it. When the opportunity is technology-based, this stage is a good one in which to pass the technology over from the originator to a commercial team. An inventor could hand over in a similar way. The exit from this stage is often the best point for the opportunity and the team to spin out from an existing organisation, if there is one.

The 'nurture' stage moves the opportunity into the real world, from a working prototype to a product or service that can be sold to real customers. It is likely that some trials will have been carried out with tame customers and the market tested. The formalities for trading will have been put in place with billing and financial systems and some expansion of the team. This is a time when the cash flow has to be carefully watched as there will be little or no income but expenditure will have begun to rise. It is possible that in this stage the enterprise moves into its own premises and sets its stall out to begin trading operations. This is a testing time for entrepreneurs but if they are good enough they will rise to the challenge and the whole thing will be great fun. The dynamic of the enterprise will begin to be created.

The 'fledgling' stage sees the enterprise operating as a business and moving into profit. The business plan for entry to this stage will be more specific than any previous ones with a clear statement of the cash flow and working capital requirements of the business on a monthly basis. It will also provide the growth strategy for the enterprise over the next three years showing how it will capture the market it has targeted. As the team grows, personnel matters will become increasingly important. Growth from ten to twenty people, and then to fifty, marks transitions in management that need to be recognised. This may require the recruitment of managers from outside and this is always a disturbing experience for those who have been involved from the start.

The output of this stage is a range of products that broadens the business base and may now be serving a number of different markets. The transition to the 'take-off' stage is probably the most difficult of all and many never make it. Instead, they stay in a kind of permanent fledgling state catering for a specific group of customers, many of whom become good friends. This is the 'stay small and stay happy' syndrome. There is nothing inherently wrong with this approach but it is the domain of the life-style entrepreneur and not the real entrepreneur who wants to go onward and upwards. Others do move from the 'fledgling' stage and mature but see no real growth. This is the manager's domain and the founding entrepreneur has often left by this time to pursue other interests.

The 'take-off 'stage is where the entrepreneur builds something of recognised value. Its output is an established position in the marketplace, preferably as market leader. One reason that this is difficult to achieve is that there has to be a fundamental shift in the view of the market. Up to this point, the market is seen as something you supply into but now it becomes something you take over and seek to control. Intel and Microsoft made this transition some years ago and, in view of the monopoly ruling against Microsoft, they have done it too well! Cisco has adopted a similar strategy to achieve dominance in the Internet market (*Business Week*, 1999).

The growth stages applied

The criteria just described for the growth stages can be used as an evaluation and decision point in the move from one stage to the other. This step can be formalised and a business plan prepared for the next stage. Most business plans are somewhat unrealistic because they have to make too many assumptions about a future that is unknown. By breaking the future down into four stages, it is possible to have business plans that become closer and closer to reality as the enterprise passes from one stage to the other. This business plan can then be used by the entrepreneur and others who have a stake in the business to decide the next step.

A formal appraisal of this kind between each stage allows the following options to be considered:

1 *Continue in business*. This will mean that there is a good continuity between the business plan for the stage just ended and the new plan for the next stage. There may be some personnel changes required and perhaps a re-negotiation of the bank overdraft, but basically it is a matter of continuing on with things according to the plan.
2 *Close the business down*. Here things will have gone wrong. The earlier business plan will have not been met and the best for all concerned is to close the operation down before things get worse. This is a difficult decision to face and most people put it off until it is unavoidable. By considering this option at the start of each stage, it minimises losses and provides a framework in which those involved can withdraw objectively and honourably.
3 *Seek additional funding*. Some of the most successful enterprises can require significant funding as they move from one stage to another. A typical high-tech business might require one or even two major funding rounds during its 'nurture' stage. This always takes time and can be a difficult and vulnerable period for the enterprise. It is important to realise the need for cash well in advance so that raising the necessary funds can be planned in plenty of time rather than being a panic measure when it is really too late.
4 *Sell off the business or part of it*. This option can be attractive to entrepreneurs who have other interests or want to concentrate on one of the many opportunities they have opened up. It may also be part of the original strategy. Technology-based companies often have technology that is of interest to the large corporation, particularly in biotechnology and the Internet sectors. It is better to plan to be taken over than simply have it happen. This option can also arise when the product or service does not provide an adequate base for a business. A company that has developed a product with a limited market size may be of interest to an existing business to supplement its product range.
5 *Seek a joint-venture partner*. The main attraction of this option is when partnership with another business can bring benefits to both parties. It is not easy to make joint-ventures work, and in reality they are often a take-over by one of the parties. However, when they do work they can strengthen the management team, improve productivity and efficiency and speed up entry into new markets.
6 *Change direction*. It is often quite difficult at the 'embryo' stage to know which of the several directions an opportunity should be developed. There can be as many

as five applications, all with potential but not the resources to follow them all up. In this case, one or two of the applications could be taken through to the 'embryo' stage with the option that if they hit problems, then there can be a change in direction and another route followed.

7 *Licensing*. This option applies mainly to technology-based businesses. It may be that a research team takes an opportunity through to the end of the 'embryo' or even the 'nurture' stage and then decides they really want to go back to being researchers. This can happen when an individual has taken sabbatical leave for a year and then has to decide between the new business and his research post. Licensing can also be an option when a number of applications with significant potential have emerged from the 'embryo' stage. One of them may be a licensing opportunity that can bring in much needed cash and allow the team to focus on the other applications. In this case one has to be careful that the application that has been licensed out does not, at a later stage, impact on the other markets that one is likely to work in.

These options can help to focus the entrepreneur and the team and ensure that some system and rigour is applied to the start-up process. It is better to face up to issues ahead of time rather than wait until there is little room to manoeuvre. Personal egos often get in the way of making clear and objective decisions at the critical points in the growth of a business. The growth stages and the above list of options to be considered as the business moves on to the next stage provide a decision framework that can minimise the influence of egos and allow people to withdraw from a situation that they might otherwise cling to.

Concluding remarks

We have presented a process model that covers the start-up and early stage growth of a business. The elements that have been described need to link together to form, as far as is possible, a smooth and continuous activity with milestones to chart and assess progress.

In principle, the model and the sequential growth methodology it employs is not limited to an enterprise or business. The social and the aesthetic entrepreneurs pass through a similar process as they build something of recognised value. Experience with social entrepreneurs shows that the *getting ready* stages are almost exactly the same as for a business but with the resource element, particularly finance, playing a more dominant role. The *building and growing* stages are similar but may need to be defined differently. The business stage definitions work well if the social entrepreneur is providing a service that is tangible and can be measured, but if there are only soft measures, this is more difficult. Even so, social entrepreneurs generally recognise the stages and find them useful in discussing their progress.

The enterprise process does not stand alone. It is set in the context of a *support infrastructure* and an *operational environment* that determine the strength and development of the process in a region. To reach a point where the process is self-sustaining, attention has to be paid to the internal elements of the process already described, and the external infrastructure and environment factors we describe in the next two chapters.

We believe that some level of critical mass can be achieved in most situations but it takes time and requires long-term commitment and co-operation from a wide range of institutions and individuals. Entrepreneurs play a key role in all this but they cannot do it without the help and support of the other stakeholders in the local economy.

References

Bolton, W.K. (1987). Securing the start-up company. 2nd International Symposium on Technical Innovation and Entrepreneurship, Birmingham, England, September.

Bolton, W.K. (1989). Growing an economic infrastructure from the university sector. 16th International Small Business Congress, Sao Paulo, Brazil, October.

Bolton, W.K. (1993). The enterprise paradigm, Latin American Seminar on the Development of Technology-based Enterprises, Rio de Janeiro, May.

Bolton, W.K. (1997). *The University Handbook on Enterprise Development*. Columbus.

Braider, D. (1967). *The Master Painter*. Bodley Head.

Branson, R. (1998). *Richard Branson: Losing my Virginity*. Virgin Publishing.

Business Week (1999). Meet Cisco's Mr Internet. 13 September.

Cambridge Science Park Newsletter (1996). Laser-scan moves from USM to Stock Exchange listing. Autumn, **32**.

Churchill, N.C. and Lewis, V.L. (1983). The five stages of small business growth. *Harvard Business Review*, May–June.

e-business (1999). Jungle fever. December, 71–73.

Financial Times (1995). Business links set sights on winners. 30 May.

Financial Times (1999). Ford set to invest £500 m in revamp at Dagenham. 6 May.

Flamholtz, E.G. (1990). *Growing Pains*. Jossey-Bass.

Forte, C. (1997). *Forte*. Pan Books.

Gardner, H. (1995). *Leading Minds*. Basic Books.

Gates, W.H. (1995). *The Road Ahead*. Viking.

Geller, D. (1999). *The Brian Epstein Story*. Faber and Faber.

Gilder, G. (1986). *The Spirit of Enterprise*. Penguin.

Greiner, L.E. (1972). Evolution and revolution as organisations grow. *Harvard Business Review*, July–August.

Hickman, C.R. (1990). *Mind of a Manager, Soul of a Leader*. John Wiley.

Jolly, V.K. (1997). *Commercialising New Technologies*. Harvard Business School Press.

Kawasaki, G. (1992). *Selling the Dream*. HarperBusiness.

Larson, J.K. and Rogers, E.M. (1986). *Silicon Valley Fever*. Unwin Counterpoint.

Levi, P. (1981). The Cambridge phenomenon. *Computer Weekly*, 19 March, 21.

McKinsey Report (1991). *Partners in Innovation*. McKinsey and Co.

Pendergrast, M. (1994). *For God, Country and Coca-Cola*. Phoenix Paperback.

Roberts, E.B. (1991). *Entrepreneurs in High-technology*. Oxford University Press.

Rose, F. (1989). *West of Eden*. Business Books.

Scott, M. and Bruce, R. (1987). Five stages of growth in small business. *Long Range Planning*, **20** (3)

Segal, N., Quince, R.E. and Wicksteed, W. (1985). *The Cambridge Phenomenon*. Segal, Quince, Wicksteed and Brand Brothers.

Steiner, R. (1998). *My First Break*. News International.

Young, D. (1990). *The Enterprise Years*. Headline.

12 How the entrepreneur can be helped and supported

Entrepreneurs, like dormant seeds, will emerge and grow if the right help and support is available. The ground has to be tilled and the soil watered. Weeds have to be kept under control and harmful insects destroyed. The Support Infrastructure that we describe in this chapter has this cultivation role. Entrepreneurs are a species. Its more hardy members grow whatever the soil condition but the rest require more friendly conditions if they are to flourish. Here we explain how those conditions can be created and a successful garden developed.

Introduction

Most of the entrepreneurs described earlier in this book simply 'got on with it'. They were very self-sufficient people and liked to do things their way. Some entrepreneurs are like this, but not all. We see around us only those entrepreneurs who have had enough courage and a strong inner ego to go it alone. These are the ones who do not need much help but they are the small percentage at one end of an axis of potential entrepreneurs. The rest have not surfaced.

The notion of an axis along which the potential entrepreneur can be positioned is an important one. Those that come forward first are at the right-hand end of the axis in Figure 12.1, and those who have to be encouraged and pushed into it are at the other end.

The initial position on the axis depends mainly upon the strength of the entrepreneur's temperament – the inner- and outer-ego character themes discussed in Chapter 2. Life experiences, opportunity and education move people along the axis in one direction or the other, making them more or less likely to emerge as entrepreneurs. The help and support discussed in this chapter can move the potential entrepreneur along the axis to the right in Figure 12.1 to the point where he or she launches out as an entrepreneur.

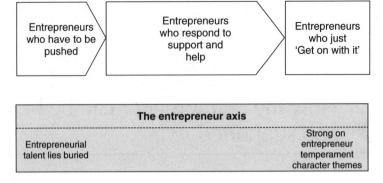

Figure 12.1 *The entrepreneur axis*

The idea of the entrepreneur axis is developed further in Figure 12.2 to illustrate how barriers in the system influence the emergence of the entrepreneur.

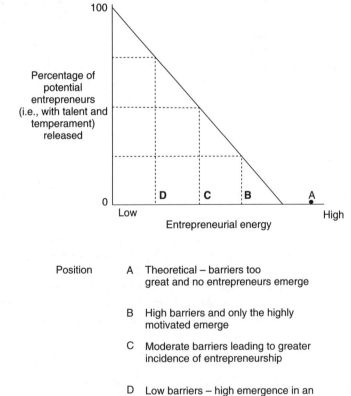

Position	A	Theoretical – barriers too great and no entrepreneurs emerge
	B	High barriers and only the highly motivated emerge
	C	Moderate barriers leading to greater incidence of entrepreneurship
	D	Low barriers – high emergence in an entrepreneurial culture

Figure 12.2 *Releasing entrepreneurial potential*

Entrepreneurs are positioned along the horizontal axis according to what might be called their 'entrepreneurial energy'. As in Figure 12.1, potential entrepreneurs who are positioned to the right along the axis will be more likely to emerge as entrepreneurs. They are the ones with the highest 'entrepreneurial energy'. Those to the left are low on 'entrepreneurial energy'. Within a particular situation, the percentage of potential entrepreneurs who will actually emerge and become real entrepreneurs depends upon the barriers that exist. As Figure 12.2 illustrates, if there are high barriers, then only those with sufficient 'entrepreneurial energy' will emerge. If the barriers are lower, then more entrepreneurs will come forward and an entrepreneurial culture can develop, which will reduce the barriers still further, releasing more entrepreneurs.

The two factors that control the release of entrepreneurial potential are the level of 'entrepreneurial energy' within an individual and the energy required to overcome the barriers. In Chapter 2 we considered the entrepreneur and the talent, temperament and technique that together provide the 'entrepreneurial energy'. In this chapter we are concerned both with how this energy can be developed further and how the barriers can be replaced by positive factors, the outcome being that the barriers in Figure 12.2 drop to position D and more entrepreneurial talent is released.

The purpose of the *support infrastructure* is not simply to support the enterprise process but to enable the continued release of entrepreneurial potential. It is the extent to which this is achieved that should be the measure of success. One of the great dangers of infrastructure projects is that they become an end in themselves and develop their own set of norms that do not serve the release of entrepreneurial potential. Business incubators can lose their original vision of being a seed-bed for start-ups and become merely a property venture from which the owners collect a rent. Seed capital firms can move away from providing seed money to become second-stage funders. These pressures are similar to the gravity effect noted in Chapter 11 whereby the Third-Wave business degrades to a Second-Wave business over time. The innovative and the dynamic are replaced by the traditional and the routine. These are the pressures that all entrepreneurial activity has to face at some time but they can be overcome by creativity and courage. Those who help and support entrepreneurs need the character themes of the entrepreneur enabler, as we described in Chapter 2, if they are to stay the course.

The support infrastructure

The support elements

Economic geographers have presented lists of factors related to 'The role of the local environment in entrepreneurship and entrepreneurial success' (Malecki, 1997). One such list by Bruno and Tyebjee (1982) has the following twelve factors: venture capital availability, presence of experienced entrepreneurs, technically skilled workforce, accessibility of suppliers, accessibility of customers or new markets, favourable government policies, proximity of universities, availability of land or facilities, accessibility to transport, receptive population, availability of supporting services and attractive living conditions.

These factors correspond well with the *support infrastructure* elements (Bolton, 1993) given in Table 12.1, where they are presented in three groups indicating their roles in the *enterprise process*.

- support related to people and potential entrepreneurs;
- support related to ideas and business opportunities;
- support related to the enterprise and its growth.

The first two groups are important in the early start-up period and relate to the *getting ready* stage discussed in Chapter 11. They provide the mechanisms that are needed to begin the *enterprise process* though they also have an ongoing role that links in with the third group that promotes the process and ensures its strength and vitality.

The 'presence of experienced entrepreneurs' on Bruno and Tyebjee's list falls within the 'business support' sector because it is in the 'clubs and associations' that the entrepreneurs meet each other and from where a peer grouping develops. The Cambridge Computer Club fulfilled this role in the early 1980s when the 'Cambridge Phenomenon' was getting underway. As the entrepreneurial culture developed, more and more groupings formed, both formal and informal, and the collective experience was openly shared.

'Accessibility of customers or new markets and favourable government policies' is part of the *operational environment* we discuss in Chapter 13, because they are not factors that can be easily influenced by either economic developers or the enterprise itself. If a start-up business is a long way from its market then it has to either move closer to it or accept the consequent difficulties that this presents. Accessibility to the

Table 12.1   *The support infrastructure*

	People	*Ideas*	*The enterprise*				
Sector	Education and training	Research and development	Property	Finance	Supply	Business support	Community development
Facility	School, college, university; training facility; entrepreneur school	Industry, university and garage	Business incubator; innovation centre; science, technology and business parks	Seed and venture capital	Sub-contractors; labour pool	Government agencies; clubs and associations; consultants and business advisers	Housing; schools; hospitals; recreation; transport; telecoms
Activity	Courses and programmes	Technology transfer	Premises and support	Equity and loans	Staff and suppliers	Training, advice and networking	Amenity provision

customer or the market, like government policies, is something that the new enterprise has to learn to live with.

Inward investment

The customer question does require some further comment at this stage because it raises the important issue of inward investment, which could be seen as a support infrastructure element. This is the policy whereby large companies are attracted into an area or region to create jobs and develop the local economy. Since the infrastructure in Table 12.1 is made up of elements that support the generation and growth of new businesses, then should the large company be included amongst them? The answer to this question is generally 'No', because there is little evidence that the presence of a large company in a region enhances the entrepreneurial culture or results in more entrepreneurs coming forward to start businesses. The best that can be achieved is that a network of sub-contractors is developed but these will be, almost certainly, small businesses run by managers and not entrepreneurs.

In the early 1960s IBM was refused planning permission to establish a research facility in Cambridge, UK. 'This indirectly triggered a chain of events that led to the establishment of the Cambridge Science Park' (Segal *et al.*, 1985). Whilst cause and effect is difficult to prove there was a view in the early 1980s, as the 'Cambridge Phenomenon' got underway, that had IBM been allowed to set up in Cambridge they would have absorbed local talent and the 'phenomenon' might not have happened. As it was, entrepreneurial and innovative talent was able to flourish resulting in a remarkable growth of indigenous businesses with a formation rate, sustained over a number of years, of around two technology-based companies per week.

Although the larger company is not included as a factor in the *support infrastructure*, there are two situations where their presence can be beneficial to the *enterprise process* and the entrepreneur. The first is when a large indigenous business is itself the result of the local entrepreneurial culture. When this happens the company often becomes a spin-off point for new businesses. For example, Nokia, the mobile phone company, has played a key role in stimulating the entrepreneurial activity that has seen Oulu in Finland become a major high-technology centre with many new businesses and more than 8000 technology-based jobs.

The second situation is when inward investment is part of an economic development strategy to develop an entrepreneurial culture around a key sector. This policy has been pursued by Highlands and Islands Enterprise (HIE) in the north of Scotland. Because of the region's relative remoteness, it required a pro-active and focused policy that was achievable. It targeted healthcare as a sector because the local hospital in Inverness was already a centre of expertise. In 1996, HIE attracted a major healthcare company as an inward investor to a site adjacent to the hospital. In 1999 a business incubator and business support centre was opened on the same site with a focus on the healthcare sector. It was hoped that this strategy would result in a clustering of healthcare start-ups in the incubator and the surrounding districts.

Application

Malecki (1997) has made the important point that entrepreneurship is a local issue. The elements listed in Table 12.1 need to be available locally and readily accessible to the enterprise. An urban area is more likely to have these resources but it does not mean that smaller urban areas and even rural areas cannot become involved in entrepreneurship, as the examples above indicate. Indeed, there is some evidence that rural areas can have an advantage in the high-technology sector where quality of life is an important factor. There has been entrepreneurial success among the orchards of Silicon Valley, in the farming district around Cambridge, England, in Oulu, Finland close to the Arctic Circle and in the hillsides north of the French Riviera at Sophia Antipolis.

The infrastructure elements listed in Table 12.1 are placed in six main sectors, from education and training to community development. These sectors have very little in common and operate with their own agendas, time scales and decision-making processes. Most crucial of all, they have quite different cultures. Herein lies one of the major difficulties faced by economic developers and those who seek to promote entrepreneurship within a region. It is not easy for these sectors to work together and align priorities even when the project is to the benefit of the majority. In an area like entrepreneurship, that is not well understood, it is particularly difficult to develop a strategy across the sectors.

The sector leaders play an important role in all this and if they are able to share a common vision then things can really happen. In one region in Wales the college principal, the head of the local authority and the head of the regional hospital came together with a shared vision and the result was an excellent technology park adjacent to the hospital. It housed hospital spin-offs, a business incubator and a number of start-up companies and succeeded in creating an entrepreneurial culture in the area.

Table 12.1 can be useful when developing a strategy for the promotion of entrepreneurship within a region. An audit of the main elements of the *support infrastructure* that are already in place is a good starting point. They can be evaluated against their actual and potential contributions to the *enterprise process* and their impact on the local entrepreneurs. From this audit, barriers to entrepreneurship, in the form of gaps in provision and inadequacies in performance, can be identified.

An entrepreneurship strategy for a region needs to focus on what is needed to promote and stimulate the *enterprise process*. It is not necessary to have all the infrastructure elements listed in Table 12.1 in place. Some are more important than others and there is also some interdependency. Thus there is little point in setting up a business incubator if there is not a supply of start-up businesses to be its tenants. There is no point in targeting a particular technology sector if the region has no research expertise in that sector. The aim is to put the infrastructure elements in place that will ensure that the *enterprise process* can flow without major blockages.

The infrastructure elements listed in Table 12.1 are now discussed by sector. The first two, the 'education and training' sector and the 'research and development' sector, correspond respectively to the activities of 'training and assessing' and 'research and evaluation' of Figure 11.3. The remainder concern the enterprise as it grows and develops.

People: educational and training sector

Universities in the USA lead the world in the area of entrepreneurship. Their experience goes back to the early 1970s, with the University of Southern California in Los Angeles starting the first course in 1971. By the mid-1980s there were over 200 universities offering courses, and by the mid-1990s this had risen to more than 500 (Vesper 1986, 1993; Kuratko and Hodgetts, 1998). This figure has now risen to 1500 according to the Ewing Marion Kauffman Foundation, Kansas.

Some of these universities have excellent entrepreneurial programmes that link in with technology transfer mechanisms, funding provision, a business incubator and technology park. Rensselaer Polytechnic Institute 'has developed since 1981 a comprehensive infrastructure for technological entrepreneurship' (Abetti and Savoy, 1991). This total package approach is important because it allows students to move easily into starting their own enterprise with appropriate support, as they develop it into a growing business. It recognises that students of entrepreneurship require a different kind of support when they leave college to those who are simply looking for a job. It is rather simplistic to say that because they are entrepreneurs they will sort themselves out. This may be true in the long run but in the early days unless they are quite exceptional they will need help to get started and make progress. One of the main purposes of support at this point is to stop unnecessary business mistakes being made.

For the entrepreneur the educational and training activities are the beginning of the journey and should be seen as such. They are not an end in themselves. Courses in entrepreneurship can be placed in one of the following three categories:

- entrepreneurship as a subject
- entrepreneurship as an activity
- entrepreneur enabling.

Entrepreneurship as a subject

The majority of courses are in this category. At worst, they are courses on small business or other traditional business school courses with an entrepreneurial spin. At best, they cover all the key areas from economic development to business plan preparation, with a major focus on the entrepreneur. The American *Success* magazine provides an annual review of entrepreneur programmes in the USA and lists the '25 Best Business Schools for Entrepreneurs'. Most offer masters and doctoral programmes.

These courses have two main difficulties, as far as the potential entrepreneur is concerned. Firstly they are *about* entrepreneurship and approach the subject as if, like most other academic subjects, it were based around a body of knowledge. The educational process is then about imparting that body of knowledge. Whilst there is certainly much that the would-be entrepreneur has to know, entrepreneurship, like medicine and engineering, has a strong 'learning by doing' element. Many courses do involve local entrepreneurs and run projects in their companies, and this should be encouraged. They are, however, curriculum-driven which means they are topic-focused and are assessed in traditional ways. There is no reason to believe that this approach will identify or develop entrepreneurs but there is a clear possibility that it might put off and constrain potential entrepreneurs and bury their talent still deeper.

The second difficulty with this approach is inherent in any new subject. Whilst it is relatively well established in the USA it is relatively new to the UK and suffers accordingly. The problem is that either the subject is ignored by the academic mainstream or else it is highjacked by one department that interprets entrepreneurship within the perceptions of its specialisms. There is a similarity here with the new subject of Contemporary Cultural Studies which Richard Hoggart (1996) told us is an area of study that can 'draw fruitfully from several disciplines: the social sciences, history, psychology, anthropology, literary study and others. Each discipline can make its case for pre-eminence. Others simply ignore it'. Hoggart quotes a Professor of English who said 'All very interesting but I don't see how to fit it in. The syllabus is already crammed'. Entrepreneurship meets similar responses. Cultural Studies found its place because the students voted with their feet. 'In 1995 Media Studies, a branch of Cultural Studies, was the subject most sought by all applicants to Higher Education courses in the UK' and it has continued to prosper. It is to be hoped that the same thing will happen with entrepreneurship.

Entrepreneurship as an activity

These courses have a different approach. They do talk *about* entrepreneurship but they are also *for* entrepreneurs. They teach a range of topics in entrepreneurship but the main focus is the preparation of a viable business plan. Students can take part on a competitive basis within their university and across universities. Some universities base their whole programme around a business plan competition and/or an Entrepreneur of the Year Award. The major business plan competition in the USA is the MOOT CORP® Award at the University of Texas at Austin which started in 1984 and went international in 1990. It has been referred to as 'The Super-Bowl of World Business-Plan Competitions' (*Business Week*, 1993) and 'The Mother of all Business-Plan Competitions' (*Success*, 1997).

The MIT Enterprise Forum has a similar business plan focus but the participants are seeking funding for real businesses. Participants make a presentation to a large audience and then are 'grilled' in public by a team of assessors. It is backed by an educational programme that seeks to promote 'the formation and growth of innovative and technologically-oriented companies'. Plans are in hand to replicate the MIT Enterprise Forum in Cambridge, England.

These courses are a good way of revealing the entrepreneurs although there can be an air of unreality about them depending on whether the business plans are 'for real'. In the early years the MOOT CORP® competition was internal to the university and was an academic assessment. As things developed some participants used the business plan as a basis for their own business and this brought a real dynamic to the programme.

The main disadvantage of this competition-based approach is that it produces a few winners and many losers, based on somewhat artificial criteria. The ability to prepare a good business plan or to stand up to a grilling from potential investors, is in itself no proof that those involved will be able to run a successful business or that the idea will turn out to be commercially viable. It can be a useful indicator but it is not a sufficiently effective instrument to do anything more than pick potential winners and it can seriously demotivate the losers.

Entrepreneur enabling

The two approaches discussed above are important and each meet different needs. The first produces people who know about entrepreneurship and the second will challenge the potential entrepreneur. Both will develop technique and understanding and the *activity*-type course will also test temperament and identify talent, though not in a structured manner.

This third type of course is concerned with potential entrepreneurs and how their talent can be identified, their temperament managed and their technique developed. Its participants have already decided that they want to be entrepreneurs. They bring a dedication and focus to the course that is motivated by their desire to run their own business. The downside is that they may discover that they are not entrepreneurs or that the opportunity they have selected is not viable, and the course needs to be structured to cope with such eventualities.

These *enabling* courses can be found in the university and the employment sectors, both public and private, though certainly not as extensively as 'subject based' courses. We profile two that have worked well, one in Holland and the other in Ireland.

In 1984 the University of Twente in Holland set up its TOP programme. It runs for one year and provides a part-time university appointment for the potential entrepreneur. This gives the person some income and the opportunity to use the resources of the university in developing the product, assessing the market and preparing the business plan. A start-up loan is available on favourable terms. Participants attend a course on 'How to become an entrepreneur' by the Twente Centre for Entrepreneurship. This centre is run by the university's Department of Graduate Studies in Management in close collaboration with a Business and Development Centre, a major Dutch bank and a firm of innovation consultants. The programme has been very successful with more than 84 per cent of participants going on to run their own businesses.

The University Industry Programme at University College, Dublin runs a similar enabling programme. Termed the 'Campus Company Development Programme' it addresses the needs of potential entrepreneurs to develop their innovative ideas, to build multi-disciplinary teams and to prepare a detailed business plan. The programme runs annually for a period of nine months and accepts a maximum of fifteen projects. In terms of the *enterprise process* model, described in Chapter 11, they see themselves as taking the idea through the *embryo stage* from 'proof of principle' to 'working prototype'. Mentors are assigned to each project team and there is a half-day interactive workshop each month with seminars on selected topics. One of the main benefits of the programme is the supportive relationship that develops between the entrepreneurs themselves. Prizes are awarded to the top three projects in each programme.

The employment sector normally sees its *enabling* courses in terms of training for self-employment. As an indication of the level of this activity, one of the leading private training providers in the north of England and Scotland was helping around 2000 people a year to start their own businesses in the late 1990s. Programmes are also available that will build business teams and assist the growing business by advice and mentoring. Most of them are based on the framework and elements of the start-up stage outlined in Chapter 11. They tend to produce well-managed businesses but not necessarily entrepreneurial ones. This is because the focus is on 'training' rather than 'enabling' the participants. This is an important distinction for those seeking to promote entrepreneurship but for the employment sector the main concern is job creation, and a well-managed business is a satisfactory outcome.

Ideas: research and development sector

Ideas always involve some form of research and development either to generate them in the first place or to turn them into practical use. Archimedes generated one of his many ideas in a bath. It was an ideal laboratory for research into hydrostatic weighing though he probably did not think of it in that way. King Hiero, ruler of Syracuse, Sicily had posed Archimedes the problem of checking whether he had been cheated by the goldsmith who had made him a new crown. The suspicion was that the gold had been alloyed with silver though the weight of the crown was correct. The story goes that Archimedes hit on the idea of hydrostatic weighing when in the public bath and was so excited by his idea that he ran home through the streets naked, shouting 'Heureka! Heureka!' ('I have found it! I have found it!').

These days we think of research and development (R&D) in more formal terms though there is still a role for the informal laboratory, especially where the entrepreneur is concerned. Hewlett and Packard in the 1930s and Jobs and Wozniak in 1970s carried out their early R&D in the family garage. Even outside of technology, R&D and ideas go hand in hand. Though the R&D stage is the domain of the inventor and researcher, many entrepreneurs pick up their ideas at this point. The entrepreneur's *support infrastructure* needs R&D facilities in some shape or form if there is to be a steady flow of new ideas.

Ideas that are as clever yet as obvious as Archimedes' raise serious problems for the entrepreneur who wants to exploit the idea commercially. If the idea comes from the entrepreneur, he wants to make sure that no one takes or steals it from him. If the idea belongs to somebody else then the entrepreneur wants access to it as cheaply as possible. We once met a would-be entrepreneur who said he had a great idea and wanted some marketing advice but he would not tell us what the idea was because someone might steal it. We got as far as finding out that it was used in the home and asked if it was a fixed item or a consumable one. To illustrate the point we asked him if it was the toilet roll holder or the toilet roll. It turned out it was a consumable item and we gave him marketing advice along that line. The inventor or entrepreneur who is obsessive about secrecy is not uncommon.

The generation and development of ideas in an R&D facility, whether bath, garage or formal laboratory and their commercial exploitation is covered by the term 'technology transfer'. It has become an industry in itself, and books, reports and conferences on the subject appear regularly. For entrepreneurs, it is the transfer that is important rather than the technology. They are really concerned with any business opportunity whether or not it has technical content. Even if there is some technical content it may be incidental to the opportunity itself. For this reason we prefer the term 'business idea transfer' even if it lacks literation. It makes the point that it is a business idea that is being transferred, and not simply technology, and implies a commercial focus. In respect of the input to the *enterprise* model it is the activity in which the idea is assessed as a business opportunity and then passed on to the potential entrepreneur, as discussed in Chapter 11.

The main aspects of 'technology transfer' that are of interest to the entrepreneur are:

- the role of the R&D laboratory
- intellectual property rights
- supporting the opportunity.

The role of the R&D laboratory

Whether in the university or in industry, the R&D laboratory is an important part of the *support infrastructure* because of its formal role in the generation of new ideas. Where these ideas are easily released they become important spin-off points for new businesses. The 'Cambridge Phenomenon' was serviced by six spin-off points. Three were the university laboratories of physics, engineering and computing, two were private contract research organisations and one was a government research centre.

The problem with most R&D laboratories is that they exist for themselves or the organisations they serve. They are not there to provide ideas for start-ups. Behind this is the long-standing debate between pure and applied researches, which over the years has be-devilled the UK government's funding priorities as first pure, and then applied research has been favoured. This very simplistic division is not shared by most researchers who see it as arbitrary and not conducive to good research (Medawar, 1984).

The situation is further compounded by the funding mechanisms employed. Funding is related to academic performance which in the UK university system is measured by the number of published papers in refereed journals. This is a peer group assessment so that the focus is on academic rigour and not commercial application. With this approach it is quite easy for the researcher to miss a commercial opportunity and publish a paper, putting the idea into the public domain for all to read and exploit. In some university departments this has become a big issue. The question is 'Do we publish in order to score validation points and secure future grants?' or 'Do we work on to the stage where the idea can be patented and forget about publishing papers and the grant money?'. A system that produces such tensions is clearly not sustainable. The danger from the entrepreneur's point of view is that the 'publish or perish' approach will prevail in academia, and ideas will remain locked in their research laboratories.

Apart from these difficulties, which can be serious, the R&D laboratory is a valuable resource for a region and can be an important component in an entrepreneur strategy. In the 1980s Finland selected certain cities to promote as mini-Silicon Valleys, and the selection criteria included the presence of a university with R&D capability.

Intellectual property rights

Intellectual property rights (IPR) are a major sub-set of technology transfer. Large companies and many universities employ people to 'capture' the intellectual property that they generate. This is usually in the form of a patent that provides legal protection against their idea being exploited by somebody else. Although this appears to be an important safeguard it is by no means a straightforward issue. Patenting can be very expensive when worldwide protection is required.

Industry tends to use IPR in a much more aggressive way than the university sector. Many large companies have technology watchers who scan scientific publications and new patents to enhance their own products and to fight the competition. In one case, a scientific discovery, with huge commercial potential, was carefully patented by the university before a paper was published. This activity was spotted by a major company that then wrote its own patent close to the original and used it to negotiate access to the ongoing research in the university. In another case, an American company sued a British competitor for patent infringement knowing that they would lose the case and it would cost them several million dollars. Their objective was to delay the entry of the competitor's product on to the American market by two years, and challenging the patent became the means of doing this.

The university approach to IPR is generally rather an ambivalent one. They want to hold on to what they consider is their IPR and yet do not have the wherewithal in terms of money to pay for patents nor do they have the human resources to follow them up and realise their full potential. This means that their claim to have IPR is something of an illusion. Intellectual property rights only exist if there is a patent that defines it. The procedures for this in most universities in the UK are significantly under-resourced.

Many universities have tightened their control over IPR in recent years in the mistaken belief that if they do not do this, others, especially their employees, will steal what is rightly theirs. This is a notion taken from industry and the UK 1977 Patent Act, where any ideas or discoveries made and developed in company time belong to the company. The difference is that in a company the employee has to work on projects that he is assigned to and it is his job to make money for the company. University researchers are in quite a different position. Their research does not have to make money for anybody so that they are not obliged to pursue its commercial application. When universities add IPR pressures to traditional career advancement pressures it is small wonder that this immense idea resource remains largely untapped.

The challenge is to find a way to release the ideas potential in the university sector. This requires at least three steps. First, give equal merit to patents and published papers in assessments of research excellence. Second, open up the IPR situation in the university so that staff and students are motivated to exploit their ideas. The third step, discussed in the next section, is to support commercial exploitation by encouraging spin-offs.

From the entrepreneurs' point of view the ideas generated within an R&D facility are only as good as the access they have to them. Intellectual property rights should be used as a tool to provide that access and ensure a fair deal for all concerned.

Supporting the opportunity

The general approach to the commercialisation of IPR generated within an R&D facility is to license it to the highest bidder. In recent years, many large industrial groups have actually set up within or adjacent to university departments to have access to the research. Most universities have a technology transfer unit (TTU) that controls all the contracts with industry and handles the licensing of technology. To have a sufficient flow of licensing opportunities, a TTU needs to be able to draw on a research base of at least £80 million. The university has to ensure that this kind of commercial activity does not adversely affect its charitable status. Cambridge and Oxford universities and Imperial College, London, all have separate companies through which this commercial activity is channelled.

Some UK universities have achieved licensing income in excess of £1 million. Whilst this is obviously welcome, the main benefactors are those who take the research and exploit it. In commercial terms, it makes little sense to receive a £1 license fee for every £100 spent on research. The universities, of course, see this as bonus money because their research has already been paid for, mainly by grant money.

Our interest is not in licensing, although some entrepreneurs have licensed research successfully. We see licensing as the easy option which returns less money to the R&D laboratory and the researcher than is their due. Stanford University's technology licensing office has been the most successful in the world. Its cumulative license income since it opened in 1970 is 'more than $300 million'. This seems an excellent figure until it is realised that 'the annual revenues of companies born at the university total more than $100 billion' (Fisher, 1998). Although the job of a university is not to run commercial enterprises, it does have an opportunity to enable the start-up of new businesses and take an equity position in return for the transfer of technology. In due time the equity holding can be realised and the capital gain passed to the university. Stanford University has enabled many companies to get started, but surprisingly until 1981, it was not permitted to take an equity position. When one considers the current valuation of the many Silicon Valley companies that owe their origins to that university, a huge commercial opportunity was missed.

The enterprise

The support elements described above are primarily, though not exclusively, concerned with the start-up stage of the enterprise. We now consider the elements that directly support the enterprise itself. The property and the financial sectors are the most important. If there is plenty of good-quality property available at reasonable cost and if seed and venture capital are readily available, then enterprises should grow and prosper.

Finally, in this chapter, we consider briefly the other three sectors listed in Table 12.1, namely, supply, business support and community development.

Enterprise: the property sector

The economic development imperative

Commercial and business property is nothing new, but specialist property for business start-ups is. It began in 1950 when Stanford University set up its park for technology and science-based businesses, as we report in Chapter 14. At that time, it was a property development initiative to raise money for the university. The idea that it might be an economic development tool and part of a range of facilities to support new businesses through their early stages of growth was not yet born. This realisation came in the USA in the early 1980s due to three factors:

- The experience of industrial re-structuring in the Boston area.
- The recognition of the important economic role of small businesses.
- The role of the business incubator and innovation centre.

Industrial re-structuring   In the period 1968–1975 the Greater Boston area was in serious decline with the loss of more than 250 000 manufacturing jobs. Recovery required a miracle, and it happened. Between 1975 and 1980 the area had its own Silicon Valley experience. The jobs lost in traditional industries, mainly textiles, were replaced by gains in technology-based businesses with MIT playing the same role as Stanford University had done in Silicon Valley. By 1980 there were more than 1600 firms in the area either in the manufacture of high-tech products or in services and consultancy (Castells and Hall, 1994).

Small businesses   There was a recognition at senior levels in government that small businesses played an important part in the economy as a creator of new jobs. A study by MIT in 1981 showed that between 1969 and 1976 nearly two-thirds of all jobs in the USA were created by firms with twenty employees or less. A report for the President by the US Small Business Administration in 1984 found that 'small enterprises with less than twenty employees generated all of the net new jobs in the economy between 1980 and 1982'.

The business incubator and innovation centre   The business incubator linked in with the importance of small firms because it was seen as one way of reducing their mortality rate. Typically, 80 per cent of start-ups in incubators survive for five years or more compared with the normal figure of only 20 per cent. The innovation centre, with its focus on technology, linked in with the first factor to promote the emergence and growth of technology-based businesses. In the 1970s the US National Science Foundation funded nine innovation centres and started this particular ball rolling (Smilor and Gill, 1986).

In the 1980s these three factors came together and the role of the research park and the business incubator in economic development was realised and promoted. In a visit to Stanford in 1989 we were told by the university office 'if we did the Stanford Research Park again we would begin with a business incubator'.

The UK situation

This progression in the USA, from property-based research and technology parks in the 1970s to business promotion initiatives in the 1980s, was mirrored in the UK 10–15 years later.

The UK's first science parks appeared in the early 1970s in Cambridge and Edinburgh, and like Stanford were property-driven, although there was an acknowledgement of their role in technology transfer. In those days the notice board at the entrance to the Cambridge Science Park simply said that it was a 'low density, landscaped site for science-based industrial development'. The real surge for science parks came in the 1980s. Although the UK Science Parks Association tried to promote the business start aspects, the majority of the science parks set up during this period were with property development motives.

In the mid-1980s business incubators began to appear based on the American model. The St John's Innovation Centre in Cambridge, proposed in 1984 and opened in 1987, was the result of visits by key people to the University of Utah Innovation Centre set up in 1978. The St John's Innovation Centre was seen, right from the start, as a means of supporting early-start technology-based businesses. It was set in the context of an Innovation Park that would offer longer-term accommodation to companies graduating from the innovation centre.

Several other incubators were established in the UK at that time but promotion of business incubators at a national level had to wait until 1996 when the government-initiated report *Growing Success, helping companies to generate wealth and create jobs through Business Incubation* (The Enterprise Panel, 1996) was published. A national centre for the promotion of business incubators has since been set up.

Business growth stages

The response of the property sector to the needs of the start-up and growing businesses is now complete in concept, if not in availability. Each of the growth stages of the start-up business is provided for, as indicated in Figure 12.3.

Ideally, the *embryo* stage should take place in the R&D laboratory. Whether this is a formal laboratory or a small garage, the emphasis is on keeping the costs down and using equipment that can be borrowed. Once there is a greater certainty that the project will go forward, then it can move into a supportive environment that is commercially oriented. The business incubator provides the ideal setting for this *nurture* stage. It offers a range of office and unit sizes in a single building with central services and business support. Because of its importance to the start-up venture, the business incubator is discussed more fully in a later section.

Once the enterprise has a product or service that it can sell and it begins to trade, it enters the *fledgling* stage. Here the property needs are similar to the previous stage in terms of central services though some larger units will be required. The business support needs will be less hands-on. Many businesses will now want to present a professional image to their clients and the building should reflect this. They also need flexibility because their space requirements can fluctuate

Figure 12.3 *Premises requirement*

as orders come and go. Two types of centre have developed to meet these needs: the 'business hotel' and the 'business home'. An excellent example of the business 'hotel' approach is the network of Regus Business Centres that operate around the world. These centres are located on prestige sites and offer fully fitted offices with professional reception and telephone and Internet services. The business 'home' approach has a different feel about it. Tenants rent units and provide their own furniture and equipment. Central services are provided in a similar way to the business 'hotels'. Business support is available to the tenants as and when required. These centres have names like Innovation or Enterprise Centre. Some carry proprietary names such as the Magdalen Centre on the Oxford Science Park.

As the company grows and reaches the *take-off* stage it will require larger premises and want its own 'front door'. At this stage it can locate anywhere but companies generally stay close to their origins and join the business community in the area. Parks and estates of various kinds offer a wide range of building sizes that meet most requirements.

The *embryo* and *nurture* stages benefit from close proximity to the source of the idea, particularly if it is technology-based. By the time the *fledgling* and *take-off* stages are reached the enterprise has a life of its own and needs to be free to develop its products and services in its own way. Even in those cases where some links with the research behind the technology are still needed, it is best if there is some separation so that a commercial, rather than a research, focus is achieved. The Cambridge Science Park is about three miles from the university laboratories and seems to provide the necessary separation.

The range of property that is now available covers the growth stages of start-up business well but the enterprise process will not flourish unless each element

Table 12.2 *Mechanisms and support facilities*

Process stage	Mechanism	Support facility
Research and development	R&D programmes with a commercial focus	University or other research laboratories
Embryo stage	Technology transfer programmes Enterprise generation programmes	Entrepreneur school Business centre
Nurture stage	Enterprise support programmes including mentoring	Business incubators
Fledgling stage	Mentoring with specialist programmes, e.g. marketing	Innovation or enterprise centre
Take-off stage	Specialist programmes, e.g. exporting	Science or technology park
Corporate stage	General consultancy support	International offices

inter-relates and the right mechanisms are in place. Table 12.2 lists the growth stages and the support facility and indicates the corresponding mechanisms that are needed. This table extends the boundaries at either ends of the growth stage model discussed earlier in order to cover the entry from the R&D stage to the exit into the corporate sector when the enterprise is an international operation. The mechanisms listed are fairly straightforward and most have been discussed earlier in this chapter. A steady flow of enterprises through these stages produces, in due time, a critical mass of indigenous businesses in a region, and the process becomes self-sustaining.

It is important to be able to identify gaps or inefficiencies in the *enterprise* process and rectify them as soon as possible. Because the support facility side is property-driven, this often attracts undue and piecemeal attention. The rush by the university sector in the UK to build science parks in the 1980s was done in isolation, and little thought was given to the idea that they were just one of the components within a process. The proposal to build an innovation centre within an innovation park that was put to St John's College, Cambridge in 1984 also included the idea of an entrepreneur school which would act as a feeder to the centre and the park. That is, the proposal was set within a process context. Despite this, the idea of an entrepreneur school was not accepted and only the centre and the park were built. In July 1999, fifteen years later, the first Cambridge Summer School for Entrepreneurs was held suggesting a new interest in completing the entrepreneur school part of the *enterprise* process.

A property model for enterprise

Figure 12.4 is a model of how the various property elements inter-relate to make a synergistic whole. The heart of the model is the business incubator and innovation centre. *Nurture* stage businesses enter the incubator from outside, perhaps fed from an entrepreneur programme and research activities in the local university. They may

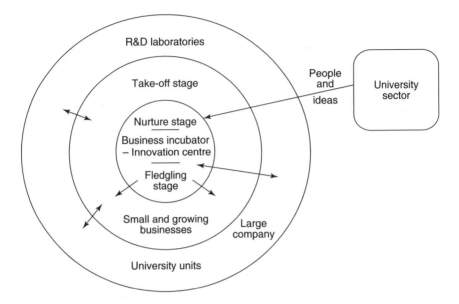

Figure 12.4 *Science or technology park model*

also come from the research laboratories or larger companies on the park itself indicated in the outer circle.

As businesses grow to the fledgling stage they move to the innovation centre. This may be the same building but the incubator and innovation centre roles are different, as we explain in the next section.

When companies leave the innovation centre they move to their own building but on the same site. They are now self-sufficient and inter-act with the institutions and larger businesses shown in the outer circle of the model. Some may even grow to the size where they can join this outer circle.

The technopolis in Oulu, Finland has used this model with considerable success.

The business incubator and the innovation centre

Because of the importance of these specialist support facilities to the start-up business we consider here:

- their role
- their advantages
- operational issues.

Their role These types of support centres were developed in the USA in the 1970s and are now common around the world. Those addressing the early needs of the start-up company, the business incubators, go by a number of different names. Other terms are 'Nursery Unit', 'Seed-bed Centre', 'Hatchery', 'Greenhouse' and 'Business Generator'. The French use the word 'Pépinière', meaning nursery or garden centre.

Support is available through training courses, the provision of advisers and mentors, help with business plan preparation and so on.

As the names imply, they incubate, nurse and tend the business until it is ready to survive on its own. This can have a negative connotation for a potential customer who is unlikely to work with a company that has health problems! The word innovation centre or enterprise centre gets around this and is often used even though the companies might not yet be trading. Because of this confusion of terminology we define the business incubator and innovation centre in respect of their function. As illustrated on Figure 12.3, the business incubator supports the *nurture* stage business and the innovation centre supports at the *fledgling* stage. Both are very similar in property terms. They provide a range of room sizes from 15 m² to 200 m², with central facilities such as reception. Though they vary in total size, experience shows that anything less than 3500 m² is not likely to be viable either in economic or social terms.

The incubator offers organised and direct support to the businesses in their care whereas the innovation or enterprise centre provides support when it is requested. Because the physical facilities are very similar there can be some businesses at the *nurture* stage and others at the *fledgling* stage in the same building. This is not a problem and can have some advantages as long as the *nurture* stage companies are encouraged to move through the process and do not develop a dependency upon the support provided. It is also important that the management of the incubator and innovation centre understand what their support role is and what stage their tenants have reached.

Their advantages From the entrepreneur's point of view these specialist facilities reduce the cost of start-up because the centre provides the reception, the telephone service and so on. A service charge is normally levied for these services but the costs are shared among the tenants, which reduces costs overall. A high-speed photocopier with collating facilities and laser printers are normally available and charged on an as-used basis but, again, the start-up company avoids the high capital cost of these items.

The 'organised' support of the incubator or the 'as required' support of the innovation centre shortens the entrepreneur's learning curve. Specialist advice is often available free of charge. The St John's Innovation Centre, Cambridge, offered free consultation one afternoon a week with a solicitor, an accountant, a patent agent and a business adviser on successive weeks.

These kind of centres attract a great deal of interest from the local business community and the media. This means that the tenant companies are soon networking with potential suppliers and customers and have the opportunity of free publicity that they can use to their advantage. Another benefit to entrepreneurs is that their credibility in the eyes of the customer is enhanced. We know of one tenant company whose customer thought that it owned the whole building and was suitably impressed! In another case, the large company was only prepared to place a contract with the start-up company if and when it was accepted by the incubator.

These are real benefits that can be easily demonstrated, but in practice they are perhaps not the most important. The St John's Innovation Centre in Cambridge was successful because it built up a community of entrepreneurs that provided mutual support and help. This was due to the 'tender loving care' (TLC) approach of the centre management and the coffee shop at the centre of the building. This feature provided a social focal point in the building and was a far more successful way of getting people to interact and meet each other, than any of the seminars or social events that were organised. Almost without realising it a community spirit developed that gave the place a special feel that visitors often commented upon. It was a fun place to work.

These benefits for the entrepreneur show themselves in the survival rates of their businesses. Data from the US National Business Incubator Association and from assessments by the UN around the world show that 80 per cent survival rates over five years are normal. The corresponding figure for the St John's Centre, Cambridge, as given in the 1996 *Growing Success* report (The Enterprise Panel, 1996) was 88 per cent.

Operational issues   There are many issues with these kind of centres that need to be understood if they are to be operated effectively (Bolton, 1997). One issue that entrepreneurs are always interested in is how much rent they have to pay and what rental liability they are taking on.

Property agents act in their own interest and impose as long a lease on the tenant as they can get away with. Because entrepreneurs are enthusiastic and often over confident they can easily be persuaded to sign up for premises which are much bigger than they need to start with. One entrepreneur of our acquaintance took a twenty-five-year lease on five large bays of a new factory unit when he really only needed two. He succeeded in expanding into four within two years and then things went wrong and he contracted down to one bay leaving the others empty. When he tried to sell the business the sticking point was always the twenty-two years still outstanding on the lease.

Business incubators and innovation centres are a very effective way around this kind of problem. Leasing terms have improved over the years so that most centres now operate an 'easy-in, easy-out' policy. This allows tenants to leave at one or three months' notice so that they are not tied into the financial liability of a long lease. Length of tenure is a more difficult matter and it is now normal for tenants to operate under a one-year renewable licence. The aim in both the business incubators and the innovation centres is that the entrepreneurs grow their businesses and then move on. Ideally, no company should stay more than three years in this kind of centre. In most cases, this is not a problem but when the company is run by a life-style entrepreneur, he can settle down in the centre blocking off a place for the next potential entrepreneur.

These facilities provide entrepreneurs with the flexibility they require but there is always the issue of cost. Commercial premises are the cheapest option but they do not offer the leasing terms, facilities, location, image or support of these specialist start-up centres. Some centres charge a premium rent that can be double or treble those charged for commercial premises. Other centres, particularly business incubators, are part of an economic development strategy so that the rent is subsidised to reduce costs for the start-up business.

Rent subsidy is a contentious issue. The argument in favour is that it helps to reduce the cost of start-up for the young business, especially if it is at the *nurture* stage and is not yet trading. The argument against is that entrepreneurs need to understand the cost of running their business, and any form of subsidy is bad for financial discipline. Rent subsidy also has a direct effect on the financial viability of the incubator itself, as its costs have to be covered. Grants given generously in the first few years have a habit of disappearing over time. Many incubators that were set up on the basis of subsidies are now simply premises-rented to the highest bidder on the longest lease possible; they have had to abandon the idea of incubating new businesses.

A business incubator in Los Angeles has a novel approach to this problem. Its aim is to promote the formation of new business in the area, and the rent is subsidised accordingly. Each tenant company knows the cost of this support in their case. If on leaving the incubator, the company locates in the local area, then the accumulated rental charges are waived but if they move outside the area then they have to pay back the amount of the subsidy in full.

The enterprise: the financial sector

There are many issues for entrepreneurs in the area of finance. In Chapter 15 we review the items with which they should be most concerned, noting the difference between working capital and investment capital and between loan and equity financing. In this section we are concerned with where the entrepreneur gets his money from in the first place and what sources of finance are open to him. At the heart of this question lies a major difference of experience between the entrepreneur who needs the money and those who provide it. Most start-ups are grossly under-funded and struggle along, finding money where they can. Yet bankers and venture capitalists say again and again that they are awash with money and that there is no shortage of funds for the right project. Both statements are true and both sides carry a share of the blame for the problem of under-funding. The attitudes and structural differences that are responsible for this perversity lie in the *Operational Environment* part of our model discussed in Chapter 13 rather than the *Support Infrastructure* being discussed here. This is because the entrepreneur cannot influence the differences in the short term. They are built into the system.

In this section we discuss the financial support elements that can be put in place to provide the potential entrepreneur with the fuel he needs to launch his enterprise. The structure of the enterprise, its people and its product are the body of the rocket but the fuel is what gets it off the launch pad and into orbit. Money is the vital fuel for the start-up business and many never have enough to really achieve lift off, let alone reach their planned orbit.

Most start-ups begin with what money the entrepreneur and other founders can scrape together from their own resources. They start on a shoestring. Data from the early 1990s of 500 successful 'star' small businesses in the USA showed that a quarter of these winners started with less than $5000, half had less than $25 000 and three-quarters had less than $100 000 – and these were growth winners.

We now consider the funding sources for the potential entrepreneur ranked in order of practical value, perhaps surprisingly venture capital sources come last!

- own resources
- high-street banks
- business angels
- credit cards
- venture capital.

Own resources

Looked at in one way, entrepreneurs are their own best source of start-up money. In 1971 the Bolton Report on Small Firms found that self-financing was the main source of funding for small businesses (Bolton, 1971). In 1982 a study showed that personal savings were the main source of funding for 56 per cent of new independent firms in the north-east of England (Storey, 1982). In 1986 a KPMG study of 280 new technology-based businesses in the UK produced a similar figure of 55 per cent (Monck *et al.*, 1988). The USA study in the early 1990s of 500 'star start-ups', quoted above, showed that personal savings, including redundancy money, was the source of funding for 78.5 per cent of them.

If one adds to these figures, 10–20 per cent for funding from family and friends, then the financial community's contribution is remarkably small. Entrepreneurs are the best providers of money because they have to be; they simply cannot get it from anywhere else. We believe that many more entrepreneurs would 'surface' if the financial supports were better structured and more readily available for start-ups.

High-street banks

The financial sector generally thinks that it is doing a good job in financing start-ups. Banks say they would like to support more start-ups but that because they carry the risk they have to be selective. They usually add that helping start-ups is not cost-effective because of the time it takes to evaluate and control them. There is clearly some truth in these comments but basically banks are risk-averse and many do not understand the start-up business. After all, few bank managers have ever started their own business.

Figure 12.5 shows the growth stages in the enterprise model in terms of risk and investment requirement. Though only qualitative, this graph shows that risks are highest when investment needs are lowest and risks are lowest when investment needs are highest. This should mean that there is the basis for a deal between the start-up company and the financial sector. The difficulty is that there is not the data to take this graph to the next level of detail. The curves would obviously be different for a manufacturing company and a software company. An Internet business would also have its own risk/investment curves. Another difficulty is that average figures only help if the investor has a sufficiently large portfolio for averages to apply. However, this approach could be adopted by high-street banks that have a wide range of clients at different growth stages. They also know the local conditions well and can keep close to a business at critical stages.

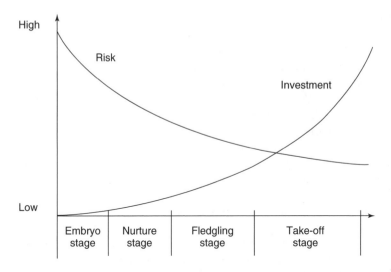

Figure 12.5 *Risk and investment curves*

In the UK, the high-street bank is the second most common source of start-up finance. The study in the north-east of England, reported above, found that 27 per cent of start-ups had bank loans and overdrafts as their most important source of funding. The equivalent figure for the KPMG study of high-technology firms was only 17 per cent suggesting that the high-street banks are wary of technology-based start-ups. Once these technology-based start-ups had a trading record, then this figure rose 25 per cent. This is clearly a matter of perception by the banks because the main funding source for 26 per cent of these technology-based start-ups with a trading record was retained earnings; they did not need the bank! By this point, personal savings, as the main source of funding, had dropped from 55 per cent down to 20 per cent.

Business angels

Since the above figures came out in the 1980s, two new sources of funding have become important for the start-up company in the UK, though both were present earlier in the USA: the business angel and the credit card. Business angels are individuals who want to use their wealth to invest in early-stage businesses. For some, the motive is to make money but for many it is simply to help the potential entrepreneur to get started. Often, they are entrepreneurs themselves who feel that life has been kind to them and they want to put something back.

In the USA a number of business incubators operate business angel 'dating' agencies in which the business angel and the business start-up are introduced to each other. In the UK most accounting firms have a list of wealthy individuals who are always pleased to talk about a new business opportunity. The interest in this area in the UK is indicated by a study published under the title *Business Angels: Securing Start-up Finance* (Coveney and Moore, 1998).

Credit cards

One accountancy firm has commented that the 'The fastest growing source of capital for small businesses is credit cards. One third of all companies with less than nineteen people use credit cards to fund themselves. These figures have doubled in the last five years'. The credit card is an easy way to raise the money and no bank guarantees are necessary. If four people get together to start a business and each has a £10 000 limit on their card then the team has £40 000 immediately available. If each person has two credit cards then they have £80 000 between them. It is that easy!

This approach to start-up funding is now quite common in the USA where credit cards are readily available and we know of one interesting case in the UK in the 1980s. A business adviser used his own credit card to provide funding at a very critical time in the early life of the business. In return, he received a minority shareholding. In due course he changed career direction and was ordained as a parish priest in the Church of England. In the meantime his investment grew significantly as the company achieved a stock exchange listing. He then sold his shares, and with the money bought an old country house in the English Lake District as a holiday home for disadvantaged children. The business adviser had become a social entrepreneur.

Venture capital

Historically, venture capital came out of the investment banking sector in the 1960s in the USA. 'Born in New York, nurtured in Boston, and almost smothered in Washington, venture capital did not really come of age until it moved to California and joined forces with the brash young technologists of Silicon Valley' (Wilson, 1986). It was the combination of talent, technology and capital that gave venture capital its early successes and put it on the world scene. Venture capitalists get their money from pension funds, major institutions, universities and wealthy individuals, and invest it on their behalf. Throughout the 1980s and early 1990s the USA venture capital industry committed between $1 billion and $5 billion every year. From 1994 onwards there has been a steady increase in this figure, which reached more than $22 billion in 1998 and climbed to $28 billion in 1999.

Davis and Rock were one of the first venture capital teams in Silicon Valley. In the 1960s they invested $257 000 in a small computer company, Scientific Data Systems. It grew rapidly reaching sales of $100 million in 1968. It was then bought by the Xerox Corporation for almost $1 billion, with Davis and Rock's investment worth $60 million. They had achieved a 233-fold return.

The venture capital industry is full of stories like this but the real question is do they actually help the entrepreneur. The answer is 'No' and 'Yes'. On the 'No' side there is the fact that very few start-ups ever get any venture fund money. The KPMG survey found that it was the main source of start-up finance for only 3 per cent of the high-technology companies they surveyed. The figure for the next stage of funding was only slightly higher at 8 per cent. This data was collected in 1986 but there is no reason to think that the situation has improved. The conclusion is that the venture capital industry is not a major source of finance for the start-up company.

Table 12.3 *Venture capital categories*

Growth stage	Embryo	Nurture	Fledgling	Take-off
Funding order of magnitude	£10 000s	£100 000s	£1 millions	£10 millions upward
VC industry classification	R&D/seed	Start-up/seed	Early stage	Development

Of course, they are all looking for winners, and given a choice between a start-up with no track record and a company that is already doing well in the marketplace, they back the latter. In the late 1980s a small high-technology venture capital company saw 340 business plans a year, made eight investments and only one of them was a start-up. They were not interested in investing less than £200 000, and the investment decision took six months. None of this is good news for the start-up company, and although these figures are from more than a decade ago the present situation is not a great deal better, though it is improving as we shall see.

On the 'Yes' side, the industry has had some remarkable success stories and the amount of money available has increased enormously. Today, there is more venture fund money available than there has ever been and the amount going to start-ups has increased accordingly. Table 12.3 gives the level of funding in order of magnitude terms for the growth stages we defined in Chapter 11. Most venture funds operate at the *fledgling* and *take-off* stages but a few are now specialising in the earlier *embryo* and *nurture* stages.

From 1987 to 1996, early-stage investment by the venture capital community in Europe was between $200 and $400 million annually. In 1997 this rose to $700 million and in 1998 it reached $1600 million. These are encouraging signs that this early-stage sector is now being serviced more effectively and the European Community has a number of schemes for supporting seed capital funds.

Table 12.3 indicates the classification used by the venture capital industry in relation to the growth stages. Seed capital and start-up funding generally mean the same thing, though sometimes seed funding is linked in with R&D funding when the business is not yet at the start-up stage. In the bio-technology sector, for example, the idea may need to be tested before a start-up can be considered.

One of the main difficulties facing venture funds is how best to exit from a funding situation. Investee companies always need more and more money and finding buyers is never easy. Figures from the USA (Wilson, 1986) show that for 10 per cent of the investments made by venture capitalists, the success is obvious and there are plenty of buyers. Fifteen per cent of investee companies fail and the investment is written off. For the remaining 75 per cent, finding a profitable exit route is extremely hard work, though this does depend on what is meant by profitable. For a venture capitalist an annual rate of return of 40 per cent is expected and so it is little wonder that entrepreneurs often call them 'vulture capitalists'!

There are of course good and bad venture capitalists. The better ones cover all stages of funding and avoid the serious discontinuities that arise by specialising in growth stages. Seed funds find it very difficult to exit from an investment because the follow-on funder wants them to keep their money in. The USA venture capitalists in Silicon Valley seem to have the best approach. When asked about how they structured their funding, we were told that they only invest if they can see that a multi-billion-dollar business will result, but that they then invest all that is necessary to achieve that end and do not bother with piecemeal funding. 'We do not just invest, we build companies. Our primary object is to grow a successful business. Capital gains are a reward, not a goal' (Wilson, 1986). These are great sentiments but experience of funding in the UK suggests that this world has still to arrive there. The main difference seems to be that in the USA there is an entrepreneurial approach to venture funding, whereas in the UK it is a banker's approach of caution and control.

The enterprise: the supply, business support and community development sectors

The remaining three sectors of the *support infrastructure* listed in Table 12.1 will normally be present within a region or district, to a greater or lesser extent. Only in specific cases of deficiency would efforts need to be made to strengthen them. As the prosperity of a region increases, these sectors develop anyway but it is helpful if they can be planned.

The supply sector

Businesses that intend to grow need access to a range of subcontractors and to a pool of suitably skilled labour. For this reason, urban areas are generally more attractive to the potential entrepreneur than rural and remote areas but there can be disadvantages as well. Old industries can leave a legacy of inappropriate skills and an inflexible work ethic.

Cambridge, England is a rural area and yet has an excellent network of small subcontractors who can turn out high-quality work with a minimum of instructions. This is because the science and engineering departments of the university have been producing technicians for generations, and some have left to set up on their own. Graduate and postgraduate students enjoy the Cambridge environment and wish to stay in the area so that there is a well-educated workforce available for the technology-based companies in the area.

Within a given region, it is possible to quantify the supply sector. The level and range of subcontractors available can be measured and the age and skill profile of the labour pool determined. This is generally done when regions seek to promote inward investment but it is rarely part of a strategy to promote indigenous businesses and encourage entrepreneurship.

These issues of subcontractors and labour availability become paramount when the start-up company begins to grow and can actually determine the growth rate that can be achieved. A Cambridge start-up that reached a stock valuation of around £500 million in about five years hit growth limits because it had absorbed a significant proportion of the software skills available in the area. When it later crashed it gave the poor performance of its major sub-contractor in the West Country as an important factor. The managing director told us that he had made a mistake in not using a local supplier whom he could have controlled more closely.

Business support sector

Over the past decade this sector has expanded considerably in the UK. When the Government Training Agency was replaced by Training and Enterprise Councils across the country and then Business Links were set up, there was a proliferation of provision for business, particularly for the small- and medium-sized enterprises (SMEs). This proliferation led to confusion and so a 'one-stop shop' approach was adopted where SMEs could get help and support from a single information point.

In principle, these organisations are there to provide the help and support that young growing businesses need. They fund a wide range of training programmes, provide business counsellors, help people to set up new businesses and many other good things. Their main draw back is that they bring bureaucracy to a support process that needs to be simple, easy to access and has real flexibility. Although there are some outstanding exceptions in the main, the personnel involved are administrators, and there is an attitude and culture clash with the entrepreneur.

Business clubs, both formal and informal, are an essential part of any business infrastructure. They provide important networking opportunities and are a source of role models for up and coming entrepreneurs. The most effective clubs or associations are those that occur naturally as the entrepreneurial culture develops. There are generally many of them and they come and go but the net effect is very beneficial.

Behind the growth of a business sector there is always an infrastructure of consultants and specialist advisers. Often there can be more advisers than there are companies to advise but they do provide an important service for the company in a hurry. Marketing and recruitment services are the most in demand, and the local networks help the start-up company to know which are the best ones to use. One of the talents of entrepreneurs is to know when they need an expert and to know how to find a good one. Without that talent, time and money can be wasted in quite large amounts because, though most consultants can tell a good tale, not all can deliver an excellent service.

Community development

This includes all the amenities that most of us take for granted: housing, schools, hospitals, recreation, transport and telecommunications. These amenities serve the community as well as the business. One of the major problems when economic success comes to a region is that it gets 'overheated' with high house prices and living costs, congested roads, crowded shops and over-stretched educational, medical and recreational facilities. Good planning can avoid most of these problems but in reality the supply is usually several years behind the demand. Just as with the lack of sub-contractors and a labour pool, these factors can seriously impact the growth rate of a business.

When an area is developing a strategy to promote local businesses, it can often influence many of these issues but it must do so to a well-thought through plan. When Milton Keynes was set up in the 1970s there was a serious mismatch between homes and jobs. People had somewhere to live but nowhere to work. When the Docklands in London was developed, most of the jobs created were for outsiders and not local people, and the transport provision was so poor that the outsider could not get to work. Even today, City Airport has no direct rail or underground link.

Concluding remarks

This review of infrastructure provision shows that many different sectors are involved. Co-ordination between them is a major problem, and so most infrastructures are a mixture of good and bad. In describing the main elements, we have tried to show how they can and should work together. If a region is seriously interested in developing a strong indigenous business base, then all parties have to co-operate. When this happens, the results can be beyond people's expectations. The opportunities for creating an entrepreneurial culture, and thereby a prosperous region, are too important for local rivalries or the attitudes of a few people to be allowed to prevent them. There can be no change without a vision but it must be a vision that everybody can feel part of and own. There is enough evidence from around the world to show that an entrepreneurial culture can become a reality and that disadvantaged regions can be turned round but there needs to be a vision and a will to make it happen. As with the individual entrepreneur, the region has to see the opportunity and then implement it.

References

Abetti, P.A. and Savoy, R. (1991). Management training of technological entrepreneurs. *International Journal of Continuing Engineering Education*, 1 (4).

Bolton, J.E. (1971). *Report of the Committee of Enquiry on Small Firms*. Cm 4811. HMSO.

Bolton, W.K. (1993). The enterprise paradigm. Latin American Seminar on the Development of Technology-based Enterprises, Rio de Janeiro, May.

Bolton, W.K. (1997). *The University Handbook on Enterprise Development*. Columbus.

Bruno, A.V. and Tyebjee, T.T. (1982). The environment for entrepreneurship. In *Encyclopaedia of Entrepreneurship* (C. Kent, D.L. Sexton and K.H. Vesper, eds), Prentice-Hall.

Business Week (1993). Special bonus issue on enterprise.

Castells, M. and Hall, P. (1994). *Technopoles of the World*. Routledge.

Coveney, P. and Moore, K. (1998). *Business Angels: Securing Start-up Finance*. John Wiley.

Enterprise Panel, The (1996). *Growing Success*. MCP 2288. HM Treasury.

Fisher, L.M. (1998). Technology transfer at Stanford University, *Policy*, 13, 76–84.

Hoggart, R. (1996). *The Way We Live Now*. Pimlico.

Kuratko, D.F. and Hodgetts, R.M. (1998). *Entrepreneurship: A Contemporary Approach*. 4th edn. The Dryden Press.

Malecki, E.J. (1997). *Technology and Economic Development*. 2nd edn. Longman.

Medawar, P. (1984). *Pluto's Republic*. Oxford University Press.

Monck, C.S.P., Porter, R.B., Quintas, P.R. and Storey, D.J. (1988). *Science Parks and the Growth of High-technology Firms*. Croom Helm.

Segal, N., Quince, R.E. and Wicksteed, W. (1985). *The Cambridge Phenomenon*. Segal, Quince, Wicksteed and Brand Brothers.

Smilor, R.W. and Gill, M.D. (1986). *The New Business Incubator*. Lexington Books.

Storey, D.J. (1982). *Entrepreneurship and the New Firm*. Croom Helm.

Success (1997). A golden future. May.

Vesper, K.H. (1986). New directions in entrepreneurship education. In *The Art and Science of Entrepreneurship* (D. Sexton and R.W. Smilor, eds), Ballinger.

Vesper, K.H. (1993). *Entrepreneurship Education*. The Anderson School, University of California, Los Angeles.

Wilson, J.W. (1986). *The New Venturers*. Addison-Wesley.

13 How the entrepreneur survives and wins

By now we understand entrepreneurs a little better and the process whereby they build something of recognised value. We have identified some of the support elements that help them along the way but it is still a journey fraught with difficulty. It is mostly an uphill fight demanding strength as well as courage. The operational environment we consider in this chapter is the background to this aspect of the journey. By giving it structure and form we hope that it will make it easier for entrepreneurs to understand their situation and deal with it. The market is the main element in an environment where the entrepreneur has to survive and win and is therefore considered in some detail. The other elements they have to learn to handle in a positive and creative way. Most entrepreneurs seem to enjoy these challenges and, if anything, run harder and faster because of them.

The operational environment

The *operational environment* is the weather through which the good ship 'Enterprise' has to sail. The ship may have been well prepared and stocked with provisions but in a severe storm all is lost. Hidden rocks, dangerous headlands, fog are all hazards. Navigation and sailing skills, good communications and weather forecasting help, but essentially it is a battle with the elements. Growing a business often feels like this. There is the sudden headline in the press aimed directly at your market. A recent one proclaimed 'Tapeless TV recorders set to make videos obsolete'. How should those in the video market respond? Is the journalist being sensationalist or has he a point? What happens when the customers read the same headline? Will they delay their purchase for a while? Is there a need to change course or does the industry just keep going?

What happens when the government suddenly changes the rules? In 1969, the US Congress raised the tax level on long-term capital gains from 28 per cent to 49 per cent and overnight halted the growing venture capital industry in its tracks. Annual private investment dropped from $171 million to $10 million. When the tax rate was returned to the 1969 level of 28 per cent nine years later and then reduced further to 20 per cent in 1981, investment rose dramatically reaching $1425 million in 1982. As Larson and Rogers (1986) comment 'That's enough money to start 2,800 small high-tech companies or 350 good-sized ones'. There was now a fair wind and the ship sailed on but the early 1970s had been very difficult years for those start-ups looking for money.

Entrepreneurs will succeed and win to the extent that they are able to cope with these vicissitudes. Just like true sailors, true entrepreneurs relish these challenges and get real satisfaction from winning through. It is often when the ship has ridden the early storms and is set on a steady course that some entrepreneurs lose interest and get bored. They look back to the excitement and challenge of it all and want to return to those days. This is one reason why entrepreneurs develop a habit of growing new enterprises. It becomes an addiction; it is what stimulates them.

Table 13.1 shows the activities that make up the *operational environment*. They determine the weather conditions. They are the things that the entrepreneur cannot change or influence easily. We identify five sectors: the market, the economy, the legal system, politics and culture. They all impact in their own way upon the start-up enterprise but there is one issue that cuts across all sectors, and that is risk. It is inherent in everything that we do in life but entrepreneurs see and handle risk in their own special way.

At first sight, these lists are somewhat daunting and can deter the faint-hearted but for entrepreneurs they are issues that must be faced up to and handled wisely. Many start-ups fail because the entrepreneurs involved have not paid sufficient attention to

Table 13.1 *The operational environment*

	The enterprise				
Sector	Market	Economic	Legislative	Political	Cultural
Activity	Risk				
	Limits to trade, e.g. tax duties, cartels	Inflation and interest rates	Company law, e.g. share ownership	Degree of stability	Attitudes towards entrepreneurs
	Market access and entry problems	Access to working capital and banking rules	Labour and factory law, e.g. union and employment rules	Short-termism National and regional policies which are politically driven	Press and the media Business and job culture; work ethic
	The market situation at local, regional, national and global levels	Government policy on zoning and taxation	Patent law and IPR rulings		University culture

them in the daily running of their business. Thus, when cash flow is under pressure and cheques begin to 'bounce', the entrepreneur must make sure that those sent to the tax man will be honoured by the bank, otherwise there will be serious trouble. Value added tax (VAT) and Companies House returns have to be made on time, or penalties will be incurred. These might seem details but they can become major irritants for the entrepreneur if they are not watched and can create unnecessary crises. The entrepreneur has to learn which matters are important and which can be left.

Before considering the sectors in turn we look at the general issues of risk. We are not concerned to provide a detailed discussion of the subject but rather to consider how the entrepreneur perceives and deals with risk.

Risk

The ordinary rate of profit rises . . . with risk.

(Adam Smith)

Sir, it's not a gamble, it's an investment.

(Punter at the Cheltenham Gold Cup)

These are the words of the 'risk aware' economist and the 'opportunity aware' gambler. The financial investor and the gambler operate in uncertain worlds. Past experience, inside knowledge and 'form', all help them understand this uncertainty but the future is essentially unknown. Both are also men of action and need to make a decision. The investor makes the decision on the basis of risk-reward considerations as per Adam Smith. The rate of return has to be commensurate with the risk being taken. The punter is seized by the opportunity and the size of the reward. Loss is not an option to be considered, even though it may be the reality half an hour later. For the punter it is not a gamble, it is an investment, as a punter once told a BBC interviewer.

Entrepreneurs who have attended a business school or are financially oriented will have the Adam Smith approach. They will find this restricts their natural inclinations to go for an opportunity and they may well miss some that they would have been able to take, had they not spent so much time in analysis. Other entrepreneurs are more like the gambler. They are seized and sometimes mesmerised by the opportunity. This gives them great focus and they storm through obstacles. They can also be foolhardy and live in a fantasy world. Even so, the gambler entrepreneur is more likely to win 'big' than is the risk-analysis entrepreneur, but then perhaps he will not win very often.

True entrepreneurs are neither investment bankers nor gamblers. They are the mountain climbers with a unique talent, temperament, technique set that they apply to what others would regard as a high-risk activity. Like climbing mountains, it is a risk that they do not have to take but somehow it is in the blood. Mountaineers know the risks because they have had friends who have died climbing. None of this deters them. Mountains are there to be climbed. Perceived opportunities are the entrepreneur's mountains. Observing them is not enough; they have to be climbed. Risk is inherent; it is the way things are. Just like mountaineers, entrepreneurs reduce risk by learning proven techniques and building experience. They take calculated risks, weighing the options carefully. They know their limitations but delight in testing themselves, always pushing the boundary so as to improve.

Most entrepreneurs see themselves as not taking undue risks; some even claim to be risk-averse. They say this because they do not perceive risks in the way that most of us do. It is not that they are not risk-averse or that they are prone to take risks. They are simply not *risk aware*. Some children take to swimming very easily. Others who are risk-aware realise that it is possible to drown in water and are much more cautious. Entrepreneurs often appear to be naïve about business risk but the truth is that they do not see it. This is one reason why they have such a hard time with bankers and financiers. They have a completely different perception of risk. This lack of risk awareness can be a serious weakness for the entrepreneur but it can also be a major strength. 'If I had realised what was involved I would probably never have started' is a sentiment often expressed by entrepreneurs but they are always glad they did. This lack of risk awareness goes hand in hand with the entrepreneur character theme of 'courage'. Without courage they would not be able to face up to the consequence of their risk-taking when things went wrong. Maybe courageous people take more risks because they know they can deal with the consequences.

There is clearly no point in entrepreneurs taking unwarranted and unnecessary risks. The basic rules of business and of profit and loss are things that entrepreneurs forget at their peril. But there is always risk in doing something that has not been done before or doing something in a new and different way. It is this category of risk that entrepreneurs take in their stride because they are not really aware of how great a risk they are taking.

When Richard Branson launched Mike Oldfield's record *Tubular Bells* he was doing something that had not been done before. An analysis would have shown that the greatest risk was in its promotion. Oldfield was an unknown and he had produced a forty-five-minute long play record, not a three-minute single. Endorsement by a disc jockey (DJ) on the radio was essential but would not be easy. Branson was turned down by BBC Radios 1 and 3 because the performance was too long. Finally he persuaded the well-known DJ, John Peel, a contact from his student days, to play it on his late night show. 'Tonight I'm not going to play a whole lot of records. I'm just going to play one by a young composer called Mike Oldfield. It's his first record and it's called "Tubular Bells". I've never heard anything like it in my life.' In his autobiography Branson recalls his anxiety as he listened to the broadcast. It was an all or nothing situation. 'I was too aware that Virgin had to sell a lot of copies to make money for next month's tax repayment.' The record was a great success and gave Virgin Records the start it so badly needed. Branson's risk in taking on Mike Oldfield had been justified but a major problem was just around the corner – one that a careful risk analysis would probably not have spotted. Branson had hired the Queen Elizabeth II Hall in London for a *Tubular Bells* concert. On the morning of the concert, Oldfield called Branson and told him he could not go through with the concert that evening. Tickets were sold, television coverage organised and now the main artist was pulling out. 'I felt a wave of despair,' recalls Branson 'I knew that Mike could be as stubborn as me when he wanted to be.' By a combination of courage and creativity, Branson solved the problem. He gave Oldfield his beloved Bentley in return for that performance (Branson, 1998).

Branson's first risk would have come out of an analysis of the market and the difficulty of market entry would have been identified. Branson knew the market well enough to take that risk. His second risk was less easy to predict but had it been, then its solution would have been in the form of a legally binding contract on Oldfield. Branson's solution was completely different. It retained the commitment of the artist and solved Branson's problem.

Risk for entrepreneurs is not a major consideration. Their approach fascinates the commentators who find it difficult to believe that they can live with such huge risks. They wonder how entrepreneurs sleep at night. As the example shows, Branson was anxious and nervous, he was in despair but he kept going and he won through. Entrepreneurs do not see risk in the normal business sense, they simply take things as they come. They are not risk-aware, and although this makes them vulnerable it is counteracted by their courage and creativity when things go wrong.

There is much that can be said about risk at the level of technique, and the risk assessment methodologies that are available can be extremely helpful. Most business plans require a section on the risk aspects of the investment and it is certainly a topic with which the entrepreneur must engage but it is lack of risk awareness that is both the entrepreneur's strength and weakness. Most things that people worry about never happen, but some do and it is better to be prepared. Entrepreneurs think differently and just get on with things dealing with problems as they arise, as Branson did.

The market sector

The market and the growth stages

The understanding of the marketplace is probably the most critical success factor for the entrepreneur. Without it he or she is unlikely to survive, let alone win. It is an understanding that has to change and develop as the business grows. Table 13.2 shows how the market and the growth stages discussed in Chapter 11 inter-relate. Concepts and visions are necessary at the *embryo* stage. Here the different possibilities are picked out and evaluated. The good entrepreneur involves his team at this early stage so that they begin to 'buy into' the enterprise. This is usually a time of

Table 13.2   *The market and the business*

	Embryo stage	Nurture stage	Fledgling stage	Take-off stage
Market stage	Concept	Focus and target	Entry	Capture and dominance
Market focus	Vision	Opportunities	Product/service	Solutions
Activity	See possibilities and evaluate	Prioritise and formulate strategy	Get close to the customer	Manage the market
Adoption	Internal adoption		Innovators	Early adopters	Early majority

dreaming dreams and seeing great possibilities. It is important not to get stuck here but to move on to the *nurture* stage to focus and target the opportunities.

'Possible' and 'probable' opportunities need to be differentiated and priorities set within a market strategy. This is a necessary preparation for market entry at the *fledgling* stage. Without it, market entry will be confused and fragmented. This is a critical stage for the business because all the market assumptions will be tested. It is much easier to generate an interest in the product or service you plan to offer than it is to land an order. Getting close to the customer is important at this stage but there must be a spread of customers to avoid bias and narrowing of the marketplace.

The *take-off* stage moves the business into a different world. This is a crucial transition for the business and the entrepreneur. It is the point at which he or she moves from being the owner manager of a small business to the builder of something of recognised value. It is the watershed between a life-style entrepreneur and the true entrepreneur. The aim is to capture the market and dominate it, as we shall see later.

The diffusion of innovation

Before discussing market entry further we need to understand the key ideas behind what has been termed 'the diffusion of innovation' (Rogers, 1995). These ideas were applied to marketing in 1969 when Frank Bass used them to describe how markets adopted new products. Since then, the methodology has been developed to monitor early sales campaigns and predict the likely take up of a new product (Mahajan *et al.*, 1990).

In the diffusion of innovation the word 'adoption' is used to describe the extent to which an innovation is taken up by the end-user and an 'innovation' is anything that is perceived as new by the user. The adoption of an innovation follows the 'diffusion' S-curve shown in Figure 13.1 (Rogers, 1995).

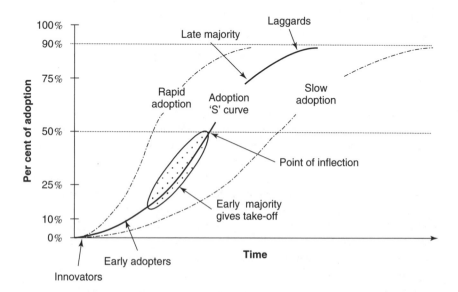

Figure 13.1 *Adoption S-curve*

The steeper the S-curve the faster the adoption, and the flatter the S-curve the slower. Fifty per cent adoption is achieved when the S-curve has reached its inflection or half-way point. It is made up of 'innovators' who are the first to adopt the innovation, followed by the 'early adopters' and then the 'early majority' up to the half-way point. Beyond that come the 'late majority' and finally 'the laggards'. Figure 13.1 suggests that around 10 per cent never adopt the innovation.

The area of real interest is the start of the S-curve. The *innovators* are the first 2.5 per cent of the users according to Rogers (1995). *Early adopters* are the next 13.5 per cent so that together the *innovators* and the *early adopters* make up 16 per cent of the customer base. The *early majority* are the next 34 per cent of customers and take the total adoption to the half-way point. These figures correspond approximately to the standard deviation multiples of the 'normal' probability distribution curve from which the S-curve is derived.

Adoption stages

Following this brief outline of 'diffusion' theory we now return to Table 13.2 and set the adoption stages on to the business growth stage model, as shown in Figure 13.2.

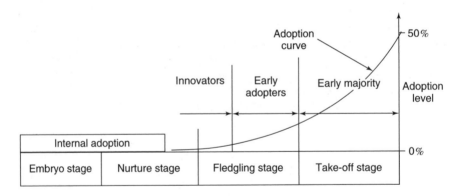

Figure 13.2   *Adoption profile*

In the early stages of the business, the market has to be 'adopted' and taken on board internally within the company. It is important for the entrepreneur to manage this internal adoption process and not to assume that it will just happen. The whole team must catch the vision and believe in the market focus and strategy.

In Figure 13.2 the external adoption follows the adopter categories proposed by Rogers (1995). The *innovators* are the potential customers that the start-up company has identified during the nurture stage and is doing business with by the start of the fledgling stage. *Innovators* will try the product out as soon as they can get their hands on it. They are the people who will respond to any publicity that is launched, as long as it emphasises newness. Margins can be high at this stage because price is not usually a factor in the *innovators'* purchase decision.

Care should be taken with the 2.5 per cent adoption figure by the *innovators* because it depends on the market being targeted. For the start-up company it really means

2.5 per cent of the market that can be realistically reached in the short term. We have seen business plans that have assumed that the new business will capture a few per-cent of a world market. This has predicted a huge sales level in the first year, which is quite unrealistic. The error in this kind of calculation is that there is no way the com-pany can ever reach that market until it is a well-established international business. The only exception to this, and it is an important one, is the Internet company which can reach the world market very easily and at low cost. But that exception apart, the start-up company must focus at this stage on the market that can be captured in the short term.

Whilst the *innovators* are prepared to take risks on the product or service the next target group, the *early adopters*, think more carefully about it and their opinion is val-ued by others. The product therefore has to function well and do what it is claimed it will do. These are the people that the fledgling company has to capture. It is pos-sible for businesses to fail because they are not able to win over these *early adopters*. The *innovators* are much more tolerant than the *early adopter* who requires products that are delivered on time and work first time.

The *innovators* and the *early adopters* together make up 16 per cent of a customer base. These customers can be in a particular geographical region or market niche and the start-up company can achieve further expansion simply by moving into new regions or applications. This can be a viable strategy in the short term and will certainly produce increased sales, but there is an important caution. The start-up com-pany must move through and out of the fledgling stage and not get stuck there. It must continue on to the take-off stage where the primary marketing task is to attract more and more of the *early majority* of adopters. These represent the next 34 per cent of a customer base. When this is done, the company is a mainstream supplier in a main-stream market with a real opportunity to establish a leadership position.

Though this approach is about the adoption of innovations it applies as much to old products in old markets as it does to new products in new markets. Innovation means anything perceived as new and this can be a new pricing or delivery approach in an old market. Shopping on the Internet is a new purchase and delivery mech-anism but the products and services have not changed. The book, video or airline ticket is still the same item. They may be old products in old markets but there is purchasing novelty and the laws of innovation diffusion apply. On-line shopping is at the *early adopter* stage and the big test will be whether or not it can cross the divide to become mainstream.

The take-off stage

The move from the fledgling to the take-off stage requires a fundamental shift in the market focus. As indicated in Table 13.2, the market focus changes as the company passes through its different stages of growth. The focus moves from the vision at the embryo stage to opportunities at the nurture stage and to product/service at the fledg-ling stage. This is a fairly natural progression that generally goes smoothly. With a real product and real customers, it is easy for entrepreneurs to think that they now have a viable and maturing business. In reality, the business has reached a critical stage. It can either grow to be a force in the industry or it can stay small with the likelihood of a slow decline. The business can either pass through to a take-off or else stay as a fledgling business. It is possible to disguise this reality by believing that the business has reached a steady state and is now mature. For some companies this 'comfort zone' can last for a number of years but sooner or later it will turn into a 'crisis zone' and the company will find it difficult to survive. To build real value, the entrepreneur has no option but to go for a take-off.

Moore (1991, 1998) has applied these diffusion of innovation ideas to marketing strategies for high-technology businesses. He sees the transition from fledgling stage to take-off stage as the move from the 'early stage' market to the 'mainstream' market. He describes the transition as a chasm that the start-up company has to cross if it is to succeed. The analogy of a chasm suggests that the gap is both deep and wide and that most who try to cross it fall to their death. Certainly the high-tech sector has a large graveyard!

Two quite different markets stand either side of this divide. Up to this stage, the start-up business has been concerned with the early market and the early adopters but now it has to enter the mainstream market and go for the early majority (Moore, 1998). This would simply mean more of the same with increased efficiency if it were not for the fact that these markets have quite different characteristics. What sells in one will not sell in the other. The early market is prepared to shop around and has a DIY approach to solving its problems but the mainstream market does not have the time or the interest. This is the reason why it is so difficult to break into a market, once it has become mainstream. The market has adopted a particular approach and will stay with it often when there are better products around. This shows the magnitude of Dyson's achievement in breaking into the vacuum cleaner market, which he did on the basis of functional excellence and not price. New products into old markets have a huge hill to climb, but as Dyson showed 'it can be done'.

This transition period has particular dangers for sales-oriented entrepreneurs. They have been very successful to date and feel they know and understand their market. They recognise that the early majority market is twice as big as the early adopter market, and are ready to go for it. But it is not more of the same. They need to recognise that a different approach is needed and that without it they will fail. There has to be a shift in focus from product to solution. This may mean new business alliances or even acquisitions if the company is to offer the customer a complete solution. This calls for new talents and skills from entrepreneurs but their courage and creativity will still serve them well. Entrepreneurs like Charles Forte and Richard Branson excelled in this take-off stage. Both demonstrated real talent for negotiating the deal and building the right alliances. They survived and won because they were not intimidated by a market environment dominated by big players. The take-off stage was where they excelled.

The market limits

There are limits to growth built into most markets due to competition. Market share is the main indicator of market performance. The Boston Consulting Group has used the idea of 'relative market share' in their well-known Growth-Share

Matrix (Thompson, 2001). This is the ratio of a company's market share to that of its nearest competitor so that a ratio of greater than 1 means that company is the market leader. For the static or declining market the matrix has a ratio of 1 as the dividing line between the cash cow product that you milk and the dog that you should kick out. Similarly for a growing market this dividing line is between the stars and the problem children. This means that only the market leader benefits from having a cash cow and star products; the rest have dogs and problem children.

This presents the start-up business with a serious problem. How can it hope to penetrate a market and achieve dominance? Part of the answer has been given above in terms of market adoption and the transition to the take-off stage. Another part is for the entrepreneur to be aware of how players in the market behave. If there is one dominant player with, say, 40 per cent market share and the rest have around 10 per cent, then a newcomer would probably go unnoticed up to about 3 per cent or 4 per cent. Thereafter, pressure will come from all except the dominant player who will simply watch the fight. This may be a open and honest competition in the marketplace but it can also be underhand and illegal. We know of one entrepreneur whose business expansion was effectively capped by the competition who 'persuaded' his supplier to limit deliveries of vital components.

In some markets the business is shared out among a group of companies so that an informal cartel operates that keeps out newcomers. In others, as soon as a business reaches a certain size there is a telephone call that offers to safeguard markets and ensure delivery for a 'consideration'. These are all problems that the entrepreneur has to be able to cope with and there is never an easy answer. Ricardo Semler, the Brazilian entrepreneur, has quoted the maxim 'You can either run a successful business or be ethical. Take your pick'. He then goes on to give examples that show that this maxim need not be true (Semler, 1993).

As we comment later, corruption affects other areas of the *operational environment* but the marketplace is perhaps the most difficult to deal with. The first big order may carry a 'commission' payment to the person placing the order which from that point on becomes the accepted way of doing business. Entrepreneurs need to decide their position on these issues before they are thrust upon them. There can be some advantage in talking things over with other entrepreneurs in the same region or area of activity so that a common stand is taken. A group of almost fifty entrepreneurs in Romania have come together in this way to develop what they term 'islands of integrity in a sea of corruption' (Murray, 1997).

The economic, legislative, political and cultural sectors

Here we present our views on how these sectors affect and influence the entrepreneur. In general, they are not particularly friendly to entrepreneurs or at least they present them with problems that they could well do without. This section has something of a lobbying tone and we present opinions, rather than facts, but we do so towards the end of a book that has tried to champion entrepreneurs and the release of their valuable talent amongst us.

The economic sector

Next to the market, this is the sector that the entrepreneur has to pay the closest attention to. The economic situation in a country has a direct bearing on the success or otherwise of the business. Most governments are trying to create the conditions that will keep the business sector in good shape and produce a healthy expanding economy. They do this against an international economy that is driven by the large trading nations such as the USA and Japan so that recession in one soon becomes a global issue. Entrepreneurs come and go in these economic cycles, and investors become more and more cautious. The net result is to suppress entrepreneurial endeavour in favour of low-risk prudent strategies.

Inflation and interest rates are economic indictors that affect the bottom line of a business, its net profit, but they are outside the control of the entrepreneur. Inflation affects both the costs of raw material and the prices that can be charged in the marketplace. If the raw material is imported or exports are a major part of the business then changes in exchange rates can almost kill a business overnight. These are serious problems but the amazing thing is that entrepreneurs still succeed and win. Ricardo Semler describes the Brazilian economy in his first eleven years running Semco 'Inflation averaged more than 400 per cent, swinging from yearly highs of 1,600 per cent to lows of a mere 100 per cent. From 1986 to 1990, the country endured five economic shock plans, knocked three zeros off its currency twice and on two occasions changed it altogether'. If this was not bad enough in 1990 a new finance minister seized 80 per cent of the cash in the country. 'Chaos does not begin to describe the reaction. Companies didn't have money to meet their payrolls, much less to conduct business. At Semco we struggled through several months of zero sales.' Despite all this, Semco, under Semler's leadership, rode the storm and came out a fitter and leaner company (Semler, 1993).

Access to working capital to run the business is a constant source of difficulty for the entrepreneur. Because of the rules that the lending banks apply, most start-up businesses simply do not have enough cash to grow and become strong. In many countries, entrepreneurs have to provide a financial guarantee well in excess of the overdraft limit allowed or the loan taken out. If they are unable to do this, then access to money is denied.

In the UK it is common for banks to require the directors of a business to provide financial guarantees. This generally involves signing the entire business over to the bank and sometimes the family home as a security in case things go wrong. Surprisingily, most entrepreneurs simply accept this and the risk does not seem to bother them.

Banks can assume powers to conduct financial audits of companies to which they have lent money. The cost of the audit has to be borne by the company. In one case, the auditors put in by the bank concluded that the company did need an increased overdraft but recommended that it be not given. This perversity is not untypical and represents the kind of unnecessary pressures that some banks put on the entrepreneur.

Taxation is another area of difficulty because it is usually imposed arbitrarily by the government without consultation. There is always a public outcry when personal taxation is increased but taxes on business often go unnoticed. Some countries find it necessary to have tax police to ensure that taxes get paid. They are empowered to come into the company at any time and see any records they wish. In some cases they confiscate everything and leave the business to carry on while they continue their investigation. This power is absolute and so can be abused. Ricardo Semler became a national hero in Brazil when he exposed corruption in a government tax department and the officials concerned received a prison sentence. He comments:

> There was no reason to rejoice. The inspector's superiors were not even brought in for questioning. A little while later one of our clerks went to a government department for a document and was told 'Tell your boss he doesn't just have one inspector to worry about, he's got 100,000 against him now'.
>
> (Semler, 1993)

Businesses, of course, are not always the innocent party and many are experts in exploiting loop holes and avoiding the payment of tax for as long as possible. Some also exploit well-meaning government policy to their own ends. The more deprived and underdeveloped regions in a country are often designated to receive grant aid of one form or another. We know of one case in the UK where the entrepreneur took advantage of this and moved to a new building in a development area. The building was rent and rates free for three years, and he received a grant for every job he created. When the three-year period was up, he closed the operation down. It appeared that he had never had the intention of setting up a permanent business in the area.

The legislative sector

There are a great many laws and regulations that the start-up business has to comply with and the entrepreneur will need legal advice right from the start. The three most critical areas are Company Law, Employment Law and Patent Law, although Property Law can sometimes be an issue. The social entrepreneur will need to comply with Charity Law if he decides to operate as a charity. It is in this legislative area that entrepreneurs will need their talent of 'using experts'. If they are strong in this character sub-theme they will know their own limits and know when to call in the experts. They will also be good at identifying experts who will not waste their time and money, and will give sound advice.

Company Law is concerned with the legal entity of the business. The entrepreneur will need to decide whether to be a sole trader, a partnership or some form of limited company. For the entrepreneur who intends to build something of recognised value, this will almost certainly mean a limited company. The social entrepreneur may need to explore the possibility of setting up as a Registered Charity. If the entrepreneur does both, then in the UK, annual accounts will need to be sent to Companies House as a limited company and the Charity Commissioners as a charity. Couple this with the complexities of setting up as a company and/or a charity and it is clear that professional advice is necessary.

Whilst legal safeguards are obviously required, they appear to be unnecessarily complex, and in practice, legal formalities can go back and forth for months delaying the start-up of the business or else the business starts without them in place and runs into trouble later on. With all these legal company matters to sort out, it is easy for the entrepreneur to forget the obvious ones like 'terms and conditions of sale' or what is legally required to be on the letterheads of the new business.

Company law in respect of shareholders is a very important area. What happens to the shareholding of founder directors who are dismissed or leave? Can they retain their shares or can they be forced to surrender them, and if so, at what value? Most start-ups face this problem within their first year or two.

These days, it is not only directors who own shares in the business. It is increasingly common for employees to be given share options. Microsoft is said to have created more millionaires among its employees than any other company. What are their rights? All these issues need to be addressed and legal advice is essential. In a litigious society like the USA most companies will go to court at some time even in their early years. The most common areas concern employees and patents. Key people leave and set up in competition or out of the blue there is a challenge to the patent upon which the product and the business are based. These are nightmare scenarios but they do happen and the entrepreneur has to be able to cope. Successful entrepreneurs build teams around them and have their experts on hand so that they are well-prepared.

In the UK, employment and labour law is becoming increasingly demanding on the business. Whilst it is there to safeguard the rights of employees, it has reduced the willingness of businesses to take on permanent employees. For this reason, start-up companies are often run below strength so that those who are employed have to work harder and longer. Entrepreneurs need more, rather than less, employee flexibility and, good though the intentions of labour law might be, it is a constraint on the start-up business.

Patent law, as we discussed in Chapter 12, is very important for the technology-based business, and venture capitalists are unlikely to invest unless the patent situation is strong. This can increase the start-up costs significantly as these days cover in the USA, Europe and Japan is almost the minimum required. Professional patent agents will be needed. It is certainly not an area where the entrepreneur should adopt a DIY approach, though some do.

Once all these matters are sorted out and the business is up and running, then a whole host of regulations have to be complied with. One entrepreneur who had started a successful business in her garden shed went to the local council to see if larger premises might be available. Their response was to say that she would have to close down because she did not have planning permission to operate a business from her garden shed. When she eventually found new premises, health and safety and environmental issues became a major problem. Such matters are now highly regulated, and whilst it may be a good thing in principle, the way they are applied often leads much to be desired.

These kind of regulations enforced by administrators may be a source of great frustration to the entrepreneur but they can also be very costly. According to the British Chambers of Commerce (BCC) the 'red-tape' burden on businesses from government legislation rose to £15 billion in 2001 and was set to increase further as new employee maternity benefits came into force in 2003. Ms Low, the regulation expert at the BCC, has commented that 'This is what really makes life hard for small firms.' It is easy to say that true entrepreneurs will rise above these inconveniences, and maybe they will, but there will not be many of them. The rest will remain buried in the woodwork waiting for better days.

The political sector

The main impact of the political situation for the entrepreneur is the degree of stability it brings to a country. The rise of entrepreneurial activity in the Renaissance period was linked with a period of relative peace and a power balance between kings, as we reported in Chapter 1. War may give some entrepreneurs a fresh opportunity but it prevents the build up of an entrepreneurial culture, and entrepreneurs can find a life's work in ruins.

The politicians' job is to create an environment that is conducive to the entrepreneur; one that encourages and rewards personal endeavour and hard work and that does not penalise the entrepreneur who has tried and failed. For example, in the matter of bankruptcy, the assumption behind British law seems to have been that anybody declared bankrupt is a bad person who deserves the worst. In truth, many have just made bad business decisions or were simply unlucky. Recent efforts by the British government to amend the law of bankruptcy are to be commended.

The electoral system in many countries means that the economic and legislation cycle is between three and five years. This leads to start-stop policies and short-termism which make life very difficult for the entrepreneur and for an agency that is trying to put in place the kind of *support infrastructure* discussed in Chapter 12. We know of a case in Brazil where the construction of a business incubator was halted because the mayor who supported the scheme was not re-elected and the new mayor stopped all building projects. Similar start-stop effects occur in universities when the principal or vice-chancellor is an elected post and the new appointee is not interested in the plans of his predecessor. Academic issues have a way of being resolved when such changes happen but peripheral things such as business incubators or special entrepreneurial initiatives always seem to suffer.

National and regional policies that are politically driven can seriously impact the entrepreneur. There may be a drive to promote employment in a difficult area and create jobs. The easy fix is to encourage a large company to move into the area, as we discussed in Chapter 12 when we commented on inward investment. Little or no thought is given to creating an indigenous business base driven by entrepreneurs. This was certainly the case a few years back but now the role of the local company is more clearly recognised by the politicians who devise these schemes. Even so, most government schemes are not user-friendly and it is normal for private sector companies working in the field of job creation to have to adjust their plans to meet the latest idea from the government. We know of one group that decided it is was just not worth the effort and used its entrepreneurial skills so that its work among young entrepreneurs was funded by a separate commercial venture, and grants were no longer needed.

Perhaps, the biggest complaint against the involvement of government agencies in entrepreneurial activity is that they are driven by the need to create jobs. Agency contracts are set up on the basis of the cost per job created. We accept the political sensitivity of employment levels but what is actually needed are sustainable jobs in viable businesses and not just any jobs. There is no virtue in a company employing more people than it needs to, simply to qualify for a grant but that is how most schemes are structured.

The cultural sector

Culture is the most deeply rooted of these environmental parameters and the most difficult to change. It varies from country to country and region to region. The USA is frequently seen as the most entrepreneurial culture in the world, which no doubt owes much to its pioneering origins, but places like Hong Kong and Singapore have developed their own brand of entrepreneurship.

Although we should not automatically assume the rate of start-up activity represents entrepreneurship, as we have defined it, it is useful to look at the conclusions from the most recent Global Entrepreneurship Monitor (GEM) – see Reynolds *et al.* (2002) – which measures start-up activity in some forty countries around the world. The highest rate of start-ups is found in Asia's developing countries, although the developed Asian countries such as Japan have a low start-up rate. The second highest cluster is Latin America, although these countries have the highest rate of necessity entrepreneurship – defined as people starting businesses because this is their best earning opportunity. Those countries that were once British colonies (Australia, New Zealand, South Africa and the US) then follow, and they are higher than Western Europe. Eastern European countries and developed Asian economies lag behind. It is interesting to also look behind these data. New Zealand, for example, has a relatively very high start-up rate, but the growth and survival rates are relatively low. Research with which we have been involved – see Frederick *et al.* (2002) – indicates New Zealanders are opportunity-takers rather than 'true' entrepreneurs. Their long-term growth and success will depend in part upon their ability to form entrepreneur teams, requiring strength in the team character theme.

The role of the small start-up has never had to be argued in many countries and regions. In some instances, it is self-evident, a product of the Chinese culture and the dominant role of the family unit (Fukuyama, 1995). Japan may have a low start-up rate and may not see itself as particularly inventive, yet it has proved to be an excellent innovator. Entrepreneurial activity can be observed in many large and successful Japanese corporations. Sony provides a wonderful example. Their managers may not be natural entrepreneurs but they are certainly outstanding project champions with remarkable focus and a strong work ethic. In Europe, there is no real culture of entrepreneurship other than in a few places. Cambridge, England and Oulu, Finland have already been mentioned but northern Italy (Porter 1990) and the Basque region of Spain around Mondragon (Whyte and Whyte, 1991) have seen significant entrepreneurial activity over the years.

The former communist countries have an anti-entrepreneurial culture at present due to their long history of centralist governments. There are signs that this is now beginning to change, though this is more likely to be to a capitalist culture than an entrepreneurial one. The Indian sub-continent, Latin America, Africa and China have huge populations, and for historic and religious reasons each has its own approach to entrepreneurship. Though it is allowed and even encouraged, it is only within certain boundaries so that it has not become the major influence that it could be. The surprise amongst these groups is that Latin America has not been more successful since its origins are not dissimilar to those of the USA. No doubt, their experience with military dictatorships and union solidarity has partially worked against individualism and the emergence of the entrepreneur. There are welcome signs that things are changing and entrepreneurship is now an increasingly important topic in their universities.

These observations present a mixed picture of how the cultures across the world relate to the entrepreneur. Though there is certainly some way to go before, our comments in Chapter 10 about a world in tune with the entrepreneur are a reality we do believe the opportunity is there and that things are moving in the right direction. Entrepreneurs are central to this culture change and the challenge is to release their potential in a positive and constructive manner to the economic and social benefit of us all.

Concluding remarks

We have made a number of assertions in this chapter as we have sought to present the entrepreneur's point of view. Most entrepreneurs are too busy running their enterprises to engage in this debate but it is a serious one. Just as the sectors in the *support infrastructure* need to understand each other so do those in the *operational environment*. The structural divisions in our society and the way career routes are organised make this difficult but unless it happens the development of an entrepreneurial culture and the release of entrepreneur talent will be seriously delayed and we will all be the losers.

References

Branson, R. (1998). *Richard Branson: Losing my Virginity*. Virgin Publishing.
Frederick, H., Carswell, P., Henry, E., Chaston, I., Thompson, J., Campbell, J. and Pivac, A. (2002). *Bartercard New Zealand Global Entrepreneurship Monitor 2002*, UNITEC Auckland.
Fukuyama, F. (1995). *Trust*. Hamish Hamilton.
Larson, J.K. and Rogers, E.M. (1986). *Silicon Valley Fever*. Unwin Counterpoint.
Mahajan, V., Muller, E. and Bass, F.M. (1990). New product diffusion models in marketing. *Journal of Marketing*, **54**, 1–26.
Moore, G.A. (1991). *Crossing the Chasm*. HarperBusiness.
Moore, G.A. (1998). *Inside the Tornado*. Capstone.
Murray, D. (1997). *Ethics in Organisations*. Kogan Page.
Porter, M.E. (1990). *The Competitive Advantage of Nations*. Macmillan.
Reynolds, P.D., Bygrave, W.D., Autio, E. and Hay, M. (2002). *Global Entrepreneurship Monitor 2002 Summary Report*, Babson College and London Business School.
Rogers, E.M. (1995). *Diffusion of Innovation*, 4th edn. Free Press.
Semler, R. (1993). *Maverick*. Century.
Thompson, J.L. (2001). *Strategic Management: Awareness and Change*, 4th edn. Thomson Learning.
Whyte, W.F. and Whyte, K.G. (1991). *Making Mondragon*, 2nd edn. Cornell University ILR Press.

14 The entrepreneurs of Silicon Valley

Silicon Valley is unique. Although the computer industry has emerged and developed in different places, and not exclusively in America, we typically think of Silicon Valley as its natural home. This story of the entrepreneurs who have started up and grown both computer and semiconductor businesses in this part of California shows how a community or region can become a collective entrepreneur – where the whole region behaves as if it was itself an entrepreneur. It also demonstrates the potential synergy when ideas, finance and talented people come together.

In principle, we believe that all regions have this potential because of the entrepreneurial talent that resides within its inhabitants. But just as this talent can lie buried within the individual entrepreneur, so it can also remain dormant within a community. Silicon Valley is the story of a number of individual entrepreneurs who were able to produce an environment that stimulated the emergence of entrepreneurial talent and most importantly attracted more of this same talent into the area.

The Silicon Valley story is not just about *individual entrepreneurs*, important though they were. It is also about the development of *mechanisms* and *infrastructure* within an *opportunity setting*. When these factors were focused to serve the entrepreneurs in the community the *collective entrepreneur* was formed.

Regions that attempt to replicate the Silicon Valley experience often fail because the *mechanisms* and *infrastructure* that have been put in place have not been within an *opportunity setting*, nor has there been a strong focus on encouraging and serving the *entrepreneurs*. These issues have already been discussed; our purpose now is to show how they combined in a small valley just South of San Francisco so that within one generation a vibrant economy was generated. Silicon Valley is an example of what happens when a community taps into its well of entrepreneurial talent – it simply takes off! There has been a similar entrepreneurial experience with IT businesses in the region around Bangalore in India. There is now an attempt to replicate this for biotechnology companies a little further north, around Hyderabad. But the important message for any economic or regional developers is clear. Entrepreneurs are needed – but they can only thrive collectively if important mechanisms and key elements of the necessary support infrastructure are in place. These sometimes require another group of entrepreneurs. The venture capitalists who funded the expansion of Silicon Valley were entrepreneurs in their own right.

> The industrial milieu or district itself can be seen as a community or collective entrepreneur with not only firms, but inter-firm associations, worker organisations, financial institutions and government agencies also playing important roles.
>
> (Malecki, 1997 – an economic geographer)

> There is nowhere else in the world we could have started this company. Silicon Valley is an attitude. We found risk capital, we found suppliers and vendors who wanted us to succeed and we found people with an attitude that made us succeed.
>
> (James Treybig, founder of Tandem Computers, quoted in Larson and Rogers, 1986)

> Silicon Valley is different from anything else I've experienced. It's like Florence must have been at the Renaissance. It's where all the bright minds are coming together and it's a place where wonderful things are going to happen.
>
> (Corporate head-hunter Gerry Roche, Chairman, Heidrick & Struggles Inc. quoted in Sculley, 1987)

The issues behind the story

There are four key issues in our story – the entrepreneurs themselves, the support mechanisms, the infrastructure and the opportunity.

The entrepreneurs

'Without Fred Terman Silicon Valley might never have happened' (Larson and Rogers, 1986). Fred Terman of Stanford University, first as Professor of Radio Engineering in 1926 and subsequently as Provost and Vice-President in the 1950s, was a key figure in the early days of Silicon Valley. He always encouraged his students to go into business, personally playing the role of coach to a generation of potential entrepreneurs, who included Bill Hewlett and Dave Packard. The now world famous Hewlett-Packard company began life in 1938 in a garage with money loaned by Fred Terman. In 1951, Fred Terman founded what became the Stanford Research Park.

'Without Bell Labs there would be no Silicon Valley' (Arno Penzias, Vice-President of Bell Laboratories, quoted in Larson and Rogers, 1986). Certainly it was at Bell Labs in New Jersey that Bill Shockley co-invented the transistor, but it was his decision to set up his new company in Palo Alto in Silicon Valley that brought the technology of the silicon chip to the area.

The 'Traitorous Eight' (Jackson, 1998) were eight young engineers who left Shockley's new company after a year to form Fairchild Semiconductor. Amongst these eight were entrepreneurs Bob Noyce and Gordon Moore who were later to found Intel Corporation, the world's leading manufacturer of microprocessors for personal computers.

From this point on, the entrepreneurs seem to emerge all over Silicon Valley. Among the classic names are Steve Jobs of Apple Computers, Gene Amdahl of the Amdahl Corporation, Nolan Bushnell of Atari, Jerry Saunders of AMD, Larry Ellison of Oracle, John Chambers of Cisco and Scott McNealy of Sun Microsystems as well as Sabia Bhatia of Hotmail and the founders of Google, Fergey Brin and Larry Page. Some, like Linus Torvalds, also rank among Silicon Valley's entrepreneurs, even though they began their work elsewhere. At the age of twenty-one in 1991, and when still in his native Finland, Torvalds started to write the Linux operating system for personal computers (PCs), using as his base the old Unix system – Linux thus being a combination of his name Linus and Unix. Though Torvalds could have located himself anywhere in the world he chose Silicon Valley. What makes Torvalds different is the fact that he is essentially an inventor who is more concerned with achievement than a personal fortune. It seems appropriate that he chose the title 'Just for Fun' for his autobiography (Torvalds and Diamond, 2001). He opted to make his system freely available through the Internet; around the world a team of like-minded technocrats continue to work on refinements and developments – all without charge for their time.

These entrepreneurs are at the heart of the IT industry that sprung out of Silicon Valley and then spread across the USA. Bill Gates returned to his home city of Seattle to develop Microsoft. Jeff Bezos also chose Seattle to be the home of Amazon.com. Michael Dell built the leading PC manufacturer, Dell Computers, in Texas. Although Silicon Valley no longer has a monopoly of the industry's leading lights, it created their opportunities.

The mechanisms

From the very early days, two essential mechanisms – spin-offs and networking – have operated consistently in Silicon Valley.

Spin-offs occur when an individual or team leaves an existing business or institution to set up a new business. Thus, Fairchild Semiconductor was a spin-off from Shockley Laboratories when the *Traitorous Eight* left to form their own company. An effective spin-off mechanism comprises a number of spin-off points, which generate a flow of new companies. We can identify three major spin-off points for Silicon Valley:

- Stanford University as early as 1912.
- Fairchild Semiconductor in the 1960s.
- The Homebrew Computer Club in the 1970s.

From the 1980s onward the process of new business generation was self-sustaining as spin-offs begat spin-offs. We elaborate later on how these spin-off points worked, but it is important to note that these three spin-off points were sufficient to get the ball rolling. This is because each was able to produce a further stream of spin-offs that multiplied themselves.

Networking is a second important mechanism. This developed naturally around people like Fred Terman and his students and then around the companies they formed. Silicon Valley, particularly in the early days, was like a big village where people networked easily. As time went on, informal groups like the Homebrew Computer Club were formed. The main talking point in these networks was the latest technology, so that they served as a very effective way of transferring and dispersing technical information. 'If a Homebrew member knew about a secret chip design at Intel, he'd be happy to share the details' (Rose, 1989).

Networking also encouraged the spin-off process as ideas were born and developed. 'The Fairchild spin-offs were often projected, discussed and decided in a nearby restaurant in Mountain View, Walker's Wagon Wheel Bar and Grill, frequented by the company's engineers' (Castells and Hall, 1994).

The infrastructure

The most important part of the infrastructure in the Silicon Valley story is Stanford University itself, but the development of part of the land owned by the University as a Research Park in 1951 was crucial in stimulating and supporting the entrepreneurial activities. Venture capitalists then moved into the area in the early 1960s and grew steadily, so that by the 1980s they were a major part of the infrastructure. They had enough money available to be able to support the growth of significant businesses – this story is not just about small business start-ups. These Californian venture capitalists have typically contributed far more than dollars and cheques to the growth of Silicon Valley. They have provided expert advice on strategy, recruitment and future financing.

As early as the 1950s, major clients and a network of sub-contractors began to develop as the Lockheed Missiles and Space Company set up in Northern California and the US Defence Department placed major contracts for semiconductors. IBM and Xerox also moved into the area and enhanced the research base.

Whilst a major university and research park, venture capital companies, customers and sub-contractors were all key parts of the infrastructure, and it was really the bars and restaurants that grew up in Silicon Valley that enabled a community of entrepreneurs to develop. This we see as the distinguishing mark of Silicon Valley and it is the part that is so often missed by those who try to replicate what happened. It was in these places, the bars and the restaurants, that the entrepreneurs met – those who were already in business and those who were thinking about it. There was a cross-fertilisation of idea and opportunity as entrepreneurs and the engineers talked together. These meeting places were essential to the development of networks and the building of an entrepreneurial community and formed an important part of the infrastructure.

The opportunity

Silicon Valley owes its remarkable growth to two technological opportunities. The general background to both was electronics, in which Stanford University had a strong reputation; but it was the silicon chip and the personal computer (including its software) that provided the two key opportunities. Although the Internet has provided a new impetus, it was these earlier opportunities that enabled Silicon Valley to become what it is today.

The transistor had been co-invented by Shockley, who moved to Silicon Valley in 1955. Two years later, Bob Noyce, at Fairchild Semiconductor, patented the integrated circuit. These inventions resulted in the first wave of companies whose business was built around the silicon chip that was to give the valley its name.

The second wave came out of Intel when Ted Hoff invented the microprocessor in 1971 and began the personal computer industry. This led to opportunities in software, computer games and now the Internet.

Without these opportunities and their enormous commercial potential, Silicon Valley would not be what it is today, namely the largest concentration of technology-based businesses in the world, with an economy greater than that of many a nation. Nevertheless, there have been disappointments and setbacks amongst the many successes. 'Silicon Valley probably produces more spin-offs than it really should. Whilst it's great to believe that anything is possible, anything ISN'T possible. But [this belief] allows some things that are possible to be realised more quickly than they otherwise would be.'

The Silicon Valley story

If you drive south down the main highway from San Francisco, in just over half an hour, depending on traffic conditions, you will come to Palo Alto and Menlo Park. This is the start of Silicon Valley and the home of Stanford University and Hewlett-Packard. The next thirty to forty miles are all Silicon Valley, with place names that will be heard later in the story – Mountain View, the home of Fairchild Semiconductor, Sunnyvale, where there were almost 800 electronic firms in 1982, Cupertino, the home of Apple Computers and Santa Clara, Intel's headquarters. At the south end of the valley is San Jose, an urban sprawl that has now spread out to extend the valley further.

Had you driven this route in 1950, you would simply have been heading for Santa Clara County, then acknowledged to be the prune capital of America. You would have seen orchards and an agricultural community. There would have been some electronic firms around in those days; indeed there were spin-offs from Stanford happening as early as 1912. Hewlett-Packard, which was formed in 1938, would also have been there – but these were all small activities compared with what was about to happen.

There are many strands that continue throughout the story of Silicon Valley, but it is possible to identify four discrete periods, each of which moved the economic activity into a higher gear. The first period takes us to the mid-1950s and lays important foundations. The second period brings the silicon chip to the valley, and the first real economic growth is seen. It was at the end of this second period, in 1971, that Don Hoefler of Microelectronics News coined the name 'Silicon Valley'. The third period from 1972 to 1985 saw the arrival of the personal computer and this is when the economy really took off. By the end of this period more people were employed in this sector than in any other. Since 1986, companies like Intel and Sun Microsystems have become world leaders, and the arrival of the Internet in the early 1990s has stimulated the emergence of a new generation of entrepreneurs.

Each period built on the previous one, such that the accumulative effect was truly remarkable. In 1959 around 7000 people worked in high-technology; by 1970 this number had increased to some 52 000; by 1980 the total was close to 180 000. Hewlett-Packard, the oldest Silicon Valley company, has remained ahead of the pack, and it was the largest company with sales in excess of $50 billion, before its recent acquisition of Compaq. The other leading businesses are Intel, Sun Microsystems, which produces servers and high-performance workstations, Oracle, world leader in database software, Cisco and 3Com, two key Internet companies and the famous Apple Corporation.

The foundation period: 1930s–1955

In reality, it is difficult to say when this period actually began because electronics was always a subject of interest at Stanford University. In 1909 a Stanford graduate set up Poulson Wireless Telephone and Telegraph Company in Palo Alto. It was funded by the School's President and based on a wireless telephone invented by a local teenager. A year later, two engineers spun-off from Poulson's and founded Magnavox to exploit a loudspeaker they had invented (Rose, 1989). In 1912, Lee de Forest, a researcher at Poulson's, by then renamed the Federal Telegraph Company, discovered that the vacuum tube could be used to amplify an electrical signal. This proved to be a discovery of profound significance to the future development of electronics. With this level of invention and innovation happening and with professors such as Harris Ryan, who was in many ways similar to Fred Terman, it is perhaps surprising that more progress was not made at that time. But the situation was some way from reaching critical mass and it took a further thirty years before things began to move.

It is from this background of opportunity that the hero of the Silicon Valley story, Fred Terman, emerged. Terman was born into an academic family. His father was a Professor of Psychology at Stanford College (as it was known in the 1920s) with a special interest in gifted children. Terman Sr developed the world's first IQ test, and its use in the evaluation of two million American service personnel in the First World War made it famous. The academic, yet practical, approach of his father is something that Fred Terman always exemplified. He studied chemistry and electrical engineering at Stanford, graduating in 1920. It would appear that he caught something of the entrepreneurial approach at Stanford and was aware of the way in which electronics companies were being set up from the university.

Terman's next step took him east, to the research excellence of the Massachusetts Institute of Technology (MIT). Here he studied for his PhD under Vannevar Bush, an outstanding academic who was also closely involved with industry and was later to be one of the four founders of the renowned electronics company, Raytheon Corporation, as well as becoming the Vice-President of MIT. In many ways, as we shall see, Terman himself emulated his mentor, Bush. For both men, research excellence and commercial application always went together, each reinforcing the other.

But for an event in 1924, Fred Terman may have stayed on at MIT and 'left his footprints' there. Perhaps he would have become the father of the high-technology developments along Route 128 in Boston, rather than of Silicon Valley. There were, of course, others who could – and did – make Route 128 happen, but only one person was available in Silicon Valley, and that was Fred Terman. This came about in a remarkable way.

After completing his PhD Terman accepted a professorship at MIT but returned home to Stanford for a vacation before he took up his new post. It was whilst he was at home that he contracted tuberculosis, which in those days was a very serious illness. It put Terman out of action for a year, at the end of which he decided it would be better for his health if he stayed in the warmer climate of California. Consequently, he took the position of Professor of Radio Engineering at Stanford University. Apart from a spell at MIT working on a military project during the Second World War, Terman then spent his whole career at Stanford University, rising to the position of Provost and Vice-President.

Fred Terman was no ordinary man. He was a visionary leader with an entrepreneurial heart. Terman influenced people to think in a different way – he set his students thinking about having their own business, based around the technology that he was teaching them in the classroom. His student laboratory became a place where students could put their ideas into practice. When Bill Hewlett, later of Hewlett-Packard fame, was a student, he built a portable radio transmitter and receiver in this laboratory.

This 'maybe I could be an entrepreneur' attitude that Terman instilled was to permeate the thinking of Silicon Valley. Bob Noyce, who co-founded Intel, came to Silicon Valley from the East Coast in 1956 and caught this same thinking. 'Suddenly it became apparent to people like myself, who had always assumed that they would be working for a salary for the rest of their lives, that they could get some equity in a start-up company. That was a great revelation and a great motivation too' (Hanson, 1982).

Fred Terman's contribution to Silicon Valley is often measured in what he achieved, most notably in helping Hewlett-Packard to get started and then in establishing the Stanford Research Park. Whilst we discuss these achievements we believe that his greatest contribution was in getting academics and students to think differently – to think entrepreneurially. He made entrepreneurship both academically respectable and socially acceptable. In that way he started to 'dig the well' so that the entrepreneurial talent in the community could be tapped and developed.

Terman assumed that the argument between pure research and applied research was over, and that subjects like engineering had to be linked with the world of industry. He therefore concentrated on what to him was the next logical step, which was spinning-off businesses from the university and the technology that it was developing. It is important to remind ourselves that this was in the 1920s and 1930s, and that Silicon Valley was grown on this foundation. Similar experiences around MIT with Route 128 and Cambridge University in the UK with the 'Cambridge Phenomenon', demonstrate that research excellence and commercial application are friends and not enemies, and also that spin-offs from the university sector can generate an entrepreneurial culture.

We now turn to consider Fred Terman's role in Hewlett-Packard and in the Stanford Research Park. The Hewlett-Packard Company (H-P) is the classic Silicon Valley story of two young men who started their business in a garage and became millionaires.

Bill Hewlett and Dave Packard met at Stanford in 1931 and their shared interest in ham radio took them to Fred Terman's classes. Terman got to know his students well and encouraged their interest in starting their own business. The opportunity came in 1938, four years after they had graduated, when Terman arranged fellowships for them so that they could return for a further year at Stanford. It was at this time that they set up a small workshop in a garage behind their lodging house, no doubt developing various electronic gadgets. The real product opportunity came from Hewlett's end of the year project to build and evaluate a variable frequency oscillator using some of the novel ideas Terman had presented in his lectures. The result was a device that was better than others that were available commercially and which cost just one tenth of the price. Terman encouraged Hewlett to join up with Packard to exploit this opportunity and organised the finance of around $1500 to get them started. After a shaky first year, they landed a big order from Walt Disney Studios to build eight audio oscillators to produce the soundtrack for the film Fantasia. In 1940 they were able to move to larger premises and by 1942 their annual sales reached $1 million.

The Second World War helped H-P to grow steadily. By 1950 they had doubled their sales to about $2 million and employed 200 people. Whilst this does not compare with the spectacular growth of some later Silicon Valley companies, H-P was still in business and well set for the future. By the mid-1980s things had really taken off. They employed almost 70 000 people worldwide and had sales of $4.4 billion. More importantly, they were the role models for other Silicon Valley Companies. The 'H-P Way' of suits, ties and professionalism might be ridiculed by some, but their personnel policies, which provided stock options, and other employee benefits, were copied by many and is the reason why there are more millionaires per head of population in Silicon Valley than anywhere else in the world.

Fred Terman had few doubts about the talents of Hewlett and Packard. As their coach and mentor he commented:

> any place in which you put them in a new environment they somehow learned what they needed to know very quickly . . . at a really superior level. So when they got into business they didn't need a teacher; they somehow learned as they went along. They always learned faster than the problems built up.
>
> (Brown, 1973)

Hewlett-Packard was not the only company that Terman helped to get on the road, but it is by far the most well known and, obviously, was important to him and to them. In 1977 Hewlett and Packard made a donation to Stanford University of almost $10 million for the construction of the Frederick Terman Engineering Center.

Fred Terman's masterstroke, however, was the founding of the Stanford Research Park, an opportunity which owes much to the history of Stanford University itself. The University and the land that surrounds it, is the result of a bequest by the parents of Leland Stanford Jr, who died tragically of typhoid in 1884, when he was just fifteen years old. His father was a self-made man who had risen from being a grocer, selling food to the hungry miners of the Gold Rush days, to the position of Governor of California during America's Civil War. He was a man of vision who was involved in the completion of the transcontinental railway. Although motivated by the death of his son, the establishment of the Leland Stanford Jr University was also a visionary step, without which the Silicon Valley story would not even have started.

Stanford left the whole of his 8800-acre estate to the university with the stipulation that it would never be sold. In the late 1940s Fred Terman, now Vice-President, and Wallace Sterling, the President, were considering how they could move Stanford up into the university super-league to be comparable with places like MIT. It may be that Terman's time at MIT during the Second World War made him see the need for such a strategy. Within the American university system the answer was a simple one – you needed enough money to attract the best people. The only asset that Terman and Sterling could turn to was the land around the university, but this was not able to be sold, and so they did the next best thing, which was to lease the land. They decided to designate 655 acres of their land as an Industrial Park. Industrial estates were not new, but what was novel here was the use of the word Park and its proximity to a university. As Terman himself put it, 'this idea of an industrial park near a university was completely foreign'.

When it was realised that such a park could promote technology transfer and stimulate university research, the name was changed to Stanford Research Park. The first company on the Park in 1951 was Varian Associates, itself a Stanford spin-off which had Terman as a Board member. Their deal of $4000 per acre for a ninety-nine-year lease on four acres has been criticised as a 'give away', but companies in those days were not 'falling over themselves' to come on to the Park and it was important to get at least one tenant. The real breakthrough came three years later, in 1954, when Hewlett-Packard took a lease and made the Park their headquarters. Hewlett-Packard became an excellent reference site that could explain the advantages of being close to the university. By 1955 the Park had seven companies, and growth continued steadily rather than dramatically. By 1960 there were thirty-two companies and by 1970 there were seventy companies. By the mid-1980s the Park was full with ninety companies in all.

The Stanford Research Park became an important flagship for Silicon Valley and the companies it attracted played an important part in building the attitudes and level of research competence that typifies the valley. The next period in the development of Silicon Valley would almost certainly not have taken place had a division of Beckman Instruments not moved on to the Park.

The silicon chip period: 1956–1970

1956 was a good year for British-born, Dr William Shockley. He received a Nobel Prize for Physics and set up his own company, Shockley Semiconductor Laboratory, in Silicon Valley. Shockley shared the Nobel Prize with two colleagues for their invention, ten years earlier, of a small device called a transistor. A transistor is an electronic switch that uses the semi-conducting properties of certain materials such as silicon. The transistor did the same job as an electronic valve but was more than a hundred times smaller, more reliable and used much less power. This was the key invention that opened up the world of electronics to a mass of applications that today we take for granted. It has been called 'the major invention of the century'. Bill Shockley was the leader of the team at the world-renowned Bell Laboratories in New Jersey that developed this fundamental device.

His own business came about when he left Bell Labs, in 1954, to exploit his invention. His first thought was to set up in the Boston area, but the larger firms there, such as Raytheon, were not interested, and so he looked elsewhere. Palo Alto in Silicon Valley was his second choice. It was his hometown and where his mother still lived. On the business side there was also an important connection. Shockley's former chemistry professor at the California Institute of Technology, Arnold Beckman, had a division of his company on the Stanford Research Park. Beckman, who had spun-off a successful business just as Shockley planned to do, was keen to help Shockley get started and provided him with financial backing.

The Shockley Semiconductor Laboratory was set up in Mountain View, in Silicon Valley, in 1956. Shockley's reputation enabled him to attract high-quality staff, some of whom came across America from the East Coast to join him. In this first year, as they were setting the research direction of the new company, a major disagreement arose. Eight of the team wanted to work on silicon transistors and saw this as the way forward. Shockley strongly disagreed and insisted on imposing his own views, namely that they should concentrate on diodes. The eight, who Shockley was to call the 'Traitorous Eight' (Jackson, 1998), decided to ignore Shockley and do their own thing. They approached a wealthy businessman on the East Coast, Sherman Fairchild, with their ideas. He backed them to the tune of $1.5 million in setting up Fairchild Semiconductor in 1957, as a subsidiary of his Fairchild Camera and Instrument Company.

Shockley Semiconductor never recovered from this defection and was eventually closed down. Shockley took an endowed professorship at Stanford in 1964. Fairchild Semiconductor, on the other hand, went from strength to strength. In 1959, one of the 'Eight', Robert Noyce, later of Intel fame, put forward his ideas of having more than one transistor on a small piece or chip of silicon and so came up with the 'integrated circuit'. In 1960, another of the 'Eight', Jean Hoerni, invented a manufacturing process that significantly increased the efficiency of silicon chip production. This made true volume production possible and put Fairchild well ahead of the competition. With these innovations, Fairchild soon established itself as a leading semiconductor company. The timing was also right as the American space programme was getting underway, spurred on by the success of the USSR. In 1957, the Soviets succeeded in putting man's first satellite into space to orbit the earth. Spending by NASA and the American Defence Department effectively bankrolled the dramatic growth of companies like Fairchild, by funding their research and development and paying them well for the products they produced.

Whilst this gave Fairchild and the rest of Silicon Valley its financial and commercial impetus, something equally important was happening – a network of spin-off companies was developing out of Fairchild and spreading across the valley. Somehow, Fairchild just replicated its own origins as a spin-off from Shockley Semiconductor. In 1961, just four years after leaving Shockley, four of the original eight, including Hoerni, moved on to found Anelco. In 1964, Hoerni left Anelco to found Union Carbide Electronics, and moved on once more in 1967 to Intersil.

This spin-off from spin-off characterised Fairchild. By 1965, there had been ten spin-offs, and in 1967 they experienced the same kind of treatment that they had given to Shockley. Their key manufacturing specialist left to form National Semiconductor. Not only did he 'hire away busloads of his former colleagues' (Jackson, 1998) he established a serious competitor. The spin-off process still continued so that now about half of America's semiconductor firms are either direct or indirect spin-offs from Fairchild (Larson and Rogers, 1986; Saxenian, 1990). Many young engineers would get their first a job in the industry at Fairchild and then move on. Larson and Rogers (1986) report a conference of semiconductor engineers held in Silicon Valley in 1969 at which 'less than two dozen of the 400 present had never worked for Fairchild'. Amongst the many passing in and out of Fairchild were some with entrepreneurial ambitions, and the conditions were right for them to at least try. An entrepreneurial culture was beginning to take root.

Intel is perhaps the most famous spin-off from Fairchild. Intel's origins lie in the deal by which Sherman Fairchild put his money in to found the company. If the company succeeded then he had the right to buy out the eight founders, at $300 000 each. He exercised this right in 1959 when the company was just two years old. Whilst this gave the eight some real money, it took away their stake in the company and meant they were no longer in control. After a while, this began to tell, and in due course six of the original eight founders left to start their own businesses. The two remaining founders were Noyce and Moore. Noyce was promoted from General Manager to be Group Vice-President of the parent company, and a successful career within Fairchild looked to be the way ahead. Gordon Moore, a close friend of Noyce, and in charge of research and development, also stayed on. Business, however, was slowing down, and the parent company on the West Coast began to impose controls that were alien to the Silicon Valley culture. This, of course, only made matters worse. Noyce and Moore decided that the time had come for them to move on, and so they planned to set up NM Electronics, using Moore's many innovative ideas and Noyce's management skills. The name was soon changed to Integrated Electronics, abbreviated to Intel.

With their excellent track record at Fairchild Semiconductor, it was not difficult to raise the $2.5 million required. By this time, in 1968, the venture capital industry was beginning to develop. They contacted Noyce's friend, Arthur Rock, the investment banker in New York who had found Sherman Fairchild for the 'Traitorous Eight', ten years before. Since then Rock had invented the term 'venture capital' and moved to San Francisco. With his contacts and the reputation of Noyce and Moore, Rock was able to raise the $2.5 million over the telephone in just one afternoon (Jackson, 1998).

Intel's main business was planned to be in memory chips. At that time, silicon chip technology had been applied to the integrated circuit that performed the calculations in a computer but not to the storage of information in the computer's memory. Intel was not the only company trying to produce a memory chip, but its funding enabled it to make real progress. The difficulty, however, was as much in the manufacturing process as in the technology itself. Tiny circuits were etched onto silicon, and in those early days only about 10 per cent of these circuits actually worked. It was essential to have a person in charge of manufacturing who could instil disciplines and give attention to detail. One of Noyce and Moore's first recruits was Andy Grove to be Director of Operations. This proved to be an outstanding appointment, and over the years Grove was able to make Intel into the powerful company it is today. It is Grove's stamp on the company that we see today, and not that of Noyce or Moore. The *laissez-faire* of the Silicon Valley entrepreneurial business has been replaced by a tough, professional regime.

The story of Intel is about microprocessors. Apart from the manufacture of memory chips, Intel was doing contract work to produce custom chips to meet special requirements. One of these was a calculator for the Japanese company, Busicom. In 1971 this led to Ted Hoff's great idea for combining the logic and memory functions required for a simple computer on the same silicon chip. Ted Hoff had invented the microprocessor. Intel's first microprocessor chip was the 4004. It was normal to assign customers the exclusive rights on the chips designed especially for them, but Intel had designed a general-purpose chip that would do more than just run a calculator. This involved some rapid renegotiating of the contract with Busicom, so that Intel could sell the 4004 to other customers.

The industry was not ready for this new innovation, nor was Intel's marketing team. Ted Hoff and his group had to spend most of 1972 selling the idea both internally and externally. In August 1973, a new, improved and faster, version of the chip, the 8080, came out. This answered all the earlier criticism and sales just took off. This innovation made Intel what it is today, but it also spawned the personal computer industry, the third phase of Silicon Valley's growth.

The personal computer: 1971–1985

IBM had been king of the mainframe computer business in the 1950s. Their competitors were known as the seven dwarfs (Wallace and Erickson, 1993). The machines they built were huge and had rooms to themselves. Then came the semiconductors and integrated circuits that we have already described, such that it became possible to provide the same computing capability with much smaller machines. When IBM decided initially not to enter this mini computer market, it was left to new companies such as the Digital Equipment Corporation (DEC). The DEC is an East Coast company that spun out from MIT in 1957 – the same year that Fairchild Semiconductor spun out of Shockley. Spin-offs in this industry were not exclusive to Silicon Valley! The DEC latched on to this minicomputer opportunity and its PDP-8, launched in 1965, established it as the market leader. Apart from offering a machine that was much cheaper and smaller than the main frame computers, it introduced the idea of using a keyboard to input data into the machine rather than the traditional punched cards.

The minicomputer spread across the USA into schools and colleges as well as industry. In 1968, an exclusive private boy's school in Seattle raised enough money to buy time on a PDP-10 owned by General Electric. This gave a thirteen-year-old Bill Gates his first access to a computer. From that time, like so many other youngsters in the USA, Gates became a computer addict and wanted a computer of his own. When Intel put the computer's central processing unit onto a small piece of silicon in 1971, and invented the microprocessor, the dream of a small computer became a real possibility.

This opportunity was not taken up by either IBM or DEC. Instead, it was the computer hobbyists who made the running. One such enthusiast was Ed Roberts, who had a small electronics company in Albuquerque, New Mexico, called MITS. Roberts designed a small computer around Intel's new and much improved microprocessor, the 8080. He did a deal with Intel on the price of the chip and arranged for his 'personal computer' to be featured in the January 1975 issue of *Popular Electronics* at a price of $397. The response from the half a million readers of this magazine was overwhelming.

Back in Silicon Valley, the computer hobbyists responded with a similar enthusiasm. In March 1975, about thirty people turned up to the first meeting of the Homebrew Computer Club, held in the garage of one of the enthusiasts in Menlo Park, close to Palo Alto and Stanford. The Club soon had a membership of 500 and became the driver for the microcomputer industry in Silicon Valley. By the mid-1980s twenty-two computer companies had been set up by club members, Apple being the most famous.

The Homebrew Club captured all that Silicon Valley stood for. It brought together an exciting and innovative group of people who networked extensively and saw all knowledge as something to be shared. They saw nothing wrong with passing around copies of the BASIC computer language that Bill Gates had written for Roberts' personal computer. The latest microprocessor chips from Intel could be *obtained*, and when Steve Wozniak designed the Apple Computer he passed out copies of the circuit to members. It was a club without rules and without formality. As the microcomputer industry began to grow, this free exchange of information gradually died away and the club was never quite the same again.

The industry itself thrived as the entrepreneurs came forward and made things happen. Steve Jobs is the classic entrepreneur of this time. He saw himself as an outlaw, a maverick, who was going to change the world by giving everybody the possibility of owning their own computer. For him, the computer was an extension of man's intellectual capabilities. It was not just a box of electronics (Sculley, 1987). For Jobs, and the team he built around him, Apple was more of a crusade than a company. Their original mission, now largely fulfilled, was 'to change the way people use information to work, learn and play'.

Jobs, the potential entrepreneur, teamed up with Wozniak, a computer 'nerd', to build a computer of their own because they could not afford the kit computer being sold by Roberts. They built their first machine in the garage at Jobs' home for their own use. When they showed it at the Homebrew Computer Club, everybody wanted one, and they realised they had a business on their hands.

The Silicon Valley network enabled Jobs to find a market outlet, The Byte Shop, and to build a team. He linked up with Mark Markkula, a millionaire at the age of thirty-eight and former marketing manager at Intel, to finance the new venture. He also recruited Michael Scott, aged thirty-three, the manufacturing director of National Semiconductor, to be President of Apple. The Apple I was replaced by Apple II in 1977 and the company really took off. Their sales growth was the fastest that US business had ever seen. In 1977 sales were $2.5 million, in 1978 $15 million, in 1979 £70 million, in 1980 $117 million, in 1981 $335 million and in 1982 $583 million.

This success alerted IBM and the competition really began. IBM released its first competing personal computer in 1981. By 1983, the IBM PC and the Apple II were neck and neck, with sales of $1 billion each. Based on the technology that Steve Jobs had seen on a visit to Xerox PARC in 1978, the Apple Mac was launched in 1984. The Macintosh featured a mouse-driven screen graphics interface and a windows-type operating system, which allowed users to view what they were doing and to switch between applications. It was launched with a sixty-second commercial during the US Super Bowl. The commercial adopted an Orwellian scene depicting the world of IBM being shattered by a newcomer; and, although it cost Apple $1.6 million, it made a huge impact. Steve Jobs, however, had involved Bill Gates and others in the development of the software for the Macintosh (Mac). Jobs saw IBM, and not Microsoft, as its key rival. When Apple launched the Mac with a premium price – which it subsequently maintained – it adopted a misjudged niche strategy and provided Gates with the mass-market opportunity he would exploit with his Windows software. In 1985, Apple revenues reached $2 billion, but in that year sales began to slide, partially because the Mac's limited memory was restricting sales growth. This resulted in the departure of Steve Jobs, the entrepreneur and co-founder. In due course, the Apple Mac was to fulfil all the hopes that Jobs had for it, and Apple sales reached $2.7 billion and gave the company a stock valuation of $7.7 billion. Apple was able to link up with Adobe to pioneer desktop publishing – Adobe had the software that would put out on a laser printer, whatever appeared on a screen. To this day, the Apple Mac remains the standard equipment for designers. For many subsequent years the Apple story is one of steady erosion of market share to the IBM PC and its clones. A decade without entrepreneurial leadership almost killed the company, and in 1997 Steve Jobs returned.[1] Almost immediately, exciting new products like the iMac began to appear.

Apple was important to Silicon Valley because it represented a new kind of exciting entrepreneurial business which others copied. It was what we have earlier called a 'third wave' company. It also spawned a whole host of businesses and new sectors such as desktop publishing that fed off Apple's success.

The first real growth in the computer industry in Silicon Valley took place between 1970 and 1980. The number employed in the industry rose from about 9000 to almost 53 000, making the computer industry the biggest employer in Silicon Valley. The semiconductor industry was second with 34 500 employees. Total high-technology employment stood at almost 180 000 in 1980.

Two other industries made important contributions to the Silicon Valley scene in this period: the video games industry, which led the microcomputer industry by about five years, and the computer software industry, that lagged it by about five years. The games industry was able to take the lead because it used the TV set and did not have to wait for the low-cost computer. Nolan Bushnell started Atari in 1972 and gave the general public its first video game, Pong – an addictive electronic table tennis game. Atari experienced instantaneous growth, shipping 200 000 home versions of Pong in its first year. By 1974 the Pong craze was over and Atari was in trouble. In 1976 the entertainment group Warner Communications (now AOL Time Warner) bought Atari, and Bushnell collected $15 million. Prior to starting Apple, Steve Jobs worked for Nolan Bushnell at Atari – whilst his partner, Steve Wozniak, was employed by Hewlett-Packard. Atari's notorious wild style, coupled with its rapid success, gave a 'California Gold Rush feel' to Silicon Valley, and this was captured by the Homebrew Club and by companies like Apple. More recently, the Gold Rush comparison has been applied to the time in early 1990s when the Internet arrived on the scene – but in truth it has never really left the Valley since it began in the early 1970s. The culture of fun and irreverence has been fundamental in driving the creativity and innovation that remains at the heart of the story and the experience.

The computer software industry developed from zero in 1970 to employing 4000 people in 1975. Thereafter, it doubled every five years to reach over 15 000 in 1985. Larry Ellison founded Oracle in 1977 to develop relational database software. Ten years later, sales reached $131 million, relatively modest by Silicon Valley standards, but since then Oracle has achieved a leading position in the market. In the next ten years, sales tripled to over $400 billion. With a personal stock-holding in Oracle worth some $6 billion, Ellison became the world's third richest software tycoon after Bill Gates and Paul Allen of Microsoft. A committed sailor, he spent millions of dollars of his personal fortune in 2002–2003 on an unsuccessful attempt to recapture the America's Cup for the United States.

The Internet period: 1986–the present day

The beginning of this period coincided with a major shift in the fortunes of companies like Apple and Intel. Here people were being laid off and sales were falling. This sent shock waves through the valley, with many thinking that the bubble must have finally burst. In addition, there were some notable changes to the culture and physical appearance of the valley. Ties and suits began to appear at places like Apple when executives with MBAs became omnipresent, and venture capitalists began to control more and more decisions and events. A transition from the dominant entrepreneur to the professional manager was taking place.

At Intel, Andrew Grove became Chief Executive and took the company from a loss-making position in 1986, a year when 7200 workers were laid off, to a position of complete dominance of the microprocessor industry, with an 80 per cent market share, ten years later. Grove is an outstandingly successful entrepreneurial leader in our earlier classification. Apple were less successful in achieving their move to professionalism and struggled throughout this period. They finally reached a performance rock bottom in 1996, though even at that time their sales was still around $8 billion. Their recent revival under a returned, and more mature, Steve Jobs has brought the entrepreneurial spirit back to Apple, and it now has exciting new competitive products.

Companies like Sun Microsystems (started in 1982) and Oracle Corporation have been the Silicon Valley success stories of this period and they are now established world leaders in their fields. They are among the largest companies in the valley.

Whilst it would have been easy to conclude, on the evidence of the late 1980s and early 1990s, that the Silicon valley phenomenon had run its course, and that it had now entered the ranks of the professional establishment, this was not the case – for two main reasons. First, the valley continues to attract young talent from all over the world, thus sustaining the entrepreneurial dynamic. For them it is still an exciting place to be; it is where the technology is leading edge and fortunes can be made. Linus Torvalds, the inventor of the Linux operating system, as mentioned earlier, left his native Finland and moved to Silicon Valley because it was a 'high tech Mecca' and because of the distinctive culture. 'Here, if you are successful, people tend to respect you. In Europe, if you're successful, people tend to envy you. Here it's easier to be rich and successful and that motivates people' (*San Jose Mercury News*, 1999).

The second reason why Silicon Valley has retained its entrepreneurial dynamic is the emergence of the Internet. The Internet was to provide a new, exciting opportunity where visionary entrepreneurs would create and drive a new future. Its development needed – and found – both the backing and the will to succeed. It was actually in October 1969 that a computer at the University of California at Los Angeles was first linked up by telephone line with a computer in Menlo Park in Silicon Valley. Though this experiment proved it could be done, it was not until 1986 that things began to move. This was when the US National Science Foundation set up the NSF net, which allowed universities to access the computing resources of super-computers in five selected universities. By 1988, there were 60 000 host computers on the Internet. With the emergence of the World Wide Web in the early 1990s, a development proposed in 1989 by Tim Berners-Lee in Switzerland, the Internet moved into the public domain.

The Internet we know today, however, needed other parallel developments, many of which have their roots in Silicon Valley. Users need web browsers, or programs that enable PC owners to view and access data on the Web. The main pioneer of web browser software was Netscape, with Navigator, but its success attracted competition from Microsoft. Bill Gates linked his browser – Explorer – to Windows, and provided it as a free extra. The third pillar was provided by Java, a programming language that enables web pages to contain imaginative programs and materials which appear as animation, sound, scrolling text and interactive features. The inventor of Java, James Gosling, was provided with development funds and working space by Sun Microsystems. The final pillar comprises access gateways or portals.

As an exciting new technology, the Internet was of huge interest to the programmers and entrepreneurs of Silicon Valley, and many new companies were spawned, each seeking to predict and influence the direction in which the Internet would move. One of these was 3Com Corporation, the networking company which was helped enormously by the success of its Palm Pilot pocket computer, a business it acquired when it bought the modem company, US Robotics, in 1997. Interestingly, in 2004, 3 Com left Silicon Valley to relocate on the East Coast. Ahead of 3Com was Cisco Systems. The driving force behind Cisco is John Chambers, who joined the company in 1991, and who presided over a stock growth of 2356 per cent in just five years. Chambers saw the opportunity for building a portfolio of Internet-related companies. By 1999 he had acquired forty young innovative companies, many of which were located in the Silicon Valley. His most costly purchase in this period was a two-year-old start-up, Cerent Corporation, with sales of a mere $10 million and for which he paid $6.9 billion in August 1999.

Yahoo!, probably the best-known provider of Internet portals, is also a resident of Santa Clara in the Valley. Unlike the focused Google, Yahoo! is diversified and provides shopping and e-mail facilities alongside games, financial information and news, and, of course, its vitally important search facilities. Search engines enable users to track down information and sites on specific topics. Yahoo! is 'about helping people find what they want and where they want to go'. Like Amazon.com (Chapter 6), Yahoo! is a brand, which can be applied successfully to several related services. It began when two Stanford PhD students produced a directory of their favourite websites in their spare time. They did not set out to build a business.

Founders Jerry Yang (born in Taiwan and an immigrant at the age of ten with his widowed mother) and David Filo were both technocrats. Reflecting the pace of growth for the Internet in the 1990s, Yahoo! had eleven employees in 1995 and 1600 in 1999 – at which time it was valued at $44 billion. The company is run by a team of three entrepreneurs – the two founders and Jeff Mallett, an MBA graduate they recruited from Novell. Recognising their own strengths and limitations, Yang and Filo were always keen to recruit the professional senior managers they knew they needed. The three work in neighbouring cubicles and get together about three times a week to discuss strategy – their acknowledged challenge lies in:

> finding a structure that allows Yahoo! to operate with the speed and flexibility of the myriad of start-ups that challenge it and every one of its main activities. The culture [of Silicon Valley] has become unforgiving. If people are not comfortable with having their ideas and practices constantly tested, they will not fit in.
>
> (Mallett)

A second challenge lies in finding more creative and innovative ways of helping meet users' information and communication needs, and linking this with new technologies. Reinforcing the significance of this last point, Oracle was one Valley organisation which sought to play a lead role when stronger links were forged between mobile telephones and the Internet. Larry Ellison identified that there were 300 million people worldwide who owned mobile phones but only 120 million owners of Internet-connected computers. In 1999, Oracle launched software which enabled web pages to be translated into a format which allows them to be displayed on the screens of mobile phones and hand-held computers. Valley resident 3Com, manufacturer of Palm pocket-size computers, formed an alliance with Nokia, the Finnish manufacturer of mobile phones to compete with the rival alliance of Microsoft and Ericsson to develop products for this growth sector of the Internet market.

Silicon Valley, then, attracts both talented young people and experienced professionals such as Cisco's Chambers, now in his mid-50s and with experience at IBM and Wang. This is a powerful combination and one of the secrets of the valley's continued success. Its mature and extensive venture capital system is another of its secrets. There are no small business attitudes in Silicon Valley. As Don Valentine, one of the valley's most successful venture capitalists, told us some years ago 'I only back a start-up if I am convinced it can become a billion-dollar business. I then put together the financial resources to make that possible'.

And what of the organisation we credit as the foundation stone – Hewlett-Packard? The company has become a computer and printer business with 40 per cent of the world market for computer printers, which are its main profit contributors. The current Chairman and CEO is Carly Fiorina and, in 2002, she decided H-P should seek to acquire Compaq to strengthen its position as a computer manufacturer. Her main opponent was Walter Hewlett, son of Bill, and a Board member but not an executive of the company. He wanted H-P to become more focused on printers. In the end, and after widespread media coverage and litigation, Fiorina won the day and the acquisition went through. Michael Capellas, a senior H-P executive was tipped to run the Compaq business within H-P, but he left to become CEO of WorldCom. Things never stand still in Silicon Valley.

Silicon Valley – the future

During the 1990s venture capital helped to spawn a constant stream of new dot.com businesses, although far more 'bright ideas' were turned down than were supported. But, as we saw with Amazon, there was considerable investment and revenue generation but very little profit. This is hardly a viable business model and hence it seemed inevitable that the bubble would eventually burst. And it did – at the end of 2000, linked to an economic recession. During 2001 and 2002, over 100 000 jobs were lost and the unemployment rate in Silicon Valley grew quickly to 7.5 per cent. There was no longer any shortage of free office space. The data given in Table 14.1 emphasises the speed of growth and the equally rapid decline. In 2002 IPOs virtually disappeared and the venture capitalists lost money for the first time.

We are left to contemplate whether the severity of such a downturn must have caused 'irreparable damage to the ecosystem that nurtured the innovation and entrepreneurship of the 1980s and 1990s' – or whether the entrepreneurs will re-emerge and bounce back once the economy properly strengthens again. For the moment, cost cutting and productivity improvement have become the focal point; expectations are lower. Optimists will argue that the whole history of Silicon Valley has been a series of waves. Each one surges and then falls away, to be replaced by another, typically one more powerful than its predecessors. The optimists have an underlying belief in renewal, but concede that 'instant fortunes' might be harder in the future. But people will never stop coming forward with imaginative new business ideas – often for niches they argue are exempt from the downturn and are about to exhibit explosive growth! Larry Ellison of Oracle, however, takes a different view. He contends 'Silicon Valley will never be the same again . . . those who believe this is merely a cyclical downturn are mad'. To Ellison, Silicon Valley is synonymous with IT, and IT is in maturity. If Ellison is proved correct, our earlier analogy of the Gold Rush might prove prescient.

Whatever the future might hold, for more than fifty years Silicon Valley has shown the world that there is such a thing as a *collective entrepreneur* and that it can be sustained. The future challenge for its entrepreneurs and venture capitalists is to maintain a leading role as the Internet leads on to more and more opportunities – and gives

Table 14.1   *Silicon Valley venture capital funding, 1995–2002*

Year	Venture capital invested in Silicon Valley ($bn)
1995	2
1996	4
1997	5
1998	7
1999	18
2000	36
2001	13
2002 (estimate)	7

Source: Thomson Financial/Venture Economics.

way to the next, discontinuous wave of developments, for which they will need to be ready. Their spirit and optimism will be critical.

Yet, for all its economic success and entrepreneurial spirit, Silicon Valley is fundamentally an urban sprawl. Silicon Valley is not one, single-organised and obvious business park in an obvious location. Instead, there are office parks with car parking everywhere, and many of the spawning businesses seem anonymous – simply people seem to know who they need to know, and where they can be found. The activity and the 'buzz' is there, but it is partially hidden. The area is clogged by traffic, and house prices have been hugely inflated. Even the richest entrepreneurs often work in cubicles. They may enjoy large houses, Porshe's and Ferrari's – and stickers which claim 'My other car is a plane' – but money is not their only driver. If it was, the multi-millionaires would not keep working, perpetually searching for the excitement of the next big opportunity.

The valley itself has really become the opportunity – to become a millionaire and to achieve something unusual and different. People have realised that equity and ownership, rather than salaried employment, hold the key to personal wealth. The valley attracts (and sometimes, but not always, rewards) young people who are willing to take risks with their lives, or who are in search of unusual lives. 'They have given up lives elsewhere to come. They come for the tremendous opportunity, believing that in no other place in the world can one person accomplish so much with talent, initiative and a good idea' (Bronson, 1999). They see the other people that have made it and conclude 'they are nothing special'. They believe that they too can do it!

For many, however, whilst Silicon Valley is a magnet and a good, creative place to work, it is not automatically a nice place. It could also be described as a multitude of cramped cubicles where people spend hours staring at screens and trying to come up with something which has never before existed. Dedication, creativity, uncertainty and the risk of failure are the essences of the lifestyle. Companies that do succeed often grow very rapidly – and then key people leave to spin-off a new venture. There is little employee loyalty – compounded by some very entrepreneurial head-hunters whose tactics for luring people away from their existing employers are ethically questionable. Many people work for performance-related pay – linked to sales they can generate or venture capital they can raise – and with a very low basic salary, but jobs are still hard to find and easy to fill. We might ask why.

Although Silicon Valley has spawned business upon business, and millionaire entrepreneur upon millionaire entrepreneur (sixty-four every day at its height), Yahoo's Jeff Mallett believes 'people do not come here for the best salary. They come here for no bureaucracy, to get their ideas heard by good people and to create something'. Clearly, the very success of the Valley, intertwined with its unique culture and promise, will in the short term, at the very least, continue to be a magnet for the best people hoping to sustain the virtuous circle of growth.

Note

1. The contribution to Apple of Steve Jobs, his departure and return, was discussed earlier, in Chapter 5.

References

Bronson, P. (1999). *The Nudist on the Late Shift – and Other Tales of Silicon Valley*. Secker and Warburg.

Brown, G. (1973). Interview with Fred Terman, Hewlett-Packard Archives. (Reference in Larson, J.K. and Rogers, E.M. (1986). *Silicon Valley Fever*. Unwin Counterpoint.)

Castells, M. and Hall, P. (1994). *Technopoles of the World*. Routledge.

Hanson, D. (1982). *The New Alchemists: Silicon Valley and the Microelectronics Revolution*. Little, Brown.

Jackson, T. (1998). *Inside Intel*. HarperCollins.

Larson, J.K. and Rogers, E.M. (1986). *Silicon Valley Fever*. Unwin Counterpoint.

Malecki, E.J. (1997). *Technology and Economic Development*. 2nd edn. Longman.

Rose, F. (1989). *West of Eden*. Business Books.

San Jose Mercury News (1999). Linus the Liberator. Special Report: Linus Torvalds, September, www.mercurycenter.com.

Saxenian, A.L. (1990). Regional networks and the resurgence of Silicon Valley. *California Management Review*, **33**, 89–112.

Sculley, J. (1987). *Odyssey: Pepsi to Apple*. Collins.

Torvalds, L. and Diamond, D. (2001). *Just For Fun*. Texture.

Wallace, J. and Erickson, J. (1993). *Hard Drive*. John Wiley.

15 Techniques for the entrepreneur

Techniques need to be applied in the right way. Techniques that are proven and linked with a recognised body of knowledge can make most people reasonably competent in the field to which they relate. But they are not sufficient to achieve excellence. Talent and temperament must be added into the equation. When talent and technique clash then talent should be the winner. Without that condition innovation and new ideas will be stifled. We therefore present this brief discussion of technique with that proviso. For entrepreneurs nothing is set in stone and they must remain free to do things their way – they probably will anyway!

Understanding the business

Business textbooks present a series of models that purport to describe the early years of a business. These are helpful in general terms but their greater value is in understanding why, how and where many companies deviate from a so-called normality. Here we discuss three common models and one that is perhaps less well known. Their links to the business adoption model (Figures 13.1 and 13.2) will be readily appreciated.

The business or product life cycle

Revenue and profit increase in the early years of the business, as shown in Figure 15.1, and then level off as things stabilise. After a period of maturity the business or product declines and dies.

For some businesses the start-up phase can last a very long time. Using our earlier terminology, businesses can get stuck at the Embryo Stage. Most of the reasons for this are linked with shortcomings of the market, the product or the people involved so that undue delay here is an important warning sign. But there can be cases when this delay is legitimate. Oxford Instruments mentioned in connection with niche markets

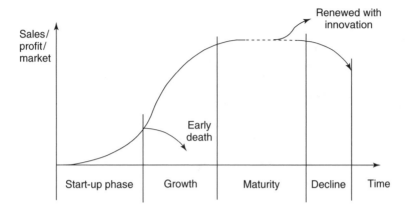

Figure 15.1 *The life-cycle curve*

in Chapter 11 is a case in point. It ran along the time axis of Figure 15.1 for ten years, until the arrival of the NMR body-scanner opened a market for its product. From then on, it moved up the life-cycle curve and is now a major international company.

Movement up the curve cannot be guaranteed and many fall to an early death, as indicated. The mature period can be short or long. Most often, it is assumed that the life expectancy of a product is short, and certainly in technology a two-year life cycle is all there may be. But some products do seem to go on forever, renewed with innovation. When the computer came on the scene, the demise of paper was widely predicted but this has not happened. If anything, computers have increased the demand for paper, rather than reducing it.

Although the precise time of movement along the life cycle track can rarely be forecast, this technique is useful for understanding the stage a product or business has reached. One final comment about the life-cycle curve is that it is rarely smooth. Instead, it can be a seesaw of ups and downs, as the business goes from crisis to crisis, with an average line that hopefully follows the curve upwards. Jolly (1997) reports seeing a 'Business Enthusiasm Curve' framed on a wall at the offices of Raychem in Silicon Valley. It was a version of the life-cycle curve ranging from 'despair' to 'ecstasy' along a time axis that zigzagged its way upwards.

Cash flow models

There are two important cash flow models. The 'break-even model' and the 'cash demand model'. Before either model can be used in a meaningful way it is important that organisations understand their costs in relation to prices and revenues. Table 15.1 gives a breakdown of the bill for around £100 in an up-market restaurant and shows where costs are incurred. Those in normal type are directly related to the individual meal – and, given good stock control, should only be incurred if meals are cooked and sold. Those in italics are overheads which the restaurant will incur regardless of the number of meals it sells.

Table 15.1 *Breakdown of restaurant costs*

Total paid by customer	**£108**
10% gratuity	10
Actual bill before gratuity	**98**
VAT included in bill	15
Cost of food and drinks consumed	25
Casual staff	7
Electricity and gas in restaurant	1
Credit card commission	2
Gross profit	**48**
Permanent staff	20
Rent, rates, insurance	8
Repairs and maintenance	4
Electricity and gas in kitchen	1
Advertising and marketing	1
Other running expenses – laundry, uniforms	6
Professional fees	1
Net profit for restaurant owner	**7**
(before interest and tax)	

The break-even model Both cash flow models in this section have the idea that there is a 'break-even' point in the sales level where the costs and the income match. Before this point, there is a loss situation, and after it a profit. Figure 15.2 depicts the break-even model.

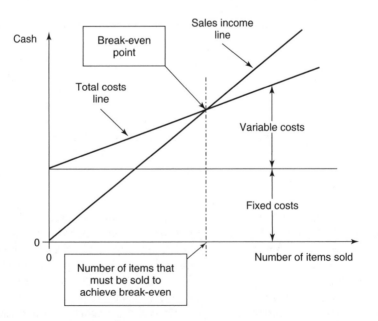

Figure 15.2 *The break-even model*

The 'fixed costs' are costs incurred whether or not anything is sold and are represented by a horizontal line in Figure 15.2. They cover the costs of the premises, the administrative staff, telephones, electricity, cars and so on. Next, there is the cost of making the products, termed the 'variable costs' that increase with the number of units made. Assuming the cost of each unit to be the same, then the 'variable costs' can be represented by a diagonal straight line as shown.

Income is the sales or turnover level. This increases as more items or units are sold. Again, assuming that each item is sold for the same amount, then this is also a diagonal straight line but starting from the origin. Break-even is achieved when the sales income equals the total costs made up of the fixed and variable costs. The number of items that have to be sold in order to break-even can be read from the graph.

This model helps to show that fixed costs or overheads have to be paid for, and that if sales are insufficient then there will be a loss. It helps to assess break-even quantities. For example, a simple calculation might show that thousands of items need to be sold every month to achieve break-even when a market analysis has indicated that the market is only likely to require hundreds a month. In this case, the business would not be viable. It can also help in assessing the potential to link some costs more closely with sales so that apparently 'fixed costs' become 'variable'.

The model is difficult to apply if there is more than one product or if the business offers a service where fixed and variable costs are hard to determine or distinguish. It is best to make a few assumptions and keep things as simple as possible. With a little juggling between the price and the fixed and variable costs it is possible to see whether or not the proposed business could be made profitable.

The cash demand model The cash demand model is shown in Figure 15.3. The vertical axis can be the actual cash or the accumulated cash – here it is the latter. The cash demand is measured over time. The curve starts off in the 'Valley of Death' in a

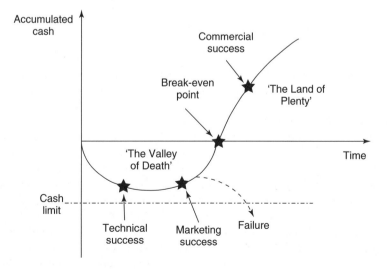

Figure 15.3 *The cash demand curve*

loss situation and moves into profit in the 'Land of Plenty'. The cross-over or break-even point is when total income to date equals total expenditure to date.

Success can be achieved in the 'Valley of Death'. 'Technical success' is reached when development costs have stopped and the product is ready for sale. In practice, these costs are often difficult to control and it can be useful to set a limit on this expenditure, as indicated in Figure 15.3. The next point is 'marketing success' when the 'innovators' buy the product and the feedback from them suggests that the 'early adopters' will not be far behind. After break-even, 'commercial success' is achieved in the 'Land of Plenty'. Profit is being generated and the market is increasing steadily.

This model is a useful control device though, in practice, the 'Valley of Death' can continue for some time with technical success, but few sales, so that income generation is low and the business never comes out of the valley and may even die there.

The soft–hard model   This is a model that conserves cash for the start-up company and enables it 'to pull itself up by its own bootstraps' (Figure 15.4). The

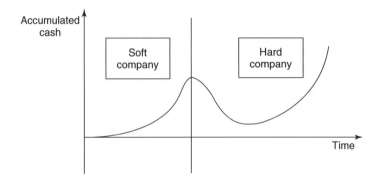

Figure 15.4   *The soft–hard model*

company starts 'soft' offering a consultancy service with low overheads. The margins are high for this kind of business so that it should be possible to put money in the bank and build up cash reserves. When it has done this for two or three years the company should be in a position to fund the development of its own products and make the transition into a 'hard' product-based business. This company then follows the cash demand curve of Figure 15.3 but the cash accumulated in the 'soft' years should enable it to pay its own way through the 'Valley of Death'.

This model was developed by Matthew Bullock, when at Barclays Bank, based on his experience with high-technology companies in Cambridge, England and a study tour of US high-technology businesses. Whilst we accept that this model describes what does happen with some start-ups, it does so because they have no other option. Were the funding available from the banks and venture capital sector in the first place, then there would be no need to waste time in consultancy when the window of opportunity may be missed. The model also presents a major personnel problem because the staff that are needed to run a successful consultancy are not the ones required for a successful product-based company. We know of companies that have successfully followed this strategy but we also know of one company that failed because it was not able to make the transition from a 'soft' contract research company to a 'hard' product-based manufacturing company.

Evaluating the opportunity

When we think of opportunity evaluation it is useful to separate the evaluation of the business proposal to exploit the opportunity from the commercial evaluation of the opportunity itself. Thus, the quality of the entrepreneur or entrepreneur team is considered when assessing the overall business proposal and the quality of the opportunity when assessing commercial viability.

Evaluating the business proposal

The measuring POLE that we introduced in Chapter 3 provides an ideal starting point. To recap, the initials relate to the following criteria:

- P = Person
- O = Opportunity
- L = Leadership and championing the opportunity
- E = Exploitation of the opportunity, resourcing it and controlling the deployment of the resources.

Drucker (1985) provided an alternative five-question evaluation test:

1 Is there a clear focus on customers?
2 Does the proposal generate a cash flow – and is there a plan for future capital needs?
3 Is the management team needed for the future in place?
4 Does the entrepreneur understand his/her role and contribution?
5 If the venture is inside an existing organisation, is it properly isolated and ring-fenced?

Evaluating the commercial opportunity

Figure 15.5 presents a very simple assessment model, based on the extent to which a market need can be demonstrated, and the ability and potential of the business and its product or service to satisfy that need and thus generate profits. However, an enterprise opportunity can be evaluated at a number of levels. Entrepreneurs who are carried along by their enthusiasm tend to do a very superficial evaluation. Others, prompted usually by their bank manager or business adviser, embark on a detailed and complex business plan and assume that when it has been completed they will have evaluated the opportunity. The truth lies between the two and here we present a short but effective way of evaluating an opportunity in greater detail. The evaluation makes the

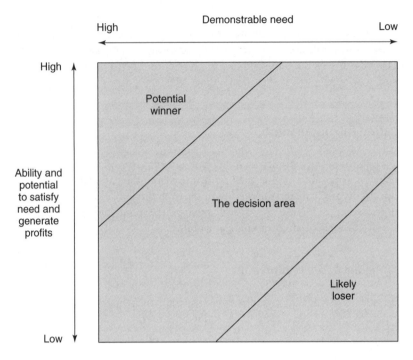

Figure 15.5   *Evaluating the opportunity*

assumption that the business is up and running, on the grounds that there is little point in working out a start-up strategy if the business is not going to be viable anyway.

For this evaluation, the entrepreneur needs three numbers with £ signs in front of them. The first is the *money in*, the second is the *money out* and the third is the *margin*. Simple subtraction of the first two will give the margin. This indicates whether or not the business will be commercially viable.

Money in   To arrive at this number the entrepreneur needs information about the market and price levels. The key questions that need to be answered are:

For the market

- How big is the market that can be reasonably reached and serviced?
- What are the main market characteristics? Are there niches, and if so, what size are they?
- What competitors are out there and how is the market shared out between them?
- What percentage of the market can be captured within a year? Anything more than 5 per cent is probably unrealistic.

The aim is to focus down on to a target market of a known size and to arrive at a realistic figure of the number of items that can be sold annually.

Pricing

- What price can be charged for each item sold?

- Will the product be sold by a third party? If so, it is reasonable to assume that the producer's price will be halved each time the product changes hands? Thus, an item selling to the end-user for £10 will be bought by the retailer for £5 from a warehouse that will pay the producer £2.50.

Unless the product or service is completely new, there will be information about the existing price structure operating in the marketplace. New products may be able to set their own prices but competition will soon arrive if the opportunity is that good. In general, the market decides the price, not the producer.

The 'money in' is the multiple of the number of items that can be sold and the price of each item. Depending on the nature of the business, this calculation can be done for a three-month period or a full year. If sales are likely to be seasonal then it should be done for the four-quarters to cover a full year.

It is possible to do these calculations on a worst, average and best case basis but that can come later. The point now is to see if the opportunity will 'stand up' commercially.

Money out   Money goes out of the business in two ways. As discussed, when we were considering the break-even graph in Figure 15.2, there are the 'fixed' costs' and the 'variable costs'. In this quick evaluation, it is sufficient to concentrate on the 'variable costs' to start with rather than spend a long time working out details of the 'fixed costs' and their allocation.

The 'variable costs' are all the costs associated with an order. Normally, this has two elements: a people cost and a material cost. The people costs are the costs of those people directly associated with the product or service. In a factory it would be the machine operatives but not the quality department. The people cost per item comes from the multiple of the total time spent making the item and the hourly rate cost (including social charges) of the people making it. The material cost per item is the cost of all materials used for that item.

The 'variable money out' is the multiple of the cost per item by the number of items to be manufactured in a given period. At this stage, it is sufficient to assume that the number manufactured is equal to the number sold, so that the item quantities from the 'money in' calculations can be used. Making for stock is a later consideration and only relevant if this assessment shows viability.

Sometimes, this 'variable money out' is termed the 'Cost of Goods Sold' or CoGS.

Gross margin   Accountants have a number of margins by which they measure a business. Here we are concerned with the 'gross margin' which is the difference between the 'money in' and the 'variable money out'. It is normally expressed as a percentage of the 'money in'.

A viable 'gross margin' depends upon the industry or market sector so that retailing is quite different from manufacturing and many new Internet businesses seem happy to operate on a negative 'gross margin'. The 'gross margins' given in Table 15.2 are for product-based businesses with some degree of manufacturing or assembly but the principle applies to all sectors. Tighter margins need better entrepreneurs and sharper businesses.

Technology-based businesses often have gross margins of 70 per cent and 80 per cent in their early years but as competition arrives prices come under pressure and

Table 15.2 *Gross margin*

Gross margin (%)	Comment
70	Anybody can run this business
50	Moderate competence required
30	Good entrepreneur required
10	Don't even try

margins are reduced. Hopefully, the entrepreneur will have learnt the techniques of running an efficient business during the 70 per cent gross margin days so that he or she can still run a profitable business when the margin falls to 50 per cent. In practice, early success with high margins can often make entrepreneurs think that running a business is easy and their ego stops them from learning as much as they should. This is one reason for the 'Founder's Disease', mentioned in Chapter 11, whereby the founder has to be replaced after a couple of years when losses begin to appear. Entrepreneurs need to see these early days as good learning opportunities.

Profit margin   This 'money in', 'money out' and 'margin' evaluation can be taken to the next level of detail by including the 'fixed costs' in the 'money out' calculation. The difference between the 'money in' and the 'total money out' (i.e. fixed costs plus variable costs) is the 'profit margin', which like the 'gross margin' is expressed as a percentage of the 'money in'. Unless the 'profit margin' comes out at around 10 per cent, the opportunity is rarely worth pursuing. Another way to approach this evaluation is to set the 'profit margin' at, say, 10 per cent and deduct this from the 'gross margin' figure calculated. The difference will be the percentage of the 'money in' that is available to cover the fixed overheads.

These overheads can be broken down into a number of areas, depending on the type of business. The running costs of the business are generally in two or three parts, normally related to the fixed costs attributable to production, administration and sales. When these are added together they must be less than the money available to cover the fixed overheads, otherwise the business will not be viable. Hopefully, some cash will be left over to fund the 'fixed costs' of research and development or an advertising campaign. If there is still money left after these extra costs, then there is probably a viable business.

Evaluation and critique   The difficulty with all financial evaluations for the start-up company is that the numbers are forecasts and estimations. The 'profit margin' is arrived at by the difference of two large numbers. If the 'money in' figure is wrong by −5 per cent and the 'money out' figure is wrong by +5 per cent then the 'profit margin' will be nearer zero rather than the 10 per cent hoped for. This is why entrepreneurs need to keep a close eye on the finances of the business, even if there is a financial specialist to do all the calculations.

Assessing the growth potential

There are four key constituents to growth:

- The strategy – the quality and potential of the business model and whether it sets the organisation apart competitively in some meaningful way.
- The structure – the quality of the entrepreneur team and their ability to work together effectively.
- Operations – the ability to deliver reliably and efficiently as the size and scale of the operation increases – this might involve licensing or franchising.
- Finance and performance – both the availability of capital and the ability to maintain a positive cash flow.

With this in mind, Hashemi and Hashemi (2002) suggest that entrepreneurs thinking seriously about growth should ask themselves four important questions:

1 Am I ready?
   Am I ready to build a team and delegate some of, and possibly a great deal of, responsibility?
2 Is the business ready?
   Are the necessary controls and systems in place?
3 Is the market ready?
   Has the business established a clear and distinct presence in the market? Are there enough customers to warrant further investment and expansion?
4 Is the business ready financially?
   Is there internal cash generation? Is additional investment capital required in the business, and if so, what are the implications?

Catlin and Matthews (2001) provide a similar set of criteria that entrepreneurs need to think about and evaluate seriously before they make a decision that commits them to further investment and growth:

- Themselves, their talent and temperament.
- Their potential to be a growth entrepreneur or leader entrepreneur.
- The way in which their role (and possibly lifestyle) would change.
- Their business and the way in which it is organised.
- Their customers.
- The business environment in which they compete.
- Their people – and not just the senior team, and what changes and developments would be required.
- Their hopes and desires for the future.

As the business moves from stage to stage in the growth process these questions need revisiting and re-assessing. The implications are different as the fundamental issues change. Early in its development, the key issue concerns the development of the product or service, but once sales begin to grow this will very quickly lead on to issues which relate to building an organisation. Future issues focus on dealing with the change agenda, when both strategic and structural/managerial change decisions have to be faced.

Growth directions and means

As organisations grow, there are two strategic issues to deal with. The first is the direction and the second is the means. A detailed treatment of this subject goes beyond the scope of this book and readers are referred to Thompson (2001) for more information. However, the following frameworks provide a brief insight into the issues.

Directions for growth The planning gap should be seen as the starting point for a consideration of growth options (Figure 15.6). Drawing a planning gap is conceptually very simple, but quantifying it is more difficult. There are two axes for the

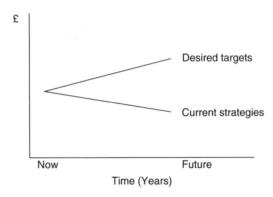

Figure 15.6 *The planning gap*

chart – the vertical axis is revenues or profits and the horizontal axis is time. The finished chart will represent a V on its side – however the lower line does not have to slope downwards; indeed it could show positive growth. The lower line indicates expected sales or profits if the organisation continues with present corporate, competitive and functional strategies; the top line represents desirable targets, which imply growth and which may or may not ultimately be realised. The difference between these two lines is the gap. Quite simply, the gap is the difference between the results which the organisation can expect to achieve from present strategies continued forward and the results that the entrepreneur or strategic leader would ideally like to attain.

Figure 15.7, developed from Ansoff (1987), provides four broad possibilities for filling the gap. The level of potential return and the level of risk is not the same for each alternative, and therefore the willingness to accept the implied risk will always be an element in the final decision about how much of the gap it makes sense to try and fill.

The least risk alternative is to seek to manage present products and services more effectively, aiming to sell more of them and to reduce their costs in order to generate increased sales and profits. This is termed market penetration in our simple growth vector. It can be extended to strategies of market and product development which imply, respectively, either new customers or even new market segments for existing products – which might be modified in some way to provide increased differentiation – and new products, ideally using related technology and skills, for sale to

	Existing products/ services	New products/ services
Existing customers/ markets	*Market penetration*	*Product development*
New customers/ markets	*Market development*	*Diversification*

Figure 15.7 *A simple growth vector*

existing markets. In this context, 'new' implies new to the firm rather than something which is necessarily completely new and innovative, although it could well be this.

The highest risk alternative is diversification because this involves both new products and new markets. Diversification might be broken down further into three distinct degrees of change:

- Replacement products and product line extensions which are based on existing technologies and skills and which represent improved products for existing customers.
- New products, based on new or unrelated technologies and skills, which constitute concentric diversification (these may be sold to either existing or new customers).
- Completely new and unrelated products for sale to new customers. This is known as conglomerate diversification and is regarded as a high-risk strategic alternative.

Thinking about the extent of the initial gap between present strategies and ideal objectives enables the entrepreneur to consider how much change and how much risk would be involved in closing the gap and achieving the target objectives. Some of the strategies considered might be neither feasible nor desirable, and consequently the gap might be too wide to close. Similarly, the degree of risk, especially if a number of changes are involved, might be greater than the entrepreneur is willing to accept. In these cases, it will be necessary to revise the desired objectives downwards so that they finally represent realistic targets which should be achieved by strategic changes that are acceptable and possible.

Ways of growing Without going into the specific advantages and disadvantages of each one, the following strategic means can all be utilised to deliver growth:

- Organic (internal) growth through investing in new resources.
- Acquisition, merger or take-over of (or with) another business.
- A strategic alliance with another organisation – if a separate business is set up, jointly funded by the two partners in alliance, this would generally be called a joint venture.

- Licensing – granting rights to other organisations to use intellectual property owned by the organisation.
- Franchising.

The scope can be national or international, depending again upon the potential and the acceptable level of risk.

The business plan

The business plan, rather like the CV, has been professionalised and to some extent sanitised. Most banks provide information guides and CDs about business plans, and there are many books that guide the reader through the process. Bankers and investors expect a certain standard of business plan and without it the start-up company is unlikely to get a hearing. The business plan is basically a selling document to obtain financial backing. It must be realistic and not over-confident. It should adopt the language of its audience. There is no point in a lengthy description of the product which is full of jargon but there will need to be plenty of numbers and facts. The layout should be clear and easy to understand with no spelling or arithmetic mistakes.

Hashemi and Hashemi (2002) provide five guiding themes to address in developing the plan:

1 What you plan to do – *the 'great idea'.*
2 Why you believe it will work, given the market, customer demand and competition – *a mixture of conviction and research.*
3 Why you are the right person to execute the plan and make things happen – *making sure you can cover any material gaps in your personal experience.*
4 How the business will make money – *prices, volumes and break-even.*
5 How much money you will need to get started – *and keep the embryo business running until you are generating a cash flow.*

Table 15.3 provides a typical and more detailed list of topics that have to be addressed.

Assessing the risks

Entrepreneurs take and, in their own way, manage risks. We have already seen that real entrepreneurs have a particular perspective on the risks involved in a venture. They take risks that many others would avoid. They believe they can manage the risk, partly because they think they understand its magnitude and partly because they believe they can manage any unexpected setbacks and challenges. Tennis player David Lloyd, who has become a millionaire businessman with a group of leisure centres, believes in taking a series of 50:50 bets – over a period, he contends, he is likely to come out on top. The most successful entrepreneurs are correct in their beliefs and assumptions; they find opportunities in crises and 'come out fighting'. Others are – or become – over-optimistic

Table 15.3   *The business plan*

Components of the business plan

- *Description of what the business is about.* This can include the background and information about the product or service that is to be offered.
- *Description of the marketplace.* This will tell the reader how well the entrepreneur understands the market and sees his or her place in it. Unless this is convincing the rest of the business plan may not be read! This section needs some hard data; generalisations will not do. It should identify the competitive advantage.
- *Explanation and reasoning behind the proposed business strategy.* This will need to include the market entry and the growth strategy.
- *Delivering the product or service.* This covers the stage that the product or service has reached at the moment and what else is needed to get it to market. What strategy will be adopted to put the product or service together and how will it get to the customer?
- *The financials.* This covers costs, pricing strategy, margins and so on.
- *The legals.* The shareholding position and the legal status of the start-up business need to be explained.
- *The people.* For investors, the people are as important as the product and its market, and they will want to know the background of the key individuals. For a start-up this can be difficult as these people may still be in their previous job waiting for the investment money to arrive before they join the new venture.
- *Risks.* A realistic appraisal of the risks of the venture is generally required.
- *What is being asked for.* The business plan needs a focus and should lead to a request for investment funding, a loan or an overdraft facility.

---

and over-confident and under-estimate the risks involved. Their risk can be metaphorically compared to climbing a tree. As the climber gets further up the tree, the branches he meets become increasingly fragile and less likely to carry his weight. Whilst it is never going to be possible to quantify every risk involved in a venture, that is no excuse for not assessing the risks. Table 15.4 provides a framework for this. It will be realised from this comprehensive list that the topic of risk is more complex than many first imagine. Every business decision, really, relates to a risk of some form.

Once they understand the risk, entrepreneurs are faced with a number of options. First, they can opt to retain the risk, logically preparing for any downside event. Second, they can transfer it by, for example, insurance. This, of course, can prove costly, which explains why some businesses turn out to be inadequately insured. Third, they can reduce the risk by investing in better controls and systems. Again, this requires investment.

Getting it right

There are many aspects to 'getting it right'. Figure 15.8 gives eight steps to a successful start-up. The good idea, the defined market opportunity, the founding team, a sound business plan and start-up capital are what puts the show on the road. That gets 25 per cent of the way; the rest is about customers and orders.

Table 15.4 *Assessing business risks*

Type of risk	Example
External environmental risks	
Supply risks	Over-dependency on a supplier
	Out-sourcing something which is strategically critical
Market/demand risks	Customer preference changes
Stakeholder risks	Misjudged priorities
Social responsibility and ethical issues	Failure to deal effectively with a chemical spill or a major incident
Politico-economic risks	Turbulence in an overseas market
Innovation risks	Misjudging market acceptance for a new idea
Competitive risks	Existing competitors 'out-innovate' the business
	Price competition
	Powerful new rivals enter the industry
Resource-based risks	
Materials risks	Need to handle/transport dangerous materials
Process risks	'Corner-cutting' to save time and money
Managerial risks	People's ability to cope with the dynamics of change in the organisation
People risks	Inadequate or inappropriate training
Commitment risks	Individuals do not 'pull their weight', especially in a crisis
Structural risks	Inappropriate balance between centralisation (for control) and decentralisation (for flexibility)
	Internal barriers to co-operation
Complexity	The spread of activities is too complex and leads to fragmentation and internal conflict
Financial risks	Under-capitalisation
	Cash flow problems
Technology risks	Inadequate information systems

These issues need to be supported by putting the right financial structures in place and careful control of the business against selected parameters.

It is a generally accepted 'rule of thumb' for venture capitalists that 'the management team is more important than the technology, which in turn is more important than the game plan'.

The right structure

This refers to the shareholding and financial structure of the business. The entrepreneur needs to decide if he or she wants to own all the business or is prepared to allow others, even the employees, to own part of the business. Most entrepreneurs already have a view on this. They either want total control or are prepared to share it and the question of which might be the best option does not come into it. The only real point to make is that if the business requires significant funding, and most do if they want to

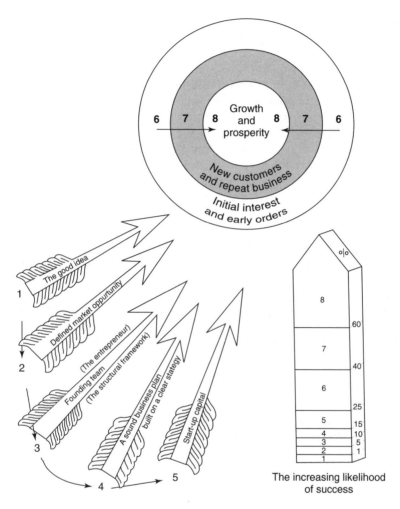

Figure 15.8 *Hitting the bulls-eye*

grow, then the founders will have to be prepared to make some of the equity available to the investors. Typically, 30 per cent is the starting point which means that the entrepreneur is passing over a third of his company in return for funding.

The financial structure of a business will be made up of borrowings of various kinds and these need to be kept in balance. Debt is something most companies carry all the time and the level of the debt will be related to the equity or value of the business. The ratio of debt to equity is termed the 'gearing'. If it is 1/1 then the company can pay off all its debts if it sold up. In practice this is rather theoretical in the case of the start-up business because it has debts but little real value. It is perhaps not surprising that bankers get nervous about start-ups.

Equity funding comes from investors who take a shareholding in the business. Equity funding stays with the company and the only cost involved is the payment of an annual dividend if that is appropriate. When shares are issued and traded in some way, their price at any given time determines the value of the business. *Loan funding* can be provided by either the investors or the banks, or both. Loans carry interest and the capital sum has to be paid off over a set period of time. The banks also provide an *overdraft facility* that enables the business to run 'in the red' as long as it does not exceed an agreed overdraft limit. Banks have their own policies for the mix of loans and overdrafts but both will cost the entrepreneur money. The loan is slightly more secure because banks can call in the overdraft at any time.

A business needs to structure the equity, loan and overdraft funding in the best way for its present and future growth. There is a difference between funding for capital equipment and for the day-to-day operations of the business. The former is referred to as *fixed or investment capital* and the latter as *working capital* though for most start-ups this distinction is rather blurred. The overdraft is meant to provide the working capital.

These are all issues that should be discussed with specialist advisers as it is very easy for a business to be under-funded, but entrepreneurs need to be sure they understand what is going on and should not simply accept the advice of the experts. We know of one entrepreneur whose investors suggested he would be better advised to have a loan from them rather than sell them equity in his business. This seemed good advice at the time but when the first year's loan was spent the venture fund called it in and the entrepreneur was given the choice of leaving or being declared bankrupt. He chose the former and the venture fund got all of the company for the price of their loan.

Table 15.5 provides a list of the factors that the banker is looking for under the acronym CAMPARI. This is a valuable evaluation tool although it might appear to be more focused on the individual borrower and the specific business than our venture capitalists' rule of thumb that put the team first. But do not be misled into thinking a banker is different from a venture capitalist. He or she will also pay great attention to the character of the person asking for the money. This first factor is likely to carry the most weight.

The right controls

Running a successful business is like a three-dimensional jigsaw puzzle. All the pieces need to be in the right place but there is a time dimension that keeps

Table 15.5   *The banker likes his CAMPARI*

C	Character of the borrower
A	Ability to borrow and repay
M	Margin of profit
P	Purpose of the loan – funding what?
A	Amount of the loan
R	Repayment terms
I	Insurance against non-payment

changing the size and shape of each piece. Table 15.6 lists the ten most important pieces of this living jigsaw. The questions asked apply to the start-up company as it sets out but similar questions need to be considered as it continues along the road.

Table 15.6 *The pieces of the jigsaw*

1 Customers	Who may have to be persuaded to try or switch?
	How long does it take to close a sale?
	Who are they?
	Where are they?
	How are they reached (selling and advertising)?
	Are your customers, your consumers?
	Paradoxically, eventual take-off can be rapid and exponential, bringing different problems
2 Suppliers	You are likely to be relatively insignificant, not in line for favours – yet you are very dependent on them
3 Distributors	Do they have to get rid of someone else to take you on?
	Credit arrangements with suppliers and distributors. Suppliers may want instant cash at first
	Logistic issues – do you need (expensive) third parties to handle you deliveries?
4 Premises	Where?
	Cost?
	Lease/purchase arrangements
5 Regulations	Anything which affects your area of activity – e.g. food, chemicals
	Don't forget your products could end up in another country
6 Team development	Where do you need help (you may, for example, not fancy the actual selling role)?
	Partners? Friends? Employees?
	Skills, trust and cost
	Why are they working for you?
7 Equipment (including IT)	What do you need?
	New or used?
	Can you beg or borrow?
	Expertise to handle it and get the best out of it
8 Money	Start-up finance
	Cash flow – getting paid
9 Time, energy and committment	Can you/should you do it full time?
	Strategy time and 'doing' time
	Are you a 70-hours-a-week person?
	Given all the people you have to meet, have you got time to produce anything?
	Can you take the disappointments?
	Who else has to make a sacrifice?
	Time out of the business
10 Credibility	You've got things to prove
	You have to keep all your stakeholders sweet

In any business, there are a number of parameters that the entrepreneur must keep an eye on. The main ones are:

Borrowing   On the financial side, the entrepreneur needs to watch the level of borrowing and to know where costs are coming from. If they are one-off costs that show the right rate of return, that is one thing, but if they are day-to-day costs then the company could be 'bleeding to death'. We know of one company in the 1970s where borrowing increased at the rate of £1 million per month and went on at that rate for eighteen months before the multinational parent took action.

Cash   The control of working capital, or rather lack of it, is the main reason why most start-ups fail. The cash position is made up of four parts that all need to be controlled, namely:

- the weekly or monthly payroll
- the money owed to others (the creditors)
- the money others owe to the business (the debtors)
- the money tied up in stock.

These regular calls on cash can be thrown by special expenditure, such as an advertising campaign or a special development project.

Various ratios are used to monitor these factors but in broad terms the following approach is recommended:

- The payroll costs should be kept to a minimum.
- The money owed to others should be stretched out as long as possible consistent with good supplier relations.
- The money others owe should be collected as promptly as possible.

In practice, because everybody is trying to do the same thing and there is a lag between when the raw materials are bought and when the finished product is sold with its added value, the business will always be owed more than it owes to others. In some industries this can mean a company is owed one-third or even a quarter of its annual turnover.

- Stock levels are always difficult to control and need to be watched carefully. They should be kept as low as possible consistent with meeting customer needs.

Numbers can be put to all these factors and it is a good idea to find out the ratios that work best and compare them with their general levels for the industry. This idea of benchmarking is now being developed extensively and can provide a useful comparison.

Sales   The entrepreneur will probably develop his or her own indicators to assess the sales position but three parameters that are useful are:

- the ratio of orders to quotations
- the size of the order book as a proportion of the annual sales
- the percentage of late deliveries.

These are industry sector specific, so the entrepreneur may not need to be too discouraged if he or she only lands one order for every seven quotations, if that is the industry average.

The entrepreneur needs to know what factors control sales. The traditional sales-person will invariably say it is price, but it is usually more subtle than that. As we discussed in Chapter 13, when a company is in the mainstream, its customers buy on service and convenience so that delivery, quality and a reputation for service are more important than price.

Market share and profit margin These two parameters work against each other and need to be held in balance. Entrepreneurs who buys market share by

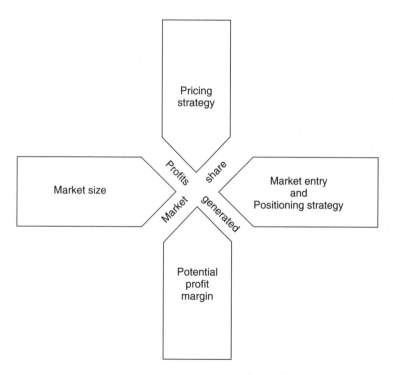

Market size £'000	Profit margin %	Market share	Net profits generated £'000
10 000	4	33	1320
10 000	8	25	2000
10 000	12	20	2400

Figure 15.9 *Market share and margin*

selling at low prices will lose their profit margin. Entrepreneurs who go only for profit can lose market share because of their higher prices. This might seem rather obvious but it does happen to the best of businesses. Apple Computers kept their profit margin high and lost market share to the IBM PC. This happened because Sculley, Head of Apple and ex-Pepsi Cola, confused the computer industry with the drinks industry. 'My theory was to price the product at a premium and then plow some of that back into advertising and build our market share. What I missed was that the key number in the business is gross margin' (Sculley, 1987). Sculley then went for gross margin and lost market share! Both must be watched and managed.

Figure 15.9 indicates these competing parameters and shows how it is possible to lose market share and make a greater cash profit. This is the trick used by the 'new broom' managing director who suddenly turns an ailing company into profit. In practice, any company that drops its market share from 33 per cent to 20 per cent is likely to be in serious trouble in the long run.

In the past, the Boston Consulting Group has argued that market share is the single most important variable in the life of a business. The British motor cycle industry died off because it lost market share without knowing it. Their steady sales level in the USA became a smaller and smaller percentage of a rapidly growing market being stimulated by motorcycles from Japan. Sales and profitability were monitored but not market share and so they did not realise they were losing their grip on the market. When the Japanese turned their attention to the UK market, British manufacturers had no answer. They were already beaten.

Concluding remarks

This final chapter has given a brief look at the techniques that are important for the entrepreneur to master. An increasing number of university programmes are available that cover this material but most have come from the traditional business school background and draw their experience from the small- to medium-sized enterprise. They therefore generally fail to provide the input that the entrepreneur, who wants to build something of recognised value, is actually looking for. In practice, business technique is learnt by doing and by making mistakes. Sculley's own admission of the mistakes he made at Apple Computers shows that despite his MBA from a prestigious US Business School he still learnt in this way. 'I had mistakenly thought . . . What I hadn't realised was . . . I should have understood . . . I discovered . . . ' (Sculley, 1987).

Sport uses the same 'learning by doing' approach and has developed the idea of 'the coach' to promote this learning process. Some businesses encourage a coaching style of management (Fortgang, 1999), which many others could do well to emulate.

Entrepreneurs certainly need this kind of coaching, as we commented in Chapter 2 when describing the role of the 'entrepreneur enabler'. At present, entrepreneurship is at the amateur level as sport was some years ago when training and coaching was rather ad hoc. Things need to change, but along the line of the sports model, rather than the academic business model. Simply, the training needs to be 'hands on' rather than 'talk about' – and entrepreneurs must be prepared to accept that they need the coaching. Perhaps this is the most difficult task of all!

References

Ansoff, H.I. (1987). *Corporate Strategy*, revised edn. Penguin.
Catlin, K. and Matthews, J. (2001). *Leading at the Speed of Growth*. Kauffman Center/Hungry Minds.
Drucker, P.F. (1985). *Innovation and Entrepreneurship*. Heinemann.
Fortgang, L.B. (1999). *Take Yourself to the Top*. Thorsons.
Hashemi, S. and Hashemi, B. (2002). *Anyone Can Do It*. Capstone Publishing.
Jolly, V.K. (1997). *Commercialising New Technologies*. Harvard Business School Press.
Sculley, J. (1987). *Odyssey: Pepse to Apple*. Collins.
Thompson, J.L. (2001). *Strategic Management*, 4th edn, Thomson Learning.

Further reading

Many of the ideas and techniques introduced in this chapter are to be found explained in greater detail in a number of good books on business planning. Readers interested in more information could usefully refer to:

Barrow, C., Barrow, P. and Brown, R. (1998). *The Business Plan Workbook*. 3rd edn. Kogan Page.
Butler, D. (2000). *Business Planning: a guide to business start-up*. Butterworth-Heinemann.
Stutely, R. (1999). *The Definitive Business Plan: The Fast-track to Intelligent Business Planning for Executives and Entrepreneurs*. Financial Times Management.

Index